A Handbook of Information and
for Disabled and Handicapped Pe

DIRECTORY FOR DISABLED PEOPLE

FOURTH EDITION

Compiled by
ANN DARNBROUGH AND DEREK KINRADE
Foreword by
The Rt Hon Alfred Morris, PC, MA, MP

Published in association with
The Royal Association for Disability and Rehabilitation

WOODHEAD-FAULKNER
(PUBLISHERS) LIMITED   ‖abdp

Member: Association of
British Directory Publishers

Published by Woodhead-Faulkner Ltd
Fitzwilliam House, 32 Trumpington Street
Cambridge CB2 1QY, England
and 51 Washington Street, Dover
New Hampshire 03820, USA

First edition 1977
Second edition 1979
Third edition 1981
Fourth edition 1985

ISBN 0 85941 255 5
ISSN 0309-4413

British Library Cataloguing in Publication Data
Directory for disabled people: a handbook of
information and opportunities for disabled and handicapped people.—4th ed.
  1. Physically handicapped—Services for—Great
  Britain—Directories
  I. Darnbrough, Ann   II. Kinrade, Derek
  362.4   HV3024.G7

  ISBN 0-85941-255-5

Library of Congress Cataloging in Publication Data
Darnbrough, Ann.
  Directory for disabled people.
  Includes index.
  1. Physically handicapped—Services for—Great
Britain—Directories.   I. Kinrade, Derek.   II. Title.
HV3024.G7D37   1985   362.4′048′02541   84-19570
ISBN 0-85941-255-5 (pbk.)

Text design by Ron Jones

Typeset by Computerset (MFK) Ltd, Saffron Walden,
Essex

Printed and bound in Great Britain by
R. J. Acford Ltd, Chichester, Sussex

About the authors
Ann Darnbrough is Project Officer of the Disability
Unit, AHRTAG (Appropriate Health Resources and
Technologies Action Group). She was also a member of
the International Year of Disabled People Voluntary
Organisations Committee (England) and Chairperson of
its Information to Disabled People Working Party (now
known as National Information Forum).
Derek Kinrade is the former Chairman of the Waltham
Forest Association for People with Disabilities.
Both are freelance writers in the field of disability and
co-authors of:
Fund Raising and Grant Aid
Motoring and Mobility for Disabled People
Handbook for Handicapped People in Waltham Forest

Whilst every effort has been made to verify the accuracy
of the information in this book, readers are advised to
make their own enquiries as to the conditions, value,
etc., of items described.

A MESSAGE FROM THE MINISTER FOR THE DISABLED

I am very happy to be given this opportunity to commend the fourth edition of the *Directory for Disabled People*. Previous editions have established an impressive reputation for presenting a wealth of information in a comprehensive and accessible way. It is difficult to think of an aspect which has not been covered, ranging from everyday activities, which able-bodied people can so easily take for granted, to the most unusual and rewarding hobbies. Like a good map it guides you to the help you want, and may reveal other opportunities you did not know existed.

I congratulate everyone concerned on the enormous care and effort they have put into compiling the Directory. As with previous editions, I am sure it will be very helpful to disabled people and those who work with them, and I wish it every success.

TONY NEWTON, OBE, MP
Joint Parliamentary Under Secretary of
State and Minister for the Disabled

FOREWORD

THE RT HON ALFRED MORRIS, PC, MA, MP

Author of the Chronically Sick and Disabled Persons Act
and Minister for the Disabled 1974–79

This is a very important book not only for disabled people and their families but also for everyone who is concerned with their problems and needs. Earlier editions have helped many thousands of individuals to improve their lot and have made the *Directory for Disabled People* a force to be reckoned with in the continuing struggle for fair treatment and equal rights for disabled people.

The book's major purpose is to bring together information which would otherwise only be available from a wide range of sources to which few disabled people have ready access. The information given in previous editions has now been scrupulously updated and there is a great deal of important new material.

As the report of the Committee on Restrictions Against Disabled People (CORAD) so clearly showed, people with disabilities are still the victims of inequality in many fields. In part this additional handicap is the result of society's attitude towards them; but in part, too, it is a handicap that derives from the lack of readily available advice and information.

This is why Rehabilitation International's *Charter for the 80s* – based as it is on the most extensive international consultation ever undertaken in the fields of disability prevention and rehabilitation – places so much emphasis on the importance of pro-

viding disabled people with full and up-to-date information on all of the benefits and services available to them.

The World Charter, like the *Directory for Disabled People*, is also concerned with the rights of disabled people and its four major aims hammer home their importance. Everyone who wants to see the Charter's aims achieved will be delighted by the care and dedication with which Ann Darnbrough and Derek Kinrade have compiled this invaluable work of reference.

The Directory provides a path round the many obstacles that face disabled people in seeking access to the information they need if they are to live full and fulfilling lives. It advises them on their rights to services and on education, travel, aids, sports and leisure activities. It also helps to put disabled people in touch with each other and with organisations whose work may be of assistance to them.

Ann Darnbrough and Derek Kinrade started this fourth edition on the day the third edition was published. They deserve our warmest appreciation, and indeed admiration, for their penetrating research and tenacity in tackling so important a job so successfully for disabled people and those who live and work with them. We have here an *Encyclopaedia Disibilitatis*.

INTRODUCTION

The fourth edition of the Directory bears a new title by which we lose those dubious words: 'the disabled'. The Directory is and always has been written for individual people, a fact which is, we hope, obvious from the way our information is presented, and from the very broad range of subject matter chosen to reflect the profusion of personal needs and tastes. We seek to bring to notice available services and opportunities to enhance the quality of life in a context of individual choice.

As always, the Directory has been revised and updated with the utmost care. But more than this, while the format remains broadly similar, within it we have tried to cover every new development, leaving no stone unturned to ensure that nothing which might be of benefit to a disabled person is missed. Each edition, we find, takes on a life of its own, reflecting the progress (sometimes, alas, cutbacks) in provision of benefits and services for disabled people. The most significant trend, which is so exciting to chronicle in this edition, is the growth of organisations which are being run by disabled people themselves. The independent living movement is gaining momentum all the time and as a result severely disabled people in increasing numbers are being enabled to live in the community in lifestyles of their own choice. In the section on House and Home we describe the Derbyshire Independent Living Project and the Hampshire Centre for Independent Living. While this edition of the Directory goes to press, similar groups are being initiated in other parts of the country. The section on Further Education also reflects a move away from specialised institutions to integrated further and higher education in colleges and universities, where many severely disabled students are pursuing studies of their choice amongst their able-bodied peers.

This fourth edition is twice the size of the first Directory, reflecting, we believe, a definite advance in the scope of facilities and the wealth of information available on living with a disability. Nevertheless, we find that many individual disabled people remain unaware of basic services and financial benefits. They are being starved of knowledge; knowledge which should be a vital part of the rehabilitation process but which so often is not. Without such knowledge, individuals suffer severe and unnecessary deprivation. While the new, emerging organisations of disabled people are in the forefront of information provision, many of the older-style voluntary organisations for disabled people still see their roles narrowly and seem not to be sufficiently aware of their members' acute needs for full and frank information.

The caring professionals, too, in their positions close to disabled people, seem not always to be aware of their patients'/clients' wider information needs. It would, of course, be very difficult for workers in this field always to have an in-depth knowledge of the complex range of services and benefits available, but very often all that is needed is a signpost or an appropriate contact who can offer detailed help and guidance.

While, as we have made clear, this Directory is written directly for and is primarily addressed to people with disabilities, we trust that it will also help all those concerned with disability who are uncertain where to look for vital information.

ACKNOWLEDGEMENTS

We can never thank enough all those people and organisations who regularly provide us with information by newsletters, leaflets, books, notices or personal contact, or indeed the hundreds of correspondents who responded to our questionnaire. As always, all of our information has been checked at source: this Directory owes its accuracy and breadth to the cooperation of so many others. We cannot mention all their names here, but particular thanks are due to Liz Fanshawe of the Disabled Living Foundation, whose encouragement is greatly appreciated; to Richard Stowell, whose advice on the section on Further Education was invaluable; to Elizabeth Dendy of the Sports Council, who again provided key information on the specialist sports organisations; and also to Ted Papps of the British Sports Association for the Disabled, who was always ready to help in this field. When we needed guidance about motoring matters David Griffiths of the Mobility Information Service and Adrian Stokes provided expert technical insights. At RADAR (Royal Association for Disability and Rehabilitation) a number of staff assisted in their specialist areas of work. Not least, helpful officers at the DHSS, the Inland Revenue, the Department of the Environment and the Manpower Services Commission provided detailed guidance on official legislation, regulations, and procedures.

Finally, we are indebted to each other. Thank you Derek. Thank you Ann. As always, it was a team effort.

Ann Darnbrough and Derek Kinrade
Little Grove, Grove Lane, Orchard-Leigh,
nr Chesham, Buckinghamshire HP5 3QL

CONTENTS

LIST OF ADVERTISERS

SECTION 1
STATUTORY SERVICES

Local Authority Services

Under a number of Acts of Parliament (*see* Section 13), local authorities, through their social services committees (which should not be confused with the social security system operated by the Department of Health and Social Security, a government body), housing authority and social workers, are required to help disabled people (as defined in Section 29 of the National Assistance Act 1948: *see* Section 13) resident in their areas in a variety of ways. In practice, the level and standard of assistance varies considerably from place to place. Some authorities appear to lack a genuine commitment to the needs of disabled people, while all have found recent economic constraints a considerable problem. Where both these drawbacks apply, the results can be disastrous. Taking the country as a whole, recent surveys by RADAR and the Disability Alliance show that between 1979 and 1983 the rate of telephone installations under the 1970 Act almost halved. There has been a similar fall in the adaptation of council houses, a reduction of over 20 per cent in the number of holidays sponsored by local authorities and cuts in such basic services as meals-on-wheels and places in day centres.

When the picture is viewed regionally, it is apparent that the variations in provision and the effect of cut-backs can be dramatic. In 1981/82, Islington spent 120 times more per head on telephones for elderly and disabled people than Dorset; Manchester 26 times more than Oldham. Only five of the 104 local authorities spend more than £100 per head on caring for the sick, frail and deprived. For 15 of them, the figure is below £30. Authorities spending least include East and West Sussex, Lincolnshire, Berkshire, Rotherham and Bradford.

Disabled people can seldom choose where they live. It is essential, therefore, that together with their carers, and organisations which seek to protect their interests, they are aware of their rights to services and are persistent and forceful in pressing for necessary help. Enquiries in the first instance should be made to the social services department of the local authority. The address will be listed in the telephone directory under the name of the local authority.

Provision is made for the following kinds of help:

Advice.

Practical assistance with, for example, housing, holidays, aids and adaptations required to bring daily living up to a satisfactory standard of safety, comfort and convenience (these subjects are more fully covered in Sections 3, 4 and 9).

Services to handicapped people (including those suffering from impaired vision or hearing). Help is available with such problems as education, mobility, vocational rehabilitation, training facilities and employment, with referral, if necessary, to the Employment Service Division (*see* Section 7). Often the social services department will liaise with relevant voluntary organisations.

Facilities to enable disabled persons to be employed under special conditions where this is necessary (*see* Section 7).

Rate relief, rent allowances, rent and rate rebates and improvement grants are available under certain conditions (*see* Section 4).

In cases of real need and isolation, help with payment for the installation or rental of a telephone may be provided (but not for the cost of calls).

Where special need arises, help may be given to obtain a radio or television, and to make use of public library facilities and other recreational activities (*see* Section 11).

Arrangements can sometimes be made for children under 5 years of age to be cared for at a day nursery, or by a registered child minder, or to attend a play-group for a few hours a day.

Many special domestic services are provided. These include home helps, meals-on-wheels and laundry services in appropriate cases.

Many authorities provide residential accommodation for the aged or mentally or physically handicapped who cannot manage in their own homes or cannot be looked after by relatives.

1

Many authorities provide day centres where there are opportunities to participate in educational, recreational and social activities and handicrafts.

Many authorities, in liaison with bus companies, can arrange for disabled people to be issued with passes allowing concessionary fares (*see* Section 8).

Local authorities are responsible for the operation of the Orange Badge Scheme, which confers a number of advantages upon disabled drivers and passengers (*see* Section 8).

In 1983 RADAR published a code of practice on the provision of services for disabled people by local authorities under Section 2 of the Chronically Sick and Disabled Persons Act 1970. Drawn up by 15 national charities, the code outlines the requirements of the law and describes the procedures the charities would like to see adopted for the provision of information on services and the assessment of need. Criteria for each of the services listed in Section 2 (and summarised above) are suggested. *Throughout the code the importance of the full involvement of people with disabilities and their families in the decisions which affect their lives is emphasised.* Copies of the code are available free from RADAR, but a s.a.e. (minimum 9 in. × 6 in.) would be appreciated.

Another guide to the Chronically Sick and Disabled Persons Act 1970 has been prepared as a leaflet by the Disabilities Study Unit under the title *Dear Councillor*. This sets out briefly what councillors must and can do for disabled people through the full and humane implementation of those sections of the Act which affect local government.

Unfortunately, the most underprivileged and vulnerable members of our society are often those least able to fend for themselves, or to receive information on rights and opportunities. This is, perhaps, especially true of our ethnic minorities, on account of both cultural and language problems. The Disabilities Study Unit has produced a brief but useful guide to services under the Chronically Sick and Disabled Persons Act which is available in Bengali, Gujurati, Hindi, Punjabi and Urdu as well as in English. We would also draw particular attention to the services offered by the Community Health Group for Ethnic Minorities detailed in Section 16, Helpful Organisations, page 299.

SOCIAL WORKERS

Social workers play a vital role in providing support in the community itself, while remaining the focal point for the essential communication between the various welfare services. They give personal help to handicapped people on a visiting basis, especially when difficulties arise through illness, stress or other domestic problems. They will advise how the best use can be made of statutory and voluntary services available in their locality. (*See* Statutory Provision of Aids in Section 3 for further details of the services provided.)

Not all services are free, but the amount an individual is expected to contribute varies in different localities, and people dependent on state benefits normally do not have to pay anything. (For further details *see* Leaflets HB 1 and HB 2 from DHSS.)

If you feel dissatisfied about, or have relationship difficulties with, a particular social worker, you are entitled to ask for a change. The first point of contact is the manager of your Area Social Work Team, but if this is unsuccessful (and area managers are notoriously resistant to such requests) you may have to go through the formal complaints procedure (*see* page 4). A precedent has been established in the case of a complaint against Norfolk County Council (Investigation 25/H/80) in which the Local Ombudsman held that the failure to recognise that the client and social worker could not work together amounted to maladministration which caused injustice to the client.

BOOKS AND PUBLICATIONS

The following publications explain the work of social services departments in greater detail:

Guide to the Social Services. This guide is published annually by the Family Welfare Association. It provides a concise source of reference for all those working in and alongside the social services and for interested members of the general public. Distributed by Bailey Bros & Swinfen Ltd, Warner House, Folkestone, Kent CT19 6PH. Price £6.25 plus 50p postage and packing, or order from good bookshops.

NCVO Newsservice (National Council for Voluntary Organisations, ten times a year). This digest of changes in the voluntary and statutory social service field is now incorporated in NCVO's magazine *Voluntary Action*. Subscription £15 per annum.

Social Services. A slide/tape set series produced by Camera Talks Ltd.

Social Services Year Book 1984/85. Published by the Longman Group Ltd. Full details of the Social Services and allied fields. Over 30,000 names, addresses and telephone numbers arranged in sections and fully indexed. Price £26.65.

REGISTRATION

People who come within the definition of Section 29 of the National Assistance Act 1948 – *i.e.* who are

3

blind, deaf or dumb, or substantially and permanently handicapped by illness, injury or congenital deformity – can apply to their local authority (social services) to be registered as disabled. If their disability is such as obviously to qualify, no medical evidence should be necessary; otherwise a statement from the applicant's GP is required. It is not obligatory to apply for registration, but certain statutory benefits, *e.g.* rate rebates, depend upon it, and some local authorities make it a pre-condition for the supply of some services. Other authorities will extend help both to registered disabled people and 'those entitled to be registered'.

Some local authorities or local borough associations for disabled people have produced guides to local services and it is well worth asking about these. A format for a basic guide was produced by the Information Working Party of the International Year of Disabled People England Committee, while a more detailed guide was produced by, among others, the London Borough of Waltham Forest.

COMPLAINTS

There are no common procedures by which local authorities deal with complaints. Clearly, the method of handling complaints as between, say, the Greater London Council and a small district council is bound to differ. However, local authorities in England are now recommended to follow a 'code of practice' worked out by the Local Authority Associations in co-operation with the Commission for Local Administration in England. This sets out guidelines which should ensure that complaints are properly and fully investigated.

In the first instance, any complaint should be raised with the department concerned or with the chief executive of the authority. If subsequent action fails to remove the grievance, the complainant can get in touch with an elected or appointed member of the authority, usually a local councillor.

If the complaint is still not cleared up, the complainant can ask a local councillor (or member of a water authority) to pass his written complaint to the Local Ombudsman. If the councillor (or member of the water authority) fails or refuses to refer the complaint, the complainant can send it direct to the Local Commissioner or Ombudsman. (A free booklet *Your Local Ombudsman* is obtainable from council offices, Citizens' Advice Bureaux or direct from the Local Commissioner at 21 Queen Anne's Gate, London SW1H 9BU (Tel: 01-222 5622). All the Local Commissioners are able to look at complaints against water authorities, as well as local councils. But it

must be stressed that the Commissioners can only investigate complaints if:

(a) they have previously been brought to the attention of the local authority and the authority has had a reasonable time to reply;
(b) the injustice is alleged to be the result of maladministration, that is, the way in which something has been handled, *e.g.* unjustifiable delay, incompetence, neglect or prejudice.

There are three Local Commissioners for England, two of whom work from the London office and the other from 29 Castlegate, York YO1 1RN (Tel: York (0904) 30151). Similar arrangements exist for Wales, Scotland and Northern Ireland. The relevant addresses are:

Commissioner for Local Administration in Wales
Derwen House, Court Road, Bridgend, Mid Glamorgan CF31 1BN (Tel: Bridgend (0656) 61325).

Commissioner for Local Administration in Scotland
3 Shandwick Place, Edinburgh EH2 4RG (Tel: 031-229 4472).

Commissioner for Complaints in Northern Ireland
Progressive House, 33 Wellington Place, Belfast BT1 6HN (Tel: Belfast (0232) 3821).

Health Services

The full range of free health and community health services is, of course, available to disabled and able-bodied people alike. Facilities which are of particular benefit to handicapped people include the statutory provision of aids (*see* Section 3), child health clinics, chiropody clinics, remedial therapy, help and advice by health visitors and home nursing by district nurses. In all cases, the primary contact is the family doctor. Financial help with fares is given to people on low incomes who have to attend hospital as a patient. (For further details *see* DHSS Leaflet H 11.) If, because of disability, patients cannot use public transport to get to hospital, or if no public transport is available, special transport arrangements can be made by the hospital concerned. Handicapped people can sometimes be admitted to hospital for short periods to give their relatives a break.

If handicapped people are worried about hereditary factors, perhaps fearing that a disability might be passed on if they were to have children, their local family doctor can refer them, if necessary, to a genetic counselling centre where expert advice is available. If there is any difficulty, write to the Great Ormond Street Medical Service Unit, Institute of Child Health, 30 Guilford Street, London WC1. There is also a useful booklet on genetic conditions,

Human Genetics, published by the DHSS (*see* Section 12).

In-patient services in hospital sometimes include purpose-built units for the care of physically handicapped people, as well as facilities for reassessment and rehabilitation back into normal life. Medical rehabilitation (as distinct from rehabilitation for employment) may involve, as well as normal medical and nursing care, the specialist help of remedial therapists. This can continue on an out-patient basis after discharge.

MEDICAL PERSONNEL

Dieticians
Can advise on specialist diets. They may be seen at local hospitals, normally on the recommendation of a doctor.

District Nurses
Are employed by district health authorities and provide help with domestic nursing care on a visiting basis. Anyone needing their services should contact their doctor.

Family Doctors
The key person and the primary contact for help or advice about health and related services and aids. You can choose your own doctor, providing he does NHS work and will accept you. (Local community health councils, post offices, libraries and Citizens' Advice Bureaux should have lists of doctors in their localities.) Simply take your medical card on your first visit. In cases of difficulty in finding a doctor, the local family practitioner committee (*see* telephone directory) will help. Also, you can change your doctor without giving a reason, though it is wise to have been accepted by your new doctor before asking to be withdrawn from your present doctor's list. Normally, each doctor simply signs your medical card and the changeover is immediately effective. In case of difficulties, or if you feel embarrassed about it, you can effect the change by sending a letter to the FPC informing the committee of your wish to transfer and enclosing your medical card. The committee will return the card with a slip affixed showing the earliest date on which the transfer can be made (normally 14 days after receipt of your letter). This can then be taken to your new doctor. If the change is caused by a move to a new district, it is necessary only to take your medical card to the new doctor of your choice.

In an emergency, you can ask *any* NHS doctor for treatment, but it is for the doctor to decide if it is a genuine emergency. Similarly, your own doctor has discretion as to whether a visit at your home is necessary.

Health Visitors
Are trained nurses employed by district health authorities. They are able to give advice and assistance on all family health and associated welfare problems.

Medical Social Workers
Are hospital based and they play a key role in helping people to sort out social problems, *e.g.* their entitlement to benefits, and make arrangements for them to receive help after discharge from hospital such as meals-on-wheels or home help. It is important that, where necessary, there is full liaison with local social services departments on behalf of patients *before* they leave hospital. They can also help patients and their families work through the emotional and social conflicts arising from disability. If necessary, they will help people to register as disabled.

Occupational Therapists
Assess the practical needs of disabled people to live and work as normally as possible. Their help should be sought through a doctor or social worker. In most areas they operate on a visiting basis to advise on any equipment, adaptations or structural alterations which may be necessary. They will also instruct disabled people in techniques for overcoming physical handicaps, to encourage the maximum possible dexterity through the performance of congenial tasks.

Physiotherapists
Help to maintain bodily movements as far as possible, by means of physical techniques. These include massage, electro-therapy and treatment by infra-red and ultra-violet light. Their services must normally be sought through a doctor, but some operate on a private professional basis. A book giving advice on moving and lifting handicapped people with dignity, under the title *Handling the Handicapped*, has been produced by the Chartered Society of Physiotherapy, published by Woodhead-Faulkner Ltd, Fitzwilliam House, 32 Trumpington Street, Cambridge CB2 1QY (price £8.50 hardback; £5.25 paperback). A film, *Moving and Lifting the Disabled Person*, on the same theme (16mm, colour, 12 minutes), made by the Multiple Sclerosis Society, is available from Concord Film Council Ltd, 201 Felixstowe Road, Ipswich, Suffolk IP3 9BJ.

Psychiatric Social Workers
Their work is particularly concerned with people who are mentally ill, helping both patients and their

families to work through their problems towards the achievement of maximum potential. In some cases, practical help is given on discharge from hospital, *e.g.* in arranging hostel accommodation and places in day centres.

Remedial Gymnasts

Are attached to rehabilitation centres in some localities. They help patients to achieve greater mobility by exercises and recreational activities.

Speech Therapists

Are specialists in helping with speech difficulties of all kinds. Serious cases will normally be referred by a doctor on his own initiative, but help is also available to improve or remove even minor impediments.

COMMUNITY HEALTH COUNCILS

These work to improve the services provided by the district health authority – hospitals, health centres, clinics and community health services and in this role represent a bridge between the public and those who administer the NHS.

Community health councils have a major part to play in informing members of the public about local health services, on such things as how to change a GP or how to register a complaint about a local service. They will guide a complainant through from the initial lodging of the complaint to accompanying him or her to a tribunal if necessary. Addresses appear in telephone directories under Community Health Council.

REHABILITATION CENTRES

In addition to the rehabilitation work done in hospitals, sometimes in special units, there are a number of purpose-built or specially adapted rehabilitation centres throughout Great Britain. They provide facilities for the rehabilitation of patients, on referral, who are suffering serious handicap as a result of injury, disease or, in some cases, age. Some, such as Mary Marlborough Lodge at Oxford and the Wolfson Centre at Wimbledon, are famous for their work with patients who have very severe physical/ neurological impairments.

Rehabilitation centres offer expert assessment and testing of functional abilities, intensive treatment, training for coping with disability in everyday activities and the provision of any necessary aids.

ARTIFICIAL LIMB AND APPLIANCE CENTRES

Strategically placed throughout the United Kingdom, Artificial Limb and Appliance Centres (ALACs) supply not only artificial limbs and ap-

pliances, but also artificial eyes, environmental controls (*see* page 61), wheelchairs and surgical appliances and equipment for home nursing. A few centres are limited to limb fitting (LFCs) or to the supply of appliances (ACs). A list is given in Appendix A of DHSS Leaflet HB 2.

Assessment and supply is invariably in response to medical referral. If a wheelchair is needed on a permanent basis, it is supplied on the recommendation of a family or hospital doctor. A range of non-powered wheelchairs (both occupant and attendant controlled), spinal carriages, pedal or hand propelled tricycles and electrically powered chairs is available. *Outdoor* electric chairs, however, are supplied only in attendant-controlled versions and only for users whose attendants cannot manage to push a wheelchair. Occupant-controlled *indoor* electric chairs are available only to users who cannot walk at all and who cannot propel themselves in a non-powered chair.

BOOKS AND PUBLICATIONS

Patients' Association Leaflets. The following leaflets are available from the Patients' Association, Room 33, 18 Charing Cross Road, London WC2H 0HR (Tel: 01-240 0671): *Rights of the Patient*, price 20p; *Changing Your Doctor*, price 20p; *Going into Hospital*, price 40p; *Using the NHS*, price 40p; *Can I Insist?*, price 40p; *Self-help and the Patient*, price £1.75 (*see* Appendix A). All leaflets are free to members.

Slide/tape sets. Camera Talks Ltd produce a series of slide/tape sets on physiotherapy, occupational therapy, speech therapy and chiropody.

A Patients' Guide to the NHS. Published by the Consumers Association with Hodder & Stoughton, 1983, price £3.95 including postage and packing. Available from the Consumers Association, it is a joint production of the Patients' Association and the Consumers Association.

Patients' Rights: A guide for NHS patients and doctors. Published by HMSO, revised version, 1983, price £1.50. Produced by the National Consumer Council, this is an admirable publication in all respects: first, on grounds of style – it is concise and to the point, with a grasp of language which makes a virtue of economy; second, it is crammed with relevant, factual information of a kind which we all need from time to time; third, it is well laid out with clear headings. It is a pity that in consolidating the editions for England/Wales, Scotland and Northern Ireland, and in changing the size and format, the index has been lost. Entries such as abortion, changing/choosing/finding a GP, complaints, confidentiality, death (right to die; use of body), drugs (addiction; consent to treatment), osteopathy and second opinion were sufficient in themselves to quicken the interest. However, the content remains and this is a publication which everyone should have to hand.

HELPFUL ORGANISATIONS

As well as the statutory services, a number of private organisations have been formed which specialise in the area of health and the welfare of patients generally. They are ready to help, guide and protect people who may encounter difficulties or who are worried about illness, diagnosis, treatment and related problems.

The Patients' Association
11 Dartmouth Street, London SW1H 9BN (Tel: 01-222 4992). The Association aims to act as 'the voice of the patient'. Also to:
(a) represent and further the interests of patients;
(b) give help and advice to individuals;
(c) acquire and spread information about patients' interests;
(d) promote understanding and goodwill between patients and everyone in medical practice and related activities.
A number of booklets are published by the Association and these are listed in the book list at the end of this section. In the booklet entitled *Can I Insist?* the following questions are posed among others, and receive helpful and informative answers: 'I'm being treated by my GP but I'm not getting any better. I'd really like to see a specialist. How can I arrange it?' 'I've been in hospital for tests but they won't tell me what the matter is or what the tests showed. Hasn't the patient got the right to know what's wrong with him?' Other questions are asked about visits by children in hospitals, dental treatment, donating body or organs, home and hospital confinement, and pregnancy tests and abortions. Apply for details of membership to the above address. Subscription £3 per annum.

The National Association of Leagues of Hospital Friends
565 Fulham Road, London SW6 1ES (Tel: 01-385 0974). Gives varied services such as running shops, helping with ward duties, entertaining and visiting lonely patients and keeping in touch with them after they have left hospital.

COMPLAINTS

The community health council (local addresses in telephone directory) will always give guidance on making a formal complaint about the health service, assisting through all stages which may be necessary to resolve the problem. In some circumstances, aggrieved people may find it desirable to seek legal advice. Again the CHC will help. Should individuals wish to pursue the matter themselves, formal complaints about family doctors, opticians, dentists or chemists should be made to the local family practitioner committee. Formal complaints about hospitals or community health services should be referred to the district administrator of the NHS district management team (ask the CHC for the address). *It is good practice always to put a formal complaint in writing and to retain a copy.*

If you are dissatisfied with the result, the Health Service Commissioner may be able to carry out an investigation. His terms of reference are, however, strictly limited by Act of Parliament, and he is precluded from investigating certain matters, for instance complaints which have been taken to a tribunal or court of law or which involve clinical judgements. Further details are given in leaflets available from the following addresses, to which complaints should also be addressed:

The Health Service Commissioner for England
Church House, Great Smith Street, London SW1P 3BW.

The Health Service Commissioner for Scotland
3rd Floor, 71 George Street, Edinburgh EH2 3EE.

The Health Service Commissioner for Wales
2nd Floor, Queens Court, Plymouth Street, Cardiff CF1 4DA.

Complaints which call into question the clinical judgement of a doctor may well involve legal action if they are of a serious nature. In less serious cases, where you are dissatisfied with an initial response, you can renew your complaint. If the matter cannot then be resolved, *e.g.* by discussion with you, there is an established procedure which provides for a review of the medical matters involved by two independent consultants who, by discussion of the whole issue with you and the medical staff concerned (possibly combined with a physical examination if you wish and if it seems appropriate), will seek to determine whether the care provided was fully appropriate to your condition and performed to a proper standard. The discussion with you will be private and completely confidential, but, if you wish, you may bring a relative or personal friend with you to the meeting. The independent consultants will then report on a confidential basis to the Regional Medical Officer, with any recommendations they wish to make, *e.g.*

on matters requiring action by the health authority. The administrator for the authority concerned will then write to you, explaining where appropriate any action it has taken as a result of your complaint.

Postal Voting

PHYSICALLY HANDICAPPED PEOPLE

If you cannot go personally to the polling station, or are unlikely to be able to do so, because of physical incapacity or blindness, or if, though able to go, you cannot vote unaided, you can apply to be treated as an 'absent voter' and to vote by post. The application should be made on form RPF 7, available from local council offices, and sent to the electoral registration officer responsible for the area where you live. The officer will allow the application if you have been registered as a blind person by your local authority or if your application has been certified by a medical or Christian Science practitioner (the officer can accept a certificate by someone else, *e.g.* a district nurse, but this is a matter for his/her discretion). Once an application has been approved, it is valid for an indefinite period. Postal voting is available at all parliamentary and local government elections except those for parish and community councils.

VOLUNTARY MENTAL PATIENTS

Special provision is made under the Representation of the People Act 1983 for the registration of electors who are patients in mental hospitals (*i.e.* 'establishments wholly or mainly for the reception and treatment of people suffering from any form of mental disorder'). The provision does not extend to patients who are detained there compulsorily by the order of a court. If, on the qualifying date for electoral registration (10 October in Great Britain), you are a voluntary mental patient and not resident anywhere other than in a mental hospital, you are entitled to be registered as an elector only in pursuance of a 'patient's declaration'. This does not apply to voluntary mental patients whose stay in hospital is only short term and who are registered for their home address in the normal way.

The patient's declaration should be made on form RPF 35, stocks of which are held in mental hospitals. You can make this declaration as a voluntary mental patient without assistance if you can do so (in this context 'assistance' does not include help necessitated by blindness or other physical incapacity). The declaration must be made in the presence of an authorised member of the hospital staff who must attest the declaration and the fact that it was made without assistance other than assistance needed because of blindness or physical incapacity. The declaration must also provide an address at which the voluntary mental patient would be resident if not in the hospital, or, alternatively, an address at which he/she has lived in the United Kingdom. The patient will be treated as registered at this address and, since it may well be at some distance from the mental hospital, he/she will be allowed to vote by post. Application to vote by post in these circumstances should be made on form RPF 36; approval, if given, will be valid for only one particular election.

Where to Find Local Sources of Help

Consult the telephone directory under the following headings:

Appliance Centres	Health and Social Security, Department of (Appliance Centres)
Citizens' Advice Bureaux	Listed as such
Community Health Councils	Listed as such
Disablement Resettlement Officers	Manpower Services Commission
Education Authorities	The relevant county, district or London borough council (Education Authority)
Family Planning	Listed as such
Income Tax	Inland Revenue
Rent and Rates	The relevant county, district or London borough council (Housing Department)
Social Security	Health and Social Security, Department of (Local Social Security Offices)
Social Services	The relevant county, district or London borough council (Social Services Department)
Voluntary Organisations	The name of the organisation (or *see* Information, Legal and Advisory Services, or Helpful Organisations, Sections 15 and 16 of this book)
Welfare Rights Officers (in some areas only)	The relevant county, district or London borough council (Welfare Rights Offices)

SECTION 2
FINANCIAL BENEFITS AND ALLOWANCES

In this section, we seek to bring to notice the main features of those benefits and allowances which are particularly relevant to the needs of disabled people, so that anyone who may be entitled to financial help may be armed with sufficient information to take their enquiries further. More detailed advice is available in a number of specialist guides which we list and commend. Where rights are not clear cut, we strongly recommend our readers to seek personal advice from one of the organisations which we mention on page 10. It is often necessary to have a one-to-one discussion to untangle the problems, and in some cases it is vital to have support in making a claim or pressing an appeal.

While acknowledging the considerable difficulties involved in understanding the benefit system and making a claim, we urge you not to give up. With the right help in filling in the forms and weighing the pros and cons, you can win through. Having given this personal advice, we believe that it is scandalous that potential claimants should face such difficulties, so that many people fail to get help which they desperately need. In a recent letter to *The Guardian*, Norman Vetter of the Welsh National School of Medicine wrote that 'according to some estimates almost half of the over 65s living at home [who] are entitled to supplementary pension do not receive it', while the School's own estimates suggest 'that only a third of those who require constant care receive an attendance allowance'. Our system of benefits can defeat even persistent enquirers. We know from experience and from numerous surveys that thousands upon thousands of people, struggling in adverse circumstances, are unaware or confused about the benefits which are available to them.

Morality is perverted when massive efforts are put into the detection of petty 'scroungers' while millions of pounds are lost to people in urgent and genuine need. In the last few years, far from being simplified, the system has become even more obscure, bureaucratic and penny pinching. It is as though, as one frustrated claimant remarked, 'someone had locked the door and thrown away the key'. The DHSS, to give it credit, publishes a considerable range of leaflets and is making some efforts to improve its advisory services, but it is the system itself which is in drastic need of overhaul.

State benefits are open to criticism on three levels: complexity, inadequacy and inequity. Their complexity is famous, massive and, as we have suggested, growing: a monument to many architects who have worked without benefit of a grand design and whose social purpose has been circumscribed by inadequate resources and sometimes by a limited recognition of social need. The result is a labyrinth, with a bewildering array of entrances – a maze which might have been designed to create the maximum of confusion and frustrate the take-up of benefits by people already restricted by physical and mental handicaps.

However, even those who manage to find their way through the system, and are actually successful in being awarded benefit, find that the rates are extremely low, so that most claimants subsist on or near the poverty line in the midst of a society which is still generally affluent. Disabled people faced with additional costs imposed by their condition and limitations are particularly ill-served; the cash levels of all the specialist benefits are plainly inadequate to meet the costs imposed by the degree of handicap which must be involved in order to qualify. This is not, let it be understood, a charge against only the present government, but against successive governments of different political persuasions (though one suspects that what used to be failure is now policy). The excuse is always one of shortage of money, though billions of pounds can always be found for obscenely destructive weaponry.

Our third complaint is that of inequity. Many of the allowances are blatantly discriminatory: the mobility allowance against older people, the invalid care allowance and the 'housewives'' non-contributory invalidity pension against married women (though, thankfully, the latter injustice is now rectified); housing benefit against the low-paid employee; the attendance allowance and the forthcoming severe disablement allowance against all but the most severely disabled people. Expediency rather than fairness is the principle upon which most benefits are based, and it is time for reform.

Helpful Organisations

A number of organisations provide help and advice in claiming benefits:

Child Poverty Action Group (CPAG)
Welfare Rights Department, 1 Macklin Street, London WC2 5NH (Tel: 01-405 5942 between 1.30 and 5.30 p.m.), or write.

Citizens' Advice Bureaux
Consult your telephone directory.

DIAL UK
Consult Section 15 for a list of local addresses.

Disability Alliance Educational and Research Association, Welfare Rights Information Service
25 Denmark Street, London WC2 8NJ (Tel: 01-240 0806, between 2 and 4.30 p.m.), or write.
They publish the famous *Disability Rights Handbook* (*see* below).

Disablement Income Group Charitable Trust
Attlee House, 28 Commercial Street, London E1 6LR (Tel: 01-247 2128/6877).

Books and Publications (for addresses *see* Appendix B)

GENERAL GUIDES

A to Z MENCAP Information Bulletin (Royal Society for Mentally Handicapped Children and Adults, 1984/85), £1.95 plus 30p postage and packing.
At the time of writing this new edition is with the printer. It is an established guide to statutory benefits.

Claim It! (Thames Television's HELP! Programme, undated), free subject to availability.
A series of eight fact sheets giving a brief guide to benefits and how to make sure you get what you are entitled to. Although necessarily lacking details, these fact sheets are admirably direct, with great writing and cartoons. A letter which accompanies the pack includes the following words which somewhat capture the spirit of the publications: '. . . remember the two golden rules: IF IN DOUBT – CLAIM, IF UNHAPPY – APPEAL. And don't forget: NEVER TAKE "NO" FOR AN ANSWER and DON'T BE FRIGHTENED TO COMPLAIN.'

Disability Rights Handbook (Disability Alliance Educational and Research Association, annually with regular updatings through the *Disability Rights Bulletin*), £2 post free (*Bulletins* extra).
A much used and much respected guide specifically for people with disabilities. It has the merit of being relatively inexpensive while being sufficiently detailed to cope with most day-to-day problems.

Disablement Income Group Advisory Service Leaflets. A series of leaflets explaining the main welfare benefits now available, together with reference to local authority provision and additional help available to those on supplementary benefit.

Greater London Association for Disabled People (GLAD) Leaflets.
Three information sheets outlining benefits for particular groups: *Families with a Handicapped Child* (August 1980); *Handicapped People of Working Age* (January 1981); *Handicapped People of Pension Age* (August 1981). All three amended May 1982, and free of charge. Very close printed, these are rather forbidding, but contain much useful information in a very short space.

A Guide to Benefits for Handicapped Children and their Families by Alison Cooper (Disability Alliance, 1981), £1.20 post free.
A 32-page booklet which supplements the annual *Disability Rights Handbook*. There are short chapters on each benefit, summarising entitlement and how to claim.

Help for Handicapped People (DHSS Leaflet HB 1, 1983; separate versions for Scotland and Northern Ireland), free. A booklet giving general guidance on benefits and services.

National Welfare Benefits Handbook (Child Poverty Action Group, annually), £2.50 including postage and packing.
One of the best-known guides, very clearly set out and covering the subject in some detail. Sections on supplementary benefit, family income supplement, health benefits, housing benefit, educational benefits and special help for disabled people. A useful index. The Handbook is supplemented by CPAG's *Welfare Rights Bulletin*, keeping subscribers up to date with changes (£6 per annum, six issues).

Rights Guide to Non-Means Tested Benefit (Child Poverty Action Group, annually), £2.50 including postage and packing.
The companion to the *National Welfare Benefits Handbook* described above. It covers benefits paid for by contributions as well as non-contributory benefits which are not subject to a means test. Like

Here are 36 pages packed with up-to-date information about cash benefits and other help for the handicapped.

So if you are disabled, or if you look after someone who is, send for this free booklet now – simply fill in the coupon below.

Organisations requiring supplies of the booklet should write to the address on the coupon saying how many copies they need.

Help for handicapped people

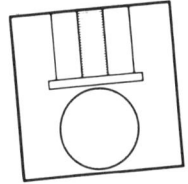

Please send me booklet HB.1, "Help for handicapped people"

Name_____

Address_____

_____

_____Postcode_____

Post coupon to DHSS Leaflets Unit, PO Box 21, Stanmore HA7 1AY

the *Handbook*, it is updated by the bi-monthly *Welfare Rights Bulletin*.

Tolley's Social Security and State Benefits by Jim Matthewman and Nigel Lambert (Tolley Publishing Co. Ltd, annually), 1984 edition £10.95.

Tolley's income tax guide is, of course, quite famous and indispensable. Now comes a hall-marked guide to benefits. The 15 chapters cover all the practical situations in which benefit may be payable, and there is a special chapter (5) on disabled and handicapped people. The discussion of each benefit is fully referenced throughout to the relevant legislation and DHSS leaflets. There is an index, tables of statutes and statutory instruments and three important appendices: Help from Independent Organisations; Social Security Decisions, Reviews and Appeals; Social Security Benefits and Medical Care in the EEC and other countries.

Particularly helpful is the systematic layout in which each benefit is analysed with a basic pattern of eight sub-headings: key points; people who qualify; period for which payable; amount payable; increases for dependants; how to claim; effect of receiving other income or benefits; position while the benefit is being received.

The book is written in clear English, avoids technical jargon, and should be invaluable to those who advise disabled people. There is a money back guarantee if you find it does not meet your requirements and it is returned in good condition within 21 days.

Which Benefit? (DHSS Leaflet FB 2, November 1982), free.

This is a 38-page guide sub-titled *60 ways to get cash help*. Its great merit is that it covers a lot of ground briefly and in a systematic way which is related to practical situations, *e.g.* 'Not enough money', 'Illness' and 'Disabled and Handicapped'. It does not tell you all you will need to know but its importance lies in its potential to act as a trigger to bring to attention benefits which may have escaped your notice. Every voluntary organisation should ensure that each of its members has a copy. Bulk supplies can be obtained from DHSS Leaflets Unit, PO Box 21, Stanmore, Middlesex HA7 1AY.

Your Rights for Pensioners (Age Concern, 1983), 55p.

A benefits guide specifically intended for women aged 60 and over and men aged 65 and over. The guide covers all the benefits, allowances, rebates and concessions which might conceivably affect elderly people. It also has chapters on the NHS, legal help, income tax and residential accommodation.

Your Social Security by Frances Bennett (Penguin Books, 1982), £1.95.

Given the complexity of the subject, this is as accessible a treatment as one could hope for, with benefits dealt with by reference to the practical situations in which people find themselves. A 'question and answer' format simplifies reading, and though much of the 'small print' is missing, this is actually helpful in achieving communication with the reader, especially the individual potential claimant. Frances Bennett stands fair and square on the side of the claimant and makes a useful contribution towards the more comprehensive take-up of benefits which are rightly due to disadvantaged people.

DHSS LEAFLETS

(Available from local DHSS offices or from DHSS Leaflets, PO Box 21, Stanmore, Middlesex HA7 1AY, unless otherwise stated.)

General

FB 2	Which benefit?
NI 196	Social security benefit rates and earnings rules
NI 208	National Insurance contribution rates
NI 105	Retirement pensions and widow's benefits: payment direct into banks or building societies
NI 146	Catalogue of social security leaflets
NI 229	Christmas bonus: paid with some social security benefits
FB 5	Social security: Service families going abroad
FB 14	National Insurance: what you pay and what you get

Not Enough Money

FIS 1	Family Income Supplement *(also from post offices)*
SB 1	Cash help: you can claim supplementary benefit
SB 8	Cash help: now you have claimed supplementary benefit
SB 21	Cash help: you can claim supplementary benefit if you are unemployed
SB 9	Supplementary benefit for unemployed people
SB 2	Supplementary benefit and trade disputes
SB 7	Supplementary benefit: living together as husband and wife

SB 17	Help with heating costs for people getting supplementary benefit
SB 12	Supplementary benefit: you can appeal
SB 16	Supplementary benefit: lump sum payments for special needs
FB 4	Help while you're working

Children

FB 3	Help for one-parent families
NI 17A	Maternity grant and maternity allowance *(also from maternity clinics)*
CH 1	Child benefit
CH 4	Child benefit for children away from home
CH 4A	Child benefit for children in the care of the local authority
CH 5	Child benefit for people entering Britain
CH 6	Child benefit for people leaving Britain
CH 7	Child benefit for children aged 16 and over
CH 11	One parent benefit for people bringing up children alone
NI 14	Guardian's allowance
NI 93	Child's special allowance

Out of Work

NI 12	Unemployment benefit *(also from unemployment benefit offices)*
NI 230	Unemployment benefit and your occupational pension
NI 55	Unemployment benefit for seasonal workers
RE 1	Re-establishment centres: how they can help you
NI 240	Voluntary work and social security benefits
NI 231	Made redundant?

Illness

NI 16	Sickness benefit
NI 16A	Invalidity benefit
NI 210	Non-contributory invalidity pension *(men and single women)*
NI 214	Non-contributory invalidity pension for married women
H 11	Your hospital fares if you're on a low income
NI 9	Going into hospital? What happens to your social security benefit or pension?
NI 212	Invalid care allowance

Health

P 11	NHS prescriptions
D 11	NHS dental treatment
G 11	NHS glasses
MV 11	Free milk and vitamins

Injured at Work

NI 2	Prescribed industrial diseases
NI 6	Disablement benefit and increases
NI 31	Pneumoconiosis and byssinosis
NI 207	Occupational deafness
NI 10	Industrial death benefits for widows and other dependants
WS 1	Supplement to workmen's compensation *(if you were injured before July 1948)*
PN 1	The pneumoconiosis, byssinosis and miscellaneous diseases benefit scheme
NI 237	Occupational asthma

Injured in War or HM Forces

MPL 120	War pensioners and widows going abroad: your pension and welfare services
MPL 153	Help for the war disabled: ex-servicemen and civilians
MPL 154	Rates of war pensions and allowances
MPL 152	War widows: war pensions, allowances and welfare services
NI 211A	War pensioners: help with transport

(The above leaflets are available only from war pensions offices, except for MPL 154 which is also available from DHSS Leaflets, Stanmore)

Handicapped or Disabled

NI 205	Attendance allowance
NI 212	Invalid care allowance
NI 211	Mobility allowance
HB 1	Help for handicapped people *(also from local social services departments)*
HB 2	Aids for the disabled
NI 219	Phasing out the invalid tricycle
NI 225	Mobility allowance: new option for vehicle scheme beneficiaries
HB 3	Payment for severe vaccine damage *(HB 3 is available only from Vaccine Damage Payments Unit, DHSS, North Fylde Central Offices, Norcross, Blackpool FY5 3TA)*
HB 4	Help with mobility: getting around
FB 18	Long-term sick and disabled: Cash help for people at home

Retired

NP 32	Your retirement pension
NP 32A	Your retirement pension if you are widowed or divorced
NP 32B	Retirement benefits for married women
NI 184	Non-contributory retirement pension for people over 80
NI 177	Was your husband over 65 in 1948? Pensions for married, widowed or divorced women
NI 92	Earning extra pension by cancelling your retirement

Widows

NP 35	Your benefit as a widow for the first 26 weeks
NP 36	Your benefit as a widow after the first 26 weeks

Death

NI 49	Death grant
D 49	What to do after a death

National Insurance Contributions

NI 40	NI contributions for employees
NI 39	NI and contract of service
NP 28	More than one job? Your Class 1 NI contributions
NI 41	NI guide for the self-employed
NI 27	People with small earnings from self-employment: NI contributions
NI 42	NI voluntary contributions
NI 48	National Insurance: unpaid and late paid contributions
NP 18	Class 4 NI contributions *(also from tax offices)*
NP 27	Looking after someone at home: how to protect your pension
NI 1	Married women: your National Insurance position
NI 51	Widows: guidance about NI contributions and benefits
NI 95	Divorced women: NI guide
NI 50	NI guide for war pensioners
NP 12	Social security: school leavers and students *(also from careers offices)*
NI 11	NI contributions for domestic workers
NI 24	Mariner's guide to NI contributions and benefits
NI 35	NI contributions for company directors
NI 47	NI guidance for share fishermen *(also from unemployment benefit offices in fishing ports)*
NI 222	NI guide for examiners and part-time lecturers, teachers and instructors
NP 21	NI contributions for ministers of religion
NP 16	NI contributions for people working in the UK embassies, consulates, or overseas employers *(and supplement Apr 81)*
NI 38	Social security abroad

Appeals

If a decision of a local DHSS office seems wrong, usually the most sensible first step to take is to *write* to that office requesting that it be reconsidered. (Personal visits are both time-consuming and generally ineffective: a degree of formality always carries greater weight.) It will help if the letter is supported or presented by an influential person or organisation. If it is a question of amount, a more detailed copy of the official assessment can be requested.

Alternatively (or if the original decision is upheld by the local office), an appeal can be made to a supplementary benefit appeal tribunal (a form for the purpose is part of DHSS leaflet SB 12, though a letter will equally suffice). Appeals should normally be submitted within 28 days of the decision, but later submissions can be accepted at the discretion of the tribunal if you can show cause for the delay. Tribunals, of course, can only operate within the law, even when that law is harsh. However, in many cases, interpretation of the law may be involved, and a tribunal examining your representations and situation in detail, and having regard to the application of the benefit rules in the widest context, may well look upon the facts in a different and more favourable light than your local office. Numerous successful appeals have not only benefited the claimant immediately concerned, but have helped to set more helpful guidelines for others.

The proceedings of tribunals are relatively informal. No one need be put off by either inexperience or awe, but the nature of the appeal and supporting facts need to be stated as clearly as possible. Legal aid is not available but assistance is; someone may accompany and/or represent the claimant and expenses may be claimed. However, personal appearances, although advisable, are not obligatory. Help in preparing an appeal may be sought from the Welfare Rights Department of the Child Poverty Action Group. General advice may be obtained from a Citizens' Advice Bureau or a local authority welfare rights or information office.

Your expenses (by the cheapest form of travel) from home to the tribunal will be paid by the clerk to the tribunal. If you have lost earnings by attending, ask the clerk for a form on which you can claim compensation; you may also be able to claim for a witness or someone who accompanies you.

BOOKS AND PUBLICATIONS

In addition to the general publications described at the beginning of this section and the DHSS Leaflet SB 12, two specialist guides are available from the National Association of Citizens' Advice Bureaux, 110 Drury Lane, London WC2B 5SN, *viz*:

I Want to Appeal – A Guide to Supplementary Benefit, £2.30, covering tribunal appeals concerning both supplementary benefit and family income supplement.

Social Security Appeals – A Guide to National Insurance Tribunals and Medical Appeal Tribunals, £2, covering medical boards, the Attendance Allowance Board, questions within the jurisdiction of the Secretary of State, and appeals to the National Insurance Commissioners.

Complaints

It is our experience that, particularly in busy urban areas, the reception and interviewing of claimants at DHSS offices is often less than satisfactory. Pressure of numbers, insufficient staff, poor accommodation, a tendency to push counter duties down to lower grades and the anger of frustrated claimants who are often obliged to wait for lengthy periods in uncongenial surroundings, all tend to create an atmosphere where it is difficult to resolve personal problems regarding benefits. In such circumstances, the dignity of privacy may be disregarded and the service become less than civil. It is our belief that complaints, where they arise, should be properly pursued. A service can only be improved if its weaknesses are brought to light. Your complaint may improve the service for others as well as redressing your own grievance.

There are, however, inappropriate ways of complaining: moaning at the hard-pressed counter clerk will not help, nor will expressing your views to other claimants. Your views need and deserve to be raised officially and at a higher level. In the ordinary way, complaints about the actions of a government department should be taken up directly with the department concerned, *e.g.* with the manager of a DHSS office. Sometimes, you may find it useful to seek the help of a local organisation (*e.g.* your Citizens' Advice Bureau or local Association for Disabled People if there is one) which can take up the cudgels on your behalf. If the matter is really

serious, you may feel it necessary to take legal advice or to seek the help of your Member of Parliament (either in writing – keep a copy – or at one of his/her local 'surgeries').

In the most serious cases – where it is claimed that injustice has been sustained through maladministration – the MP can be asked to refer the matter to the Parliamentary Commissioner for Administration, Church House, Great Smith Street, London SW1P 3BW. The scope of the Commissioner's powers exclude the investigation of certain matters, for instance complaints which have been taken to a tribunal or a court of law, or which involve local authorities, the police, nationalised industries or the Post Office. Nor can he accept a complaint directly from a member of the public. It must be made in writing to a Member of the House of Commons, and include a statement that the complainant consents to the matter being referred to the Commissioner. Further details are given in a leaflet available from the above address.

Attendance Allowance

DHSS Leaflet NI 205.

GENERAL DESCRIPTION

This is a benefit for adults and children aged 2 or more who are severely disabled, physically or mentally, and who have needed a great deal of looking after for at least six months. It does not depend on having paid National Insurance contributions, nor on your means, and is not subject to income tax. The allowance is paid at one of two rates – the higher rate is paid for those who require attendance both by day *and* by night. The lower rate is for those needing attendance either by day *or* by night.

It is an allowance which gives more trouble than most. Many disabled people still seem to be unaware of its availability, and those that do know about it appear often to have extraordinary difficulty in satisfying the conditions, which have tended to be applied in a stringent, even unsympathetic, way rather than erring on the side of generosity in the face of obvious need. What is worse, there are indications that the rules are not applied equitably or consistently.

MEDICAL CONDITIONS

The disability must be so severe that for six months you have needed:
(a) *by day*: *frequent* attention *throughout* the day in connection with your bodily functions; or *continual* supervision *throughout* the day in order to avoid substantial danger to yourself or others;

15

(b) *at night*: *prolonged or repeated* attention during the night in connection with your bodily functions; or *continual* supervision *throughout* the night in order to avoid substantial danger to yourself or others.

NOTE: 'Bodily functions' include eating, drinking, walking, keeping clean and keeping warm.

(A child of 2 or over, but under 16, must satisfy the further requirement that the attention or supervision required must be substantially in excess of that normally required by a child of the same age and sex.)

There is no provision for the Allowance to be backdated, so that it is important to claim in good time. The DHSS say that claims should be presented in anticipation of the fulfilment of the six months rule, after four months. In the case of a child under 2, who will have satisfied the conditions for at least six months on reaching the age of 2, claim at the age of 22 months.

(During the interim period of six months, a potential attendance allowance beneficiary who is entitled to *supplementary benefit* (*see* page 38) may be entitled to an additional 'requirement' for attendance needs. The amount is calculated as the cost of attendance up to £19.10 a week (November 1984), the lower rate of attendance allowance. People who do not ordinarily qualify for supplementary benefit may do so when their attendance needs are taken into account as a basic requirement.)

RESIDENCE CONDITIONS

To qualify for attendance allowance, you must:
(a) normally live in the United Kingdom or on the Isle of Man or Jersey;
(b) be so resident when you claim;
(c) have lived there for at least six months in the previous 12.
(*See* leaflet NI 205 for other residence rules applicable in special circumstances.)

WEEKLY RATES

(November 1984)
DHSS Leaflet NI 196.
Higher rate: £28.60
Lower rate: £19.10

WHO CAN CLAIM?

In the case of a disabled adult, the allowance should normally be claimed by that person, but someone can complete the claim form for you if they declare that they have done so. If, through illness or a mental condition, a disabled person is unable to manage his/her own affairs, the DHSS will appoint someone to act (this may be a legal representative).

In the case of a disabled child, the person who has care of that child should normally claim. If the child lives with both parents, the mother should claim; if with one parent, that parent should claim; if with neither parent, the person whose name appears on the order book for child benefit for that child. If, alternatively, the child lives with foster parents who receive a boarding out allowance, then the foster mother should claim.

HOW TO CLAIM AND WHAT FOLLOWS

We have pointed out that the rules governing attendance allowance are extremely restrictive and tend to be so applied. It is therefore important that applications (which must be made in writing) are accurate and clear, and give a full and proper picture of the facts. You would be well advised to seek expert help in completing the form, ideally from one of the organisations which specialise in benefits and allowances (*see* page 10).

Leaflet NI 205 incorporates a claim form DS 2. This should be sent to your local DHSS office.

The DHSS will acknowledge the receipt of the completed claim form and will usually arrange for the disabled person to be visited at home by a doctor, who will complete a medical report form on his or her attendance needs. The claim is then decided by an attendance allowance board, the result being advised to the claimant in writing. If the claim is refused or granted at the lower rate, the applicant has a right to ask for a review, and should write to the board within three months, stating clearly why he or she disputes the decision. Any new light which can be shed on the necessity for attention and its frequency should be given, if possible with examples of the problems and dangers which arise from not receiving attention at the required level. The opinion of a social worker or GP may be helpful.

If the original decision is upheld, but the claimant still feels that he or she has a just claim *in law*, he or she would be well advised to seek legal advice (*see* pages 285–87). An appeal to the National Insurance Commissioner is a possibility.

ADMISSION TO HOSPITAL OR RESIDENTIAL ACCOMMODATION

The allowance remains payable for the first four weeks. Most importantly, this allows payment to continue through short periods of respite care. Previously children going into residential care lost the allowance immediately, but regulations operative from 8 August 1983 have extended the four-week rule to bring children fully into line with other beneficiaries.

RELATIONSHIP TO OTHER BENEFITS

Attendance allowance stands on its own. It is normally paid in full and in addition to other benefits. An exception is where *constant attendance allowance* (*see* page 24) is being paid, when attendance allowance will be affected. If the CAA is the lesser, the difference between the two will be paid. Supplementary benefit, specifically, is not affected unless it includes a special payment to meet attendance needs.

Attendance allowance does not count as income when claiming means-tested benefits, *e.g.* rent rebates, supplementary benefit, free school meals, etc.

The attendance allowance may be a vital factor in deciding entitlement to invalid care allowance.

BOOKS AND PUBLICATIONS

In addition to the DHSS leaflet NI 205 and the general publications described at the beginning of this section, a specialist booklet *Attendance Allowance Checklist and Outline of Review Procedure* is available from the Disability Alliance, price 50p including postage and packing.

Blind People: Special Help for those Registered as Blind

Special income tax allowance (*see* page 22).
Television licence at reduced cost.
Free postage on items sent as articles for the blind (*see* page 272).
Travel concessions on British Rail, London Transport, local buses and internal British Airways flights on presentation of a certificate issued by the social services department of the local authority. (These concessions are sometimes limited to specific purposes and may cover a blind person's guide rather than the blind person.)
Special rates of supplementary benefit (*see* page 41).
Dog licence: no licence is necessary for a blind person's guide dog.

Dental Charges: Exemption

DHSS Leaflet D 11.
All NHS dental treatment (but not private treatment) is free if you are:
(a) under 18 (except that you have to pay for dentures and bridges if you are over 16 and not in full-time education);
(b) under 19 and still in full-time education;
(c) expecting a baby or have had a baby within the last 12 months;
(d) receiving supplementary benefit or family income supplement; in such cases exemption extends to dependants;

(e) receiving free milk and vitamins and/or free prescriptions because you are on a low income;
(f) on a low income, not much above supplementary benefit level (for details *see* leaflet D 11). If you are aged 16 or over, you can claim on grounds of your own low income even if you are still at school or college.

HOW TO CLAIM EXEMPTION

The first five categories claim exemption simply by telling their dentist that they want free treatment. If, however, you are seeking exemption on grounds of low income, you should get a form F1D from your dentist, complete it and send it to your DHSS office. If you have already paid for treatment, but were entitled to exemption under (d), (e) or (f) above, get form F6 from your DHSS office to claim a refund (low income claimants will need form F1D as well); other people should write to their local family practitioner committee for a refund.

WAR PENSIONERS

You may, of course, qualify for exemption under the normal rules described above. If not, you will have to pay the basic charges for dental treatment unless it is needed because of your war disablement, in which case you should apply to DHSS, North Fylde Central Office, Norcross, Blackpool FY5 3TA.

Employment Expenses and Training Grants

See Income Tax, page 23 and Section 7.

The Family Fund

Financed by the government and administered by the Joseph Rowntree Memorial Trust, the Family Fund exists to help those families who have children under the age of 16 (the age limit can be extended at the discretion of the trustees where a child is disqualified from receiving supplementary benefits while undergoing full-time education) who are very severely handicapped whether physically or mentally, and who, because of their economic and social circumstances, are in need of money, goods or services to relieve stress in the family while the handicapped child is at home. (During the time that a handicapped child is in hospital or a residential home, the family would be eligible for assistance only for the purpose of visiting the child or making specific provision for him.) This help is intended to complement and not to replace existing help available from statutory and voluntary services. It is for the trustees of the Fund to decide whether and what help should be provided. They will first need to establish, with the advice of professional experts, that the handicap is very severe and then establish the extent of need, and whether it can and should be met from other sources. Help may take the form of goods, services or a grant of money for some definite purpose *related to the care of the handicapped child*. The sort of help usually given includes assistance with transport problems, equipment for dealing with laundry, help with holidays where a family could not otherwise afford one and temporary help while waiting for some other payment or service to be arranged. Any grant which may be given is disregarded by the Supplementary Benefits Commission in assessing income. The Fund cannot normally consider requests for assistance towards private education, private medical treatment or private housing, nor for services which are the responsibility of statutory bodies or local authorities. Nor can the Fund give grants to reimburse previous expenditure, nor for debts not caused specifically by the needs of a handicapped child. Arrears of rent, electricity, gas charges, etc. are considered to be matters normally dealt with by local authority social workers and the Fund does not give grants for these.

Anyone who thinks the Fund could help, should write to The Family Fund, PO Box 50, York YO1 1UY, giving their name and address, the name and date of birth of their child, the way the child is disabled and the kind of help needed. One of the Fund's representatives will then call to discuss the application (any special arrangements for this – *e.g.* unsuitable dates and times – should be specified in the application). There is no means test, but general family circumstances must be taken into account, and every case must, of course, be considered on its merits.

Family Income Supplement

DHSS Leaflet FIS 1.

GENERAL DESCRIPTION

This allowance is designed for people in work and may be claimed where the total family income is below a level prescribed by Parliament. Anyone, whether single or married who is, and who is normally, in full-time paid work (*i.e.* 30 hours or more a week, 24 hours if a lone parent) including self-employment, and who has at least one dependent child in the family home, may claim. In the case of a couple either partner can claim. However, couples do not qualify if one is, and normally is, in full-time paid work while the other is receiving sickness benefit, unemployment benefit, invalidity pension, statutory sick pay, supplementary allowance or an allowance for an MSC training or rehabilitation course, *except* where the partner receiving such pay-

ment is not, and has not been for at least three months, in paid work (*i.e.* effectively in these circumstances FIS cannot be awarded unless and until the partner receiving benefit has been out of work for three months: this is to prevent an award of FIS (which lasts for 52 weeks) being made when one partner is only temporarily out of work).

FIS does not depend on National Insurance contributions and does not count as income for income tax purposes.

Income level (November 1984)

Prescribed amount (*i.e.* with one child): £90.00.
Increase in prescribed amount for each subsequent child: £10.00.

Payments (November 1984)

FIS benefit is calculated as half the difference between a family's actual gross income (excluding certain 'disregards') and the appropriate prescribed income, with the following ceiling:
Maximum payment for family with one child: £23.
Increase for each additional child: £2.

Disregards

Child benefit, one-parent benefit, attendance allowance, mobility allowance, the first £4 of a war pension, rent allowance, children's income, payment for children boarded out with the claimant and educational maintenance allowance.

HOW TO CLAIM

Complete tear-off application form which is a part of leaflet FIS 1 and send to DHSS (FIS), Poulton-le-Fylde, Blackpool FY6 8NW (free s.a.e. available at post offices).

RELATIONSHIP TO OTHER BENEFITS

Those who are entitled to FIS (or to regular supplementary benefit) and/or their dependants are also automatically entitled to the following benefits free: dental treatment and dentures, glasses, prescriptions, hospital fares, school meals, milk for the under-fives and expectant mothers. They are also likely to qualify for housing benefit, certain free legal advice (subject to level of capital/savings) and grants for extended education.

If you are a single parent working between 24 and 30 hours a week and claiming FIS, you may also qualify for some supplementary benefit and housing benefit supplement (*see* pages 21 and 38), either of which can in turn qualify you for long-term rates of supplementary benefit (*see* page 39) and single payments for exceptional needs (*see* page 42).

Further Education Grants

See Section 6.

Home Responsibilities Protection

DHSS Leaflet NP 27.

GENERAL DESCRIPTION

This is not a direct benefit, but a scheme designed for people who cannot keep up their normal National Insurance contributions because they have to look after someone at home and are therefore unable to take regular employment. It affords a measure of protection to entitlement to basic retirement pension or, in the case of a man, his wife's widowed mother's allowance or widow's pension. Any full tax year (6 April to the following 5 April) in which you qualify for HRP on the grounds set out below will be regarded as a year of 'home responsibility' and deducted from the number of qualifying years of National Insurance contributions you would otherwise need for a full pension or for a wife's benefit as a widow (though, in each case, a prescribed minimum number of qualifying years is still required).

CONDITIONS

HRP can cover any tax year after 6 April 1978 in which either you do no work at all or, though you do some work, your contributions are insufficient to count for pension purposes, provided that, for the whole tax year, you have been:
(a) getting child benefit for a child under 16; or
(b) looking after someone regularly (for at least 35 hours every week) who has been in receipt of attendance allowance or constant attendance allowance, and you do not get invalid care allowance; or
(c) in receipt of supplementary benefit to enable you to stay off work to look after an elderly or sick person at home; or
(d) covered by a combination of these conditions for the whole tax year.

NOTE: 1. A married woman or widow paying reduced NI contributions cannot qualify for HRP.
2. Even if you do qualify for HRP, you may secure a higher rate of pension if you pay Class 3 voluntary contributions (see DHSS leaflet NI 42).

Hospital Appliances and Medicine Charges: Exemption

Patients (including out-patients and day patients) are entitled to free NHS appliances and medicines if their income falls below a prescribed level. Benefit is subject to a means test and must normally be formally claimed.

The following categories of people, however, enjoy an automatic right to benefit:
(a) anyone on supplementary benefit or family income supplement;
(b) anyone in receipt of free milk or prescription because of low income;
(c) children under 16;
(d) schoolchildren over 16;
(e) war-service pensioners.
Further details (and claim forms) from the hospital.

Hospitalisation: Effect on Benefits

Leaflet NI 9 outlines the national insurance, industrial injuries and other benefits which are reduced or cease altogether when a beneficiary or one of his dependants has to stay in a hospital or similar institution provided under the National Health Service, where maintenance is provided, whether wholly or in part. The reason for such reductions is that some of the needs covered by the various allowances are, during hospitalisation, met free of charge by the National Health Service.

If either a beneficiary or a dependant is admitted to hospital:
- Supplementary benefit will be reduced immediately upon the admission of a beneficiary into hospital unless he/she leaves a dependant at home. Additions such as special diet will be stopped. After eight weeks, benefit will be reviewed and usually reduced even if you have a dependant. After 12 weeks, any supplementary benefit you continue to receive will again be reviewed. If as a beneficiary you have a child in hospital, the allowance you get for that child will be reduced after 12 weeks. After two years, supplementary benefit will be assessed separately for the needs of the person in hospital and anyone remaining at home. This can be advantageous when one partner is in a private nursing home, in that it may allow that partner to claim in his/her own right and to be treated as a 'boarder' eligible to receive supplementary benefit to cover part of the fees. There are special arrangements for lone parents.
- Attendance allowance and constant attendance allowance paid with an industrial or war disablement pension cease after four weeks. (If you normally live in a local authority home or a similar place where your costs are partly met out of public funds, attendance allowance ceases immediately on admission to hospital.)
- Sickness or invalidity benefit, non-contributory invalidity pension, widows' benefits, retirement pension and industrial injuries unemployability supplement are reduced when a beneficiary or

spouse has been in hospital for eight weeks (including lesser periods which together total eight weeks if they are not more than four weeks apart). If, as a beneficiary, you have a child in hospital, any additions for that child as a dependant will stop after 12 weeks unless you regularly spend money on the child on small necessities, gifts and visits.

After one year in hospital, if you have a dependant, you can choose either:

(a) to have your benefit paid to your dependant (or to someone looking after the dependant) less, if you wish, a basic prescribed amount to be paid direct to you; or

(b) to have only your dependant's part of your benefit paid direct to your dependant. You will only get the basic prescribed amount (*i.e.* your benefit will be reduced) but you may be able to get resettlement benefit when you are discharged.

If you do not have a dependant, your benefit, after one year in hospital, will be reduced to the basic prescribed amount, but you may get resettlement benefit when you are discharged. After two years in hospital, your benefit will be further reduced, but part of the reduction will be paid as resettlement benefit when you leave hospital. Resettlement benefit is a weekly payment to help you get back to normal life (*see* page 34).

• Invalid care allowance ceases after 12 weeks when a beneficiary who normally looks after a disabled person has to go into hospital; if the disabled person goes into hospital, payment stops after four weeks.

This is a considerable simplification of an area of some complexity. Fuller details are given in the five-page Leaflet NI 9 but this gives only 'general guidance'. The important thing is that anyone in receipt of any social security benefit (including supplementary benefit) should inform their local DHSS office immediately if they or any dependant is admitted to hospital, if they are allowed home on leave, and on discharge.

Housing Benefit

GENERAL DESCRIPTION

Housing benefit has replaced the former reliefs of rent rebates, rent allowances, rate rebates and the arrangements for meeting rent and rates as an element of supplementary benefit. Administration of the benefit scheme now lies wholly with local authorities (saving on Civil Service jobs, but causing, at least initially, extraordinary difficulties in many areas).

Eligible housing costs incurred by people on supplementary benefit are met in full; others can qualify on a means-tested basis, but benefit will generally fall short of 100% (so that, unfortunately, people in employment with low incomes are likely to be worse off than supplementary benefit claimants with comparable means). Subject to need, the scheme covers accommodation occupied as a home and is available to tenants and licensees in respect of rent and rates, and to owner-occupiers and people with comparable arrangements in respect of rates (though they may get assistance with mortgage interest as part of any supplementary benefit to which they are entitled). Boarders form a separate category and are eligible for housing benefit on accommodation costs (*e.g.* rent and rates) unless receiving supplementary benefit (which would take into account board and lodging costs).

Housing benefit is normally payable on only one home, but there are a few exceptions as when the claimant has had to leave a previous home through fear of domestic violence, or if he/she has no option but to make simultaneous payments on two homes (*e.g.* when moving house). Joint tenants and flat sharers (other than couples living together) are entitled to separate consideration, rent and rates being apportioned between them.

ELIGIBLE COSTS

The *actual* rent or rates paid should normally be taken as the eligible costs, but authorities have discretion to make reductions if they consider the accommodation to be unreasonably large, unreasonably expensive (private sector rents only), or in an unreasonably expensive area, provided that there is suitable and cheaper alternative accommodation available. Reductions on this account should not be made, however, if the applicant's personal circumstances are such that it would be unreasonable to expect him/her to move. Such circumstances include age, health, disability and special accommodation needs. If there is a registered 'fair rent' for the accommodation this will be the maximum eligible rent.

Other Reductions
Water rates (except for supplementary benefit claimants in certain circumstances).
Rent charges in respect of:

(a) sports facilities;
(b) laundering of personal items;
(c) window cleaning (except of communal areas);
(d) lighting, heating, hot water and cooking (except of communal areas, and subject to prescribed maxima* in the case of people on supplementary

benefit who have to pay a fixed charge for any of these items);

(e) business use of premises.

* NOTE: The prescribed maxima are currently (1984) as follows: heating £5.60, hot water 65p, cooking 65p, lighting 45p. Charges in excess of these amounts will not be deducted in calculating eligible rent. If the fixed charges relate to only a proportion of the facilities provided (*e.g.* 'background heating') the above figures are reduced *pro rata*.

CALCULATION OF BENEFIT

1. Supplementary Benefit Claimants

People qualifying for supplementary benefit (*see* page 38) no longer receive any allowance within that benefit for rent and rates. Instead the DHSS provides a certificate authorising local authorities to meet eligible rent and rates.

Apart from reductions in respect of non-dependent members of the household, those people entitled by certificate benefit as follows:

- Tenants of the administering authority will not have to pay rent or rates (except perhaps for residual charges).
- Owner occupiers will not have to pay rates (except perhaps for residual charges).
- Private sector tenants will receive an allowance in respect of their rent and rates.

2. Other Claimants

Anyone claiming housing benefit who does not qualify for supplementary benefit is assessed as to needs and income as follows:

(a) Needs

These are calculated in relation to the household as prescribed amounts, namely (November 1984):

single person	£45.10
couple/single parent	£66.50
single handicapped person	£50.30
couple (one handicapped) or single handicapped parent	£71.70
couple (both handicapped)	£74.15
dependent child addition	£12.85

(b) Income

Base income is taken as the applicant's (and any partner's) average gross income based on either the five weeks prior to claim (if paid weekly), or the two months prior to claim (if paid monthly). For the self-employed, net profit prior to payment of tax and National Insurance contributions is taken. Maintenance payments received and most state benefits count as income.

(c) Disregards

From the base income, deductions are allowed as follows:

Income from dependent children or non-dependants;

£18 of the claimant's earnings and £5 of his/her spouse's earnings;

attendance allowance;

mobility allowance;

£4 of any war, industrial disablement, or widow's pension, or of any charitable payments received;

maintenance payments made to former partners and any of their children not treated as dependent for the housing benefit scheme;

travel allowance and the full £40 of the MSC's away-from-home allowance received by those on TOPS or employment rehabilitation courses;

parental contributions to students in higher education (in full if assessed in respect of a student receiving a mandatory grant, otherwise up to £18.60).

(d) Assessment

Net income is calculated as base income (b) minus disregards (c) and compared with needs allowances (a). Base entitlement to housing benefit is taken at the point at which net income is equal to the needs allowance, and amounts to 60 per cent of the eligible rent and rates. This entitlement is reduced if there are any non-dependants in the household.

If the net income is above the needs allowance, the base entitlement is reduced by 29p (rent) and 9p (rates) for every £1 of the excess.

If the net income is below the needs allowance, entitlement is increased by 25p (rent) and 8p (rates) for every £1 of the deficit, except that for pensioners these amounts are increased to 50p (rent) and 20p (rates).

(e) Housing Benefit Supplement

This is a 'topping-up' allowance to compensate those who were previously better off on supplementary benefit with housing costs additions. Applicants must satisfy the basic supplementary benefit rules (*i.e.* not be in full-time employment, nor have capital of more than £2,500). The supplement is calculated as the difference between net rent/rates payable after housing benefit (calculated as at (d) above) and any income in excess of requirements calculated under the supplementary benefit rules.

3. Local Schemes

In cases dealt with under 'Other Claimants' above, authorities have discretion to enhance benefit up to 10 per cent, either generally or in particular individual circumstances. Such discretion could, for example, be used to give disabled people extra help.

In high rent areas, where the authority can show that rents are 20 per cent (council tenants) or 15 per cent (private tenants) above the national (*i.e.* England, Wales and Scotland) average, benefit can (subject to authorisation by the Secretary of State) be increased for those tenants paying rents above the thresholds. Authorities can seek authorisation for particular classes of dwelling (*e.g.* housing association schemes, sheltered housing) which have rents above the thresholds, even though the overall average rents for their area would not qualify.

HOW TO CLAIM

Supplementary benefit claimants do not need to claim, the DHSS certificate serving this purpose. Other claimants should obtain and complete a form available from their local authority.

BOOKS AND PUBLICATIONS

In addition to the general publications described at the beginning of this section, a specialist paperback book *A Guide to Housing Benefits* by Peter McGurk and Nick Raynford (Institute of Housing with SHAC, 1982, reprinted 1983), price £3.25 is available from either the Institute of Housing, 12 Upper Belgrave Street, London SW1X 8BA or SHAC (The London Housing Aid Centre), 189a Old Brompton Road, London SW5 0AR.

Housing Grants for Improvements/Repairs/ Provision of Standard Amenities

See Section 4.

Income Tax Allowances, Reliefs and Disregards

Personal Allowances
A guide to all the income tax personal allowances (Leaflet IR 22) can be obtained free from any office of HM Inspector of Taxes or from PAYE Enquiry Offices where information and help on specific problems can be obtained. Except where married couples opt for their earnings to be taxed separately (an option which is advantageous only where the joint earnings are high) a wife's income is aggregated with her husband's for income tax purposes. If the husband's income falls below the amount of his allowances (even to nil) his full allowances may nevertheless be set against the joint income of himself and his wife. If his wife works she is entitled to an 'earned income allowance' (1984/5: £2,005).

In the following notes on those allowances most likely to be of special interest to disabled people it has been assumed that married couples have *not* elected to be taxed separately, and that they are living together.

Additional Personal Allowance
The allowance for 1984/5 is £1,150. It may be available provided that:
(a) the taxpayer has a child living with him or her and is either:
　　(i) entitled to the single person's allowance as a single-parent, widow or widower; or
　　(ii) a married man whose wife is totally incapacitated by physical or mental infirmity throughout the whole of the relevant tax year; and
(b) the child is either a child of the taxpayer (including a step-child or a legally adopted child) or any other child maintained at the taxpayer's own expense.

Blind Person's Allowance
A taxpayer who is registered on the local authority's blind person's register is entitled to an allowance of £360 (1984/5). A married man may claim in respect of himself or his wife. Where both husband and wife are registered blind, the allowance is £360 each (1984/5). A registered blind person may claim the full allowance even where he or she has been registered for only part of the tax year.

NOTE: A taxpayer cannot have this relief as well as that for the services of a son or daughter.

Services of a Son or Daughter Allowance (1984/5: £55)
This allowance is available to male and female taxpayers, if, because of old age or infirmity, they have to rely on a son's or daughter's services. (A married man, however, is not entitled to the allowance unless his wife is old or infirm.) The son or daughter must be maintained by, live with and look after the taxpayer.

NOTE: A taxpayer cannot have this relief as well as the higher allowance for a housekeeper, nor as well as the allowance for a registered blind person.

Dependent Relative Allowance (1984/5: £100)
This allowance is available to a taxpayer who supports:
(a) a relative who is unable to maintain himself or herself because of old age or infirmity; *or*
(b) a mother, if she is a widow, separated or divorced, even if she is not old or infirm.
Where the taxpayer is a married man, he may claim under the above headings in respect of his own *or his wife's* relative or mother. Where the taxpayer is a single woman or a married woman living apart from her husband, she may claim a special rate of allowance (1984/5: £145). If the cost of maintaining the relative is less than £75 the allowance will be

reduced. If two taxpayers share the cost of maintaining the relative the allowance is shared. If the relative's income exceeds the basic national insurance retirement pension for a single person, the allowance is reduced by the amount of the excess. (Voluntary contributions and supplementary benefits do not count as income.)

Housekeeper Allowance (1984/5: £100)
This allowance does not depend on disability. A widow or a widower is entitled to it, if he or she has someone (male or female) living in the home as a housekeeper. If the housekeeper is a relative, the claimant must prove that no one else is claiming an allowance. No allowance is due if the relative acting as housekeeper is a married man who is claiming the married man's allowance. If the housekeeper is not a relative, the claimant must be his or her employer.

NOTE: A taxpayer cannot have this relief as well as the additional personal allowance for children, nor in addition to the allowance for a son's or daughter's services.

One-Parent Families
Leaflet IR 29 gives details of the special tax position of lone parents.

Pensioners
Leaflet IR 4 *Income Tax and Pensioners* answers many of the questions pensioners ask about their income tax. It gives first some general explanation on matters which often cause misunderstandings. It goes on to describe some of the tax allowances which may be claimed and the way in which National Insurance pensions and other pensions are taxed. Finally it deals with the taxation of other kinds of income.

Widows
Leaflet IR 23 *Income Tax and Widows* explains how income tax affects widows, especially those recently bereaved.

Tax Relief for Expenses Incurred by Self-employed People
In calculating the profits of a trade, profession or vocation which fall to be taxed under Schedule D, the extent to which expenses may be deducted is governed by Section 130 of the Income and Corporation Taxes Act 1970 (as amended). The rules are of great complexity, and in practice each case is judged on its merits, but the underlying principle is to limit relief to expenses 'wholly and exclusively' for the purposes of the trade. In general, an expense whose purpose is to overcome a physical disability of the trader does not meet this condition. However, individual circumstances may sometimes produce a different result. For example, a shopkeeper who was fit might be able to cope single-handed with the number of customers patronising his shop. If some disability reduced his mobility, he might find it necessary to engage an assistant to do some of the work. The direct and exclusive purposes of paying wages to the assistant would then be a trade purpose, even though in the absence of the disability the necessity would not have arisen.

A similar distinction is to be found in the case of medical expenses. If a trader has to have medical attention, its cost is not exclusively for the purposes of his trade and is not allowable as tax relief. But if he has to engage a *locum tenens* to run the business during his absence owing to illness, the fee payable to the *locum* is allowable as being exclusively for the purposes of the trade.

Relief for Expenses Incurred by Employees
To qualify for this relief, the expenses must be incurred 'wholly, exclusively and necessarily' in the performance of the duties of the employment. Expenses incurred in order to put a person in a position to do his job do not, unfortunately, qualify for a tax allowance; neither do expenses arising from his personal circumstances as distinct from those which are inherent in his duties. On these criteria (which have been upheld by the courts in a number of cases) expenditure arising from a person's disability is not within the admissible category and cannot, therefore, be allowed.

Early Retirement Through Disability
The Inland Revenue has issued a Statement of Practice that payments on retirement made on account of injury or disability are not chargeable to tax whether the cause of the disability was a sudden affliction or a gradual decline in physical or mental ability caused by chronic illness.

Benefits, Grants and Allowances
The following benefits count as taxable income:
  industrial death benefits in the form of pensions and allowances paid to a widow or parents of the deceased person;
  invalid care allowance;
  retirement pension;
  statutory sick pay;
  unemployment benefit;
  widow's National Insurance benefits, *viz.* widow's allowance and supplementary allowance, widowed mother's allowance, widow's pension and widow's basic pension.

Supplementary benefit paid to unemployed people is also normally taxable. But if you are in one of the following groups you do not have to make yourself available for work in order to get supplementary benefit, and the supplementary benefit is not taxable:
a man aged 65 and over;
a woman aged 60 or over;
a single parent with a child aged under 16;
a man aged 60 or over who is entitled to the long-term scale rate of supplementary benefit;
someone who has to stay at home to look after a severely disabled person.
The following benefits do *not* count as taxable income:
attendance allowance;
child benefit;
child dependency additions paid with taxable benefits;
child's special allowance;
Christmas bonuses paid with National Insurance pensions or allowances;
death grant;
disablement benefit and special allowances;
family income supplement;
guardian's allowance;
housing benefit;
industrial death benefits in the form of lump-sum gratuities paid to the dependants of deceased people;
invalidity benefit (but this may become taxable later);
maternity benefit and allowance;
mobility allowance;
non-contributory invalidity pension;
private car allowance;
sickness benefit (but this may become taxable later);
war pensioners' mobility supplement.

Industrial Injuries and Diseases: Disablement Benefit

DHSS Leaflets NI 2 (Prescribed Industrial Diseases), NI 3 (Pneumoconiosis and Byssinosis), NI 6 (Industrial Injury Disablement Benefit and Increases), NI 207 (Occupational Deafness), NI 237 (Occupational Asthma).

GENERAL DESCRIPTION

Benefit in respect of absence from work through incapacity is now normally covered by the schemes for statutory sick pay (*see* page 37) or sickness/invalidity benefit (*see* pages 26 and 35). Where incapacity arises from an industrial accident or a prescribed disease (*see* leaflets NI 2 and NI 3) you

may be awarded benefit even if you have not paid National Insurance contributions.

Disablement benefit is a separate grant available if you are still incapacitated as a result of an industrial accident or prescribed disease after a period of 15 weeks (90 days, excluding Sundays) from the date of your accident or the onset of the disease. (If this date was before 5 April 1983 different rules apply; ask your DHSS office for further information.) Disablement benefit is paid in addition to any sickness/invalidity benefit you may be getting, or whether or not you have been able to return to work. It may take the form of a weekly pension or a lump-sum grant depending on the degree to which you have suffered a loss of physical or mental faculty causing impairment of your power to enjoy a normal life (this can include disfigurement). The loss of faculty is assessed by comparing your condition as a result of the accident or disease with the condition of a normal healthy person of the same age and sex. The assessment is expressed as a percentage, up to a maximum of 100 per cent. No benefit is payable where the loss of faculty is assessed at less than 1 per cent.

In addition to the basic disablement benefit, there may be an entitlement to one or more of the following increases:
Special hardship allowance if you are unable to return to your regular job or to do work of an equivalent standard because of the injury or disease. The allowance and your disablement pension cannot total more than the adult 100 per cent disablement pension.
Hospital treatment allowance if your disablement is assessed at less than 100 per cent and you are receiving treatment as an in-patient in hospital. The allowance raises benefit to the 100 per cent rate.
Unemployability supplement if you are likely to be permanently unable to work or unable to earn more than a limited prescribed amount (£1,170 in November 1983) in a year. You cannot get special hardship allowance; unemployment, sickness, invalidity or injury benefit; non-contributory invalidity pension; retirement or widow's pension at the same time as you get the supplement.
Constant attendance allowance if the disease or injury has caused disablement so serious that you receive the 100 per cent rate of disablement benefit and need constant care and attention, whether or not the attendance is given by a relative and whether or not it is given on a paid basis.
Exceptionally severe disablement allowance if your disablement resulting from the injury or disease is exceptionally severe and you are already entitled to the constant attendance allowance at a rate above the

normal maximum, where the need for attendance is likely to be permanent. The benefits for injuries arising from industrial accidents apply only where the accident occurred on or after 5 July 1948 and arose out of and in the course of the employee's work, and only to persons who were covered for industrial injuries benefits at the time of the accident (most people who work for an employer for wages or salary are so covered, but members of the forces are not).

There are similar conditions for benefits in respect of the prescribed diseases. Normally, it must be established that the claimant in fact suffers from a prescribed disease and has been employed in the relevant prescribed occupation after 4 July 1948; *e.g.* sufferers from cadmium poisoning must have worked in an occupation involving exposure to cadmium fumes.

In the case of occupational deafness, benefit is payable for deafness resulting from noise at work. Claimants must have been employed for a total of not less than ten years in one or more of a number of prescribed occupations, and must be suffering from substantial permanent hearing loss as legally defined. Disablement benefit and increases do not count as income for income tax purposes.

WEEKLY RATES

(November 1984)
DHSS Leaflet NI 196.

Disablement benefit (100 per cent
assessment)   £58.40
(lower assessments are roughly pro-rata,
claimants under the age of 18 get roughly
61 per cent of the adult rate)
Increases:
    special hardship allowance   £23.36
                                         (maximum)

    hospital treatment allowance – as
    required to raise benefit to 100 per
    cent
    unemployability supplement   £34.25
    (increases for dependants can also be
    claimed and will be the same as those
    payable with invalidity pensions)
    constant attendance allowance   £23.40
                                 (normal maximum)
    exceptionally severe disablement
    allowance   £23.90
    (payable with constant attendance
    allowance up to a joint maximum of
    £46.80)

NOTE: If the disablement is assessed at less than 20 per cent, benefit is a gratuity which will normally be paid as a lump-sum.

If the assessment is 20 per cent or more, benefit is always paid as a weekly pension.

HOW TO CLAIM

Use form BI 100A for accidents, BI 100(Pn) for pneumoconiosis and byssinosis, BI 100(OD) for occupational deafness, BI 100(OA) for occupational asthma and BI 100B for other prescribed diseases. Forms are obtainable from and should be returned to your local DHSS office.

EMPLOYMENT BEFORE 5 JULY 1948

If your disablement is the result of an accident or disease due to your employment before 5 July 1948, you are not entitled to disablement benefit. You may, however, qualify for an allowance under either the Workmen's Compensation Supplementation Scheme (*see* DHSS leaflet WS 1) or the Pneumoconiosis, Byssinosis and Miscellaneous Diseases Benefit Scheme (*see* DHSS leaflet PN 1).

LOSS OF LIFE

If the accident or disease causes death, a widow or other dependants may be entitled to industrial death benefit (*see* DHSS leaflet NI 10).

Invalid Care Allowance

DHSS Leaflet NI 212.

GENERAL DESCRIPTION

The only state benefit specifically for carers, but a miserable, constrained one. It is available to a minority of people (in 1982, only 7,600) under pension age (60 for women, 65 for men) who are unable to work because they have to stay at home to look after a disabled person. In order for the carer to qualify for invalid care allowance, the person being cared for must be receiving, and therefore have satisfied the stringent qualification rules of, either attendance allowance (at either the higher or lower rate) or constant attendance allowance (at the maximum rate). As if this were not restrictive enough, however, the detailed benefit rules overtly discriminate against married and cohabiting women (estimated to number 110,000, *i.e.* the majority of carers) on the dubious, ill-founded, old-fashioned premise that they could not be expected ordinarily to be in paid employment, but are financially dependent on men. The Equal Opportunities Commission has commented: 'If ... the ICA is regarded not simply as a substitute for lost earnings but as a recompense for the service performed by carers, the cost of which would otherwise fall on the state, then there can be no argument for excluding anyone at all.'

CONDITIONS

You must:

(a) be spending at least 35 hours a week caring for a disabled person as described above. (The constant attendance allowance can be one that is paid in association with any one of the following benefits: war pension, industrial disablement pension, workmen's compensation, an allowance under the Pneumoconiosis, Byssinosis and Miscellaneous Diseases Benefit Scheme);

(b) be aged between 16 and 60 (women) or 16 and 65 (men);

(c) not be earning (nor expecting to earn) more than £12 a week (as to what counts/does not count as earnings see leaflet NI 212);

(d) not be attending a full-time course of education;

(e) be resident in the United Kingdom, and have been resident here for 26 weeks out of the 52 preceding your claim.

As a woman, you cannot get the allowance if you:

(a) are married and living with your husband; or

(b) are separated from your husband, but receiving maintenance of at least the amount of the current rate of invalid care allowance (see below); or

(c) live with a man as his wife.

WEEKLY RATES

(November 1984)
DHSS Leaflet NI 196.

As a substitute for lost income, the rates are absurdly low. The basic rate is £21.50 a week. In addition, £12.85 a week may be payable for a wife or housekeeper, and £7.65 per week for each dependent child of the family. There are, however, conditions attaching to payments for dependants and the additions may be disallowed or reduced (see leaflet NI 212 for details).

HOW TO CLAIM

Complete form DS 700 which is attached to leaflet NI 212 and send it to the Controller, DHSS, Invalid Care Allowance Unit, Central Office, Norcross, Blackpool FY5 3TA (free s.a.e. available at your local DHSS office). The decision is notified in writing with advice as to your right of appeal and necessary action. Claims can be backdated, but not normally by more than three months.

RELATIONSHIP TO OTHER BENEFITS

Even if you qualify under the above rules, you cannot get invalid care allowance if you are already in receipt of the same amount or more from one of the following benefits for yourself:

(a) sickness or invalidity benefit;

(b) non-contributory invalidity pension;

(c) unemployment benefit;

(d) unemployability supplement (paid with an industrial disablement or war pension);

(e) training allowance or training grant paid out of government funds (including payments from the Manpower Services Commission);

(f) industrial injury benefit;

(g) maternity allowance;

(h) widow's benefit (including industrial or war widow's pension), but see under heading *National Insurance Credits* below;

(i) retirement pension.

If the amount received from the above benefits is less than the invalid care allowance, the difference may be claimed.

Anyone in receipt of supplementary benefit who qualifies can claim the invalid care allowance, but the allowance if granted will be deducted from supplementary benefit. If the amount of invalid care allowance exceeds the supplementary benefit it is clearly better to claim the former, but even where the invalid care allowance is the same or slightly less than supplementary benefit, it may be preferred, because it is non-means-tested and also gives credits for National Insurance contributions.

Neither the disabled person's attendance allowance, mobility allowance nor any other benefit received by the person being cared for is affected by payment of invalid care allowance.

NATIONAL INSURANCE CREDITS

Class 1 National Insurance contributions will normally be credited to you for each week you receive invalid care allowance, but to get contribution-related benefits you will need to have paid contributions as well. If necessary, this can be achieved by paying voluntary contributions (see DHSS leaflet NI 42). If you are receiving widow's benefit, it will normally exceed the rate of invalid care allowance, so that you cannot be paid invalid care allowance as well. However, you can *claim* ICA solely to get National Insurance credits.

Invalidity Benefit

DHSS Leaflet NI 16A.

GENERAL DESCRIPTION

This benefit depends, like sickness benefit, on your National Insurance contribution record (for Non-Contributory Invalidity Pension see page 31). It consists of (a) invalidity pension and (b) invalidity allowance (not to be confused with Invalid Care Allowance). It does not, at the time of writing (1984), count as income for income tax purposes, but it is planned to tax it at a future date to be announced.

The rules are difficult to understand, not least the strange official definition of a 'period of interruption of employment', which is not what it appears to be, but a period in which only certain of those days when you are not working count. Periods when you are claiming unemployment, sickness or invalidity benefit count, but days when you get statutory sick pay do not. Any qualifying 'periods of interruption of employment' which are not more than 8 weeks apart (including any when you were not paid benefit because you did not have enough contributions) are treated as 'linked', *i.e.* treated as one claim.

(a) *Invalidity Pension* replaces sickness benefit when you have been incapable of work for 28 weeks (168 days excluding Sundays, but including the three 'waiting days' at the start of your incapacity – *see* Sickness Benefit, page 35). This period is reduced to 20 weeks (120 days excluding Sundays, but including 'waiting days') if you have been due your full entitlement to statutory sick pay (*i.e.* eight weeks in one tax year or in a period of incapacity spanning two tax years), *and* your claim to sickness benefit followed on straight after your statutory sick pay ran out or is 'linked' with your last spell of statutory sick pay.

The linking rules are quite complex. Basically, spells of incapacity for work covered by sickness benefit can be linked (*i.e.* treated as a single period) if they are not separated from each other (or from an intervening period of unemployment) by more than eight weeks (*see* page 36). Periods covered by statutory sick pay can also be linked if they are not more than 14 calendar days apart (*see* page 37). Statutory sick pay periods, as we have sought to explain, do not count as a 'period of interruption of employment'. However, for the purpose of the 168 (or 120) day rule, a spell of statutory sick pay can be linked with a spell of sickness benefit if not separated by more than eight weeks.

Invalidity pension is paid at a standard rate for women under 60 and men under 65 with increases for dependants. If, however, you have become entitled to invalidity benefit since 6 April 1979, you may be entitled to an addition based on the earnings-related (Class 1) National Insurance contributions you paid as an employed person from 6 April 1978 (for details of how this is calculated *see* DHSS leaflet NI 16A, page 5).

(b) *Invalidity Allowance* is payable in addition to invalidity pension if you are under 55 (women) or 60 (men) on the first day you became incapable of work in a 'period of interruption of employment'. For this purpose, days for which you were covered by statutory sick pay are excluded from the 'period of interruption of employment'.

Widows and Widowers

There are special provisions which make it possible for widows and widowers who are incapable of work to qualify for invalidity benefit, even though they may not have been qualified for sickness benefit. As a widow, you may qualify for invalidity pension if your widow's allowance or widowed mother's allowance ended since 6 April 1979 and at this time you were not capable of work and not entitled to a widow's pension (or entitled only at a reduced rate, being under 50 when your husband died or when your widowed mother's allowance ended). If you remain, or have already been, incapable of work for 168 (or 120) days (in the circumstances described above), you may qualify for an invalidity pension. *See* DHSS leaflet 16A, page 3 as to the rate of payment. Invalidity allowance will also be payable to you as a widow according to your age when you became incapable of work. If as a widow you qualify for invalidity benefit under these provisions, it can be paid for any spell of incapacity in that 'period of interruption of employment', until you retire or reach the age of 65. It will then be replaced by a retirement pension of at least the same amount.

As a widower, you may qualify for invalidity pension if your wife died since 6 April 1979 and you were incapable of work at the time of her death or became so within 13 weeks, and if your incapacity lasts for 168 (or 120) days. Again, short periods of incapacity can be linked as described above. The invalidity pension will be based on either your own contribution record or that of your late wife, whichever is the more favourable to you. Invalidity allowance will also be payable to you as a widower if you were under 60 when you became incapable of work. If as a widower you qualify for invalidity benefit under these provisions, it can be paid for as long as your incapacity in that 'period of interruption of employment' lasts, until you retire or reach the age of 70. It will then be replaced by a retirement pension of at least the same amount.

Women over 60 and men over 65

If you do not retire at 60 (women) or 65 (men) or if you cancel your retirement before you reach 65 (women) or 70 (men), you can get invalidity pension for periods when you are incapable of work up to age 65 (women) or 70 (men) if, when you do retire, you will receive a retirement pension either on your own contributions, or under the widows'/widowers' arrangements described above. *But* any day for which you are paid invalidity pension will not count towards any extra pension you may get for deferring your retirement. (*See* DHSS leaflet NI 16 A, pages 4/5 as to rates of payment.)

You cannot get invalidity pension after your final retirement, nor after age 65 (women) or 70 (men). However, your retirement pension will be permanently increased by the amount of any invalidity allowance to which you have been entitled if:

(a) you are entitled to a retirement pension based on your own contributions; or

(b) your retirement pension is one which has replaced entitlement to invalidity pension under the special widows'/widowers' arrangements described above; and

(c) you were entitled to invalidity allowance on a day which is not more than eight weeks before your 60th birthday (women) or 65th birthday (men).

MEDICAL AND OTHER CONDITIONS

These are the same as for sickness benefit (*see* page 35).

WEEKLY RATES

(November 1984)
DHSS Leaflet NI 196.

Invalidity pension	£34.25

Invalidity allowance payable in addition for incapacity beginning before:

age 40	£7.50
age 50	£4.80
age 55 (women) or 60 (men)	£2.40

For increases in respect of dependants, *see* DHSS leaflet 196, in conjunction with leaflet NI 16A, pages 6 to 8.

HOW TO CLAIM

If you become entitled to invalidity benefit during a period of sickness it will be awarded to you automatically without further claim. If, however, you qualify for invalidity benefit at the start of a separate but 'linked' period of sickness, you can claim in the same way as for sickness benefit. Keep sending sick notes from your doctor promptly to your DHSS office, if necessary via your employer (*see*

sickness benefit, page 36 for advice as to sick notes). If you think you might qualify under the special provisions for widows and widowers described above, write to your DHSS office without delay, enclosing a sick note.

RELATIONSHIP TO OTHER BENEFITS

As for sickness benefit (*see* page 36).

PAYMENT WHILE IN HOSPITAL

As for sickness benefit (*see* page 36).

NATIONAL INSURANCE CREDITS

While you are receiving invalidity benefit, you will normally be credited with a contribution for each complete week of incapacity for work. However, a married woman who retains the right to pay reduced contributions cannot be so credited. Contributions credited during periods of incapacity normally count towards satisfying the contribution conditions for basic benefits, but there are some conditions as to their use for sickness benefit (leaflet NI 16), unemployment benefit (leaflet NI 12), or maternity allowance (leaflet NI 17A).

From 6 April 1983, there are special credit provisions for people aged 60 or over, or who will reach 60 in the current tax year (6 April to the following 5 April). For details *see* DHSS amendment *Special provisions for people approaching, or over, age 60.*

WORK WHILE RECEIVING BENEFIT

This may be permitted in certain limited circumstances (*see* Therapeutic Earnings Rule, page 43).

Mobility Allowance

DHSS Leaflets 211 and 225.

GENERAL DESCRIPTION

This non-means-tested cash benefit, introduced on 1 January 1976, can now be claimed by severely disabled people (male or female), irrespective of whether they drive, aged from 5 to 64 inclusive (it may not be too late to claim if you: (a) have not yet reached your 66th birthday and (b) missed the opportunity to claim before you reached 65, but you will have to establish that you satisfied the qualifying conditions before you reached age 65). If the allowance is awarded, it will be for a stated period, at most until you are 75. From 24 November 1984 the weekly rate of payment is £20. This is paid in addition to other social security benefits and is not subject to income tax.

There are indications that not everyone entitled to mobility allowance is claiming it, and this seems particularly true of women in the 60–65 age group. On 31 December 1981, only 25,800 women aged 60 or more were in receipt of the allowance, compared with 39,900 men in the same age range.

It also seems likely that there are many 'borderline' situations in which people are either reluctant to claim or fail to present a fully accurate picture of their condition when they do. Although the criteria are quite strict, it is apparent to us that some people, by their sheer determination to cope with a disability, present a more favourable impression of their difficulties than is justified by the facts. Certainly the view of the doctor carrying out the first examination can be wrong. *A high percentage of applicants* who are turned down are awarded the allowance after a Medical Board or Appeal Tribunal.

RESIDENCE CONDITION

You must be living in the United Kingdom, and must have been living there for at least 12 months in the 18 months preceding the date of claim.

MEDICAL CONDITIONS

1. You must be suffering from physical disablement such that you are either unable to walk or virtually unable to do so. This requirement will be regarded as satisfied if your physical condition *as a whole* (without special factors peculiar to where you live or work or the nature of your work) is such that:
    (a) you are unable to walk; or
    (b) your ability to walk out of doors is so limited, as regards the distance over which or the speed at which or the length of time for which or the manner in which you can make progress on foot without severe discomfort, that you are virtually unable to walk; or
    (c) the exertion required to walk would constitute a danger to your life or would be likely to lead to a serious deterioration in your health.
    If, however, the habitual use of a suitable artificial aid or prosthesis overcomes or would overcome your inability or virtual inability to walk, then you may not qualify.
2. You must be likely to remain unable or virtually unable to walk for at least a year.
3. You must be able to make use of the allowance, *i.e.* you must be able to be moved without danger to your life and must be capable of appreciating your surroundings.

The Mobility Allowance Regulations were amended in 1979 to clarify the entitlement of people who, although apparently physically able to walk, cannot or do not do so to any significant extent because of a mental handicap which results from their physical condition. More recently, the allowance was awarded, on appeal, to a blind man whose hearing and sense of balance are severely impaired as a result of a head injury sustained in an accident. It was held that 'ability to walk' meant to 'move effectively and in an intended direction on one's feet' and this view was subsequently upheld by Social Security Commissioner, Mr D. Reith, who said that although 'the claimant's legs are capable of making the movements required in the activity of walking, he is in fact unable to walk to any place to which he desires to go without help and guidance from another person'.

Early in 1983, a further tribunal ruled that 'the need for assistance in walking (guidance, supervision or support) is a facet of the manner in which a person can make progress on foot and is to be taken into account by the medical authorities in conjunction with any other matters in determining whether ... the person concerned is virtually unable to walk'. The Tribunal accepted a submission that 'it is proper to take account of the fact that a major purpose of walking is to get to a designated place. It follows that if a person can be caused to move himself (/herself) to a designated place only with the benefit of guidance and supervision and possibly after much cajoling, the point may be reached at which he (/she) may be found to be virtually unable to walk. There may be other factors such as blindness and deafness ... to be taken into account in addition.'

Practice suggests that claims from people who are non or scarcely ambulant other than in a straightforward way will continue to be resisted, and interpretation of 'special cases' is far from settled or agreed, but we dare to hope that the law will be applied in a generous spirit to those who have genuine mobility problems, whether they arise from physical impairments, mental inhibitions or lack of orientation.

HOW TO CLAIM

The Mobility Allowance leaflet NI 211, with the claim form attached, is available from DHSS offices and appliance centres or from the DHSS Mobility Allowance Unit at North Fylde Central Office, Blackpool FY5 3TA. Completed forms should be sent to this address (but *see* below for special arrangements applicable to beneficiaries under the pre-1976 vehicle scheme). If a medical examination is necessary (and it usually is) before the claim is decided, it will be arranged as near to your home as possible.

Travelling and subsistence expenses can be claimed. Alternatively, if you are unable to travel, a home visit can be made. There is a right of appeal in the event of your claim being disallowed. Full details of how and to whom an appeal should be made will be sent with the notification of the decision not to grant the allowance.

The Mobility Allowance Regulations were amended on 29 August 1983 to allow a right of appeal against the period of an award if it is for less than the maximum period (*i.e.* ceasing before you reach the age of 75). This will be particularly important where the period of an award is less than $4\frac{1}{2}$ years and therefore not long enough to enable the beneficiary to obtain a car through the Motability hire purchase or leasing schemes. Your appeal must, however, be made within 28 days unless there is 'good cause' for the delay.

RELATIONSHIP TO OTHER BENEFITS

Mobility allowance is generally disregarded in assessing income for supplementary benefit, family income supplement, rent and rate rebates and free school meals and milk. Receipt of the allowance is not affected by 'travel to work' assistance under the Employment Service Division Scheme. It is, in short, something extra which can go some way towards restoring personal mobility. No check is made on how the allowance is spent unless the beneficiary is a child. Then the person who looks after the money has to sign an undertaking to apply the allowance for the benefit of the disabled child.

The allowance can also confer other financial advantages; some suppliers of goods and services accept entitlement to mobility allowance as the basis for offering special discounts and other concessionary terms.

PAYMENT WHILE IN HOSPITAL OR RESIDENTIAL CARE

Mobility allowance continues to be paid to eligible disabled people who enter hospital or residential accommodation whatever the length of stay. The allowance is not subject to hospital down-rating but remains in payment at the full rate. Many disabled people are able to manage their own affairs, although on entry to hospital or residential care some of them may be incapable of actually collecting the money themselves and need someone else known as a 'signing agent' to collect the allowance on their behalf. The 'signing agent' would, however, have no power or responsibility for the spending of that money.

Others may not be able to manage their own affairs and there may already be alternative arrangements in existence for the management of their benefit money. If not, then someone should be appointed to receive and manage the mobility allowance payments on the beneficiary's behalf to ensure that the disabled person derives the maximum benefit and enjoyment from his/her allowance, rather than the money being allowed simply to accumulate – unless, of course, the saving is for a definite purpose.

Where a relative or friend is willing to act as such an appointee, an application for an appointeeship should be made to the DHSS Mobility Allowance Unit at Norcross, Blackpool. Alternatively, a receiver, with power to receive benefit, can be appointed by the Court of Protection. Enquiries about this arrangement should be addressed to the Chief Clerk, The Court of Protection, Staffordshire House, Store Street, London WC1E 7BP (Tel: 01-636 6877).

If no one can be found who is willing to act, then the Health Authority or person in charge of the residential accommodation will probably be asked to become the person appointed. There have, in the past, been some problems arising from this situation, mobility allowance money building up without benefit to the entitled disabled people. The Department of Health and Social Security advise us that, following responses to a consultative document, the Department is considering the revision of Guidance to Health Authorities on Patients'/Residents' Money (HM (71)90) which is expected to cover the spending of mobility allowance for the benefit of the disabled people concerned (among many other aspects).

BENEFICIARIES UNDER EARLIER SCHEMES

Certain disabled drivers, who were beneficiaries under the pre-1976 vehicle scheme, have a right to switch to mobility allowance, regardless of their age and without any automatic cut-off at age 75.

This special option applies to:
(a) those who currently have a car, 'trike' or private car allowance provided under the pre-1976 vehicle scheme (*i.e.* in response to an application made up to 1 January 1976);
(b) those who had a provided car, 'trike' or private car allowance on 1 January 1976 and, although they do not have one now, remain medically eligible;
(c) those who were beneficiaries under the invalid vehicle scheme both before and after 1 January 1976 who have already switched to mobility allowance under the normal arrangements.

The main medical conditions for the mobility allowance will be deemed to be satisfied and medical examinations will not normally be required. The allowance will normally be payable throughout the rest of the person's lifetime. It will cease only if his or her condition improves to such an extent that he or she no longer meets the old vehicle scheme medical conditions, or if the condition deteriorates to the extent that he or she is unable to benefit from outdoor mobility.

Details and application form are contained in DHSS leaflet NI 225 (*not* NI 211) available as follows:

England and Wales: DHSS, Disablement Services, Warbreck Hill Road, Blackpool FY2 0UZ.

Scotland: Scottish Home & Health Department, St Andrews House, Edinburgh EH1 3DE.

Northern Ireland: DHSS, Castle Grounds, Stormont, Belfast BT4 3SG.

A special provision (The Mobility Allowance (Amendment) Regulations 1981) allows certain disabled people to keep their 'trikes' for a period not usually exceeding six months while first claiming mobility allowance. This overlap applies to people who need mobility allowance to buy a car and need to learn to drive. It is intended to enable anyone in this position to retain independent mobility during the period of acquiring and gaining proof of competence in driving an ordinary car.

A small number of people received 'trikes' in response to applications made after 1 January 1976. Though they can retain the vehicle after retirement age, they do not enjoy the special option described above and do not have reserved rights to further mobility help when their vehicles wear out. Thus by retaining the vehicle after the age of 64 they would find themselves debarred from applying for mobility allowance under the ordinary conditions because of the age qualification. The mobility allowance scheme does not affect the continued issue of wheelchairs nor does the free issue of wheelchairs affect the allowance.

TEMPORARY MOBILITY ALLOWANCE

Both war pensioners and beneficiaries under the pre-1976 vehicle scheme may be able to get mobility allowance on a temporary basis during any period when they lose the use of a DHSS vehicle and a replacement cannot be immediately provided. This includes periods when the vehicle is off the road for repairs, and unavoidable delay in its return can be foreseen. The allowance can be paid in addition to 'fares to work'. If you find yourself immobilised and your local Approved Repairer cannot help, you should get in touch at once with your local Appliance Centre, who should advise you about what can be done to assist you.

WAR PENSIONERS

A special allowance, War Pensioners' Mobility Supplement (*see* page 45) is available to disabled war pensioners.

Non-Contributory Invalidity Pension

DHSS Leaflet NI 210.

GENERAL DESCRIPTION

This is a non-means-tested benefit for men and single or unsupported women of working age who meet a residence qualification and have been incapable of work for at least 28 consecutive weeks immediately before the date for which they claim, but whose National Insurance contributions are insufficient for them to qualify for sickness or invalidity benefit. Entitlement begins at the age of 16, but those under 19 years and still at school or college are excluded unless they are having education or training especially arranged for them as disabled or handicapped people (*e.g.* at special schools).

You cannot qualify if you are a woman:

(a) living with your husband;
(b) separated from your husband but receiving maintenance from him; or which is the same or more than the weekly rate of NCIP; or
(c) living with a man as his wife.

But *see* next entry, Non-contributory invalidity pension for married women. NCIP does not count as income for income tax purposes.

CONDITIONS

On the first occasion of claim, you must have been continuously incapable of work for the 28 weeks immediately before the date from which you claim. During those 28 weeks you must have lived in the United Kingdom, but if you have been abroad during those weeks for not more than 28 days you will still satisfy this rule. If you claim on a subsequent occasion and were entitled to NCIP less than eight weeks ago, you can claim without having to wait another 28 weeks.

You must be at least 16, but if you are still at school or college full-time you cannot get NCIP until age 19, unless you are having education or training especially arranged for you as a disabled person.

You must be under 60 (women) or 65 (men) when you qualify for NCIP for the first time. You must live in the United Kingdom and have been present in the United Kingdom for at least 26 weeks in the 12 months before payment starts, and you must also have lived in the United Kingdom for a total of at least 10 years during the past 20 years (or, if you are under 20, for a total of 10 years since birth).

31

WEEKLY RATES

(November 1984)
DHSS Leaflet NI 196.

Man or single woman	£21.50
Increase for wife or adult dependant	£12.85
Increase for each child	£7.65

HOW TO CLAIM

Complete form BF 400 which is attached to leaflet NI 210 and send it to your local DHSS office (post-free addressed envelopes can be obtained from post offices).

RELATIONSHIP TO OTHER BENEFITS

If you are receiving any of the following benefits – *viz.* sickness benefit, invalidity benefit, invalid care allowance, injury benefit, unemployability supplement, maternity allowance, widow's benefit (including industrial or war widow's), training allowance – the amount of any such benefit will be deducted from the NCIP and may, of course, offset it altogether.

If the claimant is getting supplementary benefit (or someone else is getting it for him or her) it will be reduced if NCIP is granted. There are nevertheless, advantages in drawing NCIP in the shape of more generous earnings rules and the crediting of National Insurance contributions.

NATIONAL INSURANCE CREDITS

While you are receiving NCIP you will be credited with Class 1 contributions. But credited contributions can only help you to get benefits like sickness, unemployment or invalidity benefit if you have *paid* contributions as well.

BOOKS AND PUBLICATIONS

NCIP, 16–19 Years and 'Normal Schooling', is a leaflet produced by the Disability Alliance which looks at the problems which commonly arise over the interpretation of the rule which excludes young people between the ages of 16 and 19 still at school or college, unless they 'are having education or training especially arranged for disabled or handicapped people'.

NOTE: In November 1984, this allowance was replaced by the severe disablement allowance. Existing NCIP beneficiaries will qualify, but new applicants over the age of 20 will be excluded from benefit unless they are assessed as being 80 per cent or more disabled. *See* page 34.

Non-Contributory Invalidity Pension for Married Women
DHSS Leaflet NI 214.

GENERAL DESCRIPTION

Commonly known as HNCIP (Housewives' NCIP). No benefit has evoked greater or more sustained controversy, a fact which is hardly surprising given that the rules are blatantly discriminatory. The pension is specifically for the following categories of women, excluded from the main NCIP:
(a) married and living with husband; or
(b) married and living apart from husband who is paying maintenance to his wife (he must be contributing at least as much as the weekly rate of NCIP); or
(c) living with a man as his wife.
The qualifications follow those of NCIP, with one highly objectionable exception: whereas the test for NCIP is continuous incapacity for work for at least 28 weeks, the rule for HNCIP requires that a woman within any of the above categories must be (for the same period):
(a) continuously incapable of paid work; *and*
(b) continuously incapable of normal household duties.
The term 'household duties' has proved notoriously difficult to define and the application form goes into intrusive detail in ascertaining to what extent you can carry out a range of tasks: moreover, a medical examination is normally required to determine incapacity for the said household duties and the qualifying conditions are very strict, having been reinforced by amending regulations. Thus women in the above categories have to meet a condition which applies to no one else, based, it would seem, on the anachronistic assumption that a woman's place is in the home, her role not involving paid work and thus not contributing financially to the resources of the household. Thus, in this perception, there is no need for compensation unless the claimant is quite incapable of doing housework!

NOTE: In November 1984, this allowance was replaced by the severe disablement allowance. Existing HNCIP beneficiaries will qualify, but new applicants over the age of 20 will be excluded from benefit unless they are assessed as being 80 per cent or more disabled. Thus, although discrimination against married and cohabiting women will be ended, discrimination by degree of disablement will be introduced! *See* page 34 for further details.

WEEKLY RATES

DHSS Leaflet NI 196.

As for NCIP. A wife can now get an increase for her husband if his earnings are less than the short-term benefit dependency addition.

HOW TO CLAIM

Claim on form BF 450 which forms part of leaflet NI 214, and send it to your local DHSS office.

BOOKS AND PUBLICATIONS

In addition to the DHSS leaflet NI 214 and the general publications described at the beginning of this section, the following specialist books are available:

HNCIP Checklist published by and available from the Disability Alliance, price 80p including postage and packing.

Appealing about Refusal to Grant HNCIP, published by and available from The Disablement Income Group (send a foolscap s.a.e.).

After Working All These Years by Caroline Glendinning, published by and available from the Disability Alliance, price £1.10 post free: a response to the report of the National Advisory Council on the 'household duties' test.

Optical Charges: Exemption

DHSS Leaflet G 11.

You can get NHS glasses free if you are:

(a) under 16;
(b) over 16 and under 19, but still in full-time education (only standard children's frames: for adults' frames you would have to qualify on grounds of low income);
(c) in receipt of supplementary benefit or family income supplement;
(d) in receipt of free milk and vitamins and/or free prescriptions on grounds of low income;
(e) on a low income, not much above supplementary benefit level (for details *see* leaflet G 11). If you are aged 16 or over, you can claim on grounds of your own low income even if you are still at school or college.

HOW TO CLAIM EXEMPTION

Groups (a) and (b) should obtain a certificate from the head of their school, college or university department confirming that they are students there. The certificate is then given to the optician.

Groups (c) and (d) can get the necessary form from the optician.

Group (e) should obtain form F1 from the optician and send it to the local DHSS office.

NOTE: Those in group (e), even if they don't qualify for free glasses, may be entitled to help with part of the cost, especially if the charge is high. However, you cannot get help with the cost of private frames or glasses.

GLASSES COVERED

Opticians can supply you with glasses under the NHS or privately as you wish. You can have:

(a) NHS lenses in an NHS frame;
(b) NHS lenses in a suitable private frame;
(c) private lenses in a private frame.

But *not* private lenses in an NHS frame.

The range of NHS frames available is illustrated in DHSS leaflet G 11. You can have NHS lenses fitted to:

(a) a new frame from this range;
(b) a new private frame if it is the right shape and is otherwise suitable for the lenses;
(c) a frame you already have if it is suitable for the lenses and in good condition.

If you qualify for exemption or help with costs, it will apply to:

(a) standard NHS lenses;
(b) any special lenses or frames prescribed by the hospital eye service;
(c) frame No. 524 from the NHS range.

If you have any of the other NHS frames by choice, you can get help only up to the charge for frame No. 524. If children have NHS lenses in a private frame, both the lenses and the frame have to be paid for.

WAR PENSIONERS

You may, of course, qualify for exemption under the normal rules. If not, you will have to pay the basic charges for NHS glasses unless they are needed because of your war disablement, in which case you should apply to DHSS, North Fylde Central Office, Norcross, Blackpool FY5 3TA.

Prescription Charges: Exemption

DHSS Leaflet P 11.

Children under 16 and adults at or over pension age (women 60, men 65) do not have to pay prescription charges. Exemption is claimed simply by completing the back of each prescription form before going to the chemist.

The following categories of people are also exempt, but they must first obtain an *exemption certificate*, and also complete the declaration on the back of each prescription form before going to the chemist:

Those who suffer from a continuing physical disability which prevents them from leaving their home without someone's help (use form C in DHSS leaflet P 11).

War service pensioners, when the prescription is for the accepted disability (exemption certificate is issued by the War Pensions Branch of DHSS).

Those receiving supplementary benefit or family income supplement; in such cases the exemption extends to dependants. (Exemption certificates are included in the pages at the back of order books. If you don't have one, ask the chemist for a receipt form FP57 (EC57 in Scotland) when you pay. Then claim a refund as instructed on the receipt. If you are not paid by order book but need prescriptions regularly, ask your DHSS office for an exemption certificate.)

Expectant mothers (use form FW8 from your doctor, midwife or health visitor).

Mothers who have a child under 12 months old (use form A in DHSS leaflet P 11).

Those who suffer from one of the following conditions:

permanent fistula (including caecostomy, colostomy, laryngostomy, or ileostomy) requiring continuous surgical dressing or an appliance.

the following disorders for which specific substitution therapy is essential:

Addison's disease and other forms of hypoadrenalism;
diabetes insipidus and other forms of hypopituitarism;
diabetes mellitus;
hypoparathyroidism;
myasthenia gravis;
myxoedema.

Epilepsy requiring continuous anti-convulsive therapy (use form C in leaflet P 11 and ask your doctor to sign it).

Those who have an income below prescribed limits set out in leaflet P 11 (*i.e.* not much above supplementary benefit levels). If you are aged 16 or over, you can claim on grounds of your own low income even if you are still at school or college.

Normal prescription charges are currently £1.60 per item. Those who do not qualify for exemption and who need to have more than 15 items dispensed in a year (or more than five items in four months) may like to consider using a prescription 'season ticket'. These cost £24 a year (or £8.50 for four months) and cover any number of items dispensed in the period covered by the pre-payment. Leaflet FP 95 (EC 95 in Scotland) includes an application form and is available from post offices, chemists and DHSS offices.

Prescription charges do not apply to items sup-plied and personally administered by either prescribing or dispensing doctors (from 1 September 1983).

Resettlement Benefit

DHSS Leaflet NI 9.

GENERAL DESCRIPTION

This is a weekly payment to help you get back to normal life after a long stay in hospital. It is paid from money set aside by reducing your normal benefits during your second and any subsequent years in hospital. You may be able to get this benefit:

(a) provided that your personal benefit (but not supplementary benefit) was reduced to the basic prescribed amount after a year in hospital; *and*

(b) you do not go into accommodation provided by arrangement with a local authority or government department (but not including council housing or temporary accommodation if you are homeless).

Severe Disablement Allowance

GENERAL DESCRIPTION

This new social security benefit was introduced in November 1984. It replaces the Non-Contributory Invalidity Pension (*see* page 31) and the Non-Contributory Invalidity Pension for Married Women (*see* page 32).

Although all existing recipients of NCIP will be eligible for the new benefit so long as they remain incapable of work, new applicants have to satisfy more restrictive conditions. Anyone over the age of 20 is excluded from benefit unless assessed as being 80 per cent or more disabled. Married women are treated on equal terms with others, but those terms are generally less favourable. One form of discrimination has been replaced by another! And married women who have failed the household duties test or who have been unwilling to submit themselves to the indignity of it, are still not entitled to benefit unless they satisfy the condition of severe disablement.

CONDITIONS

The severe disablement allowance is payable to:

(a) those already incapable of work by the age of 20, on a simple test of that incapacity;

(b) those becoming incapable of work after that age, if they are also 80 per cent or more disabled (by reference to the measure of loss of faculty already used in the industrial injuries and war pensions schemes – *see* Note below);

(c) all existing recipients of non-contributory invalidity pension, or non-contributory invalidity pension for married women.

NOTE: The basis for assessing disability currently operated regards someone who is completely blind or completely deaf as 100 per cent disabled, someone who has had a leg amputated at the hip as 90 per cent disabled.

WEEKLY RATES

The new benefit will be in line with the present NCIP and other non-contributory maintenance benefits (currently £21.50 a week) with annual review.

Sickness Benefit

DHSS Leaflet NI 16.

GENERAL DESCRIPTION

This is a benefit which depends on the claimant's record of National Insurance contributions. It is for people who are incapable of work because of sickness or disablement. It does not count as income for income tax purposes.

Subject to adequate contributions having been paid, it is available to the following people:

Employed people who have either run out of entitlement to statutory sick pay (see page 37), or who are excluded from that scheme, or whose sickness or disability is the result of an industrial accident or a prescribed disease.

People who are self-employed, unemployed or non-employed.

The reduced rate of NI contributions paid by some married women does not entitle them to benefit. Normally, benefit is not paid for a period of incapacity which lasts less than four days (not counting Sundays); nor is it paid for the first three days in any period which does qualify. These are treated as 'waiting days'. There are, however, some exceptions:

'Waiting days' will not be attributed to you if you were due statutory sick pay at any time in the eight weeks prior to your claim to sickness benefit.

Benefit can be claimed for a period of less than four days if you cease to be entitled to statutory sick pay shortly before you are due to return to work.

Benefit may be allowed for absences of less than four days where they occur as a regular weekly pattern because you need treatment by dialysis, radiotherapy, or chemotherapy with cytotoxic drugs (this concession does not extend to statutory sick pay).

Sickness benefit is paid for only a limited period (maximum 28 weeks, i.e. 168 days excluding Sundays). Thereafter, if the incapacity continues, invalidity benefit (see page 26) is paid instead. This may be after the maximum 28 weeks, or, if you have exhausted your entitlement to eight weeks statutory sick pay and that happened eight weeks or less before your sickness benefit started, after 20 weeks.

CONTRIBUTION CONDITIONS

Cover for sickness benefit is provided only by Class 1 contributions (paid by those who work for an employer) or Class 2 contributions (paid by the self-employed). There is a lower earnings limit at which contributions become due (see leaflet NI 208; 1981/2 £27 a week, 1982/3 £29.50 a week, 1983/4 £32.50 a week; 1984/5 £34 a week) and the rate of contribution varies with your earnings.

There are two contribution conditions:

(a) that in any one tax year since 6 April 1975, Class 1 and/or Class 2 contributions have been paid which give a total of at least 25 times the contributions payable on earnings at the lower earnings limit for that year (this condition will be regarded as satisfied if you paid 26 flat-rate contributions before 6 April 1975);

(b) that in the tax year relevant to the claim (see below) Class 1 or 2 contributions have been paid or credited which give a total of at least 50 times the contributions payable on earnings at the lower earnings limit for that year. (If you have less than 50 but more than 25 times the contributions, you may be entitled to a reduced rate of benefit.)

Condition (b) may be eased for those who cannot satisfy it because they have only recently left school, college, university, youth apprenticeship or MSC training course (see leaflet NI 16, part 2, section C).

NOTE: The 'relevant tax year' (see (b) above) is the last complete tax year (6 April to the following 5 April) before the start of your 'benefit year'. Your 'benefit year' (commencing on the first Sunday in January) is the year in which the first day of your period of interruption of employment occurs. Confused? Then turn to the heading 'Linking' below for further trouble.

OTHER CONDITIONS

While you are receiving sickness benefit:
(a) you must not do anything which might stop you getting better as soon as possible;
(b) you should leave word where you can be found if you go away from the address you have given;
(c) you must not do any work unless you have asked your DHSS office whether it can be allowed (see heading 'Work while receiving benefit' below).

WEEKLY RATES

(November 1984).
DHSS Leaflet NI 196.

Beneficiary under pension age:	
Single person	£27.25
Wife or other adult dependant	£16.80
Beneficiary over pension age:	
Single person	£34.25
Wife or other adult dependant	£20.55

NOTE: The earnings-related supplement to sickness benefit ceased to be payable after 3 January 1982. Increases for dependants are payable, but are subject to detailed conditions (*see* leaflet NI 16, part 2, section D).

HOW TO CLAIM

This varies with circumstances:

If you are not entitled to statutory sick pay, make sure your employer gives you form SSP 1(E). This should be submitted to your local DHSS office *without delay*. If a doctor's certificate is not immediately available (*e.g.* because it is needed by your employer) send it later.

If you have or are about to run out of statutory sick pay, make sure your employer gives you form SSP 1(T). Send it promptly to the DHSS as advised above.

If you are self-employed, unemployed or non-employed, obtain form SC1 (from doctors' surgeries, hospitals or DHSS offices). Complete and send it to your local DHSS office promptly on the day advised by the form. If you can't get a form, simply write to indicate that you wish to claim benefit, giving as far as you can, name, address, date of birth, NI number and first date of illness. A doctor's certificate will be needed only if your sickness lasts longer than a week (they are not issued for the first week).

If you have regular weekly treatment by dialysis, radiotherapy or chemotherapy by cytoxic drugs, and this makes you incapable of work on two or three days each week, you can claim sickness benefit for those days, even if you are otherwise covered by the statutory sick pay scheme as an employee. Complete form SC1 (doctors' surgeries, hospitals or DHSS offices) to show the first day of incapacity for work and send it with a doctor's statement and a letter explaining the circumstances of your treatment to your local DHSS office. The doctor's statement should show the treatment you are receiving, on which days of the week you will be incapable of work and how long the treatment will last.

In the first three cases described above, if you continue to be incapable of work beyond the period covered by the initial claim, it will be necessary to submit doctor's certificates to cover continuing sickness. These may be 'open', *i.e.* interim certificates to cover you to a stated date when you will need to see your doctor again, or 'closed', indicating that you should be fit for work on a stated date. If you want to return to work during the currency of an open certificate, you should see your doctor first and obtain a closed certificate. If you decide to return to work before the date given on a closed certificate, you should advise your DHSS office without delay.

RELATIONSHIP TO OTHER BENEFITS

You cannot be paid sickness benefit at the same time as:

(a) any other weekly national insurance benefit (*e.g.* unemployment benefit, retirement pension, widow's benefit or maternity allowance);

(b) benefits for industrial injury;

(c) an unemployability supplement of any kind; or

(d) a training allowance from public funds (this includes an allowance under the Youth Opportunities Programme);

(e) statutory sick pay.

If you are entitled to more than one state benefit at the same time, you will normally get an amount equal to the greater, or greatest, of them (but *see* Mobility Allowance). Attendance allowance for severely disabled people, maternity grant, or basic war or industrial disablement pension or gratuity do not affect benefit.

A widow, getting a war widow's pension, or an industrial death benefit, may in some circumstances get full sickness benefit on the basis of her own Class 1 contributions paid. You cannot get sickness benefit for any period for which you are covered by the SSP scheme. But sickness benefit is not affected if you get salary, wages or occupational sick pay from your employer or benefit from a Friendly Society or Trade Union while you are sick.

If, notwithstanding sickness benefit, you don't have enough money to live on, or if payment of sickness benefit is delayed, you may be entitled to supplementary benefit (see page 38).

PAYMENT WHILE IN HOSPITAL

If you are admitted to a hospital where you receive treatment and your keep free of charge, sickness benefit is unaffected for eight weeks, but thereafter will be reduced. Increases for dependants may also be affected if they go into hospital.

LINKING

Periods for which you claim sickness or invalidity

benefit (but not statutory sick pay) which occur at intervals not more than eight weeks apart are treated as *linked*. This includes any period for which you made a claim but did not get benefit because you did not have enough contributions. This is significant in that linked claims are treated as one claim, and it is the first day of the earlier/earliest period which determines your 'benefit year'. As explained above (contribution condition (b)), this also fixes the 'relevant tax year'. Your benefit, and indeed your qualification for benefit, will be based on your National Insurance contributions during the tax year so determined.

WORK WHILE RECEIVING BENEFIT

This may be permitted in certain limited circumstances (*see* page 43).

NATIONAL INSURANCE CREDITS

While you are receiving sickness benefit, you will normally be credited with a contribution for each complete week of incapacity for work. However, a married woman who retains the right to pay reduced contributions cannot be so credited. Contributions credited during periods of incapacity normally count towards satisfying the contribution conditions for basic benefits, but they count for sickness, unemployment and maternity allowance only if special conditions are met (*see* DHSS leaflet NI 16, page 28). Since 6 April 1983, there have been special credit provisions for people aged 60 or over, or who will reach 60 in the current tax year (6 April to the following 5 April). For details *see* DHSS amendment *Special provisions for people approaching, or over, age 60*.

Statutory Sick Pay

DHSS Leaflets NI 16 and NI 244 (NI 227 for employers)

GENERAL DESCRIPTION

The arrangements for benefit when you are unable to work through sickness or physical or mental disability have changed considerably since the third edition of this Directory was published. Since 6 April 1983, most people who work for an employer and pay Class 1 National Insurance contributions (including those married women who pay reduced contributions) have received flat-rate minimum 'sick pay' direct from their employers for up to eight weeks in any tax year (employers are recompensed by the government by reduced National Insurance contributions). This is called statutory sick pay. There must, however, be at least four consecutive days (including Sunday and any holiday) of incapacity for work to qualify for SSP, and even then the first three

qualifying days (normally the first three working days) are treated as 'waiting days' for which no SSP is payable. If you have more than one qualifying period of sickness and the interval between the end of one period and the start of the next is not more than 14 calendar days, they are treated as linked, whence the attribution of 'waiting days' is limited to three in relation to the periods taken together.

Statutory sick pay is separate from any private sick pay arrangements which your employer may operate. Occupational sick pay can be used towards an employee's SSP entitlement, but SSP cannot be paid as a supplement to occupational sick pay. Thus if for a particular day you are due £7 SSP and £10 occupational sick pay, you will only get £10 in all. SSP counts as income for income tax purposes, is liable for National Insurance contributions if the rate paid is above the lower earnings limit, and may be subject to any deductions which your employer normally makes from your pay.

If and when your entitlement to SSP is exhausted, and you remain or again become unable to work through sickness or disability, you will normally qualify for sickness benefit (*see* page 35), and, in the case of long-term incapacity, invalidity benefit (*see* page 26).

Some people, including those who do not work for an employer, or who are unemployed, are excluded from the statutory sick pay scheme, but may be alternatively entitled to sickness benefit. Details of excluded groups are given in leaflet NI 16. These include:

(a) women over 60 and men over 65;
(b) people who don't pay National Insurance contributions because their pay is below the lower earnings limit;
(c) people who were claiming sickness benefit, invalidity benefit, maternity allowance or non-contributory invalidity pension eight or less weeks ago;
(d) people taken on by their employer for three months or less;
(e) people whose first day of sickness is during a trade dispute at their place of work, in which they are taking part, or from which they expect to gain;
(f) people who are in legal custody;
(g) people who fall sick outside the European Community (except aircrew based in the United Kingdom, and people who work on the continental shelf);
(h) women whose sickness occurs in the period starting 11 weeks before they are due to have a baby and ending six weeks after the birth.

WEEKLY RATES

SSP is paid at one of three weekly rates, depending on your average earnings. There are no additions for dependants, nor earnings related supplement. Rates are given in leaflet NI 208 and are reviewed annually, any change applying from 6 April. Rates for 1983/4:

Weekly earnings	Weekly rate of SSP
£68.00 or more	£42.25
£50.50 to £67.99	£35.45
£34.00 to £50.49	£28.55
Less than £34.00	Nil – employee is excluded from SSP

HOW TO CLAIM

Employers will normally have their own procedures for the notification of sick absence and you should be careful to observe these to avoid any possibility of loss of entitlement. Your employer may want evidence that you are incapable of work. This may be a form of self-certificate (for periods of sickness up to seven days, including a Sunday) or a doctor's or other professional's certificate (for absences in excess of seven days).

RELATIONSHIP TO OTHER BENEFITS

Receipt of SSP does not rule out the possibility of claiming supplementary benefit if, with other income, you do not have enough on which to manage.

BOOKS AND PUBLICATIONS

In addition to the DHSS leaflets NI 16 and NI 244 and the general publications described at the beginning of this section, a specialist booklet, *Guide to Statutory Sick Pay* is available from the Disability Alliance, price £1.20 including postage and packing.

Supplementary Benefit

DHSS Leaflets SB 1(brief guide), SB 2 (supplementary benefit and trade disputes), SB 7 (living together as husband and wife), SB 8 (general guide), SB 9 (unemployed people), SB 12 (appeals), SB 16 (lump sum payments for special needs), SB 17 (help with heating costs), SB 18 (the capital rule), SB 19 (weekly payments for special needs), SB 21 (unemployed people).

GENERAL DESCRIPTION

This benefit does not depend on National Insurance contributions and does not count as income for income tax purposes. It is referred to as supplementary allowance for men under 65 and women under 60; thereafter it is called supplementary pension. It is intended to provide cash help for adults (16 and over) whose income falls below basic minimum standards set by the government. It is particularly important in providing for those of limited means who, for one reason or another, fail to qualify for other benefits. The amount is related to an assessment of the claimant's need within prescribed limits, after taking any other income into account.

In the case of couples, from 21 November 1983, either partner can now claim provided he or she can show over the six months prior to claim 'contact with the employment field' (*e.g.* working eight hours or more a week), or a good reason for being out of it (*e.g.* being available for work but unable to find it, sickness, looking after a sick relative, receiving education or training, in prison, absent from the United Kingdom). Couples are now also entitled to supplementary pension when either partner is 65 or over.

The new supplementary benefit scheme, unlike the previous discretionary system, is based on detailed legal rights. Regulations spell out entitlement and allowances and provide a more precise (and more restrictive) scheme. The regulations are equally binding on supplementary benefit officers, appeals tribunals and on the Social Security Commissioner. The intricacies of the scheme are considerable. We outline here mainly those allowances which arise from disability, but cannot deal with all the many circumstances which may affect your entitlement to benefit, either at the basic level or in relation to special additions. We urge anyone in need who thinks that they may qualify for benefit, or who, though receiving benefit, may qualify for extra help, to consult the *Supplementary Benefits Handbook*, the *Disability Rights Handbook*, or the *National Welfare Benefits Handbook* (*see* page 10).

It is important to be aware that you are entitled to have, on request, an advice of your assessment (form A 124) from your local DHSS office, so that you can check what has been allowed/disallowed, and whether any relevant factors have been omitted or incorrectly assessed.

CONDITIONS

You must be aged 16 or over.

You must be normally resident in the United Kingdom.

Normally, you must not be in full-time work (30 hours or more a week – in some circumstances even when you work fewer hours, *e.g.* when you are on holiday or absent from work without good reason). However, if you are disabled and your average earnings are not more than 75 per cent of what a fit person would earn in the same job, you can work part-time up to 35 hours and still, subject to assessment, be entitled to supplementary benefit. You can also exceed the 30-hour rule without losing the right to benefit if:

(a) because of your disability, you earn as a self-employed person substantially less than a fit person doing the same sort of work (however many hours you work); or

(b) in some circumstances you are the only person caring for someone who is severely handicapped and cannot be left alone.

It is a normal requirement that claimants under pension age should be 'available for work' and attend regularly (usually fortnightly) at their local unemployment office (compulsory registration at Jobcentres ceased to be required from October 1982). But certain groups are excepted from this rule. These include:

(a) men aged 60 or more;

(b) people who, on the evidence of a current doctor's statement, are incapable of work;

(c) disabled people who are working part-time up to the limit of their capabilities;

(d) disabled people who are self-employed and working full-time but whose earning capacity is substantially reduced compared to that of a fit person in the same job;

(e) people who are necessarily looking after someone who is severely disabled and in receipt of attendance allowance or whose claim for that allowance is under consideration;

(f) blind people who are incapable of performing work for which eyesight is essential and who are not used to working outside the home;

(g) people who, because of a physical or mental disablement, have no further prospect of finding work;

(h) people who are caring for a partner who is ill and there are no alternative means by which that partner could be cared for.

In other cases, the requirement to attend the unemployment benefit office may be relaxed to a quarterly basis, *i.e.*:

If you have been unemployed and receiving benefit for a year, but have been 'closely handicapped' in your search for work by mental or physical disability;

If you are over 50 and have been unemployed and receiving benefit for a year.

These special exceptions from attendance at the unemployment benefit office may be crucial to your entitlement to move on to long-term scale rates (*see* below).

CALCULATION OF REQUIREMENTS

1. Basic scale rates are prescribed as below and are reviewed annually. They are extremely low, but are nevertheless supposed somehow to cover 'all items of normal expenditure on day-to-day living' other than housing costs (now largely met by Housing Benefit – *see* page 20). The weekly rates are as follows:

	Ordinary rates	Long-term rates
Married couple	£45.55	£57.10
Single person paying rent or living in own house	£28.05	£35.70
Any other person:		
– age 18 or over	£22.45	£28.55
– age 16 to 17	£17.30	£21.90
Plus:		
For each dependent child:		
– age 18 or over	£22.45	£28.55
– age 16 to 17	£17.30	£21.90
– age 11 to 15	£14.35	
– age under 11	£9.60	

2. Long-term Scale Rates

In a variety of circumstances, claimants may be eligible to have their basic requirements assessed on a higher long-term scale rate. The following are so eligible:

(a) single people aged 60 or over;

(b) couples where either party has reached age 60 (whether or not the claimant is required to be available for work);

(c) people who have received a supplementary allowance or a long-term incapacity benefit (invalidity benefit, non-contributory invalidity pension, unemployability supplement to an industrial or war disablement pension) for 52 weeks without being required to be available for work. (In calculating the 52-weeks period, breaks in entitlement of eight weeks or less are ignored; and, in the case of a disabled person who is exempted from the requirement to be available for work because he/she has no further prospects of employment, any prior period during which attendance at the unemployment benefit office was relaxed to quarterly intervals counts towards the qualifying period.)

NOTE: A claimant who is currently required to be available for work can qualify only for the ordinary-scale rates, even if he/she has previously been on the long-term rates.

3. Additional Requirements

Given that the basic-scale rates are set so low, the possibility of getting regular additional help is of great importance. You can qualify for additional allowances in a variety of circumstances, details of which can be found in the *Supplementary Benefits Handbook*, the *Disability Rights Handbook* or the *National Welfare Benefits Handbook* (*see* page 10), or a special guide to additional payments, *Disability Care and Counting the Costs* (*see* page 43). Official guidance (intended for supplementary benefit officers) is contained in the so-called S Code (*see* page 43) or in special guidance notes published by the DHSS, available for inspection at local DHSS offices or for purchase, price 95p, from DHSS Leaflets, PO Box 21, Stanmore, Middlesex.

The following notes outline those additions which may be of particular interest to disabled people (the rates quoted are again those in force from 23 November 1984).

NOTE: For people on the long-term scale rates, 50p may be taken off certain of the additional payments, because the long-term rates are intended to meet these extra expenses. This does not, however, affect additions for:

(a) age;
(b) heating;
(c) blindness;
(d) a dependent child for his/her special diet, attendance expenses, extra baths, heavy wear and tear on clothing, or expenses in visiting a patient in hospital.

Age
Claimants aged 80 or over, or whose partner is aged 80 or over get an extra 25p. If both partners are 80 or over, the addition is 50p.

Special Diets
(a) £9.60 a week if you, your partner or child is on a kidney machine.
(b) £3.35 a week if you need a special diet for:
diabetes
a peptic ulcer (including a stomach or duodenal ulcer)
ulcerative colitis
a form of tuberculosis which requires treatment by drugs
a throat condition which causes serious difficulty in swallowing
an illness which requires a diet similar to those above.
(c) £1.45 a week if you are convalescing from a major operation or illness; or
if you need a diet which, although not qualifying under (b) above, involves extra cost; or for each dependant living in the same accommodation as someone who suffers from a form of respiratory tuberculosis which requires treatment by drugs.
(d) If you suffer from a condition other than one specified in (b) above which requires a special diet involving an extra cost substantially in excess of £3.35 a week, you may be able to get a higher allowance. Where this can be supported (*e.g.* by a doctor or hospital) a claim based on the real cost should certainly be pressed.

Extra Heating
£2.10 a week:
if you or your wife or one of your dependants has difficulty in walking (*e.g.* through age or frailty) or has a chronic illness which would be helped by extra heating;
if you are a householder and live in accommodation that is difficult to heat (*e.g.* because it is damp or has very large rooms);
if you are a householder and either you or your partner are 70 or over, or a member of the family is under 5;
if you are a householder and live in a centrally heated home with up to four rooms (not counting the bathroom)
£4.20 a week:
if you are a householder and live in a centrally heated home with five or more rooms (not counting the bathroom);
£5.20 a week:
if you or your partner or one of your dependants is seriously ill, bedridden, or housebound;
if you or your partner or one of your dependants gets attendance allowance, constant attendance allowance, or mobility allowance or a DHSS 'trike' or other government vehicle, or a private car allowance from the DHSS. Whereas heating additions are normally limited to one amount per household, additions under this heading can be claimed for each person who qualifies;
if you are a householder and live in accommodation that is *exceptionally* difficult to heat (*e.g.* because the house is very old or is in a very exposed position).

NOTE: If you pay a fixed charge for full or partial central heating, any allowance should be claimed as Housing Benefit (*see* page 20). Tenants who pay a fixed charge for full central heating cannot then get any other supplementary benefit heating additions.

Laundry
An addition to cover average weekly costs over 45p can be claimed in a variety of circumstances, including:
(a) if your laundry cannot be done at home because every adult member of the household is ill, disabled or infirm; or
(b) the amount of laundry you have to do is substantially greater than would be normal, *e.g.* because of incontinence.

Domestic Assistance
An addition can be claimed for reasonable payments made for essential private domestic help if you and any partner cannot cope with housework, through old age, ill-health, disability or heavy family responsibilities. The amount you pay must be for ordinary domestic tasks. Oddly, these exclude errands and window cleaning. You won't get the addition if your helper is a close relative who incurs only minimal expenses or a local authority home help.

In cases of severe disablement, where you need a permanent helper (*e.g.* a community service volunteer – *see* page 80 – or even two if the need arises) a weekly amount not exceeding twice the ordinary scale rate for non-householders can be allowed, *i.e.* up to £44.90. Attendance allowance is not affected.

Attendance Needs
This addition can be claimed over and above the cost of any domestic assistance if you (or any member of your family over the age of 2) needs throughout the day or night either:
(a) frequent attention in connection with bodily functions; or
(b) continual supervision to avoid substantial danger to yourself or others;
and you are likely to need such attendance for at least six months. These conditions are similar to those for attendance allowance (*see* page 15) and indeed the addition is designed for people who have applied for or are waiting the prescribed six months to qualify for that allowance.

Blindness
If you (or one of your family) is 16 or over and is so blind as to be unable to perform any work for which eyesight is essential, or you have been blind but have regained your sight during the last six months while on benefit, you can usually get an addition of £1.25 a week.

Baths
If your doctor certifies that you need more than one bath a week on medical gounds, an addition of 25p per bath can be claimed.

Extraordinary Wear and Tear on Clothing
If you (or one of your family) wears out clothes more quickly than is usual because of physical or mental disability, you can receive either a regular weekly addition or an occasional lump-sum grant. The amount is not fixed but should be related to the real cost involved.

4. Housing Costs
Most housing costs are now covered by Housing Benefit (*see* page 20). Costs excluded from that scheme – such as water rates, mortgage interest (but not capital repayments), repairs and insurance (a prescribed annual sum, £88.40), ground rent, sewerage charges – can, however, be taken into account for supplementary benefit. The costs are averaged as a weekly requirement, which may be reduced if:
(a) you are sub-letting part of your home; or
(b) your housing costs are considered to be too high by the DHSS; or
(c) someone lives in your household who is not dependent and who could be expected to contribute to your housing costs, *e.g.* an adult son or daughter.

5. Boarders
The scale rates do not apply to boarders. If you are staying in a boarding house, private house or hostel, your full board and lodging charge will be taken into account unless it is considered by the DHSS to be unreasonably high. To this is added an amount for personal expenses, *viz*:

	Ordinary rates	Long-term rates
Couple	£18.50	£20.60
Single person	£9.25	£10.30
Dependent children aged:		
18 to 19 inclusive	£8.85	
16 to 17 inclusive	£5.30	
11 to 15 inclusive	£4.55	
under 11	£2.95	

CALCULATION OF RESOURCES

The income of your household includes all money which you, your partner or your children have coming in, but for supplementary benefit purposes there are a number of allowable deductions. The following sources of income are counted in full:
(a) most social security benefits (but *not* housing benefit, mobility allowance, attendance allowance (or its equivalent paid because of an injury at work or a war injury));
(b) maintenance payments (except for occasional gifts up to £100);
(c) occupational pensions and weekly redundancy payments.
The following expenses connected with work are allowed as deductions:
(a) income tax;
(b) National Insurance contributions;
(c) fares to work;
(d) child-minding fees while you are at work;
(e) trade union subscriptions;

(f) meals at work (up to 15p!);

(g) other reasonable expenses, *e.g.* cleaning of overalls.

And part of your remaining income is also disregarded:

(a) £4 of any weekly earnings you receive;

(b) £4 of any weekly earnings your partner receives;

NOTE: lone parents get the first £4 of any earnings, plus half of any weekly earnings between £4 and £20.

(c) £4 a week of the total of any other money you receive, such as disablement pension or payments from a charitable fund;

(d) attendance and equivalent allowances;

(e) mobility allowance;

(f) housing benefit;

(g) approved adoption allowances (but only to the extent that the amount of the allowance exceeds the total weekly amount of normal and additional requirements of the person in respect of whom it is payable).

CAPITAL

If you and your partner have capital of more than £3,000, you are not entitled to supplementary benefit. If your children's savings take the family's capital over £3,000, you may nevertheless get some benefit. Capital means most kinds of savings but excludes the house you live in and your everyday possessions, and (from November 1983) the first £1,500 surrender value of life assurance policies.

If you have capital of £3,000 or less it is ignored, and neither the capital itself nor any income from it (such as interest) affects the amount of weekly benefit.

CALCULATION OF BENEFIT

This is simply the sum total of requirements less the sum total of reckonable income.

HOW TO CLAIM

Complete form SB1 (from post offices or your DHSS office) or, if you are registering as unemployed, form B1 (from unemployment benefit offices). It cannot be emphasised too strongly that you must be sure to bring all relevant facts to the notice of the supplementary benefits officer. Check carefully to see if there are special factors which might entitle you to extra help and claim accordingly.

SINGLE PAYMENTS

Over and above the weekly payments of supplementary benefit, which may include provision for special (but regular) expenses, it is possible to claim lump-sum grant payments to cover 'exceptional needs'. The circumstances in which such payments shall be made are precisely defined in regulations. The payments are intended to meet essential needs not covered by the ordinary rates and are available both to people on weekly supplementary benefit *and those who would be immediately entitled if they claimed.* You may be able to get lump-sum payments in a variety of circumstances in respect of such items as clothing, things for a new baby, travel costs to hospital, expenses in starting work, funeral costs, removal expenses, furniture, bedding, fuel bills, repairs and redecoration. You will, however, be expected to use any savings you may have in excess of £500, and the conditions under which payments are allowed are strict. Disability can sometimes be a crucial factor in securing a grant, *e.g.*:

Clothing

The ordinary rates are supposed to cover replacement of clothing and footwear, but a lump-sum grant may be made where the need arises other than by normal wear and tear. Examples of this are heavy wear and tear on clothing resulting from a disability, or a particular or extra item needed because of an illness or disability.

Bedding

A special payment is possible either if you do not have enough bedding, or if you need extra, *e.g.* because someone in the household is incontinent or suffers from a condition which necessitates extra warmth (if you are elderly or infirm, you can claim for a covered hot water bottle).

Fuel Bills

There are a number of circumstances in which you can claim special help with unpaid fuel bills which you cannot pay out of your weekly income, including:

(a) if you (or a member of your family) has had a period of severe illness for which extra heating was needed but you did not get a weekly addition;

(b) if as a result of a period of exceptionally severe weather you have had to use more fuel than usual and your fuel costs are therefore greater than the amount you have set aside for them.

Removal Expenses

You may get a special grant to pay for your removal costs if you have to move house, *e.g.* because it is unhealthy or unsafe, and you don't qualify for help from your local authority. One of the circumstances which may necessitate such a move is so that a close relative can live with you, in order to give him/her better care. To qualify, it must be reasonable for you to provide accommodation for your close relative (which includes a step-child), and the relative must be either:

(a) over pensionable age, chronically sick or mentally or physically disabled; or
(b) a patient; or
(c) in the care of a local authority; or
(d) living in local authority provided, residential accommodation.

Furniture and Household Equipment
The cost of furniture and household equipment is not covered by the scale rates; but only certain groups can qualify for single payments for such costs. Among the grounds on which you can claim a special grant for essential items is the situation where you or someone in your family is mentally or physically disabled or chronically sick.

Travel Costs
You may get help with fares (and in some circumstances necessary overnight accommodation) on several grounds including when:

(a) costs are incurred when you or a member of your family has to visit a close relative in hospital;
(b) costs are incurred associated with a child travelling to stay with relatives or friends because one of its parents has to go into hospital.

BOOKS AND PUBLICATIONS

In addition to the DHSS leaflets and the general publications described at the beginning of this section (the *Disability Rights Handbook* and the *National Welfare Benefits Handbook*, it should be noted, deal with supplementary benefit in some detail), there are a number of specialist guides:

Supplementary Benefits (Requirements) Regulations 1983 (SI 1983: 1399, HMSO)

Supplementary Benefits Handbook (HMSO, 1983), £2.50

The Law Relating to Supplementary Benefit and Family Income Supplement (HMSO, regularly updated), £41.00 plus extra for updating supplements. Loose-leaf, often called *The Yellow Book*.

Guidance issued by the Chief Supplementary Benefit Officer (DHSS)
Various leaflets including: *Additional Requirements*, 95p; *Single Payments*, 85p; *Voluntary Work*, 20p; *Resources*, £1.70; *Single Payments for Redecoration*, 25p; *Urgent Cases*, £1.00; *Single Payments for Fuel Costs*, 44p; all available from DHSS Leaflets, PO Box 21, Stanmore, Middlesex HA7 1AY.

DHSS Supplementary Benefits Procedure Manual (*'S' Manual*) (DHSS, 1983), £22.50. An interpretation of the law, primarily written for the guidance of supplementary benefit officers.

Disability Care and Counting the Costs by Linda Avery (Disability Alliance and RADAR, 1983), 80p plus 20p postage and packing from either the Disability Alliance or RADAR. A guide to supplementary benefit additions based on a survey of fifty-one real claims. It shows that supplementary benefit officers are themselves often totally ignorant about entitlements and that persistence can bring reward, especially in the area of clothing and diets.

Supplementary Benefit and the Elderly (Age Concern, 1982), £2.50 including postage and packing. The second edition of a step-by-step guide to the calculation of supplementary benefit. Although the book is aimed primarily at people over the statutory retirement age and unemployed men over the age of 59 who do not intend to return to full time work, its advice is applicable to younger people on long-term rates and should help anyone who is bemused by the system.

An Element of Rough Justice: Disabled People and the new supplementary benefits scheme by Diana Robbins (DIG Charitable Trust, 1981), 45p. A critical look at the inadequacy of the supplementary benefits scheme in relation to disabled people. A very good paper with a number of worthwhile recommendations.

Making Ends Meet by Scott Kerr (Bedford Square Press, 1983), £4.50 plus 55p postage and packing. An investigation into the reasons underlying non-claiming of supplementary pensions. The author considers non-claiming as a problem of motivation. Based on a series of studies in Edinburgh between 1976 and 1982, the author's analyses show clearly that, although factors influencing behaviour may vary from individual to individual, the underlying process of decision-making is the same for all pensioners.

The implications of these findings for government policy are discussed, and two essential factors are identified in relation to the non take-up of benefits generally: the provision of comprehensible information to those for whom it is relevant, and changes in the assessment procedure to make claiming both more acceptable and easier.

Therapeutic Earnings Rule

Claimants may, in certain circumstances, derive earnings from work without affecting their entitlement to sickness, injury, invalidity or non-contributory invalidity benefit. The local social security office will advise whether the work concerned falls within this concession. Full details must be given, including whether the claimant's doctor approves the work. For this purpose, earnings must not exceed £23.50 (November 1984) a week, after the deduction of allowable expenses.

Vaccine Damage Payments Scheme

DHSS Leaflet HB 3 (available only from the Vaccine Damage Payments Unit, address below).

This scheme provides a lump sum of £10,000, free of tax, in respect of a person who has suffered severe damage as a result of vaccination and who meets the conditions laid down.

In greater detail, the following people qualify:

(a) those who are severely damaged as a result of having been vaccinated against one of the following diseases – diphtheria, tetanus, whooping cough, tuberculosis (BCG), poliomyelitis, measles, rubella, smallpox; *and*

(b) who were vaccinated in the United Kingdom or the Isle of Man on or after 5 July 1948 (where the vaccination was against smallpox, it must have been given before 1 August 1971, by which date it ceased to be recommended for routine use); *and*

(c) who have reached the age of 2 years.

Permanent residence in a hospital or special home, etc., need not prevent a person from qualifying, but special conditions may apply as to the circumstances in which, and to whom, payment may be made.

As regards (b) above, there are special provisions covering families of members of HM Forces accompanying them during service abroad.

The criterion of 'severe' damage is 80 per cent disability or more. (The principles of assessment are those which apply for the purposes of industrial injuries disablement benefit.) Whether the severe damage can be attributed to vaccination will be determined in accordance with medical advice.

The scheme does not cover persons who died before 9 May 1978.

HOW TO CLAIM

A claim form is obtainable from the Vaccine Damage Payments Unit, Department of Health and Social Security, North Fylde Central Offices, Norcross, Blackpool FY5 3TA.

After completion it should be returned to the same address. Any supporting medical evidence may also be submitted, but the claim should not be delayed on that account, nor because some of the information asked for in the form is not readily available. The claim can be made either by the disabled person in his or her own right if aged 18 or over, or by a parent or guardian on behalf of any entitled person under that age. A disabled adult should complete the claim form personally, but, if this is not possible, it may be completed by someone else on his or her behalf.

Decisions are notified in writing and there is a right of appeal which is explained at the time.

War Disablement Pension

DHSS Leaflets MPL 153 and 154 (rates) (available only from War Pensions offices).

GENERAL DESCRIPTION

You may get Disability Retired Pay or Pension if your disablement was due to, or made worse by, service in the 1914 war, or at any time since 2 September 1939. If you were an officer or member of the Naval Auxiliary Services or Merchant Navy, you may get a pension for disablement due to a 1939 war injury or a war risk injury, or to detention during the 1939 war. Similar arrangements apply to some Merchant Navy officers and seamen of the 1914 war.

Pensions can also be awarded to civilians for serious and prolonged disablement caused by a war injury, or to civil defence volunteers for a war service injury, suffered during World War II (3 September 1939 to 19 March 1946). The scheme is similar to that for industrial injuries, with a basic disablement pension (which is related to the severity of disablement and your rank during service) and a number of special allowances. The basic pension for 100 per cent disablement for a private is £58.40 (November 1984). Less than total disablement is expressed as a percentage depending on the severity, and the basic entitlement is calculated *pro rata*. If the disablement is assessed as less than 20 per cent, the pension takes the form of a lump-sum gratuity.

Benefit does not depend on National Insurance contributions, and does not count as income for income tax purposes.

HOW TO CLAIM

Write to DHSS, North Fylde Central Office, Norcross, Blackpool FY5 3TA for a claim form. Although there are no time limits for claiming war disablement pension, there are considerable advantages in making a claim for disablement arising from service in the armed forces within seven years of the end of such service.

RELATIONSHIP TO OTHER BENEFITS

Basic war disablement pension does not affect the payment of National Insurance benefits. Of the supplementary allowances, only unemployability supplement and constant attendance allowance affect other benefits (*see* DHSS leaflet NI 50 for details).

War Pensioners' Mobility Supplement

DHSS Leaflet MPL 155

GENERAL DESCRIPTION

A cash benefit intended to help those war pensioners who have difficulty in walking. It is similar to mobility allowance (*see* page 28) but *is paid at a higher rate and without age limitation*. Subject to qualification (*see* below), the supplement can be claimed by war pensioners who are currently receiving mobility allowance or who have a DHSS vehicle on loan, but it cannot, of course, be paid as well at the same time. (Vehicles are no longer being issued, and the supplement will, in any event, progressively replace existing vehicles supplied under the war pensioners' vehicle scheme.)

The supplement does not count as income for income tax purposes. If you are turned down, you can ask the DHSS to review its decision. If you are still dissatisfied with their response, you can ask the War Pensioners' Committee for your district to discuss the matter with you.

SERVICE CONDITIONS

The supplement is available only to people who are receiving a war pension for disablement arising from service in the forces, either in the 1914 war or at any time after 3 September 1939 (this includes civilian, Polish, and some Mercantile Marine Scheme war pensioners) and whose walking problems are caused wholly or mainly by the pensioned disablement.

MEDICAL CONDITIONS

Subject to the above service conditions, you can qualify for the supplement if you are either:
(a) a war disablement pensioner with double leg amputations, one above or through the knee; or
(b) a war disablement pensioner who to all intents and purposes is unable to walk.

Those covered by (a) above qualify automatically without medical examination. For qualification under (b), if you have some ability to walk, the DHSS may require a medical examination and will take into account the way, how far, how fast and the length of time for which you can walk without feeling severe discomfort, and whether the exertion needed to walk would put your life at risk or be likely to lead to a serious deterioration in your health. Where appropriate, account will be taken of your walking ability with aids you can use, such as an artificial limb or a walking stick. Your problems must be such that you are likely to remain unable, or for all practical purposes unable, to walk for at least a year.

WEEKLY RATES

(November 1984)
DHSS Leaflet MPL 154; £22.25

HOW TO CLAIM

Write to: War Pensioners' Mobility Supplement Section, Department of Health and Social Security, North Fylde Central Office, Norcross, Blackpool FY5 3TA, quoting your war pensions reference number. If currently you have a DHSS vehicle on loan under the War Pensioners' Vehicle Scheme, it will be necessary for you either to buy or surrender the car before the supplement can be awarded. If you wish to do so, write to: Disablement Services Branch, Department of Health and Social Security, Warbreck Hill, Blackpool FY2 0UZ or, in Scotland, to the Scottish Home and Health Department, St Andrew's House, Edinburgh EH1 3DE.

PAYMENT WHILE IN HOSPITAL

The supplement will continue to be paid if you go into hospital (or, indeed, if you go abroad).

RELATIONSHIP TO OTHER BENEFITS

If notwithstanding your war pension and mobility supplement you haven't enough money to live on, you may be entitled to supplementary benefit (*see* page 38). If you are already receiving supplementary benefit, and are awarded the war pensioners' mobility supplement, you may be eligible for a heating addition.

Neither National Insurance benefits, nor Industrial Injury benefits are affected by payment of the mobility supplement. Mobility Allowance cannot be paid at the same time as the mobility supplement.

SECTION 3

AIDS: THEIR PROVISION AND AVAILABILITY

Aids are a perfectly normal feature of everyday living. *They can make the impossible possible*. Try, if you will, to remove a screw without a screwdriver! For those whose physical powers are impaired, aids have a vital role to play in helping to overcome the limitations imposed by the handicap. A vast range of aids and appliances is available, from sophisticated electronic equipment to an elastic band wrapped round a pencil to afford a better grip to shaky hands. However, just as it is necessary for a craftsman to match the right tool to a particular job, so must handicapped people be equipped with the aids most suited to their needs.

There are significant problems in this area: a great danger that disabled people will buy or accept aids, even high-cost equipment, not fully appropriate or suitable to their needs and without weighing the pros and cons. The disabled consumer is often in a situation which makes it difficult to compare one aid with another, to try them out, to find out how his/her needs can best be met and to evaluate products. He/she often lacks access to or is unaware of sources of advice, or is advised by people who are themselves inexpert. Thus many aids are acquired which are found in practice to be either unsuitable, ineffective, inoperative, non-durable or unacceptable to the user. It is important to realise that even if one can be satisfied as to the quality of a product (a matter which unfortunately cannot be taken for granted), aids which are made to a standard design may suit one individual but not another. Wherever possible, it is wise to visit one of the increasing number of aids centres (*see* page 55) to see a range of aids and to enlist the advice of a trained occupational therapist or adviser. If this is impracticable, much helpful guidance as to what is available and the functional application of the various items of equipment and clothing can be gained from an information service (*see* page 53), from travelling exhibitions (*see* page 60), from books (*see* page 62) or from helpful organisations or local authorities. If you can, have the aid on approval to see if it works for you.

Reliefs from Value Added Tax and Car Tax

Relief is governed by Group 14 of the Zero Rate Schedule (Value Added Tax Act 1983, Schedule 5), as amended by the Value Added Tax (Handicapped Persons) Order 1984 (SI 1984/489). The reliefs are, broadly, as follows:

Item 2
Zero rate applies to the supply (including supply by letting on hire) to a handicapped person (defined in law as someone who is 'chronically sick or disabled') for domestic or his/her personal use, or to a charity for making available to handicapped persons (whether by sale or otherwise) for domestic or their personal use, of the following goods:
(a) Medical or surgical appliances designed solely for the relief of a severe abnormality or severe injury.
(b) Electrically or mechanically adjustable beds designed for invalids.
(c) Commode chairs, commode stools, devices incorporating a bidet jet and warm air drier and frames or other devices for sitting over or rising from a sanitary appliance.
(d) Chair lifts or stair lifts designed for use in connection with invalid wheelchairs.
(e) Hoists and lifters designed for use by invalids.
(f) Motor vehicles designed or substantially and permanently adapted for the carriage of a person in a wheelchair or on a stretcher and of no more than five other persons.
(g) Equipment and appliances not included in paragraphs (a) to (f) above designed solely for use by a handicapped person.
(h) Parts and accessories designed solely for use in or with goods described in paragraphs (a) to (g).

NOTE: Item 2 is deemed to include, so far as they relieve a severe abnormality or injury or are otherwise designed solely for the use of a handicapped person, the following:
(i) clothing, footwear and wigs;
(ii) invalid wheelchairs, and invalid carriages other than mechanically propelled vehicles intended for use on roads

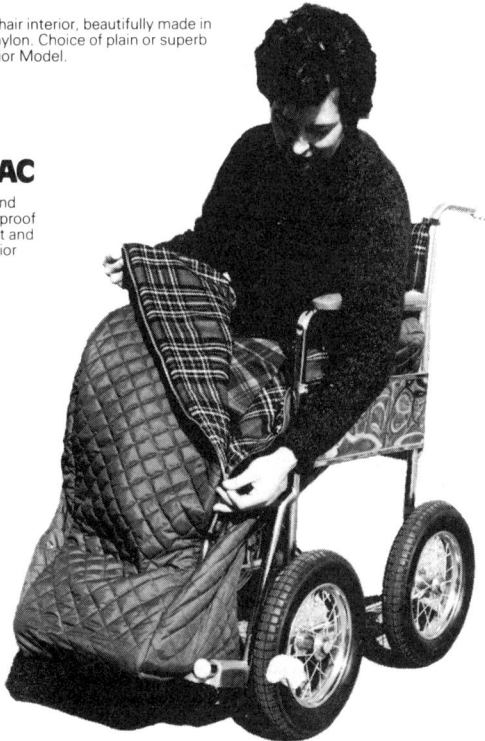

47

(but see comment below);

(iii) renal haemodialysis units, oxygen concentrators, artificial respirators and other similar apparatus.

Exceptions

The following goods are specifically excluded from relief under Group 14 (but are normally eligible for the lesser relief of exemption under item 1 or 2 of Group 7 of the Exemption Schedule):

hearing aids (except those designed for the auditory training of deaf children);

dentures;

spectacles;

contact lenses.

Item 3

The supply to a handicapped person of services of adapting goods to suit his/her condition.

Item 4

The supply to a charity of services of adapting goods to suit the condition of a handicapped person to whom the goods are to be made available, by sale or otherwise, by the charity.

Item 5

The supply to a handicapped person of a service of repair or maintenance of any goods which were supplied to him/her, or to a charity, where the supply was of a description specified in items 2 or 6.

Item 6

The supply of goods in connection with a supply described in items 3, 4 or 5.

Item 7 (from 1 June 1984)

The supply to a handicapped person or to a charity of services necessarily performed in the installation of equipment or appliances (including parts and accessories therefor) specified in item 2 and supplied as described in that item.

Item 8 (from 1 June 1984)

The supply to a handicapped person of a service of constructing ramps or widening doorways or passages for the purpose of facilitating his/her entry to or movement within his/her private residence.

Item 9 (from 1 June 1984)
The supply to a charity of a service described in item 8 for the purpose of facilitating a handicapped person's entry to or movement within any building.

Item 10 (from 1 June 1984)
The supply to a handicapped person of a service of providing a bathroom, washroom or lavatory for the first time on the ground floor of the building where he/she has his/her private residence and where such provision is necessary by reason of his/her condition.

Item 11 (from 1 June 1984)
The supply of goods in connection with a supply described in items 8, 9 or 10.

Comment: It will be seen that the scope of the relief now effectively covers virtually any goods which are *designed solely* for use by a handicapped person and supplied to that person or to a charity for the use of handicapped people. Some goods qualify because they are of a description such as to be invariably for use only by handicapped people; in other cases it will

be a matter for consideration whether they meet the relevant criteria. Essentially, the goods must have specialised design features which make them clearly belong to the category in question; the relief does not apply to general purpose goods used by disabled people. Thus an ordinary walking stick for example, is not entitled to relief, since it is commonly used by able-bodied people, whereas crutches and walking frames would obviously qualify.

The liability of vehicles is rather difficult to understand. A legal note to item 2 clarifies that it includes as indicated 'invalid wheel chairs, and invalid carriages *other than* mechanically propelled vehicles intended or adapted for use on roads'. The implication appears to be that road-going mechanically propelled invalid carriages are outside the scope of relief. We are advised, however, that this exclusion does not extend to motor cars designed solely for use by a handicapped person, and that each vehicle will be considered on its merits. For a vehicle to be zero-rated under this item, it must have been designed from the beginning as a specialised vehicle for use by

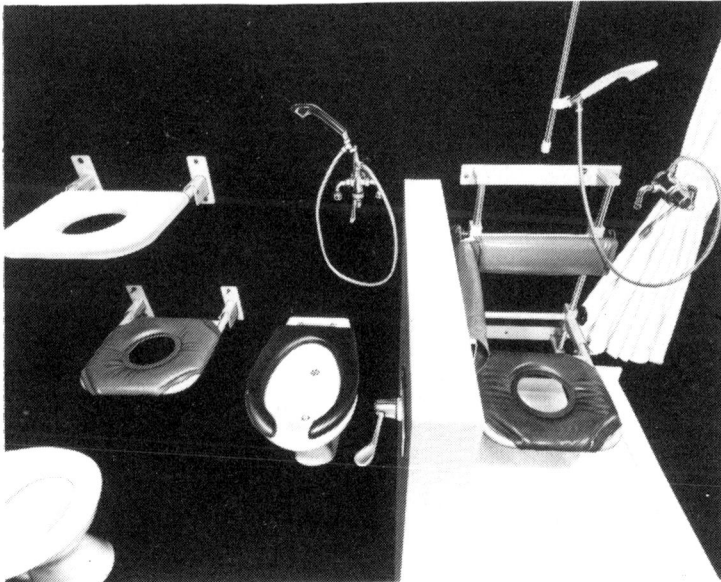

a disabled person. However, the 'designed solely' requirement does not mean that the vehicle can only qualify if it is a single seater. Provided that the primary, essential purpose of the vehicle is to afford a means of transport for a disabled person, others (up to five) may benefit from secondary use, as either passengers or driver. (The Salamander and the Elswick Envoy have already been accepted as qualifying for zero-rating under Group 14, item 2.)

In addition, there can be relief for standard production models which are adapted for use by a disabled person. If the adaptations are relatively minor, such as the modification of controls, then the adaptation may qualify but not the car itself. However, if it is 'substantially and permanently' adapted for carrying a disabled person in a wheelchair or on a stretcher, then the whole vehicle may qualify. Such a vehicle must have permanent features to load and secure the wheelchair or stretcher and design features which make it clearly belong in this category. Provided it meets these conditions, up to five other people can be carried. Obviously, in practice, there will be areas of doubt. If you intend to build vehicles specially designed for disabled people, or to convert or adapt a vehicle to this end, you should contact your local office of Customs & Excise in advance.

It should also be recognised that if you, as a private individual not 'registered' for value added tax purposes, buy a vehicle and pay the appropriate VAT, it cannot subsequently be reclaimed because of its conversion/adaptation. To enjoy the benefit of zero-rating on the vehicle and its conversion/adaptation, it would be necessary for the specially designed vehicle to be built, converted or adapted and supplied by a person/company registered for value added tax.

Where only the adaptation qualifies for zero-rating, and the car and its adaptation are ordered at the same time from the same supplier, the car (standard-rated) and adaptation (zero-rated) should be ordered and invoiced separately.

Similarly, when considering the repair or maintenance of an adapted car, zero-rating would apply only to work done and parts supplied in relation to the adaptation, and not to general repairs, etc., to the car, and each should be separately invoiced.

It is our understanding that the relief for repair and maintenance applies whether or not the goods concerned were eligible at the time of first purchase, provided that they are eligible now, and are owned by a handicapped person.

HOW TO OBTAIN ZERO-RATED SUPPLIES

A supplier who is registered under VAT law is liable for tax on his supplies if the conditions for relief are not fulfilled, and there is a danger that if there is any doubt, or if he is unaware of the provisions of Group 14, he will charge tax. It may be necessary for the customer to represent to him that the supply is entitled to zero-rating, and he will in any event require a declaration from the customer. These forms are not supplied officially, but the following models are taken from the Customs and Excise leaflet 'Aids for Handicapped Persons' (701/7/84 dated April 1984), which also gives details of obtaining relief on imported goods which are eligible under Group 14.

It is no longer necessary that the supply be to the order of a doctor, nor that the recipient be under the care of a doctor.

AIDS FOR HANDICAPPED PERSONS:
SUPPLY TO AN INDIVIDUAL

I (full name)...
of (address)...
declare that I am chronically sick or disabled, and that I am receiving from

....
(name and address of supplier)
(a) the following goods which are being supplied to me for domestic or my personal use:
....
(description of goods)
OR
(b) the following services to adapt goods to suit my condition:
....
(description of goods and adaptation)
OR
(c) the following services of repair or maintenance of goods:
....
(description of goods and service)
OR
(d) the following alterations to my private residence:
....
(description of alteration)
and I claim that the supply of these goods or services is eligible for relief from value added tax under Group 14 of the Zero Rate Schedule to the Value Added Tax Act 1983.

.... (Signature)
.... (Date)

AIDS FOR HANDICAPPED PERSONS:
SUPPLY TO A CHARITY

I (full name)...
(status in charity) ....

of (name and address of charity) ....
declare that the charity named above is receiving from

....

(name and address of supplier)

(a) the following goods which are to be made available to one or more handicapped people for domestic or personal use:

OR

(b) the following services to adapt goods to suit the condition of a handicapped person:

....

(description of goods and adaptation)

OR

(c) the services of constructing ramps, widening doorways or passages in:

....

(address of building)

to enable a handicapped person to enter or move within the building;

and I claim that the supply of these goods or services is eligible for relief from value added tax under Group 14 of the Zero Rate Schedule to the Value Added Tax Act 1983.

.... (Signature)
.... (Date)

NOTE: Specimen forms for the relief of vehicles from VAT and Car Tax are included in Customs & Excise Notice No. 670 (April 1984).

Goods which are eligible for relief as described in this Section, and certain other goods, are eligible for relief under certain conditions when donated or, in some cases, sold, to certain institutions. For details see Customs and Excise leaflet No. 701/6/82 'Donated Medical and Scientific Equipment, etc.' Leaflets can be obtained from any local VAT office (*see* telephone directory under Customs and Excise) who will also advise or refer for Head Office advice any questions of doubt concerning eligibility.

CAR TAX

The March 1984 Budget announced that the relief for vehicles for disabled people from Car Tax (not to be confused with Vehicle Excise Duty) would be parallel with the zero-rating described under item 2 above, with effect from 1 May 1984. The legislation is the Car Tax Act 1983, section 2(2)(c) as amended by the Car Tax (Vehicles for the Handicapped) Order 1984, SI 1984 No. 488. This relieves 'prison vans, ambulances and vehicles designed or substantially and permanently adapted for the carriage of a chronically sick or disabled person in a wheelchair or on a stretcher and of no more than five other per-

sons.' Further details are in Customs & Excise Notice No. 670 (April 1984). Car Tax enquiries should be addressed to your local Customs & Excise (Excise) office, not to the VAT office.

Relief from Import Duty for Articles Imported for Blind and Other Handicapped People

New regulations which have been applicable from 1 July 1984 involve some variation of the relief as set out in the third edition of this directory. The main change is that blind and handicapped people are now able to apply directly for duty relief on their own behalf, as well as through approved organisations. Changes are italicised.

EEC regulations *which have applied from 1 July 1984* allow certain articles to be imported free of customs duties otherwise due under the European Community's Common Customs Tariff (CCT) if:

(a) *they are intended for either blind persons themselves for their own use*;

(b) they are intended for approved organisations which are concerned with educating or assisting blind people;

(c) *they are intended for handicapped persons themselves for their own use*;

(d) they are intended for approved organisations which are principally engaged in the education of, *or the provision of*, assistance to handicapped people.

Relief is conditional upon the imported goods being used only by lending, hiring out or transferring to blind or handicapped people on a non-profit-making basis, or to other approved organisations with the prior consent of the Department of Trade.

BLIND PEOPLE AND ORGANISATIONS FOR BLIND PEOPLE

The articles concerned are:

braille paper;

white canes;

typewriters adapted for use by blind or partially sighted people;

equipment for the mechanical production of braille and recorded material;

television enlargers for partially sighted people;

electronic orientation and obstacle detection appliances;

teaching aids and apparatus specifically designed for the use of blind and partially sighted people;

braille watches (other than those with cases of precious metal); record players and cassette players specially designed or adapted for blind and partially sighted people;

talking books, magnetic tapes and cassettes for the production of braille and talking books;

electronic reading machines;

table games and accessories specially adapted for the use of blind and partially sighted people;

all other articles specially designed for the educational, scientific or cultural advancement of blind or partially sighted people;

spare parts components and accessories specifically *or identifiably* intended for all the above articles *and tools to be used for the maintenance, checking, calibration or repair of all the above articles*.

NOTE: Books and other matter printed in relief for blind and partially sighted people are not included, because they are free of duty to anyone.

HANDICAPPED PEOPLE AND ORGANISATIONS FOR HANDICAPPED PEOPLE

The relief is for any articles specially designed for the education, employment and social advancement of physically or mentally handicapped people. It also covers spare parts, components *and* accessories specifically or identifiably intended for such articles, *and tools to be used for the maintenance, checking, calibration or repair of all the above articles*.

However, with some minor exceptions, the relief is granted only when it will not prejudice the production of equivalent goods in the EEC.

APPLICATION

Relief from CCT duties, where granted, is given by HM Customs and Excise, against certificates issued by the Department of Trade, to whom application should be made on special forms (DFA(BW) for goods for blind and partially sighted people; DFA(H) for goods for other handicapped people), obtainable from the Department of Trade, Room 432A, 1 Victoria Street, London SW1H 0ET (Tel: 01-215 5968). There is no need for organisations to apply to the Department of Trade for prior registration as an approved body. Each application for relief will be considered on its merit at the time. In no circumstances can applications be accepted from agents, distributors or other commercial organisations.

NOTE: Fuller details of conditions and procedures are given in Notice 371 obtainable from the above address or from any local Customs and Excise office (but *not* VAT office).

Statutory Provision of Aids by Local Authorities

Under the Chronically Sick and Disabled Persons Act 1970, local authorities are required to inform themselves of the numbers and needs of handicapped people in their area and to meet those needs.

Various kinds of help available to a disabled person are set out in Section 2 of the Act and include: 'assistance . . . in arranging for the carrying out of any works of adaptation in his home or . . . any additional facilities designed to secure his greater safety, comfort or convenience'. Local authorities also have the power to provide or help to obtain special aids to hearing for deaf people known as environmental aids, *e.g.* flashing doorbells, vibrator pillows and induction loop systems.

There are similar requirements to provide for or to help a disabled person to obtain 'wireless, television, library or similar recreational facilities' and 'a telephone and any special equipment necessary to enable him to use a telephone'. It is important to recognise, however, that these provisions apply only where the authority is 'satisfied' that such action is 'necessary' to meet the needs of the disabled person, and are subject to the general guidance of the Secretary of State. In practice, local authorities vary considerably in the extent to which they provide aids and assistance, and in their interpretation of the Act. However, in any case where a real need is felt for help with aids, gadgets or adaptations to assist daily living, an approach should be made through a doctor or social worker for help by an occupational therapist or social worker in the local social services department. A home visit may be arranged to make practical suggestions about ways of doing things, about aids and, if necessary, alterations to the house.

Statutory Provision of Aids by the National Health Service

In general, aids required in connection with medical and nursing care at home are supplied through the National Health Service. These include ripple beds, cushions, hoists and aids for incontinence. General practitioners have lists of aids which may be prescribed where necessary. They can also recommend to the Department of Health and Social Security that large items be prescribed even though they may not be on the regular list. In the case of hearing aids, doctors can refer their patients to a special clinic in the local hospital for examination. If a hearing aid is found to be necessary, patients are then referred to a hearing aid centre, where the appliance will be fitted and supplied. Hearing aids are also available on free loan. NHS aids are serviced, maintained and supplied with batteries free of charge. (A range of medium-power BE (behind-the-ear) aids is available to all new patients, but owing to the heavy demand there is a waiting period at some centres.)

If a person is attending a rehabilitation department

of the local hospital, the occupational therapist will assess the patient and prescribe whatever aids are needed. A number of rehabilitation centres, both NHS and voluntary, offer highly specialised programmes of rehabilitation with assessment and training to maximise the individual's ability to cope with everyday activities at home and elsewhere, and to provide expert advice on aids. Whether or not you are under medical care, it may be possible to secure a referral to such a centre from your doctor or therapist.

A wide range of body-worn surgical appliances can be obtained on the recommendation of a hospital consultant. These include surgical footwear, colostomy and ileostomy appliances and arm, neck and head appliances.

Artificial limbs are supplied, maintained and, if necessary, replaced under the National Health Service free of charge. NHS hospitals will arrange for the patient to visit an artificial limb and appliance centre or a limb fitting centre to make the necessary arrangements (a list of such centres is given on Leaflet HB 2, pages 14–16).

Not all aids supplied under prescription are free, but where they are for the domestic or personal use of a disabled person they generally carry a zero-rated VAT (for details see VAT – Zero-rating, page 46). For particulars relating to the supply of invalid vehicles and wheelchairs, see Section 8.

Advice on the problems of incontinence should be sought from health visitors, district nurses or social workers. Both district health authorities *and* local authority social service departments can supply incontinence pads to people who live in their own homes. However, while DHAs may not charge for them, LASS departments may do so, according to local policy. They cannot be prescribed by GPs nor dispensed by chemists under the NHS and it is left to the discretion of the supplying authority to decide the type of pad to be provided, to whom they will be supplied and how they are delivered.

Statutory Provision of Aids by Local Education Authorities

Aids for use in connection with education may be supplied by local education authorities for use in schools or colleges.

Statutory Provision of Aids for Employment

The Manpower Services Commission can provide, on free permanent loan, any aids necessary to enable disabled people to perform their particular duties which they need only because of their disability. These include modifications to machines, purpose-built desks and seating, counter-balanced drawing boards, electric typewriters, keyboard guards, telephone aids and accessories, reading and writing aids and braille measuring devices.

The Commission can also make grants up to a maximum of £6,000 to help employers who need to make essential adaptations to premises to take on, or retain in, employment a disabled person. The adaptation must relate to the needs of a specific employee, and the employer is then expected to keep the disabled person concerned in the job for as long as he or she is capable of doing it satisfactorily.

Disabled employees or potential employees may well wish to bring these opportunities to the notice of their employers, who can get further information from MSC Leaflet EPL 71 or by contacting the local Disablement Resettlement Officer.

Provision of Aids by Voluntary Organisations

With the limited resources of local and national government spending, provision of aids can never be entirely satisfactory and disabled people would do well to approach voluntary organisations if their needs cannot be met by statutory provision. Section 16 gives details of many such organisations, but in addition to these there are many trusts, both local and national, which exist to help disabled people. Perhaps the best guide to such bodies is the *Directory of Grant-Making Trusts*, published by the Charities Aid Foundation and available in reference libraries.

Information Services

General information services are described in Section 15; a number, however, specialise in information about aids, often in association with Aids Centres (see page 55).

Disabled Living Foundation

This comprehensive service is designed for use by those professionally concerned with disabled people, voluntary organisations and other groups and individuals requiring up-to-date information about aids, equipment and services. Information is provided in response to individual requests or on a regular basis by subscription. Subscribers receive a complete and back-dated set of information lists and subsequent bi-monthly bulletins. Each list is updated at least once a year.

Any member of a subscribing group is entitled to make unlimited use of the enquiry service. Enquiries on any relevant subject, apart from purely medical matters, are answered by telephone or letter, including any appropriate trade literature and information. Subscribers are also entitled to borrow DLF publications. Information lists cover the following subjects:

List No.

1A *Beds*
including beds and accessories, mattresses, bedding, waterproof bed protection, anti-pressure equipment, self-lifting aids, bed and cantilever tables.

1B *Pressure Relief*
material and equipment for pressure relief.

2 *Chairs*
including geriatric, adjustable and mobile chairs, self-lift seats, raising blocks, footstools and cushions.

3A *Communication A*
including reading aids (incl. page turners), writing aids, speech aids, deaf aids; tape recorders and radios, and organisations concerned with sensory and speech impairment.

3B *Communication B*
including remote control apparatus, emergency call systems, intercoms, and telephone aids.

4 *Eating and Drinking Aids*
including cutlery, plates, trays, egg-cups, non-slip materials, drinking aids and bibs.

5 *Hoists and Lifting Equipment*
including portable, fixed and electric hoists, manual lifting aids, lifts and stairclimbers, bath hoists and car hoists.

6 *Leisure Activities*
including music, drama, gardening, sport, holidays, libraries, sewing aids, crafts, hobbies and clubs.

6 App *Sport and Physical Recreation (facilities for disabled people)*
including details of organisations and clubs, etc., concerned with sport for disabled people.

7A *Personal Toilet*
including WCs, WC aids, commodes, bedpans, urinals and waste disposal units.

7B *Personal Care*
including washing, dressing, cosmetic and hygiene aids; rails, baths, bath aids, showers, wash basins, hairwashing units.

8 *Transport*
including bicycles and tricycles, car, van and coach conversions; accessories; hire of vehicles, tuition and information.

9 *Walking Aids*
including frames and trolleys, walking aids, sticks and seat sticks, crutches and standing aids.

10 *Wheelchairs*
including self-propelled and push chairs, electrically operated chairs, carrying chairs, accessories including ramps and harnesses; information and hire.

11A *Household Equipment*
including kitchen utensils, small cooking appliances, taps, trolleys, steps and stools, laundry and cleaning equipment; reaching aids (pick-up-sticks).

11B *Household Fittings*
including kitchen/storage units, sinks, cookers, flooring, doors and door furniture, wall protection, windows, and electrical switches.

12 *Incontinence (aids and protective pants)*
including notes on day- and nightwear, protective garments and liners, female urinals and male appliances; bed pads.

12 App *Notes on Incontinence*
including details of equipment, notes on management of incontinence, and details of deodorants and neutralisers.

13 *Clothing*
including daywear, nightwear, underwear, swimwear, hosiery, notes for wheelchair users and people with stiff hips, dressing aids.

14 *Footwear*
including odd-sized shoes, extra-large and small sizes, shoe conversions, shoes suitable for use with calipers, etc.

15A *Children's Aids*
including eating/drinking aids, wheelchairs, mobility aids, walking aids, tricycles, car seats, harnesses, personal toilet aids, educational toys.

15B *Children's Furniture*
including chairs, beds, desks, tables, workbenches, easels, floor-level furniture; standing aids; playground equipment.

Index

Enquiries, which need to be as specific as possible, to: The Information Officer, Disabled Living Foundation, 380–384 Harrow Road, London W9 2HU (Tel: 01-289 6111).

(A tape-slide sequence (16 minutes) describing the information service has been prepared. It shows how the information is collected, stored and made available to users. Available from Graves Medical Audiovisual Library, PO Box 99, Chelmsford, Essex CM2 9BJ (Tel: Chelmsford (0245) 83351)).

The Foundation also provides advisory services on

incontinence, clothing, visual impairment, music, physical recreation and skin. All these advisory services can give information and guidance in response to enquiries from those affected, their families and all those professionally concerned with these particular subjects. Lectures and demonstrations can be arranged and publications and some training kits are available. Further details on the work of these advisory services available from Disabled Living Foundation.

Blind Centre for Northern Ireland (The)
65 Eglantine Avenue, Belfast BT9 6EW (Tel: Belfast (0232) 664544).
This Centre was established in 1978 to fill the gaps not covered by statutory services. It covers the whole of Northern Ireland, with special information units in Belfast, Londonderry, Dungannon and Newry. Another is planned for Co. Antrim. At these units, visually handicapped people can learn about the latest aids, examine new apparatus and also learn about available services for blind people.

The Blind Centre also offers administrative and secretarial support to all Northern Ireland's other organisations for blind people. Information is also provided through tape magazines (*see* Section 14). Other activities now include holidays, social clubs, day care activities, seminars and workshops.

British Database on Research into Aids for the Disabled (BARD)
Handicapped Persons Research Unit, Newcastle upon Tyne Polytechnic, 1 Coach Lane, Coach Lane Campus, Newcastle upon Tyne NE7 7TW (Tel: Newcastle upon Tyne (0632) 326002 ext. 4211).
This is a computerised register of 'non-manufactured' aids and related research projects. It contains descriptions of current design and development projects, prototypes, one-offs, latest developments, as well as surveys, evaluations and research in the use of aids. The database complements information provided by other organisations whose emphases lie in manufactured and commercially available aids.

The aim of BARD is to facilitate the exchange of ideas, a process which is central to the research and development stage of producing aids for handicapped people. Each entry in the database contains a description of the project together with the name and address of maker, aid function and type of handicap. Information is supplied through print-outs in response to specific enquiries, and through reports on particular descriptions of aids, *viz.* Therapy and Training; Prosthetics and Orthotics; Personal Care; Mobility; Household and Daily Living; Furniture and Fixtures; Communication and Environmental

Control; Aids for Handling Other Products; Leisure and Sports; Building/Environmental Design; Education; Workplace; Communication and Education.

BARD is keen to hear from those working in this field, with specific details of their work.

Northern Ireland Information Service for Disabled People
2 Annadale Avenue, Belfast BT7 3JH (Tel: Belfast (0232) 640011 or 649555).
A comprehensive information service, including aids. Subjects for enquiry cover a similar area to that of the Disabled Living Foundation but with a Northern Ireland orientation where this is possible.

Enquiries by letter, visit (by appointment) or by telephone are dealt with free of charge from 10 a.m. to 5 p.m. on Mondays to Fridays.

An annual subscription ensures regular dispatch of relevant updating and general Northern Ireland information, and is used extensively by professionals and others concerned with disabled people in the Province.

Scottish Council on Disability
Information Department, 5 Shandwick Place, Edinburgh EH2 4RG (Tel: 031-229 8632).
It provides information to disabled people resident in Scotland and those working with them. There is a free enquiry service and a bi-monthly newsletter available on subscription. Regularly updated information lists are produced on a range of topics and are available to subscribers. The lists are available to non-subscribers at 75p each including postage, and they are free to disabled people and their families.

Information Lists
1 *Beds*
2 *Chairs*
3 *Communication Aids*
4 *Eating and Drinking Aids*
5 *Hoists and Lifting Equipment*
6 *Leisure Activities*
7 *Sport and Physical Recreation*
8 *Baths and Showers*
9 *Toilets and Commodes*
10 *Personal Aids*
11 *Transport – Vehicles and Accessories*
12 *Transport – Information and Regulations*
13 *Walking Aids*
14 *Wheelchairs*
15 *Household Equipment*
16 *Household Fitments*
17 *Incontinence Clothing and Protection*
18 *Notes on Odour Control and Incontinence Management*

19   *Clothing for Adults*
20   *Voluntary Organisations concerned with Disabled People*
21   *Children's Aids and Equipment*
22   *Furniture for Disabled Children in Schools*
23   *Holidays*
24   *Employment and Training*

NOTE: Many organisations exist to meet the needs of those who suffer from specific disabilities, and will give advice on aids and specialised clothing (*see* list of organisations in Section 16). Branches of the British Red Cross Society often have items of equipment available for short-term loan.

Aids Centres

In recent years, there has been a considerable growth in aids centres: they seem to be springing up in various parts of the country even as we write.

The centres listed below are exhibitions where a selection of aids for disabled people can be seen and tried out. They have been set up to provide information to disabled people, their friends and relations, and those professionally concerned with disability.

Intending visitors should always contact the centre in advance; an appointment is usually necessary. As the centres vary considerably in size and scope, it is also sensible to check that the purpose of the visit can be fulfilled.

Belfast: Aids Demonstration Centre
Prosthetic Orthotic and Aids Service, Musgrave Park Hospital, Stockman's Lane, Belfast BT9 7JB (Tel: Belfast (0232) 669501 ext. 560).
A permanent display which includes a wide range of aids for disabled people of all ages. Open Mondays, Wednesdays and Fridays 9 a.m. to 4 p.m. by appointment.

Belfast: The Blind Centre for Northern Ireland
65 Eglantine Avenue, Belfast BT9 6EW (Tel: Belfast (0232) 664544).
Services cover the whole of Northern Ireland, with special information units in Belfast, Londonderry, Dungannon and Newry. Another is planned for Co. Antrim. At these information bureaux visually handicapped people can learn about the latest available aids, examine new apparatus and also learn about available services in their own community. The Blind Centre itself has over one hundred aids – household, technical, electronic and low visual, available for individuals to borrow and assess.

Annual one week provincial tour to show electronic aids (October).

Birmingham: Birmingham Disabled Living Centre
Broadgate House, Broad Street, Birmingham B1 2HF (Tel: 021-643 0980).

A permanent display, information and assessment centre for disabled people and their families. Provision is made for the handicapped person and the professional to see and try the aids and assess if they are suitable for individual needs. There are sections dealing with activities of daily living and some leisure pursuits.

Birmingham: Breakthrough Trust Deaf/Hearing Integration
Charles W. Gillett Centre, Selly Oak Colleges, Birmingham B29 6LE (Tel: 021-472 6447).
The Link Room at the above address provides a wide array of information for hearing impaired people and those concerned with deafness. The permanent display includes details of organisations, study books, library services, home equipment aids, hearing aids and the telephone for deaf people. (*See also* Section 16.)

Bristol: Assistive Communication Aids Centre
Speech Therapy Department, Frenchay Hospital, Bristol BS16 1LE (Tel: Bristol (0272) 565656 ext. 204).
The aims of the Centre are:
(a) to train speech therapists in the selection and use of communication aids;
(b) to act as a resource centre for demonstration, training and trials of aids;
(c) to examine the needs of this selected population;
(d) to assess and treat patients using assistive communication devices;
(e) to develop expertise on how best to introduce and train patients to use communication aids;
(f) to keep in contact with those using communication aids and assess their changing needs;
(g) to investigate the funding of aids, given the high cost of much of this equipment.
Day seminars are run on a regular basis, free of charge, for speech therapists and associated professions, to familiarise themselves with communication aids currently on the market. A free booklet *The Acquisition of Aids for the Speech Impaired* is available.

There is now a growing number of Communication Aids Centres in various parts of the country: the Disabled Living Foundation (*see* pages 53–54) will advise.

Caerphilly: Aids and Information Centre
Wales Council for the Disabled, Caerbragdy Industrial Estate, Bedwas Road, Caerphilly, Mid Glamorgan CF8 3SL (Tel: Caerphilly (0222) 887325/6/7).
An aids exhibition centre has been established

together with an extensive information bank on all aspects of aids and equipment for disabled people. Visits can be arranged by appointment, with a qualified physiotherapist in attendance.

Dudley: Aids and Assessment Centre
1 St Giles Street, Netherton, Dudley, West Midlands (Tel: (Dudley Social Services Department) Dudley (0384) 55433 ext. 5839).
This Centre is one of the more recent facilities for disabled people and serves people living in the Dudley Metropolitan Borough. It provides a permanent exhibition of aids and equipment which may be supplied, under the Chronically Sick and Disabled Persons Act 1970, by the Social Services Department (following a professional assessment by an occupational therapist to determine exact needs). Disabled people and their relatives will be shown how to use the equipment by trained, professional staff, and, where necessary, aids will be constantly reviewed, renewed or replaced.

The Centre is in ground floor accommodation with easy access and adequate parking nearby. Because of space limitations, however, wheelchairs cannot be displayed.

An appointment can be made by contacting Social Services at the above telephone number.

Edinburgh: South Lothian Aids Centre
Astley Ainslie Hospital, Grange Loan, Edinburgh EH9 2HL (Tel: 031-447 9200).
Provides a permanent standing exhibition of a comprehensive range of aids and equipment with a supporting information service for aids, techniques, financial benefits, services and facilities not displayed; acts as an educational centre where staff and volunteers working with disabled people may learn about these aids and services. Special exhibitions of particular types of aid are held on a regular basis.

The Centre is open Monday to Friday, *by appointment*. Special arrangements can be made to open outside normal working hours.

Glasgow: Aids Information Centre for Disabled People
26 Florence Street, Glasgow G5 (Tel: 041-429 2878).
Set up by The Greater Glasgow Health Board and Strathclyde Regional Council Social Work Department to serve the whole of the Strathclyde Region. Provides information on aids supply, manufacture, adaptation, prices and statutory provision. Also provides advice and contacts in the fields of housing, transport, employment and voluntary organisations.

In addition the centre organises seminars for pro-

fessionals covering a broad range of issues concerning disabled people.

Hours of opening are Monday to Thursday 9 a.m. to 4.30 p.m. and 9 a.m. to 3.45 p.m. on Friday.

Leeds: William Merritt Aids and Information Centre for Disabled People
St Mary's Hospital, Greenhill Road, Armley, Leeds LS12 3QE (Tel: Leeds (0532) 793140).
Two occupational therapists and a physiotherapist provide practical information and advice to disabled people, their families and those professionally concerned with disability.

A permanent exhibition of aids gives the visitor the opportunity both to view and to try out equipment covering all aspects of disability. There is a DIAL service housed in the same building (*see* page 281).

Visits to the centre should be arranged by prior appointment. Day courses and seminars are held bi-monthly and details are available on request.

Leicester: British Red Cross Society, Leicestershire Aids Centre for the Trent Regional Health Authority
76 Clarendon Park Road, Leicester LE2 3AD (Tel: Leicester (0533) 700747).

Liverpool: Merseyside Aids Centre
Youens Way, East Prescot Road, Liverpool 14 2EP (Tel: 051-228 9221).
The Merseyside Aids Centre is a permanent display of a comprehensive range of aids for disabled people of all ages. The Centre provides space for the display of over 1,500 pieces of equipment which is constantly under review. Visitors are welcome by appointment. Individual assessments are carried out, groups are shown round, and instruction is given in the use of aids and equipment.

London: The Disabled Living Foundation
380–384 Harrow Road, London W9 2HU (Tel: 01-289 6111).
A permanent exhibition of aids and equipment is provided. Although the centre is primarily for those professionally concerned with disability, disabled people and their relatives are also welcome. The equipment displayed covers aids to help with every aspect of disablement. Visitors will be shown around the centre by demonstrators who are professionally qualified in the care of disabled people. Aids are not on sale at the centre, but information on sources of supply, cost, etc., is available. In all cases, visits should be arranged beforehand by appointment.

The centre is open Monday to Friday 9.30 a.m. to

5.30 p.m.; no charge is made to disabled visitors, but there is a fee for those who are professionally concerned and to students. *An appointment is essential.* All enquiries to the Head Demonstrator. Day courses (for those professionally concerned) on various ranges of equipment are held at bi-monthly intervals.

London: Psychiatric Rehabilitation Association Aids Exhibition
The Halls, Mitchley Road, London N17 (Tel: 01-808 2833).
A permanent exhibition of a wide range of aids displayed in typical home settings. The selection for display is guided by the Disabled Living Foundation and local occupational therapists and is constantly updated. Some articles can be purchased from stock; otherwise, aids can be ordered. There is now some scope for supplying certain aids to individual requirements. An appointment is desirable, when an occupational therapist can be present to offer guidance. .

London: Spastics Society Aid and Equipment Exhibition
16 Fitzroy Square, London W1P 5HQ.
In addition to its Visiting Aids Centre (*see* page 60), the Society has a permanent centre at the above address where a wide range of products is exhibited. There is also a back-up of information sheets and address lists displayed in a carousel at wheelchair height, and a selection of helpful books.

Although the exhibition room is specially geared towards children, it is open to any cerebrally palsied person in the country. In order to visit, you can ask to be referred by your family doctor, contact one of the Society's regional offices, or write direct to Fitzroy Square.

Manchester: Manchester Centre for Disabled Living
Director, Jane Hugall, The Cripples Help Society, 26 Blackfriars Street, Manchester M3 5BE (Tel: 061-832 3678).
No other details made available.

Newcastle upon Tyne Council for the Disabled
MEA House, Ellison Place, Newcastle upon Tyne NE1 8XS (Tel: Newcastle upon Tyne (0632) 323617).
As the leading co-ordinating body for disabled people in the north-east, the Council provides a forum for consultation amongst and co-operation between voluntary, professional and statutory organisations. It undertakes research into the unmet needs of disabled people in the area and has initiated several projects to fulfil some of these needs such as a trans-port study, speech after stroke groups and a volunteer drivers' service.

There is an information and advisory service available to answer queries on cash benefits, services, facilities and sources of help, from disabled people and those who care for them.

The aids centre has a comprehensive range of aids for disabled people and is a major project of the Council. The centre's main purpose is to provide practical information and a means of demonstration to members of the medical, paramedical and social services, and also to organise seminars, etc. Visits to the centre should be arranged by prior appointment by letter or telephone to the above address. Aids are not on sale at the centre but information on sources of supply, cost, etc., is available.

An Incontinence Advisory Service has been established for the understanding and management of incontinence. The Continence Adviser is a qualified nurse and health visitor who has made a special study of this subject and is available to advise and train professionals of all disciplines in the methods and aids available for maintaining continence. Individual patient referrals are accepted.

Sheffield: Sheffield Aids Centre
Family and Community Services, 87–89 The Wicker, Sheffield 3 (Tel: Sheffield (0742) 737025).

Southampton: Southampton Aids Centre
West Ward Block, Southampton General Hospital, Tremona Road, Southampton SO9 4XY (Tel: Southampton (0703) 777222 ext. 3414 or 3233).
At this centre, the Southampton and South-West Hants District Health Authority provides an advice, information and demonstration service on aids and equipment to anyone who requires it. You do not need a doctor's referral but you must have an appointment. Open Monday to Friday 8.30 a.m. to 4.30 p.m.

Stockport: Stockport Aids Centre
St Thomas' Hospital, Shaw Heath, Stockport, Cheshire SK3 8BL (Tel: 061-480 7201 ext. 15).
Houses a permanent display of a comprehensive range of aids and services for disabled people of all ages, living in their own homes or other domestic settings.

Practical information and demonstrations are available to disabled people and their families, and to professionals involved in the care of disabled people.

Some of the smaller aids are on sale at the centre, and for others information can be given as to cost and source of supply.

Open Monday to Friday 9.30 a.m. to 4.00 p.m.

except closed on Wednesday afternoon. In all cases visits are by prior appointment only.

Swindon: Swindon Aids Centre
The Hawthorn Centre, Cricklade Road, Swindon SN2 1AF (Tel: Swindon (0793) 43966).
The centre has a permanent display of a wide range of aids and equipment for disabled people. There is supporting information on benefits, facilities and services for disabled people and illustrated literature on aids not on display.

Disabled people and those involved in their care are able to try out, or to see demonstrated, equipment relevant to their particular needs. Because the centre is not a commercial organisation, it allows a range of different manufacturers' equipment to be assessed and compared and impartial advice to be given.

Another important function is the education of paramedical staff and students. They may not be involved in the provision of aids themselves, but should be aware of the wide range of equipment that is available for disabled people and know where to refer them for help and advice on aids.

Aids on display range from simple, inexpensive gadgets to more complex electrical equipment. Aids are not on sale, but information is available on manufacturers and prices, and also on the provision of aids through the statutory authorities and the facilities offered by voluntary organisations.

Open Monday to Friday. Parking facilities are available. Visitors are seen by appointment with an occupational therapist, but you are welcome to seek advice by telephone before making an appointment.

Wakefield: National Demonstration Centre
Pinderfields General Hospital, Pinderfields, Wakefield WF1 4DG (Tel: Wakefield (0924) 375217 ext. 2510 or 2263).
A small standing exhibition of aids, mainly paediatric, with special exhibitions at regular intervals and an information service.

Touring Aids Exhibitions

Mobile Aids Centre (MAC)
MAC travels throughout Scotland with information and an exhibition of aids for disabled people. It is organised by the Scottish Council on Disability. For further information contact the Secretary, Mobile Aids Centre, Scottish Council on Disability, 5 Shandwick Place, Edinburgh EH2 4RG (Tel: 031-229 8632).

The RADAR Travelling Aids Exhibition
Demonstrations are given by an occupational thera-

pist of over 400 individual items of aids for dressing, feeding, housework, etc. The exhibition is accessible for wheelchairs. For information of locations to be visited, contact the Royal Association for Disability and Rehabilitation (RADAR), 25 Mortimer Street, London W1N 8AB (Tel: 01-637 5400).

The Spastics Society's Visiting Aids Centre
This mobile exhibition, which is financed by the Department of Health and Social Security and run by the Spastics Society, travels all over the country. The range of aids and information available on it is not exclusive to spastic people but caters for the needs of a whole range of disabilities. It incorporates items for visitors to try, and an illustrated index system gives comprehensive information about aids and equipment and where to obtain them. There is also a reference library, and audio-visual facilities for slides and films include an outside projection screen. The trailer has a tail-lift enabling wheelchair-bound visitors to have easy access to the Centre. An occupational therapist is in attendance to give help and advice.

Details of sites to be visited may be obtained from The VAC Department, 16 Fitzroy Square, London W1P 5HQ (Tel: 01-387 9571).

Purpose-made Aids

ACTIVE
Seabrook House, Darkes Lane, Potters Bar, Herts. EN6 2HL (Tel: Potters Bar (0707) 44571).
This organisation moved into partnership with the Toy Libraries Association (*see* Section 11, Sports and Leisure Activities) in January 1981. It was founded in 1975 and brought together an informal group of teachers, therapists and toy designers, meeting regularly to exchange ideas, to share and solve problems, and to produce new toys and play aids for handicapped children. Later, ACTIVE widened its frame of reference to include disabled adults as well as children, communication and learning aids as well as play aids. The membership has also widened to include disabled people themselves, their relatives and others with a professional or personal interest in ACTIVE's aims. It collects practical information about adaptations to and designs for toys, games, equipment and communication aids, and encourages their development and use.

ACTIVE's approach is one of 'do-it-yourself' with help, ensuring that *individual* needs are met appropriately, quickly and at minimum cost. Good ideas are passed on through *Ark* (the journal of the Toy Libraries Association – now Play Matters – published three times a year), through conferences and

DISABLED LIVING FOUNDATION

HOW CAN WE HELP?

By providing:–

1. An information Service on any matter to do with disabled people of any age and with any disability or handicap. This is free to disabled people and their relatives but on a subscription basis to local and health authorities.

2. Advisory Services on particular problems arising out of or related to disability, for example Clothing, Incontinence, Physical Recreation, Music, Visual Handicap and Skin Conditions.

3. A comprehensive collection of aids, equipment and design criteria which can be viewed by appointment. (Regional Aids Centres, although autonomous, are similar in concept and a list of these is available from DLF).

4. Publications on many aspects of daily living which provide solutions to the problems experienced by disabled people.

The Disabled Living Foundation
380-384 Harrow Road, London, W9 2HU.
Tel. No. (01)-289 6111

courses, and through an emerging network of local groups.

ACTIVE publishes a series of worksheets giving instructions for making a range of play, leisure and communication aids.

Rehabilitation Engineering Movement Advisory Panels (REMAP)

REMAP offers engineering help, advice and research on aids for disabled people. It brings together engineers who, advised appropriately by members of the medical and paramedical professions, design and make items of equipment, or modify commercially available equipment, to suit the special needs of handicapped individuals. REMAP operates through over 90 local panels which will make every attempt to solve problems which have not been overcome by standard equipment. By taking a fresh look at difficult problems, these panels are often able to devise ingenious solutions. The number of panels continues to grow.

Its work is voluntary though a charge may need to be passed on if raw materials, usually donated, have to be bought. Such charges may be borne by the local social services department.

The *REMAP Yearbook* is one of the best of its kind – inspiring, encouraging, and worth every penny of its cover price of £1. It gives examples of all kinds of equipment, shows exactly what REMAP is about and how others can help its work. Warmly recommended.

All enquiries should be made to REMAP, 25 Mortimer Street, London W1N 8AB (Tel: 01-637 5400).

Rehabilitation Engineering Unit, Chailey Heritage Hospital and School

North Chailey, Lewes, East Sussex BN8 4EF (Tel: Newick (082 572) 2112 ext. 99).

As well as marketing a range of aids developed at the Unit (*see* page 63), it is sometimes possible to respond to requests for one-off aids or personalised equipment for children. However, it is imperative in such cases that a member of the medical therapy staff, responsible for treatment, accompanies the child on any appropriate appointment.

Electronic Aids

The development of electronic control equipment is increasingly helping people with severe physical disabilities to gain a measure of control over their environment, and thereby returning to them a certain amount of independence. Possum Controls Ltd, Middlegreen Road, Langley, Slough, Berkshire SL3 6DF (Tel: Slough (0753) 79234), were pioneers in

this field. The earliest system was called a patient operated selector mechanism, and the initials for it, POSM, came to be pronounced as 'possum'. Fortuitously, there is a Latin word 'possum', meaning 'I can' or 'I am able' and this became a by-word in the care of severely disabled people. The Possum PSU3 environmental control system is available through the National Health Service free of charge to people approved by medical assessment (the initial application must come through your GP). It provides control of alarms, intercoms, telephones, lighting, heating, television, radio, electrically operated curtains and beds and the like.

Other Possum systems provide means of communication and basic learning which open up new opportunities for disabled people. The Possum ZX81 and Spectrum Computers enable people with severe disabilities to operate computers for education or personal use, as well as in employment.

Many other manufacturers are now active in this field, and there is an ever-increasing range of remote control, environmental and communication aids specially designed to meet the needs of people with physical handicaps, or who are affected by defects of sight, speech or hearing. A number of these incorporate visual displays, either integrally or through domestic television receivers, or can reproduce language in tactile forms; others link to standard equipment from everyday household devices through to mini and mainframe computers.

These developments are of immense importance to disabled people and it is for this reason that we single out electronic aids for special mention. But their range and scope is far too great to contain within these pages. We refer the reader to specialist sources of advice below, while the literature on communication aids is reviewed on page 65. Some of this equipment is now available under the NHS, or the cost may be met, or partly met, by Social Services Departments.

Progress, of course, has not been confined to equipment specifically designed for people with disabilities. Many advances which have been of more general benefit have nevertheless had particular spin-offs for disabled people. Obvious examples are cordless telephones, Prestel and similar information systems, and the marvellously versatile word processor. Electronic filing with access through a desk top visual display unit means that information in an office can be stored and retrieved as easily from a wheelchair as by a fully mobile staff member. New technology generally is pushing us into an age when a wide spectrum of human activity is controlled and facilitated by sophisticated electronic equipment.

Goods are manufactured, trains controlled on their journeys, and information stored, transmitted and reproduced virtually without human intervention. In such a context, the disadvantage of disability recedes, and we may look to a future when even profoundly disabled people can control their environment and work on equal terms with able-bodied colleagues with comparative ease.

Advice on Electronic Aids, Communicators and Microcomputers

Aids, Communications and Electronics (ACE)
ACE is a newsletter on communication aids published (four times a year) by The Group for Technology and Disability, Neath Hill Professional Workshop, 1 Fletchers Mews, Neath Hill, Milton Keynes, Bucks. It aims to be a 'clearing house' for up-to-date information and a forum for initial discussion on effectiveness, design and use of aids using the new technology. *ACE* is also developing a register of technical specialists who are willing to help 'tailor' equipment to meet individual needs. Annual subscription £5.50 (UK), £7.50 (overseas).

Roger M. Jefcoate
Willowbrook, Swanbourne Road, Mursley, Bucks MK17 0JA (Tel: Mursley (029 672) 533).
Roger Jefcoate is adviser on electronic aids to many of the major organisations concerned with disability, including the Spastics Society, Multiple Sclerosis Society, Muscular Dystrophy Group, Leonard Cheshire Foundation, Arthritis Care, Motor Neurone Disease Association and Manpower Services Commission. He travels throughout the United Kingdom and widely overseas, visiting severely disabled people, adults and children, at school, home or work, giving advice and help on the practical application of electronic technology to increase independence. He is sometimes able to assist disabled people to obtain financial help towards the cost of appropriate aids and equipment.

As well as helping individuals, Roger has established several projects which provide technical help on a wider scale. In 1975 he founded ACTIVE (*see* page 60) and an annual residential course at Castle Priory College; later, the Electronic Aids Loan Service (*see* below), Toy Aids Projects and the Aids for Disabled Fund.

Electronic Aids Loan Service for Disabled People

In 1978 Roger Jefcoate (*see* above) started an 'electronic aids loan service' whereby underused or unused electronic aids may be lent free of charge to others in need. The loan period is usually for a minimum of two months and sometimes much longer (even indefinite) according to demand. Items most usually available for loan include electronic and electric typewriters, portable communicators, page turners, microcomputers, dictation machines and other miscellaneous items.

The borrower must collect the item and return it to Mursley when no longer required, pay for all maintenance and repairs while retaining it, and insure it with the Special Aids Insurance Scheme (*see* below) *before* collection (£15 to £25 a year – a proposal form is provided). Small items such as communicators can be sent by post for £3. Stock changes frequently and a list of current items, updated every two months, is available. However, this is only a guide: if you do not see what you want it is nevertheless worth making a specific enquiry. Only written requests enclosing a 9 in. × 4 in. s.a.e. will be considered.

Insurance of Communicators, Typewriters and Microcomputers
The Sun Alliance Insurance Group operate a *Special Aids Scheme for Disabled People* which covers electronic aids used by disabled people (whether or not owned by them) at home, school or work. It is also available to organisations, special schools, etc. The scheme offers protection against fire, theft and accidental damage (including in transit) anywhere in Britain. It is available only through the Aylesbury office of Sun Alliance. The premium is likely to be between £15 and £25, according to the total value and type of items to be insured.

For further information and an application form, write to: Mr A Bayes, Sun Alliance Insurance Group, 12 Rickford's Hill, Aylesbury, Bucks HP20 2RX.

Books and Publications (for addresses *see* Appendix B)

AIDS IN GENERAL

ACTIVE Worksheets. ACTIVE (*see* page 60) publishes a series of worksheets covering a wide range of play, leisure and communication aids for severely disabled children and adults. The designs are submitted by ACTIVE members, parents, therapists, teachers, etc., and they are tested and drawn up in worksheet format by the ACTIVE design team, so that the aid can be made up for individual needs. The worksheets are categorised according to the skills and facilities needed. They range from simple 'kitchen table' woodwork to sophisticated electronic, woodwork, or metalwork designs. Contact Judy Denziloe, ACTIVE, c/o Play Matters, The

Toy Libraries Association, Seabrook House, Darkes Lane, Potters Bar, Herts EN6 2HL.

Aids and Adaptations by Ursula Keeble, published by Bedford Square Press, 1979. Price £5.95
This is not by any means a lay person's guide to aids and adaptations for use, but rather a study of the provision of aids in the United Kingdom. Chapters 2–7 cover the legislative background to the Chronically Sick and Disabled Persons Act 1970 and its financial implications, especially in the Greater London boroughs, the structure of the social services department, types of aids and appliances, sources of supply, the safety and storage of aids. Chapters 8–13 cover 'action research' on getting aids to clients, including ordering, delivery, installation, etc., types of adaptations and getting them done in public sector housing, GLC policies and adaptations in the private sector.

Aids for the Disabled, edited by Mary Manning (Community Care/IPC Business Press Ltd, Quadrant House, The Quadrant, Sutton, Surrey, 1982), £4.75: a compact 128-page paperback, with sections on broad classifications of aids, each listing relevant suppliers/manufacturers, with a brief indication of their products.

Aids for the Disabled. DHSS booklet HB2 available from local DHSS offices, Citizens' Advice Bureaux, etc., free of charge. Provides information about aids for use by individual disabled and elderly people. It describes the arrangements which exist to provide information about the aids which are available and the ways in which aids are provided by statutory bodies. It also briefly refers to the work being done in the research field and the part played by voluntary bodies and other organisations.

Aids for Independence. A sales catalogue of aids produced at the Rehabilitation Engineering Unit, Chailey Heritage Hospital and School, North Chailey, Lewes, Sussex BN8 4EF (Tel: Newick (082 572) 2112 ext. 99).
The aids were designed to overcome some of the problems experienced by children at Chailey Heritage Hospital, but are likely to have a wider application. In some instances the designs have been taken up by recognised manufacturing and marketing outlets, but other aids are available only from the Chailey Unit. The catalogue illustrates both batch-produced and one-off designs and thus also serves to disseminate ideas.

Aids to Independence. This includes drawings for the making of aids and suggestions for overcoming han-

dicaps. Available from RADAR. Price 65p plus 35p postage and packing.

DLF Information leaflets (*see* page 53).

Equipment for the Disabled compiled at Mary Marlborough Lodge, Nuffield Orthopaedic Centre, Oxford and published by the Oxfordshire Health Authority on behalf of the Department of Health and Social Security. A series of fully illustrated books which constitute the most authoritative guide to date to the wide range of aids and equipment available today. Specially designed, manufactured equipment and everyday consumer goods, as well as simple aids which can be made at home by the amateur are included. Advice is offered on selection, and solutions to various problems suggested. Most of the equipment shown has been used by a disabled person and its use assessed by a therapist.

Books are revised on a rota system and publication of new editions is announced in professional journals and those of voluntary organisations, as well as through an extensive mailing list. A box binder to hold all 11 books is available.
Titles are:

Wheelchairs	(*see* Section 8);
Outdoor Transport	(*see* Section 8);
Hoists and Walking Aids	(*see* Section 8);
Communication	(*see* this section);
Housing and Furniture	(*see* Section 4);
Home Management	(*see* Section 4);
Personal Care	(*see* Section 4);
Clothing and Dressing	(*see* this section);
Disabled Mother	(*see* Section 4);
Leisure and Gardening	(*see* Section 11);
Disabled Child	(*see* Section 4).

Each book costs £3.50, postage and packing extra. Binder £3.30, postage and packing extra. Orders should be sent to Equipment for the Disabled. Send no money with order: you will be invoiced.

Everyday Aids for the Disabled. Available from RADAR. Price 35p plus 20p postage and packing.

Easy-to-make Aids for your Handicapped Child by Don Caston, published by Souvenir Press Ltd. Contains simple instructions and diagrams showing how to make 60 aids for the handicapped child from basic materials with simple tools. Available from good bookshops, price £4.95 (paperback) plus 90p postage and packing.

Home-made Aids for Handicapped People. This booklet is full of cheap and simple ideas and costs 50p from the Supply Department, British Red Cross Society, 4 Grosvenor Crescent, London SW1X 7EJ (Tel: 01-235 5454).

Rehabilitation Today edited by Stephen Mattingly. Sections 12 and 18 by P. J. R. Nichols and E. Williams give a brief outline of a variety of aids, including those associated with severe disability. (For details *see* Appendix A.)

The Use of Technology in the Care of the Elderly and Disabled edited by Jean Bray and Sheila Wright, published by Frances Pinter (Publishers) Ltd. This book presents a collection of papers from two international conferences sponsored by the Commission of the European Communities which examine the provision of aids, especially technical aids, from a variety of standpoints, including research, design and development, testing and selection and the opportunities presented for the application of recent technological advances. It looks in depth at ways and means of putting better and more appropriate products at the service of disabled people and considers the contribution which industry could make to improve provision. Available from good booksellers or, in cases of difficulty, from the publisher, price £12.50 plus 95p postage and packing.

Which Aid? – On TV describes an experiment in which a number of selected aids were demonstrated on ATV's *Link* programme. Viewers were invited to write in about their own practical experience of the aids, and the results of these consumer views and of laboratory testing were then collated and broadcast. The aim of the project was not simply to show the various aids that are available, but to give advice on choosing aids to meet individual needs; to show which models work best and which stand up to hard use; and to give advice on self-help alternatives. This new book describes the objectives of the trial, explains how it was set up, reports on feedback from viewers and manufacturers and gives twelve individual reports on aids such as tin openers, special cutlery, bed hoists and walking frames. It will serve as a useful guide to choosing aids to suit individual requirements, and it is hoped will stimulate the provision of a continuing and much needed service for disabled people in their selection of aids. Available from the publisher, the National Fund for Research into Crippling Diseases.

With a Little Help compiled by Philippa Harpin (Muscular Dystrophy Group of Great Britain, Nattrass House, 35 Macaulay Road, London SW4 0QP, 1981), £7.50 inc. p & p: a guide, in eight volumes, to aids and adaptations written primarily for people with muscular dystrophy and allied neuromuscular diseases, but actually helpful to many people with other disabilities. The eight volumes are spirally bound for ease of handling and come in a none-too-strong box file. Taken together the package (about 4 inches thick) is rather cumbersome, but individually the books are neatly divided by subject:

Introduction and Adaptation
Bedroom and Clothing
Bathroom
Household and Seating
Communication
Mobility
Leisure
Index, Price Guide, Addresses

Each part is well illustrated with drawings, and contains much helpful, practical advice.

AIDS FOR BLIND AND PARTIALLY SIGHTED PEOPLE

Aids and Games for the Blind. This is an illustrated catalogue produced by and available from the Royal National Institute for the Blind. All kinds of aids for communication, employment and leisure are included. RNIB sells at subsidised prices to blind people almost 500 specially designed or adapted goods for school and home, work and leisure. It runs a London Resource Centre where people can try out goods sold by RNIB and commercial manufacturers.

DLF Fact Sheet about the full range of optical aids for low vision, with information about how to obtain them, is available from the Disabled Living Foundation, price 50p. Details of demonstration collections of such aids and advice about individual problems can be obtained by telephone on Tuesdays, Wednesdays and Thursdays from 10 a.m. to 2 p.m. (01-602 2491 – Mrs Scarr).

In Touch, a book taking its title from the BBC Radio 4 programme for blind listeners (*see* Appendix A for details), contains much useful information on aids available to blind and partially sighted people.

So You're Partially Sighted is a free leaflet detailing the help available for the visual problems of partially sighted people and includes information on low-vision magnifying aids. Available free from Optical Information Council, Walter House, 418–422 Strand, London WC2R 0PB (Tel: 01-836 2323). Please send s.a.e.

CLOTHING

Clothes Sense for Handicapped Adults of All Ages by P. McCartney, MBAOT. This book has been prepared primarily to help handicapped people in the community and those who shop and care for their clothes. There are details of many useful items of clothing available on the mass retail market and of a few specialised garments which are obtainable. There are also suggestions for simple adaptations which can be undertaken at home for those who are unable to buy suitable clothes in the shops. There is a very helpful chapter on aids to independence, including fastenings, dressing techniques and aids. Available from DLF (Sales) Ltd. Price £3.50.

Clothing and Dressing for Adults is one of the books in the series *Equipment for the Disabled*. It contains general information; metrication in fabrics and clothing, laundering and dry cleaning codes; selection of clothes; fastenings; foundation garments; underwear; nightwear; incontinence clothing; socks, stockings and shoes; women's wear; men's wear; trouser adaptations for men and women; dressing aids; solving problems; select bibliography; metric comparison tables; addresses/telephone numbers; alphabetical index.

Available from Equipment for the Disabled. Price £3.50 plus postage and packing (send no money with order).

Clothing. This is one of the many information leaflets available from Disabled Living Foundation.

Clothing for the Handicapped Child. Fully illustrated. An investigation of the problems presented by their garments and footwear to children having physical and mental disabilities and some suggested solutions. Available from DLF (Sales) Ltd. Price £2.50.

Dressmaking for the Disabled. A booklet describing how to adapt paper patterns to an individual's physical disabilities. Available from Disabled Living Foundation. Price 80p.

Footwear and Footcare for Disabled Children. A handbook for parents and those without medical, nursing or therapy qualifications (though also of value to relevant professionals and students). Available from DLF (Sales) Ltd. Price £5.25.

Footwear for Problem Feet by M. D. England, Lecturer Emeritus, London Foot Hospital. This book contains a great deal of useful advice on general problems in relation to foot health and comfort. However, this booklet is not intended for those with acute foot problems who require orthopaedic shoes or chiropodist treatment. Fully illustrated. Available from DLF (Sales) Ltd. Price £2.50.

How to Adapt Existing Clothing for the Disabled. Sewing notes with illustrations. Available from DLF (Sales) Ltd. Price £1.10.

Ways and Means – Taking the difficulty out of dressing, a do-it-yourself guide to adapting clothes for those who are slightly disabled, published by the WRVS, 17 Old Park Lane, London W1Y 4AJ.

COMMUNICATION AIDS

ACE. A newsletter on communication aids: *see* page 61.

Communication is one of the books in the series *Equipment for the Disabled*. It contains speech aids; call systems; environmental controls; telephones and telephone aids, radio and television; taped/large print books; bookrests and reading frames; manual, mouth and electric page turners; magnifiers; prismatic spectacles; writing aids and writing tables; typewriters, typing aids, typing tables; blind aids; deaf aids; solving problems; select bibliography; select list of associations concerned with different aspects of communication; metric comparison tables; addresses/telephone numbers; alphabetical index. Available from Equipment for the Disabled. Price £3.50 plus postage and packing (send no money with order).

Communication A & B. Two of the information leaflets available from the Disabled Living Foundation.

Communication Aids for Blind and Partially Sighted People. An information sheet compiled (August 1979) by the Greater London Association for Disabled People. Covers reading aids, talking books and newspapers, writing aids, telephone aids, intercom door openers and alarm systems, general aids and finance and help with relevant addresses. Free to disabled people in response to an s.a.e.

Communication Aids for Deaf and Hard of Hearing People. An information sheet compiled (January 1980) by the Greater London Association for Disabled People. Covers basic and special aids to hearing, methods of face-to-face communication, telephone and television aids, daily living aids and finance, with relevant addresses. Free to disabled people in response to a s.a.e.

Communication Aids for Physically Handicapped People. An information sheet compiled (January 1983) by the Greater London Association for Disabled People. Covers the range of communication aids currently available for disabled people under the following headings: remote control switches and environment control systems; intercoms and door openers; alarm systems; telephones; speech aids; writing aids; reading aids; finance.

RNID booklets.
Alarms and Indicators (duplicated sheet). Details of environmental aids.

Current Hearing Aids. A list of hearing aids on the market, giving details of price and performance.

Hearing Aids: Questions and Answers. A simple question and answer account of modern hearing aids.

Induction Loops in Public Places. Installation guidelines for engineers.

NHS Hearing Aids. A review, as at January 1983.

Radio Microphone and Infra-Red Hearing Aid Systems. For educational use.

TV and Radio Adaptors and the Loop System. Information on special devices to help those with hearing problems.

Visual Doorbell Systems.

These, and other booklets and leaflets, can be obtained free of charge (single copies) from the Royal National Institute for the Deaf, but a stamp would be appreciated.

General Guidance for Hearing Aid Users (DHSS booklet, 1982) available from LASS/SH2C, Alexander Fleming House, Elephant and Castle, London SE1 6BY, free of charge. Intended to help you to get the best use from your hearing aid. It does not, however, cover the special problems of hearing aid use by infants and children.

Hearing Impairment: A guide for people with auditory handicaps and those concerned with their care and rehabilitation by Kenneth Lysons. This book is a complete source of reference on the subject, covering everything from the different causes and types of hearing impairment to its psychological consequences. Expert advice is given on services, aids, rehabilitation procedures, educational facilities and special aspects of work with the hearing impaired. Available from good bookshops or, in case of difficulty, from the publishers, Woodhead-Faulkner (Publishers) Ltd, Fitzwilliam House, 32 Trumpington Street, Cambridge CB2 1QY. Price £7.95 paperback; £11.95 hardback, plus postage and packing.

Induction Loop Systems Installed in Greater London. An information sheet compiled (December 1981) by Greater London Association for Disabled People.

Explains how induction loops work and gives a list of places in London where a loop is installed.

List of Members of the Hearing Aid Industry Association is available from the Association at 16A The Broadway, London SW19 1RF (Tel: 01-946 3389). Members of the Association subscribe to a professional code of ethics. The list is free, but a s.a.e. is essential.

Rehabilitation Today edited by Stephen Mattingly. Section 22 by D. Garfield Davies includes useful basic information on hearing aids. (For details *see* Appendix A.)

Sound Advice – how you can help deaf people. A free leaflet issued by the Health Education Council. It is aimed at staff of retail stores and covers four key points in dealing with customers with a hearing problem.

DOMESTIC AIDS

See Section 4.

ELECTRONIC AIDS

Aids for the Severely Handicapped edited by Keith Copeland of the Bio-Physics Department of University College, London (Sector Publishing Ltd, 1974). A technical book, dealing with sophisticated electronic aids, in which 29 authors describe devices that they have designed to assist people who have lost – completely or partially – the use of their arms and legs, and who may also be unable to speak. The aids are intended to enable severely disabled people to use residual physical activity, not only to control most of their domestic environment, but also to communicate. There are also contributions on do-it-yourself aids. Price £10.95.

GARDENING AIDS

See Section 11.

INCONTINENCE AIDS

Bowel Management: A manual of ideas and techniques. Includes: methods to facilitate bowel evacuation; considerations such as frequency, timing, diet, water intake, exercise, use of laxatives, position, use of medications, toilet aids and cleaning; programmes from three rehabilitation centres; and ideas from readers of *Accent on Living*. Available from Accent Special Publications. Price $3.50 plus $0.85 postage and packing.

The following publications are obtainable from DLF (Sales) Ltd. Order forms and current prices on request.

Incontinence and its Management. Edited by Dorothy A. Mandelstam, published by Croom Helm Ltd, 1980. A textbook consisting of contributions by specialists in a range of disciplines dealing with the incontinent patient. Also of use to the informed lay person.

Incontinence: A guide to the understanding and management of a very common complaint by Dorothy A. Mandelstam, published by Heinemann Health Books for the DLF, 1977.
A practical illustrated handbook of value to incontinent people and those who care for them.

Incontinence: A burden for families with handicapped children by Jonathon Bradshaw, published by DLF, 1978. A study of the effects of incontinence and an examination of the availability of help. Based on research into the work of the Family Fund carried out at the University of York and intended for those professionally responsible for incontinence services.

Childhood Incontinence by Dr Roger Morgan. Subtitled 'A Guide to Problems of Wetting and Soiling for Parents and Professionals', this book outlines the normal working of the bladder and bowel, and gives a detailed analysis of training for continence, the problems of bedwetting, daytime wetting, urgency and faecal soiling. It describes a range of self-help and more formal treatment approaches. The book also includes sections on incontinence and the handicapped child. It is based firmly on the premise that something *can* be done about most children's incontinence problems, and provides a source of guidance to reduce the all-too-common disappointment of routines and treatments that fail through lack of information about the techniques and details of their practical use. Bill Brennan has provided clear and detailed illustrations.

The Management of Incontinence by Dorothy A. Mandelstam. A tape/slide presentation in two parts: Causes and Treatment, and Management. Obtainable from Camera Talks Ltd.

Portable Urinals and Related Appliances by Eric Ryckmans. A tape/slide presentation. Obtainable from Graves Medical Audiovisual Library.

ACA Directory of Aids. A comprehensive directory of aids and appliances for the management of incontinence, with supply details and guide prices. Compiled in 1983 by members of the Association of Continence Advisors, a multidisciplinary special interest group of health care professionals. Price £5 including postage and packing. Order forms obtainable from Incontinence Advisory Service, Disabled Living Foundation.

A leaflet on incontinence is available free of charge from The Health Education Council.

Incontinence. An information sheet compiled (January 1979) by the Greater London Association for Disabled People. It reviews incontinence wear for ambulant and wheelchair- and bed-bound people and also considers protection at night. There are sections on commodes, odour control and hygiene, financial help available and helpful organisations. Free in response to a s.a.e.

NOTE: A bibliography on the subject of incontinence is available from DLF (Sales) Ltd. *See* Appendix A for details.

LEISURE AIDS

See Section 11.

LIFTING AIDS

Handling the Handicapped: A guide to the lifting and movement of disabled people (second edition) edited by the Chartered Society of Physiotherapy. A completely updated edition of what has become the standard text on this subject. This book illustrates the professional methods of lifting and moving disabled people in day-to-day situations. Including over 100 photographs, it explains how to help them when they get up, and methods of transfer from bed or seat to wheelchair, into the bath, car or swimming pool, and even on to a horse are described. Also included are sections on choosing beds, wheelchairs, hoists and other aids for disabled people. Published by Woodhead-Faulkner Ltd. Price £5.25 paperback; £8.50 hardback plus postage and packing.

Hoists and their Use by Christine Tarling. Published by Heinemann Medical Books. As well as describing the various hoists now available, the author, a principal occupational therapist, explains how the heavy job of lifting can best be done, so that those caring for disabled people can use hoists without fear of damaging their backs. Disabled people are encouraged, wherever possible, to manage their own hoists and lift themselves. Available from DLF (Sales) Ltd. Price £8.75 including postage and packing.

Hoists and Lifting Equipment. One of the information leaflets available from the Disabled Living Foundation.

MOBILITY AND MOTORING AIDS

See Section 8.

READING AIDS

Library Association Leaflet. This free leaflet includes details of reading aids of all kinds: bookstands, mag-

nifying glasses and page turners. Available from A. E. L. Hobart, Library Association, 7 Ridgmount Street, London WC1 7AE. (Send s.a.e. 9 in. × 12 in. minimum.)
See also Communication Aids, page 65.

SEXUAL AIDS

See Section 12.

SPORTS AIDS

See Section 11.

TELEPHONE AIDS

See Section 4.

WHEELCHAIRS

See Section 8.

Audiovisual Material

Aids and Adaptations in the Home. A two-part tape/slide set produced and distributed by Camera Talks Ltd.

Challenge, 16 mm, colour, 27 minutes. Produced by Le Court (a home for severely disabled people at Liss, Hampshire) in 1967. Presents the inability to do normal things the normal way as a challenge, in the face of which human ingenuity is boundless. Shows a number of simple gadgets and techniques, and the transformation that electric-powered mobility effects. Available on hire from Concord Films Council Ltd.

No Limit, 16 mm, colour, 20 minutes. Another film by Le Court. It shows some of the ingenious gadgets evolved there, and presents a moving record of the cheerful courage and enterprise of the disabled inventors. It has won a variety of awards. Available on hire from Concord Films Council Ltd.

Words Without Hands, 16 mm, sound film in colour. A film which shows the simplest to the most sophisticated aids to writing and reading. Narrated by Robert Robinson. Available on hire from Concord Films Council Ltd.

Graves Medical Audiovisual Library, Holly House, 220 New London Road, Chelmsford, Essex CM2 9BJ (Tel: Chelmsford (0245) 83351). This library carries a large stock of tape/slide programmes available for hire and sale. These include a number relating to aids (catalogue number in brackets):

Aids for People Who Have Had a Stroke (78/7, etc.). A series of six tape/slide programmes designed for those people who have had a stroke, their relatives and the people professionally concerned with their rehabilitation. Prepared by the Disabled Living Foundation, the programmes, each lasting about 35 minutes, cover aids for personal independence, aids to communication, clothing and dressing aids, aids for mobility, aids for housework and aids for leisure.

Aids and Appliances for Rheumatoid Arthritis (78/ 61). Covers mobility, leisure and daily living. Prepared by the Arthritis and Rheumatism Council, the programme lasts 18 minutes.

Simple Electric Aids for the Handicapped and Elderly (74/12). By electronics expert, R. M. Jefcoate. De-scribes simple aids for mobility and independence. Lasts 12 minutes.

Clothing for the Disabled (72/41–42, 73/62–63). Four programmes made in association with the Disabled Living Foundation. They cover incontinence protective garments (22 minutes), clothing (28 minutes), incontinence protective clothing for children (38 minutes), and how to adapt clothing for handicapped children (29 minutes).

Home Aids for the Patient with Arthritis (72/7). De-scribes a wide range of equipment, appliances and gadgets to help a disabled person overcome problems in the home. Lasts 25 minutes.

HOUSE AND HOME

A home of one's own: a simple right and necessity for all of us, but in this overcrowded island what problems this can present! Then, in addition, for disabled people there is the difficulty of finding specialised accommodation to tie in with their tastes and requirements. A badly designed home for a disabled person can be at best a further handicap, at worst an inhospitable prison. Then there is the expense. This section sets out to pinpoint the various services and organisations which may ease the path of the aspiring disabled home-maker. How to find that indispensable roof over your head, then how to have it adapted, or how to arrange your own home which has become so difficult to manage. It has to be said that these adaptations are seldom easily won, but sheer sticky persistence may well bring its reward.

For many people with disabilities, help with daily living activities and household chores is as important as a suitable building and comfortable surroundings. In the United States, Centres for Independent Living have shown that given the right assistance, tailor-made for and directed by individual disabled people, an independent life-style is possible – even for those who are severely disabled. We describe in this section some of the initiatives being developed along these lines.

We hope that these projects will inspire many others around the country.

Housing Standards

Mobility Housing

This is built to 'normal' space standards, but includes such features as a ramped entrance and wide doors; it may be provided for those who can walk a little and do not need to use a wheelchair all the time.

The important feature of mobility housing is that it can be lived in without the need to cope with steps or stairs. 'No steps or stairs' mobility housing can be achieved with: bungalows; ground-floor flats in low-rise blocks; flats with lifts to upper levels; two-storey houses with a bathroom and bedroom at ground level; two-storey houses with a suitable staircase, enabling a stairlift to be installed so that upper rooms can be reached without climbing the stairs.

Wheelchair Housing

This housing is specially planned for people confined to wheelchairs. Important design considerations are: a level or slightly ramped approach to the entrance with no threshold obstruction; internal planning for wheelchair manœuvre, with passageways 1,200 mm wide and suitable doors – either 900 mm doorsets or sliding doors with a 775 mm opening; a kitchen planned for wheelchair manœuvre, with space to turn the wheelchair and access to equipment and storage; a bathroom planned for use from a wheelchair, with a shower or bath allowing a person to transfer from a wheelchair; a lavatory planned for transfer from a wheelchair; switches, window controls, door furniture and other fittings placed so as to be comfortably reached from a wheelchair; windows placed to give views out for wheelchair users; a garage or carport (if provided) with undercover access to the dwelling; a flexible and economic central heating system.

British Standards Institution Codes of Practice.

Design of housing for the convenience of disabled people – the British Standards Institution's Code of Practice BS 5619: 1978. Price £6 to non-members. The principle behind this Code of Practice is that whenever practicable, ordinary housing should be convenient for disabled occupants or visitors. Three main areas are considered. First are design recommendations for the approach to a dwelling (including ramps, lifts, parking, garden paths and entrance doors). Second are recommendations for interior features such as circulation spaces and internal doors, floors, windows, kitchens, bedrooms, WCs, bathrooms and stairs. Finally, the Code deals with the design of services; electricity, heating, controls and refuse disposal.

The level of disablement considered is that of people using wheelchairs who are not so disabled that they need special housing. The guidelines set down in the Code are to encourage good practice.

The recommendations are to be regarded as a list of desirable provisions, which, according to circumstances, should be observed wherever practicable. The Code, drawn up by experts in the field of building together with government and voluntary organisations including the Royal Association for Disability and Rehabilitation, Disabled Drivers' Association, Disabled Living Foundation, Joint Committee on Mobility for the Disabled, RNIB, RNID, Age Concern and Spastics Society, is a considerable landmark in the campaign for integrated housing. It goes a long way to establishing that housing built to such standards need not be considered exclusive but is more comfortable and convenient for a very wide range of people. Now it is essential that we all continue to press these standards on all those responsible for building our houses.

Other British Standard codes include:
Powered stairlifts BS 5776: 1979. Price to non-members £10.50.
Powered homelifts BS 5900: 1980. Price to non-members £14.

Manually driven balanced personal homelifts BS 5965: 1980. Price to non-members £10.50.
Access for the Disabled to Buildings BS 5810: 1979. Price to non-members £10.50. (For details *see* Appendix A.)

It would now be reasonable to expect compliance with these codes for relevant equipment. Copies of British Standards may be obtained from British Standards Institution, Sales Department, 101 Pentonville Road, London N1 9ND (Tel: 01-837 8801).

Statutory Provisions

Under the provisions of the Chronically Sick and Disabled Persons Act 1970, local authorities are required to consider housing needs in their areas in respect of the special requirements of registered disabled people, and to provide assistance to such persons to adapt their homes and to provide any necessary extra facilities to secure their greater safety, comfort or convenience.

While wide powers are available to both housing and social services authorities to undertake or to

provide assistance with adaptations, it has to be emphasised that local authorities vary widely in their interpretation of the needs of disabled people. There has been in the past a confusion of responsibilities between the housing and the social services departments. In order to make matters clearer a government circular defined the areas of responsibility:

Housing authorities should be responsible for structural modifications to dwellings owned or managed by them. These modifications include extensions or alterations to provide a bathroom, WC or bedroom, etc., with level or suitable ramped access, replacement of steps with ramps, widening or rehanging of doors, alterations to electrical and heating systems, and alterations to bathroom and WC fixtures. These responsibilities lie alongside the housing authorities' role in the provision of mobility and wheelchair housing.

Social services should be responsible for non-structural features and the provision of aids and equipment. In addition social services are responsible for identifying, assessing and advising on the needs of disabled people, including the need for adaptations to their homes.

Advice should be sought from the local social services department, or housing department.

OWNER-OCCUPIERS AND PRIVATE TENANTS

Alternatively, under the Housing Act 1974 (as amended by Housing Rents and Subsidies Act 1975) house renovation grants (i.e. improvement and intermediate grants) may be available to disabled people to meet their special needs. Owner-occupiers who qualify (see Section 13) may find it advantageous to choose this method of securing adaptations and financial help rather than the less well-defined arrangements operated by the social services authority, as described above. The decision will, of course, hinge upon the relative cost of the alternative schemes to the person concerned: the cost under social services arrangements will depend to a large extent on the financial circumstances of the applicant, whereas in the case of grants there is a prescribed percentage to be paid by the applicant (though in certain circumstances the social services department may help with this cost).

COMPULSORY PURCHASE

If a dwelling which has been constructed or adapted to meet the needs of a disabled person is compulsorily purchased, compensation may be based on the reasonable cost of equivalent reinstatement (Land Compensation Act 1973: see page 260).

LOCAL AUTHORITY TENANTS

The local authority may be able to provide a council house to rent, and, if it is necessary and practicable, the home may be adapted to suit a particular disability. Tenants who need major adaptations to their homes should go to their housing department or social services department for help. They will not be required to contribute to the cost if the housing department carries out the adaptations, but their rent could be affected. However, if the social services department carries out the adaptations, then tenants may be asked to contribute to the cost.

HOUSE RENOVATION GRANTS

The grants are intended for the improvement and upgrading of older housing and are not normally available for houses built after 2 October 1961, but since this restriction has no relevance to the provision of facilities for disabled people the Secretary of State has directed that local authorities may entertain applications in respect of works needed for a disabled occupant regardless of the age of the dwelling. Applications should be made to the Housing Improvement Officer at your local council office. In certain cases the social services authority may help to meet the applicant's share of the cost. It is important to wait until the local authority has approved your application for grant because you may be disqualified from assistance if the work is started before the application is approved. Make sure also that you have the right approval notice. Approval for building regulation or planning purposes is not the same as grant approval.

How much grant you get depends on the rate of grant approved by the local authority and the cost of the work accepted by the local authority as eligible for the particular grant applied for (known as the 'eligible expense'). The maximum rates of grant are:

For priority cases (see below) in all areas	75 per cent
For houses in general improvement areas	65 per cent
For all other cases	50 per cent

The priority categories of case are:

Houses in housing action areas, and
Houses that are unfit (lacking one or more of the standard amenities, or in need of substantial and structural repair).

The 75 and 50 per cent rates may be increased by the local authority to 90 and 65 per cent respectively in cases of hardship.

Who can apply?

The applicant must be the freeholder or leaseholder (including both owner-occupiers and landlords), or a regulated or secure tenant who may wish to do the work himself. The right of a tenant to apply does not affect his right in certain circumstances to ask the local council to require the landlord to improve the dwelling if it lacks one or more of the standard amenities. More information about the grants is given in the booklet *Home Improvement Grants*, available from local rent offices, council offices, housing aid centres and Citizens' Advice Bureaux.

Are conditions attached to the grants?

Owner-occupiers and landlords have to supply a certificate of future occupation and conditions are attached to the grants to ensure broadly that for a period (normally of five years) the dwelling is used in the manner described in the certificate. If a condition is breached, the local authority may demand repayment of the grant, but owner-occupiers can now sell without breach of condition. Tenants cannot be asked to repay, but the local authority may require an undertaking from the landlord that he will continue to let the dwelling, before approving an application from a tenant.

Value added tax

Since 1 June 1984 most building alterations have been liable at the standard rate of VAT, along with repairs and maintenance, which always have been. The following alterations, however, are specifically zero-rated:

(a) the supply to a handicapped person of the services of constructing ramps, widening doorways or passages to enable him/her to enter or move within his/her private residence;

(b) the supply to a charity of the services of constructing ramps, widening doorways or passages to enable a handicapped person to enter or move within any building;

(c) the supply to a handicapped person of the service of providing, for the first time, a bathroom, washroom or lavatory on the ground floor of his/her private residence;

(d) goods supplied in connection with any of these services.

If VAT does apply to any works carried out under the House Renovation Grants scheme, it may be included in the costs to which a grant applies. Any charge for building regulations approval is also eligible.

HOME IMPROVEMENT GRANTS

These are made at the discretion of the local authority and they are intended to help improve homes to a good standard, or (if you own a property) to provide additional homes through conversions.

For disabled people, improvement grants are available for work to adapt a house for the accommodating, welfare or employment of a disabled occupant, who may be yourself or another person who is disabled and is living in your home. They are not intended to help with improvements to modern houses or fully equipped houses in good repair, or normally to enlarge a house to provide more bedroom space, and you will not get a grant for the installation of central heating unless it forms part of a major scheme of improvement.

If you are an owner-occupier you will not qualify for an improvement grant to improve your house if its rateable value is more than £400 in Greater London or £225 elsewhere. These limits do not apply if you live in a housing action area or are applying for a grant to improve a home for a disabled person.

In non-priority cases the eligible expense limit is £6,600 outside London or £9,000 in Greater London. In priority cases (*see* above) the normal limits are £10,200 outside London and £13,800 in Greater London. Higher limits apply for some conversions, and for improvements to listed buildings.

Intermediate grants

These are available as of right for the provision of missing standard amenities so long as the basic condition, that the dwelling shall be fit for human habitation, is met (and even this requirement may be waived in some cases). Application may also be made to provide extra standard amenities for a disabled occupant to whom existing amenities may be inaccessible. The eligible expense limits are:

	In Greater London £	Elsewhere £
Fixed bath or shower	450	340
Wash-hand basin	175	130
Sink	450	340
Hot and cold water supply at		
bath or shower	570	430
wash-hand basin	300	230
sink	380	290
Water closet	680	515
Total	3,005	2,275

Repairs are also eligible within the limits of £4,200 in Greater London and £3,000 elsewhere (or a smaller

amount for minor repairs only may be claimed).

Repairs grants

These are now available generally (not just in housing action areas and general improvement areas). They are made for substantial and structural repairs to pre-1919 dwellings within specified rateable value limits and at the discretion of local authorities. The eligible expense limit is £4,800 outside London and £6,600 in Greater London.

Special grants

These are for the provision of standard amenities and means of escape from fire, together with repairs, in houses in multiple occupation. Landlords can apply, but not tenants. The eligible expense limits are the amounts per standard amenity to be provided, as set out above; for means of escape £8,100 outside London and £10,800 in Greater London; and for repairs £3,000 outside London and £4,200 in Greater London.

DEPARTMENT OF EMPLOYMENT GRANTS

Through the Business on Own Account Scheme limited facilities are occasionally provided under Section 15 of the Disabled Persons (Employment) Act 1944 to enable severely disabled people to work on their own account if all other possibilities of employment have been found unsuitable and where the suggested business seems a viable economic proposition. Each case is considered on its merits and the scheme is likely to be recommended only if no other option for employment seems possible.

RELIEF FROM RATES IN RESPECT OF SPECIAL FACILITIES FOR DISABLED PEOPLE

A new scheme of relief on rates payable by certain disabled persons came into force on 1 April 1979. The Rating (Disabled Persons) Act 1978 clarifies the circumstances in which rate relief is available to disabled people; it provides for relief to be given in the form of a deduction from the rate bill. It specifies certain facilities required for meeting the needs of a disabled person, the amount of relief to be paid, and extends the types of institution which are eligible. Despite the fact that the new legislation is still rather complicated, it throws welcome light on an area which has remained confused by anomalies and inconsistencies, and it provides a sensible framework in which disabled people may claim rating relief for home necessities which justly serve to lighten a harsh environment. The new legislation owes much to Neville Vandyk who, being severely disabled himself, proposed that his entire flat should be relieved of rates because of adaptations he had made. The Greater London Central Valuation Court decided that two rooms only should be exempt, but on appeal to the Lands Tribunal, the whole flat was removed from the valuation list. The Court of Appeal upheld this decision, but on further appeal by the valuation officer to the House of Lords, the decision was reversed and the flat at full valuation was restored to the list.

It could be said that while the battle was lost, the war was won as evidenced by the more enlightened thinking leading to the new Act.

The Provisions of the Rating (Disabled Persons) Act 1978
For more precise details *see* Section 13.

On properties which include specified facilities required for meeting the needs of a disabled person, a rebate may be awarded on a specified amount at the rate applicable to the property in question, and for the period for which the relief applies.

The facilities attracting rebates do not have to be installed with the particular disabled person in mind in respect of whom the claim is made. Premises may

have been moved into because they had the facilities needed by the incoming disabled person. A claim can accordingly be made even though the new arrival, or the person entitled to a rebate, did nothing to equip the accommodation with the facilities. A claim may be made in respect of more than one residence for the same disabled person. Any rate rebates given under provisions of the Local Government Act 1974 will be adjusted to take account of any rebate granted under the Rating (Disabled Persons) Act 1978.

In England and Wales relief is allowed according to the declared rate in the £ on the following specified amounts (a rating authority has discretion to increase these amounts by one-fifth):

(a) a room other than a bathroom or lavatory predominantly used by the disabled person whether for providing therapy or for other purposes – £30;
(b) an additional bathroom – £20;
(c) an additional lavatory – £10;
(d) sufficient floor space to permit the movement of a wheelchair used by the disabled person – £30;

(e) (i) a garage – £25*;
     (ii) a carport – £15*;
     (iii) a parking space – £5*.

* The applicant has the option to have the rateable value separately assessed.

Central heating systems and other facilities (*e.g.* a lift or escalator) will attract relief if the valuation officer is able to attribute a rateable value to them and issues a certificate accordingly.

In Scotland, with one exception (*see* page 262), the rebate is calculated as that much of the rates chargeable on the property for the rebate period as is attributable in the opinion of the assessor to the particular locality.

In Northern Ireland (*see* page 263) the District Valuer has to certify the value of any facility qualifying for a rate rebate, even on 'sufficient floor space for use of wheelchair'.

Making a claim

A rebate can only be granted by a rating authority after the receipt of an application from the person entitled to it. Applications will have to be renewed annually, but it is expected that rating authorities will make provision to avoid a full re-application where there has been no change of circumstances.

Home Adaptations and Equipment

There are many aids and a wide range of useful equipment to enable disabled people to adapt the environment of their home to their own special needs and requirements. By the addition of a lift or stair-climbing apparatus it may be possible to continue to live in a house which has become unsuitable or to buy a house in an area where a single-storey building is not available. It would obviously be necessary to ensure that there was a suitable position for the lift or that the stairs were suitable to take the stair-climbing apparatus. There are also a number of prefabricated rooms available such as purpose-built bathrooms and toilets, which from a practical point of view are relatively easy to install, and provide the necessary amenities with the minimum of fuss. Adaptation of existing accommodation has an important part to play in the provision of housing suitable for the needs of disabled people. It has the advantage, not always possible with new housing, of enabling people to remain close to friends and relations, and in familiar surroundings. For further details *see* Aids Centres, Section 3.

NEW HOUSING BENEFIT SCHEME

This scheme, which had a partial start in November 1982, was fully implemented in April 1983. It replaces the old system where people requiring help with housing costs had to make a choice between claiming supplementary benefit from the DHSS or applying to their local authority for rent rebates and rent allowances. For full details *see* Section 2.

LOFT INSULATION GRANTS

Householders with uninsulated lofts, or lofts that have less than 1 inch of insulation, can obtain grants towards the cost of installing loft insulation, also to cover the insulation of water tanks and pipes in the roof-space and the provision of a jacket to insulate a hot water tank. The value of the grant is normally about two-thirds of the cost up to a maximum of £69. If you are elderly or severely disabled and on a low income the grant could cover 90 per cent of the cost up to a maximum of £95.

Those who may be entitled to a 90 per cent grant include:

A man over 65 or a woman over 60 getting a supplementary pension or allowance, a rent/rate rebate or rent allowance – together known as housing benefit. A person (or a dependant living in the same house) receiving mobility allowance and/or attendance allowance or constant attendance allowance.

Further information in leaflet *Save Money on Loft Insulation* available from council offices, housing aid centres and Citizens' Advice Bureaux.

GAS AND ELECTRICITY IN THE HOME

Gas checks

Arrangements have been made to institute free gas checks for elderly people who live alone or registered handicapped users of any age. Only those whose names are given by the local authority social work department or an organisation representing handicapped people will be included in this scheme. British Gas Home Service advisers will call on people with disabilities or special problems and provide advice free of charge. Minor replacement parts up to the cost of £1 will be provided free. Any part connected with rubber tubing and push-on ends will have such connections replaced with more suitable ones free of charge. Special tap handles for gas cookers, fires and central heating radiator control valves, can be obtained at £2 plus VAT per appliance. Special braille thermostats are available for most gas cookers together with braille cooking charts to help those with failing sight or blindness.

Gas accounts

Savings schemes are available and monthly payments may be made based on estimated consumption.

Meters can be repositioned at a more convenient height. There is a standard charge of £3 plus VAT for this service.

Electricity accounts
All electricity boards offer monthly budget payment schemes by cash, bank Giro, or monthly standing order. A settlement is made annually and then the level of monthly payments is also reviewed. Quarterly accounts advise the consumer of the amount of electricity he has used and enable him to check that all payments have been credited to his account. Interim payment schemes are similar but settlement is made quarterly.

Most boards also offer payment schemes at their shops where the customer can pay an amount and collect a personal card or book of payment receipts. All boards offer a savings stamp scheme with stamps of various denominations available from their shops.

Free booklets
Gas Aids for Disabled People is available from British Gas showrooms.
Making Life Easier for Disabled People gives brief advice on heaters, cookers, mixers, clothes and dishwashing appliances, refrigerators and freezers. Also included are details of some of the special controls which can be fitted to appliances such as cookers. The leaflet is available free from Electricity Board showrooms.
Electricity and Gas bills for your home: How to pay them, how to get help if there is real hardship. A Code of Practice issued by the Electricity and Gas Industries.
The Gas Consumers' Council's *Guide to Special Services and Benefits for Elderly and Disabled People*.

Independent Living

An increasing number of disabled people are choosing to live independently and to maintain homes of their own. Even those people with severe disabilities, who need help for most of their daily living activities, are not only rejecting the institutional style of life, but also arranging their domestic lives so as not to rely more than absolutely necessary on able-bodied relatives. These include single people with disabilities and couples where both partners are disabled. In her book *Living Independently*, Ann Shearer looks at the lives of nine severely disabled people who have established homes of their own in the community. (For details of this book *see* page 89.)

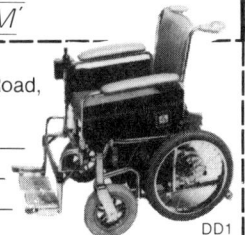

We describe below some of the projects and support services which very often, in combination, can make a home of one's own a practical possibility. Section 2 in this Directory describes the financial benefits which may be juggled around to offset the not inconsiderable cost of living independently. In particular, it is important to note that supplementary benefit is available to cover the 'reasonable cost' of visiting domestic help if this is not provided by the local authority.

See also details of specialist housing associations who, in addition to building appropriate accommodation, may provide wardens on their estates who are on call for emergencies, and, in the case of Habinteg, a community assistant who provides personal care and support. *See* page 83.

SOCIAL SERVICES

Home helps
Domestic and other help, where this is needed to relieve the domestic situation in the home when someone in the household is sick or handicapped, may be provided by a local authority. Most local authorities make a charge for this service, and this is often based on the means of the household and the number of hours the home help is in attendance.

The service, on its own, is intended to provide back-up help and cannot usually be stretched enough to enable a severely disabled person to live independently.

Laundry service
Local councils may provide a laundry service to help households where there is a handicapped person. However, a charge may be made according to the means of the household. For further information contact the social services department, family doctor, district nurse or health visitor.

Meals-on-wheels
These are administered by local authorities and may be delivered by volunteers. There may be a charge.

HEALTH SERVICE

District nurses
Are employed by district health authorities and provide help with domestic nursing care on a visiting basis. They may help with getting up and going to bed, and with bathing among their general duties. Anyone needing their services should contact their doctor.

CENTRES FOR INDEPENDENT LIVING

These Centres in the United States have been in the forefront of the movement initiated and built up by disabled people who are determined to maintain maximum control over their own lives. While it would hardly be possible to translate them exactly as they are to the United Kingdom, given the very different social conditions, they have been a great source of inspiration to disabled people in this country who espouse similar principles of independence. A number of projects are being planned and we describe three of them.

Derbyshire Independent Living Project (DILP)
(as developed by the Derbyshire Coalition of Disabled People) Victoria Buildings, 117 High Street, Clay Cross, Chesterfield, Derbyshire (Tel: Chesterfield (0246) 865305).
The DCDP has been much involved with working out ways of developing 'Centres for Independent Living' in the United Kingdom, somewhat on the lines of existing CILs in the United States. (As these terms are registered trade marks they will not be used when a final decision is made on naming the Derbyshire and other initiatives.)

The problem in Derbyshire has been to decide how best a CIL and Mixed Ability Co-op could thread into the tapestry of existing statutory and voluntary service provision at local level. The DILP project has progressed so far with the co-operation of the County Council through a joint working party.

A CIL is about independent, integrated living and thus gives a vital sense of direction both to the way resources are allocated and to the way existing services are utilised. The prime objective of any CIL is the provision of care attendants and in Derbyshire one of the first programmes will be to compile a detailed register of all disabled people in the county and also a register of people who would be willing to become paid care attendants. The disabled person, as in the United States, will define what help he or she requires, the frequency and at what times. They will also have the right not only to select their own care attendants, but also to hire and fire and to actually pay them personally for their services.

Other support services provided by a CIL will include transport services, full specialist and information advice services, workshops to produce home adaptations, make one-off gadgets and to service and repair all types of wheelchairs, aids and equipment. There will be an aids and equipment showroom, and a half-way house to provide temporary accommodation for one or two families or single disabled people while they adjust and learn to cope with their disability. Peer counselling will be an important part of the service.

Such initiatives mark a breakthrough for disabled people in establishing their right to independent life-styles of their choice.

Hampshire Centre for Independent Living
Formerly known as Project 81 – a scheme devised to help severely disabled people to find alternative accommodation and support outside residential care. It was started by a group of residents from Le Court Cheshire Home, most of whom are now living independently in the community. HCIL is a group of like-thinking people, most of whom have disabilities, who seek to promote an approach for the philosophy, support and practice of independent living for people with disabilities. HCIL was established to promote the following aims:

(a) to enable persons with disabilities to live independently in the community;

(b) to help people with disabilities plan and implement the decisions that affect their lives;

(c) to foster an image of people with disabilities that expresses their true value and potential as equal members of society;

(d) to propagate the philosophy of independent living for disabled people.

Activities include working with locally based people to encourage them to become active and involved in their area and establishing an effective and distinctive, organised voice as a balance to orthodox agencies as well as acting as a spokesperson for like-thinking people.

Programmes seek to advance the education of the public about the needs and potential of disabled people and the part that such people can play in society generally. Also to protect and promote the physical, mental and psychological health of disabled people, particularly through the provision of a skilled counselling service appropriate to their individual needs, through peer support and advice by peer models and to provide assistance with care and housing matters.

Further information from: John Evans, Le Court, Liss, Hampshire GU35 6HD or Philip Mason, 4 Plantation Way, Whitehill, Bordon, Hampshire GU35 9HD.

SHAD (Sheltered Housing Assistance for the Disabled)
c/o Battersea Arts Centre, Old Town Hall, Lavender Hill, London SW11 5TF (Tel: 01-350 1721).
SHAD was established so that severely disabled people could have the opportunity to live in their own houses, enabling them to lead independent and full lives, working or studying, as members of the community.

The first project is in Wandsworth, London, where SHAD aims to establish homes for severely disabled women and men. Priority is given to local people. Prospective tenants must be between 18 and 35, severely physically dependent and intellectually and emotionally independent, *i.e.* capable of work or of undergoing training that will lead to work. Initially, three houses are being converted, providing one SHAD flat per house for a disabled person among accommodation for other single people. Each house is in a different area of Wandsworth and like any other in its street, except for the special conversions to meet the needs of the disabled occupant. The first SHAD flat was opened in March 1982. The next two were expected to be ready in 1984.

A vitally important area of SHAD's work is the provision and co-ordination of volunteers who will live with and assist the disabled tenants. SHAD has therefore appointed a Volunteers Organiser to co-ordinate the recruitment and placement of the volunteers, to liaise with them on their projects in the community and to act as their supervisor, available for support.

SHAD is hoping to facilitate independent living-type schemes in other London boroughs and possibly further afield.

HELPFUL ORGANISATIONS

British Council of Organisations of Disabled People (BCODP), c/o Yeoman's House, 76 St James's Lane, Muswell Hill, London N10.
The BCODP, in assessing their members' needs, felt that housing must be a priority area for their consideration. As a result the Housing Standing Committee was formed. This committee seeks to involve disabled people at local level in the planning and provision of suitable housing to meet individual needs.

BCODP believes that every disabled person has a right to make their own decisions regarding their housing preferences and to be involved at planning and other stages. The Council seeks to avoid, as far as possible, any suggestion that a disabled person should be forced to live in an institution against their will and inclination. BCODP has joined up with Shelter to develop a project which operates in ten areas: Cardiff, Leeds, Leicester, Liverpool, North London, South London, Newcastle, Nottingham, Salford and Walsall. For the project to be successful it is essential that disabled people in these areas take part. BCODP has found that the most successful housing schemes have been those in which disabled people have been involved in the planning right from the start.

Shelter is producing a report on local authority housing practices, with an introduction by BCODP. It is likely to be available by the time this Directory is published. Further information from the BCODP Housing Standing Committee at the above address. For further details of BCODP *see* page 295.

Centre on Environment for the Handicapped
126 Albert Street, London NW1 7NF (Tel: 01-482 2247)
CEH provides a specialist information and advisory service on the environmental needs of all handicapped people. Its aim is to make that environment better so that handicapped people can, as individuals, make the most of their potential for living. CEH services are used by architects, occupational therapists, health, social services and housing authorities, housing associations, voluntary organisations and individual handicapped people.

While CEH's principal focus is on the built environment, and it is therefore primarily concerned with the contribution made by architects, it recognises that the provision of good environments for handicapped people is not simply a matter of buildings but is often, more importantly, one of attitudes and relationships and of the policies and controls which are exercised by local authorities and central government.

A Register of Housing and Care Support Schemes
Recognising the need to draw together all the information on means for living as independently as possible in the community, CEH, together with the Long Term and Community Care Team at the King's Fund Centre, is compiling a register on the full range of housing and care support schemes available to physically handicapped people.

The information is intended primarily for those professionally interested in the provision of such services, but disabled people may also write to Diana Twitchin at the King's Fund Centre if they are interested in learning about the availability of such schemes in particular areas.

CEH publications are informative and are imaginatively produced. A new publication *Buying or Adapting a House or Flat: a consumer guide for disabled people*, price 50p, is a delight. Not only does it abound with information which is clearly set out but also it combines the witty presentation we are coming to expect from CEH. Its own brand of cartoons are a joy. CEH members receive discounts on all CEH services. Corporate membership £25 p.a. Individual membership £18.50 p.a. CEH services include the following:

Information and consultancy service
Library and current awareness service
CEH Register of Buildings
CEH/King's Fund Centre joint register of housing and care support schemes for physically handicapped people
Seminars on topics of current concern
Publications (list available)
CEH journal *Design for Special Needs*. Annual subscription UK and overseas surface mail £8.50; overseas mail £10.50.

See also Access Committee for England (page 289).

Community Service Volunteers – Independent Living Scheme
237 Pentonville Road, London N1 9NJ (Tel: 01-278 6601) (for further details of CSV *see* page 125).
The Independent Living Scheme is a flexible and broadly applicable form of non-professional care which seeks to match volunteers with individuals and families who need a particularly high and concentrated level of support to enable them to remain within the community and to live as independent a life as possible. Some 'projects' work on a contractual basis, running for a specified period of time. Others are long-term, and as one volunteer completes his/her period of service, arrangements are made for another to take his/her place.

Families and individuals in all sorts of difficult situations can find the scheme useful. A few of these may be disabled people wanting to live independently in their own homes; disabled people needing help to complete courses in further education; mentally handicapped people needing special care within day centres or hostels, or in the community; people disabled through injury who need support to create new life-styles.

CSVs are young, untrained people, committed to helping where they can. Their role is to enable, not to impose care. They can undertake physical care and offer genuine support, but they need expert direction from the individual or family with whom they are working.

Projects are expected to be organised through and supported by the local social services, health authority or other statutory or voluntary agency. Potential users are asked to consider how much care is required, then to judge the number of volunteers needed. An external project supervisor with an overall view of the project is nominated to offer regular support for the CSV before any placement can begin. The CSV's pocket money (at £13 a week), board (or food allowance of up to £15 a week), lodging and travelling expenses and the placement fee (£50 a month) must be met by the appropriate agency and/or the CSV user.

Crossroads Care Attendant Scheme
See page 292.

The following four aids and information centres provide practical help and advice on all aspects of living with a disability, including housing and help in the home:

Disabled Living Foundation
380–384 Harrow Road, London W9 2HU (Tel: 01-289 6111).

Northern Ireland Information Service for Disabled People
2 Annadale Avenue, Belfast BT7 3JH (Tel: Belfast (0232) 640011 or 649555).

Scottish Council on Disability
Information Department, 5 Shandwick Place, Edinburgh EH2 4RG (Tel: 031-229 8632).

Wales Council for the Disabled
Caerbragdy Industrial Estate, Bedwas Road, Caerphilly, Mid Glamorgan CF8 3SL (Tel: Caerphilly (0222) 887325).

Family Fund
Full information on the Fund's help for families with a disabled child is given on page 17. We would just mention here that help can sometimes be made available to help with the installation of a telephone where the social services cannot help. Grants sometimes include an amount for the first year's rental of the telephone, but no help is given towards the cost of calls. Help with the cost of heating may also be available.

Home Assessment and Advisory Services
Westcroft, Scatterdells Lane, Chipperfield, Kings Langley, Hertfordshire (Tel: Kings Langley (092 77) 63676).
Two state registered occupational therapists provide this private service within a 30-mile radius of the above address. Their leaflet says: 'The Service offers a prompt and practical response with individually designed programmes to promote maximum independence to help solve the problems posed by disability, and to ease the care for each person concerned.'

Leonard Cheshire Foundation
26–29 Maunsel Street, London SW1P 2QN (Tel: 01-828 1822).

The Foundation has set up Family Support Services around the country. In these a network of 'carers' is available to respond to requests for help. Each Service aims to provide practical help where this is needed. For further details of the services and the areas covered contact the above address.

National Homes Network
Refuge House, Watergate Row, Chester CH1 2HL (Tel: Chester (0244) 316695).
This is a network of estate agents who have agreed positively to help disabled house seekers by promoting those properties which have been specially adapted. Disabled people are encouraged to search for their special requirements through an NHN member. An index of NHN estate agents is available from the above address.

New Homes Marketing Board
82 New Cavendish Street, London W1M 8AD (Tel: 01-580 5588).
The Board has compiled a list of house builders throughout the country who will adapt their houses for disabled people. The list is available to enquirers.

Royal Association for Disability and Rehabilitation (RADAR)
25 Mortimer Street, London W1N 8AB (Tel: 01-637 5400)
RADAR has a very helpful housing department ready to offer advice and guidance. RADAR also adopts a research policy to appraise in depth all aspects of housing for disabled people and then to bring pressure to bear on the various authorities and organisations to build more accommodation of the type and standard required. (*See also* Books and Publications in this section.)

SHAC (The London Housing Aid Centre)
189A Old Brompton Road, London SW5 0AR (Tel: 01-373 7276).
A housing aid centre for people living in the Greater London area, SHAC offers information, advice and help to those who are homeless, threatened with eviction, living in bad conditions or needing general advice on housing. SHAC advises on landlord/tenant and public health law, financial problems including rent and mortgage arrears, and on options for rehousing through councils, house purchase, housing associations and 'New Towns' outside London.

Shelter, National Campaign for the Homeless
157 Waterloo Road, London SE1 8XF (Tel: 01-633 9377).
Scotland: 6 Castle Street, Edinburgh EH2 3AT.
Northern Ireland: 16 Howard Street, Belfast BT1 6PA.

Shelter is a charity which helps homeless and badly housed people through its local housing aid centres, local housing projects and campaign work. Since 1981, it has been looking specifically at housing opportunities for disabled people and the development of community care.

Spastics Society
12 Park Crescent, London W1N 4EQ (Tel: 01-636 5020).
The Society has established a special scheme in the new development town of Milton Keynes to provide independent living for up to 45 handicapped people along the lines of the FOKUS development in Sweden. (*See also* Habinteg Housing Association (page 83), which is independent of the Society but continues to receive some help from it.)

Spinal Injuries Association
Yeoman's House, 76 St James's Lane, Muswell Hill, London N10 (Tel: 01-444 2121).
The SIA recognises that increasing numbers of severely disabled people are choosing to live independently – that is, in a home of their own with appropriate support from the community. The SIA Welfare Officer will support, encourage, advise and put people in touch with those who have done it already. SIA will maintain up-to-date information on all aspects of independent living. As well as advising on rights and helping individuals to get the best out of their local social services, SIA is actively involved in projects to widen the choice of housing available to members.

SIA also plans to set up a Care Attendant Agency for members. This would aim to provide helpers for people in four categories: for short periods in emergencies; to enable someone to attend a conference, for example; for holidays; to help members to find long-term care assistance.

Housing Associations and Trusts

Housing associations are non-profit-making organisations which provide accommodation, generally to rent. Under the arrangements of the Housing Act 1974 registered housing associations may be funded by the Housing Corporation or local authorities to provide housing facilities for special needs groups.

We suggest you contact your local housing department or housing aid centre to ask about housing associations in the area who include specialist housing in their developments.

Often the associations work in co-operation with specific voluntary organisations. Some of the housing associations cater for both able-bodied and disabled people on an integrated basis. Most of them require an interview and assessment after the initial application forms have been completed. The great advantage that housing associations have over local authorities is flexibility. They do not have to be tied to strict allocation procedures and restrictive residential requirements. Local authorities have a responsibility to provide accommodation for a wide cross-section of the community. Housing associations, on the other hand, can choose either to concentrate on certain specialist fields or to provide more general family accommodation, or, indeed, to combine the two. As a flexible alternative to local authority housing they are in a position to complement provision made by the authorities, and also to provide housing for those who, for one reason or another, are not or cannot be provided for by the authorities to any extent. Among these special need groups who can benefit from the voluntary housing movement are one-parent families, the elderly and disabled people. Some social services departments refer applicants to these associations on recommendation. It is the specialist housing asssociations which have led the way in developing housing alternatives to institutions for the disabled.

Anchor Housing Association
Central Office: Oxenford House, 13–15 Magdalen Street, Oxford OX1 3BP (Tel: Oxford (0865) 722261).
Warden-supported housing in the form of self-contained flats for those of retirement age and over. Priority is given to those in poor housing conditions, in distress through loneliness and of limited income. Most schemes are designed to full mobility housing standards and some include a specially designed flat for a disabled elderly person. Regional offices in Altrincham, Bath, Bradford, London and Newcastle.

The Disabled Housing Trust
6 Oakenfield, Burgess Hill, West Sussex RH15 8SJ (Tel: Burgess Hill (044 46) 41955).
The Trust is now firmly established in Burgess Hill with 10 of the 17 bungalows already occupied by disabled people and their families. A fund raising campaign has been launched for the Hostel, which will house bedsits and flats for 22 young disabled people. It will also have communal areas, laundry and restaurant facilities. The Trust forms links with the local community through a neighbourhood care scheme as well as social activities and it also hopes to promote employment opportunities for disabled people.

John Grooms Housing Association
10 Gloucester Drive, Finsbury Park, London N4 2LP (Tel: 01-802 7272).
Specialises in wheelchair housing. Fourteen developments are in operation or planned for the near future – with or without warden care – situated in southern England and Wales. (*See* Films, page 88.)

Habinteg Housing Association
Habinteg Housing Association Ltd, 6 Duke's Mews, London W1M 5RB (Tel: 01-935 6931).
Northern Ireland Habinteg Housing Association (Ulster) Ltd, 4 Redburn Square, Holywood, BT18 9HZ (Tel: Holywood (023 17) 6731).
Sponsored originally by the Spastics Society to tackle some of the problems and to study the issues involved, Habinteg has a housing philosophy that recognises the fundamental needs of its disabled tenants. It is a national organisation, registered as a charity, operating in England and Wales and has a sister organisation operating in Northern Ireland.

Any disabled person (and his or her family) requiring an architectural and/or care solution to their housing problem is eligible for accommodation through Habinteg developments with the exception of those who need continuous medical or nursing care. However, Habinteg schemes do provide personal care and support, falling short of continuous nursing care, through trained community assistants who supplement the normal domiciliary services of a local authority.

All developments are mixed in terms of able-bodied and disabled tenants and while percentages vary from development to development according to the size and nature of the dwellings, disabled tenants usually represent a maximum of 9–11 per cent of the total number of tenants.

Habinteg's objectives are:
(a) the provision of housing facilities for handicapped people, their families and others in need;
(b) the study of new approaches to housing, in terms of both environment and building design, and the provision of help and advice in this field to others;
(c) the dissemination of information about housing for disabled people generally to promote improved housing conditions;
(d) the provision of personal support services to supplement local authority provision, and, where appropriate and possible, support to individuals in need of improved housing.
Other housing associations incorporating specialist housing include the following:

Key Housing Association Ltd
13 Elmbank Street, Glasgow G2 4QA (Tel: 041-226 4868).
Key Housing Association has a range of accommodation for mentally handicapped people throughout central and west Scotland. This consists of various types of housing, including hostels, sheltered housing with warden support, self-contained bedsits, flats and houses. Most developments provide for both mentally handicapped and non-handicapped tenants.

Margaret Blackwood Housing Association
32 Inglis Green Road, Edinburgh EH14 2ER (Tel: 031-443 5634).
The Association specialises in the provision throughout Scotland of flats and houses for disabled people. These are grouped in developments of about 35 dwellings, each of which is designed to cater for a wide range of disabilities. A comprehensive alarm call system is also provided and a warden is on call 24 hours a day. Schemes are open at Dundee, Edinburgh, Peebles and Wishaw and others are planned or being built in Glasgow, Rutherglen, Leith, Aberdeen and Kirkcaldy.

Raglan Housing Association
Jolliffe House, West Street, Poole, Dorset BH15 1LA (Tel: Poole (0202) 678731).
Housing for disabled people in various locations in the east Midlands and southern England.

The Royal British Legion Housing Association Ltd
PO Box 32, Unit 2, St John's Industrial Estate, St John's Road, Penn, High Wycombe, Buckinghamshire HP10 8JF (Tel: Penn (049 481) 3771).
Provides housing for elderly ex-service personnel or their elderly dependants in 300 schemes in England, Scotland and Wales. Although not specifically designed for disabled people there are built-in bathroom aids which make the accommodation suitable for the more active elderly who have someone local to help them. The housing is of a high standard and has won several architectural awards. Applications through the local Branch Service Committee of the Royal British Legion or, if there is no local Branch, enquiries should be made direct.

Shaftesbury Society Housing Association
112 Regency Street, London SW1P 4AX (Tel: 01-834 7581).
This Association provides blocks of flatlets for elderly and disabled people throughout the country. All tenants must be able to look after themselves, but within the schemes there are wardens who answer to

a call alarm system which is installed in every flat and who help out in emergencies. In each scheme one or two flats are provided which are designed for wheelchair users. Communal facilities are always available including lounge, television room, guest bedroom, laundry.

Hostels for those who are frail and elderly have recently been added to the Association's work, together with those for the mentally or physically handicapped person. Care and dining facilities are provided.

Sutton Housing Trust
Sutton Court, Tring, Hertfordshire HP23 5BB (Tel: Tring (044 282) 4921).
The Trust is a non-profit-making charitable organisation providing rented accommodation throughout England for people in the lower income group. There is accommodation especially designed for disabled people on Trust estates in Birmingham, Bolton, Bradford, Hemel Hempstead, Hull, Leeds, Leicester, London, Manchester, Middlesbrough, Plymouth, Salford, South Shields, Stoke-on-Trent, Tamworth, Warrington and Widnes.

Books and Publications

Access Data Sheets have been produced by RADAR (Royal Association for Disability and Rehabilitation) giving extracts from BS 5810: 1979 *British Standard Code of Practice for Access for the Disabled to Buildings*. Each of the six sheets sets out clearly extracts of specific recommendations from the Code as follows:
1. Approach to buildings.
2. Doors.
3. Internal circulation areas.
4. Lifts.
5. Internal staircases.
6. Lavatories.
Available from RADAR, 25 Mortimer Street, London W1N 8AB (Tel: 01-637 5400). Price 40p a set of six including postage and packing.

Buying or Adapting a House or Flat by Sarah Langton-Lockton and Rosalind Purcell. This useful publication written and produced in the usual lively CEH style (with all those lovely Louis Hellman cartoons) covers all the practical information needed to fulfil the promise of the title. There are plenty of names and addresses of further sources of help. Published by the Centre on Environment for the Handicapped, 126 Albert Street, London NW1 7NE. Price 50p including postage and packing.

Buying a House or Flat. In 'question and answer'

format, this guide sets out clearly and authoritatively basic legal and practical information. It contains information for council tenants about additional costs and responsibilities to take into account when assessing the wisdom of purchase. There is a handy chart of steps which need to be taken prior to and during purchase. Published by Bedford Square Press, National Council of Voluntary Organisations, 26 Bedford Square, London WC1B 3HU (Tel: 01-636 4066). Price £1.50.

Cooking Made Easy for Disabled People One of the Sainsbury's Food Guides written by Audrey Ellis. It is designed for people with reduced manual dexterity and includes sections on kitchen layout, equipment, shopping and nutrition as well as a small recipes section.
Available from Sainsbury's checkouts, price 30p or from RADAR, 25 Mortimer Street, London W1N 8AB. Price 50p including postage and packing.

Department of the Environment Publications DoE Circular 59/78: *Adaptations of Housing for People who are Physically Handicapped*.
DoE Circular 21/80: *Housing Acts 1974 and 1980 Improvement of Older Housing*.
DoE Circular 36/81: *Housing Acts 1974 and 1980 House Renovation Grants for the Disabled*.
Housing Booklet number 14: *Home Improvement Grants*.
Housing Booklet number 15: *Shared Ownership*.
Film Information Pack: *Housing for the Disabled* (this pack supplements a film with the same title made by the Department in 1981).

Designing for the Disabled by Selwyn Goldsmith, MA, RIBA. This is not a reissue of the original book by Selwyn Goldsmith, one of this country's leading authorities on the subject, but a total revision. It is the most comprehensive guide yet produced to the planning and design of provision for disabled people in buildings. The text takes account of recent legislation and the increasing amount of evidence about disabled people and their problems, both in the home and outside it. This new edition is seen by the author as a consultancy service at the side of the practising architect's drawing board, informing him on every aspect of designing for disabled people: from anthropometrics and wheelchair circulation spaces, through ramps, doors, lifts, kitchens, bathrooms and WCs, to provision in public buildings such as cinemas, theatres, hotels, swimming pools and libraries, to employment, transport and educational buildings and on to the planning of housing, residential homes and hospital accommodation; it gives straightforward practical recommendations and comment. Available from RIBA Bookshop, 66 Portland Place, London W1N 4AD for personal callers only. Correspondence to Finsbury Mission, Moreland Street, London EC1V 8VB (Tel: 01-251 0791). Price £25.

The Directory of Residential Accommodation for the Mentally Handicapped in England, Wales and Northern Ireland (1982). Available from MENCAP, The Bookshop, 123 Golden Lane, London EC1Y 0RT. Price £5.95 plus £1 postage and packing.

Disabled Living Foundation Publications are available from: DLF (Sales) Ltd, Book House, 45 East Hill, Wandsworth, London SW18 2QZ. The DLF has a bibliography of publications relevant to the design of housing for disabled people. Also a list entitled *Long Stay Accommodation for Handicapped People of All Ages*, which includes addresses of organisations providing various types of accommodation.

Also available from the DLF:

(a) *Kitchen Sense for Disabled and Elderly People* by Sydney Foott, Marian Lane and Jill Mena. This book aims to make cooking and catering for the handicapped home-maker, whether in a wheelchair, on crutches, unsteady, ill co-ordinated or one-handed, an easier and happier task. Also included is information on choice of equipment, kitchen planning and cleaning and maintenance. (This book is being updated.)

(b) *The Disabled Schoolchild and Kitchen Sense* by Sue Handscombe, Sydney Foott and Marian Lane. This is a logical successor to the above book, in that the schoolchild of today is the home-maker of tomorrow, who will wish and need to live independently. The book is intended for all those who are involved with the teaching of physically disabled children. Price £2.35.

(c) *Handicapped at Home* by Sydney Foott, published by the Design Council. This book, fully illustrated by photographs and line drawings, suggests ways in which a home may be shared by able and disabled people, whatever the age or disability. It is aimed at maximum independence and sharing of enjoyment and responsibilities. Price £2.85.

(d) *An Introduction to Domestic Design*. Includes seven pages of line drawings. Price £2.50. Also *Four Architectural Movement Studies for the Wheelchair and Ambulant Disabled*. This book which is fully illustrated by diagrams, deals with circulation space, doorway manœuvres, ramp gradients, and disabled drivers and their vehicles. Price £2. Both books are by Felix Walter.

Equipment for the Disabled Mary Marlborough Lodge, Nuffield Orthopaedic Centre, Headington, Oxford OX3 7LD (Tel: Oxford (0865) 750103).

Five of the books in this series are described below. Each book contains a wealth of precise information (regularly updated) regarding the aids and equipment described, all of which are illustrated. Each is priced at £3.50 plus postage. (Send no money with order, you will be invoiced.) For further details of this series see Section 3.

(a) *Housing and Furniture*. General housing information, suggestions concerning design and layout; garages; ramps; external steps and lifting tables; flooring, doors and door furniture; handrails and methods of wall-fixing; stairlifts; home lifts; windows; electrical fittings; environmental controls; heating; refuse disposal; storage; sanitary ware; beds: domestic, variable height, adjustable, electric, water; bed accessories: boards, backrests, cradles, lifting aids, mirrors, raising blocks; chairs: high seat, reclining, riser, dining; chair accessories: leg rests and raising blocks; work chairs and stools; tables; select bibliography.

(b) *Home Management*. General information: advice labels, gas and electric aids; safety; environmental controls; reaching aids; trays; trolleys; bed making; electric blankets; cleaning equipment; laundry equipment; kitchen furniture; sinks, taps and tap turners; water heaters; dish washers; refuse disposal; cooking equipment; food preparation: stabilising, cutting/peeling, weighing/measuring, mixing/blending equipment; opening/undoing aids; kettle and kettle tippers; eating and drinking: tableware, cutlery, drinking utensils; solving problems; select bibliography; metric comparison tables; addresses/telephone numbers; alphabetical index.

(c) *Disabled Mother*. Contains information on: cots, carrycots; bedding; nightwear; nappies; potties; trainer seats; feeding bottles; cups and plates; bibs; high chairs; bathing arrangements; baths and washing; suitable styles for easy dressing; methods of lifting and carrying a small baby; prams and pushchairs; playpens; safety precautions: gates, cooker guards, fireguards, harnesses, latches, sockets; alarms; laundry; shopping; ways of solving various problems; select bibliography.

(d) *Disabled Child*. Contains information on: furniture: corner seats, chairs, play tables; beds and bedding; mobility aids: baby carriers, crawling and walking aids, trolleys, tricycles, go-karts, children's wheelchairs and tricycles, including those supplied by the DHSS in the United Kingdom; car harnesses and safety seats; bath and toilet aids; incontinence appliances; protective pants; feeding bottles, cups, mugs, plates; clothing styles for independent dressing; therapy equipment; communication equipment including environmental controls; toys and select list of toy manufacturers; associations concerned with disabled children; select bibliography.

(e) *Personal Care*. Contains information on bathroom design; prefabricated bathroom modules; grooming: hair care, specially designed handles for brushes, combs, toothbrushes, razors; washbasins and taps, washing aids; baths, bath seats, boards, lifts, rails; shower units, thermostatically controlled valves, shower seats; WCs, support rails, raised WC seats, toilet aids; commodes; bedpans and urinals; incontinence: protective pants and pads, male fitted appliances; welfare associations; pressure sore prevention aids; solving problems concerning personal care; stoma care; select bibliography.

A Handbook of Housing for Disabled People by John Penton, AADipl, RIBA. An ideal first reference book for the designer who is faced with the problem of producing housing for disabled people. The second edition has been expanded to include sections on adaptations, housing in the private sector and housing for elderly people. Published by the London Housing Consortium and available from Royal Association for Disability and Rehabilitation, 25 Mortimer Street, London W1N 8AB (Tel: 01-637 5400). Price £4.45.

Housing Adaptations for Disabled People by Terence Lockhart is a practical, fully illustrated manual which outlines different types of disablement and describes in detail the building alterations, aids and equipment needed to cater for each of them. The adaptations range from simple bathroom grab rails to the complicated installation of special lifts and hoists. Each item of equipment is described in detail. Procedures for obtaining finance and permission are simply explained, while detailed case studies illustrate the practicalities of obtaining finance, dealing with committees and ensuring that the building work is carried out. Addresses of organisations concerned with disablement and of world-wide information sources are listed in the appendices. Available from The Architectural Press, 9 Queen Anne's Gate, London SW1H 9BY. Price £8.95 cloth (£9.85 including postage and packing).

Housing and Care Support for People with Physical Disabilities. A report of a conference organised by the Greater Manchester Housing and Disability Group on 30 September 1982.

The day conference and the video film prepared for it were the first steps taken by the Group actively to promote consideration of alternatives to institutional care. The Group had realised that the main problem of independent living was not bricks or mortar but care support in the home. They found that information on new ways of providing both housing and care support was very poor, and that both statutory authorities and disabled people themselves were unaware of many of the experiments in providing alternatives to institutional care.

Copies of this report are available at £1 including postage and packing. The video mentioned above entitled *Independent Living – The Alternatives to Segregated Residential Institutions for Physically Disabled People* is available at £5 plus postage and packing. For further information contact the Greater Manchester Council for Voluntary Services, St Thomas' Centre, Ardwick Green North, Manchester M12 6FZ (Tel: 061-273 7451).

Housing the Disabled by John Hunt and Lesley Hoyes. Published by Torfaen Borough Council. A report of a project carried out to identify and meet the housing needs of disabled people living in the borough of Torfaen. While this nicely illustrated book is principally of interest and encouragement to planners and architects, its practicality makes it of use to disabled people who may want to impress local authorities with their understanding of the problems and the ways in which their housing needs can be met. For instance, Part II is entitled 'Providing Solutions' and has a section on 'Making the Policies Effective'. References to Department of the Environment circulars and other publications abound – a useful resource for both the professional and general reader. Available from Torfaen Borough Council *(Housing the Disabled)*, Gwent House, Town Centre, Cwmbran, Gwent. Price £3.95 plus 90p postage and packing.

Housing for the Handicapped. The housing problems of handicapped children and disabled people are examined in two reports, *Handicapped Children: their homes and lifestyles*, HDD Occasional Paper 4/78 (price £1.40 plus 39p postage and packing) and *Housing Services for Disabled People*, HDD Occasional Paper 3/78 (price £1.10 plus 33p postage and packing). Both are available from the Department of the Environment, Room N9/03, 2 Marsham Street, London SW1P 3EB.

Housing Year Book. A reference directory of the individuals and organisations involved in housing in the United Kingdom. Its 660 pages contain information on national and local government, housing advisory bodies and pressure groups, housing aid and building centres, the media and research and training organisations. Price £24 (1984 edition). Available from public libraries or from the Longman Group Ltd, 6th Floor, Westgate House, The High, Harlow, Essex CM20 1YQ.

Living Independently by Ann Shearer. This book looks at the lives of nine severely disabled people who, against all the odds, have established homes of their own in the community in a way and a place which they have chosen and for which they are responsible. Descriptions of their daily lives show the variety of help they have drawn on and the difficulties they encountered in finding out what was possible.

All sorts of assumptions are challenged: that severely disabled people are not capable of running their own lives; that disability automatically means a state of total dependency; that custom-built houses are the only answer. Ann Shearer points out that, among the nine people, the houses that worked best were not purpose-built at all but were adapted and, in fact, the house that worked least well was the one that was purpose-built.

The book is very practical in that it clearly describes how each person manages their daily routine and does not gloss over the difficulties they encountered. Each story includes a plan of the living accommodation, not only showing the layout but also giving details of the fittings. The knotty problems of finance are clearly described. One of the householders reckoned that it took her five years to work out the benefits and allowances due to her.

In addition, in an endpiece entitled 'Implications', information is given on support services, including Neighbourhood Support Schemes, Crossroads and the Community Service Volunteers' One-to-One Scheme. Published by the Centre on Environment for the Handicapped (CEH) and King Edward's Hospital Fund for London and available from CEH, 126 Albert Street, London NW1 7NF. Price £5 including postage and packing.

Made to Measure, a very helpful booklet published by the Cheshire County Council Department of Architecture. It describes in a fairly informal way domestic extensions and adaptations carried out by this department and in so doing provides a good deal of helpful advice and information. The booklet contains drawings, sketches, photographs, brief chapters on ramps, doors, showers, kitchens, check-lists of

firms and a list of books for further reading. Available from Department of Construction Services, Cheshire County Council, Goldsmith House, Hamilton Place, Chester CH1 1SE. Price £2.50 including postage and packing.

New Rights for Tenants. A guide to the Housing Act 1980 for council, housing association and new town tenants. Published by the National Consumer Council, 18 Queen Anne's Gate, London SW1H 9AA. Available free.

SHAC 189A Old Brompton Road, London SW5 0AR (Tel: 01-373 7276).
SHAC produces the following guides: *Buying a Home*, price 75p; *Rights Guide for Home Owners* (being updated); *Your Rights to Repairs* (two volumes, one for council tenants and the other for private and housing association tenants), each 35p; *Homeless, Know Your Rights*, price 35p; *A Guide to Housing Benefits*, price £3.25 (a very detailed guide aimed principally at people advising claimants). The following three simple claimants' guides are 50p each: *Home Owners: Your Guide to Housing Benefits; Council Tenants: Your Guide to Housing Benefits; Private and Housing Association Tenants: Your Guide to Housing Benefits*.

Shelter Publications, 157 Waterloo Road, London SE1 8XF (Tel: 01-633 9377).
Ferndale. A caring repair service for elderly home-owners. With many elderly home-owners facing the prospect of spending their last years in houses scarcely fit to live in, there is a need to consider the particular repair problems which face elderly people. This report looks at a pioneer Shelter/Help The Aged project in the Rhondda Valley and its implications for housing policy. Price £2.50.
Housing and Campaigning. A complete up-to-date guide for the housing problems of the 1980s and what you can do about them. Price £3.

A report of current provision of housing for disabled people, based on a survey of local authorities and new-build statistics. This covers all aspects of local authority involvement and includes the results of a survey of the housing circumstances of disabled people.
Roof, Shelter's housing magazine, appears every two months. Annual subscription £7, single copies £1. It is an excellent source of information, debate and ideas for the housing professional or for the interested lay person.
Shelter's Progress Report, published annually, is available free – just send a large s.a.e.

Your Home and Your Rheumatism. This booklet

shows how to manage around the home generally, in the kitchen, in the bathroom, cleaning, getting in and out of a chair, writing, dressing, etc. It is available from the Arthritis and Rheumatism Council, 41 Eagle Street, London WC1R 4AR. Price 25p inclusive of postage and packing.

Films

No Steps to Conquer, 16 mm, colour, 20 minutes. This film describes the John Grooms Housing Association development at Princess Crescent, Finsbury Park, London N4.

The single building of 13 dwellings is designed for use exclusively by 15 disabled people in wheelchairs able to go out to work. Many of the special features incorporated into the design – particularly in the kitchen – will make this film of interest to all who appreciate the advantages of a well-planned home. Available from: John Grooms Housing Association, 10 Gloucester Drive, London N4 2LP (Tel: 01-802 7272). Available on loan in return for a donation.

Tape and Slide Programme

Home Adaptations for the Disabled (24 minutes) by Elizabeth Fanshawe. Adapting home, handrails, kitchens, toilets, baths, hoists, telephones, garden. Also available six programmes illustrating different ranges of equipment for people who have had a stroke. Available on hire and for sale from Graves Medical Audiovisual Library, Holly House, 220 New London Road, Chelmsford, Essex CM2 9BJ (Tel: Chelmsford (0245) 83351).

EDUCATION

It is the inalienable right of every child, despite any disability, to receive appropriate education to encourage and develop potential abilities. Gradually, over the years, this right has been strengthened by legislation, most recently by the Education Act 1981, which followed many of the progressive recommendations of the 1978 Report of the Warnock Committee. In particular, it has been accepted that categorisation of children by specific handicaps is inappropriate. As a government White Paper put it: 'no system of classification can readily describe simultaneously the medical, psychological, educational and social aspects of a child's needs; and a medical diagnosis does not provide an adequate assessment of a child's educational requirements'. Instead, Warnock's concept of 'special educational needs' has been adopted, allowing a much broader recognition of children with 'learning difficulties'. Certain children whose difficulties are particularly severe – perhaps 2 per cent of the school population – will, after careful multi-professional assessment, have their special educational needs defined by a statement under Section 7 of the Act. In practice, these are children broadly corresponding to those hitherto 'ascertained' under previous legislation as requiring special educational treatment, but the new arrangements have two main advantages: first, it should be possible to define individual needs more accurately and to specify the action proposed for meeting them with a view to safeguarding the proper education of the children concerned; second, parents are now accorded rights at all stages of the legal process to make representations and contest decisions made about their children.

Perhaps the most fundamental aspect of the new legislation is the requirement that, except in certain prescribed circumstances, local education authorities and others concerned in making special educational provision are to secure that children protected by a statement under Section 7 of the Act are educated with children who do not have special educational needs, *i.e.* in ordinary schools, provided always that parental wishes have been taken into account. This provision is of enormous importance, for it establishes integrated education as the norm and segregated education as the exception. In practice, unfortunately, there is ample scope for local education authorities to evade this central principle. Segregated education can be preferred in any individual case if the authority considers that 'mainstreaming' would be incompatible with the child receiving the special educational provision he or she needs, with the provision of efficient education for other children or with the efficient use of resources. Undoubtedly, there will continue to be children for whom, in the words of the White Paper, 'association, or full association, with other children is the wrong solution' and for whom special arrangements will be necessary, including education in special schools, at home or in hospital. But equally, in some cases, children with severe problems can be educated in ordinary schools if there is the necessary will, understanding and back-up. Special units in ordinary schools have been found to be successful in a number of areas and these allow greater flexibility in maximising integration wherever this is possible. At a time when falling rolls are prompting a reorganisation of educational provision in many areas, it is opportune to re-examine the future of special education. For some years the trend has been *away* from integration. Department of Education and Science statistics show that between 1960 and 1979 the number of pupils in special and hospital schools rose by over 100 per cent, against an increase of less than 13 per cent in the total number of pupils in full-time education. In the same period, the number of special schools rose from 788 to 1,599 (about 103 per cent).

The 1981 Act, in practical terms, does little to reverse this trend. In failing to back up ideology with practical resources and by providing grounds to permit the avoidance of integration, it gives latitude to unprogressive authorities simply to maintain the *status quo*. There will be some, alas, who because they have set up costly special schools, with special equipment and special staff, will wish to justify their investment and ensure their continued use. Others will simply shrink from the difficulties involved in integration, and persist with special, segregated education as the more convenient alternative. A survey conducted jointly by the Advisory Centre for Education (ACE) and the Spastics Society revealed that only one-third of local education authorities had displayed a willingness to alter existing arrangements in line with the integration principle expressed in Section 2 of the Act. While only two authorities (Barking and Barnsley) admitted to having no policy at all on integration, the remainder made it clear, by stressing the let-out clauses in Section 2, that changes following the Act would be confined to questions of assessment and the role of professionals, and would *not* include a re-examination of existing segregationist policies. Given these attitudes, it is vital that parents should, as the 1981 Act allows, be closely involved in the decision-making process and make determined use of their rights.

Educational Alternatives

If early and accurate assessment of special educational needs is essential to the development of educational programmes appropriate for individual children, then no less vital is that the various kinds of special education necessary to meet differing needs should be available in practice. Without such provision the 1981 Education Act cannot be effective.

It is important for parents to be aware of their rights, in particular to appreciate that under the new legislation education authorities, having made a statement of a child's special educational needs under Section 7 of the Act, are placed under an obligation to meet those needs. This may call for the provision of long-term specialised education in a special school or short-term remedial provision in an ordinary school. *Provision should be related to individual need and should in no circumstances be regarded as a final solution.*

Education authorities operate their own special schools with specialised facilities and suitably trained staff and some run special units and classes attached to ordinary schools. There is an increasing recognition that more can be done to accommodate handicapped children, in suitable cases, in ordinary primary and secondary schools. This calls for an improved provision of special facilities in ordinary schools, for a greater understanding on the part of teachers, and for the more flexible use of specialist staff.

If an authority cannot conveniently place a child in a suitable school in its own area, it may arrange for the child to attend a school in another area or in a non-maintained school, many of which are run by voluntary organisations. There is legal provision, in such cases, for the payment of fees and of board and lodging if residence is necessary. Transport must be provided, or reasonable travelling expenses met.

Integration or Specialisation

In 1944, as expressed in the Education Act of that year, the thinking of Parliament was that special education should, as far as possible, be provided for seriously disabled pupils in appropriate special schools. Only if this was impracticable, or if the disability was not serious, might education be provided in an ordinary school. It could be said that special schools were regarded as the normal solution to significant handicap, and integration in ordinary schools exceptional. Over the years, attitudes have changed. A powerful movement, not limited to this country and certainly not confined to education, has urged that disabled people are not to be treated as 'different'; that facilities should be provided so as to allow them to join in the mainstream of life alongside their able-bodied peers. Thus, in education, it is argued that handicapped children should not be separated off from other children, but should be educated in a common setting towards the day when they may take their place in ordinary society and share the opportunities enjoyed by able-bodied people.

We have seen that the government, at least in principle, now espouses this approach, but with some qualifications. Not everyone, in fact, is fully convinced of the merits of the case for integration. Teachers warn of the harm which can be done if integration is 'forced' without adequate support services. There are also those who believe that there will always be children who will benefit from the specialised facilities and care which a special school is built, staffed and equipped to offer, and who will develop better in a somewhat protected environment. Philippa Russell in *The Wheelchair Child* (*see* page 335) expresses the view that 'for many children integration will not be achieved without a preliminary period in special education' and points to the advantage of a special school in providing special services for special need as being 'that it is developed to offer a much more individual educational approach to children's needs than would be possible in the larger classes of the normal school'. Warnock, while looking forward to a shift of emphasis towards greater integration and improved provision for special education in ordinary schools, at least in England and Wales, cautions that we must safeguard the interests of those whose needs cannot be so met.

To the champions of total integration, segregation is an anachronism, a hangover from a benighted past, an affront to the principles of equality of opportunity and fraternity, an obstacle to handicapped young people taking their proper place in the mainstream of life, something to be phased-out as soon as possible through the input of increased resources into ordinary schools and the more flexible deployment of staff.

It may well be that the best, as well as the most appropriate, way ahead lies in the development and expansion of special units within ordinary schools, retaining the policies and expertise vital to the needs of handicapped children, but breaking the rigid isolation imposed by a special school in a separate building, and making possible, at the same time, a greater flexibility and opportunity for movement and transfer between special unit and ordinary classes as may be appropriate. Above all, we would urge that future policy be guided by the best interests of individual children rather than by dogmatic rigidity, political expediency or what is convenient to the public purse.

NOTE: A brief, but excellent, statement of the case for integration is contained in a fact sheet *Integration – the main arguments*, available from the Centre for Studies on Integration in Education, The Spastics Society, 12 Park Crescent, London W1N 4EQ (Tel: 01-636 5020).

Assessment Procedures and Parental Rights

The 1981 Education Act places a wide obligation on local education authorities to secure that adequate provision is made for *all* children with special educational needs. Department of Education and Science Circular 1/83 to local education authorities indicates that the main focus should be on the child rather than on his/her disability, and that the assessment of special educational needs (which must be seen as a continuous process) is not an end in itself, but a means of arriving at a better understanding of a child's learning difficulties for the practical purpose of providing a guide to his/her education and a basis against which to monitor progress. 'In looking at the child as a whole person', the Circular points out, 'the involvement of the child's parents is essential.'

'Assessment should be seen as a partnership between teachers, professionals and parents.' Close relations should be established and maintained with parents, *'and can only be helped by frankness and openness on all sides'* (our italics). Moreover, 'the feelings and perceptions of the child concerned should be taken into account.'

In most cases, the procedures for assessment will be a matter for local education authorities, though always with parents being involved and kept informed. However, the 1981 Act lays down more formal procedures for the assessment of children whose needs are, or probably are, such as to require local education authorities to determine their special educational provision and it gives such children the protection of a Statement. Circular 1/83 indicates that such formal procedures should be initiated where, at first sight, there are grounds to suggest that a child's needs are such as to require provision additional to, or otherwise different from, the facilities and resources generally available in ordinary schools in the area under normal arrangements. The deciding factors in making this decision will vary from area to area, depending on the range of provision which is normally available to the authority, but the Secretary of State for Education has indicated that he expects local education authorities to afford the protection of a Statement to all children who have 'severe or complex learning difficulties which require the provision of extra resources in ordinary schools, and in all cases where the child is placed in a special unit attached to an ordinary school, a special school, a non-maintained special school or an independent school approved for the purpose'.

A summary of the legal process of assessment is given in Section 13 on page 256. Briefly, in respect of children aged 2 or more, local education authorities are required to identify any who require special educational provision and then to assess their special educational needs in accordance with Regulations, taking all necessary advice to do so. Parents can request an assessment on their own initiative and such a request must be met unless the local education authority concerned thinks it unreasonable. If the child, after assessment, is determined as needing special educational provision, the authority must make and maintain a Statement of his/her special educational needs and the provision to be made to meet those needs, setting out the representations, evidence, advice and information taken into account in the assessment. Having done so, it is bound to make that provision unless suitable arrangements have been made by a parent. In respect of children under 2, the authority *may* assess with parental consent and *must* do so at the parent's request. Assessment in such cases can be made in whatever manner the authority considers appropriate, whereupon it *may* make a statement of the child's special educational needs and thereafter maintain it as it considers appropriate.

Assessments of children aged 2 or more are made under Section 5 and Schedule 1 of the 1981 Act, and the Education (Special Educational Needs) Regulations 1983. Parents are afforded rights at each step of the process, and it is of considerable importance that these are known and fully utilised:

1. When a proposal to assess is made (and this must be notified in writing), there is a right to make representations and to submit written evidence. The authority must take these views into account, and must notify the parent whether or not it has decided to assess. Circular 1/83 goes further. It indicates that the serving of a formal notice under Section 5 should not be the first indication to a parent that a child has learning difficulties, and that, before a notice is served, 'every possible effort' should be made to effect initial contact between teacher, or any other professional making the referral, and the child's parent. There is also a right to information. Section 5(3) of the Act provides that parents should be informed of the procedures to be followed in assessment, and given the name of an officer of the authority from whom further information can be obtained.

2. If the authority, as part of an assessment, requires a child to be examined, the arrangements must be notified and parents have a right to attend and submit any information they wish. This right does not extend to an assessment by observation over a period of time in the classroom or elsewhere, but, as Circular 1/83 points out, it remains part of a process of maintaining good relations with parents for all professionals to involve them in the process of assessment.

3. In making an assessment, the authority must take account of any views expressed by the parent. When they seek professional advice under the Act, local education authorities must provide their advisers with copies of any representations or evidence submitted by the child's parent, including any written summary or oral representations. Circular 1/83 properly points out that 'the relations between professional advisers and parents during the process of assessment are of crucial importance'.

If, having made an assessment, an authority concludes that it need not determine special educational provision, then it must notify the parent, who has a right of appeal to the Secretary of State for Education. If, on the other hand, it determines a need for special educational provision, it must serve the parent with a copy of the proposed Statement, specifying the child's special educational needs, the provision proposed to meet those needs and the advice, etc., on which the proposals are based. The parent then has a right to make representations about the content of the proposed Statement and can request a meeting to discuss it. If, after such a meeting, a parent disagrees with any part of the assessment, there is a further right to require the authority to arrange additional meetings as they consider will enable the parent to discuss the professional advice on which the proposed statement is based, as far as it relates to the disagreed matters. The authority must thereafter decide whether or not it will make a Statement and, if so, whether in the original or a modified form. This decision must again be notified in writing and there is a right of appeal. The Secretary of State for Education has expressed the hope that appeals will be seen only as a last resort.

4. Where a Statement is being maintained, parents may request a re-assessment which, if an assessment has not been made within the previous six months, must be complied with unless the authority is satisfied that a further assessment would be inappropriate.

Further Information (for addresses *see* Appendix B)

STATUTORY

Scottish legislation (*see* page 258) imposes a duty on education authorities to disseminate information in their areas as to the importance of the early discovery of special educational needs and the statutory opportunities for assessment. There is no such general requirement in the law as it relates to England and Wales, but Section 8 of the Education Act 1980 requires certain information about schools to be provided by local education authorities, and this includes a wide range of information about special educational provision, the arrangements for the identification and assessment of children with special educational needs, and the involvement of parents (see Section 13, Legislation, page 257). Reference copies should be available at local education authority offices, schools and public libraries. Personal copies can be obtained by parents free of charge, *but must be requested*. Little is provided centrally

(which is a pity), but the Department of Education and Science, Elizabeth House, York Road, London SE1 7PH (Tel: 01-928 9222) has produced a number of circulars relating to the education of children with special educational needs and to the provisions of the Education Act 1981, although these are not normally available to the public at large. General information about special education can, however, be found in Reports on Education No.69 *The Last to Come In* (1971) and No.77 *Special Education – A Fresh Look* (1973). Booklists about children with particular handicaps or learning difficulties will be supplied on request from the DES library, Elizabeth House, York Road, London SE1 7PH. The following further publications are available from Her Majesty's Stationery Office:

Pamphlet No. 60 *Educating Mentally Handicapped Children*.

The Warnock Report *Special Educational Needs* (1978), £5.65.

Meeting Special Educational Needs (a shortened version of the Warnock Report), 85p.

The Educational System of England and Wales (October 1982), free booklet.

List of Addresses of Local Education Authorities, free booklet.

The Education Act 1981, £2.30.

OTHER

Books and other literature published by specific organisations are listed under Helpful Organisations in this section.

Elisabeth Anderson, *The Disabled Schoolchild* (Methuen, 1973), £5.95: a study of integration in primary schools.

A. Bowley and L. Gardner, *The Handicapped Child* (Churchill Livingstone, fourth edition, 1980), £8.75: educational and psychological guidance; children with cerebral palsy, spina bifida, deafness, blindness or autism.

Wilfred Brennan, *Changing Special Education* (Open University Press, 1981), available from MENCAP Bookshop, £4.95.

W. K. Brennan, *Shaping the Education of Slow Learners* (Routledge & Kegan Paul Ltd, 1974), available from MENCAP Bookshop, £2.50.

Janet Carr, *Helping Your Handicapped Child* (Penguin, 1980), £1.95 plus 45p postage and packing.

Chazan, Laing, Shackleton Bailey and Jones, *Some of our Children* (Open Books Publishing, 1980), available from MENCAP Bookshop, £5.95: the early education of children with special needs.

Christine Cope and Elisabeth Anderson, *Special*

Units in Ordinary Schools (Heinemann Educational Books, 1977), £3.95 plus £1 postage and packing: an exploratory study of special provision for disabled children.

R. N. M. Crosby with R. A. Liston, *Reading and the Dyslexic Child* (Souvenir Press, 1983), £5.95 (paperback): a revised and updated edition, published for the first time in paperback. The book is aimed at teachers and parents concerned with teaching dyslexic children to read, with a specific approach to the needs of each individual child.

W. B. Dockrell, W. R. Dunn and A. Milne, *Special Education in Scotland* (Scottish Council for Research in Education, 15 St John Street, Edinburgh EH8 8JR, 1978), £2.50: a wide-ranging review of the growth, current practice and future development of special education in Scotland.

Early Education of Physically Handicapped Children at Schools (31 minutes): a tape/slide sequence available for hire or sale from Graves Medical Audiovisual Library.

The Education Authorities Directory and Annual (The School Government Publishing Co. Ltd, 1983), £26.00: standard work of reference on the educational facilities available throughout the United Kingdom; includes details of both statutory and non-maintained schools for handicapped children. Available at good reference libraries.

Education Year Book (Longman Group Ltd, 1984), £25: full details of education offices, services and statistics; complete listing of all middle, secondary and special schools including independent schools; sections on higher education, careers, visits and teachers' associations.

B. Furneaux and B. Roberts, *Autistic Children* (Routledge & Kegan Paul Ltd, 1977), £6.95 hardback; £3.95 paperback: concerned with the special needs of autistic children and everyday aspects of dealing with them. The book is aimed at teachers and parents, but is also important reading for professionals involved in the diagnosis and care of these children. The overall viewpoint is one of optimism. The contributors believe that with efficient and co-ordinated professional, parental and community involvement, much more can be done to help autistic children to become self-supporting adults.

R. Gulliford, *Special Educational Needs* (Routledge & Kegan Paul Ltd, 1971), available from MENCAP Bookshop, £3.95.

Seamus Hegarty, Keith Pocklington and Dorothy Lucas, *Educating Pupils with Special Needs* (NFER-Nelson Publishing, 1981), £14.45.

Seamus Hegarty, Keith Pocklington and Dorothy Lucas, *Integration in Action* NFER-Nelson Publishing, 1982), £10.95: written as a companion to *Educating Pupils with Special Needs in the Ordinary School* (*see* above), this book considers the issues and problems raised by the integration of handicapped children into mainstream education.

Beve Hornsby and Frula Shear, *Alpha to Omega* (Heinemann Educational Books, 1980), £4.50: recommended as a highly effective remedial programme suitable for use with individuals or small groups from primary level right up to adult literacy classes.

D. M. Jeffree and R. McConkey, *Let Me Speak* (Souvenir Press, 1976), £2.95 paperback: offers a complete teaching programme for children who are slow in acquiring language, through learning games designed to be played with their parents. Also valuable to teachers and therapists professionally involved with such children.

D. M. Jeffree and M. Skeffington, *Let Me Read* (Souvenir Press, 1980), £5.95 hardback; £3.50 paperback: provides teaching games and exercises evolved primarily for young people with severe learning difficulties, and designed to be used by parents as well as by teachers (the authors particularly recommend co-operation at vital stages between home and school).

D. M. Jeffree, R. McConkey and S. Hewson, *Teaching the Handicapped Child* (Souvenir Press, 1977), £3.95 paperback: a handbook for teachers, professionals and parents showing how to formulate teaching objectives for each individual child according to his or her level of development and skills, how to design and carry through individualised teaching schemes and to monitor both the progress of the child and the effectiveness of the scheme.

Judith Jenkins, David Felce, Jim Mansell and Ursula De Kock, *Bereweeke Skill-Teaching System* (Graves Medical Audiovisual Library): a tape/slide sequence (50 slides) which describes, with examples, a system for running systematic teaching programmes for mentally handicapped people in residential care. Available for hire or sale.

Chris Kiernan, Barbara Reid and Linda Jones, *Signs and Symbols* (Heinemann Educational Books, 1982), £5.95: reviews the extensive literature on non-vocal communication systems for severely handicapped children and adults, reports on surveys of their use, discusses the findings and makes recommendations.

C. Kiernan, R. Jordan and C. Saunders, *Starting Off* (Souvenir Press, 1978), £4.50 paperback: details techniques for helping to develop the skills of severely handicapped children and adults, written in such a way as to allow teacher or parent to decide on the best programme for each child and to adapt the schemes for individual use.

Julia Leach and Gillian Nettle, *Read, Write and Spell* (Heinemann Educational Books, 1977/78), £3.80 (four staged workbooks), £12.20 (four staged flashcard sets): a systematically structured remedial programme of workbooks and flashcards designed to develop and reinforce the linguistic confidence of any pupil who experiences difficulty with basic language skills. It is likely to be particularly useful in junior remedial work.

James Loring and Graham Burn, *Integration of Handicapped Children in Society* (Routledge & Kegan Paul Ltd, 1975), £7.95 plus postage and packing: contributors from a variety of countries present their findings and views on the scope for bringing handicapped children into mainstream schools and for social integration. It looks at the problems of the multiple handicapped child and includes a survey of disabled students at universities and polytechnics in Great Britain.

T. R. Miles, *On Helping the Dyslexic Child* (Methuen, 1970), £2.40.

T. R. Miles and E. Miles, *More Help for Dyslexic Children* (Methuen, 1975), £2.95.

F. Morgenstern, *Teaching Plans for Handicapped Children* (Methuen, 1981), £3.95: intended to give a basic understanding of the effects of a handicap on a child's development, to help teachers to develop a theoretical framework and to illustrate how the theory can best be used to plan detailed teaching programmes to stimulate and help children to fill in the gaps in the learning process which result from a particular handicap.

Philippa Russell, *The Wheelchair Child* (Souvenir Press, revised edition, 1984), £6.95 paperback (for details *see* Appendix A).

Ann Shearer, *Integration: A New Partnership?* (ACE/Spastics Society, 1983), £1.50: this conference report suggests that there are four main barriers to progress in the education of children with special needs:

    ignorance and misinterpretation;
    inadequate and unequal provision;
    conflict between professionals;
    conflict between parents and professionals.

The report examines the issues raised at the conference, comments on them, and looks to the future for possible patterns of change.

The Snowdon Report – *Integrating the Disabled* (*see* Appendix A) has some very useful overviews of integration in primary, secondary and further education.

Will Swann, *The Practice of Special Education* (Blackwell, 1981), available from MENCAP Bookshop, £4.95.

A. E. Tansley and R. Gulliford, *The Education of Slow Learning Children* (Routledge & Kegan Paul Ltd, 1960), available from MENCAP Bookshop, £3.50.

Tom Wakefield, *Special School* (Routledge & Kegan Paul Ltd, 1977), £3.50: a personal account of the staff and children of a school for 'disadvantaged' children which tells how care, concern and sympathetic co-operation between adults and children can help handicapped young people to find themselves through communication with each other. It offers much practical advice about bringing up children at home and school, and offers hope and encouragement to educationists, social workers and parents.

John Welton *et al.*, *Meeting Special Educational Needs – the 1981 Act and its Implications* (University of London Institute of Education, 1982), £1.95: introduction by Mary Warnock.

A. A. Williams, *Basic Subjects for Slow Learners* (Methuen, 1970), available from MENCAP Bookshop, £3.95.

Jessie Francis-Williams, *Children with Specific Learning Difficulties* (Pergamon Press, 1974), available from MENCAP Bookshop, £4.40.

Films

Concord Films Council Ltd
201 Felixstowe Road, Ipswich, Suffolk IP3 9BJ (Tel: Ipswich (0473) 76012).
For a general note on this company *see* Appendix B.

Films available for hire include a considerable range and number of educational documentaries. There are many helpful films concerning the special problems of blind, deaf, mentally handicapped and disabled children. Most films are in 16 mm and many have been transferred on to video cassettes.

National Audio-Visual Aids Library
Paxton Place, Gipsy Road, London SE27 9SR (Tel: 01-670 4247). Publishes a catalogue of its Film Library for Teacher Education which includes a number of films and video tapes about special schools dealing with children with cerebral palsy, mental subnormality, blindness and multiple handicaps. Two films available are: *In the Mainstream*, an American film made by CBS News (16 mm, colour, 14 minutes), examines the workings of an American federal law that, wherever possible, handicapped children should be 'mainstreamed', *i.e.* educated in the classroom with other children. The film allows teachers and relatives to give their views, which are, perhaps, weighted to the idea that handicapped children are being 'dumped' into regular classes. Nevertheless,

the film is a useful starting point for discussion.

People You'd Like to Know, another American series for classroom showing, covers in short (10 minutes) colour films three schoolchildren with different impairments – reading difficulty, deafness and cystic fibrosis – and points out the problems and solutions involved.

Helpful Organisations

The following list is not exhaustive. Other organisations concerned with disability will advise on educational matters affecting their members with special regard to the particular handicap involved (*see* Section 16).

Advisory Centre for Education (ACE) Ltd
18 Victoria Park Square, London E2 9PB (Tel: 01-980 4596).
The Centre provides information and advice for all those involved in the education service, primarily through its magazine *Where to find out more about education*. It aims to help people to become more involved in education and to make more effective choices. It encourages closer home-school relations and urges greater consideration of the views of parents and students in educational decisions, as well as seeking a generally more open and responsive system. As well as its many advisory publications, ACE runs conferences on topical issues for parents, students, teachers and administrators.

Publications include:
Where to find out more about education, a magazine on education. Published ten times a year, £7.50 per annum (£7 by banker's order).
Where to look things up (third edition, 1983), an A-Z of the sources on all major educational topics, £3.
Booklets for school governors:
Special Education Handbook: the 1981 Education Act explained for parents of children with special needs;
School Choice Appeals;
Choosing a School.
Many other booklets and information sheets are available. Free publications list on request.

Association for All Speech Impaired Children (AFASIC)
347 Central Markets, Smithfield, London EC1A 9LH (Tel: 01-236 3632/6487).
For a general note *see* Section 16.
The following AFASIC booklets are available:
Educational Facilities for Speech and Language Impaired Children.
The Assessment and Diagnosis of Children with Speech and Language Disorders – Notes for Parents.

Children with Speech and Language Disorders – A Brief Guide to the Law concerning their Education.
These booklets are free to members, prices on application to non-members.

Association of Professions for the Mentally Handicapped
126 Albert Street, London NW1 7NF (Tel: 01-267 6111). *See* Section 16.

Association for Spina Bifida and Hydrocephalus
22 Upper Woburn Place, London WC1H 0EP (Tel: 01-388 1382).
A general note on the Association is given in Section 16. The national office is always willing to give advice on all aspects of education, and in addition has begun social independence courses for children and young people with spina bifida and/or hydrocephalus.

The Association publishes the following booklets on aspects of educating children with spina bifida and hydrocephalus:
The Handwriting of Spina Bifida Children (1979).
Children with Spina Bifida at School, 30p plus postage (for teachers and students).
Further publications deal with other aspects of the handicaps, and the Association provides a list of suggested reading on the subject.

The British Association for Early Childhood Education
Montgomery Hall, Kennington Oval, London SE11 5SW (Tel: 01-582 8744).
The Association is concerned with all aspects of children's development and learning from birth to the age of about 8 to 9 years. It believes that education in the early years is vital, and presses for the provision of adequate facilities of high standard. It recognises a need for team work in terms of closer collaboration with parents and a wider interdisciplinary concept of education.

It recognises that a disturbing number of children are disadvantaged through poor housing, overcrowding, isolation, poverty, ill-health and other handicapping conditions, and is concerned to ensure that the health, education and well-being of all young children are advanced wherever they may be. The teacher in the nursery class often has the opportunity to help with the early diagnosis of a disability.

BAECE publishes inexpensive leaflets on child care and child development, and welcomes enquiries from parents, either by telephone or letter. Please send s.a.e. for reply.

British Dyslexia Association
See Section 16.

British Epilepsy Association
Crowthorne House, Bigshotte, Wokingham, Berkshire RG11 3AY (Tel: Crowthorne (0344) 773122).
For a general note *see* Section 16. The Association publishes a guide in leaflet form of Schools and Centres for Epilepsy, price 25p. Literature lists and film guide available on request. Association staff provide health education talks to schools, organisations and professional bodies.

British Institute of Mental Handicap
Wolverhampton Road, Kidderminster, Worcestershire DY10 3PP (Tel: Kidderminster (0562) 850251)
See Section 16. Publications include:
Curriculum Planning for the ESN(S) Child, Skills Analysis Model. An effective curriculum for children with severe learning difficulties.

The Campaign for Mentally Handicapped People
16 Fitzroy Square, London W1P 5HQ (Tel: 01-387 9571). *See* Section 16.
CMH publications, available from 8 Church End, Gamlingay, Sandy, Bedfordshire SG19 3EP, include:
Meeting mentally handicapped people, an introductory leaflet, single copies 5p, larger orders 2½p each.
Parents' Choice by Tony Booth and June Statham (1982), a description of how, on the initiative of a group of parents, a unit for mentally handicapped children was set up in an ordinary school. Introductory chapter on the 1981 Education Act and its effect on parents' choice.
Schools for All by P. Beresford and P. Tuckwell, an examination of the present system of special schools and integrated alternatives in both England and the United States, showing how integration into ordinary schools can be achieved (1977), £1.20 (published jointly with MIND).

Centre for Studies on Integration in Education (CSIE)
The Spastics Society, 12 Park Crescent, London W1N 4EQ (Tel: 01-636 5020).
The Spastics Society set up this Centre in July 1982 to raise public, professional and political awareness of the issue of integration and to promote good practice. It aims to encourage local education authorities, individual schools, parents, governors and others to establish effective and successful integration schemes for children with special needs, and to ensure that any re-evaluation of policy will be considered an integral part of a *whole* education service. As well as exchanging information relating to integration, and

linking those already running successful schemes and those who wish to do the same, the Centre will lobby central and local government to help to speed up change, arrange conferences and study days on various aspects of integration and specific problems and will publish relevant information. The literature so far produced is most impressive – admirably clear, direct, and well written. This includes fact sheets, a report of the conference held in 1982, *Working Towards Integration* and a useful *Selected Reading List*. A publications list is available free of charge and is recommended to parents and any others concerned about integration.

The Children's Society

Church of England Children's Society, Old Town Hall, Kennington Road, London SE11 4QD (Tel: 01-735 2441).
See Section 16. Halliwick Further Education Centre, Winchmore Hill, London, has residential and daycare places including independence training for those aged 16 and above. North London Physically Handicapped Independence Units have places where young people learn to live on their own without supervision. The young people attend a variety of local further education centres.

Cystic Fibrosis Research Trust

5 Blyth Road, Bromley, Kent BR1 3RS (Tel: 01-464 7211).
See Section 16.

Dr Barnardo's

Tanners Lane, Barkingside, Ilford, Essex IG6 1QG (Tel: 01-550 8822).
London Division, Divisional Office, Tanners Lane, Barkingside, Ilford, Essex IG6 1QG (Tel: 01-551 0011), runs two residential schools for maladjusted children and one residential school for severely physically handicapped children.
Yorkshire Division, Divisional Office, Four Gables, Clarence Road, Horsforth, Leeds LS18 4LB (Tel: Leeds (0532) 582115), one residential school for maladjusted/ESN(M) children and another for physically handicapped children.
South Wales and South West Division, Divisional Office, 177 Newport Road, Cardiff (Tel: Cardiff (0222) 485592), a residential school for physically handicapped children.
Scottish Division, Divisional Office, 22 Drumsheugh Gardens, Edinburgh EH3 7RP (Tel: 031-226 5241), two residential schools for maladjusted children.

Dyslexia Institute

Head Office: 133 Gresham Road, Staines TW18 2AJ (Tel: Staines (0784) 59498).
A non-profit-making voluntary organisation providing professional assessment and teaching for dyslexic children and adults, an advisory service for parents and teachers and training for teachers of dyslexic children and adults. Centres have been established throughout England. Write to the Head Office for full list of centres and services.

Home and School Council

81 Rustlings Road, Sheffield S11 7AB (Tel: Sheffield (0742) 662467).
For a general note *see* Section 16. Publications include:
The Child with a Medical Problem in the Ordinary School, which covers a wide range of problems, such as asthma, eczema, loss of limbs, spina bifida, partial deafness and diabetes, which may be met in an ordinary classroom situation, and offers guidance to teachers; 50p, including postage and packing.

Invalid Children's Aid Association

126 Buckingham Palace Road, London SW1W 9SB (Tel: 01-730 9891).
The Association's work (*see* Section 16) includes the provision and running of four schools:
Dawn House, Helmsley Road, Rainworth, Nottinghamshire (speech and language disorders);
John Horniman, 2 Park Road, Worthing, Sussex (speech and language disorders);
Meath, Brox Road, Ottershaw, Surrey (speech and language disorders);
Pilgrims, Firle Road, Seaford, Sussex (senior boys with severe asthma, asthma/eczema).
Children are taken from all over the United Kingdom on referral from local education authorities.
   The Association's publications include:
Assessment and Teaching of Dyslexic Children (Dr White Franklin and S. Naidoo), £1.75 plus postage and packing.
Three papers on language therapy (80p, 80p and £1.35 plus postage and packing).
Developmental Aphasia (Pauline Griffiths), 60p plus postage and packing.
In addition, an ICAA research report *Specific Dyslexia* is published by Pitmans, £3.

MENCAP – The Royal Society for Mentally Handicapped Children and Adults

123 Golden Lane, London EC1Y 0RT (Tel: 01-253 9433).
For a general note on the Society *see* Section 16.

MIND (National Association for Mental Health)
22 Harley Street, London W1N 2ED (Tel: 01-637
0741).
MIND is active in the field of education in several
ways:
(a) It does continuous campaigning work aimed at
improving the educational services for both
mentally ill and mentally handicapped children
and adults.
(b) It has regular training courses, workshops and
conferences for mental health professionals.
MIND's training programmes aim to give mental health workers access to specialist skills.
(c) It runs a pioneering residential school for children with emotional problems, Feversham
School, near Newcastle.
See also Section 16.

The National Autistic Society
276 Willesden Lane, London NW2 5RB (Tel: 01-451
3844).
A general note on this Society is given in Section 16.
One of its primary functions is in the field of education. It aims to provide and promote day and residential centres for the care and education of autistic
children and to help their parents.
The Society's advisory service for parents specifically offers help with educational placement, and its
information service provides a resource for professional workers on the nature of childhood autism
and the type of service and teaching methods
needed. It also publishes and distributes literature on
the management and education of autistic children.
The Society runs six schools:
Radlett, Harper Lane, Radlett, Hertfordshire;
Dedisham, Slinfold, Horsham, Sussex;
Gulworthy, The Old Rectory, Gulworthy, nr
Tavistock, Devon;
Helen Allison, 29 The Overcliffe, Gravesend, Kent;
Storm House, 134 Barnsley Road, Wath-on-Dearne,
Rotherham, South Yorkshire;
Sybil Elgar, 10 Florence Road, Ealing, London W5.
All, except Radlett, offer residential facilities.
In addition, NAS local societies run eight schools
at Nottingham, Colchester, Southampton, South-
port, Sunderland, Christchurch, Alloa and Newton-
le-Willows. A list of all these schools together with
local authority and other independent schools for
autistic children is available from the Society, price
50p.

The National Centre for Cued Speech
London House, 68 Upper Richmond Road, Putney,
London SW15 2RP (Tel: 01-870 5335).

Cued speech is a language tool designed for use with
and amongst the deaf. It is also used to teach hearing-
dyslexic children. Eight hand shapes, used in close
proximity to the lips, reflect the elements of spoken
language in such a way that the observer is forced to
watch the lips, thus developing oral language clarify-
ing lip reading and assisting speech production.
The National Centre for Cued Speech exists to
advise schools, clinics, local education authorities,
voluntary organisations, individuals and the government on the method. It provides lectures, literature,
films, visual aids and lesson materials, and organises
regional conferences. It offers courses of instruction
for parents, teachers and any other interested people, and group instruction to parents and staff of any
school wishing to adopt cued speech techniques. A
certificate of proficiency in cueing is offered in conjunction with the City Literary Institute Centre for
the Deaf.

National Children's Bureau
8 Wakley Street, London EC1V 7QE (Tel: 01-278
9441).
See Section 16. The Bureau stocks bibliographies
covering the educational implications of various
forms of handicap: asthma, cerebral palsy, cardiac
disorders, diabetes, haemophilia, spina bifida,
orthopaedic handicaps; and Ronald Gulliford's
Helping the Handicapped Child at School (NFER
Publishing Company, 1975). All books can be consulted in the Bureau's library.

National Children's Home
85 Highbury Park, London N5 1UD (Tel: 01-226
2033).
Provides five non-maintained special residential
schools:
Hilton Grange, Old Bramhope, Leeds, Yorkshire;
Crowthorn, Broadhead Road, Turton, nr Bolton,
Lancashire;
Bourne Place, Nizels Lane, Hildenborough, Ton-
bridge, Kent;
Penhurst, Chipping Norton, Oxfordshire;
Elmfield, Ambrose Lane, Harpenden, Hert-
fordshire.
Penhurst is for physically handicapped children,
Elmfield for maladjusted children, while the others
cater for children with learning difficulties. The NCH
also run three community homes with schooling on
the premises and three intermediate treatment
centres. For further information please contact the
NCH Education Officer at Highbury Park.

National Council for Special Education
1 Wood Street, Stratford-upon-Avon CV37 6JE (Tel: Stratford-upon-Avon (0789) 205332).
An organisation formed from the Association for Special Education, the College of Special Education and the Guild of Teachers of Backward Children. The Council exists to further the education and welfare of all who are in any way handicapped, whether in ordinary or special schools, and whether the handicap is mental, physical, emotional or environmental. Membership consists mostly of specialist teachers in the field, but administrators, medical personnel, social workers, psychologists and therapists are also welcome. There are some 50 branches with a membership of over 4,500.

A variety of books and pamphlets is available, though these are aimed at the professional worker rather than parents.

National Deaf Children's Society
45 Hereford Road, London W2 5AH (Tel: 01-229 9272/4).
For a general note *see* Section 16. The Society's activities in the education field are:
(a) to provide information and advice to parents regarding educational provision in the United Kingdom;
(b) to liaise and co-ordinate with schools, special schools and units and local authorities;
(c) to provide information to general enquirers about education facilities and methods for hearing impaired children;
(d) to campaign for improvements in services, the need for which is brought to light by parents and/or education committees.

National Elfrida Rathbone Society
11A Whitworth Street, Manchester M1 3GW (Tel: 061-236 5358).
For a general note *see* Section 16.

Elfrida Rathbone devoted her life to helping mentally handicapped and educationally backward children in north London, and the modern Society has grown out of her work. It exists to help, as far as it is able, those children of lower intelligence unhappily labelled ESN(M), and is active in London, the midlands and the north.

A publications list is available and includes reports and studies on pre-school needs and provision, training for childminders, help for parents, education and adjustments for work and further education. The Society's newsletter, *Rathbone News*, gives up-to-date information on all aspects of work in this field.

Royal National Institute for the Blind
224 Great Portland Street, London W1N 6AA (Tel: 01-388 1266).
For a general note *see* Section 16. RNIB publishes booklets *One step at a time* for parents of blind babies and *Blind children at school* which describes schools and centres run by RNIB and by other organisations.

RNIB's Education Advisers are all qualified and experienced teachers of blind children. They are based round the country and on request they will visit parents, teachers and others concerned with bringing up young blind children to give practical help and advice about the future. The service covers the whole of England and Wales (exept where local authorities have their own service), most of Scotland and occasionally Northern Ireland by special request.

Some young blind children, especially those with other handicaps, too, may benefit from a period away from home. At RNIB's four Sunshine nursery schools the children develop their independence and begin the early stages of their education. They may go on to Rushton Hall (primary) near Kettering and Condover Hall (secondary) near Shrewsbury, RNIB's schools for blind children with other physical, mental or emotional handicaps. At RNIB's Worcester College for boys and Chorleywood College for girls pupils study for O and A levels and most leavers go on to university, college or professional training. School leavers who are unsure what to do next can go to Hethersett College in Surrey. Here staff assess their aptitudes and interests and suggest suitable training and employment.

Royal National Institute for the Deaf
105 Gower Street, London WC1E 6AH (Tel: 01-387 8033).
For a general note *see* Section 16. RNID's technical department has produced a variety of aids to assist the education of deaf children. These aids are marketed commercially, but details are available from RNID.

Royal Schools for the Deaf
Stanley Road, Cheadle Hulme, Cheadle, Cheshire SK8 6RF (Tel: 061-437 5951).
A non-maintained school with residential facilities for hearing impaired children with additional handicaps or children requiring total communication. There is also a centre providing a free assessment and advisory service. Vocational training in City and Guilds courses in catering, bakery and joinery is provided for young people from 16 to 18 years of age.

The Schools publish a wide variety of papers written by members of the teaching, clinic and technical staff at the Royal Schools. They are made available at cost and provide expert advice and guidance for students, teachers, audiologists and other professionals. Publication list available from the Publications Secretary.

Scottish Epilepsy Association
48 Govan Road, Glasgow G51 1JL (Tel: 041-427 4911).
The Association's Education Department employs full-time training officers who provide training in relation to epilepsy for students and professional personnel in the fields of health, education, social work and the employment services. Seminars, talks, film shows and discussion groups can be arranged. The Association's headquarters in Glasgow have been developed as a national resource centre for epilepsy. A wide range of educational materials are available.

Shaftesbury Society
See Section 16.

The Spastics Society
12 Park Crescent, London W1N 4EQ (Tel: 01-636 5020).
The Society runs seven residential schools for children of differing abilities from the ages of 5 to 8. They are:
Rutland House, Nottingham, which caters for severely mentally and physically handicapped children who, because of the multiplicity of their handicaps, are not being provided for elsewhere.
Ingfield Manor School, Five Oaks, Billingshurst, Sussex. The school is for slow-learning spastic children. It has a unit for the partially hearing. An additional wing carries out 'conductive education' (Peto method) for 12 severely handicapped children from 3 to 7 years of age.
Meldreth Manor School, Meldreth, Royston, Hertfordshire, caters for children who are severely intellectually handicapped. There is also a unit for behaviour-disturbed pupils which uses behaviour modification techniques under the direction of the psychologist.
Craig-Y-Parc, Pentyrch, Cardiff CF4 8NB. This school is for handicapped children of average intelligence.
Thomas Delarue School, Tonbridge, Kent. Handicapped pupils at this school are in the average ability range. Comprehensive education is provided and courses offered may lead to CSE, and O and A level GCE.
Hawksworth Hall, Hawksworth, Guiseley, Leeds, has exceptional facilities for the long-term assessment of children who are so severely handicapped that the level of their ability cannot be clearly determined.
Trengweath School, Plymouth, Devon, provides education for children of differing intellectual abilities. Those within the average ability range may transfer to other schools, but secondary education for the mentally handicapped is provided here until the age of 16.

The Society's substantial publications list includes the following:
Art and Cerebral Palsy by T. Jeavons (1974), 55p plus 25p postage and packing, a practical booklet on the teaching of painting and sculpture.
Conductive Education and Cerebral Palsy by E. Cotton (1975), 50p, an introduction to conductive education.

Voluntary Council for Handicapped Children
National Children's Bureau, 8 Wakley Street, London EC1V 7QE (Tel: 01-278 9441).
See Section 16. The Council's information services range over mental, physical, sensory and social handicap and include expert advice on educational matters. The Council's Senior Officer, Mrs Philippa Russell, is author of *The Wheelchair Child* (revised edition, 1983), one of the most comprehensive and up-to-date works on the subject of handicapped children.

SECTION 6

FURTHER EDUCATION AND TRAINING

Broadening the mind can be a fascinating business, opening up interests and horizons which produce enrichment for a lifetime. Acquired skills and knowledge can also mean the difference between a life-sapping, mundane round of drudgery known as earning a crust, and a fulfilling involvement as a happily employed person. For a person who becomes disabled, further education of one sort or another may be essential in order to alter course to accommodate specific handicaps. Those who have grown up with a handicap may well find that a low assessment is placed on their potential, and may wish to seek further or higher educational opportunities to improve their performance as well as to seek much needed qualifications and self-confidence.

There has been a growing awareness over recent years of the tremendous importance further education has for young people with special needs. In fact, it is a legal duty of local education authorities (LEAs) to provide education at school or college for all 16 to 19 year olds who require it, as prescribed by the Education Act 1944 (*see* page 253). However, there is no doubt that not all LEAs are meeting these commitments and there is shown to be a further failure on the part of most LEAs to inform young people and their parents of what is available.

A survey of LEA provision for 16 to 19 year olds with special needs, undertaken by the National Union of Teachers (NUT) in 1982, showed that a substantial number of authorities were not fully meeting their obligations. Only 17 per cent gave an unconditional 'yes' to a question asking whether they guaranteed a place, either at college or at school, for every handicapped young person wishing to continue his or her education beyond compulsory school age. Others pointed to limited resources as a reason for not providing places.

In 1983 a campaign was launched by a number of organisations who believed that 'there are quite irrefutable educational, social and economic reasons for establishing in practice the right that has long existed in law: the right of every young person with special needs to appropriate full-time education up to

the age of 19'. They go on to say: 'Lack of resources is not an excuse for breaking the law. The right of access of a 16 year old to full-time education is no less than that of an 8 or 12 year old. What the NUT survey reveals, then, is widespread illegal discrimination – discrimination, moreover, against young people who are already disadvantaged by their physical or intellectual disabilities.'

The campaign is outlined in a pamphlet *After 16: the education of young people with special needs*, prepared by a small working group drawn from: the Greater London Association for Disabled People, the Royal Society for Mentally Handicapped Children and Adults (MENCAP), the Royal Association for Disability and Rehabilitation (RADAR), the Spastics Society, the National Bureau for Handicapped Students, the National Association of Teachers in Further and Higher Education and the National Union of Teachers (NUT). Other organisations have also provided their endorsement.

We hope that the information provided in this section of the Directory will help young people and their parents to take advantage of the further education and also higher education opportunities which may suit their own individual needs and aspirations.

Studying Independently

Colleges and universities are slowly making it possible for disabled students to attend in greater numbers. The matter of access is at last being taken seriously by at least some of the establishments of further and higher education, allowing less disabled students who can look after themselves the opportunity to follow courses on an equal and integrated basis with their able-bodied peers. Traditionally, disabled students have chosen or have been directed to study at specialist residential colleges. Some still prefer the automatic provision of special facilities these can provide, while others are choosing to study independently in mainstream establishments backed up by appropriate services.

Severely disabled students who, in addition to access facilities, need personal care services and possibly help with taking notes and getting from room to room for lectures, have found admission much more difficult. However, largely thanks to the pioneering work of the National Bureau of Handicapped Students and of a few enlightened college and university administrations, necessary services, though in severely limited supply, are becoming established parts of general welfare procedures.

However, before taking final decisions about continuing education it is essential to consider all the options of venue, course, general support services, personal care support and financial implications. The National Bureau of Handicapped Students exists to provide advice and to offer practical help through their knowledge of the establishments concerned and through their many contacts. As a first step you could do no better than send for their information sheet No. 4 *Meeting the Personal Care Needs of Severely Physically Handicapped Students at College* (*see* page 118).

Living Independently by Ann Shearer also studies the options of disabled people who have chosen to live in their own homes. A good deal of the information is equally valuable to students needing personal attention, particularly in residential situations. (For details *see* page 87.)

Specialist Careers Officers for the Handicapped

These officers can provide a valuable link between a student seeking to continue his/her education and all the various bodies who can help in these endeavours. They may often help by advising on any grants available and how to approach social services with requests for financial help, say to fund the costs of having a personal care helper. (*See also* page 80.)

College advisers for disabled students

Many colleges of further and higher education, polytechnics and universities now have a member of staff who has special responsibility for advising disabled students. Some even have advisory committees making sure that the disabled student can move smoothly into an ordinary college. The Regional Advisory Councils for Further Education produce guides for handicapped students and list local advisers, together with other useful information (*see* page 109). Alternatively, the National Bureau for Handicapped Students keeps a list of local advisers. Arrangements for personal care tend to follow one of two models:

1. Specialist colleges or training establishments.

These are set up solely for the benefit of disabled students and are usually residential. We describe a number of them in this section. Some are run by voluntary societies. They will provide all the care support needed as an integral part of the tuition.

2. Mainstream colleges and universities.

These exist to serve the community at large and therefore provide facilities on that basis. Some are beginning to realise that disabled students require more personal attention if they are to pursue studies of their choice and that they should not be excluded from continuing education because of this. As a result they have appointed specialist staff, who may themselves help with personal care and provide extra tutorial support. In the main, this pattern is only available at non-residential colleges of further education. In the few residential colleges of higher education where specialist services are provided, personal care helpers who are not members of a staff team are more likely to be made available. Care provided in Southampton and Sussex Universities is described below, as well as facilities provided at Taylor House, Oxford, and Bridgend College of Technology.

Southampton University

Accommodation for disabled students will be provided in a university residence. Those students needing extra personal care may be accommodated in Clarkson House, the only residence on the main site, being purpose built to provide accommodation for five to six severely disabled students, a greater number of lightly disabled students and an even larger number of non-disabled students. Care is provided on a 24-hour basis by a team of care assistants. The building is well equipped so that the disabled students can help themselves as far as possible. Many items of equipment have been selected to permit students to gain experience of what to choose (or not to choose) for their own accommodation in the future. The house is, in principle, self-catering but the care assistants and non-disabled students provide necessary help.

Further information from: The Adviser to Disabled Students, The University of Southampton, University Road, Highfield, Southampton SO9 5NH (Tel: Southampton (0703) 559122 ext. 344).

Sussex University

Kulukundis House is a small purpose-built residence, attached to another student residence, providing personal care and accessible facilities for either four severely disabled students or a mix of disabled and able-bodied students, depending on applications. The residence is centrally situated near to shops, banks and eating places.

From October 1983, personal care has been arranged with a variety of paid helpers for specific sessions, *i.e.* 7.30 a.m. to 9.30 a.m., 8.30 p.m. to 11.30 p.m., weekends, etc., and also for volunteers for emergency and other day-care sessions as required. From October 1984 it is likely that a CSV care system (*see* page 80) will be used, depending on potential application needs which can be discussed with the student.

Costs for personal care will, it is hoped, be met by negotiation with the applicants' home social services department, and the University will assist with these discussions. If a student is provisionally accepted through the UCCA system, the student will be invited to visit the University, including Kulukundis House, but we are assured that informal visits and enquiries are always welcome.

Other on-campus integrated ground-floor accommodation is also available for less severely disabled students, who can discuss personal care needs. Further details from Ann Eyles, Welfare Officer, University of Sussex Union, Falmer House, Falmer, Brighton, Sussex (Tel: Brighton (0273) 698111).

Bridgend College of Technology
Cowbridge Road, Bridgend, Mid Glamorgan EF31 3DF (Tel: Bridgend (0656) 55588).
The college offers residential accommodation on a weekly basis to up to 28 physically handicapped students, in order that they may attend appropriate courses on further education. The hostel is fully staffed and supplemented by specialist support services, including a community nurse, speech therapist, physiotherapist, etc. Those students eligible to attend mainstream college courses on an integrated basis are offered the essential physical and counselling support, but in addition two special courses are offered:
1. Foundation Course – an effective lead-in to further education or vocational training opportunities.
2. Extension Course – continued education towards a greater degree of personal independence.
Although the course is normally of one year's duration, exceptionally students may continue on to more advanced further education courses. Informal enquiries are welcomed, but application is normally made via specialist careers officers. While priority is given to Mid Glamorgan school-leavers, applications are accepted from all local authorities within the region, including Avon and Somerset.

In addition to the above, the college now offers day courses for hearing-impaired students, including specialist support for those able to attend mainstream courses; also a Social Development Course for school-leavers with learning difficulties. Fees, including accommodation charges, are normally met by the student's home education authority, whose approval should be granted before a place can be offered.

For further information contact the Tutor in charge of the Special Education Section.

Oxford Hostel for Disabled Students
Taylor House, 16 Osler Road, Headington, Oxford (Tel: Oxford (0865) 68620).
Here, young men and women with severe physical disabilities may study for degrees or diplomas at one of Oxford's many places of higher or further education. The hostel provides domestic and medical care, while allowing for maximum self-help and independence for those who would not otherwise be able to come into residence. The hostel also invites applications for holiday bookings in April, July and August. For further information contact the Warden.

The services we have described at Bridgend, Taylor House and Southampton and Sussex Universities are those that provide specialist staff. However, it is worth remembering that this is not the only option: the majority of even the most disabled students are studying and training in ordinary colleges using other forms of support.

Student-Arranged Care Service
1. District Nurse.
Some students manage by arranging for the district nursing service to come in on a regular basis. A nurse may help, for instance, with taking baths, with getting up or going to bed, or with any medical requirements. District nurses will also be able to advise on borrowing equipment such as ripple mattresses, incontinence aids, etc. They could provide details of possible help with laundry. It would be important to discuss your needs with the college medical staff to see whether this form of help would be sufficient to help you study independently.
2. Living-in Helper.
This degree of help may be provided by a Community Service Volunteer or by a private-care helper. We give details of the CSV Independent Living Scheme on page 80.

Some students may have sufficient funds to employ a private-care helper. This option can be very expensive indeed and involves the student in finding and appointing the helper and being completely responsible for all the arrangements surrounding the appointment.

Financial Help Available

Certain awards are mandatory, that is they are made under statutory regulations and, provided certain conditions are met, an award is automatic. The following courses attract mandatory awards: degree and courses prescribed as equivalent to degree; teacher training; Higher National Diploma in Higher Education; the Higher Diplomas of the Technician Education Council and the Business Education Council. To be eligible for these awards students must have been ordinarily resident in the United Kingdom for the three years before 1 September of the year their course begins. In addition, students must not have attended certain courses in the past.

The main rate of grant (1984/85) for students living away from home in London is £2,100, for students living away from home other than in London £1,775 and for students living at home £1,435. Additional allowances may be paid in respect of travel (some disabled students have heavy travel costs which can be met in this way), additional weeks of study, extra equipment, dependants and, in the case of students aged 26 or over, a mature student's allowance. These awards are normally means-tested on parental income unless the student is independent, *i.e.* over 25 or has worked for three years before the start of his course.

Full details of these awards are given in the National Union of Students leaflet No. 4 *Grants and Awards. See* page 118.

Special Allowance for Disabled Students

The extra allowance for disabled students in 1984/85 is a maximum of £540 per annum and Local Education Authorities are empowered by the Secretary of State for Education and Science to pay up to this amount to any of their award-holding students who are disabled. The statutory instrument relating to this provision reads: 'In the case of a disabled student where the authority is satisfied that he is obliged by reason of his disability to incur additional expenditure in respect of his attendance at the course ... such sum not exceeding £540 as the authority considers appropriate.' It is a disabled student's right to claim this grant if she/he incurs extra financial costs as a result of disability. These costs may relate to such items as tape recorders for blind students, extra heating and dietary needs in certain circumstances, use of readers and amanuenses and other extra aids.

Supplementary Benefit

Students on a grant are not usually eligible for supplementary benefit during term-time because they cannot meet the conditions for benefit of being unemployed and available for work. Moreover, the payment of supplementary benefit during vacations is usually restricted to the summer vacation only. However, severely handicapped students may qualify if their handicap is such that they would be unlikely to obtain a job within a reasonable period of time if they were not in further education, and at the same time their income was less than they would otherwise receive in supplementary benefit. Disabled students applying for supplementary benefit during term-time will probably be required to produce medical certificates from their doctor at regular intervals. When assessing the benefit of these students the DHSS should: ignore £2 a week of the vacation element of the grant; ignore all or any additional grant from the local authority to cover extra expenses because of a disability; and make good any shortfall in the full grant where the student's parents do not pay their assessed contribution in full. (For further details on supplementary benefit *see* Section 2.)

Educational Grants Advisory Service

Family Welfare Association, 501–505 Kingsland Road, London E8 4AU.

EGAS endeavours to put students in touch with sources of charitable and other help. Where required and possible, it also advises students in their negotiations with local education authorities and other official bodies. Enquiries should be in writing.

Snowdon Award Scheme

A special award scheme to help disabled students has been set up by Lord Snowdon. Applications are invited for these awards from physically and sensorily handicapped young people who have been offered an opportunity for further education or training and who must demonstrate financial need in order to take advantage of such an opportunity. Applicants should be at least 17 years of age and preferably under 25 at the start of the period of education or training to be supported.

Each award will be for a period of one or two years and will not, in normal circumstances exceed £1,000 a year. Application forms are available from:

The Snowdon Award Secretary, Action Research – The National Fund for Research into Crippling Diseases, Vincent House, North Parade, Horsham, West Sussex RH12 2DA.

It may be possible to receive an award from the local education authority, but such awards are discretionary in the light of all relevant circumstances. However, all necessary costs must be reimbursed. In the case of a disabled student, it may be possible for a claim to be supported by a social worker, and the National Bureau for Handicapped Students (*see* below) may also make representations on a student's behalf. In some areas, the social services department of the local authority may be prepared to help.

Young Persons Railcard (and older students)
Anyone who is under 24 years of age at the time of purchase of the Railcard *or* a student of any age who is in full-time education attending an educational establishment for over 15 hours weekly and for at least 20 weeks, can buy this Railcard costing £12 and covering a 12 months' period.

Severely disabled people may qualify for the Disabled Persons Railcard for the same price. For those who do qualify, the Disabled Persons Railcard can be a better buy because it also allows an accompanying adult to travel for half-fare. For further details see page 164.

EXAMINATION CONCESSIONS

Concessions may be made for disabled students taking examinations on the understanding that they compensate for the purely practical restrictions imposed by a handicap. Additional time may be needed. You may require an amanuensis to copy what you dictate which will also necessitate a separate room in which to take the examination plus an extra invigilator. If you are unsure of the practical arrangements needed, it would be useful to have a trial run using an old examination paper. This would also provide very practical guidance for your tutors.

The National Bureau for Handicapped Students would be glad to advise. For those who are visually impaired, the Bureau together with the RNIB have produced guidance notes for students and staff entitled *Blind and Partially Sighted Students in College*, including information on examination concessions. (Details on page 118.)

For those who are hearing impaired the National Study Group on Further and Higher Education for the Hearing Impaired has produced a revised list of examination concessions made by the various examining boards for the pre-lingually hearing impaired. For details *see* page 107.

Helpful Organisations and Services

Students are recommended to contact any organisation which exists specifically to cater for their particular handicap. As well as advising, such bodies may be able to help with fees and the cost of necessary special equipment. For tape-recording equipment and services *see* Section 14.

The Armchair Book Service
The Cleuch, Twynholm, Kirkcudbright, Scotland DG6 4SD (Tel: Twynholm (055 76) 215).
This is a personal book service for customers in the United Kingdom and overseas who do not have access to a good bookshop. The main business is in new rather than second-hand books, but any available book can be supplied to order. The service operates six days a week by mail order only.

Association of Disabled Professionals
The Stables, 73 Pound Road, Banstead, Surrey SM7 2HU (Tel: Burgh Heath (073 73) 52366).
The Association exists to secure improvements and to provide advice on educational and employment opportunities for disabled people. Membership fee is £6 per annum and £2 for disabled students. There is an occasional newsletter and a quarterly house bulletin.

CRYPT
The Crypt Foundation, 21 Plover Close, East Wittering, Chichester, West Sussex PO20 8PW (Tel: Bracklesham Bay (0243) 670000).
Creative Young People Together (CRYPT) is a new charitable trust which sets out to help disabled people develop their creative talents. The Trust aims to buy and equip bungalows for young disabled people, who will be provided with workshop areas where other disabled people with talent could share in the creative work on a daily basis. Helpers will be appointed for the special needs arising from disability, and tutors/aides to further the creative work.

Disabled Living Foundation
380–384 Harrow Road, London W9 2HU (Tel: 01-289 6111).
Provides a general information service on aids and services for disabled people (*see* Section 3). Details of specific aids will be supplied on request. The Foundation also publishes an information leaflet on tertiary education for physically disabled people.

The Library Association
7 Ridgmount Street, London WC1E 7AE (Tel: 01-636 7543).
A leaflet has been prepared for visually handicapped people and others with reading problems. It provides information on the publishers of large print books, talking newspapers and reading aids of all kinds. For a free copy send s.a.e. (minimum 9 in. × 12 in.) to Ms Ann Hobart at the above address.

National Bureau for Handicapped Students
40 Brunswick Square, London WC1N 1AZ (Tel: 01-278 3459).

The aims of the Bureau are to improve opportunities in further, higher and adult education for handicapped people. The Bureau is concerned with the whole range of physical, sensory and mental handicap. In fact, it covers all people with 'special educational needs' (*see* Education Act 1981, page 91) including those with learning difficulties who may have an intellectual handicap or dyslexia.

It runs a national information and advice service on all aspects of education and handicap. It aims to co-ordinate the work of organisations and institutions working in the field by organising conferences, and the development of its network of voluntary regional co-ordinators who have links at the local and regional levels.

Membership is open to all interested institutions and individuals. Members receive a regular journal, *Educare*, three times a year which covers news and information on all aspects of the handicapped student.

Further details on membership and a full publications list are available on request from the Bureau. For details of publications, *see* page 117.

The National Study Group on Further and Higher Education for the Hearing Impaired

Peter Greenwood, Thorn Park School for the Deaf, Bingley Road, Bradford, West Yorkshire BD9 6RY. The Group was set up by teachers working with deaf students in colleges of further and higher education in 1976. It has a broad range of objectives, including: to promote the exchange of views and experience of all those concerned in further education and higher education for the hearing impaired; to liaise with schools and careers services; to improve facilities; and to promote co-operation between further education and higher education, and industry, commerce and training boards on the education and employment of those who are hearing impaired.

The group has produced a list of examination concessions made by the various examining boards for the pre-lingually hearing impaired. Available for 25p with a foolscap s.a.e. Also available, a *Directory of Courses* which lists courses and tutors for the hearing impaired nationwide. Price, 50p plus stamps.

Rehabilitation – Great Britain (The Rehabilitation Trust of Great Britain)

PO Box 23, Hailsham, Sussex.
Rehab's objectives are to advance study, teaching and research in the rehabilitation of disabled people. They operate a personal tuition service to help individuals who need extra coaching in academic or vocational training subjects, particularly where such help should lead to employment opportunities.

Rehab (GB) has founded the Institute of Agricultural Medicine and Rehabilitation in order to concentrate more fully upon the needs of the rural worker.

Research and Policy Development, National Union of Students

461 Holloway Road, London N7 6LJ (Tel: 01-272 8900).
Publishes a number of leaflets including *Financial Assistance for Handicapped Students*, a brief guide for disabled persons wishing to enter further or higher education and *Guide to Provision for Students with Locomotor Disorders in Halls of Residence*. Available free with s.a.e.

Open University Adviser to Disabled Students

Derek Child, The Open University, Walton Hall, Milton Keynes MK7 6AA (Tel: Milton Keynes (0908) 653442).

Royal National Institute for the Blind

224 Great Portland Street, London W1N 6AA (Tel: 01-388 1266).

The RNIB makes grants available to visually handicapped students following a wide variety of approved courses of study. These grants are intended to help with the cost of aids and material, readers' fees and other special expenses incurred by the visually handicapped student which are not adequately covered by statutory provision. The RNIB stresses that on no account should a student limit his reading needs because of lack of resources. Also, in some towns, they point out, there are local reading groups who will read anything from novels to weighty texts.

The RNIB student advisers contact each student at least once during the academic year and offer to visit; during this visit they can give advice about study methods, equipment, etc., and they will also be happy to meet teachers and lecturers to discuss any problems which may have arisen. The advisers may be contacted at the above address.

RNIB grants: For O and A level courses a grant of £300 is available. For full-time degree, OND, HND and teacher training courses there is an initial grant of £400, which can be extended by a further grant of £400 as necessary in approved cases. For higher degrees, PGCE and post-graduate qualifications a further grant of up to £400 is available. (For grants for Open University courses *see* page 115.)

Royal National Institute for the Deaf

105 Gower Street, London WC1E 6AH (Tel: 01-387 8033).
RNID has a list of further education courses for deaf people.

Spastics Society
12 Park Crescent, London W1N 4EQ (Tel: 01-636 5020).
The Society's Family Services and Assessment Centre is housed at 16 Fitzroy Square, London W1P 5HQ (Tel: 01-387 9571). It offers a helpful service providing a homely environment where children, adolescents and adults are assessed by a small panel of professional staff. (*See also* Beaumont College and Dene College on page 113.)

(*See also* Beaumont College and Dene College on page 113.)

LIBRARY SERVICES FOR BLIND PEOPLE

Before leaving school, any student with a serious visual handicap who intends to undertake a course of further education is advised to apply for membership of the RNIB Students' Braille Library, the National Library for the Blind and the RNIB Student Tape Library (which incorporates membership of the British Talking Book Service).

General information on these and allied services is given in the booklet *Blind and Partially Sighted Students in College* available from RNIB, 224 Great Portland Street, London W1N 6AA (Tel: 01-388 1266). Students are also strongly advised to get their names on the mailing list of the braille *Monthly Announcement* or to subscribe to the print edition of the *New Beacon*. (For further details of taped books and tape services see Section 14.)

RNIB Students' Braille Library
Braille House, 338–346 Goswell Road, London EC1V 7JE (Tel: 01-837 9921).
The service includes the loan of books, and transcriptions into braille of examination papers, selected texts and short documents.

The National Library for the Blind
Cromwell Road, Bredbury, Stockport, Cheshire SK6 2SG (Tel: 061-494 0217/8/9).
The lending service is free, and post free. The library holds the largest stock of books in braille and Moon types in the United Kingdom. It also stocks some large print books.

RNIB Student Tape Library
Braille House, 338-346 Goswell Road, London EC1V 7JE (Tel: 01-837 9921).
The Student Tape Library exists to provide books on tape for blind and partially sighted students, teachers and other professional people. Once in the library, books may be borrowed by any other visually handicapped people who are interested. Recordings are made on C90 compact cassettes, mostly in the stan-
dard two-track way. However, some titles are on C90s with four tracks recorded at half-speed, while titles produced before July 1978 are on Clarke & Smith Talking Book cassettes. Contact the above address for further details.

Public Libraries
These provide commercial recordings on disc and tape.

Tape Organisations and Services
See Section 14.

LARGE PRINT BOOKS
See Appendix A.

OTHER RESOURCES FOR BLIND AND PARTIALLY SIGHTED STUDENTS

Learning to type
In some areas, typing is taught to newly blind people either at home or in a local rehabilitation centre. Where these facilities are not provided by the social services it may not be too difficult for a blind person to follow instruction at an ordinary sighted typing class, as all students are taught to type by touch alone. A braille version of Pitmans *Teach Yourself Typewriting* is available from the Royal National Institute for the Blind, 224 Great Portland Street, London W1N 6AA (Tel: 01-388 1266).

In addition, some blind people may be prepared to teach themselves with the aid of a cassette typing course. Available free of charge, but requests must be accompanied by four blank C60 cassettes and a self-addressed label, from Charles Cadwell, MBE, Tape Recording Service for the Blind, 48 Fairfax Road, Farnborough, Hampshire GU14 8JP (Tel: Farnborough (0252) 47943).

Talking calculators
There is a range of talking calculators now becoming available for educational and vocational use, including the teaching of mathematics. There is a full voice read-out of input and output, and of the result of every stage of the calculation. The calculators are 8/12 function calculators which provide visual display, voice read-out and print-out for the basic four functions, plus all numeral entries and results. All number keys are in a separate group, the arithmetic and per cent key in another group and the additional function keys in a third group to simplify location. Prices range from £65 to £230. Details available from the Employment Services Manager at the RNIB.

ORGANISATIONS PROVIDING DIRECTORIES OF
EDUCATIONAL OPPORTUNITIES

Association of British Correspondence Colleges
6 Francis Grove, London SW19 4DT.
The Association aims to safeguard the interests of all
students taking correspondence courses and to ensure that its members provide a high standard of
tuition and an efficient service. It also operates an
advice and information centre on matters pertaining
to correspondence education, in which context it
offers, free on request, a broadsheet that details its
member-colleges and lists the subjects in which, as
well as the examinations for which, correspondence
instruction is available from them.

*COPE – the Compendium of Post-16 Education in
Residential Training Establishments for Handicapped Young People*
Price, £5 from the National Bureau for Handicapped
Students.
   In addition to the many hundreds of ordinary
colleges of further and higher education who are now
willing to assist disabled students, there are still a
number of independent residential colleges for those
who need or prefer this form of further education
and training. A full list of these colleges is provided in
COPE.

*Council for the Accreditation of Correspondence
Colleges*
27 Marylebone Road, London NW1 5JS (Tel: 01-935
5391).
The Council is the only organisation in the United
Kingdom officially recognised as responsible for the
award of accreditation to correspondence colleges.
The principal objects of the Council are:
(a) to promote education by setting standards for all
     aspects of tuition, education or training con-
     ducted wholly or in part by post, to investigate
     the manner in which such activities are carried
     out and to grant, where appropriate, the award
     of accreditation stating that the activities of the
     college conform to such standards;
(b) to protect the educational interests and progress
     of students and to ensure that a satisfactory and
     responsible service is provided by accredited
     correspondence colleges, having regard to the
     distinctive characteristics, traditions and needs
     of both.
The process of accreditation is carried out by panels
of independent qualified assessors appointed by the
Council. The assessors' reports, supplemented by
the reports of members or officers of the Council, are
finally considered by the full Council before a decision as to accreditation, or otherwise, is made. Accreditation is subject to periodic review.
   A list of accredited correspondence colleges is
available from the Council's offices.

National Institute of Adult Education
19B De Montfort Street, Leicester LE1 7GE (Tel:
Leicester (0533) 551451).
Acts as a co-ordinator for local authorities, universities, voluntary organisations and other agencies,
including broadcasting and television. (For further
details, *see* Section 9.)

*Regional Advisory Councils for the Organisation of
Further Education – Guides for Handicapped
Students*
These guides provide useful information covering all
colleges of further and higher education in each of
the regions, with the names of co-ordinators to
whom enquiries about opportunities for handi-
capped students should be directed. Details of
specialist teaching staff as well as other relevant
details are included.
   Details of the guides are as follows:
*East Midlands – Further Education for Handicapped
People*
Available from: The Secretary, Regional Advisory
Council for the Organisation of Further Education in
the East Midlands, Robins Wood House, Robins
Wood Road, Aspley, Nottingham NG8 3NH. Free
but please enclose a 12 in. × 9 in. addressed en-
velope, stamped for 3 oz per copy.
*London and Home Counties – A Guide to Specialist
Facilities and Courses for Handicapped People: In
Post School Educational Establishments.*
Available from London and Home Counties Regio-
nal Advisory Council for Technological Education,
Tavistock House South, Tavistock Square, London
WC1H 9LR. Price £2.
*West Midlands – Specialist Facilities and Courses in
Further Education for Handicapped People in the
West Midlands.* Occasional Paper No. 5.
Available from West Midlands Council for the
Disabled, Mosely Hall Hospital, Birmingham B13
8JZ. Price £1.
*Yorkshire and Humberside – Further Education for
the Handicapped in Yorkshire and Humberside.*
Available from Chief Officer, Yorkshire and Hum-
berside Association for Further and Higher Educa-
tion, Bowling Green Terrace, Leeds LS11 9SX.
Price £1.
See also *A Directory of Open Learning Opportunities
in Scotland* (page 117).

Travelling Fellowship

The Winston Churchill Memorial Trust offers Churchill Travelling Fellowships for people to make studies overseas related to their trade, profession or interests, in order that they might bring back knowledge and experience for the benefit of the community. Each year applications are sought from UK citizens, with no age limits and no special qualifications required. Categories of subject change each year. A number of disabled people are now Fellows having successfully completed their travelling fellowships. For further information apply to: The Winston Churchill Memorial Trust, 15 Queen's Gate Terrace, London SW7 5PR.

Vocational Guidance and Training

LOCAL EDUCATION AUTHORITY CAREERS SERVICE

See Section 7.

YOUTH TRAINING SCHEME (MANPOWER SERVICES COMMISSION)

This scheme came fully into operation in September 1983. It is a permanent programme which is intended to provide a bridge between school or further education and the world of work. It generally offers 12 months of training and linked work experience. The training usually takes place with an employer, in a training workshop or community project or in a local college.

Young disabled people may stay on YTS for up to 26 weeks longer than the normal 52-week maximum if more time would significantly improve their prospects of employment, or training which might lead to employment. This extension of stay might be taken at the end of a normal 52-week programme, or up to 13 weeks of it might be taken to accommodate a period of special assessment/preparation prior to entry to a full YTS programme. Young people of 16, or sometimes 17, years of age may join the scheme, while disabled young people may join at up to 21 years old. A flat-rate allowance of £25.00 per week, which includes any travel costs, is paid. In addition, young disabled people may claim the cost of taxi fares.

Details of the scheme can be obtained from any Careers Office, Employment Office or Jobcentre, though it is perhaps best to contact your local Specialist Careers Officer for the Handicapped. The MSC also has a Disabled Persons Liaison Officer in each Area Office whom local Jobcentres can contact for advice. The National Bureau for Handicapped Students is making a special study of YTS and they can also offer help and advice.

TRAINING DIVISION (MSC)

Section 7 explains in some detail the role of the Employment Division (ED) and this section describes the Training Division (TD). They co-operate to provide training suited to individual needs, and this includes special provision to meet the needs of disabled people. They provide a service to those who are interested in opportunities for training or who are seeking advice on careers. Disabled people can find out more about training opportunities from Jobcentre staff or from the Disablement Resettlement Officer (DRO).

The following paragraphs outline the training facilities which are currently available. (*See also* ED booklet EPL 37 *Rehabilitation, Retraining, Resettlement*.)

TRAINING OPPORTUNITIES SCHEME (TOPS)

Of special interest to disabled people is the Training Opportunities Scheme, which offers free training with weekly tax-free allowances to men and women who want to develop their skills in order to improve their job prospects. TOPS provides full-time courses at TD Skillcentres, at colleges of further education, at private colleges and at employers' own premises.

TOPS courses cover such diverse subjects as business administration, secretarial and commercial work, craft and technical courses in engineering and construction, automotive skills, television and industrial electronics and many other skills. Many people train as operators in a wide variety of industries. Most courses at Skillcentres last six to nine months, while courses at colleges of further education and at employers' premises may be shorter or longer. For technical or administrative subjects the training could last up to a year. Graduates over 27 may be eligible for postgraduate courses at universities and polytechnics.

There are, of course, eligibility conditions, but these are less stringent for disabled people; admission to training can be at any time after school-leaving age and a second course may be given in less than three years where a person's state of health makes this necessary. All TOPS courses are free and, in addition, trainees receive allowances to enable them to maintain themselves and their dependants during training. These allowances are tax-free, and National Insurance contributions are credited without charge. In addition, where the trainee has to stay away from home, free accommodation or a living-away-from-home allowance is provided. Mid-day meals are free, or a weekly allowance is given if they are not available.

As well as training under TOPS the TD also offers disabled people special training opportunities under its Other Training Arrangements (OTA) and under its Professional Training Scheme (PTS). OTA may involve training of longer than 12 months, including on-the-job training by an employer who is asked to offer wage-earning employment after training is completed. A disabled person may be accepted for part-time training or for training by means of a correspondence course, including those of the Open University. Arrangements are made with the Royal National Institute for the Deaf (RNID) to train *profoundly deaf people* in electronic wiring, painting and decorating, general building, carpentry and joinery and horticulture. A few profoundly deaf people who have overcome communication problems are trained in Skillcentres.

Further information is contained in the leaflet *Training for a better job with TOPS* (TSD N100) and further information on how the scheme operates for handicapped people is given in *Training opportunities for disabled people* (TSD N121). Allowances available for TOPS trainees are detailed in TD N103 (the allowances paid under OTA are the same). These leaflets are available from Local Employment Offices.

Full details of TOPS for handicapped people can be obtained from Disablement Resettlement Officers who can be contacted through any Jobcentre, Employment Office or TD office.

RESIDENTIAL TRAINING (MSC)

As is the case with further education, *most* disabled people undergo training in ordinary training establishments and workshops. However, for those who, for one reason or another, require special provision, four residential training establishments have been set up by the Training Division (TD) of the MSC.

These are independent voluntary organisations and are located in rural surroundings at Durham, Mansfield, Leatherhead and Exeter. For many years they have provided a variety of vocational training courses for disabled people (but not blind people), who are recruited through Jobcentres, Employment Offices and local education authority careers services. Courses are planned in consultation with the TD, and are aimed at preparing disabled people for ordinary employment in industry or commerce. Their duration is varied according to subject and to individual learning difficulties. Accommodation is provided on a seven-day-week basis (except for public holidays) and is of a high standard, with purpose-built toilet and bathroom facilities, and easy access. Each college has residential nursing staff

(who are available by day and night) and a welfare officer. Medical attention can be obtained promptly.

The cost of both training and accommodation at the residential training colleges is met by the TD. In addition, trainees receive allowances to enable them to maintain themselves and their dependants during training. These allowances are tax-free, and National Insurance contributions are credited without charge. Free travel warrants are issued to allow trainees to return home on public holidays or any periods of leave to which they may be entitled, and for travel from and to home at the beginning and end of courses.

Further information is contained in the TD leaflet *Residential training for disabled people* (TSD N278) available from Employment Offices or Jobcentres, or from TD district offices. Allowances are described in more detail in Leaflet TD N103. The colleges and the courses they provide are as follows:

Finchale Training College
Durham DH1 5RX (Tel: Durham (0385) 62634).
Offers training to disabled persons from 16 to 58 years. Courses may be arranged in the following subjects: bench joinery; assistant quantity surveying; domestic service engineering (domestic electrical appliances); horticulture; production engineering workshop skills; watch and clock repairing; typewriter mechanics; business studies (general office skills, book-keeping, wages and accounts, using manual and computerised systems, audio and copy typing, shorthand, word processing). A course in electronics servicing is being introduced in the near future.

All trainees are sponsored by the Manpower Services Commission and further information on all courses is obtainable from Jobcentres.

Portland Training College for the Disabled
Harlow Wood, Mansfield, Nottinghamshire NG18 4TJ (Tel: Mansfield (0623) 792141).
Offers the following facilities to all categories of disabled people (with the exception of the totally blind) between the ages of 16 and 60 years:
(a) *Assessment/Development Centre*. For the multi-handicapped school-leaver.
(b) *Further Education Department*. Incorporating further and remedial education for handicapped school-leavers, and literacy/numeracy courses for all ages.
(c) *Vocational Training Department*. In two sections, the following are available:
  (i) *Business Studies*. Basic office skills; office procedures and use of machinery; book-keeping and accounts; copy/audio typing.

(ii) *Technical Studies.* Basic technical skills; three electronics modules covering wiring and assembly, industrial electronics and radio, television and electronic servicing; light engineering; horology; horticulture.

(d) *Multi-purpose Unit.* Intended to cater as a preparatory form of training for the very severely handicapped.

(e) *Sheltered Employment Workshops.* Employment is offered to those handicapped people not able to work in the open market on a series of assembly operations.

For further information, apply to the Principal at the above address.

Queen Elizabeth's Training College for the Disabled
Leatherhead, Surrey KT22 0BN (Tel: Oxshott (037 284) 2204).
The College offers residential training in technical, clerical and practical courses for disabled men and women of all ages from 16 upwards, leading to normal competitive employment. All disabilities other than total blindness are accepted.

There are 192 places (150 men and 42 women). New students are admitted throughout the year as vacancies arise, there being no academic terms. As the training courses run continuously, instruction is given on an individual or tutorial basis. The instructor can thus bias the course towards the needs of each individual. The instructor's close link with the student, together with a system of tests throughout the course, ensure that the best possible results are achieved. Whenever practicable, courses are directed towards recognised examinations such as those of the Royal Society of Arts, the City and Guilds of London Institute and Pitman's Institute.

Courses may be arranged in the following subjects:
Business studies. Commerce; book-keeping; accounting; basic office skills; word processing; computer programming; copy/audio typing; shorthand or speedwriting; reception.
Technical studies. Bench carpentry; builders' quantities; electric arc welding; engineering draughtsmanship; gardening.
Industrial training and work experience. Electric/electronic wiring; sewing machining (leather/plastics); light electrical servicing (domestic appliances, etc.); spray painting (motor vehicles).

Pre-vocational assessment may also be undertaken primarily for disabled school-leavers.

St Loye's College for Training the Disabled for Commerce and Industry
Fairfield House, Topsham Road, Exeter, Devon EX2 6EP (Tel: Exeter (0392) 55428).
For young people there is an assessment, pre-training and work-preparation unit for 16-18 year olds. For adults, courses are run in the following subjects: practical accounting; telephony and reception duties; typewriting, audio typewriting and shorthand; cookery (industrial); horticulture; electronics servicing; electronic wiring; engineering inspection; light electro-mechanical fitting; light precision engineering; joinery; storekeeping; watch and clock repair. The College also operates a sheltered workshop.

TRAINING FOR BLIND PEOPLE

Residential courses for computer programmers and for commercial employment in shorthand and typing, audio typing and telephony are available at the Royal National Institute for the Blind Commercial College in London. Similar course facilities, excluding computer programming, exist for people living in Scotland at the Royal Blind School, Edinburgh. The RNIB North London School of Physiotherapy has a three-year residential course leading to the qualifying examinations of the Chartered Society of Physiotherapy. Training as piano tuners, on courses lasting two years or more, is available at the London College of Furniture and the Royal National College for the Blind (see page 114).

Queen Alexandra College in Birmingham runs a two-year course in machine operating and inspection, and one on bicycle repair. The Letchworth Skillcentre (TD) provides introductory courses in light engineering, machine operating, repetitive assembly and inspection training for blind people. Hostel accommodation is provided. The TD also works with the Royal National Institute for the Blind.

TRAINING FOR PROFESSIONAL EMPLOYMENT (MSC)

Disabled people with the necessary educational background and ability who wish to train for a professional career, including a university degree, are normally able to secure an educational grant as students. If not, the TD's Professional Training Scheme for disabled people may be able to provide financial assistance for an approved course likely to lead to resettlement in work of a professional nature. Those accepted have to follow the normal methods of training for the profession concerned (except in the case of training for blind people at the RNIB School of Physiotherapy in London). A maintenance grant may be provided during training, and fees for tuition and examinations may be paid. Entitlement depends on individual financial circumstances and whether or not the trainee can live at home during training.

OTHER RESIDENTIAL COLLEGES

Beaumont College of Further Education
Slyne Road, Lancaster LA2 6AP (Tel: Lancaster (0524) 64278).
Offers a residential two-year course for physically handicapped young people (16 to 19). Most students are of below average academic ability, have moderate to severe learning difficulties and are immature in terms of their personal and social development. Individual programmes of learning are offered from within an integrated social learning curriculum in response to the particular needs of each student.

Dene College
Shipbourne Road, Tonbridge, Kent TN11 9NT (Tel: Tonbridge (0732) 355101).
Offers a two-year course for multi-handicapped spastic young people over 16. The course covers broadly the same subjects as those described under Beaumont College, but takes account of the more limited ability of the students. It aims at planned dependency since students are unlikely to be capable of earning their own living.

Derwen Training College for the Disabled
Oswestry, Shropshire SY11 3JA (Tel: Oswestry (0691) 661234).
The College provides comprehensive assessment for one term, followed by further education and vocational training for young people over 16. The aim of the College is to assist all students to reach their maximum level of independence and skill with a view to placement in open industry or sheltered workshops. All students must be sponsored by their local authorities.

Hereward College
Bramston Crescent, Tile Hill Lane, Coventry CV4 9SW (Tel: Coventry (0203) 461231).
The College, which is closely linked with a normal college of further education on the same campus, provides courses for disabled young people similar to those provided in technical colleges generally, to prepare students for employment or for entry to more advanced courses. A fundamental aim of the College is to assist each student to achieve a high level of competence and independence. There are adequate sporting and recreational facilities available. Specialised transport for students using wheelchairs is provided and good garaging facilities are provided within the College grounds. Because of the special circumstances of the students no precise entry requirements are laid down. The College will consider applicants of either sex within a wide range of physical handicaps. Application forms and further information may be obtained from the Principal at the above address.

Nash House
Coney Hill School, Croydon Road, Hayes, Bromley, Kent BR2 7AG (Tel: 01-462 2017).
A Shaftesbury Society extended education centre for disabled school-leavers, seeking to provide an educational and social environment where physically handicapped school-leavers learn the basic skills of independent living. Two flats are on the site as bases for practising these skills and students have several sessions living in them. The curriculum is broadly based and tailored to meet individual needs. It includes literacy, numeracy, household management, craftwork, music, health management, social life, mobility and work experience. Facilities for learning to drive are available for suitable candidates after assessment. The course aims to bridge the gap between school and adulthood by developing to the fullest any potential skill or aptitude and, at the same time, helping the young people mature socially and emotionally so that they can take their place in society confidently. Each student (16 places available) has his or her own bed/study room.

National Star Centre for Disabled Youth
Ullenwood Manor, Cheltenham, Gloucestershire (Tel: Cheltenham (0242) 27631).
The College caters for disabled students of 16 and over who are considered to have a level of potential attainment sufficiently high to allow them to benefit from the programme of further education provided. The College is a recognised examination centre for the Associated Examining Board, the Royal Society of Arts and the City and Guilds of London Institute, Pitmans, London Chamber of Commerce, and the English Speaking Board.

The course structure allows for GCE studies, pre-vocational courses including commercial studies, computer studies and a range of other work areas as well as a series of general courses including remedial studies. Speech therapy, occupational therapy, physiotherapy and work experience are also available. The College provides a residential environment strongly encouraging personal independence.

Royal National College (Further Education for the Blind and Partially Sighted)
College Road, Hereford HR1 1EB (Tel: Hereford (0432) 265725).
Formerly known as the Royal Normal College, it is the only Further Education College in this country geared to the needs of the visually handicapped, and offers two- to three-year courses in business studies, computer programming, music, piano tuning and general studies. All students are taught mobility, living skills, and typewriting. The business studies course includes shorthand typing or audio typing, telephony and word processing and the BEC general diploma. The piano tuning course includes piano repairs and also book-keeping, as many piano tuners eventually set up their own businesses. The general studies course offers a choice of 15 O and 10 A level subjects, in preparation for higher education, physiotherapy, etc. Students are accepted from the age of 16 and there is no upper age limit for most courses. The fees are normally met by discretionary awards from local authorities. Mature students are sometimes funded by the Manpower Services Commission.

Home Study Courses

THE OPEN UNIVERSITY

Open University courses are specifically designed for home-based study. Courses are offered in arts, educational studies, mathematics, science, social science and technology. No entry qualifications are required and the University is open to all over the age of 21 who are resident in Britain. In some circumstances applicants can be admitted under 21. Entry is on a 'first come, first served' basis; hence early application is advisable, but applications from disabled people may receive special consideration.

The Undergraduate and Associate courses are at different levels. Six credits are required for an ordinary degree, eight for an honours degree, although if you study as an Associate student you can study a particular course that interests you without any further commitment. There are also community education courses that are not at degree level, are shorter, do not have examinations and which do not involve the full range of support services such as tutoring and counselling.

The main element of study is the specially written course material. In addition, courses may utilise television and radio, records and tape cassettes, slides and home experiment kits. Though study at home is the basis of Open University study there are opportunities for tuition and group discussion at local study centres. Tuition and counselling are also carried out by telephone or letter.

Many courses run week-long residential summer schools at conventional university campuses. If need demands, disabled persons may take a personal assistant, or the summer school's office will find such a helper. This will incur no extra cost for the student. In certain circumstances students may be excused summer school attendance.

The United Kingdom is divided into 13 regions, and within these regions there is a member of staff with an interest in and responsibility for disabled students. All students are appointed a tutor counsellor in their first year of study, who also remains a contact person in subsequent years of study. Tuition at higher course levels is undertaken by course tutors.

The Open University provides certain advice and services specifically to meet the needs of disabled students. These include: assistance at summer schools; cassette tapes of course material for those unable to deal with written text; transcripts of broadcasts; study weekends for persons with particular handicaps; advice on the accesssibility of courses to those with specific disabilities and advice on study techniques. These services come from different areas within the University and an Adviser on the Education of Disabled Students has been appointed to both advise and liaise with these departments and outside bodies.

If you would like further information about admission and registration for undergraduate courses write to: The Undergraduate Admissions Officer, the Open University, PO Box 48, Milton Keynes MK7 6AB. For further information on admission and registration for associate student courses write to the Open University, PO Box 76, Milton Keynes MK7 6AN.

The Open University Students' Association (OUSA)
Sherwood House, Sherwood Drive, Bletchley, Milton Keynes MK3 6HN (Tel: Milton Keynes (0908) 71131 ext. 298).
The Association offers many facilities and a back-up service for disabled students, including recruiting helpers for those who need assistance at summer schools.

There is a regionally operated welfare scheme with a representative in each region who will be available for anyone (disabled or able-bodied) with problems, to contact.

In addition, the Open University Students' Association has a Trust Fund, which is designed to assist disadvantaged students of the University.

Applications for aid should be addressed to the Secretary for the Trust, at the central office address given above.

Among the many societies organised by OU students, there is OUMPAS (the OU Mixed Physical Ability Society). This Society is made up of about half handicapped students and half able-bodied students. They organise social events, visits to museums and study weekends in different parts of the country.

OU financial help – grants and awards
In the first instance local education authorities' social services departments or local education authorities should be approached for financial assistance relating to:
(a) preparatory studies;
(b) tuition fees;
(c) kit deposits;
(d) set books;
(e) summer school attendance;
(f) summer school assistant's travelling expenses;
(g) travel to tutorials.
Those handicapped students who belong to an organisation related to a particular disability may find they can apply for assistance with fees. In the event of an undergraduate being unsuccessful with an application for funds from the local education authority then he or she may apply to the Open University Financial Assistance Fund for a grant or a loan.

RNIB grants
The RNIB makes an initial grant to those students taking OU degree courses of £300 raised by £250 at second level study and extended by a further grant of up to £250 at the third level.

For degree level courses in open education there is a grant of £400 which can be extended if necessary.

Further information from RNIB Education Department, 224 Great Portland Street, London W1N 6AA (Tel: 01-388 1266).

NATIONAL EXTENSION COLLEGE, CAMBRIDGE (NEC)

This is a non-profit-making educational trust founded to provide adults with high-quality home study courses. It provides correspondence courses for Open University preparatory and GCE O and A levels, as well as special interest courses. It also provides a correspondence tuition service for London University external degrees and diplomas and for certain professional examinations. For further information apply to National Extension College, 18 Brooklands Avenue, Cambridge CB2 2HN (Tel: Cambridge (0223) 63465).

Fresh Start courses
These courses are suitable for any adult returning to study after a long period away from education. They include courses on study skills, writing skills, elementary maths and beginner's language courses.

GCE courses
NEC provides GCE O and A level courses in most subjects examined by GCE Boards. Any adult can study at home with NEC for a GCE O and A level examination and then enter the examinations through a GCE Board. Full details of the examination entry procedure are sent to students by NEC.

Open University preparatory courses
NEC provides preparatory courses for intending Open University students. These courses cover preparation for the OU Foundation Courses A101, D101, S101 and M101. A detailed leaflet on preparatory courses is published by NEC.

London external degrees and diplomas
Anyone with the appropriate academic qualifications may register with London University for an external degree. London University does not provide any tuition for its external students, who must arrange such tuition themselves. The National Extension College provides such a tuition service for most London external degrees. Those who think they may be eligible for registration with London University for an external degree or diploma should write to the University Entrance Requirements Department, London University, Senate House, Malet Street, London WC1E 7HU for a copy of *Regulations Relating to the University Entrance Requirements*.

While NEC has no power to admit an intending student to registration with London University as an external student, the NEC student advisers can often help with an application for registration, so it is advisable to write to NEC when also writing to London University.

Grants
Most handicapped students studying with NEC get grants from their local education authorities. Before applying for a grant for an NEC course it is advisable to contact the Head of Student Services at NEC for advice on how to phrase the application.

Further information
About correspondence courses: write to NEC for their free *Guide to Courses*. About tuition for London external degrees and diplomas: write for the free NEC *Degree and Professional Booklet*.

115

RADAR, 25 Mortimer Street, London W1N 8AB
(Tel: 01-637 5400).
The Education and Training Bureau, previously
known as the Preparatory Training Bureau, was
established by the British Council for the Rehabilitation for the Disabled and is now administered by
RADAR. The aim of the Bureau is to provide
education and training opportunities for people who,
because of their disabilities, are unable to take advantage of the normal further education facilities.
The Bureau can provide financial assistance for
correspondence courses (from colleges which are
approved by The Council for the Accreditation of
Correspondence Colleges) and also arranges home
tuition for people living in the Inner London Education Authority area. Similar services are administered by the Midlands Council for the
Preparatory Training of the Disabled and the Scottish Council for the Tuition of the Disabled in their
regions. Anyone who is physically handicapped and
over the age of 16 is eligible to apply for assistance
from the Bureau. Courses are generally in basic
English and mathematics but a wide range of other
subjects can be studied. In some instances courses
are taken with the view to assisting people to find
employment; others are taken for their therapeutic
value. A Disablement Resettlement Officer (DRO)
or other professional is usually required to support
applications.

Further details and application forms may be obtained from RADAR. Enquiries from the Midlands
should be sent to Mrs R. Wolf, The Midlands Council for Preparatory Training of the Disabled, 14
Barlows Road, Edgbaston, Birmingham B15 2PL,
and enquiries from Scotland should be sent to The
Scottish Council for the Tuition of the Disabled,
Edinburgh University Settlement, Student Centre,
Bristo Street, Edinburgh EH8 9AL.

Scottish Centre for the Tuition of the Disabled
Queen Margaret College, Clerwood Terrace, Edinburgh EH12 8TS (Tel: 031-339 5408).
The SCTD is a recently established educational information, advice and tutorial service for disabled
men and women over the age of 16 in Scotland. It
provides, through a network of regional organisers,
information and advice on current educational and
leisure opportunities locally and nationally. Anyone
may apply and there is no selection process. The
Centre tries to provide help for every applicant,
although, being more aware of the opportunities
available, they may advise a different path than the
student first envisaged.

There are two broad categories of student – those
seeking tuition for employment purposes, and those
seeking tuition for leisure purposes. Tuition from the
SCTD can be a bridge to college attendance, either
by reintroducing the study habit, or by bringing the
student to the level at which he or she can cope with
the proposed course. Where appropriate, the Centre
will provide individual one-to-one tuition in
academic/leisure/craft subjects, at home or in hospital, using volunteer tutors. The service is free.

*Scottish Co-ordinating Committee for Distance
Learning Schemes in Vocational Further Education*
22 Great King Street, Edinburgh EH3 6QH (Tel:
031-557 4555).
The schemes provide a system of directed private
study for students aged 20 years or more who find it
difficult to attend a college on a normal basis. They
take the form of college-based correspondence
courses reinforced with generally three-day face-
to-face sessions.

Some handicapped students may well be able to
attend the three-day residential periods. Others may
find this quite impossible and, if so, a letter should be
sent to the Secretary of the Co-ordinating Committee who will try to arrange for an equivalent measure
of face-to-face tuition to be given to these students in
their own homes by visiting college tutors.

Information about tuition and examination fees,
together with estimates of residential accommodation costs, are given on the separate leaflets for each
course. Courses on offer cover business studies,
distribution studies, printing and public administration, and lead to the awards of the Scottish Business
and Technical Education Councils.

A wide variety of correspondence courses is offered
on cassette or braille by a correspondence school for
the blind in the United States. Courses are free of
charge to blind students all over the world. Details
from the Hadley School for the Blind, 700 Elm
Street, Winnetka, Illinois 60093, USA.

Local education authorities publish each year a full
prospectus of all local part-time, day and evening
classes. Where a particular subject is not covered, if a
number of people get together and make a request a
class can usually be arranged. Handicapped students
can nearly always be accommodated, if necessary by
making special arrangements. Many local authorities
will waive charges for those who are receiving supplementary benefit.

Holiday Courses

See Section 9.

Books and Publications

Able to Work by Bernadette Fallon. (For further details *see* Section 7, page 131.)

Directory of Courses. Lists courses and tutors for those who are hearing impaired nation-wide. Price 50p plus stamps. Available from the National Study Group on Further and Higher Education for the Hearing Impaired, Peter Greenwood, Thorn Park School for the Deaf, Bingley Road, Bradford, West Yorkshire BD9 6RY.

Also available is a list of examination concessions made by the various examining boards for the pre-lingually hearing impaired. Price 25p with a foolscap s.a.e.

Directory of Further Education 83/84 (Careers Research and Advisory Centre), published by Hobsons Press (Cambridge) Ltd, Bateman Street, Cambridge CB2 1LZ. Details of all full-time, part-time, block-release and day-release courses: degree, professional, BEC, TEC, national City & Guilds, regional colleges, GCE A level/SCE H-grade plus entrance requirements, college announcements and addresses (apparently no special advice for disabled people).

Price £35 plus postage and handling. Also available in libraries and careers offices.

Directory of Educational Courses for Mentally Handicapped Adults edited by Victoria Shennan. Available from MENCAP, The Bookshop, 123 Golden Lane, London EC1Y 0RT. Price £3.95 plus 75p postage and packing.

A Directory of Open Learning Opportunities in Scotland. This Guide lists over 190 different courses designed for students who cannot attend conventional courses for a variety of reasons.

'Open Learning' is a term used to describe courses flexibly designed to meet individual circumstances which may prevent you attending more traditional courses. The courses will differ in many ways, but broadly speaking 'you should be able to study what you want, where you want, when you want, at a speed suitable to yourself without the necessity to join a group of a specific size'. There are many variations, but for ease of classification the courses are divided into:

Courses where most of the learning takes place in a learning centre of some kind or another.

Courses where most of the activity is at home, or away from a learning centre.

The Guide may be obtained post-free to addresses in Scotland from Peter Gartside, the Scottish Council for Educational Technology, 74 Victoria Crescent Road, Glasgow G12 9JN.

The Education Authorities Directory and Annual. (For details *see* page 94.)

The Education Year Book. (For details *see* page 94.)

Have Wheels: Will Travel. A first study tour of Rome by Open University disabled students. The aim of the tour was to extend to OU disabled students parity of educational opportunities – in this instance to join fellow humanities students for course studies in Italy. The reporting, by the students themselves, is both frank and informed, and there is sound advice for future disabled travellers – what to take, how to cope with incontinence and practical problems, and guidance on accessibility difficulties in Rome. Available from OUSA office, Sherwood House, Sherwood Drive, Bletchley, Milton Keynes MK3 6HN (Tel: Milton Keynes (0908) 71131). Price £1.20 including postage.

Living Independently. See page 87.

MSC leaflets available at your Jobcentre
Training Opportunities for Disabled People – TSD N121.

Residential Training for Disabled People – TSD N278.

All that Counts is Ability – TSD L109.

40 Brunswick Square, London WC1N 1AZ (Tel: 01-278 3459/3450).

The Bureau has a range of very helpful and informative literature which includes:

After 16: what next? Published by the Family Fund and available from the Bureau. Price: £1.75 including postage. A general guide for young people with disabilities as they reach their sixteenth birthday. Also helpful to their parents and advisers. Information is included on: further education, employment, benefits, aids and adaptations, holidays, independent living and mobility.

An Educational Policy for Handicapped People (1977). This leaflet outlines the Bureau's general philosophy on the provision of educational opportunities for handicapped people and on the attitudes which should be adopted by those agencies primarily concerned with making such opportunities available, mainly local education authorities and institutions of further and higher education.

Further Education Training and Employment Opportunities for Handicapped People (1981). This publication sets out the various options available to the handicapped school-leaver and the handicapped adult, and attempts to show the links between the various levels of education, training and employment. Price £1.50 including postage and packing.

A set of information sheets:

1. *Students with Disabilities* (updated each year). This sheet is published jointly with the National Union of Students. It provides valuable information on sources of financial assistance as well as a limited amount of general information. Price 60p including postage and packing.

2. *Directory of Specialist Careers Officers for the Handicapped*. A most useful list for all those seeking a contact with whom they can discuss their special needs. The Bureau's aim in producing this directory was to identify a contact within each local education authority to whom enquiries by and on behalf of handicapped young people might be referred, and to give some indication of the function of the specialist. Price 70p including postage and packing.

3. *Applying to Higher Education*. Some notes for disabled students, their parents and advisers. Answers many of the questions disabled people seeking entry to higher education have brought to the Bureau's information service over the years in a simple 'question and answer' format. Price 50p including postage and packing.

4. *Meeting the Personal Care Needs of Severely Physically Handicapped Students at College*. This information sheet shows how many students have been able to make arrangements to meet their personal care needs. The sheet will be helpful to current and potential students, their parents and advisers. The options discussed are intended to help both students and those who advise them to make informed and detailed enquiries for themselves, based on the pooled experience of others who have faced similar difficulties. Price £1.50 including postage and packing.

5. *Deaf Students in College* (in conjunction with the National Study Group in Further and Higher Education for the Hearing Impaired). Provides guidance and support – both tutorial and technical – which can enable a deaf student to complete a college course with confidence. Price 50p including postage and packing.

6. *Blind and Partially Sighted Students in College* (in conjunction with the Royal National Institute for the Blind). This sheet offers a wide range of information on aids and support for visually handicapped students. It is intended for college staff with little experience of their study needs and for students themselves. Price 50p including postage and packing. A set of leaflets costs £3.50 including postage and packing. Single copies of the information sheets are free to handicapped students (a stamped addressed A4-size envelope for reply is appreciated).

NOTE: At the time of writing (1984) a guide is being prepared to all the Universities, Polytechnics and Colleges of Higher Education. Information will include the name of a contact, special provision available, facilities, accessibility and general information.

The National Bureau for Handicapped Students, in association with the National Union of Students, publishes:

Students with Disabilities. This leaflet has a wealth of information relating to sources of financial assistance and provision in colleges for students with disabilities. Available free from the NBHS. Please send a s.a.e.

The National Union of Students publishes a number of other leaflets and reports, including *Guide to Provision for Students with Locomotor Disorders in Halls of Residence* and leaflet No. 4 *Grants and Awards*. Available free with s.a.e.

Never Too Late to Learn by Judith Bell and Gordon Roderick. Published by Longman Group Ltd, Retail Services Dept, 4th Avenue, Harlow, Essex. (Tel: Harlow (0279) 29655).

A well-indexed guide to adult education. Details of courses, grants and sponsorships are well covered. Guidance is also given on job prospects and there is a list of books on how to study.

Typewriting Exercises for One-handed People by Jean Kempthorne. The author is a qualified typing teacher with a special interest in the difficulties of handicapped students. While this book is published primarily for the teacher's use, there are sufficient explanatory notes for the student working alone. Available from St Albans College, St Albans, Hertfordshire. Price £2.40 including postage and packing.

SECTION 7
EMPLOYMENT

On a cold and wet Monday morning, we all want to turn over and pull the blankets up higher, rueing the fates who have in their cruelty decreed that we must earn our living. In fact, of course, it is a privilege so to do, and a privilege to which all of us have a right to aspire. For those who are disabled, the right to work can be difficult to achieve and, in fact, requires a good deal more initiative and determination than many able-bodied people ever show. There was the disabled housewife who telephoned a local firm offering to do a home-based telephone-selling job for them; they replied that they had never employed someone in this capacity before. 'Isn't it about time you did?' she said, and got the job.

This section attempts to set out the statutory assistance there is available and also to provide some general ideas. It definitely helps to be talented, but those of us who cannot aspire to creative writing or painting should not despair; persistence and determination are also talents and they can be cultivated. There are a good many aids available, including an increasing range of sophisticated electronic equipment, which for many disabled people can provide the means to earn a living.

This section should be read in conjunction with Section 6 on Further Education, for who knows where a few acquired skills may lead, certainly to greater opportunities and to a confidence which in itself seems to produce opportunities.

Statutory Services

Statutory provision for the employment and training for employment of disabled people is based on the Disabled Persons (Employment) Acts 1944 and 1958. These Acts are summarised in Section 13 on Legislation. Training is dealt with in Section 6 on Further Education. The following paragraphs describe in broad outline the practical employment services which are now available.

THE MANPOWER SERVICES COMMISSION (MSC)

This Commission was set up under the Employment and Training Act 1973 and is responsible for public employment and training services. The MSC operates through two divisions: the Employment Divison (ED), and the Training Division (TD), discussed in Section 6.

EMPLOYMENT DIVISION (ED)

The ED runs the network of local Employment Offices and Jobcentres; in addition, it offers some specialist services for particular groups of employees and for particular industries. The services include the Disablement Resettlement Officer Service and Professional and Executive Recruitment (PER). Included in these services is the administration of sheltered employment for the disabled and the provision of an employment rehabilitation service for those who have suffered illness or injury.

THE LOCAL AUTHORITY CAREERS SERVICE

The Employment and Training Act 1973 also places a legal obligation on each local authority to provide a vocational guidance and employment placement service, known as the Careers Service, for young people leaving school. Under these arrangements all Careers Officers have a duty to assist young disabled people, and most local education authorities have appointed Careers Officers to specialise in this field. As a normal feature of the work Careers Officers maintain close co-operation with the ED's Jobcentres, local authority social workers and specialist voluntary organisations, as appropriate.

REGISTRATION

Disabled people over the statutory school-leaving age (at present 16 years) may apply to their local Employment Office or Jobcentre for registration under the Disabled Persons (Employment) Act 1944 (see Section 13). A Disablement Resettlement Officer will arrange, in suitable cases, for medical certification of this disablement before finding the person eligible. Registration in this way may, in some cases, be an aid to employment because large firms are required by law to employ a certain quota of people on the register. Certain other facilities also, in

particular sheltered employment, are limited to those who are registered. The three main conditions of registration are:
(a) that the applicant is substantially handicapped in finding and keeping suitable employment;
(b) that the disability is likely to last for at least 12 months;
(c) that the applicant wants a job and has a reasonable prospect of obtaining and keeping one.
(Full details from any Employment Office or Jobcentre. Leaflet DPL 1.)

NOTE: Registration as described above should not be confused with registration under Section 29 of the National Assistance Act 1948.

COMPANIES' DIRECTORS' REPORTS

Many companies will now have to state their policies in the annual reports regarding their employment of disabled people. For further information *see* page 259.

PROFESSIONAL AND EXECUTIVE RECRUITMENT (PER)

PER is the specialist branch of the MSC which provides a recruitment service for employers who wish to engage professional, executive, managerial, scientific and technical staff, and assists people seeking employment at this level. PER operates nationally through a network of offices and offers a comprehensive recruitment service which includes selection, interviewing and advertising. The service is free to job-seekers while employers are charged a fee based on the type of service used.

When a disabled person enrols, he or she is invited to a joint interview with a PER Candidate Consultant and a Disablement Resettlement Officer (DRO).

EMPLOYMENT REHABILITATION CENTRES

The ED runs a network of 27 Employment Rehabilitation Centres (ERCs) which provide facilities for those who have been ill or injured or are handicapped in some way to return to working fitness. Courses aim to restore a person's physical capacity, restore confidence and assess his or her abilities so as to give a practical and considered recommendation as to the type of work most likely to offer permanent employment. This is achieved with the help of a team of specialists who examine clients' social, medical and psychological circumstances as well as technical ability.

Courses last on average about six to eight weeks, though they may be as short as two to three weeks or as long as 26 weeks depending on individual need.

There are also Short Assessment Courses of up to two weeks especially for people who just need a clearer idea of what type of work they can do. In addition, most ERCs provide 13-week Young Persons Work Preparation Courses designed for handicapped school-leavers. These courses aim to combine practical work and assessment with further education directed towards the needs of young people entering employment.

Three ERCs have residential provision, although most ERCs are able to arrange lodgings in hostels or private accommodation for those unable to travel to the ERC daily. People attending ERCs are generally entitled to tax-free allowances and assistance with fares, and, where necessary, the expenses involved in living away from home.

In addition to ERCs, ED supports a number of agency centres run by local authorities and voluntary bodies specialising in the employment rehabilitation of the blind, the cerebrally palsied and the mentally ill.

People are generally referred to ERCs through the DRO or Employment Adviser (EA) at their local Jobcentre or Employment Office. However, direct references by doctors and employers are encouraged. (For further information see Leaflets EPL 86 and EPL 57 (or EPL 97 for young people).)

MSC EMPLOYMENT SERVICES FOR DISABLED PEOPLE

Wherever possible disabled people make use of existing Jobcentre provision, including the self-service vacancy displays. However, for those disabled people with more complex employment problems related to disability, Disablement Resettlement Officers (DROs) provide advice and guidance through counselling on suitable job opportunities and the special MSC facilities available.

Jobcentres will give advice to handicapped people about facilities for assessment, guidance and further training, including, where necessary, residential courses. They can also advise on special aids and equipment needed to help a disabled person at work, and can make arrangements for financial help with the cost of travel to work in certain cases.

Blind Persons Resettlement Officers (BPROs), as the title implies, help blind and some partially sighted people. There are Blind Persons Training Officers (BPTOs) who carry out initial training on the job and advise on technical matters and aids for blind people in employment. They also visit employers' premises in an attempt to identify suitable work for blind and partially sighted people.

Some DROs are based at large hospitals and are

At Remploy we're more concerned with ability than disability.

Since Remploy is well known as Britain's biggest employer of severely disabled people, this may strike you as a little strange.

But in fact, it's no more than the way it should be.

Because though Remploy is primarily in business to employ severely disabled people, it's by no means a charity.

It's a major industrial company. And it has to be competitive, like any other.

So rather than provide our disabled employees with some kind of diversionary employment, we provide them with the training to do a worthwhile job of work.

And they do it extremely well.

In 94 production units, in communities all over the country, they're helping to produce over 100 quality products and services, many of which are vital to British industry.

And last year alone, their efforts paid off to the tune of 42 million pounds in sales.

Clearly, to a greater or lesser extent, we have to put our skills and experience to work to accommodate each individual's particular handicap.

But as we see it, our real job is to help them make the most of their skills. Which they do with a great deal more enthusiasm than many fit people.

Our success as a business depends on the abilities of the 8,700 severely disabled people we employ.

And they'd be the last ones to want it any other way.

Remploy

Britain's biggest employer of disabled people means business

121

known as Hospital Resettlement Officers. They are concerned to help people leaving hospital with a disability and to improve liaison with the rehabilitation services. (See also ED Leaflet EPL 37.)

DROs also operate the quota scheme whereby employers with 20 or more employees have a duty to employ a quota of registered disabled people (at present 3 per cent of their total staffs). This scheme is under review.

We have been informed that a new Disablement Advisory Service, comprising small specialist teams at ED area level, will encourage and give practical advice to employers about the adoption of 'progressive personnel practices for disabled people and the retention of those employees who become disabled'.

SHELTERED WORK

The minority of disabled people who are so severely disabled as to be unable to cope with employment under ordinary conditions, but who are nevertheless able to carry out productive work, may benefit from suitable 'sheltered' work. Advice and information can be obtained from Disablement Resettlement Officers. Help may be obtained with fares and this payment is not taxable. This type of work is provided in three ways:
(a) by Remploy;
(b) by local authorities;
(c) by voluntary organisations, *e.g.* Queen Elizabeth's Foundation for the Disabled.

REMPLOY

Remploy is a government-supported company set up under the provisions of the Disabled Persons (Employment) Act 1944 to provide employment for severely disabled men and women in England, Scotland and Wales who are unable to obtain or retain work in open industry.

The Secretary of State for Employment appoints the 15 men and women who sit on the Board of Directors. Its turnover is in the region of £50 million and it employs over 8,700 severely disabled people in 94 production units. Many disabled people are employed in supervisory, managerial or administrative positions. Remploy has three trade groups, namely: Furniture and Medical Equipment; Leather and Textile Products; and Packaging and Assembly.

A disabled person seeking employment with Remploy must be registered with the Manpower Services Commission. He will then be referred, at the discretion of the Disablement Resettlement Officer, to the nearest Remploy factory. Part-time medical officers assist Remploy factory managers in

assessing the work capabilities and functional limitations of potential employees, and the candidate will undergo a three-month trial period during which he will receive training and further assessment as to the job most suitable for him. Emphasis in Remploy factories is on meaningful employment under industrial conditions as near normal as possible. Conditions are very similar to those in any other industrial concern, while the industrial environment is designed to meet the employment needs of disabled people. The 39-hour working week compares with the normal basic working hours of other British companies. Since the start of Remploy in 1946 over 50,000 disabled people have been provided with employment. Remploy sells its goods on quality and price, the latter being based on the manufacturing costs in normal industry. The products are diverse and include fashion knitwear, packaging of nationally known consumer goods, leather goods, furniture and hardware. In addition, the company provides a contract service for major industrial organisations.

LOCAL AUTHORITY AND VOLUNTARY BODY WORKSHOPS

Some 5,300 severely disabled people are employed in 132 workshops run by local authorities and voluntary bodies. Employees in sheltered workshops are engaged in a wide range of activities and are employed under contracts of service, receiving wages and paying income tax and National Insurance contributions. The MSC provides financial assistance in the form of capital grants towards expenditure on land, building and equipment and capitation grants to help meet actual workshop losses. For further information see Leaflets DPL 11 and EPL 99.

SHELTERED INDUSTRIAL GROUPS (SIGS)

Sheltered Industrial Groups offer the opportunity for small groups of severely disabled people to work under special supervision alongside able-bodied colleagues in an otherwise ordinary working environment. The severely disabled workers are sponsored by a local authority, a voluntary body or Remploy Ltd; the sponsor acts as the employer and pays the SIG workers' wages while the firm on whose premises the SIG operates pays the sponsor for the amount of work done and provides all the necessary equipment and material for the job.

As with the sheltered employment facilities described above, the statutory authority for financing SIGs is derived from the Disabled Persons (Employment) Act 1944. Local authority and voluntary body sponsors receive a revenue grant from the MSC to help offset the cost of operating the scheme while the cost to Remploy is met by its normal government subvention.

As well as offering the opportunity for severely disabled people to become integrated within an ordinary working environment, SIGs can provide sheltered employment in less densely populated areas where the setting up of a workshop could not be justified. SIGs in current operation include a number of schemes set up by local authority parks and gardens departments providing outdoor work for severely disabled people with mental handicap or epilepsy as well as other schemes providing laundry and kitchen work, book refurbishing and assembly work in the light electrical engineering industry. The minimum output requirement for severely disabled people in SIGs and sheltered employment is one-third that of an able-bodied employee with a 60 per cent requirement in the case of outdoor schemes. (See Leaflet EPL 95.)

GRANTS, ALLOWANCES AND AIDS

Assistance to look for and move to take up work
There are two schemes to assist people in finding and moving to a new job. An unemployed person who is looking for work beyond daily travelling distance may be helped with fares and temporary living expenses through the Job Search Scheme. Having found a job at a distance, an unemployed or redundant person may qualify under the Employment Transfer Scheme for financial help with the cost of working and living away from home and the cost of moving permanently to the new area. The schemes are run through Jobcentres. There are several qualifying rules to be satisfied before assistance can be given. One of these rules is that all applications for assistance must be made at a Jobcentre before travelling to the interview (Job Search Scheme) or before starting the job or moving to the new area (Employment Transfer Scheme).

Assistance with fares to work
This is available to registered disabled people who, because of their disability, are unable to use public transport for all or part of their journey to and from work and therefore incur travelling costs over and above those of an able-bodied person making the same journey. The financial assistance provided is normally in respect of taxi fares, at a rate of three-quarters of the total cost, and is normally subject to a maximum weekly amount of £55 for five-day-week workers. Applications by disabled people for assistance with extra costs, other than taxi fares, will be considered.

People in receipt of a mobility allowance or private car allowance may be included if they are permanently or temporarily unable to drive. People in sheltered employment may also now be eligible.

Applications for assistance under this scheme should be made in the first instance to local Disablement Resettlement Officers, who can be contacted through any local Jobcentre or Employment Office. (See also Leaflet DPL 13.)

Aids to employment
These may be supplied on free permanent loan; the scheme covers any aids necessary to enable disabled people to perform their particular duties but which they would not need if they were not disabled. Examples of the type of aid that can be issued are: special purpose jigs and fixtures, modifications to machines, special fitments for tools, purpose-built desks, seats and benches, including counter-balanced drawing boards and tilting stands and tables, electric typewriters, telephone aids and accessories, reading and writing aids, braille measuring devices such as braille rulers and micrometers. Application in the first instance should be made to the local DRO who can be contacted through any Jobcentre or Employment Office. (See also Leaflet EPL 71.)

ADAPTATIONS TO PREMISES AND EQUIPMENT

Grants of up to £6,000 can be made by the MSC to employers towards the costs of adaptations to their premises and equipment. The adaptations, such as installation of ramps and special toilet facilities, must be for the benefit of a specific disabled employee. Application should be made in the first instance to the local DRO who can be contacted through any Jobcentre or Employment Office.

PERSONAL READER SERVICE

This service is intended to support blind people who are unable to progress in their work because they lack adequate help in dealing with paperwork. It is to help those who lose their sight to retain their jobs, as well as to help blind people starting or even applying for a new job. The scheme is being administered by the RNIB on behalf of the Manpower Services Commission. Application for the Reader's Allowance should be made to Chris Croft at the RNIB, 244 Great Portland Street, London W1N 6AA (Tel: 01-388 1266).

JOB INTRODUCTION SCHEME

This scheme enables the MSC to make a grant of £45 per week to employers who engage a selected disabled person for a trial period of usually six weeks but up to a maximum of 13 weeks. It operates at the discretion of the DRO and is designed to encourage employers to allow disabled people the opportunity of proving their ability to perform a particular job, where doubts are expressed by the employer.

THERAPEUTIC EARNINGS RULE

Disabled persons may, in certain circumstances, derive earnings from casual work without affecting their entitlement to sickness, injury, invalidity or non-contributory invalidity benefit. (For further details *see* Section 2.)

COMMITTEES FOR EMPLOYMENT OF DISABLED PEOPLE

There are 87 Committees for Employment of Disabled People (CEDPs) established under the Disabled Persons (Employment) Act 1944 to advise Ministers on matters relating to the employment, or undertaking of work on their own account, of disabled people in their area. In practice they work largely with MSC staff on the following functions: marketing, such as 'Fit for Work' presentations to employers; surveying disabled people's employment and training needs; stimulating improvements in services to meet those needs; quota and registration functions under the 1944 Act. CEDP membership brings together high-level representation from both sides of industry and other people, including doctors, with practical experience of resettlement.

CEDPs are complemented at a very local level by members of the local community, called Recognised Local Contacts (RLCs), who give MSC staff practical help in their work of assisting disabled people obtain and retain employment.

Self-employment

Self-employment can be a most satisfying way to earn a living and many independently minded people would rather accept a lower income and be their own boss than sell themselves to the vagaries of employers. However, working for yourself usually means working harder and for longer hours than those who suffer the 9 to 5 routine. For disabled people self-employment may very well be the answer to a number of problems and, when all is said and done, there is a marvellous satisfaction at the end of the day, when the work produced is all of your own making. There is no room in this section to outline all the possibilities and opportunities. We have merely provided a few pointers, but there is also valuable information in the books we describe at the end of this section.

Income tax allowances – self-employed

Self-employed people may claim tax relief for expenses they incur wholly and exclusively in connection with their trade or profession. This in practice may include a wide range of expenses which the new 'tycoon' may not have anticipated – for instance, business travel expenses including the cost of hiring a car, some subscriptions to magazines and professional or trade associations, use of home as an office, where a proportion of heating, lighting, rent, rates, cleaning and insurance may be offset against tax. Much useful information is given in the Inland Revenue booklet IR 28 *Starting in Business*, which is available free of charge from the office of any HM Inspector of Taxes or from PAYE Enquiry Offices. People setting up on their own should consider engaging an accountant, not just for dealing with tax matters but for general advice about running a business and keeping records. His fee may also be included in the deductible expenses. When starting a business even while self-employed, it is essential to inform the local Inspector of Taxes, whose address appears in the local telephone directory under 'Inland Revenue'. (*See also* 'Tax Relief for Expenses Incurred by Self-Employed People' under Income Tax in Section 2.)

VAT

Value added tax is chargeable on a wide range of goods and services in the United Kingdom and is therefore of significance to anyone who contemplates starting a business. A trader not registered for VAT pays VAT on his purchases (as part of the price to be paid to suppliers), but does not have to account for VAT on sales. A registered trader does charge VAT on sales and must account for this to Customs and Excise, but is allowed to offset VAT paid on purchases (with certain exceptions). Registration is obligatory for anyone whose taxable turnover exceeds, or is likely to exceed, £18,700 per annum (March 1984), but voluntary registration can be sought by smaller traders if this would be to their advantage. However, you will need to show that you have a compelling and continuing business need for registration.

Customs and Excise publish a useful booklet *Should I be Registered for VAT?* This leaflet and others is available from local VAT offices, which may be found in your local telephone directory under Customs and Excise.

National Insurance contributions – self-employed

Self-employed people must pay Class 2 National Insurance contributions (Leaflet NI 41) unless they are:

(a) over pension age; *or*

(b) their earnings are below a prescribed level. In addition, married women and some widows who chose, before 5 April 1978, not to pay Class 2 contributions may continue with this exemption. This choice is no longer available. In order to qualify for the low earnings exception it is necessary to apply for a certificate of exception each year by filling in form CF 10 which is part of Leaflet NI 27A available from social security offices. But it is important to note that in this case entitlement to the full range of contribution-based benefits will cease, and if no contributions are paid over a period of time any advantage of previous contributions may be lost. This is a situation which must be studied very carefully. Those who consider their state of low income may not last very long, and who wish to preserve their entitlement to some of the benefits (particularly retirement pension) may decide to pay Class 3 contributions (for further details see Leaflet NI 42).

It is important to note that sickness and invalidity benefit is only awarded to those who pay Class 1 (employed) or Class 2 (self-employed) contributions.

Self-employed grants
See Department of Employment Grants in Section 4, page 74.

Small Firms' Service
This is an information and counselling service provided by the Department of Industry to help owners and managers of small businesses with their plans and problems. It also acts as an advisory service to those thinking of starting their own business. The service, which operates through a nation-wide network of Small Firms' Centres, is designed to encourage business efficiency. There is no limit to the type of business the service will help.

Through the Small Firms' Service you can get information on any business problem from finance, diversification and industrial training to exporting, planning, technological advances, industrial relations and marketing.

The information service is free. For counselling, after one free exploratory session, a modest charge is made for the second and subsequent sessions. Apart from the 11 Small Firms' Centres, counselling is available at over 50 Area Counselling Offices around the country.

To make contact with your local Small Firms' Centre dial 100 and ask the operator for Freefone 2444. The Small Firms' Service in Scotland is oper-

ated through the Scottish Development Agency. In Wales the information service is provided by the Welsh Office and the counselling service is operated by the Welsh Development Agency. An information service is provided by the Department of Commerce in Northern Ireland.

Volunteering

Community Service Volunteers (CSV)
237 Pentonville Road, London N1 9NJ (Tel: 01-278 6601).
CSV places volunteers in a large number of projects each year, and each project is different. The purpose and role of CSV is to match the generous spirit of giving and serving, latent in most people, with every kind of social need which contemporary pressures generate. In translating thought into action, CSV has kept firmly in mind that in the modern context, social service must be a two-way process of benefit to give as well as receive; not only does CSV accept every volunteer between 16 and 35 but also positively encourages physically, socially or culturally disadvantaged people who wish to offer their services. CSV take pride in pointing out that a good deal of their effort goes in matching the volunteer to the project, in fact they would see this as their main skill as an organisation.

The CSV Able-to-Help Scheme is designed specifically to offer the opportunity of volunteering to people with physical disabilities. All volunteers involved on the Scheme serve under the same terms and conditions as all other CSVs, but a special effort is made to secure uniquely appropriate project settings. The Scheme employs a specialist worker who, through close consultation with individual physically handicapped volunteers, attempts to find and design a project which suits their physical limitations and abilities as well as capitalising on their individual strengths, positive interests and skills. The Scheme is a specialist service, dealing with a relatively small number of volunteers and offering a high degree of support to participants. Projects are available in a volunteer's home area or away from home, with or without residential board provided. The Able-to-Help Scheme offers a flexible programme to potential volunteers and attempts to start positive work from what they can do, while accepting those things they cannot do. The normal full range of types of project and settings available to all CSV volunteers is offered on the Able-to-Help Scheme. No one is rejected, whatever their handicap. Enquiries should be made to the Able-to-Help Scheme worker at the above address.

For details of the Independent Living Scheme *see* page 77.

Advisory Organisations

The Association of Blind Piano Tuners
224 Great Portland Street, London W1N 6AA.
Recognised and known by many people in the piano and music trade, the ABPT is now a nation-wide organisation of highly trained, qualified people with branches where members can meet to discuss new ideas in the piano world, ways of improving the service which members offer to clients and any problems which they may encounter.

Association of Disabled Professionals
The Stables, 73 Pound Road, Banstead, Surrey SM7 2HU (Tel: Burgh Heath (073 73) 52366).
Founded by Miss Mary Greaves, MBE, the ADP was formed because it was felt that very little of the statutory provision for the rehabilitation, training and employment of disabled people was geared to the particular needs of professional people, disabled in childhood or adult life.

At an inaugural meeting in January 1971, it was agreed that the Association would be concerned, among other issues, with:

(a) improving the rehabilitation, education and training facilities and opportunities of disabled people, assisting them by encouragement and example of its disabled members to develop their physical and mental capacities to the full and promoting their entry into the professions and their full participation in and contribution to society;

(b) improving the employment opportunities and career prospects of disabled people, and assisting them by encouragement and example in finding and retaining employment commensurate with their abilities and qualifications;

(c) educating the public regarding the problems, needs and capabilities of disabled people and how to assist in compensating disabled people for their physical, mental or financial handicaps in relation to education, employment and recreation.

There are now over 500 members, some 90 per cent of whom are disabled (about one-tenth of these are students). The other 10 per cent non-disabled are qualified professionals working in the field of disablement or having an interest in this area. The Association has disabled members from both Houses of Parliament and also includes amongst its members solicitors, barristers, engineers, computer programmers, dentists, actuaries, writers, editors, librarians, social workers, economists, statisticians, doctors, university lecturers, psychologists, scientists, educational technologists, accountants, teachers, graphic designers, hospital administrators and civil servants.

The ADP has a growing Register of Professional Advisers; members qualified and practising in professions, who have volunteered their help to those who need advice on employment prospects in particular fields. A large proportion of the work of the Association is concerned with educational and employment problems and members are frequently put in touch with organisations and individuals who might be able to help them. In many cases the ADP will take up issues with outside organisations on members' behalf.

The ADP submits evidence regularly to the appropriate government departments who in turn consult the Association in its specific areas of interest. It is a fundamental aim of the Association that a battle fought successfully by one disabled person shall be a victory for all and that those who follow in the successful path of existing members shall encounter fewer obstacles and far more encouragement and help on the journey. Membership fee is £6 per annum and £2 for disabled students, but if there are financial difficulties the subscription may be deferred. There is an occasional newsletter and a quarterly house bulletin.

Association for Spina Bifida and Hydrocephalus
22 Upper Woburn Place, London WC1H 0EP (Tel: 01-388 1382).
The Association has a specialist advisory staff. The Employment Officer is always willing to support and advise individuals and their families, and liaise with DROs and Careers Officers. In some areas there are local field workers who are able to visit people at home. Advice can also be given on matters such as aids and incontinence management.

AVHOW – Association of Visually Handicapped Office Workers
Secretary: Miss E Siekmann, 14 Verulam House, Hammersmith Grove, London W6 (Tel: 01-749 1372, evenings only).
AVHOW (formerly the Visually Handicapped Typists' Group) aims to work for the benefit of blind and partially sighted office workers. It offers membership to all visually handicapped people in office occupations.

AVHOW publishes a quarterly magazine on compact cassette and holds occasional meetings in London and elsewhere to exchange information and ideas for working in the office.

CoSIRA – Council for Small Industries in Rural Areas
141 Castle Street, Salisbury, Wiltshire SP1 3TP (Tel: Salisbury (0722) 6255).

CoSIRA is charged with improving the prosperity of small businesses in English country areas, by providing a local source of advice backed up by technical and management services, supervised training and loans. CoSIRA has representatives (known as small industries organisers) who are stationed in every English county. In addition to their own knowledge of small rural businesses they can call upon the experience and support of a local voluntary committee and thus can provide assistance with a wide variety of problems affecting the small firm. CoSIRA operates only in the rural parts of England. Similar services to small businesses are offered in the United Kingdom.

The Welsh Development Agency (Small Businesses Unit)
Treforest Industrial Estate, Pontypridd, Mid Glamorgan CF37 5UT (Tel: Treforest (044 385) 2666).

Scottish Development Agency
120 Bothwell Street, Glasgow G2 7JP (Tel: 041-248 2700).
Small Business Division, 102 Telford Road, Edinburgh EH4 2HP (Tel: 031-343 1911).
The Scottish Development Agency offers a wide range of assistance to people wishing to start up or develop a business in Scotland. Assistance is available through the Agency's Small Business Division, with headquarters in Edinburgh and area offices in Aberdeen, Dumfries, Dundee, Glasgow and Edinburgh. The following services are offered:

A counselling service covering management, finance and investment.

An information service to put small businesses in touch with the right person to help with any business problem.

A marketing service to advise companies on market research, marketing problems and exporting. The service also organises a programme of trade visits and exhibitions in the United Kingdom and abroad to promote the goods of small Scottish companies.

A range of technical advisory services including instruction in various trades, contacts with customers for sub-contract work and assistance with production problems.

Financial assistance in the form of loans of up to £150,000 to assist companies to develop their products or services. These can be made in respect of buildings, equipment and working capital.

Advice in all aspects of financial management.

An advisory and information service on all matters relating to crafts including publications, exhibitions, advice on conservation.

Grants for craftspeople towards setting up in business, equipment, workshop and exhibition costs and a crafts fellowship scheme for research. Training schemes for established and trainee craftspeople and those involved in conservation work.

Crafts Council
12 Waterloo Place, London SW1Y 4AU (Tel: 01-930 4811).
The Council has a very helpful information service covering craft courses, craft shops, galleries, exhibitions, supplies of materials and equipment, museums featuring crafts and crafts publications. Also available for consultation is a non-selective register of craftspeople in England and Wales, in which any craftsperson may be listed. In addition, slides are held on a wide variety of craft subjects. Lecturers and organisations can hire sets of slides for a nominal charge. The Council publishes *Crafts* magazine six times a year with features on crafts activities in the United Kingdom and overseas, and a calendar of related events.

A range of grant and loan schemes has been designed to help the artist-craftsperson at various stages in his/her career. Applicants in each case must be resident in England or Wales (*see also* Scottish Development Agency above).

Workshop training. Master craftspeople who are able to provide training for art school graduates and others may apply to the Crafts Council for a grant under the Workshop Training Scheme. The grants help to provide a living wage for the trainee and usually extend over one year.

New craftspeople grant. Within two years of acquiring premises of their own young craftsmakers may apply for a new craftspeople grant. The grant is specifically for financial assistance towards the purchase of equipment and general maintenance.

Loans. A loan scheme has been introduced to help those who want to enlarge an existing workshop (which has been in production for a number of years), expand production and develop their work, or set up a new workshop.

Special projects. Societies, organisations or individual craftspeople can apply for a grant or a guarantee against loss under the Special Projects Scheme.

In the case of regionally oriented projects, however, enquiries should first be made to the appropriate regional arts association to see whether the project is eligible for grant-aid direct from the Regional Arts Association. An address list is available from the Crafts Council. Further information on these schemes as outlined may be obtained from the grants and loans office at the Crafts Council.

The Welsh Arts Council

Museum Place, Cardiff CF1 3NX (Tel: Cardiff (0222) 394711).

With financial support from the Crafts Council (*see* above) the Welsh Arts Council gives grants and itself organises projects of particular interest to Wales and Welsh craftspeople. The scheme does not duplicate those of the Crafts Council and individual craftspeople working in Wales can apply for any of the Crafts Council schemes already described. Details of the Welsh scheme are available from the Crafts and Design Department of the Welsh Arts Council.

Disabled Living Foundation

380–384 Harrow Road, London W9 2HU (Tel: 01-289 6111).

Aids can be vital to employment. The DLF Information Service and Aids Centre (which includes a photographic display of aids to employment) offers helpful advice as to the range of equipment available, including the different kinds of wheelchairs which may be more suitable for office or factory use. (*See* Section 3 for further details.)

Medical Division, Health and Safety Executive

Head Office: 25 Chapel Street, London NW1 5DT (Tel: 01-262 3277).

This is a national government service of doctors and nurses trained in occupational health, whose main functions are to help to prevent ill health caused by work and to advise on medical aspects for fitness for training or employment in relation to both mental and physical disabilities. Employers may wish to consult the service about the ability of individuals to cope with a particular type of work, or the health pattern of certain disabilities. The Medical Division will also advise disabled people on suitable employment, and work closely with DROs.

Home Opportunities for Professional Employment (HOPE)

96 Greencroft Gardens, London NW6 3PH.

HOPE is a small committee of the Association of Disabled Professionals set up to provide information and ideas on non-manual occupations for people who have had to give up their professional careers and must work at home, but who are not necessarily completely housebound. It is intended to help both those people who became disabled after starting their careers, and those disabled people who have recently acquired professional qualifications. It must be stressed that HOPE is in no way an agency, and cannot provide jobs. What it does provide, however, is assistance in the form of concrete ideas, information, advice and useful contact addresses. HOPE is geared towards the provision of money-making employment, although it does also offer suggestions for non-income-producing work which could eventually become financially rewarding.

HOPE is concerned with employment at the professional level, and covers all the professions as well as a whole range of allied activities. Although HOPE has in the past produced detailed information sheets on a variety of home-based occupations such as proof-reading, indexing, translating, etc. (and it is expected that further sheets will be produced in due course), the main emphasis is on individual contact with information designed to suit the needs of each applicant. Contact Ronald Gerver at the above address.

Mouth and Foot Painting Artists

9 Inverness Place, London W2 3JF (Tel: 01-229 4491).

Any person without the use of hands (through illness or accident) who paints by holding the brush in the mouth or with the feet and who is seriously interested in art as a way of earning a living should apply in writing, giving biographical details, disability, any art training, etc. Examples of work will be requested and assessed by the Association.

MENCAP – The Royal Society for Mentally Handicapped Children and Adults

MENCAP Centre, 123 Golden Lane, London EC1Y 0RT (Tel: 01-253 9433).

MENCAP has a number of schemes to help mentally handicapped people integrate into a normal working life. It advocates and encourages local adult training centres to include such subjects as horticulture in their training programmes and to be more adventurous in their plans for more services for mentally handicapped people. In addition, MENCAP has a unique work training scheme known as Pathway. The scheme revolves around the MENCAP Pathway placement officer, who is based at the Society's regional office. An individual social education and training programme is worked out for every Pathway trainee, based on a panel of experts' assessment of his abilities and potential. Once the trainee has successfully completed his or her pre-work preparation course the placement officer co-operates with the local Disablement Resettlement Officer and careers specialists to find the trainee a suitable job with a sympathetic employer.

Royal National Institute for the Blind

224 Great Portland Street, London W1N 6AA (Tel: 01-388 1266).

The RNIB runs a rehabilitation centre where people

who have lost their sight can learn new skills for coping at home and at work, and a Commercial Training College teaching shorthand and audio typing, switchboard operating and computer programming. RNIB's employment officers help to find commercial and professional jobs. *Looking for work*, free from RNIB in print, braille and on tape, describes the services available to help blind job-seekers. *See also* Personal Reader Service page 123.

RNIB Student Tape Library
Braille House, 338–346 Goswell Road, London EC1V 7JE (Tel: 01-837 9921).
Careers tapes are available on a number of subjects including technical work, social work, higher education, Civil Service careers, law, teaching English as a foreign language and so on. Material recorded during training and on the job's location is included. For further details of the library *see* page 108.

The Spastics Society
12 Park Crescent, London W1N 4EQ (Tel: 01-636 5020).
The Society operates eight industrial units which produce under the name of Beaumont Products. The aim is to enable spastic people to fulfil their potential in the work of the units.

Earning Opportunities

WORKING WITH COMPUTERS

The British Computer Society – Committee for Disabled
13 Mansfield Street, London W1M 0BP (Tel: 01-637 0471).
The principal objectives of the Committee are:
(a) to secure the increasing involvement of severely disabled computer people with all sections of the computing community;
(b) to study and publicise the special needs of the severely disabled in computing;
(c) to draw the attention of other severely disabled persons to the possibilities of engaging in computer practice.

Buretire UK Limited
c/o The Employment Fellowship, Drayton House, Gordon Street, London WC1 (Tel: 01-387 1828).
Buretire is an employment bureau which aims to obtain part-time employment for retired and disabled people, in work related to their skills and experience. The service aims to cover all occupations and people from all walks of life. The service is nation-wide and there is a planned and phased programme to open more Buretire centres throughout the country.

Eosys Limited
Clove House, The Broadway, Farnham Common, Slough, Berkshire SL2 3PQ (Tel: 02814 5123).
This company is involved with setting up a Department of Industry scheme for the establishment of micro-computers, computer terminals or similar equipment in the homes of unemployed disabled people subject to an employer being willing to employ each person to perform the function which the computer system enables. The computer system remains the property of the Department of Industry, but is lent to the employee/employer combination for a minimum of three years (probably, in fact, for an unlimited duration). Ongoing costs stand to be paid by the employer.

The people who have already been employed on this scheme have a variety of disabilities, but in the main share the common problem of severely restricted mobility which makes it impracticable to journey to and from a place of work and cope physically with the day. The person is employed full-time or part-time under a standard contract of employment.

The scheme, we understand, is likely to be taken over by the MSC, probably some time in 1985. Eosys would be glad to answer any queries from individual disabled people interested in the scheme.

Pamela Woodman Associates Ltd
Head Office: Edengrove, Dairsie, Cupar, Fife, Scotland KY15 4RP (Tel: Balmullo (0334) 870265).
Pamela Woodman Associates Ltd is an established software house and has been operating since 1972 throughout the United Kingdom. The company provides a comprehensive range of consultancy, systems and programming services to industry, commerce, central/local government and scientific establishments.

PWA standard services comprise business consultancy; feasibility studies; equipment selection; systems design; systems consultancy; programming; programming consultancy; programming conversions; programming maintenance. Specialist services offered include implementation of technical and project control standards, project management and MAPCON consultancy. PWA operates on a project basis and staff are based in strategic locations throughout the United Kingdom, which enables the company to allocate management, consultancy and technical staff local to the client in the majority of cases. PWA has a very low turnover of staff and is therefore able to offer long-term continuity to clients.

PWA has approximately one hundred consultancy, technical and managerial staff, with an average of 12 years' experience in the computer industry, working on a full-time and part-time basis. PWA's operation is geared towards the effective use of skilled computing professionals who wish, for domestic reasons or otherwise, to work on a consultancy basis. Some consultants work from home on a part-time basis whilst others work on-site on the clients' premises.

In the case of programming, it is generally necessary for staff to be sufficiently mobile to attend on-site for program testing, within a reasonable travelling distance. However, recently there has been some interest shown by clients in program testing, either via remote portable terminals linked directly to the client's computer or via micro-computers from the home base. Naturally progress in this direction is governed by equipment costs and the availability of client computers with the relevant communications hardware/software.

PWA would give favourable consideration to disabled persons provided that they had the required technical skills, together with an ability to communicate accurately with PWA's management. All candidates applying must have a minimum of four full years' computing experience, and they must be prepared to have at least 15 hours a week to spare for PWA work. Candidates should write in the first instance for an application form to Pamela Woodman at the Head Office address.

OTHER OPPORTUNITIES

British Printing Society
38 North Drive, Orpington, Kent BR6 9PQ (Tel: Orpington (0689) 53846).
The Society will advise disabled people regarding printing opportunities and will assist them to overcome problems perhaps by advising on the use of special tools or techniques.

Countrywide Workshops
17c Earls Court Square, London SW5 9BY.
This new venture is aimed at promoting quality goods produced by blind, partially sighted and physically or mentally handicapped people. The emphasis is on employment rather than fund raising. The lush catalogue (£1.50) underlines the quality of the products which range from stylish and attractive garments, knitted sweaters and socks, men's hats and ties, engraved glass, goods in leather, wood, china, wax and much more. Any disabled producer of quality goods looking for further outlets should contact Valerie Wood-Gaiger at the above address.

Glove Corporation Ltd
North Street, Milborne Port, Sherborne, Dorset DT9 5ER (Tel: Milbourne Port (0963) 250338).
The operation of this company is geared to dealing with the individual who wishes to knit or crochet for pocket money. Approximately 1,000 knitters and crocheters make gloves for the firm and it is emphasised that this is intended to bring in a little extra income and is not suitable for anyone who seeks a major contribution to their income. On request a sample pack is sent and the intending knitter is asked to make a trial pair of gloves which is then returned for approval. For further information write direct to the firm.

Mail Order Firms
These can always be approached through their advertisements in the national press to ask if there is scope for an agent in the relevant area. Through showing the catalogue to friends and acquaintances a small remunerative hobby can be built up.

Women's Institutes
39 Eccleston Street, London SW1W 9NT (Tel: 01-730 7212).
The movement offers to its members the opportunity of extending their horizons in all directions by making new friends, becoming involved in public questions and learning or improving skills in cooking, crafts, the arts and sport.

WI markets are held usually once a week in towns and villages easily accessible to rural producers. Home-grown and home-made produce of good quality and crafts are sold direct to the general public. The WI markets are subject to the usual trading regulations and goods are sold at reasonable prices according to the locality. They are registered under the Industrial and Provident Societies Act and are run by committees elected by shareholders. Men and women who are not WI members may apply to become shareholders and sell their produce through the markets, provided it comes up to the standard required. The money from the sale of goods (less a small commission deducted for overhead expenses) goes back to the producers. Produce which may be sold at a market includes vegetables, flowers and plants, fruit, herbs, preserves, fruit syrups, cakes, cookies, breads, savouries, sweets, eggs and craftwork. New producers should consult the controller of their nearest market to find out what can be sold locally and how and when to bring it in.

Wherever possible producers help in running the market. For a complete, free list of markets in England, Wales and the Channel Islands, for marketing details and for a copy of *Marketing for Pleasure and Profit* (£1.25 by post) apply to the NFWI Market Adviser at the address above. For free literature please send a s.a.e. If you would like information on how to join the Women's Institutes write to the Administrative Secretary, Organisation Department, at the above address.

Books and Publications

Able to Work by Bernadette Fallon. This guide for the disabled person has been produced to provide a straightforward explanation of those services which have been set up to help disabled people in the fields of training and employment. This system is, by its very complexity, imperfectly understood by just those people who need to benefit from it, and who therefore miss opportunities which may be open to them. While it was written with paraplegics and tetraplegics in mind, it is equally useful to those with other disabilities, particularly severe ones. It covers, among other topics, preparation for work, statutory help available, training of various kinds in special centres and in colleges of further education, correspondence courses, the particular problems of professionally qualified disabled people and self-employment. Available from the Spinal Injuries Association, Yeoman's House, 76 St James's Lane, Muswell Hill, London N10. Price £3 including postage.

Creating Your Own Work by Micheline Mason. This imaginative and practical book (completely revised and updated in 1983) is a must for those contemplating self-employment. She provides the whys and wherefores and supplies a good many ideas. The text is laced with stories of people who have made it on their own in a wide variety of enterprises. She starts at the beginning with the acquiring of skills and training courses. She goes on to outline the accounting and administrative skills essential to a business enterprise under such headings as 'estimates and invoices', 'chasing debts', 'tax allowances', etc. There is a most useful chapter on 'structures' which is guaranteed to give people ideas on working arrangements – she describes the use of a trade name, working in partnership, starting a limited company, setting up a co-operative. She also describes a system of common ownership and how to start a charity. In addition, there are chapters on 'marketing', 'statutory regulations' and 'helpful organisations'. Available from Gresham Books, PO Box 61, Henley-on-Thames, Oxfordshire RG9 3LQ (Tel: Wargrave (0735) 223789). Price £2.95 plus 50p postage and packing.

Disabled People – A Right to Work? By Richard Grover and Francis Gladstone, published by Bedford Square Press/NCVO, 26 Bedford Square, London WC1B 3HU. Price £3.50
This report examines existing programmes for access to open employment, vocational training and rehabilitation as well as sheltered work. It proposes a number of ways of improving work opportunities for disabled people, calling for initiatives by employers, voluntary organisations and government.

Disabled People and their Employment: a review of research into the performance of disabled people at work by Melvyn Kettle (1979). Price £2.50 including postage and packing. Available from Peggy Marchant, General Secretary, Association of Disabled Professionals, The Stables, 73 Pound Road, Banstead, Surrey SM7 2HU. The review cites over 100 references concerning research into the performance at work of people who are in wheelchairs, ambulant disabled people, blind or deaf people, mentally handicapped people and others suffering from a variety of other complaints including epilepsy. The research reviewed by Dr Kettle destroys the myths still believed by too many employers; myths that add up to the erroneous idea that to employ someone with a disability is to employ a liability. Dr Kettle's research proves the contrary: that disabled people are reliable, loyal, conscientious and productive workers.

Employment for Handicapped People: Bibliography compiled by Struan Simpson covers such subjects as architecture and design, community and group work, employment, epilepsy, history, income and earnings, job classification, legislation, mental handicap and mental illness, rehabilitation and sheltered employment. Published by Reedbooks, Chertsey and available from Disabled Living Foundation (Sales) Ltd, Book House, 45 East Hill, Wandsworth, London SW18 2QZ. Price £7.

Employers' Guide to Disabilities by Bert Massie and Melvyn Kettle. Published by RADAR, 25 Mortimer Street, London W1N 8AB. Price £5. A useful little book for employers, briefly describing various disabilities. No need for a potential employer to be baffled with medical terms. The book aims to give a realistic assessment of the effects of a disability upon an individual and how any difficulties can be overcome in the chosen field of employment.

Epilepsy and Getting a Job. A leaflet available from British Epilepsy Association, Crowthorne House, New Wokingham Road, Wokingham, Berkshire RG11 3AY (Tel: Crowthorne (0344) 773122). Price 10p.

Getting to Work by Edward Whelan and Barbara Speake. The authors of this book set out to identify and develop the knowledge, attitudes and abilities necessary for the young handicapped person seeking employment. It is intended to help instructors, teachers, counsellors and parents, and draws on the experience of workers in the field, as well as that of employers. The importance of 'job satisfaction' is discussed, as well as the range of jobs open to such youngsters and the necessity of helping them to make their own choices. There are sections on pre-vocational training and on the facilities available for learning specific skills. The authors include advice on applying for a job, creating a favourable impression at the interview, job-rehearsal and starting work. Published by Souvenir Press as one of the 'Human Horizons Series', price £6.95 hardback; £4.95 paperback.

Get Yourself Going – An Action Handbook for the Handicapped Office Worker by Henry Mara and Penny Thrift. This is a book of useful information for thousands of handicapped people who want to earn a living in an office or run a business from home. It is for men and women who are seeking jobs in competition with able-bodied colleagues and who want to gear themselves up to handle the job, or for those who already have office jobs and want to keep up with their colleagues to hold those jobs and gain promotion. It should be of considerable interest to employers and also to Disablement Resettlement Officers. The book is immensely practical giving full details, plus illustrations, of a wide variety of equipment and should be compulsive reading for the disorganised, disabled or otherwise. Two illustrations say it all. The first shows the author's totally chaotic room before improvements; the second shows a simply splendid uncluttered work station, with everything to hand. These particular authors are lost in admiration. Available from Royal Association for Disability and Rehabilitation, 25 Mortimer Street, London W1N 8AB (Tel: 01-637 5400). Price £1.30.

KOGAN PAGE LIMITED

120 Pentonville Road, London N1 (Tel: 01-837 7851).
This company publishes a number of books concerned with self-employment and small businesses. We recommend you send for their catalogue which also includes other titles. To give you the flavour we describe two of the books listed under small businesses:

Raising Finance: the Guardian Guide for the Small Business by Clive Woodcock. A guide to the wide range of sources of finance now available to the small business. From starting up to expansion, development and eventually to the public issue of shares, case studies illustrate the various ways in which these sources of finance can best be used. It shows you how to go about getting finance, what the advantages and disadvantages of each type of finance are and who is involved in providing it. It also considers important factors such as interest rates and how to benefit from the tax system. Finally, for easy reference, there are directories of names and addresses of all the various sources together with an index and section on further information. Price £4.95.

Working for Yourself: The Daily Telegraph Guide to Self-Employment by Godfrey Golzen, sixth edition. Sets out clearly basic techniques required for setting up your business and lists some 35 different opportunities in self-employment. It provides a crash course in planning cash flow, raising money, keeping records and pricing the product or service on offer. Available from Kogan Page Ltd, 120 Pentonville Road, London N1. Price £4.95 plus postage and packing.

Looking for Jobs. This booklet is an introduction to the rights of blind and partially sighted people. It discusses finding a job, rehabilitation, training, office work, special aids and so on. There is also a list of workshops for blind people. Published by National Federation of the Blind of the United Kingdom, it is available from Jill Allen, 59 Silver Sea Drive, Westcliff-on-Sea, Essex (Tel: Southend (0702) 74059). Please enclose a s.a.e. $8\frac{1}{2}$ in. × 6 in.

MSC Employment Services leaflets available from Jobcentres or Employment Offices:
Employment Rehabilitation Centres – EPL 86 and EPL 30 (or EPL 97 for young people).
The Disabled Persons Register – DPL 1.
Rehabilitation, Retraining, Resettlement, Employment Series for Disabled People – EPL 37.
Employment in Sheltered Workshops – DPL 11.
Assistance with Fares to Work Scheme for Severely Disabled People – DPL 13.
Aids & Adaptations for Disabled Employees – EPL 71.
Job Introduction for Disabled People – DPL 15.
Sheltered Industrial Groups – EPL 95.
Sheltered Employment and You – EPL 99.
Job Search Scheme – EPL 66.
The Employment Transfer Scheme – EPL 103.

Employment Rehabilitation Allowances – EPL 57.
Employing Someone who is Deaf or Hard of Hearing – EPL 38
Employing Someone with Epilepsy – EPL 40.
Employing Someone who is Mentally Handicapped – EPL 44.
Employing Someone who is Blind or Partially Sighted – EPL 63.
Employing People who have had a Mental Illness – EPL 93.
Employing Someone with Haemophilia – EPL 98.
Employing Disabled People – EPL 100.
Employing Someone with Multiple Sclerosis – EPL 102.
Royal National Institute for the Blind have issued three leaflets: *Looking for Work*, *Blind People at Work* and *Computer Programming*. The first of these is available in print, braille or on tape and is for blind job-hunters; the second describes for employers the sort of jobs blind people do and the aids and support services available; and the third explains how blind people train and work in data processing.

Single copies free (enclose s.a.e.) from RNIB, 224 Great Portland Street, London W1N 6AA.

What of my Future? Re-employment of Disabled Professional People by Enid M. Dell, BSc(Econ), DPA highlights the widespread lack of information about the employment needs of newly-disabled professionals and executives. The report underlines the vital importance of co-operation between the various services involved and includes recommendations for possible action by hospitals, professional bodies and employers to improve this situation. Published by Disabled Living Foundation and available from Disabled Living Foundation (Sales) Ltd, Book House, 45 East Hill, Wandsworth, London SW18 2QZ. Price £4.25.

Woman's Own Reader Service, King's Reach Tower, Stamford Street, London SE1 9LS (Tel: 01-261 5000), have published two very helpful leaflets. *Earning Money at Home (Craftwork)* covers flowers, photography, pottery, woodwork, metalwork and bookbinding, gives details of national craft associations and county local craft groups, and contains a wealth of information on marketing and selling produce and on understanding antiques. *Working from Home* gives advice and information on caring for children, typing and office skills, cooking, sewing and hairdressing for profit together with other suggestions and a host of very relevant business information. The leaflets are free, but requests *must* be accompanied by a large s.a.e.

Working at Home for Profit by Joanna Johnson. This book provides a detailed description of every aspect of working at home for profit. It deals in depth with 36 different occupations ranging from animals and antiques to typing and writing and including art and craft, computer programming, hairdressing, market research, printing, selling, teaching and so on. It guides the would-be home worker towards sources of help and advice and opportunities for further study, and it gives a useful reading list. The advantages and disadvantages of home work are examined in detail and there is advice on avoiding the most common pitfalls. Published by Basil Blackwell and available from 108 Cowley Road, Oxford OX1 4HB (Tel: Oxford (0865) 72214). Price £3.95.

Writers' and Artists' Yearbook published annually by A. & C. Black, 35 Bedford Row, London WC1R 4JH. This reference book (available in paperback, price £4.50, 1984 edition) has an extensive list of journals and magazines both in this country and abroad, together with other useful information about publishers, copyright, etc. The details about journals and magazines include the type and length of articles or stories which are normally published.

Films

Get the Picture, 16 mm, colour, 43 minutes. Told through the eyes of a severely disabled trainee photographer, this film demonstrates once again that it is considering the ability of the disabled person that is all-important. The film shows the co-ordinated work of voluntary and statutory organisations responsible for the training and employment of disabled people. Prince Philip sums up the film by saying 'ability is where you look for it'. Available for sale at £290 plus VAT or hire for one showing at £15 including postage and packing plus VAT from Cinexsa Film Productions Ltd, 209 Manygate Lane, Shepperton, Middlesex TW17 9ER (Tel: Walton-on-Thames (093 22) 25950).

How to Survive in an Occupied Country, 16 mm, 30 minutes. Produced by Cinexsa Film Productions Ltd. Concerned solely with the employment of mentally handicapped people, this film demonstrates very clearly how many such people, given the right training, are able to carry out useful jobs in open employment and through group living schemes can successfully live together in normal living conditions while, at the same time, integrating well with their neighbours. Available from the Concord Films Council, 201 Felixstowe Road, Ipswich, Suffolk IP3 9BJ (Tel: Ipswich (0473) 76012).

The Right to Work, 16 mm, colour, 25 minutes. Produced by the Spastics Society in 1974, this film illustrates the problems experienced and the practical difficulties encountered by physically handicapped people, not only in securing employment but also in obtaining suitable working conditions. Their keen desire to be self-supporting and useful is demonstrated. Available on free loan from Concord Films Council Ltd, 201 Felixstowe Road, Ipswich, Suffolk IP3 9BJ (Tel: Ipswich (0473) 76012).

Ready, Willing and Disabled, 16 mm, colour, 30 minutes. Produced by Granada TV in 1972. Reports on the problem of the 100,000 disabled people who want a job but cannot find one. Available on hire from Concord Films Council Ltd, 201 Felixstowe Road, Ipswich, Suffolk IP3 9BJ (Tel: Ipswich (0473) 76012).

SECTION 8
MOBILITY AND MOTORING

The power of mobility through motoring can be heady indeed and of course all the more so when wheels are quite literally replacing unresponsive limbs, making distance no object and difficult or impossible public transport a system of mobility to be disregarded without a qualm. The car, because it is a machine, is capable of having an infinite variety of mechanical alterations made to its various parts to make it driveable by people who have considerably limited movement and powers of control. Engineers have been most ingenious in the various adaptations they have made available to disabled motorists. In addition to adaptations to the engine and the mechanics of driving, a variety of swivel seats and mobile hoists have made the tricky business of getting in and out of the car an altogether easier task.

From cars to ships, planes and trains, increasingly, handicapped people are proving that obstacles are to be overcome and that travel is not only possible but actively to be pursued. Airlines have led the way in providing helpful facilities. Now Access to the Skies (see page 207) is seeking to make the planes themselves more accessible. Railways are improving their services and hopefully there will be fewer and fewer guards' van travellers tumbling about among the baggage. Somehow or other we need to devise accessible lavatories on trains.

It is sadly true that public transport in Britain so often lags behind the best in modern design thus making its use difficult even for nimble travellers and well nigh impossible for many disabled people. Trying to board a pay-as-you-enter bus – up the steep steps, through the narrow entrance, while fumbling for change and clutching parcels, children, walking stick, crutches – requires the agility of a mountain goat. It is interesting to note that in San Francisco the newly constructed underground system is completely accessible to wheelchair users, and a number of United States bus companies are substantially adapting parts of their fleets to take into account the needs of disabled travellers. Now in England we have the splendid example of the Tyne & Wear Metro which is accessible and usable by people in wheelchairs and those with sight difficulties, not to mention parents with prams or pushchairs.

The biggest obstacle to acquiring the freedom of mobility is, of course, finance, and the mobility allowance designed for disabled drivers and others is the statutory answer. With some extra outlay it is now possible to use the mobility allowance to help in the leasing or hire-purchase of a car at fairly reasonable terms through Motability. However, there are still many regrets at the decision to phase out the trikes, since they had proved very suitable for certain disabled drivers who find standard cars too inconvenient to manage, and not suited to their needs. For many people the ownership of a car is impossible and for these the growing number of Dial-a-Rides provides a welcome opportunity to get out and about.

Integration is a meaningless concept without mobility, and mobility to become a reality depends on cash, imagination and determination: cash to cater for individual needs, imagination to see past steps and other artificial barriers and determination to continue to press for much needed action to overcome the difficulties.

Mobility by Car

THE MOBILITY ALLOWANCE

For details *see* page 28.

VEHICLE EXCISE DUTY

(a) *Those receiving mobility allowance* – since 1 December 1978 a mobility allowance beneficiary (or a person appointed to act for him) with a car of his or her own has been eligible for exemption from vehicle excise duty (sometimes called road tax). If he/she does not have a car of his/her own, he/she may nominate someone else for exemption. The vehicle to be exempted must be used by, or for the purpose of, the mobility allowance beneficiary. The DHSS automatically sends an application form for a VED exemption certificate to all those receiving the mobility

135

allowance. A certificate issued in response to a valid application may then be used as proof when applying for a 'tax-exempt' disc at the local vehicle licensing office of the Department of Transport.

(b) *Those* not *receiving mobility allowance* exemption from VED extends to disabled people (including children between the ages of two years and four years nine months) who do not already enjoy exemption as mobility allowance beneficiaries, if they:
   (i) are unable or virtually unable to walk; and
   (ii) need to be driven; and
   (iii) need to be cared for by a constant attendant (this condition is satisfied if attendance allowance at either the higher or lower rate is in payment); and
   (iv) have a vehicle that is registered in their name and is suitable for their use (special arrangements about registration apply in the case of children).

How to claim

First, ask for form MHS 564 from Disablement Services Branch, Department of Health and Social Security, Block 1, Government Buildings, Warbreck Hill Road, Blackpool FY2 0UZ. Complete and return it to the same address. If satisfied, the DHSS will issue certificate MHS 330 which constitutes the required evidence of disability. Next, complete form V 10 (application for a vehicle licence), obtainable from any local vehicle licensing office or main post office, and send or take it to the LVLO with the vehicle registration document, insurance certificate or cover note, the certificate MHS 330 and the MOT certificate if appropriate. If satisfied, the LVLO will issue a 12-month exempt licence and exempt licence disc. The licence disc must be displayed in the vehicle and renewed on expiry like the ordinary tax disc.

Provided that the vehicle is registered in the disabled person's name, and is used for his/her purposes, a refund of duty may be claimed on a normal licence in the same way as for Mobility Allowance beneficiaries.

MOBILITY SUPPLEMENT FOR DISABLED WAR PENSIONERS

The vehicle scheme for severely disabled war pensioners is being progressively phased out. No cars have been issued since 21 November 1983. Eligible war pensioners now have the choice of claiming the Mobility Supplement (*see* page 45) and giving up their present car, or waiting until their car becomes unroadworthy. The Supplement is not taxable and will be paid for life. It is set at a rate of £2.15 above that of the civilian mobility allowance, which means that the Supplement amounts to £22.25 as at November 1984 and will be up-rated annually.

VEHICLE LICENSING REGULATIONS

When applying for a driving licence, the nature of any disability must be declared in the appropriate section of the application form. The licensing authority may then ask the applicant to consent to his doctor being contacted for further details. The term of licence to be issued is dependent on the medical facts, *i.e.* one year, two years, three years, etc. It is important to bear in mind that where there are no indications to the contrary, *i.e.* that the disability is not recurring nor likely to be progressive, the new long-term licence may be issued, that is up to the age of 70. After considerable pressure by members of disabled groups, the Department of Transport decided in 1978 that drivers paralysed by spinal cord injuries may be granted driving licences valid until the age of 70. It was finally accepted that provided medical investigation shows that the condition of drivers injured in this way has stabilised, and that they are not suffering from secondary complications, the period of the licence should not be restricted. They are, of course, under the same obligation as all licence holders to notify the Licensing Centre of the onset of a disability or the worsening of an existing condition. Licences may be renewed after age 70 but will run for three years or less, depending on the circumstances – though with the possibility of further renewals.

Those people who hold a full licence which only authorises them to drive an invalid carriage or restricts them to a vehicle of special construction or design do not have provisional entitlement to drive any other type of vehicle. If they wish to drive a vehicle of a type not covered by the full licence, they must first apply for the appropriate provisional entitlement to be added to the licence. After the initial cost of a licence has been paid, there are no further charges for those who have to reapply having only been granted a restricted-term licence.

Drivers who become disabled must inform the Licensing Centre without delay regarding any disability which is likely to last more than three months and which is or may become likely to affect the ability to drive, whereupon the same procedure will be followed as above. Regulations are variable to take into account the different circumstances of an individual's disability. Should a re-test be necessary, there will be no charge and test centres will now automatically give priority to disabled applicants.

Licences are issued by the Driver and Vehicle Licensing Centre, Swansea SA6 7JL. Application forms for driving licences are obtainable at main post offices.

DRIVING AND EPILEPSY

People who have epilepsy may be issued with a licence to drive if they fulfil the following conditions:

(a) he/she has been free from any epileptic attack during the period of two years immediately preceding the date when the licence is to have effect (or, if not, that he/she has had such attacks only whilst asleep during a period of three years immediately preceding the date when the licence is to have effect); and

(b) the driving of a vehicle is not likely to be a source of danger to the public.

BUYING A CAR

Assistance and Independence for Disabled People (AID)
AID Centre, 182 Brighton Road, Coulsdon, Surrey, CR3 2NF (Tel: 01-645 9014) or contact: Consumer Insurance Services, 2 Great Marlborough Street, London W1V 1DE (Tel: 01-439 0065).

AID is a brand-new service designed in co-operation with disabled people for disabled people. It provides a flexible service to enable disabled people to buy their own cars, together with any adaptations they may need. There is a choice of over 50 models to choose from on a no-deposit basis at discounted rates. Your vehicle will be delivered to your door with any necessary conversion already fitted. The person delivering will give any necessary explanations on use, controls, etc.

Finance terms will be arranged at competitive terms with a major international organisation. The AID package will include a specially tailored motor insurance package underwritten at Lloyd's. Included will be a 24-hour legal advisory service, £5,000 of motorist legal protection and a full uninsured loss recovery service. Existing no-claims discounts will be honoured. A disabled driver emergency rescue service offers an at-home service, roadside repair and recovery of vehicle, driver and any passengers. Life insurance cover will operate to avoid any financial hardship to surviving family in the event of the death of the disabled driver.

At the end of your finance term, or at any time during the term, you may wish to change your vehicle. AID will professionally dispose of your vehicle and pay the disabled driver any profit achieved over the agreed settlement figure.

In addition, an advice centre (manned by disabled people) operates 8 a.m. to 8 p.m., Monday to Friday, giving advice and information on vehicle terms, delivery, finance and insurance.

MOTABILITY

Motability, Boundary House, 91-93 Charterhouse Street, London EC1M 6BT (Tel: 01-253 1211).
Motability Finance Ltd, Tabard House, 116 Southwark Street, London SE1 0TA.

Motability is an independent charitable organisation whose main objective is to enable people who receive mobility allowance (drivers and passengers, including children) to use this to lease a new standard production car or to hire-purchase a new or second-hand production car which may be, where necessary, adapted for special needs. In order to provide favourable terms, Motability has negotiated discounts with motor manufacturers, insurance brokers and others. Motability has also arranged favourable hire-purchase terms for certain electric and non-powered wheelchairs from a range of companies.

Before coming to a decision, you need to look at the schemes very thoroughly, first of all to decide which Motability option may be the most useful to you (leasing or hire-purchase, new or secondhand), or indeed whether there may be another source of funding which may suit you better. In our book *Motoring and Mobility for Disabled People* (1983) the subjects of choosing a car on the open market as well as alternative means of finance are fully discussed (*see* page 167).

FINANCIAL HELP AVAILABLE

Charitable funds are available to help people who find difficulty in paying for those extras not covered by the leasing or hire purchase arrangements. For instance, the cost of adaptation or the deposit on hire-purchase or extra rental on a lease. However, as funds are limited, it will be necessary to show you need what you have asked for, whether it is a more expensive car, an automatic gearbox or adaptation, and also to show you cannot pay for these items yourself.

LEASING OR HIRE PURCHASE

The Motability Leasing Scheme
Who is eligible? All recipients of mobility allowance including children.

How long may I lease? Initially for a period of three or four years; the period depends on the make of car you choose. After that you can apply to lease another car at the rentals then current. You would also have

.

to pay a further lump-sum down payment. Any adaptations you had made to your first leased car would have to be removed, at your expense, at the end of the lease. Depending on the type of equipment, it might be mechanically possible to transfer this to your second leased car but this would be by no means certain.

What are the costs of leasing? Provided you have an award of mobility allowance for more than the next three years, Motability may be able to arrange for you to lease a new car for three or four years – the period depends on the make of car. You will then, for that period, arrange to have your mobility allowance paid as rental to Motability Finance Ltd. Any increase in mobility allowance occurring during the period of the lease must be paid over.

Who pays for what? The arrangements are as follows:

(a) The whole of the mobility allowance must be paid over to Motability Finance Ltd for the full term of the lease (three to four years). This includes any mobility allowance increases which will have already been taken into account.

(b) Any extra cost of leasing not covered by your mobility allowance has to be paid in a lump sum at the start of the lease.

(c) The cost of any necessary conversion equipment must usually be borne by the person leasing the car.

(d) Insurance is paid by the person leasing the car. A block insurance scheme has been arranged with the Zurich Insurance Company, through whom all arrangements must be made.

(e) The car will be maintained and repaired under the terms of the lease, but the prices quoted do not include replacement tyres for Minis and Metros.

(f) As mobility allowance is taxable, it remains so when paid direct to Motability Finance Ltd for a leased car.

What are the choices?

Leasing	Hire-purchase
You will not own the car when the lease ends and the car must go back to the dealer	You will own the car at the end of the HP contract
The whole of your mobility allowance, including increases, is paid over to the finance company throughout the term of the lease	Any increases in the allowance during the term of the HP contract will be paid to you direct by DHSS
Maintenance and servicing are included in the rental	You pay for your own maintenance and servicing
There are mileage charges for each mile over 10,000 miles a year	There are no mileage charges
You are responsible for insurance cover which must be with the Zurich Insurance Company. Proposed drivers must have good driving records	You are responsible for all the cost of insurance cover, and must make your own arrangements (for help with this *see* page 000)
The range of adaptations which you can have made to a leased car is necessarily limited. Also they have to be removed at the end of the lease at your own cost	You are freer to choose your adaptations made to a car on hire-purchase, since it will be yours at the end of the agreement
In a two-mobility-allowance family, you may use part of the second allowance to obtain a Motability loan to pay for the lump-sum advance rental	The second mobility allowance may be used to offset the cost of the deposit only by arrangement with Motability where one person has control of two allowances
You are limited to a specified list of cars	You have a wider choice of cars

(g) For all the cars within the scheme, annual charges will be made for mileage in excess of 10,000 miles a year.

(h) Where there are two mobility allowances in one family, one may be used to pay the rental of your leased car, while arrangements may be made to use part of the second mobility allowance to arrange a loan to cover the cost of advance rental needed as a lump sum at the start of a Motability leasing agreement.

The Motability Hire Purchase Scheme
Normally, Motability are only able to offer for hire-purchase those vehicles listed by them including cars produced by British Leyland, Ford, Talbot and Vauxhall. (For details on HP arrangements on electric vehicles and wheelchairs *see* page 162.) However, if you want to take a new vehicle on HP which is not mentioned in the list and you are able to negotiate with a dealer hire-purchase terms similar to those provided by the Motability Hire Purchase Scheme,

Motability will do its best to help you obtain finance, but they cannot guarantee being able to do so.

Who is eligible? All those people including children who have an award of mobility allowance which will run for four and a half years from the time the hire-purchase agreement is signed.

Who pays for what?
(a) Under the Motability Hire Purchase Scheme you will arrange to have your mobility allowance paid over direct to Motability Finance Ltd at the rate then prevailing. Increases in the rate of mobility allowance during the four and a half years will be paid direct to you by the Department of Health and Social Security (Department of Health and Social Services in Northern Ireland).
(b) Unfortunately, the mobility allowance does not cover the whole cost of any car and a deposit ranging from £15.94 for a Mini Mayfair to £1,633.64 for a Talbot Solara automatic will be payable (October 1983 prices).
(c) The cost of buying and installing any necessary equipment or controls is your responsibility. You may receive help with this cost (*see* page 137).
(d) You will need to arrange and be responsible for insurance.
(e) People receiving mobility allowance may be exempt from paying vehicle excise duty (*see* page 135).
(f) In a situation where someone is entitled to draw another person's mobility allowance as well as their own, for instance in the case of a disabled parent and child or where a parent is responsible for two disabled children, then, provided the two allowances added together are less than the cost of hire-purchasing the car, they may be used together to pay the cost of the hire-purchase terms.

Unfortunately, where two individuals are separately responsible for drawing their own mobility allowances, even though they live in the same household and where they have agreed to use one of the allowances to pay the cost of Motability HP terms, it is not possible to use the second allowance to arrange a loan with Motability to also offset the cost of the deposit. This ruling is not of Motability's making but arises out of existing consumer law designed to protect individual consumers from exploitation.

Bank Loans
Personal loans offer an increasingly popular alternative way to finance car purchase. The principal advantage is that you are not tied down to the credit terms offered by any particular dealer. You have an unlimited choice of suppliers and the opportunity to look for a bargain. It is important to remember for those who are nervous about approaching banks for cash, seeing themselves, perhaps, as not very creditworthy, that a mobility allowance can change all that. Bank managers are inclined to look very favourably on those receiving a nice predictable and regular source of income like mobility allowance. Normally you will approach your own bank, but it is worth knowing that some banks will lend money to applicants who do not have an account with them. You can generally vary the repayment period, up to a specified maximum, to suit your own financial circumstances. Details of banks' lending policies are given in *Motoring and Mobility for Disabled People* (*see* page 167).

Hire-purchase other than Motability
Many garages are able to make arrangements with finance companies to provide hire-purchase facilities for their customers. It is worth asking and worth shopping around for the most favourable terms. A number of car manufacturers also will recommend to dealers special discounts for disabled customers. We describe these on page 145.

Abbey National Finance
Disabled people who either own their home or are buying it with the help of an Abbey National mortgage, may be able to borrow an additional amount to cover the purchase or conversion of a car for their own use. Primarily the scheme is intended for adaptations to a home needed to meet the requirements of a disabled person, but applications in respect of adapted cars would be considered.

This scheme is designed to help severely disabled and blind people with mobility and parking problems by allowing them special privileges in the form of parking concessions. Present regulations allow badge holders to leave their vehicles, without charge or time limit, at parking meters and restricted parking spaces. Drivers with blind passengers may also benefit from the concessions. Badge holders in England, Wales and Northern Ireland may park for up to two hours on yellow lines except where there is a ban on loading and unloading in force at the time;

in Scotland they may park on yellow lines without time limit where there is no ban on loading or unloading. To control this entitlement, a special orange parking time disc (provided by the issuing authority) must be displayed and set to show the time of arrival. In the case of broken yellow lines the parking disc need be displayed only when the restrictions are for more than two hours and are in operation when the period of parking begins. Vehicles may also park free of charge at certain ancient monuments and sites of historic buildings.

Who is eligible? The badge, which may be used on any motor vehicle (including taxis or hired cars) driven by or carrying a badge holder, is now available only to disabled people over two years of age who are either:
(a) recipients of mobility allowance; or
(b) blind; or
(c) using vehicles supplied by government departments or receiving grants towards their own vehicle; or
(d) have a permanent and substantial disability which makes them unable to walk or to have very considerable difficulty in doing so.

Orange badges are issued by local authorities and are universally recognised except within certain areas of central London as follows: City of London, City of Westminster, Royal Borough of Kensington and Chelsea and part of the London Borough of Camden south of, and including, the Euston Road, where authorities issue their own parking badges for the use of disabled persons resident or working in their respective districts. Wardens are generally sympathetic to disabled people visiting these areas, and by exercising tact and discretion orange badge holders will usually be treated generously. Able-bodied people who try to pass themselves off as badge holders are liable to a maximum fine of £200.

Badges are issued by local authorities (normally the Social Services Department) for a period of three years from the date of issue. They remain the property of the authority which is entitled to charge a fee, but this may not exceed £2. Applicants within categories (a), (b), and (c) will need to prove their entitlement, but this should be possible with the minimum of formality, *e.g.* by producing an official letter confirming award of mobility allowance, the payment book or a vehicle excise duty exemption certificate (MHS 330). In the case of applicants under category (d), the decision rests with the local authority, but it may wish to have medical advice in reaching that decision. This is likely to be sought in the form of a standard medical certificate, on a confidential basis.

For reciprocal 'orange badge' concessions with other European countries see page 209.

TYRE, BATTERY AND EXHAUST SYSTEM CONCESSIONS

The following companies provide price concessions on tyres to disabled motorists in receipt of the mobility allowance. Special discount cards are available on application. Motorway Tyres also offer concessions on batteries and National Tyre Service on exhaust systems.

Motorway Tyres & Accessories Ltd
National Sales Office, Crown House, Crown Street, Reading, Berkshire RG1 2SL.

National Tyre Service Ltd
Retail Marketing Department, 80-82 Wellington Road North, Stockport SK4 1HR.

TOLL CONCESSIONS

A number of tunnel and bridge authorities waive their charges for disabled travellers provided they meet certain requirements. For those holding orange badges these include the Severn Bridge, the Erskine Bride, the Forth Road Bridge, the Tay Bridge, Tamar Bridge and Torpoint Ferry. For Tamar and Torpoint, vouchers must be obtained in advance on an application form available from: City of Plymouth, City Treasury, Guildhall, Plymouth PL1 2AA.

For the Tyne and Dartford tunnels, exemption may be obtained for any disabled person whose vehicle is exempt from vehicle excise duty. In the case of the Mersey Tunnel only the following categories of people are eligible for exemption: (a) disabled drivers with a DHSS vehicle or in receipt of the Private Car Allowance whose application must be accompanied by form MHS 330 currently dated by the Tax Authority and (b) disabled drivers who are over 65 years of age and have an orange badge whose application must be accompanied by their orange badge and proof of age, for example, birth certificate or retirement pension book. Applications should be made to the County Engineer, 4th Floor, Steers House, Canning Place, Liverpool L1 8JW. (Tel: 051-227 5234).

For the Humber Bridge, exemption is granted to a 'trike' driver (who need make no special application) or a disabled driver in possession of either a tax exemption certificate MY 182 or a MHS 330 following the completion of an application form available from: The Bridgemaster, Administration Building, Ferriby Road, Kessle, North Humberside HU13 0JG.

It is always worth enquiring about possible concessions which may be available if you are likely to be travelling regularly where there is a toll charge, since it is not possible to list all the concessions, and regulations are liable to change.

FERRY CONCESSIONS

See Section 10.

MOTORING INSURANCE

As any disabled driver knows, securing motor insurance at an affordable price can be a thorny problem; it is always best to 'shop around' and to beware of possible dangers hidden away in the small print. It is not unusual for a quotation to include a premium loading, even for a mild disability which is easily overcome by adaptation of the vehicle. If this happens to you, you would be well advised to take your custom elsewhere. There should be no real difficulty in a disabled driver obtaining 'fair' insurance, but there are no hard and fast rules and many insurers insist on treating each case on what they see as its merits. Those who automatically regard disability as a risk are unlikely to be sympathetic and are best avoided.

Equally, of course, you have a responsibility to declare the full facts about your disability, and failure to do so could well invalidate any future claim. You must also be sure to inform your insurers about *all* alterations made to the insured vehicle. The cost of motor insurance depends on many variable factors, principally the scope of the policy, your age, whether you enjoy 'no claims' discount, the area in which you live and the type of car you wish to drive.

Specialist Insurance Companies
The following companies have recognised the reliability of the average disabled driver and accordingly provide reasonable insurance cover. You would be wise always to seek a number of quotations before signing on the dotted line, and to consider carefully whether the cover offered is adequate, should you be unfortunate enough to be involved in an accident. Third-party insurance is a good deal cheaper than comprehensive, but it does not cover your own vehicle and you will be at a loss in this respect in the event of damage for which you are responsible or in circumstances which effectively preclude compensation from a third party. If your car is pretty old this may be a risk you are prepared to

take, but another important point is that third-party insurance includes no cover for personal injury. A comprehensive policy, by contrast, will cover your own as well as other vehicles and will normally provide some element of indemnity against personal injury. But even here, it should be noted that many companies will delete personal accident cover if their client is disabled.

Chartwell Insurance Brokers (incorporating Disabled Drivers' Insurance Bureau)
292 Hale Lane, Edgware, Middlesex HA8 8NP (Tel: 01-958 3135).
This firm operates a special scheme for disabled drivers through a panel of underwriters. They advise us that they are able to place motor insurance for disabled people *without any additional premium loadings being imposed in respect of their disability*.

This company also offers a personal accident policy for disabled drivers as a supplementary cover to their motor insurance. The premium in 1983 was £15 a year.

Consumer Insurance Services
2 Great Marlborough Street, London W1V 1DE (Tel: 01-439 0065). A 'vehicle-related' insurance package has been designed which combines (a) motor insurance, (b) legal advisory and motoring prosecution defence, (c) vehicle accident/breakdown recovery services.
(a) The motor insurance is underwritten by Lloyd's of London and provides a choice of cover: comprehensive, third party fire and theft or third party only. No loadings are applied for disabled drivers and a simplified rating structure will honour any existing no-claims bonus.
(b) The legal advisory and motoring prosecution defence cover. This section provides:
    (i) a 24-hour advisory service on any personal problem;
    (ii) up to £5,000 per incident of legal expenses in defending the disabled driver against possible motoring prosecution;
    (iii) recovery of uninsured losses as a result of a motor accident.
(c) Vehicle accident/breakdown recovery emergency services. Provides a 24-hour emergency rescue service for disabled drivers. Cover includes:
    (i) roadside repairs (including assistance with punctures);
    (ii) vehicle recovery;
    (iii) passenger 'get you home' service (up to five people);
    (iv) at-home service.
For information/details/quotations apply as above.

CVM (Company of Veteran Motorists)
1 East Grinstead House, East Grinstead, West Sussex RH19 1UF (Tel: East Grinstead (0342) 24444).
This is primarily a road safety organisation, the main aim of which is to promote safety via the high driving standard of its members, of whom there are about 80,000. The CVM also aims to bring about a better understanding between the insurers and the insured, and is always pleased to help members who have insurance problems. CVM (Agents) Ltd will act on behalf of members for the placing of private motor car insurance with first-class companies. In addition to the basic CVM policy which is available to members at 15 per cent discount, there are three special schemes:
(a) Insurance against mechanical failure (covering engine, rear axle, steering, fuel system, gearbox, transmission, brake and electrical systems) for cars which are less than five years old and have covered less than 50,000 miles. The annual premium is £30.
(b) An insurance-based breakdown/recovery. This is unlike the major services in this area in that instead of the driver just calling for help, he organises whatever is necessary – roadside repair or lift home for vehicle and passengers – and reclaims the cost. The annual premium if £9.95.
(c) Legal expenses insurance. For an annual premium of £12, CVM members can take out a 'Family Motor Legal Protection Policy'. This will cover costs involved if you have to protect your legal rights in and out of Court up to a maximum of £10,000 for each claim.

M. J. Fish & Co., Insurance Brokers
1–3 Slater Lane, Leyland, Preston, Lancashire PR5 3AL (Tel: Leyland (077 44) 22401/24841).
This company has recently arranged a special scheme of motor insurance for disabled drivers, underwritten by certain Lloyd's underwriters on 'non-loaded' terms.

The main features are: a simplified rating structure; specially negotiated premiums; no loadings for young/inexperienced drivers; any disabled driver accepted at the quoted rates irrespective of disability, provided the condition is not a deteriorating one (individual consideration will, however, be given in such cases); medical certificates not required; common rates irrespective of age from 16 to 65; common rates for the majority of family saloons.

Personal accident cover is usually deleted from the motor insurance policies for disabled motorists, and the main scheme offered here is no exception. However, a separate low-cost Personal Accident policy is available to disabled people who hold a current driving licence and are aged 16 to 65. Cover will normally cease at age 70. The annual premium is £20 and gives a wide range of benefits up to £10,000 in the event of death or certain severe injuries.

Greenway Insurance Brokers (UK) Ltd

20 Eastcheap, London EC3 (Tel: 01-623 1033).
This company has recently set up a Disabled Insurance Programme ('d.i.p.'), and will be glad to answer telephone enquiries on the special 'd.i.p.' line as above without any obligation or 'follow-up', unless requested, by a representative. They will also be glad to send details.

Under Greenway's programme, other covers are available, such as life insurance, travel, personal accident and artificial limbs.

Hartley Cooper UK Ltd (incorporating Duveen & Walker)

PO Box 25, Hartley House, Eaton Road, Enfield EN1 1NR (Tel: 01-366 6551).
This firm are brokers to the Department of Health and Social Security in connection with vehicles on loan to disabled people. The firm advises us that they have arranged a special motor insurance scheme which offers a discount of 20 per cent off schedule rates.

STANDARD PRODUCTION CARS

With the phasing out of the 'trike', more and more disabled motorists are having to look to the standard range of production cars to meet their needs, adapting the car of their choice as appropriate to their particular disability. In this market, mistakes are expensive, and care needs to be exercised. A second-hand car, provided that it is in reasonable condition, will often give better value for money than buying new. Pound for pound, the disabled motorist may be able to buy a car which is roomier, more comfortable, more easily accessible, which has ample storage space and, if necessary, power-assisted steering. In our book *Motoring and Mobility for Disabled People* (*see* page 167), we examine the general considerations governing the choice of a car in some detail and give the vital specifications of nearly 50 models. We describe the advantages afforded by automatic transmission, assisted braking and steering, storage space, seating, width and height of doors, all of which may be critical to the disabled driver or passenger.

Perhaps the most important advice is to take your time in making your choice. There is no substitute for trying out the car you have in mind to be sure that it suits your individual physique and disability.

SPECIALISED VEHICLES

With the phasing out of the trike and the manufacturers of standard production cars doing so little to accommodate disabled drivers, it is no wonder that people turn hopefully to new specialist cars provided by the ingenious brainwaves of the inventors. The problem as always is finance. The initial, substantial costs of development and testing, including type approval, are very difficult to recoup when, however well designed, the market for which such a vehicle is designed will remain strictly limited. Only a small proportion of disabled drivers will find any one design meets individual needs.

It is, nevertheless, very encouraging to see the progress made by the Elswick Envoy and the Salamander after all the years of planning and development which have gone into producing the vehicles, which are now available to us to drive.

The Trike

By phasing out the vehicle scheme (war pensioners who were not included in the phasing out operation of 1976 are now also to have their vehicles phased out) and introducing the mobility allowance, drivers and passengers were, for the first time, treated equally.

However, thousands of people still prefer to retain their trike (rather than switch over to mobility allowance) which they feel cannot be replaced by mobility allowance with or without Motability. These drivers have been assured that the Department of Health and Social Security expects to be able to continue maintaining, and, where necessary, replacing three-wheelers at present in service for those who want to keep them for at least some years yet. We are told that there are adequate stocks of serviceable vehicles for use as replacements and that access will continue for some years to sources of supply for spare parts.

In order to encourage trike drivers to change over to mobility allowance it has been made easier for them to plug the gap between losing the trike and being able to drive a car. Those invalid three-wheeler users without a full licence who wish to change over to mobility allowance may, subject to certain conditions, retain the three-wheeler while at the same time receiving mobility allowance (or having a Motability car) for an overlap period not usually exceeding six months, or until the driving test is passed, whichever is the sooner.

The Elswick Envoy

Elswick Special Vehicles Ltd, The Mill, Kings Coughton, Warwickshire B49 5QG (Tel: Alcester (0789) 763711).

The Envoy is, the manufacturers believe, the only car in the world specifically designed to be driven from a wheelchair and to be fully type approved. This car was originally designed by GKN Sankey and was then taken over by Elswick.

One of the biggest problems for wheelchair drivers is the business of stowing their awkward and heavy wheelchairs and then transferring in and out of their cars. The time this takes and the discomfort which can be caused in the process make for added difficulties in the pursuit of personal mobility. Elswick claim to have solved this problem. With their vehicle and the wheelchair of Vessa manufacture, a chairbound driver may enter, drive and leave his car without having to move from his wheelchair. The driver, in his wheelchair, enters the vehicle by means of a counterbalanced tail ramp. He then uses the special anchorage provided to secure the chair in position in front of the centrally situated steering wheel, from where he has excellent vision through a large flat inclined windscreen providing a commanding view of his surroundings. In addition, there are sliding side windows and a rear window.

The car has an automatic gearbox and hand controls which are mounted on the left-hand side of the steering column. No foot pedals are fitted. Push-button hydraulics lower the car rear to allow easy access up the low-angle ramps. The bonnet lid, hinged at the front, is detachable allowing wheelchair-level access to distributor, plugs, battery and dipstick.

Not all wheelchair users want to drive from a wheelchair. In such cases, Elswick will be happy to fit a normal car-type driver's seat whilst providing facilities to carry a wheelchair.

Accommodation for two passengers is provided in the form of two inward-facing foldaway seats at the rear of the car, which flap up to give easy access for the driver's wheelchair. The bodywork is in fibre glass (a rust-free bonus) and the shells are built by Reliant. The finished product is available in a range of colours. The engine, automatic gearbox and transmission are those of the Metro 1000, while the mechanical components are standard British Leyland manufacture.

The Envoy is claimed to have a top speed of 70 m.p.h. and a touring fuel consumption of 36 m.p.g. Price: £7,228 including self-propelling Vessa wheelchair. Optional extras include: power assisted steering £875; remote-controlled powered rear door

and ramp £890.00, rear door only £665.00; powered wheelchair £1,296.00, less an allowance when the self-propelled is not accepted with the car.

The Salamander

PK Specialist Vehicles Ltd, 12 Muslin Street, Salford, Manchester M5 4NE (Tel: 061-737 9758). The Salamander was conceived by the School of Design at the Institute of Advanced Studies at Manchester Polytechnic. It is financed by the City of Salford, and has been developed primarily to fill the need of the people of Salford at the demise of the 'trike'. The vehicle has an 1100 cc engine with automatic transmission. The one model has two seating options (a) one occupant where the disabled person gets in from the offside, slides across and then raises the wheelchair into the vehicle by means of an electrically operated lift (b) two fixed seats are included for passenger and driver. The seats will, of course, recline and also move backwards and forwards to accommodate leg requirements. The car has an exceptionally wide door opening with the door moving through a full 90 degrees.

While continuing to meet the need of Salford residents, the company is expanding production to sell the Salamander nationally and possibly, in the future, internationally. The price for the double-seater is £5,995. Salford residents may claim a 50 per cent non-repayable grant towards the cost of the car from the City Council.

CAR PURCHASE DISCOUNTS AND OTHER CONCESSIONS

A number of the leading car manufacturers have recently introduced schemes allowing special terms to disabled drivers or to the immediate family of those qualifying disabled people who do not drive.

Most of these schemes rely on the goodwill of dealers who are encouraged to sell certain models at reduced prices, but for whom there is no overall ruling. Dealers will, in any case, not usually consider offering special discounts in trade-in situations, so intending customers who wish to take advantage of any discount scheme may be better advised to sell their existing cars privately rather than seeking a part-exchange deal.

Intending purchasers are recommended to visit showrooms, find out what discounts are available and discuss their particular needs. A guide to some of the schemes is given below.

BL Cars Ltd (Austin Rover Group)

International House, Bickenhill Lane, Birmingham B37 7HH.
BL operate a special mobility scheme for disabled people in receipt of the mobility allowance, the private car allowance, or who hold DHSS 'trikes'. It can be claimed either by themselves as drivers, or, if they cannot drive, by a relative. Discounts vary on the different models, from $12\frac{1}{2}$ per cent to $18\frac{1}{2}$ per cent.

There are special order forms for this scheme and these can be obtained in advance from the Mobility Department, BL Cars Ltd, Longbridge, Birmingham B31 2TB. In addition, BL operate a special credit plan for disabled drivers, allowing the discounted price plus car tax and VAT to be paid over a period of up to four years. A deposit of not less than 20 per cent is required, after which the balance plus interest can be paid in up to 47 monthly instalments with a final payment of 10 per cent of the credit taken plus the sum of £3. An advantage of the plan is free accident life benefit of £10,000 for the driver and each passenger.

Fiat

Discount of 15 per cent allowed on basic list prices of cars. Available to any person in receipt of mobility allowance. Full details from Fiat dealers. In case of difficulty contact National Sales, Fiat Auto (UK) Ltd, Great West Road, Brentford, Middlesex TW8 9DJ (Tel: 01-568 8822).

Ford

Financial concessions are a matter of negotiation with the supplying dealer in the case of a cash sale, but a discount of up to 15 per cent is offered on all Fiestas (manual transmission only) and Escort models purchased through the Motability Hire-Purchase Scheme. Further details from dealers or from Ford Motor Company Ltd, Eagle Way, Brentwood, Essex CM13 3BW (Tel: Brentwood (0277) 253000).

Mazda

Mazda operate a disabled drivers' scheme offering 15 per cent discount off the basic price to purchasers who are in receipt of mobility allowance or registered as disabled. Consideration will also be given to those who though not disabled themselves purchase a car for the benefit of a disabled person. The scheme has been initiated in conjunction with Mazda's network of 240 dealers and has their full back-up in providing necessary preparation work and after-sales service. Adaptations can also be arranged. Details from dealers or from Mazda Car Imports (GB) Ltd, Longfield Road, North Farm Industrial Estate, Tunbridge Wells, Kent TN2 3EY (Tel: Tunbridge Wells (0892) 40123).

Saab

Additional support is given to Saab dealers so that disabled drivers may negotiate more attractive part exchanges. Assistance is also given to dealers which will enable drivers to negotiate preferential prices on a straightforward new car purchase. Details from dealers or from Saab (Gt Britain) Ltd, SAAB House, Fieldhouse Lane, Marlow, Buckinghamshire SL7 1LY (Tel: Marlow (06284) 6977).

Talbot

Discount of 15 per cent allowed on new cars. Available to any person in receipt of mobility allowance. Full details from local dealers or from Talbot Motor Co. Ltd, PO Box 46, London Road, Ryton on Dunsmore, Coventry CV8 3DZ (Tel: Coventry (0203) 303030).

Vauxhall

Discount of 15 per cent allowed on certain new cars. Available to any person in receipt of mobility allowance but not where a vehicle is taken in part exchange. Full details from local dealers or from Vauxhall-Opel, Vauxhall Motors Ltd, PO Box 3, Luton LU2 0SY (Tel: Luton (0582) 21122).

Volkswagen

Most of Volkswagen dealers offer a $12\frac{1}{2}$ per cent discount from the basic price of any vehicle in the range to those in receipt of mobility allowance. Full details from dealers or from Volkswagen (GB) Ltd, Yeomans Drive, Blakelands, Milton Keynes MK14 5AN (Tel: Milton Keynes (0908) 679121).

Volvo

Dealers are encouraged to allow 15 per cent discount on the automatic versions for disabled people, but this is discretionary and may depend on whether another car has to be taken in part exchange. Further details from dealers or from Volvo Concessionaires Ltd, Lancaster Road, Cressex, High Wycombe, Buckinghamshire HP12 3QE (Tel: High Wycombe (0494) 33444).

CAR HIRE

Hertz

(Administrative offices) Radnor House, 1272 London Road, Norbury, London SW16 4DQ (Tel: 01-679 1799).
Hand controls (at no extra charge) in the United Kingdom are available for drivers with lower limb disability only. The car offered is the Vauxhall Astra 1.3L automatic. It is available from central London, Gatwick and Heathrow. Reservations on request with minimum seven days advance notice. The con-

trols are fitted to the brake and accelerator pedals; no attachment is fitted to the steering wheel.
Hertz Reservation Centres: Manchester (Tel: 061-437 8321); Birmingham (Tel: 021-643 8991); Glasgow (Tel: 041-248 7733); London (as above).

Kenning Car Hire

This company has been providing automatic cars equipped with full hand controls for several years. Depots are in London (Tel: 01-882 3576); Sheffield (Tel: (0742) 71141); and Edinburgh (Tel: 031-343 3377). These specialise in cars for disabled drivers so contact should be made to the one nearest your home, however Kenning has a nation-wide spread of depots to ensure full back-up service.

A variety of hand controls are available at what we are informed are competitive prices. $17\frac{1}{2}$ per cent discount is available on non-hand control cars and vans to those giving evidence of receipt of mobility allowance. Further information can be obtained from the depots as listed or from Central Reservations Office, Kenning Car Hire, Manor Offices, Old Road, Chesterfield, Derbyshire S40 3QT (Tel: Chesterfield (0246) 77241).

Regent Street Motors (Wrexham) Ltd

Regent Street, Wrexham, Clwyd LL11 1RE (Tel: Wrexham (0978) 56822).
This firm will provide an automatic three-door Renault 5 with Bekker hand controls. The car is available for daily or weekly hire at normal rates with no additional charge for hand controls.

Wadham Stringer

This firm is offering a 10 per cent discount on the hire of its cars to anyone in receipt of the mobility allowance or to anyone who is a member of the DDA, DDMC or DMF. Enquiries to Mr R. B. J. Wheeler, Director and General Manager, Granada Road, Southsea, Hampshire PO4 0RF (Tel: Portsmouth (0705) 735311).

C.B. RADIO

See page 217.

GARAGE RATES EXEMPTION

Garages, carports and car spaces accommodating a vehicle needed by a disabled person may attract rate relief. In England and Wales the amount of relief is calculated in one of two ways, which the claimant can elect:
either
(a) (i) £25 for a garage;
     (ii) £15 for a carport;
     (iii) £5 for land;

or

(b) So much of the rateable value of the property as a whole as is attributable to the garage, carport or land as certified by a Valuation Officer. (If the accommodation for the vehicle is rated in its own right, the rebate would be equal to the rates chargeable for the period of relief.) Where the facility is also used for other purposes, the rating authority can reduce the rebate under this option.

In Scotland, relief is that part of the rates chargeable on the property for the rebate period which is attributable to the special facility, as certified by the Assessor. Application should be made to your local rating authority.

For further information on Rates Relief (including Scottish regulations) *see* Section 13.

CONVERSION OF VEHICLE – RELIEF FROM VAT

The VAT position on 'personal' ambulances, specialised vehicles, conversions to suit the condition of a handicapped person, goods supplied for such conversions, and the repair or maintenance of such goods is described on page 48 of Section 3.

MOTORING CONVERSION COMPANIES

It would be impossible to give a comprehensive list of firms who specialise in this type of equipment; however, the following are leaders in this field. The conversions and adaptations can very often be specially tailored to suit the driver's own particular needs.

Further information may be obtained from the individual motoring organisations or from Disabled Living Foundation, 380–384 Harrow Road, London W9 2HU (Tel: 01-289 6111). See also our book *Motoring and Mobility for Disabled People*, referred to on page 167.

General and special conversions
Ashley Mobility, Hay Road, Hay Mills, Birmingham B25 8HY (Tel: 021-772 5364). Also at: Derwent Close Industrial Estate, Langdale Drive, Warnden, Worcester (Tel: Worcester (0905) 28575); and 45 Swiss Road, Weston-super-Mare (Tel: Weston-super-Mare (0934) 26011).
Provides a range of conversion services to cover any degree of leg disability for most types of cars, automatic or manual gearbox models. Conversions

are undertaken in the firm's workshops in Birmingham, but a nation-wide collection and delivery service is available. Mini Autos and Metro Autos can be converted at your own garage by Ashley's own fitters. This firm has a Mini 1000 converted to hand controls which is available to enquirers in the West Midlands area for demonstration and assessment services.

Adaptacar, Cooks Cross, South Molton, North Devon EX36 4AW (Tel: South Molton (076 95) 2785).

Provides three different types of hand controls. In addition the firm will carry out many other minor adaptations as required. They cover Cornwall, Devon, parts of Dorset and Somerset, collecting and delivering cars at a cost a little over the expenses involved.

Automobile and Industrial Developments Ltd, Queensdale Works, Queensthorpe Road, Sydenham, London SE26 4PJ (Tel: 01-778 7055).

Provides hand controls for most makes of car.

AutoMobility Limited, Scottish Disabled Drivers Centre, 630 Keppochill Road, Glasgow G22 5HS (Tel: 041-332 7467/7441).

Provides a range of services described in their 'Yellow Page' *Guide for Disabled Drivers*, in which they describe how they 'tailor' the car to fit the driver or passenger and modify the car or controls.

Alfred Bekker, The Green, Longtoft, nr Driffield, North Humberside YO25 0TF (Tel: Driffield (0377) 87276).

Makes and markets hand controls for any make and model of car, either in kit form for the local garage to fit or for fitting at workshops while you wait, for a small extra charge.

Alfred Bekker provides an assessment service (around his own equipment) and will also make available overnight accommodation.

BRIG-AYD Controls, Warrengate, Tewin, Welwyn, Hertfordshire AL6 0JP (Tel: Tewin (043 871) 4206).

Provides two separate hand control system conversions and will also build to customers' requirements where necessary.

Cowal Mobility Aids Ltd, 32 Newpond Road, Holmer Green, nr High Wycombe, Buckinghamshire HP15 6SU (Tel: High Wycombe (0494) 714400).

This firm specialises in conversions to a range of vehicles; also supplying hand control kits.

Eurostag (Leeds) Ltd, Wellbridge Industrial Estate, Wellington Bridge, Leeds 12 (Tel: Leeds (0532) 444765).

Hand controls and other conversions for all types of cars to suit individual requirements. All conversions made in Leeds.

Feeny & Johnson (Components) Ltd, Alperton Lane, Wembley HA0 1JJ (Tel: 01-998 4458/9).

This firm provides a variety of conversions to suit individual needs, including four kit sets to suit most vehicles, automatic or manual. All controls apart from one to control the throttle only must be fitted by Feeny & Johnson or their accredited agents.

D. G. Hodge & Son Limited, Feathers Lane, Wraysbury, Staines, Middlesex (Tel: Wraysbury (078 481) 3580).

This firm specialises in providing at its own premises a wide variety of driving controls to suit an individual person's needs, including foot steering by means of a rotating plate positioned on the floor rotating in the same way as does the steering wheel. They also fit joy-stick steering. A demonstration car is available to show customers an example of hand controls. This firm has a reputation for providing very helpful advice, innovative ideas, and a degree of personal assessment.

Midland Cylinder Rebores, Torrington Avenue, Coventry CV4 9BL (Tel: Coventry (0203) 462424).
Provides a one-handle control kit of brake and accelerator designed to fit any car. A throttle conversion kit is available for most makes of car, also brake and throttle conversion. Other modifications may be provided according to individual requirements. The firm is an agent for Feeny & Johnson.

Motor Services (Manchester) Ltd, Royal Works, Canal Side, Edge Lane, Stretford, nr Manchester M32 8HS (Tel: 061-865 6922).
Provides a range of conversions and adaptations for cars having automatic and manual transmission. Also agents for Feeney & Johnson.

Reselco Invalid Carriages Ltd, 262 King Street, London W6 0SS (Tel: 01-748 5053).
Provides a variety of special controls for most makes of car whether automatic or with a manual gearbox and offers a free consultation service at the premises for people who are undecided in the type of controls suited to their disability.

Ross Auto Engineering Ltd, 2-3 Westfield Road, Wallasey, Cheshire L44 7HX. Also at: Banastre Road, Southport, and Athlone Road, Warrington (Tel: 051-652 9224; Southport (0704) 35757; Warrington (0925) 34289).

This firm provides a range of services for disabled people including adaptations to cars, hand-control conversions, and wheelchair sales, service and hire.

In the Wallasey works there is also a static Chevette Automatic transmission-type car (less engine and wheels). It is adapted for hand controls which provide for simulated speed and braking. To test physical ability to brake, servo-assisted brakes and hydraulic pressure read-out are installed. Overcam park braking, twin-pedal acceleration and other aids are also shown.

S.W.S. Motor Bodies, Unit 9, Hartford House, Newport Road, Weston Street, Bolton, Lancashire (Tel: Bolton (0204) 395660).
In addition to converting Fiat 127 Fiorino vans into purpose-built vehicles to take wheelchair passengers, this firm also fits cars with hand controls and undertakes a range of other modifications where necessary.

Seat conversions
Elap Engineering, 43 King Street, Accrington, Lancashire (Tel: Accrington (0254) 36042).
This firm manufactures a conversion kit consisting of a swivel mechanism which can be fitted to the basic frame of a car seat, enabling the seat to rotate around and beyond the doorway of the vehicle at a right angle. To operate, a release lever is situated at the side of the seat – the seat being locked automatically in position until released by the lever. A number of conversion firms provide special seating arrangements, including Ashley Repairs, Cowal Mobility Aids Ltd and D. G. Hodge & Son Ltd.

Conversions to allow access and travel for drivers (or passengers) without leaving wheelchair.
Car Chair Sales Ltd, Station Road Industrial Estate, Hailsham, Sussex BN27 2ES (Tel: Hailsham (0323) 840283).
This innovative unit, the brain-child of Brian Waite, consists of a special wheelchair and a unique lift-transfer mechanism which together eliminate the need for the difficult transfer between wheelchair and car seat as well as the problem of wheelchair stowage. The disabled person remains in the car chair throughout. The system is suitable for both passengers and drivers (who drive from the chair). It can be fitted to operate on either side of most two-door family saloons.

The special wheelchair, which is designed for ordinary use both indoors and outdoors, is extremely sturdy and is available either in attendant-controlled or electrically powered versions. The lifting mechanism is easily fitted to the car with virtually no modification. When it has been lowered, and the transfer mechanism extended from the car, the wheelchair is reversed up to the open doorway and aligned so that a pick-up point locates into the chair. It is then lifted off the ground – whether flat or cambered kerbing – complete with occupant, and all four wheels are retracted. It transfers in two stages to lock automatically into a front seat position. The mechanism can be removed and transferred to your next car without affecting the resale value of the first vehicle.

Gowrings Mobility International, The Grange, Lower Way, Thatcham, Newbury, Berkshire RG13 4PH (Tel: Thatcham (0635) 64464).

The new Freelancer system enables a chairborne person to get into and out of a standard car without leaving his/her wheelchair, without assistance and, if appropriate, to drive from it.

Freelancer is at present fitted to a three-door Ford Escort and consists of a specially designed wheelchair, a beam and base frame and an electrical control system. The front seat of the car is removed and replaced with the base frame. The beam which is attached to the base frame swings in and out of the car as required. Entry to the car (whether as a driver or passenger) is achieved by connecting the wheelchair to the beam, electrically raising the wheelchair wheels, thereafter swinging into the car and adjusting the position as required. Entry and exit can be achieved in a matter of two to three minutes.

The car's construction or design is not affected in any way. As a consequence the entire system can easily be removed and thereafter transferred to another car.

Conversion to allow access and travel for passengers without leaving wheelchairs
Gowrings Mobility International (as above).
Gowrings have produced the Chairman Metro conversion to enable a disabled passenger to travel without leaving his/her wheelchair. A non-slip ramp affording entry to the rear of the vehicle (1 in 5 gradient) doubles as the back door. The conversion can be carried out on your own vehicle or as part of a package deal with a new car.

Gowrings have also developed conversions based on the BL Mini van and Transit, the latter including a hydraulic tailgate lift and room for up to four people in their wheelchairs.

Liningtons (Portsmouth) Ltd, (Atlas Conversions), Milton Road, Portsmouth, Hampshire PO4 8PW (Tel: Portsmouth (0705) 815151).

The Renault Mobility Wheelchair Ambulance is based on a Renault Trafic T800 van, the front wheel drive version of which has a very low floor height (18

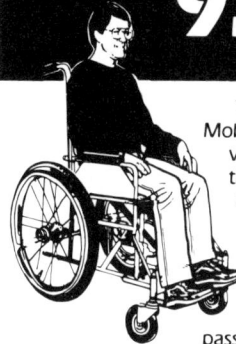

in.) facilitating wheelchair access by ramp. The vehicle is available in a number of versions with short or long wheelbase and standard or high roof.

Mellor Coachcraft, Bodybuilding Division, Durham Street, Rochdale OL11 1BY (Tel: Rochdale (0706) 355355).

As well as vehicles built for multi-occupation, Mellors also undertake conversions of the Ford Escort van to accommodate one or two wheelchairs. As far as possible, Mellor undertake to build to the customer's own specification.

Neill & Bennett, 7 Wyngate Road, Cheadle Hulme, Cheshire SK8 6ER (Tel: 061-485 3149).

The Renault Trafic van is available as a front-wheel drive, manual gearbox vehicle, in long or short wheelbase versions, with high or standard height roof and a choice of petrol or diesel engines. A $31\frac{1}{2}$ in. wide side door combines with a low-level uninterrupted floor to allow easy wheelchair access by a self-stowing ramp.

A motor caravan conversion with elevating roof comes fully equipped for up to four people, including a wheelchair user, with flushing lavatory, sink and cooker. Other makes of van can be similarly converted to order.

Victor W. Poynting, Coachbuilder, Faraday Road, Churchfields Industrial Estate, Salisbury, Wiltshire SP2 7NR (Tel: Salisbury (0722) 6048).

The conversion is based on the standard British Leyland Mini van or Clubman estate and is designed to accommodate a wheelchair-seated passenger in the rear of the vehicle with adequate side and forward vision. A universal anchor bracket is fitted for holding the wheelchair stationary.

Similar conversions are based on the VW Golf, Ford Fiesta, Ford Escort van and the Talbot Rancho. The Rancho retains its normal four to five seating capacity making this a good family car.

Rootes (Maidstone) Ltd, Mill Street, Maidstone, Kent ME15 6YD (Tel: Maidstone (0622) 53333).

Various vehicles for transporting passengers in wheelchairs with capacities of one to 20 occupied wheelchairs, or up to 42 seated passengers.

Smulders Systems, PO Box 8, Oxted, Surrey RH8 0TZ (Tel: Oxted (088 33) 3350).

Smulders convert two vehicles, the Talbot Matra

Rancho and the Talbot High-top van. Both vehicles will carry one wheelchair-bound person in the rear and one slightly less disabled person on a special rotating front passenger seat available as an optional extra.

S.W.S. Motor Bodies, Unit 9, Hartford House, Newport Road/Weston Street, Bolton, Lancashire (Tel: Bolton (0204) 395660).

The Fiat 127 Fiorino conversion allows access for a disabled person in a wheelchair through the rear doors, and travel in the rear section of the vehicle without leaving the wheelchair.

B. Walker & Son Ltd, Gammons Lane, Watford, Hertfordshire WD2 5BZ (Tel: Watford (0923) 25816).

For individual wheelchair users the company offers a number of conversions. The largest are based on the Bedford CF and Ford Transit short wheelbase panel vans which offer room for a wheelchair, a companion's seat and extra equipment or seating. Also suitable for conversion (although smaller) are the Toyota Hi-Ace and the Mitsubishi Colt L300.

Devices to assist access to a car with separate wheelchair loading

Autobility Ltd, Unit 1A, North Tyne Industrial Estate, Whitley Road, Longbenton, Tyne and Wear NE12 9SZ (Tel: 0632 700880).

The Autobility Astra is a conversion facilitating transfer between wheelchair and car and stowing the chair with minimum effort on the inside front door of the car.

The wheelchair is specially designed to fold up small and to release one of its wheels. When stowed, the other wheel fits neatly into a recess in the driver's door and the chair is anchored, firmly and automatically, against the door.

After fully opening the car door, the wheelchair is manœuvred as close to the car as possible. By using a small catch, the car seat is released to slide outwards over the door sill and automatically locks in this position. Having removed the left armrest from his wheelchair, the disabled person slides on to the car seat which is level with his chair. The chair is now folded and brought up to the open door. By tilting it slightly it can be hooked on to a hoist arm on the door, and the handles folded down. A switch activates the chair hoist which raises the chair into its storage position. Fully raised, the wheelchair is automatically locked in position below window level. The outer wheel can now be easily removed and stowed within the car. The seat is returned to lock in its normal position, and with the door closed there is ample space to drive. The car seat retains its normal fore and aft travel adjustment. Leaving the car involves the same procedure in reverse.

The driver-side conversion fits only on an automatic 3-door Astra. But if the driver can efficiently and permanently operate the clutch pedal with one foot, or if the conversion required is on the passenger side, then it may be fitted to any 3-door manual Astra. D. G. Hodge & Son Limited, Feathers Lane, Wraysbury, Staines, Middlesex (Tel: Wraysbury (078 481) 3580).

A very useful system to help a disabled driver with access to the driver's seat from the passenger side, while at the same time providing easy stowage for the wheelchair, is a combination of a narrow 11 in. seat set on runners (in place of the normal passenger seat) which, on transfer from wheelchair to car, acts as a carrier to get across the car to the driver's seat, together with electric gear to lift the wheelchair (which must be folded) into the empty passenger space where it is then secured. The unused passenger seat can be stored and the car returned to standard condition at any time.

ASSESSMENT CENTRES

Learning to drive a car can be a daunting business to anybody. However, before we can learn to drive it may be necessary to have an assessment, first of ability to drive, and second of the sort of controls and equipment we will need to help overcome any physical limitations. Advice of this sort is still in short supply but we are delighted to be able to give details of assessment centres which are now able to provide tailor-made individual assessment and advice services.

We are, of course, not forgetting that disabled drivers themselves have always been the greatest source of help to fellow aspiring drivers. Through the various disabled driver organisations a 'matching' process has long been in action, when by way of network schemes of members a would-be driver is put in touch with an established driver with a similar disability who is able to guide and help through his/her own personal experience. Very often this means having the opportunity to try out vehicles with the special controls needed to compensate for certain specific physical difficulties. The DDMC have Area Representatives who seek to 'match' in this way while the DMF and DDA perform a similar service through their local clubs.

Banstead Place Mobility Centre
Park Road, Banstead, Surrey SM7 3EE (Tel: Burgh Heath (073 73) 56222/51756).
The Mobility Centre forms part of the Assessment Centre for disabled school leavers operated by the Queen Elizabeth's Foundation for the Disabled at Banstead. The Centre includes a demonstration area and workshops and also features an open-air tarmac road system which has been marked out authentically to resemble normal driving conditions. It includes a roundabout, crossing, junctions and varying kerb heights.

The Centre, which is available to members of the general public, is equipped for the following:
1. To provide an information service which may include advice on eligibility for and use of the mobility allowance, facilities offered by Motability and availability of appropriate car adaptations for drivers and passengers. Advice on wheelchairs and motorised pavement vehicles is also available. In addition, counselling on the correct use of equipment can be provided.
2. To demonstrate the available range of powered outdoor wheelchairs.
3. For assessment and recommendation on car adaptations.
4. For a comprehensive examination of suitability to apply for a driving licence.

How to contact the service:
Clients are welcome to refer themselves to this Centre. While an appointment must be made before a visit can be made to the Mobility Centre, anyone may contact Banstead Place by telephone or in writing for general information. An application form will be sent to all prospective clients for wheelchair or car assessments; on receipt of this, the applicant's General Practitioner will then be contacted for background medical information.

Types of assessment:
1. Demonstration – clients can try out models from the range of equipment available in simulated road conditions. Qualified therapists consider the medical aspects of posture, controls and transfers so they may offer suitable advice. Instruction on use and maintenance of the vehicle selected is included in this type of asssessment, which usually lasts two to three hours.
2. Car adaptation – the need for suitable adaptations to standard production vehicles can be investigated and recommendations made. This service is considered most applicable to new drivers and those whose disability is recently acquired or changing. Such clients are assessed on a car assessment unit incorporating fully adjustable seating, reaction timing equipment and a variety of controls which help to assess strength, co-ordination and joint range in each limb. Access, seat and controls are investigated

153

by a therapist and a disability driving consultant. This assessment takes up to two hours and a full written report is sent to the client and his/her General Practitioner.

3. Driving ability – this type of assessment is recommended for those individuals whose damage involves neurological damage which may affect their safety in modern road conditions. Many of these applicants have the basic ability to use modified car controls but possible impairment of their speed reaction, perceptual, visual and reasoning skills suggest that further investigation is necessary. This group will include those suffering from damage or abnormalities of the central nervous system resulting from hydrocephalus, cerebral palsy, traumatic head injury or a stroke. Those suffering from certain progressive conditions such as multiple sclerosis which affect vision and motor response could also benefit from this more complex form of assessment. A whole day is taken up with the necessary testing and investigations which are carried out by a team consisting of the Medical Consultant, Psychologist, Orthoptist, Driving Consultant and Therapist. At the conclusion of the assessment they exchange findings and a written report is sent to the client and his/her General Practitioner.

Fees: The information service is free of charge. Otherwise charges are as in the table (November 1983):

1. 4 m.p.h. pavement vehicles assessment with written report £15
2. Car adaptation assessment with written report £30
3. Full day's driving ability plus car adaptation assessment with written report £65

In certain circumstances fees are recoverable from other agencies and further advice on this is available on application.

Derby Disabled Driving Centre
Derwent Hospital, Old Mansfield Road, Derby DE2 4BB (Tel: Derby (0332) 47141 – ask for Derwent Hospital ext. 363).
This is a new Centre for disabled drivers and would-be drivers providing an enthusiastic and flexible assessment service. The assessment facilities are backed up by a workshop where disabled drivers can have their vehicles (cars, vans, farm vehicles, etc.), converted, often paying only for the cost of the components. However, if welding or spraying is involved a charge will be made to cover this service.

Driving assessment is provided on a module (a Mini cut in half) with interchangeable hand controls and a variety of seats and hand brakes. In addition, there is a reaction testing meter in conjunction with a computer to test braking sequence application.

A full team of rehabilitation specialists is available if required including doctors and eye specialists. Individual disabled people are welcome to telephone with queries or to make an appointment. Your doctor may need to be contacted if there are queries about medication or surgery.

In the future it is hoped to build a test track for motorists to try out a vehicle which has already (1984) been made available.

Mobility Information Service
Copthorne Community Hall, Shelton Road, Shrewsbury, Shropshire SY3 8TD (Tel: Shrewsbury (0743) 68383).
The MIS offers an assessment service, advising disabled drivers on individual needs. In addition, a specially designed mobile driving simulator unit capable of assessing the needs of the majority of disabled people prior to trying an adapted car is operated in conjunction with MEDLI (see below) and is available on loan to rehabilitation centres, aids centres, schools and similar units on a rota basis when not required at the centre. The simulator is able to test reaction for braking by hand or foot and physical effort available. It is also equipped with a variable resistance steering mechanism and a wide range of adjustments.

The unit is completed by the addition of the towage vehicle, a fully automatic transmission saloon car suitable for and driven by a wheelchair user, fitted with hand controls. Thus, not only are disabled people given the opportunity to assess their potential as a driver on the machine, but also, if found suitable, they will be able to see and try the real thing at the same time.

There is always a car on the premises fitted with hand controls for demonstration purposes. In cases where this car is not suitable, advice can nevertheless be given. Transport to Copthorne can be arranged, where necessary, through the MEDLI scheme but this can only be done on a referral basis. *Anyone wishing to visit the Service must make an appointment in advance to ensure that they will receive proper attention.*

For further details of MIS see below and for their publications see page 167.

Vehicles for the Disabled Centre
Astley Ainslie Hospital, Grange Loan, Edinburgh E109 2HL (Tel: 031-447 6271).
Facilities at the Centre include a circuit for driver training and also arrangements for assessment of potential ability to drive and then, if all goes well, assessment of adaptations needed and advice on controls.

The first stage in the assessment of ability to control a vehicle involves a clinical and functional examination including degree of power, co-ordination, reaction time, eyesight and so on. This assessment will include use of a test rig and may also involve an in-car assessment.

Individuals may refer themselves, but they are asked to consult their GP and to obtain a covering letter. The service is free.

Assessment and Information Centre for Disabled Drivers
Road Safety Headquarters for the County of South Glamorgan, Briadene, North Road, Cardiff (Tel: Cardiff (0222) 43693).
This new centre is building up its resources with the aim of providing assessment and information services for disabled motorists. Assessment facilities will be geared to suit individual need. These will include the use of a simulator with hand controls. Results of the assessment will be clearly set out in a personal booklet which will also include general motoring information. On the basis of the results applicants may, if they wish, be guided in their choice of vehicle and any necessary controls or equipment.

The information part of the centre will be available to provide disabled motorists with a wide range of knowledge, and it is to be managed by an information officer who will be disabled. The service of the centre will be built up through 1983 and 1984.

Wales
For details of services, *see* Welsh Disabled Motorists Club, page 160.

MOTORING ASSOCIATIONS

Automobile Association
Fanum House, Basingstoke, Hampshire RG21 2EA (Tel: Basingstoke (0256) 20123).
For drivers of Ministry three-wheel vehicles there is an annual membership fee of approximately £6.50 and no joining fee. These concessions do not apply to privately purchased cars, even if converted to a particular disabled person's needs. (*See* page 164, *AA Guide for the Disabled.*)

AA Relay is a special service for uplifting vehicles and drivers in the case of travel breakdown and is available to disabled DHSS trike-driver members as part of their membership fee. The enrolment fee of £4 is also waived for drivers whose cars have been obtained through Motability.

CVM
1 East Grinstead House, East Grinstead, West Sussex RH19 1UF (Tel: East Grinstead (0342) 24444).

The Company of Veteran Motorists is a road safety organisation with a current membership of nearly 80,000 experienced motorists (some of these living abroad). It also incorporates the Association of Good Motorists (AGM), and encourages the enrolment of motorists with less experience to this ancillary organisation.

CVM publishes a general motoring magazine *Good Motoring* covering all matters relating to members' responsibilities as motorists, and particulars of, and amendments and additions to, the Road Traffic Act, Licensing and Traffic Regulations and insurance requirements.

CVM provides all members with free legal, technical and insurance advice on all aspects of motoring. Membership is open to all motorists who hold a full driving licence, and have been free of convictions for any serious driving offence, for the following periods reckoned from the starting date of their first Provisional Driving Licence.

Membership of the CVM – over ten years

Membership of the AGM – under ten years

CVM also operates an insurance scheme which includes an insurance-based breakdown/recovery service.

The British School of Motoring
Disability Training Centre, 81-87 Hartfield Road, Wimbledon, London SW19 3TJ (Tel: 01-540 8262). The Centre provides an assessment service which includes use of a reaction test unit. Driving tuition can be arranged in the owner's specially converted car. Alternatively, the Centre has two Metros fitted with hand controls for clients' use. Advice will also be given on types of conversion appropriate to overcome a particular disability.

If it is impossible to attend the Centre in Wimbledon for a detailed assessment, it is usually possible to arrange for a home appointment with a consultant to discuss the best course of action to take. Cost of assessment is £19.50. There is a seven to eight week waiting list for an appointment.

In addition, a number of the 179 BSM branches have cars (all Metros with automatic transmission) with partial or full hand controls: some of them have reaction test units.

Disabled Drivers' Association

Ashwellthorpe, Norwich NR16 1EX (Tel: Fundenhall (050 841) 449). London office (base for the Appeal Co-ordinator and Principal Executive): Drake House, Creekside, Deptford, London SE8 3DZ (Tel: 01-692 7141).

The Association will help and advise physically disabled people, who are fully paid up members, whether drivers or not, on all matters of mobility including vehicles and conversions, ferry concessions, insurance, legal requirements and government and local authority help.

Members are organised into about 70 local groups in 14 'areas' and each group enjoys a good deal of autonomy in the range of its activities. All receive the Association's quarterly magazine the *Magic Carpet* and enjoy a number of concessions such as cheap travel on certain ferries. The DDA also actively campaigns for improved government help in the mobility field and for improved facilities for disabled people. The headquarters, Ashwellthorpe Hall, is also a holiday centre set in 18 acres of ground providing ideal accommodation for wheelchair members of the DDA; for non-members there is a slight extra charge. Annual subscription £3.50.

Disabled Drivers' Club (Peterborough & District)

5 Donegal Close, Gunthorpe, Peterborough PE4 6TH (Tel: Peterborough (0733) 71550).

This Club, while only serving a localised area, that of Peterborough and surrounding districts, has nevertheless attracted national interest from the wide spread of its activities and its pioneering achievements. The Club distributes a quarterly newsletter *Wheels* which provides detailed information on such matters as local parking facilities, the orange badge scheme, mobility allowance, etc.

The Club also distributes a *Members' Handbook*: *see* page 167. Membership is not limited to those living in the Peterborough area. The annual subscription is £1.50. An application form will be sent on request, provided a stamped addressed envelope is received.

Disabled Drivers' Motor Club Ltd

1a Dudley Gardens, Ealing, London W13 9LU (Tel: 01-840 1515).

Members can seek help and advice on motoring problems, ferry concessions, vehicles, conversions and statutory help either from their Area Representatives or from Head Office where there is a 24-hour answering service. Members are kept informed on motoring matters through a bi-monthly newspaper the *Disabled Driver* and a *Year-book* (*see* page 165). The DDMC also has a full time General Secretary.

Members are also entitled to certain ferry concessions, discounts on RAC subscriptions, and to the benefit of a special insurance scheme run in conjunction with the Disabled Drivers' Insurance Bureau.

The DDMC have appointed voluntary area representatives in 38 areas throughout England, Scotland and Wales, who may have lists of people with converted cars which they are willing to demonstrate to new drivers.

There are two classes of membership: full (disabled people) and associate (those who are interested in promoting the welfare of disabled people and in furthering the aims of the Club). Subscriptions are £3 a year.

Disabled Motorists Federation

Copthorne Community Hall, Shelton Road, Shrewsbury, Shropshire SY3 8TD (Tel: Shrewsbury (0743) 68383).

The DMF was founded in June 1973 by a group of experienced disabled people who believed that there was a need for an organisation to give representation to individual groups of disabled motorists without affecting their independence in any way.

Currently, 23 clubs are linked in this way, as far apart as Swansea and Strathclyde, and have been conspicuously active within their local areas in securing improvements in the arrangements for disabled motorists. An excellent quarterly journal *Flying Mat* is published for members, keeping them up to date with technical and policy developments in the field of mobility, and providing a forum for passing on personal experiences and solutions to motoring problems.

The Mobility Information Service is an offspring of the DMF. This is an excellent service and we describe it briefly below. For information on your nearest group contact David Griffiths at the above address.

The Institute of Advanced Motorists

IAM House, 359-65 Chiswick High Road, London W4 4HS (Tel: 01-994 4403).

The IAM is out to promote skill with responsibility and it maintains that if every driver had the ability to pass the IAM test and the self-discipline to employ its standards at all times, there would be a dramatic drop in the number of road casualties. Of the 248,000 motorists who have taken the test 60 per cent have passed.

The IAM makes the point that the Government's driving test is a very basic, elementary examination, and the Institute feels that passing it should be seen as simply the starting point in the acquisition of mature driving skills. The Institute welcomes disabled motorists, who take the test on exactly the same terms as able-bodied drivers, providing they use a suitably adapted car. There are 114 members' groups throughout the country who can, if required, give assistance to disabled drivers and who will welcome them as members when they have passed the test.

The test costs £12.50 and if you pass you will become a member of the Institute for an annual subscription of £7.50 including VAT.

Motability
(For details *see* page 137.)

Mobility Information Service
Copthorne Community Hall, Shelton Road, Shrewsbury (Tel: Shrewsbury (0743) 68383).
This specialist service offers personal guidance and advice on mobility problems, including motoring (choice of car, controls, etc.), wheelchairs, mobility allowance, leasing, parking privileges and financial concessions. The information officers have personal experience of disability and have an extensive knowledge of many kinds of disabilities. They are concerned to deal with enquiries on a specialised individual basis, tailoring their practical advice and action to suit each person's needs. They are glad to help those with slender resources meet their mobility needs in the most economical way possible. The MIS offers an assessment service; there is always a car on the premises fitted with hand controls. In cases where this car is not suitable, advice can nevertheless be given.

Transport to Copthorne or a home visit can usually be arranged. MIS co-operates closely with the MEDLI scheme (*see* below). Those wishing to visit the Service must make an appointment in advance to ensure that they will receive individual attention.

The Service has published a series of leaflets on many aspects of mobility for handicapped people. Also available a complete information pack covering all aspects of the Service and containing a wide selection of manufacturers' and other brochures. For details *see* page 167.

No charges are made for services, but if your enquiry is in writing it would be appreciated if you could send sufficent postage for a reply. (*See also* MIS Assessment Service, page 154.)

Royal Automobile Club
RAC, RAC House, Lansdowne Road, Croydon CR9 2JA (Tel: 01-686 2525).
Membership is available at a reduced subscription fee of £1 per year, to disabled drivers of Ministry-issued three-wheel vehicles. For all other vehicles members pay the normal subscription fee.

Association for Spina Bifida and Hydrocephalus
22 Upper Woburn Place, London WC1H 0EP (Tel: 01-388 1382).
ASBAH has a Mobility Adviser who is based at Banstead Place Mobility Centre, Park Road, Banstead, Surrey (Tel: Burgh Heath (073 73) 56222).

The adviser will give information and advice about all kinds of mobility problems to people suffering from spina bifida and/or hydrocephalus. She is also a member of the team of assessors at Banstead Place. Some of the matters she can help with include: how to use the mobility allowance; Motability schemes for buying outdoor powered wheelchairs and for buying or leasing new or second-hand cars; how to apply for a driving licence; special facilities to provide assessment and help for young people who want to learn to drive; details of driving schools with motor cars fitted with hand controls; taking the driving test; choosing a car; adapting a car; information about manufacturers providing special car controls, seats, powered wheelchairs, etc.

The adviser works part-time at Banstead Place and all enquiries should be directed to her there, either by letter, or by telephone call on Thursdays only, 9 a.m. to 3.30 p.m. Details of Banstead Place Mobility Centre are given on page 153.

British Red Cross Society
9 Grosvenor Crescent, London SW1X 7EJ (Tel: 01-235 5454).
The British Red Cross Society branches situated in every county in the United Kingdom will help and advise disabled people concerning travel arrangements within this country. This may take the form of providing escorts to travel with disabled people on public transport, or the provision of private transport by car or ambulance. Enquiries should be made to the local branch of the British Red Cross Society (address in telephone directory) or to the home division national headquarters at the above address.

DIAL UK (National Association of Disablement Information and Advice Services)
Dial House, 117 High Street, Clay Cross, Derbyshire (Tel: Chesterfield (0246) 864498).
DIAL is a growing organisation encompassing local groups who provide a free, impartial and confidential service of information, advice and, in some cases, practical help provided by people with direct personal experience of disability.

Local DIALs are able to help with queries surrounding every aspect of disability and will be particularly knowledgeable about local resources. Information naturally includes the subject of mobility and where specialist advice may be sought in the locality.

Disabled Living Foundation
380–384 Harrow Road, London W9 2HU (Tel: 01-289 6111).
The DLF operates a comprehensive information service (*see* page 53) and houses a permanent collection of aids of all kinds, including a wide range of mobility equipment. A useful publication list is also available. Enquiries will be dealt with by telephone or letter. Before visiting the Aids Centre, it is necessary to make an appointment when expert assistance will be given in discussing and assessing the individual needs of a disabled person.

The Family Fund
PO Box 50, York YO1 1UY.
Since the introduction of the mobility allowance the Fund does not help with mobility problems to the same extent as previously. However, the Fund tries to ensure that where a child's handicaps cause a grave mobility problem, it will seek to make it possible for the family to get out for recreational purposes. Sometimes this may mean making a grant towards driving lessons in order to allow a parent to use an existing family car. In exceptional circumstances, and where a child does not receive the mobility allowance and travelling by public transport is virtually impossible, the Fund may be able to help with the costs of maintenance of the family car, where these are only modest. It may also be possible to arrange car hire for limited periods.

For full details of the Fund and how to apply *see* page 17.

Joint Committee on Mobility of Blind and Partially Sighted People
224 Great Portland Street, London W1N 6AA (Tel: 01-388 1266).
The Committee, in its concern with the problems of the mobility of visually handicapped people, seeks to consider ways in which blind people may be enabled to move more safely and independently and how the environment can be improved for this purpose.

The Committee is also concerned to make the general public more aware of ways in which they can improve the quality of life for blind people in matters relating to mobility and to seek government support to achieve these aims whenever possible.

Joint Committee on Mobility for the Disabled
Hon. Sec. Tim Shapley, 9 Moss Close, Pinner, Middlesex HA5 3AY (Tel: 01-866 7884).
Co-ordinates, collects and disseminates expertise on all aspects of mobility for disabled people, and represents their interests to the government and its statutory organisations. Details of publications are given on page 167.

MEDLI (Motoring Experience for the Disabled by Lions International)
This imaginative scheme to help disabled people attain personal mobility has now developed into a national service. Help may be given with additional driving experience or by assisting with other motoring difficulties.

Calls for help may be on behalf of individuals already having professional driving lessons, but needing additional practice to get them through the test. Others may need to be taken to and from the professional lessons.

MEDLI have emphasised that they wish to remain flexible in the service they offer to drivers and would-be drivers, helping disabled people in very practical ways to attain and maintain the goal of personal mobility.

For many people the need of assessment is vital, to decide whether it really is feasible for them to drive before they go to the expense of acquiring a car. In this case MEDLI will be able to transport the person to a suitable centre.

In addition, MEDLI operate, in conjunction with the Mobility Information Service (*see* Assessment Centres, page 153) a specially designed mobile simulator. Off the road help should also be possible; helping to teach the Highway Code, to apply for the test, etc.

MEDLI will only accept calls for help on behalf of individuals from one of their co-organisers: Motability, Mobility Information Service, Disabled Drivers' Motor Club, and the Disabled Drivers' Association. On no account should a disabled individual contact their local Lions club direct.

Northern Ireland Council for the Handicapped
2 Annadale Avenue, Belfast BT7 3JH (Tel: Belfast (0232) 640011).
NICH provides a forum for voluntary and statutory organisations working for disabled people in Northern Ireland. It aims to focus attention on the needs of handicapped people and the services available to them. It operates an information service (*see* page 55) and has published a *Guide to Mobility Assistance for Disabled People in Northern Ireland* (*see* page 168).

Rehabilitation Engineering Movement Advisory Panels (REMAP)
c/o RADAR, 25 Mortimer Street, London W1N 8AB (Tel: 01-637 5400).
The Panels are concerned with problems affecting every aspect of disabled living, naturally including hoists and lifting equipment, walking aids, wheelchairs, children's aids and equipment and also transport. Some devices created by Panels for transport needs include: driving mirror for a client with a locked neck; truck for amputee to use in garden; transferable car seat for disabled child; driving seat for very short person; Citroën car handbrake extension; for a client with rheumatoid arthritis, help to open car door and lift handbrake. For further details of REMAP *see* page 60.

Royal Association for Disability and Rehabilitation
25 Mortimer Street, London W1N 8AB (Tel: 01-637 5400).
RADAR will advise on all aspects of mobility. Contact the Mobility Officer.

St John Ambulance
Provide two mobility services to disabled or sick people: an escort service and an ambulance transport service. For either service adequate notice (not less than a week) is essential. For escorting, the escort's fares must be met, plus the cost of any necessary over-night accommodation. For transport, a charge is made for running costs (which would include any return journey after taking the passenger to his or her destination). Apply to nearest local county office of the St John Ambulance Brigade.

Scottish Council on Disability
5 Shandwick Place, Edinburgh EH2 4RG (Tel: 031-229 8632).
The Council provides a means of consultation and joint action among voluntary and statutory organisations working for disabled people in Scotland. It operates an information service (*see* page 55) and a mobile aids centre.

The Council has also set up the Scottish Committee on Mobility for the Disabled which comprises representatives of voluntary and statutory organisations, and which aims to provide within the Scottish Council on Disability a focus of interest, concern and action on all matters affecting the mobility of disabled people, with particular reference to transport services in Scotland. The Committee also aims to encourage the growth and development of local groups with a similar focus. For further information on the Council *see* page 324.

SEQUAL (Special Equipment and Aids for Living)
(formerly known as Possum Users' Association)
27 Thames House, 140 Battersea Park Road, London SW11 (Tel: 01-622 3738).
SEQUAL runs a most inspired and imaginative vehicle scheme for its members. The organisation owns a number of specially adapted Mini vans and Commer vans which are placed strategically around the British Isles. Each vehicle is loaned to a particular member with the condition that they allow other disabled people in their area to borrow it provided they have their own driver. It is expected that those using the vehicles pay for petrol and general maintenance and SEQUAL pays tax (where applicable) and insurance. Such a scheme provides disabled people with their own specialised and personal transport at relatively small cost. For further details of SEQUAL *see* page 326.

Spinal Injuries Association
Yeoman's House, 76 St James's Lane, Muswell Hill, London N10.
The SIA links paraplegics and tetraplegics, providing information on spinal cord injury and rehabilitation. The Association is expert in the problems of mobility and the needs of disabled drivers and, in our view, outstanding in the provision of relevant and practical information.

Through their LINK Scheme SIA are able to put members in touch with each other for mutual help and encouragement. In matters of mobility this can be particularly helpful, with some members being prepared to show the car adaptations which they have found useful whilst encouraging new drivers to try out the controls before committing themselves to inappropriate conversions. For further details of SIA *see* page 328.

Welsh Disabled Motorists Club
32 Caerau Road, Ely, Cardiff CF5 5JQ (Tel: Cardiff (0222) 591284).
The WDMC is a member of the Disabled Motorists' Federation and is affiliated to the Wales Council for the Disabled. The Club operates over a wide area of Wales but concentrates its activities mainly in South Wales. It provides practical advice, services and information for individual disabled motorists and also seeks to improve conditions and services for disabled motorists generally. Assessment of disabled drivers and their potential abilities can be arranged by appointment. The Club works closely with other organisations having similar aims.

Help with Travel Costs

CONCESSIONARY FARES

Local authorities have powers to operate a concessionary fares scheme for travel on local buses – free or at reduced rates – and disabled people may benefit under these schemes. To find out what concessions you may be entitled to locally ask your social worker or enquire at the Town Hall.

ATTENDING OR VISITING HOSPITAL

Those people who are hospital in-patients or out-patients and who are drawing supplementary benefit or family income supplement, or who are on a low income, and who must attend hospital for treatment, may have their fares and petrol costs paid to and from hospital. If your fares are paid, and the hospital agrees that you need someone to travel with you, your escort's fares will be paid as well. For further details and for the application form see DHSS leaflet H 11.

If you are not the patient, but you are visiting someone in hospital, you should ask your social security office if you can get help with your fares.

Fares of schoolchildren may be met by the local education authority.

EMPLOYMENT TRAVEL

Assistance with fares is available to severely disabled people in ordinary employment who, because of their disability, incur excessive costs in travelling to work, for example, by having to use taxis. (*See* Section 7.)

Mobility Equipment

There is a wide range of aids to mobility available, including walking aids, grab rails, stair lifts (including a 'stair driver' for independent negotiation of stairs whilst in a wheelchair), hoists, ramps and wheelchairs. Detailed information on this equipment can be obtained from: Disabled Living Foundation, 380–384 Harrow Road, London W9 2HU (Tel: 01-289 6111). (*See also* Section 3.) Wheelchairs are normally obtained from appliance centres (*see* below) whereas walking aids are more generally arranged through the district nurse, health visitor or occupational therapist. For further details on provision of aids *see* Section 3.

WHEELCHAIRS

If a wheelchair is needed for a short time – for example, because of a broken leg – the hospital arranging for treatment will also arrange to provide a wheelchair. If a wheelchair is needed for long-term or permanent use, the Department of Health and Social Security supply and maintain it (through appliance centres) on the recommendation of a hospital consultant or general practitioner. The first step, therefore, if a wheelchair is required is to see the general practitioner. Ideally the doctor should arrange for a home visit by the local authority occupational therapist to assess the need not only in relation to the person but also the home environment. The doctor sends the recommendation to the local appliance centre of the DHSS who will arrange the supply. (The Red Cross will sometimes loan wheelchairs to tide people over where there may be a gap of provision.)

The non-powered wheelchairs supplied by the DHSS include not only the more conventional types but also hand and foot propelled tricycles. Their range covers the needs of all ages. More than one non-powered wheelchair may be supplied if these are really necessary – for example, one needed for home and the other for work or school use, or two different types required for differing uses, although the DHSS tries to provide one that will be suitable for all needs. Most wheelchairs can be equipped with accessories or alternative items, such as leg rests, backrest extensions and trays.

ELECTRIC WHEELCHAIRS

The Department of Health and Social Security also provides two different types of powered wheelchairs on the recommendation of the general practitioner or hospital consultant. For those who are unable to walk and unable themselves to propel an ordinary wheelchair, they will provide a powered occupant-controlled wheelchair for indoor use providing the home circumstances are such that the user will benefit from having a powered wheelchair; these wheelchairs are for use indoors or within the grounds of the residence. For those who need to be pushed out of doors in a wheelchair, but whose usual attendant cannot push an ordinary wheelchair because of the hilliness of the area or because of health reasons, the DHSS will provide an attendant-operated powered wheelchair. If the DHSS provides a powered wheelchair, they will also provide the batteries and arrange maintenance; when necessary they will also provide a shed to house the chair.

The Department of Health and Social Security does not provide powered outdoor wheelchairs for control by the occupant.

Leaflet HB 1 *Help for Handicapped People* lists appliance centres and certain details of services and facilities.

WHEELCHAIR HIRE PURCHASE

Motability
Boundary House, 91–93 Charterhouse Street, London EC1M 6BT (Tel: 01-253 1211).
Will arrange favourable hire-purchase terms with a small deposit for certain electric vehicles including wheelchairs from: Batricar, BEC Mobility, Carters (J and A), Downs Surgical Ltd, Everest and Jennings, Lion Rock Holdings Ltd, Meyra-Rehab, Neill and Bennett, NV Distributors Ltd (Dudley Power Plus), Raymar, Vessa.

REGULATIONS REGARDING THE USE OF POWERED WHEELCHAIRS ON PAVEMENTS

Since 1970 it has been legal to use certain powered wheelchairs on pavements, footpaths and footways, to cross roads in them and drive along where there are no pedestrian sidewalks. No driving test, licence or number plates are required. This concession applies whether vehicles are controlled by the occupant or by an attendant and to disabled adults or children using mechanically propelled tricycles, powered wheelchairs or powered 'Go-Karts'. However, if a qualifying vehicle is being used during the hours of darkness, on a road which had no pedestrian sidewalk, it must have a single white light in front and a single red light plus a red reflector at the back, and both lights and reflector must be in good working order. Otherwise lights need not be fitted and no lights are needed if the vehicle is being used during the hours of darkness on a pavement or crossing a road from one pavement to another.

To qualify for this concession the vehicle must be incapable of being driven faster than four miles per hour on level ground under its own power. Such a vehicle must have an efficient braking system in good working order, capable of bringing it to rest and holding it stationary on a gradient of 1 in 5. The vehicle's unladen weight must not be more than 250 lb.

Those vehicles which qualify are exempt from the compulsory insurance requirements of the Road Traffic Act 1960. However, the disabled person would do well to consider carefully the desirability of obtaining suitable insurance cover.

WHEELCHAIR INSURANCE

James Yarrow, Young & Company Ltd
327 Station Road, Harrow, Middlesex HA1 2XN
(Tel: 01-863 5577).
This company is able to arrange cover against various
eventualities. Basic cover includes the following:
(a) Loss or damage to your wheelchair and/or its
accessories by accidental damage, fire or theft
(excluding the first £5 of any claim). Maximum
sum insured £2,500.
(b) Legal liability for accidental damage to the
property of, or injury to, third parties, arising
from the use of the wheelchair. Indemnity
against any one accident £500,000.
(c) 'Get You Home' – travelling expenses to your
residence following accidental damage, fire or
theft of your wheelchair. Up to £100 one event.
Maximum amount in any one period of insurance £500.
The company is usually able to arrange with insurers,
on payments of an additional premium, for the
wheelchair to be covered during holidays abroad.

Mobility by Rail

SPECIAL FACILITIES – TRAINS

(*See* under country headings in Section 10 for special
rail services in Belgium, Holland and Norway.)

In recent years there has been considerable improvement in the design of trains, and British Rail
have been at some pains to provide and incorporate
reasonable facilities for disabled passengers. However, before setting out on a journey, it has to be
borne in mind that it is still often necessary for
wheelchair-bound passengers to travel in the guard's
van, and toilet facilities on trains, for practical
reasons, are still and are likely to remain inaccessible
to wheelchair travellers in this country.

BRITISH RAIL

Motorail
The Motorail network criss-crosses the country and
terminals are located at Aberdeen, Bristol, Carlisle,
Crewe, Edinburgh, Inverness, London, Newcastle,
Newton Abbot, Penzance, St Austell, Stirling.

It can be rather expensive as normal Motorail fares
apply, however holders of British Rail's Disabled
Persons Railcard making a Motorail journey on
specified year-round services, whether the driver or a
passenger, will qualify for a £10 discount on a return,
or £5 on a single journey. The British Motorail
system links up with similar rail systems throughout

Europe. The Car Ferry Centre, Victoria Station,
London SW1 (Tel: 01-730 3440), will advise on Continental Motorail services.

It is important that you give good notice to British
Rail (or any other railway company) of any special
help needed in transferring from your car on to a
train and vice versa in order that they may be able to
help where this is needed. For British Rail this would
be the Area Manager at your departure station and
the details most needed are:
(a) date and time of train;
(b) destination station and any intermediate changing points;
(c) nature of disablement (*i.e.* wheelchair-bound,
can be transferred to seat, can walk with aid of
sticks, blind, etc.);
(d) any special need to be accommodated near a
lavatory;
(e) if wheelchair is required at stations;
(f) accompanied or travelling alone.
A number of facilities and services are provided for
disabled people travelling by train. At most Motorail
terminals standard wheelchairs are available and at
larger stations, *e.g.* Kings Cross, Paddington, Crewe,
Edinburgh and York, British Rail are able to provide
a 'Mobyle' folding wheelchair for those people who
may be transferred to a seat. They can be lifted with
the occupant into a coach and pushed along the
gangway/corridor to a seat.

Full details of Motorail services, routes and fares
are contained in a special brochure obtainable from
Travel Centres or stations or from British Rail
appointed travel agents.

INTER-CITY SERVICES – NEW FACILITIES

In the latest design of first-class coaches there is a
removable seat and table at one end of the saloon.
This enables a wheelchair traveller to stay in their
own chair, provided it does not exceed 622 mm ($24\frac{1}{2}$
in.) in width. Vestibule doors and areas afford access
from the platform by means of lightweight ramps
kept at stations served by the trains. Inter-City 125
High Speed Trains also offer this facility.

Half the ordinary second-class single or return fare
is charged to a disabled person travelling in this way.
The same rate is charged for one travelling companion. Prior notice is needed for these facilities to be
available.

In the latest second-class coaches a table has been
omitted from one group of seats nearest the entrance
and next to the lavatory. These seats are being
especially signed and, if needed, should be requested
when reserving a seat.

INTER-CITY SERVICES – OTHER TRAINS

On many other Inter-City trains, coaches also have wide doors for easier access and handy grab rails, but unfortunately it is not possible to travel while remaining in a wheelchair unless you are prepared to travel in the guard's van. For those people who can transfer to a seat, it is often possible for a wheelchair to be taken on board the train and positioned close to the train seat. Some British Rail stations also have special narrow chairs for carrying people aboard trains to transfer to a normal seat. Otherwise wheelchairs are carried free of charge in the guard's van.

TRAVELLING IN THE GUARD'S VAN

If you have to travel in the guard's van because you cannot leave your wheelchair, it is necessary to obtain a permit unless you have a Disabled Person's Railcard. There are separate forms and permits for frequent travellers covering journeys over a period (Form BR 25559/1) and for single journeys (Form BR 25559/2). The traveller (and a companion) is charged half the second-class single or return fare.

INTER-CITY SLEEPERS

Second-class compartments have twin berths, one above the other, and if a disabled person is travelling alone the lower berth may be reserved.

First-class single-berth compartments have communicating doors with the adjacent compartment which may be convenient for a severely disabled traveller who needs to be in close contact with a companion. However, normal berth fees apply.

Guide dogs accompanying blind people may be taken into sleeper compartments if prior booking is made and suitable space is available. Normally the blind passenger and guide dog travel in a single-berth compartment, but pay only a second-class fare and berth fee.

LAVATORIES

An increasing number of main line stations now have lavatories accessible to wheelchair users. British Rail is now part of the National Key Scheme – for details *see* page 186.

Regrettably, lavatories on trains are still all inaccessible to wheelchair-bound travellers.

TRAVELLING REFRESHMENTS

On a number of trains full meals are served to passengers in first-class seats, otherwise drinks and light refreshments may often be brought to passengers in their seats in either class.

Guide dogs may be taken into Travellers-Fare buffets and restaurants at stations and on trains, at the discretion of the manager or chief steward.

FARES FOR BLIND PEOPLE

Only one adult fare is charged when a registered blind person travels with a companion for any of the following purposes:
(a) on business;
(b) to organisations for blind people to discuss a change of employment or training facilities for employment;
(c) to hospitals or specialists for treatment or consultation;
(d) between the blind person's home and the Centre at which he/she is receiving rehabilitation, education or training.

Only ordinary single, ordinary return and season tickets are covered by this facility.

DISABLED PERSON'S RAILCARD

This card entitles people who qualify to half-price rail fares. In order to qualify, permanently and severely disabled people must be:
(a) registered with their local authority as blind or partially sighted;
(b) receiving attendance allowance or mobility allowance;
(c) receiving private car allowance or a DHSS car or be the driver of a DHSS three-wheeler, or be leasing or buying a vehicle through Motability;
(d) receiving War or Service Disablement Pension for 80 per cent or more disability;
(e) entitled to Industrial Disablement Benefit (where paid with Constant Attendance Allowance).

Full details about the railcard, including how to apply, are contained in the leaflet *Half Price Train Travel for Disabled People*, available from stations, travel centres, and at any Post Office. For details of the leaflet *British Rail and Disabled Travellers*, *see* below.

Books and Publications

AA Guide for the Disabled gives information on accommodation throughout the British Isles, with very detailed descriptions of the amenities, *i.e.* steps if any, number of rooms on the ground floor, type of doors, turning space in toilets, room service, etc. There is also information on suitable restaurants, parking and all the usual motoring information. This guide is available free to members, but there is a charge of 95p to non-members. Available from the Automobile Association (Hotel and Information Services Department), Fanum House, Basingstoke,

Hampshire RG21 2EA (Tel: Basingstoke (0256) 20123). The general guide *Hotels and Restaurants in Britain* includes the access symbol for appropriate establishments.

Access to Cars (1982) published by Age Concern England and available from its Training Department, 60 Pitcairn Road, Mitcham, Surrey CR4 3LL. Price £9.75 including postage and packing. A training kit devised as a basic training course for volunteer drivers, relatives and indeed anyone faced with the problem of assisting frail or disabled people in and out of a vehicle. Incorporating slides and a written commentary, *Access to Cars* can be used independently or in conjunction with formal training provided by occupational therapists, the Red Cross, or St John Ambulance. It gives detailed guidance, illustrated step by step, on various techniques which can be used to manœuvre the frail or disabled person in and out of the vehicle.

British Rail and Disabled Travellers. This leaflet was issued in conjunction with the Joint Committee on Mobility for the Disabled and includes useful information on Inter-City sleeper and Motorail services and concessions for blind passengers. Available from the Royal Association for Disability and Rehabilitation, 25 Mortimer Street, London W1N 8AB. Price 15p.

Access to the Southern Region. A new guide issued by British Rail Southern giving details of all railway stations in that area is now available from RADAR as above. Please send a stamped addressed envelope (22 cm × 11 cm).

Disabled Drivers' Association Information Leaflets These DDA leaflets are currently available free to fully paid up members.
Titles include:

Ferry Concessions: a booklet.

Mobility is the Key to Independence: a brief review of vehicles and conversions.

Buying your car: a guide for disabled drivers and passengers. Available on receipt of a large s.a.e. from the DDA, Ashwellthorpe, Norwich NR16 1EX.

Disabled Drivers' Motor Club Handbook. This useful publication presents its information in a succinct and logical way. It ranges not only over specific guidance on motoring questions, but touches on wider issues such as benefits and allowances and helpful organisations in the field of disability. The format does not permit a great amount of detail, but

the basic clues are provided for you to follow up. The Handbook costs £1 plus postage and packing (free to members on receipt of a 10 in. × 7 in. envelope with 33p stamps) and is available from the Disabled Drivers' Motor Club Ltd, 1a Dudley Gardens, Ealing, London W13 (Tel: 01-840 1515).

Disabled People and the Tyne and Wear Metro – a Field Evaluation. The evaluation provided by the Handicapped Persons Research Unit, Newcastle upon Tyne Polytechnic, describes in detail this first rapid transit system designed and built within the United Kingdom which specifically includes provision for disabled and elderly people from the early planning stages. A description is given of the planning and design decisions that have made it accessible to people with a wide range of disabilities. Sketch layouts for each station of interchange together with an outline of the ticketing system are provided. The report is to be updated and extended when further stations are opened or major changes made. Special versions of the report (audio or tactile) for the blind and partially sighted are planned. Available from the Handicapped Persons Research Unit, Newcastle upon Tyne Polytechnic, 1 Coach Lane, Coach Lane Campus, Newcastle upon Tyne NE7 7TW (Tel: Newcastle upon Tyne (0632) 664061). Price £4.50 including postage and packing.

Door to Door, A Guide to Transport for Disabled People. This is a free 72-page guide published in 1982 by the Department of Transport. It is admirably laid out and remarkably wide ranging, covering benefits, mobility aids, personal and public transport (local, national, and international). Naturally, in a book of this size, the information is basic – a starting point – but its succinct style permits the inclusion of a huge amount of material, which is accurate and reliable. Appendices give details of organisations which can provide more detailed advice or help, both nationally and locally. Available from Department of Transport, Building 3, *Door to Door Guide*, Freepost, Ruislip, Middlesex HA4 0BR.

Equipment for the Disabled
A series of illustrated books compiled at Mary Marlborough Lodge, Nuffield Orthopaedic Centre, Headington, Oxford OX3 7LD (Tel: Oxford (0865) 750103), and published by the Oxfordshire Health Authority on behalf of the DHSS. Three of the books in the series are listed below. (Others are described on page 63.) Each book is priced at £3.50 plus postage.

Wheelchairs. Information: obtaining a wheelchair, wheelchair assessment, wheelchair features, handling a wheelchair, simple home maintenance, methods of wheelchair propulsion, mobility allowance, VAT exemption, Motability; DHSS *Handbook on wheelchairs* (leaflet MHM 408); summary of 'Notes for guidance' and 'Notes on availability', ALAC addresses, approved repairers' addresses, details of chairs supplied by DHSS: occupant-controlled, push chairs, indoor electric chairs, accessories; commercially available self propelling chairs, push chairs, children's chairs, elevating chairs, sports chairs, electric chairs, cushioning, support systems, chair accessories; movable and portable ramps; step lift; chair carrier; select bibliography; metric comparison tables; addresses/telephone numbers; alphabetical index.

Outdoor Transport. General information: mobility allowance, orange badge scheme, Motability, vehicle hire-purchase and hiring concessions, exemption from VED, motor insurance, concessions available, driving licences, driving tuition and tests, motorists' clubs, information services, transport and escort services, British Rail and disabled travellers, British Airports Authority facilities; choosing a car; car conversions; specially designed cars; control conver-sions; car accessories; transfers and seating; car safety seats; vehicle conversions; wheelchair restraint systems; passenger restraint harnesses; garages, doors and remote-control door operators; pedal and hand-propelled tricycles, electric tricycle, electric scooters; outdoor electric wheelchairs; wheelchair covers; portable ramps; select bibliography; metric comparison tables; addresses/telephone numbers; alphabetical index.

Hoists and Walking Aids. Carry seats; transfer techniques and aids including sliding boards; hoist assessment; portable hoists; overhead hoists, including electric; overhead tracking and gantries; bathroom and hydrotherapy hoists; car hoist; types of slings; slinging techniques; advice on hoist/sling selection. Adult and children's: axillary, elbow and gutter crutches, walking sticks and quadrupods; 'pick-up', folding and pushing walking frame; accessories; standing aids; select bibliography.

Esso Petroleum have published a guide to service stations all over the United Kingdom where disabled people can count on some assistance from the operators. All the Esso stations listed have indicated their

willingness to assist disabled drivers and they will be displaying a blue and white wheelchair symbol in the forecourt. The 47-page booklet is free and copies are available from the Scottish Council on Disability, Princes House, 5 Shandwick Place, Edinburgh EH2 4RG.

How to Push a Wheelchair by David Griffiths and David Wynne, with illustrated sketches by Ross Murcott, gives a lot of useful hints on all aspects of wheelchair usage from pushing to parking and putting it into the boot of a car. Published by the Disabled Motorists' Club, Copthorne Community Hall, Shelton Road, Shrewsbury. Price 17p.

Joint Committee on Mobility for the Disabled (*see* page 159). Publications include: *Disabled People and Driving Licences*; *Orange Badge Scheme for Disabled Drivers and Disabled Passengers*; *Pedestrian Precincts and Disabled People*; *Exemption for Vehicle Excise Duty for Disabled People*; *Transport Act 1978 and Disabled People*; *Use of Powered Wheelchairs on Pavements by Physically Disabled People*. All available from the Royal Association for Disability and Rehabilitation, 25 Mortimer Street, London W1N 8AB. Please include a s.a.e. with your request.

Managing a Wheelchair (1982) published by Age Concern, England and available from its Training Department, 60 Pitcairn Road, Mitcham, Surrey CR4 3LL. Price £9.75 including postage and packing. A training kit suitable for training volunteers, relatives and others who work with elderly and disabled people. Incorporating slides and a written commentary, *Managing a Wheelchair* can be used independently as part of a wider training course.

The kit describes techniques for moving a passenger in and out of a wheelchair and gives advice in manœuvring the chair over a variety of everyday obstacles. Handout diagrams of different wheelchair models are included to give an understanding of the main mechanical features and how these affect handling; there is also advice on maintenance.

Mobility Information Service publications
Copthorne Community Hall, Shelton Road, Shrewsbury, Shropshire SY3 8TD (Tel: Shrewsbury (0743) 68383).

Wheels Under You by David Griffiths. A booklet covering forms of personal transport for handicapped people, aimed chiefly at those who are young or newly disabled. Advice is offered on choosing a car in relation to specific disabilities and on the adaptations required in order to drive a vehicle. Price 40p

including postage and packing (cash with order please).
The MIS leaflets include:

Motoring Accessories	s.a.e.
Hand Controls	s.a.e.
Mobility Information Service	s.a.e
Insurance	s.a.e.
2 and 3 Door Automatics	s.a.e.
Discounts and Concessions	s.a.e.
Wheelchair Accessories	s.a.e.
How to Push a Wheelchair including postage and packing	17p
Road Test: Datsun Cherry	s.a.e.
Road Test: Volvo 66 Estate	s.a.e.
Road Test: Disabled Drivers' Escort	s.a.e.
Road Test: Renault 5 Automatic	s.a.e.
Road Test: Honda Accord Automatic	s.a.e.
Road Test: Vauxhall Chevette Automatic	s.a.e.
Road Test: Mini Metro Automatic	s.a.e.
Road Test: Ford Cortina Automatic 1600 Disabled Drivers' Model	s.a.e.

A complete information pack covering all aspects of the Service and containing a wide selection of manufacturers' and other brochures is available, price £2.50 including postage and packing.

Motoring and Mobility for Disabled People by Ann Darnbrough and Derek Kinrade. This book explores the theme of personal mobility and is the first to cover the subject in real depth. Subjects covered include a run-down on standard cars giving all those measurements not included in the brochures but so necessary to disabled motorists (both drivers and passengers); details of specialist controls including recent innovations; motoring accessories; financial allowances, driving tests and lessons; orange badge scheme, pedestrianisation, problems of incontinence while travelling or simply of being 'caught short'; specialist organisations including Motability; useful books and publications. A further section is devoted to information on wheelchairs and wheelchair accessories. Details are also given on the various buggy-type vehicles available. Information for children describes not only standard wheelchairs but also a wide range of play vehicles including trolleys, karts and stylish racing-car-type vehicles for play and mobility at ground level. Published by and obtainable from RADAR, 25 Mortimer Street, London W1N 8AB (Tel: 01-637 5400). Price £2.50 including postage and packing.

Peterborough Disabled Drivers' Club Handbook. This is a locally produced guide which not only provides information about Peterborough's facilities for the motorist, but also examines more general matters such as the orange badge scheme; buying, adapting, licensing, insuring, driving, financing, and maintaining a car; wheelchairs; holidays and recreation, and many other useful matters of interest to the disabled motorist. The handbook is free to members, otherwise £1.50 including postage. Available from the Club's treasurer and membership secretary: Sylvia Goodacre, 17 Pembroke Avenue (Lady Lodge Estate), Orton Longueville, Peterborough PE2 0EY (Tel: Peterborough (0733) 031527).

RAC Guide and Handbook includes the access symbol where appropriate and details of facilities in motorway areas. Available from RAC, RAC House, Lansdowne Road, Croydon CR9 2JA (Tel: 01-686 2525) or from local offices. Price to members £4.50 including postage and packing.

RADAR (Royal Association for Disability and Rehabilitation)
25 Mortimer Street, London W1N 8AB (Tel: 01-637 5400).
Produces an invaluable publications list, free of charge, containing a number of books, pamphlets and other literature relating to mobility and travel, as well as the whole range of disability information. Send a large s.a.e. with your request.

REMAP Year-book. First published in 1982, this year-book of the Rehabilitation Engineering Movement Advisory Panels (*see* page 60) reflects the ingenious work of the organisation in designing aids to meet individual needs, and includes examples from the REMAP case lists. These include a number of mobility aids, modifications and adaptations with helpful illustrations. Most importantly, the year-book contains details of local REMAP contacts, whose help can be sought where a problem arising from disability cannot be adequately solved by any standard aid.

Published by and available from RADAR, 25 Mortimer Street, London W1N 8AB (Tel: 01-637 5400). Price £1 plus 30p postage and packing.

See Section 9 on Holidays in Britain for Access Guides.

Disabled Living Foundation Information Sheets
380–384 Harrow Road, London W9 2HU (Tel: 01-289 6111).
The DLF Information Service provides regularly updated, detailed information lists on aids, equipment and services for disabled people. These include:

List 5: *Hoists and Lifting Equipment*
List 8: *Transport* (publications, allowances and concessions, driving controls and conversions, accessories, insurance, etc.)
List 9: *Walking Aids*
List 10: *Wheelchairs* (adult)
List 15: *Children's Aids and Equipment* (including wheelchairs, pushchairs and other mobility aids).

Information is provided free of charge to members of the general public in response to individual requests or, on a regular basis, by subscription. For further details *see* page 53.

Scottish Council on Disability Information Sheets
5 Shandwick Place, Edinburgh EH2 4RG (Tel: 031-229 8632).
A range of information is available including:

List 5: *Hoists and Lifting Equipment*
List 11: *Transport – Vehicles, Accessories and Adaptations*
List 12: *Transport – Information and Regulations*
List 13: *Walking Aids*
List 14: *Wheelchairs* (including battery operated)

For further details of this service *see* page 55.

Northern Ireland Council for the Handicapped
2 Annadale Avenue, Belfast BT7 3JH (Tel: Belfast (0232) 640011).
NICH has published a *Guide to Mobility Assistance for Disabled People in Northern Ireland*. Topics covered include: access guides, parking badges, car seats and hoists, car discount schemes, hand controls, mobility allowance, Motability, public transport, wheelchairs, travel to work, options for trike drivers, remote control garage doors, road tax exemption, discounts on tyres, car ferry concessions, organisations concerned with mobility and a list of relevant publications.

HOLIDAYS IN BRITAIN

One man's holiday is another's assault course, particularly where there are difficult access problems, but the possibilities and opportunities of activity holidays for handicapped people are growing every year. Facilities are becoming available to suit almost every individual taste, and to cater for a wide range of disabilities. Many of these facilities are listed below, but no handicapped holidaymaker should be put off if his particular desert island is not mentioned. Increasingly, standard tour operators, holiday organisers and others are accepting disabled participants on an integrated basis. Similarly, many ordinary accommodation guides now use the access symbol to denote establishments with suitable access facilities. The golden rule is to contact the airline/railway/ferry/accommodation well in advance, stating the nature of the disability and mentioning any special requirements. If is, of course, essential that a disabled person provides him/herself with all necessary equipment and does not rely on hotels to provide these extras. For those who require personal help it is essential that they are accompanied by a friend, as staff in hotels, guest houses and holiday camps cannot give this type of personal assistance. On the other hand, there are a number of group holiays for unattended disabled people where there are voluntary helpers to provide the necessary help (*see* information on voluntary organisations on page 176).

(*See* Section 8 for general travel advice and ferry concessions, and Section 10 for information on air travel. Section 10 also has information on helpful travel agents, etc.)

Finance

Under the Chronically Sick and Disabled Persons Act 1970, the social services departments of the local authorities are empowered to assist financially, registered disabled people to have a holiday and, where necessary, to suggest suitable locations and provide transport. However, the amount of help given varies greatly from area to area. Relevant charities and trade and professional organisations may also be approached for help and many of these bodies own holiday homes, bungalows, caravans, etc., which are available at very reasonable rates (*see* Voluntary Organisations on page 176, and also Section 16).

The Family Fund may help with holidays for severely handicapped children, under 16, who normally live with their families. This Fund is at present administered by the Joseph Rowntree Memorial Trust, PO Box 50, York YO1 1UY.

Insurance

For further details *see* page 189 in Section 10.

Interest and Specialist Holidays

The Askrigg Foundation
Low Mill Youth Centre, Askrigg, Leyburn, North Yorkshire DL8 3HZ (Tel: Wensleydale (0969) 50432).
This residential youth centre is in the heart of Wensleydale, situated in the Dales National Park on the edge of the village. Low Mill offers facilities for groups of young people to spend a weekend or a midweek period in a rural community. A special feature of Low Mill is the New Wing which is specially equipped for physically disabled visitors. The Centre is keen to include handicapped people with those who consider themselves fit.

Bookings must be made in groups – 20 is the minimum (26 maximum), and 10 in the New Wing as a minimum (14 maximum).

Price: Able-bodied accommodation £75, New Wing £50.

The interest from a capital bursary account is used to provide free places for 'particularly deserving' youngsters. The Warden would be glad to advise.

Bendrigg Lodge
Old Hutton, Kendal, Cumbria LA8 0NR (Tel: Kendal (0539) 23766).
The centre is open for use by a wide range of groups and organisations including mentally and physically handicapped people, one-parent families, com-

munity associations, community contact police officers, intermediate treatment groups, pensioners, pre-retirement clubs and Manpower Service groups.

The building is a converted hunting lodge with seven acres of land, fully equipped to take one or two mixed groups of up to 40 people for stays of two to ten days. The grounds consist of 4½ acres of woodland, a smallholding and a games field. The wood contains an adventure playground and campsite. There is a range of facilities and equipment for disabled people.

Groups using the centre are usually assisted with catering and have their own leaders who plan for their visit with the Bendrigg staff. A wide range of activities is available to groups, led by qualified staff. They include fell walking, basic rock climbing, caving, canoeing, sailing, horse riding, grass skiing, archery, orienteering, swimming, camping, photography, painting, drawing, music workshops, craftwork, weaving, drama, games and living skills. Other options may be available.

The Brecon Beacons Mountain Centre
Brecon Beacons National Park, Glamorgan Street, Brecon, Powys LD3 7DP (Tel: Brecon (0874) 4437). A centre from which to enjoy the beauties of the National Park. Wheelchairs have access in all parts of the building. Suggestions for local walks with wheelchairs can be obtained from the information desk.

Calvert Trust Adventure Centre
Little Crosthwaite, Underskiddaw, Keswick, Cumbria CA12 4QD (Tel: Keswick (0596) 72254). The Trust was formed to enable disabled people to enjoy the Lake District National Park in the same way as able-bodied people. The Adventure Centre is sited near Keswick in an area of outstanding natural beauty overlooking Bassenthwaite Lake and below the mountain range of Skiddaw. It is open from mid-January to mid-November for archery, angling, birdwatching, riding, hill walking, mountaineering and nature trails, while between April and October sailing and canoeing are added to the programme. Camping is also available as well as orienteering.

Included in the equipment and materials available for use by visitors are Wayfarer dinghies, a Drascombe lugger, and single-seater, four double-seater and two Canadian canoes. Two 14-seater Bedford Dormobiles provide transport and a large number of books form an excellent library. An indoor riding school, heated swimming pool and games room are also part of the facilities. Accommodation is in two, three and four-bedded rooms. Disabled

visitors should bring a helper with them if their disability warrants it.

Costs in 1984 were £100 for a six-day course, £68 for a four-day course, £34 for a two-day course (weekend), all plus VAT. These prices include food and tuition. Further information from the Warden.

Northumbria Calvert Trust
Kielder Adventure Centre, Low Craneleugh, Kielder Water, Hexham NE48 1BS (Tel: Bellingham (0660) 50232).
Readers may well be familiar with the Calvert Trust and the Adventure Centre at Keswick. Now the Kielder Adventure Centre of the Northumbria Calvert Trust is following in the same footsteps and will follow similar pursuits. In 1983 day activities were offered and residential facilities are planned for 1984. Activities include: guided tours, archery skills, navigation and orienteering, rock climbing, camping, fishing, swimming, sailing, canoeing, riding, pony driving, bird watching and nature walks. Costs for residential courses are likely to be similar to the Calvert Trust at Keswick.

Multi-Activity Adventure Centre
YMCA National Centre, Fairthorne Manor, Curdridge, Southampton, Hampshire SO3 2GH (Tel: Botley (048 92) 5228).
Contact Mr W. J. Wilson, Director. Offers one-week courses (and weekend courses in the off-season) in sailing, canoeing, archery, riding and golf. Qualified instruction. Age group 10 to 18 years. Handicapped guests should be escorted. Excellent adaptations include ramps, special toilets and ground-floor dormitories. Total accommodation for 190 in dormitories, 120 in tents.

The Pines Trust
Contact for bookings: Mrs Lewis, The Bungalow, The Pines, Bishop's Castle, Shropshire (Tel: Shrewsbury (0743) 222242).
The Pines house and grounds on the outskirts of the little town of Bishop's Castle in the heart of the border hill country of southern Shropshire provides opportunities for groups and individual disabled people to enjoy weekends and holidays camping in the house and grounds. Visitors look after themselves with the help of a specially adapted kitchen, lavatory and washing accommodation.

A range of other facilities is available in the surrounding area including fishing, riding, canoeing and gliding.

Charges: Outdoor camping – £1.20 per person over 16 years per night, 60p per person over 6 and under 16 years per night. These charges cover tent pitches and use of indoor washing/toilet/kitchen accommodation. A limited number of four-berth tents are available at a charge of £1 per night. Indoor camping – £1.50 per person over 6 years per night.

Share

Share Centre, Smith's Strand, Shanaghy, nr Lisnaskea, Co. Fermanagh (Tel: Lisnaskea (036 57) 22122).

Share is a residential activity centre, situated on the shores of Upper Lough Erne. It is designed for use by both able-bodied and handicapped people. It is open all year round and in the summer months it concentrates on organised activity holidays for both families and individuals. The Centre occupies a beautiful eight-acre site with direct access to the lake and to an adjacent beach. It has its own jetty from which to canoe, sail or windsurf, and the scores of wooded islands in the lake are ideal for picnics, barbecues and overnight camps.

Spastics Society

Sailing, canoeing and other sports are arranged by the Spastics Society. For further details contact the Sport and Recreation Officer, 16 Fitzroy Square, London W1P 5HQ (Tel: 01-387 9571).

The Trefoil Holiday and Adventure Centre for the Handicapped

Gogarbank, Edinburgh EH12 9DA (Tel: 031-339 3148 (Warden); 031-339 3629 (guests)).

The Centre is set in the countryside seven miles from Edinburgh, and is specially designed to cater for up to 45 physically handicapped people with their helpers, either in groups or as individuals. The house is centrally heated throughout and has a bar, shop, TV room and three well-stocked games rooms; indoor heated pool; minicoach with lift. Rambler cars are available for guests to explore the grounds, gardens and woods. Barbecues and discos are organised; advice is given on suitable outings and other activities.

Rates: High season (1983): £92.50 per person per week, full board, in groups of 10 or more; Low season (November 83 to March 84): £73.50, as above.

Colour brochure and full tariff details from the Warden.

Registered Guide

William Forrester, 1 Belvedere Close (off Manor Road), Guildford, Surrey GU2 6NP (Tel: Guildford (0483) 575401).

William Forrester was the first person in a wheelchair to succeed in becoming a London Tourist Board Registered Guide. He is now also a Round-Britain Tour Guide. Having specialised in history and taught the subject for several years he brings English heritage and traditions to life.

He provides a unique service of particular benefit to the disabled individual or group. Having had to survey the places of interest in and around London and around the country personally he has exact, up-to-the-minute experience of wheelchair accessibility. He knows where that ramp is, what to advise for a visitor and, above all, where those elusive lavatories are! Though many excellent guide books for the disabled visitor exist, it often happens that the site may not have been checked with a wheelchair or that vital information has been omitted.

William likes to help you tailor your visit and itinerary especially to suit you and to accompany you as he is needed. He can also offer an advice service. He will visit you in your hotel to help make an informal plan so that you can get the best from your holiday. If required, slides of the principal places that can be visited in this country will be shown to help you choose what to do. This service particularly benefits those who wish to go their own way yet require accurate and concise information to help them. Or if you prefer, let William plan a special itinerary just for you or your group before you set off.

Fees will be discussed on application.

CAMPING

David Griffiths is an enthusiastic camper with a great deal of experience (good and bad!) which he is prepared to share with other intrepid adventurers. He has camped extensively in the United Kingdom and on the Continent and never allows his wheelchair to stop him, although he admits he has never discovered anyone yet who has managed to erect a tent from a wheelchair! He points out that quite a proportion of Britain's camp sites have accessible washing and toilet facilities, and on the Continent there are few inaccessible camp sites.

David has compiled a number of guides to camp sites including Britain, West Germany, Switzerland, Holland and Spain. The membership subscription to *Camping for the Disabled* is £2 covering a family of up to five members. It entitles you to receive all camp site lists published by them and a reduction in the camp site charges. Contact David at *Camping for the Disabled*, 20 Burton Close, Dawley, Telford, Shropshire TF4 2BX. (Tel: Telford (0952) 507653).

CARAVAN HOLIDAYS

(*See* under Voluntary and Specialist Holiday Organisations.)

COMPUTER HOLIDAY FOR THE DISABLED

Wardle & Wardle MAPs Ltd, 37 University Road, Highfield, Southampton SO2 1TL (Tel: Southampton (0703) 558621).
With the support of the Department of Industry this holiday in 1983 was available at a cost of £70 per week instead of £160. This is for tuition, the use of the computers and self-catering accommodation in Clarkson House (*see* page 103, Southampton University). While this holiday was only a pilot scheme it is hoped that further such opportunities will be available in future years. It would be worth enquiring.

RIDING

Riding for the Disabled Association
National Headquarters, Avenue R, National Agricultural Centre, Kenilworth, Warwickshire CV8 2LY (Tel: Coventry (0203) 56107).
Riding holidays for disabled children and adults are organised by headquarters and local groups of individuals. Priority is given to those who ride with an RDA member group. For details of holidays and for member groups write to the above address.

Knight Bridge Riding School
Sway, Lymington, Hampshire (Tel: Lymington (059 068) 2271).
Contact Mrs T. M. Harris. Weekly courses and holidays all year except Christmas, for those aged 10 to 18. Suitable ponies available for disabled children. Accommodation at centre in four-berth bedrooms or at a nearby farmhouse. Camping and caravanning facilities nearby in the New Forest. Hats provided.

SAILING AND CRUISING

(*See also* the Spinal Injuries Association in Section 16 for details of their narrow boat *Kingfisher*.)

Medina Valley Centre
Dodnor Lane, Newport, Isle of Wight PO30 5TE (Tel: Newport (0983) 522195).
We are informed that the Centre is designed in such a way that handicapped people have few mobility difficulties. The Director and his staff are always glad to help staff who bring organised groups.

Groups can use the Centre as a base for their own activities on the Isle of Wight, or they can join in with Centre organised activities which include sailing, art courses, wildlife and environmental studies, and a programme of channel cruises. Sailing courses for disabled people are provided using purpose-designed single-seat Trimaran and Seastar dinghies.

The Centre is run as a Christian home and some time is given each day to examining Christian beliefs. Prices vary according to type of course, but start at £148 per seven-day stay (1984 price – including accommodation and VAT).

Staffordshire Narrowboats Ltd
The Wharf, Newcastle Road, Stone, Staffordshire ST15 8JW (Tel: Stone (0785) 816871) or Blake's Canal Cruisers (Tel: Wroxham (060 53) 3221).
Doubloon is a 'family' boat for those who want to take a cruising holiday while also having special facilities for a disabled family or group member. There is full access throughout for most wheelchairs plus other useful adaptations including a lift and special toilet facilities. *Doubloon* is centrally based at Stone on the Trent and Mersey Canal, giving access to the Cheshire Ring, the Four Counties Ring and the Caldon Canal.

Peter Le Marchant Trust
Colston Bassett House, Colston Bassett, Nottingham NG12 3FE (Tel: Kinoulton (094 97) 205).
The Peter Le Marchant Trust arranges free day trips and short holiday trips for handicapped people of all ages on their broadbeam boats, *Symphony* and *Serenade*. *Symphony* is used for day trips and can take 28 people including helpers, while *Serenade* provides the short holiday trips and can carry 12 handicapped people, plus wheelchairs if necessary. Each boat is equipped with hydraulic lifts, large shower and toilet areas, resuscitation equipment and radio telephones. All trips take place between April and October from the Derby Road moorings at Loughborough. For details apply to Clare Hanmer, Trustee.

SKIING

The British Ski Club for the Disabled
Corton House, Corton, nr Warminster, Wiltshire (Tel: Warminster (0985) 50321).
For further details *see* page 227 in Section 11.

GENERAL STUDY COURSES

A wide range of educational courses is available, including some with facilities for disabled people, details of which are published every January and August by the National Institute of Adult Education, De Montfort House, 19B De Montfort Street, Leicester LE1 7GE (Tel: Leicester (0533) 551451) in *Residential Short Courses*. Price 90p inclusive of postage and packing.

The following colleges and course centres are among those which can accept some partially disabled students for suitable courses. In general, this does not mean that these centres are suitable for students who cannot walk at all, although there may be some facilities, *e.g.* ground-floor bedrooms and lifts.

Those who need personal help would need to be accompanied. However, Maryland College does have special facilities for non-ambulant disabled students and its Principal will give further details. Intending students should indicate the nature of their disability and their special needs when applying for a place. Early application is strongly recommended since suitable accommodation is usually limited.

The Earnley Concourse
Nr Chichester, Sussex PO20 7HL (Tel: Bracklesham Bay (0243) 670392/670326).
For those aged 16 plus. A variety of courses including painting, music, crafts, yoga, caring for antiques and modern languages (French, German, Spanish and Italian).

Halsway Manor Society Ltd
Crowcombe, nr Taunton, Somerset (Tel: Crowcombe (098 48) 274).
Folk holiday weeks.

The Hill Residential College
Pen-y-Pound, Abergavenny, Gwent NP7 7RP (Tel: Abergavenny (0873) 5221).
Courses include pottery, crafts, history, social science, languages, flower arranging, anthropology and nature courses.

Knuston Hall
Irchester, Wellingborough, Northamptonshire (Tel: Rushden (0933) 312104). Contact Mr I. F. Fraser, Principal.
Short residential courses all year. Subjects include arts, literature, music, archaeology, education, crafts and languages. For those aged 18 plus.

Maryland College
Woburn, Milton Keynes MK17 9JD (Tel: Woburn (052 525) 688).
Gardening, architecture, photography, languages, nature studies, writing, lace making, painting and art, antiques, film making, crafts and literature courses.

Millfield Village of Education
Millfield School, Street, Somerset (Tel: Street (045 84) 42291 ext. 45).
In addition to 250 courses, and over 60 sport and

creative activities, there is also a communication course for young hearing impaired people and their families.

Westham Adult Residential College
Barford, Warwickshire CV35 8DP (Tel: Barford (0926) 624206).
Painting, literature, languages, music and other courses.

FIELD STUDIES AND OUTDOOR PURSUITS

Churchtown Farm Field Studies Centre
Lanlivery, Bodmin, Cornwall (Tel: Bodmin (0208) 872148).
This Centre provides field study and linked education/adventure holiday courses for all types of handicapped children and adults. Accommodation is in a mixture of purpose-built residential blocks and converted, traditional stone barns. There is a well-equipped laboratory, library and photographic darkroom as well as a range of audio-visual aids. A feature of the development is an indoor heated swimming pool. All the buildings and facilities are linked by the imaginative use of ramps and a covered concourse. Churchtown Farm can accommodate 50 students plus the necessary visiting staff in small student and staff bedrooms. All the accommodation has been specifically designed for the handicapped visitor.

Courses are provided in natural sciences, rural studies, adventure pursuits including sailing, canoeing, rock climbing and a wide variety of leisure activities. The Centre is situated close to the coast, river and moor and has its own nature reserve and nature trail. There is an educational farm which includes animals, greenhouses and a kitchen garden.

Groups may attend with their own teachers and/or care staff. The Centre is able to take single bookings but this will depend on the degree of care required by the individual.

Transport is available both for courses and to collect parties from the local railway station. Courses start and finish on Wednesdays. Applications should be made to the Warden, either by heads of schools or centres or by private individuals.

The charge for a one-week course in 1984 including all residential and tuition fees is £88 for those under 18 years or in receipt of full-time education, and £110 for adults. Visiting staff accompanying students, accommodation fee only £64.

Preston Montford Field Centre
Montford Bridge, Shrewsbury SY4 1DX (Tel: Shrewsbury (0743) 850380).

Painting, design, flower illustration, creative writing, photography, local history, architecture, heraldry and natural history.

The Scottish Field Studies Association Ltd

Kindrogan Field Centre, Enochdhu, Blairgowrie, Perthshire PH10 7PG (Tel: Strathardle (025 081) 286).

The Association is interested in encouraging disabled people to use the Centre. However, they point out that their facilities are somewhat limited especially access for wheelchairs. Notwithstanding these difficulties the Association is keen to arrange special courses for groups of disabled people. It would be possible to adapt courses like 'Natural History in the Highlands' and 'Exploring Tayside'. A wide range of environmental and countryside courses are arranged – the programme is a delight to browse through.

Quaker Workcamps

Friends House, Euston Road, London NW1 2BJ (Tel: 01-387 3601).

A programme of about 20 international workcamps is arranged each year, in which a group of people come together for a couple of weeks to live and work together on some socially useful project (children's playschemes, in hospitals, manual work, etc.). It is not necessary to have any connection with Quakers to take part. Disabled volunteers are welcome to apply and will be given advice as to the most suitable workcamp for each individual.

HOLIDAYS FOR CHILDREN

Association For All Speech Impaired Children (AFASIC)

347 Central Markets, Smithfield, London EC1A 9NH (Tel: 01-236 3632/6487).

AFASIC organises activity week holidays every summer in which volunteers and children are linked on a one-to-one basis. Details from Mr J. Richards, Chairman, AFASIC Creative and Outdoor Activities subcommittee, 21 Rhos Avenue, Middleton, Manchester M24 1EG.

BREAK

20 Hooks Hill Road, Sheringham, Norfolk NR26 8NL (Tel: Sheringham (0263) 823170/823025).

Provides a wide range of short-stay residential care, designed to be very flexible and covering most needs from holidays to emergency admissions. Individual and group placements of both mentally and physically handicapped children (including pre-school ages), mentally and multi-handicapped adults and families with special needs. In the case of groups, accompanying staff can be accommodated if re-quired. There are two centres on the Norfolk coast open all the year round and placements can be from long weekends to several weeks. A good ratio of experienced staff is provided giving both day and night cover. Parents are most welcome to accompany their child or children but should know that each centre is organised around the needs of its handicapped guests. However, there is plenty of opportunity for parents to follow an independent programme, leaving their children in the care of staff or alternatively they can join in the programme organised by the centres. A wide range of activities is provided in a holiday atmosphere and these include frequent outings in specially adapted transport. Independence training, counselling, observation and assessments can be embraced if required. Both centres are furnished and decorated like family homes. Escort facilities are available from and to most parts of the country.

Buckets & Spades

Lancaster Road, Hollington, St Leonards on Sea, Sussex TN38 9LX (Tel: Hastings (0424) 52119).

The home is open all the year round, providing short-term holidays for mentally handicapped children up to 18 years who are normally resident at home. January to March is usually reserved for adult mentally handicapped guests.

Inter-School Christian Fellowship

Activities Secretary, 130 City Road, London EC1V 2NJ (Tel: 01-250 1966).

Organises holidays for handicapped and able-bodied young people of 14 plus.

Holiday Care Service

The Service provides a number of information sheets on holidays for disabled children. These include: *Holidays for Mentally and/or Physically Handicapped Children and Young People*; *Special Interest and Activity Holidays Suitable for Disabled Children and Young People*; *Other Holiday Ideas for Mentally or Physically Handicapped Children or Young People*; *Hotels where Parents with Handicapped Children are Welcome*; *Holidays for Unaccompanied Children and Young People*; *Outdoor Activity Holiday Centres Accepting Deaf Young People*; and *Activity Holidays for Sight Impaired Youngsters*.

For further details of Holiday Care Service *see* page 176.

Jane Hodge Holiday Home

Trerhyngyll, Maendy, nr Cowbridge, South Glamorgan CF7 7TN (Tel: Cowbridge (044 63) 2608/2972).

Varied and interesting holidays are provided designed to improve the quality of life, broaden the outlook, strengthen the confidence and encourage the independence of handicapped children. The holidays provided include trips to places of interest, *e.g.* beaches, bird and wildlife sanctuaries, zoos, museums, etc. Amenities include a hydrotherapy swimming pool with aqua roundabouts, a well-equipped playroom, music/television room, lake, roundabouts, putting green and croquet lawn. A full leisure programme is organised under trained supervision. Every application is considered on its merits and there are no fixed age limits. Prices vary in seasons and for other reasons, but as a guide the total cost of a week's holiday for a child during the peak period could be £140. Applications should be made to the Director to obtain a quotation or an acceptance of an intended booking. *See also* Les Evans Holiday Fund for Sick and Handicapped Children, page 202.

Voluntary Council for Handicapped Children
National Children's Bureau, 8 Wakley Street, London EC1V 7QE (Tel: 01-278 9441).
Free fact sheet available on holidays for handicapped children.

HOUSE EXCHANGE SCHEME FOR HOLIDAYS

Handihols
12 Ormonde Avenue, Rochford, Essex SS4 1QW (Tel: Southend-on-Sea (0702) 548257).
Joan Humphrey and Rhona Thring, realising the need, through personal experience, for disabled people to have homely facilities and where possible special adaptations when they are on holiday, have compiled a register of families who wish to exchange their homes for a break, be it a weekend, several days or one or more weeks. There is a registration fee plus £3 for each successful introduction. People and their houses are matched to similar accommodation catering for similar needs as far as possible, so that

the disabled holidaymaker may remain as independent as possible. Please send s.a.e. with enquiries.

VOLUNTARY AND SPECIALIST HOLIDAY ORGANISATIONS

Many of the organisations catering for people with specific handicaps or problems either run their own holiday facilities from caravans and chalets to bigger accommodation, or are able to advise prospective holidaymakers on the type of accommodation where they may enjoy a holiday suited to their needs and their tastes. Some are listed below, but this list is by no means exhaustive. We recommend you look through Section 16 on Helpful Organisations and make enquiries to the appropriate association or group.

Arthritis Care
6 Grosvenor Crescent, London SW1X 7ER (Tel: 01-235 0902).
The Association has five specially adapted holiday centres for the use of members, four in England (Lancashire, Devon, Dorset and Kent) and one in Scotland (Nairn).

The British Association for Sporting and Recreational Activities of the Blind
Mr Frank McFarlane, 11 Ovolow Road, Liverpool L13 3DR (Tel: 051-220 2516).
The Association will provide information on activity or study holidays.

The British Diabetic Association
10 Queen Anne Street, London W1M 0BD (Tel: 01-323 1531).
A list of hotels and boarding houses is available free. Educational holidays are run annually for diabetic children, also holidays abroad.

British Epilepsy Assocation
Crowthorne House, Bigshotte, Wokingham, Berkshire RG11 3AY (Tel: Crowthorne (0344) 773122).
The Association operates a specialist children's holiday unit during the summer months. Details will be sent on request.

British Polio Fellowship
Bell Close, West End Road, Ruislip, Middlesex HA4 6LP (Tel: Ruislip (089 56) 75515).
The Fellowship runs a residential/holiday establishment as well as self-catering accommodation, *i.e.* a bungalow, holiday flat and holiday caravans.

British Red Cross Society
9 Grosvenor Crescent, London SW1X 7EJ (Tel: 01-235 5454).

Many of the Society's branches organise holidays for handicapped people either open to general applicants or to applicants from the area of the branch. Branches also provide information on holidays available through other organisations and it is usually possible to borrow equipment such as wheelchairs, commodes, etc., for use on holiday, but early application is advisable. In addition, holiday camps are organised through the Youth and Junior Red Cross where youth members of the Society entertain handicapped children. All enquiries should be made to the county branch of the British Red Cross Society in the area concerned (*see* local telephone directory).

The Disabled Drivers' Association
Ashwellthorpe Hall, Ashwellthorpe, Norwich, Norfolk NR16 1EX (Tel: Main Office: Fundenhall (050 841) 449; holiday enquiries: Fundenhall (050 841) 324).
The Association runs a moated Tudor country house holiday hotel in Norfolk offering excellent facilities in the midst of 22 acres of delightful grounds near the Norfolk Broads and Yarmouth.

In addition, local groups have funded the purchase of properties in Belfast, Bournemouth, Glasgow, and Llanelli, and some groups own holiday caravans. For further details of the DDA *see* page 157.

Elizabeth FitzRoy Homes
Caxton House, Station Approach, Haslemere, Surrey GU27 2PE (Tel: Haslemere (0428) 52001).
Elizabeth FitzRoy Homes provide Christian residential care for mentally handicapped children and adults for life in small family units, enabling them to obtain their full potential development.

Long-term and short-term care is offered in nine homes in Essex, Richmond upon Thames, Norfolk, Worcestershire, Birmingham, Manchester and Hampshire (three homes). This Trust also organises summer holidays for physically handicapped boys and girls (8 to 18) in schools, etc. Chair-bound and incontinent people accepted.

Holiday Care Service
2 Old Bank Chambers, Station Road, Horley, Surrey RH6 9HW (Tel: Horley (029 34) 74535).
The Service has established itself as a most valuable resource providing a wide range of information on holidays for several thousands of disabled people each year. While most of their enquiries are for holidays in the United Kingdom, they also help with details of places around the world.

The Service has an extensive range of leaflets available to enquirers. These are too numerous to list here but a selection includes:

Holidays in the UK – *Companies Involved in the Provision of Holidays in the UK and Ireland for Disabled People*; *Access Guides*; *Self Catering Accommodation for Disabled People*; *Special Interest Weaving, Pottery and Cooking Holidays*; *Painting Holidays and Courses for Disabled People*; *Farm Holiday Accommodation in England with Ground Floor Bedrooms*; *Hotels and Guest Houses* (sheets covering different areas of the United Kingdom); *Hotel Accommodation for Disabled People on a UK Tour*; *Hotels in the South East for Disabled People, Suggested for Spending a Honeymoon*; *Holiday Camps and Centres Suitable for Disabled People*; *Accommodation where Nursing or Personal Care is Provided*; *Beach Access for Disabled People*; *Bird Watching for Disabled People*; *Organisations or Companies Offering Specially Adapted Narrow Boats*; *Special Diets* (lists of hotels and guest houses in England and Scotland which are able to cater for special diets); *Hotels where Epileptic Guests are Accepted*; *Hotels and Guest Houses Accepting Mentally Handicapped or Ill Guests*; *Voluntary and Paid Escorts on Holidays for Disabled People*; *Holiday Information for Visually Handicapped People*; and *Holiday Facilities for Hearing Impaired People*. Holidays overseas – *Holiday Insurance Cover*; *Companies Involved in the Provision of Holidays Abroad for Disabled People*; *Cruises*; *Independent and Inclusive Self-Catering Holidays Abroad*; *Overseas Spa Holidays*; *Car Hire in the USA*; *Abroad Sheets* (each sheet covers hotels considered suitable for disabled people in various towns and countries); *Holidays in Paris Suitable for Disabled People*; *Paying Guest Holidays in France*; and *Self-Catering Accommodation in France for Disabled People*.

Additional sheets provide information on holidays for disabled children.

John Grooms Association for the Disabled
10 Gloucester Drive, Finsbury Park, London N4 2LP (Tel: 01-802 7272).
At Minehead, Somerset the Promenade Hotel provides purpose-planned accommodation for wheelchair users and their families/escorts. At Llandudno, North Wales, the West Shore Hotel provides similar accommodation. Both hotels have received awards from the British Tourist Authority. On sites in 12 other areas there are self-catering holiday units, including a motor caravan with tail-lift, a narrow boat, and bungalow all adapted for people in wheelchairs. There is also a holiday flat available for hire in London N4.

MENCAP – The Royal Society for Mentally Handicapped Children and Adults
123 Golden Lane, London EC1Y 0RT (Tel: 01-253 9433).
Holiday queries (enclosing large s.a.e.) to Holidays Officer, MENCAP, 119 Drake Street, Rochdale, Lancashire OL16 1PZ.

MENCAP publishes a *Holiday Accommodation List* showing independent hotels, boarding houses, self-catering flats, chalets and caravans where families may be together. In addition the Society arranges a variety of provisions for mentally handicapped children and adults. Adventure holidays can accommodate children with a quite severe degree of handicap. On special care holidays, priority is given to guests in wheelchairs and those with mobility difficulties. A qualified state registered nurse always accompanies each special care holiday.

The Multiple Sclerosis Society of Great Britain and Northern Ireland
England: 286 Munster Road, Fulham, London SW6 6AP (Tel: 01-381 4022/385 6146).
Scotland: 27 Castle Street, Edinburgh EH2 3DN (Tel: 031-225 3600).
Northern Ireland: 34 Annadale Avenue, Belfast BT7 3JJ.
The Society has a number of holiday homes in Ipswich, Kent, Exeter, Worthing, Leamington Spa, North Berwick, the Cairngorms and Co. Antrim. In addition local branches own bungalows, caravans and chalets for the use of members at very reasonable rates. The Society will sometimes help with the cost of members' holidays where necessary.

Norman Wilkes Tours
2 Lower Sloane Street, London SW1 (Tel: 01-730 5407).
Exclusive tours described as Britain with flair. Itineraries include visits to stately homes, famous gardens and historic buildings. Tours range from £1,167. Send for itinerary of accessible holidays.

PHAB (Physically Handicapped and Able-Bodied)
Tavistock House North, Tavistock Square, London WC1H 9HX (Tel: 01-388 1963).
Northern Ireland: Northern Ireland PHAB, Hampton House, Glenmachan Road, Belfast BT4 2NN (Tel: Belfast (0232) 768603).
Besides the 400 PHAB Clubs throughout the United Kingdom, PHAB organises a full programme of residential courses catering for all ages and for families.

The activities on the courses include: art, pottery and other crafts, music, drama, photography, sailing, riding, swimming, canoeing, outings to places of interest, visits to the theatre, discos, etc.

Project Phoenix Trust – Overseas Study Tours for the Disabled
68 Rochfords, Coffee Hall, Milton Keynes MK6 5DJ.
The Trust organises group study tours and interest holidays for adults of mixed physical abilities who want to share a common interest, say art or history, and who want to make this the focal point of their holiday. It is for those who enjoy learning something new in company with other like-minded people. For many disabled people it could be impossible to arrange this on their own. They may need some physical help to make the visit possible and they may need some financial assistance to take part.

Most groups number between 12 and 20 people, with a ratio of one/two able-bodied helpers to one handicapped participant. All the visits are accompanied by a group leader, at least one tutor, sometimes two, and at least one SRN in addition to other assistants. According to the resources of the Trust Fund sponsorship may be offered to individuals from time to time. It is, in any case the intention to keep the maximum cost for any visit to around £350 per person.

A number of guides have been published to Rome £1, Florence £1, Tunisia £1, Bruges 25p, Leningrad and Moscow 25p and Athens £1 (all enquiries to be sent with a 10 in. × 7 in. s.a.e.). The information is based on actual experience, and does not contain lists of hotels (unless they are personally known to the Trust). It is therefore selective information based on what study groups have done (what they were not able to do), what they have seen and why they went to see it. The information will be of interest to those holidaymakers who want something more than just sitting on a beach.

Royal Association for Disability and Rehabilitation
25 Mortimer Street, London W1N 8AB (Tel: 01-637 5400).
The Association has a Holidays Officer and publishes an annual holiday guide, *Holidays for the Physically Handicapped*, as well as a wide selection of Access Guides (*see* Specialist Guides, page 182).

Royal National Institute for the Blind
224 Great Portland Street, London W1N 6AA (Tel: 01-388 1266).
The RNIB has four hotels, in Scarborough, Llandudno, Blackpool and Eastbourne, for which application should be made early in January direct to the manager of the selected hotel. Other holiday accommodation is available in Hove and Burnham-on-Sea. Christmas bookings begin in April. Further details are available from the Social Services Department, RNIB.

Scottish Epilepsy Association
48 Govan Road, Glasgow G51 1JL (Tel: 041-427 4911).
The Association has over 30 years' experience in providing group holidays for adults and children with epilepsy, both in Scotland and abroad. Several holidays are organised each year, some designed for the energetic and adventurous holiday-maker, and others for those who require less demanding timetables.

Application should be made early in the year through the Association's Social Work Department.

The Association also has an eight-berth caravan available to families or small groups.

Scout Holiday Homes Trust
Baden-Powell House, Queen's Gate, London SW7 5JS (Tel: 01-584 7030).
The Trust provides fully furnished six-berth caravans and chalets for any family with a handicapped member, all of which have specially constructed wheelchair ramps. They all have their own toilets and all sites have excellent facilities.

Caravans at Exmouth, Devon; Paignton, Devon; Felixstowe, Suffolk; Fleetwood, Lancashire; Berrow, Somerset; Seton Sands, Longniddry, Scotland. Chalets at Westward Ho!, Devon; Eastbourne, Sussex; Ferryside, Kidwelly, South Wales; New Milton, Hampshire.

Servas
PO Box 17, Hayes, Middlesex UB3 5BZ (Tel: 01-897 8231/584 2978).
An organisation concerned with promoting peace by encouraging people to travel in the cause of peace and to visit others in different countries with similar views. Travellers, unless invited to extend their visit, stay for two nights and are asked to rely on their various talents and to offer assistance where it is needed. Travellers must carry an approved Letter of Introduction, a current Servas list, a sheet sleeping-bag or sleeping-bag, and a towel. The hosts, for their part, are not expected to go to a lot of trouble and expense to look after their Servas travellers.

At present Servas has contacts with more than 80 countries in six continents, and is still trying to encourage people to travel seriously and thoughtfully, rather than fast and far, and to turn their minds to building peace. Servas members are kept informed about the progress of the organisation by periodic issues of *Servas International News* and the national newsletter. These are sent free to all members. From time to time there are meetings in hosts' homes to which all members and interested friends are invited.

The USA group already lists those hosts who are able to offer special provision for members with various types of physical disability. The British group is at present involved in a survey of hosts.

The Visitors' Club

Juxon House, 94 St Paul's Churchyard, London EC4M 8EH. The purpose of forming the Club is to be of help to disabled people wishing to stay away overnight (or longer) in London.

Arrangements have already been made for special facilities to be available at the London Tara Hotel, Scarsdale Place, London W8. Ten rooms on the mezzanine floor are being specially adapted by the Club to meet the requirements of those in wheelchairs or otherwise disabled. Each room has a specially equipped bathroom. Adjoining rooms with communicating doors are available for able-bodied friends or members of the family.

Although these rooms will be available to any disabled person, the London Tara Hotel has also agreed to make them available at a concessionary rate to anyone booking through this organisation. Room rates will inevitably vary from time to time but in 1983 the full rate for bed and breakfast for a shared room is about £25 per person and the concessionary rate is £16.50 per person per night. For a room in single occupation the full rate is about £36 per person and the concessionary rate is £20.40 per person per night.

Membership subscription to the Visitors' Club is £1. The Club hopes to be able to arrange further facilities in other hotels in time.

Winged Fellowship Trust

2nd Floor, 64–66 Oxford Street, London W1N 0AL (Tel: 01-636 5575/5886).
The Trust provides holidays for severely physically disabled people and welcomes those who have additional problems such as incontinence and speech defects who might have difficulty in finding holiday accommodation. They cater for 100 holidays a fortnight in their three centres in Essex, Nottinghamshire and Surrey which are staffed by both qualified people and volunteers. They offer a varied programme of entertainment and a generally informal atmosphere.

The Spastics Society

Family Services and Assessment Centre, 16 Fitzroy Square, London W1P 5HQ (Tel: 01-387 9571).
The Society maintains two holiday hotels by the sea – one at Bognor Regis and one at Clacton-on-Sea. Handicapped guests need not be accompanied as the staff are trained to deal with their personal needs.

Another hotel for handicapped children is run by the Stars Organisation for Spastics in Bexhill-on-Sea.

Advice and help with arranging holidays is also available by contacting the Assessment Centre as above.

Spinal Injuries Association

Yeoman's House, 76 St James's Lane, Muswell Hill, London N10.
SIA offers holidays afloat or by the sea. Their Kingfisher narrowboats, which they claim are the first such boats in the world which can be skippered from a wheelchair, are available for hire with reduced charges for members.

The narrowboats, based at Rugby and Gilwern, sleep seven and five respectively. They have two hydraulic lifts, one in the bow to enable people to get their wheelchairs on and off and down to the galley, and the other at the stern to raise a wheelchair from the galley to the back deck level or up to a position where a clear view can be had over the top of the cabin while taking over the controls of the boat.

Prices per week including VAT are about £327 in the low season and £378 in the high season. You are also charged £10 for full tuition before you set off to adventure through the British canal system.

The SIA caravan is based at a holiday centre in Selsey on the Sussex coast and is also available for hire. Prices range from about £40 to £90 depending on the season.

Young Disabled on Holiday

66 Kingston Deverill, Warminster, Wiltshire BA12 7LH (Tel: Warminster (0985) 3281).
An organisation which caters for physically handicapped people between the ages of 16 and 30. Active holidays are arranged in this country and abroad. Please send s.a.e. when applying for details.

Youth Hostels Association (England and Wales)

National Office: Trevelyan House, 8 St Stephen's Hill, St Albans, Hertfordshire AL1 2DY (Tel: St Albans (0727) 55215).
Many YHA hostels are suitable for people with certain degrees of disability, but it is essential that intending hostellers enquire about possible facilities in advance. Broad Haven Youth Hostel, Haverford-

west, however, is the first hostel in the country to be specially designed to cater for people with physical disabilities. The whole building is on one level with easy routes to the sandy beach. Facilities for field work at Broad Haven are available for the study of marine biology, geography, geology, ornithology, geomorphology, etc. Address: YHA, Broad Haven, Haverfordwest, Dyfed SA62 3JH.

A list of hostels detailing the degrees of accessibility is given in the RADAR book *Holidays for the Physically Handicapped* (*see* below).

GENERAL HOTELS

Best Western Hotels International
26 Kew Road, Richmond, Surrey TW9 2NA (Tel: 01-940 9766).
The hotels within the Best Western organisation are, in the main, independently owned and run, meaning that hotels have to apply to join and to maintain certain standards. Their glossy brochures show hotels throughout the United Kingdom and abroad. Among the welter of symbols indicating facilities are two wheelchair symbols, one showing access for wheelchairs in all areas and the other showing access for wheelchairs in some areas.

Country Holidays: Self-Catering Northern England
Gargrave, Skipton, North Yorkshire, BD23 3RW (Tel: Gargrave (075 678) 776).
The brochure, giving details of a wide variety of properties, is a delight to browse through. The line drawings provide tempting glimpses of holiday residences. The facilities are well described and give a much better idea than having to plough through a sea of symbols. Included are details of those places considered accessible for people in wheelchairs. Country Holidays itself is a holiday booking organisation specialising in self-catering holidays in the Yorkshire Dales, the Lake District and Northern England. The brochure costs 50p.

Holiday Inns – Each hotel in the United Kingdom has a room (if possible on the ground floor) with access facilities incorporating a bathroom, and including helpful details such as handrails, low mirrors, etc. Details from Holiday Inn, 128 King Henry's Road, London NW3 3ST (Tel: 01-722 7711).

Novotel
This chain of hotels assures us that all their hotels have facilities for disabled visitors. Each hotel has two bedrooms with private bathrooms which are specially fitted out for people in wheelchairs to use. There are no steps up from the car park into the hotels.

Further information from: Novotel UK Division, Wilsons Lane, Longford, Coventry (Tel: Coventry (0203) 365000).

Specialist Books and Publications

AA Guide for the Disabled. Recently updated, this Guide gives information on accommodation throughout the British Isles, which has been checked for accessibility and is considered suitable for disabled visitors confined to wheelchairs. Details are given of such features as steps, number of ground floor rooms, type of doors, turning space in toilets and room service.

There is also guidance on regulations affecting disabled drivers, available concessions, toilet facilities at motorway service areas, picnic sites and, in towns throughout the United Kingdom, nature trails recommended for people in wheelchairs. Wheelchair repair and appliance centres are listed.

The Guide is available free to AA members, but otherwise costs 95p. Published by and available from the Automobile Association, Fanum House, Basingstoke, Hampshire RG21 2EA. (Tel: Basingstoke (0256) 20123).

Also available from the AA: *Hotels and Restaurants in Britain*, which identifies facilities for disabled people with the access symbol. Price £5.95 plus £1.45 postage and packing.

Holidays for the Physically Handicapped is a wonderfully comprehensive guide to every type of accommodation available in the United Kingdom with very detailed descriptions of available amenities for disabled holidaymakers. The guidebook is updated every year and contains an enlarged section on overseas holidays and a section on activity holidays. Accommodation is classified under such headings as:
(a) Specially designed or adapted.
(b) Limited personal help given.
(c) Takes some incontinent guests.
(d) Night attention given.
(e) Nursing care given.
(f) Group accommodation.
(g) Self-catering flats, caravans, etc.
(h) Taking children, young persons.
Published by the Royal Association for Disability and Rehabilitation. Available from booksellers, including branches of W. H. Smith & Son Ltd. Price £1 or £2.35 by post from RADAR.

Holiday Care Service. The Service provides a wide range of very helpful leaflets on holidays abroad and in the United Kingdom (*see* page 176), also details of holidays for children (*see* page 174).

Motoring and Mobility for Disabled People (second edition) by Ann Darnbrough and Derek Kinrade. The book includes a chapter on holiday motoring, giving information on ferries, Motorail, toll concessions, etc. For full details of the book *see* page 167.

Help! Thames Television's Access Pack to London containing:
1. *Access Notes* by William Forrester, a registered London guide who himself uses a wheelchair. He writes interestingly and with personal knowledge of places of interest as well as of facilities including stations, loos, taxis, etc.
2. *GLC Wheelchairs in Theatres and Cinemas* leaflet.
3. *Museums* also by William Forrester.
The pack is available free, subject to availability, from: Thames Television Limited, 149 Tottenham Court Road, London W1P 9LD (Tel: 01-388 5199).

London for the Disabled Visitor. A splendidly illustrated and well-documented guide to the exciting sights of old and new London with something to suit everybody's taste. For keen explorers the guide is stimulating and invaluable. It ranges from street markets to Bond Street and Kensington, from all the famous sights to little-known museums, from Cockney cabaret and Music Hall to Elizabethan banquets. If your energy holds, there is plenty to do and the guide sets the information out clearly and helpfully. A whole range of symbols are used to signify accessibility, parking, lifts, facilities for visually handicapped or deaf people and so on. London has a serious lack of accessible lavatories, but the guide has done its best to pinpoint those suitable for disabled people. This is a London Tourist Board/ British Tourist Authority guide, available from London Tourist Board, 26 Grosvenor Gardens, London SW1W 0DU. Price £1.20 including postage and packing.

See also the Visitors' Club for information on visiting London.

ENGLAND

Access in London: A Guide for Disabled People (1984). Published by Nicholsons. Compiled by boys and old boys from the Hephaistos School near Reading and St Paul's School, Barnes. The compilers, some of whom are handicapped (including a number in wheelchairs) carried out the research and survey work. Practically all the places included in the Guide – public buildings, theatres, cinemas, shops, sights, hotels, etc., have been walked in and wheeled over by one of the survey teams.

At the time of writing, the book is with the publishers, but we can safely anticipate that it will be thorough in its coverage and will be written in the usual encouraging and informal style as the other guides in the same series. Widely available, but may also be obtained from Pauline Hephaistos Survey Project, 39 Bradley Gardens, West Ealing, London W13. Price £2.25.

Ancient Monuments and Historic Buildings in England. The Department of the Environment has compiled a list of the ancient monuments and historic buildings in England open to the public, which are in its care and which are accessible to disabled people. The list also indicates those sites where parking is available.

The list is available from the Department of the Environment, Room 112, 25 Savile Row, London W1X 2BT.

English Tourist Board, Department D, 4 Grosvenor Gardens, London SW1W 0DU.
The following free leaflets provide information for hotel and guest house proprietors on how to meet the needs of disabled visitors.
(a) *Providing for Disabled Visitors.*
(b) *Providing for Visitors with Impaired Hearing.*
(c) *Providing for Visitors with Impaired Vision.*

NORTHERN IRELAND

Get Away with Ye, 1984 Guide for holidays for disabled people, provided by voluntary organisations. In addition to details of provision by 27 voluntary organisations, there are sections on air travel, transport services, parking, toilets and travel concessions. General holiday information covers finance, holidays for carers, insurance notes for organisations, travel agents and guides and publications. Available from the Northern Ireland Council for the Handicapped, Northern Ireland Council of Social Service, 2 Annadale Avenue, Belfast BY7 3JH (Tel: Belfast (0232) 640011). Price £1 plus 25p postage and packing.

The Northern Ireland Tourist Board, River House, 48 High Street, Belfast BT1 2DS (Tel: Belfast (0232) 246609). The Board produces two publications of special interest to disabled people
(a) An *Information Bulletin* listing accessible public lavatories throughout the Province. Available free.
(b) A booklet (in co-operation with the Northern Ireland Council for the Handicapped) describing places to stay and things to do for disabled tourists. Price 20p.

SCOTLAND

Access in Dumfries. Available from DIAL, Loreburn Hall, Newall Terrace, Dumfries DG1 1LN (Tel: Dumfries (0387) 65599).

Guide to Public Toilets in Scotland – Accessible to People in Wheelchairs. Published by and available from the Scottish Council on Disability, 5 Shandwick Place, Edinburgh EH2 4RG (Tel: 031-229 8632).

Providing for Disabled Visitors in Glasgow. A leaflet listing buildings open to the public, museums and art galleries, theatres, concert halls, cinemas and public lavatories giving details of access. Available free from the Information Bureau, George Square, Glasgow G2 1ES (Tel: 041-221 7371).

Scottish Council on Disability.
5 Shandwick Place, Edinburgh EH2 4RG (Tel: 031-229 8632).
Among its information lists is one on holidays including sections on holiday places providing nursing assistance, group and activity holidays and other specialist information. List free to disabled people.

WALES

Europe for the Handicapped Traveller – Wales. This guide is one in a series produced by Mobility International including very useful information on where to go and stay, helpful organisations, transport, etc. Available from Mobility International, 62 Union Street, London SE1 1TD.

ACCESS GUIDES FROM RADAR

Available from: Royal Association for Disability and Rehabilitation, 25 Mortimer Street, London W1N 8AB (Tel: 01-637 5400). Prices include postage in the United Kingdom.

Access to Public Conveniences 1980 (throughout England and Wales). Price £1.50.

Access to the Underground 1981. A guide for elderly and disabled people. Published by London Transport. Available from RADAR. Price £1.20.

Countryside and Wildlife for the Disabled by Anthony Chapman (1983). Price £1.60.

Just the Ticket – Access to Theatres and Cinemas in Central London. List compiled by the Greater London Council and available from RADAR, price 25p.

COUNTY/TOWN/CITY/GUIDES IN THE UNITED KINGDOM FROM RADAR

Price including postage

ENGLAND	
AVON	
BATH (1982)	20p
WESTON-SUPER-MARE (1981)	75p
BEDFORDSHIRE	
LEIGHTON-LINSLADE (1982)	45p
LUTON (1980)	25p
BERKSHIRE	
READING (1982)	30p
WINDSOR (1981)	40p
BUCKINGHAMSHIRE	
AMERSHAM AND CHESHAM (1980)	20p
HIGH WYCOMBE (1982)	40p
CAMBRIDGESHIRE	
WISBECH (1982)	20p
CHESHIRE	
KNUTSFORD	45p
MACCLESFIELD (1981)	55p
WILMSLOW (1981)	55p
CLEVELAND	
MIDDLESBROUGH (1982)	20p
CORNWALL	
CORNISH TOWNS (1981)	25p
HELSTON (1981)	20p
CO. DURHAM	
DURHAM (1981)	80p
DEVON	
DARTMOOR (1980)	30p
NEWTON ABBOT AND BOVEY TRACEY (1981)	30p
TEIGNMOUTH AND DAWLISH (1980)	40p
TIVERTON (1982)	15p
TORBAY (1981)	60p
DERBYSHIRE	
DERBY (1981)	20p
DORSET	
BOURNEMOUTH (1981)	80p
BRIDPORT AND WEST BAY (1982)	25p
WEYMOUTH (1980)	20p
ESSEX	
CASTLEPOINT (1982)	25p
HARWICH AND DOVER COURT (1981)	15p
GLOUCESTERSHIRE	
GLOUCESTERSHIRE (1981)	20p
GREATER LONDON	
CHINGFORD (1982)	25p
KENSINGTON AND CHELSEA (1982)	75p
LONDON (1981)	£1.10
RICHMOND UPON THAMES (1981)	35p
SUTTON (1981)	30p
HAMPSHIRE	
BROCKENHURST (1982)	20p

Price including postage

Price including postage

PORTSMOUTH AND SOUTHSEA (1981)	65p
SOUTHAMPTON (1980)	70p
HEREFORD AND WORCESTER	
HEREFORD (1981)	20p
HERTFORDSHIRE	
CHESHUNT AND WALTHAM CROSS (1979)	45p
HEMEL HEMPSTEAD (1982)	40p
HITCHIN (1981)	25p
HUMBERSIDE	
BRIDLINGTON (1982)	35p
SCUNTHORPE (1980)	35p
ISLE OF WIGHT	
ISLE OF WIGHT (1982)	75p
KENT	
ASHFORD (1981)	£1.05
CANTERBURY (1981)	65p
GRAVESHAM (1982)	30p
MEDWAY AREA (1982)	80p
THANET (1980)	50p
TUNBRIDGE WELLS (1981)	35p
LANCASHIRE	
CHORLEY (1981)	20p
DARWEN AND BLACKBURN (1981)	15p
WEST LANCS (1982)	30p
LEICESTERSHIRE	
LOUGHBOROUGH (1981)	45p
LINCOLNSHIRE	
SPALDING (1981)	15p
MANCHESTER	
MANCHESTER (1981)	60p
SALFORD (1981)	15p
STOCKPORT (1982)	30p
WIGAN (1980)	65p
MERSEYSIDE	
LIVERPOOL (1982)	85p
SOUTHPORT (1982)	80p
NORTHUMBERLAND	
BLYTH (1981)	20p
OXFORDSHIRE	
EYNSHAM (1982)	70p
OXFORD (1981)	70p
SOMERSET	
SEDGEMOOR (1982)	70p
TAUNTON (1982)	25p
WELLINGTON (1982)	20p
YEOVIL (1981)	75p
STAFFORDSHIRE	
NEWCASTLE UNDER LYME (1981)	95p
SUFFOLK	
BURY ST EDMUNDS (1981)	25p
IPSWICH (1982)	35p
SURREY	
GUILDFORD (1981)	40p
MOLE VALLEY (1982)	20p

SUSSEX	
ARUN (INCLUDING ADUR DISTRICTS AND THE DOWNS AND WORTHING) (1983)	90p
BRIGHTON (1982)	90p
CHICHESTER DISTRICT (INCLUDING BOGNOR REGIS) (1983)	90p
CRAWLEY (INCLUDING HORSHAM AND SURROUNDINGS) (1983)	90p
EASTBOURNE (1980)	70p
HASTINGS AND ROTHER (1980)	80p
HOVE AND PORTSLADE (1980)	55p
LEWES AND WEALDEN (1980)	90p
LITTLEHAMPTON (1980)	25p
MID SUSSEX (INCLUDING BURGESS HILL, EAST GRINSTEAD AND HAYWARDS HEATH) (1983)	90p
TYNE AND WEAR	
SUNDERLAND (1982)	45p
WARWICKSHIRE	
WARWICK, KENILWORTH AND ROYAL LEAMINGTON SPA (1982)	30p
WORCESTERSHIRE	
STRATFORD-UPON-AVON (1980)	50p
YORKSHIRE	
BARNSLEY (1981)	35p
BRADFORD (1982)	£1.10
KEIGHLEY AND HAWORTH (1982)	80p
SCARBOROUGH (1981)	35p
YORK (1980)	60p
YORKSHIRE AND HUMBERSIDE (1981)	45p
NORTHERN IRELAND	
CO. ANTRIM (1978)	65p
CO. ARMAGH (1978)	45p
CO. DOWN (1978)	55p
CO. LONDONDERRY (1978)	50p
CO. TYRONE AND FERMANAGH (1978)	50p
SCOTLAND	
ABERDEEN (1982)	15p
EDINBURGH AND LOTHIAN (1978)	95p
ISLE OF LEWIS (1980)	45p
WALES	
BRECON (1980)	55p
WALES (1982)	20p

OTHER ACCESS GUIDES

Bournemouth: A Guide for the Disabled. Available from the Department of Tourism and Publicity, Westover Road, Bournemouth BH1 2BU (Tel: Bournemouth (0202) 291715). Price 50p.

Northumberland National Park and Countryside Sites: A Disabled Visitor's Guide. Available from: Northumberland County Council, National Park and Countryside Department, Eastburn, South Park, Hexham, Northumberland NE46 1BS (Tel: Hexham (0434) 5555).

Museums. Two special lists have been compiled by the Museums Association – one showing those museums having access facilities and one showing facilities for blind people. Available free but enclose a large s.a.e. from the Museums Association, 34 Bloomsbury Way, London WC1A 2SF (Tel: 01-404 4767).

The National Trust – Facilities for the Disabled and Visually Handicapped. This booklet should be used alongside *National Trust Properties Open* (*see* page 186) which gives full opening details of each property. The National Trust, 36 Queen Anne's Gate, London SW1H 9AS (Tel: 01-222 9251). Available free on receipt of a long s.a.e.

Uttoxeter for the Disabled. Available free from Uttoxeter Help Centre, Hawthorn House, High Street, Uttoxeter, Staffordshire.

Wheelchair Walks in West Sussex is available from: The County Secretary, West Sussex County Council, County Hall, Chichester, West Sussex PO19 1RQ.

Guide to the Isle of Wight for the Disabled. Available from Isle of Wight Tourist Board, 21 High Street, Newport, Isle of Wight PO30 1JS (Tel: Newport (0983) 524343). Price 60p plus 25p postage and packing.

Forest Freedom for the Disabled: A Short Guide to Selected Forests in Hampshire, Kent and Sussex. Available free from the Forestry Commission, 1 Southampton Road, Lyndhurst, Hampshire SO4 7NH (Tel: Lyndhurst (042 128) 3141).

GENERAL GUIDES

(Now incorporating the wheelchair access symbol for those establishments having suitable facilities for disabled people.)

The AA publish *Hotels and Restaurants in Britain*. Available from major bookshops. Price £4.25. (*See also AA Guide for the Disabled* page 180.)

All the Places to Stay (Northern Ireland). Among the general accommodation listed there are plenty of hotels, guest houses and farm or country houses which are suitable for disabled visitors. These are indicated by a symbol. Available price £1 from Northern Ireland Tourist Board, River House, 48

High Street, Belfast BT1 2DS (Tel: Belfast (0232) 246609).

The Cornwall Tourist Board produces a colour guide to Cornwall and a register of approved accommodation. Each of these contains a key to facilities indicating those properties which cater for handicapped persons. Both publications are available from Cornwall Tourist Board, County Hall, Station Road, Truro, Cornwall (Tel: Truro (0872) 74282 ext. 60). Colour guide 50p, register of accommodation 25p.

Egon Ronay's 1984 Guides. Published in association with Mitchell Beazley.

Egon Ronay's Lucas Guide 1984 to Hotels, Restaurants and Inns Great Britain and Ireland. Price £7.50 plus postage. The 1984 edition, contains over 2,500 hotels and restaurants. It is entirely newly compiled and written for 1984, with many new recommendations replacing former entries after careful inspection. It contains many well-known features: '1001 Bargains', country house hotels, grading of wine lists, hotels with sporting facilities, etc. The wheelchair symbol is awarded to those places where the management say it is suitable.

Just a Bite: Egon Ronay's Lucas Guide 1984 for Gourmets on a Family Budget. Price £3.95 plus 50p postage and packing. This is the sixth annual edition of this guide to informal meals to be found in some 1,000 carefully selected places such as tea rooms, coffee shops, wine bars, cafés and vegetarian restaurants. Amongst its features is a section devoted to establishments serving good food on and near motorways. Those considered accessible by the management are marked with the usual wheelchair symbol. Available from bookshops or direct from Egon Ronay Organisation, Greencoat House, Francis Street, London SW1P 1DH.

ENGLISH TOURIST BOARD AND REGIONAL GUIDES

We are assured that the following guides display the access symbol where appropriate.

Where to Stay accommodation guides. Available from the English Tourist Board, Admail 14, London SW1W 0YE or from bookshops and most Tourist Information Centres. The following regional guides cost 95p each plus 40p postage (plus 15p for each additional guide): *Northumbria*; *North West England*; *Yorkshire and Humberside*; *Heart of England*; *East Midlands*; *Thames and Chilterns*; *East Anglia*; *London*; *South of England*; *South East England*. The *English Lakeland – Cumbria* and *West Country* guides cost £1.10 each plus 40p postage (plus

15p for each additional guide). In addition to the regional guides there are three all-England guides: *Hotels in England*, price £3.25 plus 95p postage; *Self-Catering Accommodation in England*, price £2.65 plus 75p postage; *Farmhouses and Bed and Breakfast in England*, price £1.85 plus 50p postage.

Also available from the English Tourist Board (address as above) is *Let's Go*, a free guide to hotels offering reduced-rate breaks during autumn, winter and spring, and the English Tourist Board, Department D, 4 Grosvenor Gardens, London SW1W 0DU offers *Activity and Special Interest Holidays in England 1984*, price £1.25 plus 25p postage. Both of these guides include information on suitability for disabled visitors.

Visit an English Garden is a guide to gardens open to the public which includes the access symbol where appropriate. One page describes gardens of special interest to visually handicapped visitors. Price 75p plus 20p postage, available from the English Tourist Board.

North West Tourist Board. In addition to the regional guide mentioned above, the Board also produces *Ideas for Party Visits* (Cheshire, Greater Manchester, Lancashire, Merseyside, Derbyshire (High Peak)). This free guide depicts a wide variety of places to visit and includes the access symbol to show they are considered to be manageable for disabled visitors. This symbol is also included on a picturesque and useful map of the region which graphically pinpoints the local places of interest. Available free from the North West Tourist Board, The Last Drop Village, Bromley Cross, Bolton, Lancashire BL7 9PZ (Tel: Bolton (0204) 591511).

Glasgow. The following two guides are available free from the Information Bureau, George Square, Glasgow G2 1ES (Tel: 041-221 7371).
1. *Wining and Dining in Glasgow*. This little leaflet lists restaurants in the central area. It does not attempt to cover snack bars, cafés or pubs. Those restaurants considering themselves accessible to disabled people are indicated; unfortunately it is only on the last page, on which restaurants within hotels are listed, that the symbol appears. Apparently there are no facilities in any restaurant outside a hotel. Hungry wheelchair users beware!
2. *Accommodation in Glasgow* provides a guide to hotels, guest houses and other serviced accommodation. The wheelchair access symbol denotes those establishments considered manageable for physically handicapped guests.

Good Food Guide no longer includes a wheelchair symbol, but does, nevertheless, continue to indicate establishments which claim their facilities are suitable for disabled people. Published by the Consumers Association and available from them at Castlemead, Gascoyne Way, Hertford SG14 1LH. Price £7.50 (1983).

The Good Museums Guide (second edition) by Kenneth Hudson. The Guide assesses and describes 1,600 museums of the British Isles, 900 of them having been personally visited by the editors. The wheelchair symbol is used where facilities exist for physically handicapped people. Published by Papermac, 4 Little Essex Street, London WC2R 3LF (Tel: 01-836 6633). Available from bookshops, price £4.95.

Historic Houses Handbook by Neil Burton. This is a delightful book including information on access for disabled visitors. It does not restrict itself to symbols but gives basic information about obstacles or the lack of them, also mentioning lavatory facilities or otherwise. The 550 houses regularly open to the public are described, ranging from great palaces and castles to tiny cottages and ruins. In addition, for the architectural enthusiast, there are specialist descriptions of over 300 houses open to the public only by appointment. A useful glossary is included to remind us of all those architectural terms which serve to conjure up the rich tapestry of building styles through the ages. A set of drawings give us the basic styles on which to build our knowledge. Published by Papermac, 4 Little Essex Street, London WC2R 3LF (Tel: 01-836 6633). Available in bookshops, price £1.95.

Isle of Man. This guide of places to stay and places to visit includes a few hotels which are considered suitable for wheelchair visitors. Available free from the Isle of Man Tourist Board, 13 Victoria Street, Douglas, Isle of Man (Tel: Douglas (0624) 4323).

Isle of Wight. This guide indicates a fair proportion of hotels, motels, guest houses and other serviced accommodation, which have suitable amenities for disabled visitors. Available from Isle of Wight Tourist Board, 21 High Street, Newport, Isle of Wight PO30 1JS (Tel: Newport (0983) 524343). Price 50p.

London is for Children is an imaginative little booklet listing museums, funfairs, parks, farms (surprisingly there are five of them), ships, brass rubbing centres, zoos, cinemas, theatres and even places where dinosaurs and monsters may be seen. Facilities for access to disabled visitors (or otherwise) are described. Published by the London Tourist

Board, and available from Tourist Information Centres in London or by post from Sales Department, London Tourist Board, 26 Grosvenor Gardens, London SW1W 0DU. Price 60p including postage and packing. Telephone Information Service 01-730 0791.

Michelin Red Guide to Great Britain and Ireland. Uses the wheelchair access symbol. Available from bookshops or direct from Hachette Bookshop, 4 Regent Place, London W1R 6BH (Tel: 01-734 5259/5633). Price £4.95 plus £1.55 postage and packing.

Michelin Guide to Greater London obtainable from Hachette Bookshop as above. Price: £1.30 plus 75p postage and packing.

National Trust Properties Open (England, Wales and Northern Ireland). There are many properties listed which indicate their suitability for wheelchair users. One symbol indicates that one or more wheelchairs are available for visitors' use, another symbol indicates that visitors are welcomed in their own wheelchairs, but there are none for hire. Free admission will be given to any individual necessarily accompanying a disabled or visually handicapped person to any Trust property. Most properties now admit guide dogs for the blind, unless otherwise stated in the individual entries in the booklet. Additional information is given on such items as accessibility of lavatories, availability of braille guide books, lifts, special nature trails, etc. Available from the National Trust, 36 Queen Anne's Gate, London SW1H 9AS (Tel: 01-222 9251). Price 35p plus 25p postage and packing.

The National Trust – Facilities for the Disabled and Visually Handicapped (*see* page 184) is to be used alongside the above publication.

The National Trust for Scotland Year Book. Among financial and general reports this book also includes information on Trust property giving details of visiting arrangements and indicating those properties which are practicable for wheelchairs. Available from the National Trust, 5 Charlotte Square, Edinburgh EH2 4DU (Tel: 031-226 5922). Price 60p plus 20p postage and packing.

RAC Guide and Handbook includes the access symbol where appropriate and details of facilities in motorway areas. Available from the RAC, RAC House, Lansdowne Road, Croydon CR9 2JA (Tel: 01-686 2525) or from local offices. Price to members £3.50 (£4.50 with postage and packing).

The Scottish Tourist Board, 23 Ravelston Terrace, Edinburgh EH4 3EU (Tel: 031-332 2433) publish two *Where to Stay* guides which include the access symbol where appropriate. *Where to Stay in Scotland, Hotels and Guest Houses* and *Where to Stay in Scotland, Bed and Breakfast*. Available from booksellers for £1.20 and 90p respectively or direct from the Scottish Tourist Board for £1.60 and £1.30 respectively including postage.

Self-Catering Holidays. This is a useful guide for all those people who want to do their own thing in their own way. Ideal for those accompanied by children or dogs, the book provides scope for individual holidaymakers to indulge their own timetables and whims without upsetting the landlady or hotel manager. The guide covers England, Wales, Scotland and Southern Ireland, and includes houses, chalets, flatlets, caravans, bungalows, cottages, farms and flats. A symbol shows where somebody considers the accommodation suitable for disabled guests. Published by Pastime Publications Ltd, 1 Huntly Street, Canonmills, Edinburgh EH3 5HB (Tel: 031-556 1105). Price 95p plus 42p postage and packing.

VOLUNTARY WORK OPPORTUNITIES

Guides to voluntary work: (a) *Long-term Places*, free but send a large s.a.e. (33p stamp); (b) *Short-term Places*, free but send a large s.a.e. (27p stamp). These guides, published by the National Youth Bureau, provide information for young people who would like to spend a part or the whole of their holidays engaged in a community service project. The guides include a number of projects which welcome handicapped volunteers depending on the nature of the disability and of the work involved in the project. Copies of the guides are available from the National Youth Bureau, 17–23 Albion Street, Leicester LE1 6GD (Tel: Leicester (0533) 554775).

ACCESSIBLE LAVATORIES

The National Key Scheme provides disabled people with keys to special lavatories throughout the country. Keys may be obtained from your local social services department or, in case of difficulty, enquiries about the scheme should be sent to RADAR, 25 Mortimer Street, London W1N 8AB (Tel: 01-637 5400). RADAR will also be glad to send you a list of those areas taking part in the scheme and the lavatories involved. Lavatories on British Rail stations are included. Please enclose a large stamped, addressed envelope.

SECTION 10

HOLIDAYS ABROAD

For general guidance please see the relevant information in Section 9 on Holidays in Britain, realising that the suggestions made are doubly important when related to foreign travel. In addition to taking all possible equipment that may be needed, it is essential to remember to take an adequate supply of any necessary medication.

Financial Help Available

Some local authorities' social services departments may be willing to consider giving financial support for a disabled person's holiday abroad, up to the amount they would allocate for a holiday in this country. Some social services departments and voluntary organisations also arrange group holidays abroad, thus bringing the costs down fairly considerably. Young people may choose to take part in an educational visit or exchange for which grants are sometimes available. The Central Bureau for Educational Visits and Exchanges will advise individuals and groups on suitable contacts, also on sources of partial funding for specific projects (*see* page 201).

For information on motoring and mobility, *see* Section 8.

IYDP Holiday Fund

The IYDP Holiday Fund exists to provide towards the costs of helpers of severely disabled people on holidays abroad where these costs can be met by neither the helper nor the disabled person and where the disabled person would be unable to go on holiday without someone to help him or her with everyday needs.

The Fund was inaugurated in 1981 by the IYDP Working Group on Leisure. As a result, a scheme to collect small change in foreign currency from travellers returning from abroad has been put into operation by the International Association of Tour Managers, whose members change the donated currency into sterling. In order to get the scheme off the ground Thomson Holidays, one of Britain's leading tour operators, also donated a number of their own holidays together with a sum of money.

Funds are limited and applications can only be received from individual disabled people or from groups who plan to travel abroad but cannot afford to pay helpers' expenses. There are separate application forms for individuals and for groups. Individual applications must be supported by a bona fide organisation or doctor willing to verify that they meet the scheme's requirements. The minimum age for applicants is 17 years.

The closing date for applications for assistance towards holidays being taken between 1 October and 31 March is 1 July and for holidays being taken between 1 April and 30 September the closing date is 1 January. Further information and application forms are available from the Honorary Secretary, Cottleston, 39 Cranbrook Road, Thornton Heath, Surrey CR4 8PQ.

SOCIAL SECURITY BENEFITS

Attendance allowance and mobility allowance
You can go on receiving attendance allowance or mobility allowance during a temporary absence abroad for up to six months. You may be able to get an allowance for longer if your absence abroad is for the specific purpose of getting treatment for an illness or disabling condition which began before you left the United Kingdom. For further details contact the attendance allowance unit or the mobility allowance unit, Norcross, Blackpool FY5 3TA before you go.

Child Benefit
You can usually continue to receive child benefit for the first six months of a temporary absence abroad.

Family Income Supplement
If you are already receiving FIS when you go abroad, you can go on getting it to the end of the 12-month award time. Before you go abroad write to DHSS (FIS), Poulton-le-Fylde, Blackpool FY6 8NW about payment.

Invalid Care Allowance
You can go on receiving ICA if you are temporarily absent abroad. Send your order book to the ICA

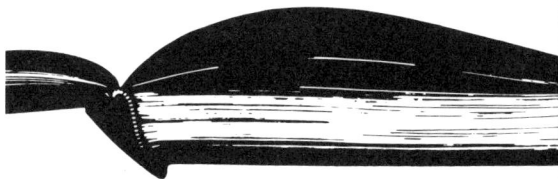

Unit, DHSS, Central Office, Norcross, Blackpool FY5 3TA and tell them you are going abroad.

Insurance

There are basically two types of policy – package and selective. A 'package' offers cover for a variety of events such as illness or accident, loss of baggage, costs arising from holiday cancellation and, possibly, personal liability. In almost every case, the client has to sign a form indicating that he is free from illness or disability, and, in principle, a disabled person cannot therefore make a claim under *any* section of the policy. However, most holiday firms now include details of insurance as part of their package deals and some of them offer policies without the exclusion clause relating to pre-existing disability. It is worth browsing through the brochures, not only for the best holiday, but also for the best insurance deal.

We would recommend you read the small print very carefully indeed. Some of the companies operating apparently helpful schemes are as follows:

Europ Assistance Ltd
252 High Street, Croydon CR0 1NF (Tel: 01-680 1234).
Europ Assistance offer two standard schemes. Their Personal Service applies world-wide, covering the full range of medical emergencies, providing comprehensive repatriation facilities and incorporating medical expenses insurance. Conventional travel insurance covering baggage cancellation risks, personal accident and the public liability is included in both motoring and personal services. Public liability is available as an optional extra package if required.

A Motoring Emergency Service caters for the special needs of the motorist abroad in addition to the medical protection outlined. Repatriation of disabled vehicles, car hire benefits, location and transport of replacement parts, and assistance with roadside repairs are some of the features of this service.

Europ Assistance are, naturally, unable to cover anyone who is likely to be ill abroad, and they require of both individuals and groups that the nature of any disability is declared when the application is made. They will, however, give complete cover to many individuals who have previously been excluded, in particular, those who are disabled, but who are normally in good health. Their booklet *Assistance Advice Guide* provides useful information on services.

Those who subscribe to the GB Assistance scheme are entitled to a 10 per cent discount on the published rates for the Europ Assistance Foreign Motoring Services.

Extra Sure Travel Insurance
The Association of British Travel Agents have put together what they consider to be 'comprehensive travel cover combined in one inexpensive policy'. ABTA point out that there are no exclusions for pre-existing medical conditions, unless travelling against a doctor's specific advice. A 24-hour Emergency Telephone Service is operated for the benefit of insured persons, so that, in the event of an emergency, medical problems covered by the insurance and help and advice will be given. If necessary, emergency repatriation will be arranged. Your ABTA travel agent will advise you, or contact Kersley, Prockter & Day Ltd, Lloyd's Avenue House, 6 Lloyd's Avenue, London EC3N 3AX (Tel: 01-488 9341/480 6871).

Lyle Gibson and Partners Ltd
Mid-Sussex House, 66A Church Road, Burgess Hill, West Sussex RH15 9AS (Tel: Burgess Hill (044 46) 5106 or Caledonian House, Betts Way, Crawley, West Sussex RH10 2XA or 12 Princes Square, Glasgow G1 3JU (Tel: 041-204 2161).
This firm will provide holiday care insurance underwritten by Bishopsgate Insurance Company for all ages but 'in respect of insured persons over 70 years of age, the insurers shall not be liable for any claim arising from pre-existing physical or mental defects, illnesses or diseases which have required consultation within six months prior to validation of the insurance'.

In addition, 'No holiday or journey shall be undertaken against the advice of a medical practitioner'.

Lyle Gibson also provides the Novaplan Holiday Insurance for clients of Blue Skies Holidays. Among its 'special features' Novaplan states that it is not subject to the usual age limits nor the exclusion of pre-existing physical or mental defects, illness, disease and pregnancy. The special cover is underwritten by Norwich Union insurers.

C.R. Toogood & Co. Ltd
Duncombe House, Ockham Road North, East Horsley, Leatherhead, Surrey KT24 6NX (Tel: East Horsley (048 65) 4181).
This company informs us that it has facilities for placing travel insurance on a world-wide basis, both at Lloyd's and in the company market, without exclusion of pre-existing medical condition. Leaflets and details of cover and rates together with proposal forms are available on request. Cover includes sections for baggage and personal effects, personal liability, cancellation or curtailment, personal accident, and medical and other expenses. Under the Lloyd's contract, cover is also available for loss of or

damage to wheelchairs up to £300 for a modest additional premium.

We are assured that the company is able to deal with all classes of insurance and is always pleased to discuss insurance arrangements with disabled individuals or with disability organisations.

Royal Association for Disability and Rehabilitation 25 Mortimer Street, London W1N 8AB (Tel: 01-637 5400).
RADAR has arranged a special master policy for standard insurance and at a premium in line with normal market rates.

Medical Treatment Overseas

SICKNESS BENEFIT DURING A TEMPORARY VISIT TO A MEMBER COUNTRY OF THE EEC

Most UK citizens covered by the UK National Insurance scheme, and their dependants, are entitled to immediately necessary medical treatment if they become ill while visiting another EEC country.

Persons covered by the regulations who are on holiday or otherwise staying temporarily in a Community country will be entitled to medical treatment for sickness or accidents which require urgent attention on the same basis as insured nationals of that country. It must be borne in mind, however, that treatment available in the Community countries is that provided under their own domestic legislation, and in some, but not all of them, persons receiving medical treatment have to pay part of the cost. Medical benefits available under these schemes are dependent upon certain insurance conditions and *are available only on production of a certificate of entitlement to medical benefits* (form E111). To apply for this certificate it is necessary to complete an application form CM 1 (at least a month in advance of the holiday) which you will find at the end of Leaflet SA 30, obtainable from social security offices or from DHSS Leaflets Unit, PO Box 21, Stanmore, Middlesex HA7 1AY. Leaflet SA 30 explains your entitlements in the various countries. Full details, including how to get refunds, are in Leaflet SA 36. This will be sent to you with your form E111.

SICKNESS BENEFIT AND VACCINATION REQUIREMENTS DURING A TEMPORARY VISIT TO COUNTRIES OUTSIDE THE EEC

Leaflet SA 30, as well as providing brief details on travelling to EEC countries as a temporary visitor, also provides brief information on visiting Bulgaria, the Channel Islands, Czechoslovakia, Finland, East Germany, Gibraltar, Hong Kong, Hungary, Iceland, Malta, New Zealand, Poland, Portugal,

Romania, Sweden, USSR and Yugoslavia. The leaflet is available from social security offices and most travel agents. We mention some entitlements under the countries concerned. These apply if you fall ill or have an accident but don't apply if you go to a country to be treated for an illness which you already had when you left the United Kingdom.

Notice to Travellers – Health Protection (Leaflet SA 35).
Information for people travelling overseas – especially to hotter climates. It gives details of compulsory vaccinations and other useful health care measures – well worth consulting to be on the safe side. Available from social security offices or from DHSS Leaflets Unit, PO Box 21, Stanmore, Middlesex HA17 1AY.

Vaccination Certificate Requirements for International Travel and Health Advice to Travellers.
Published by the World Health Organisation and available from HMSO Publications Centre, 51 Nine Elms Lane, London SW8 5DR (Tel: 01-211 3000). Price £4.80 plus postage and packing.

This is an official handbook intended for those who have to advise travellers regarding the risks they might encounter when visiting other countries. The information is detailed and therefore not for the casual traveller who does not venture far afield. However, for the adventurous among us, it makes interesting armchair reading as well as providing practical information covering, in addition to vaccination requirements, some health risks to which travellers may be subject including environmental effects, risks from food and drink, sexually transmitted diseases and hazards from insects and animals; geographical distribution of potential health hazards to travellers in Africa, the Americas, Asia, Europe, and Oceania; precautions against certain diseases and injuries.

Helpful Organisations

A number of voluntary organisations will help and advise on holidays; these are listed in Section 9.

Country by Country

The following list includes details of Access Guides and other facilities where they are known. The leading address given in each country is the one, to the best of our knowledge, to apply to for general information. We make every effort to check these entries but inevitably foreign addresses are more difficult to keep up to date with. We suggest you also try the various countries' national tourist offices or embassies in London.

AUSTRIA

Austrian National Tourist Office, 30 Saint George Street, London W1R 9FA (Tel: 01-629 0461).
Hotels Guide for Disabled Persons. A guide in English listing hotels, guest houses and pensions and describing in detail accessibility to the various parts of the establishments. Available from the address above.
Also available from this address, a sheet entitled *Accommodation for Handicapped Travellers*. This briefly lists some accommodation as well as travel agencies specialising in tours for those who are physically handicapped.
A Hotel Guide for handicapped travellers is on file at:
Verband der Querschnittgelahmten Osterreichs, A-8144 Tobelbad, Styria.
Verband der Querschnittgelahmten Osterreichs, Liechtensteinstrasse 61, A-1090 Wien.
A special hotel guide for disabled visitors to Vienna is available.
Michelin Red Guide to Austria. This guide, which in 1983 is in the course of preparation, will use the wheelchair access symbol. It will be available from Hachette Bookshop, 4 Regent Place, London W1R 6BH (Tel: 01-734 5259/5633).
Europe for the Handicapped Traveller (section on Austria) – for details see under Mobility International, page 203.
Orange badge scheme, reciprocal arrangements, *see* page 209.

Medical treatment on holiday

Citizens of the United Kingdom and colonies who require urgent medical treatment as hospital in-patients while in Austria can normally obtain this free on the same terms as Austrian nationals. Admission to a public hospital is arranged by the local social insurance offices (Gebietskrankenkasse für Arbeiten und Angestellten) on production of a UK passport.

BELGIUM (EEC)

Croix-Rouge de Belgique, Chaussée de Vleurgat 98, 1050 Bruxelles, Belgium (Tel: (010 32 2) 647 10 10 ext. 316). The Belgian Red Cross Society has published a booklet listing (in French and Flemish) information on town halls, cultural buildings, sports clubs, churches, hotels, restaurants, shops, banks and hospitals. Price BF 50.
Hotels. This general guide to accommodation also lists many hotels which are accessible to disabled

visitors in all parts of Belgium. Available from the Belgian National Tourist Office, 38 Dover Street, London W1X 3RB (Tel: 01-499 5379).
Europe for the Handicapped Traveller (section on Belgium) – for details see under Mobility International, page 203.
Project Phoenix Trust Fund – Overseas Study Tours for the Disabled, 68 Rochfords, Coffee Hall, Milton Keynes, MK6 5DJ. The Trust has compiled a leaflet on Bruges (1983). The information is based on actual experience, and does not contain lists of hotels (unless they are personally known to the Trust). It includes selective information based on what study groups have done (and what they were unable to do), what they have seen and why they went to see it. The information will be of interest to those holiday-makers who want something more than just sitting on a beach. The leaflet costs 25p and enquirers are asked to send a 10 in. × 7 in. s.a.e.
Belgian National Railways, 22–25 Sackville Street, London W1X 1DE (Tel: 01-734 1491). A number of facilities are available on Belgian Railways for handicapped travellers. Details of these may be obtained by writing to the above address. A list of stations will be supplied giving details of the facilities at each station and information will be given on the availability of wheelchairs.

Medical treatment on holiday

You will have to pay for treatment but about 75 per cent of the cost and of approved medicines will be refunded. A refund of a percentage of the cost of hospital treatment will also be made.
Further information about refunds, etc., may be obtained from: Regional offices of the Auxiliary Fund for Sickness and Invalidity Insurance (Caisse auxiliaire d'assurance maladie-invalidité) usually located in each provincial capital. (*See* leaflet SA 36, details on page 190.)
Orange badge scheme, reciprocal arrangements, *see* page 209.

BENELUX (EEC)

Michelin Red Guide to Benelux. Uses the wheelchair access symbol. Available from Hachette Bookshop, 4 Regent Place, London W1R 6BH (Tel: 01-734 5633) and other bookshops. Price £4.95 plus £1.55 postage.

BERMUDA

Bermuda Department of Tourism, 9/10 Savile Row, London W1X 2BL (Tel: 01-734 8813).
The *Access Guide to Bermuda for the Handicapped*

Traveller is available from this office, together with lots of sun-soaked brochures. Also available an information sheet *Handicapped Visitors – Facilities in Bermuda* (1980). In addition, we were sent a paper entitled *Handicapped Travellers can be Comfortable in Bermuda* which went into useful details in a nice, informal way.

Medical treatment on holiday
Full costs will have to be paid.

CANADA

Canadian Paraplegic Association, 520 Sutherland Drive, Toronto, Ontario, Canada M4G 3V9 (Tel: (010 1 416) 422 5640). The Association will respond to travel questions about Canada or refer to the appropriate source.

British Columbia – Travel Guide for the Disabled (1981). Available free from Province of British Columbia, Ministry of Tourism, 1112 Wharf Street, Victoria BC V8W 2Z2, Canada.

Burlington: An Accessibility Guidebook of Burlington (1981). Available free from Burlington Social Planning Council, 760 Brant Street, Burlington, Ontario L7R 4B7, Canada.

Calgary: Handbook '81: Calgary (1981). Available free from Calgary Action Group of the Disabled, 815 1st Street SW, Room 604, Calgary, Alberta T2P 1M3, Canada.

Cambridge: Freewheeling Through Cambridge (1982). Available for 50 cents from Mrs Ruth Galway, 14 Jarvis Street, Cambridge, Ontario N1R 1G8, Canada.

Dryden: A Guide for the Physically Disabled and The Elderly in the Dryden Area. Available free from Len Lotecki, Handicapped Action Group, c/o 18A Queen Street, Dryden, Ontario P8N 1A2, Canada.

Durham: Access Guide for the Disabled – Durham Region (1979). Available free from Ontario March of the Dimes, 141 Thornton Road South, Oshawa, Ontario L1J 2Y1, Canada.

Edmonton: Handibook '81 Edmonton (1981). Available free from Calgary Action Group of the Disabled, 815 1st Street SW, Room 604, Calgary, Alberta T2P 1M3, Canada.

Guelph: An Accessibility Guidebook of Guelph (1978). Available free from Volunteer Department, St Joseph's Hospital, 80 Westmount Road, Guelph, Ontario N1H 5H8, Canada.

Halifax – Dartmouth: Guide for the Handicapped (1977). Available free from Canadian Paraplegic Association, 5599 Fenwick Street, Halifax, Nova Scotia B3H 1R2, Canada.

Kingston: A Guide to Kingston for the Handicapped (1979). Available free from Zonta Club of Kingston, 60 Brock Street, Kingston, Ontario K7L 1R9, Canada.

Montreal: A Guide for the Handicapped. Available from the Quebec Paraplegic Association, 4545 Queen Mary Road, Montreal, Quebec H3W 1W4, Canada. (Tel: (010 1 514) 344 3890).

Montreal: Access Montreal (1982). Available from Junior League Office, 366 Victoria Avenue, Montreal H3Z 2N4, Canada.

Niagara Falls: An Accessibility Guide for the Physically Disabled (1981). Available for $1.50 from Social Planning Council, 5017 Victoria Avenue, Niagara Falls, Ontario L2E 4C9, Canada.

Oakville: Oakville Care-a-van, published by and available from Oakville Social Planning Council, 168 Lakeshore Road, Oakville, Ontario, Canada.

Ontario (two publications) 1. *Accommodation*. 2. *Travel Guide for the Disabled* (1982). Available from Ontario Travel, 900 Bay Street, Queens Park, Toronto, Ontario M7A 2E5, Canada.

Ottawa: Accessibility Guide for Ottawa-Carleton. Available from the Rehabilitation Institute of Ottawa, 1400 Clyde Avenue, Nepean, Ontario K2G 3J2, Canada. In English and French.

Peel: Access to Peel Region (1978). Available free from Peel Association for Handicapped Adults, Tomken Senior Public School, 3200 Tomken Road, Mississauga, Ontario L4Y 2Y6, Canada.

Peterborough: Peterborough Guide for the Physically Handicapped (1976). Available for 50 cents from Disability Resource Centre, St Joseph's General Hospital, Peterborough, Ontario K9H 7B6, Canada.

Quebec: Quebec in a Wheelchair (1976). Available for 50 cents from Henriette Germain, 1725 rue Dunant, Sherbrooke, Quebec J1H 4A3, Canada. In English and French.

St Catharine's: Access 79 – St Catharine's. Available from Ontario March of Dimes, 160 Main Street East, Welland, Ontario, L3B 3W8, Canada.

St John's: Access: St John's Region (1982). Available free from The Hub, Box 4397, St John's, Newfoundland A1C 6C4, Canada.

Sault Ste Marie: Accessibility Sault Ste Marie (1977). Available free from March of Dimes, 180 Gore Street, Sault Ste Marie, Ontario P6A 1M2, Canada.

Saskatchewan: Guide to Saskatchewan (1979). Available free from Canadian Paraplegic Association, 325 5th Avenue, Saskatoon, Saskatchewan S7K 2P7, Canada.

Saskatoon: Guide to Saskatoon for the Handicapped Visitor (1979). Available free from Canadian Paraplegic Association, 325 5th Avenue North, Saskatoon, Saskatchewan S7K 2P7, Canada.

Toronto: Toronto With Ease (1980). Available free from Ontario March of Dimes, 90 Thorncliffe Park Drive, Toronto M4H 1M5, Canada.
Vancouver: Guide to Vancouver (1979). Available for $1.50 from the Canadian Paraplegic Association, 780 SW Marine Drive, Vancouver BC V6P 5Y7, Canada.
Windsor/Essex County: An Accessibility Guide for the Physically Handicapped (1978). Available free from Ontario March of Dimes, Suite 601, Metro Plaza, 2260 University Avenue West, Windsor, Ontario N9B 1E5, Canada.
Winnipeg: Easy Winnipeg Wheeling. Available from the Canadian Paraplegic Association, 825 Sherbrook Street, Winnipeg, Manitoba R3A M5, Canada.
York: Spokes Access Guide to York Region for the Disabled (1977). Available free from Ontario March of Dimes, 90 Thorncliffe Park Drive, Toronto, Ontario M4H 1M5, Canada.

CANARY ISLES

On the island of Lanzarote the Norwegians have designed and built what is described as a garden hotel at Casas Heddy which has special facilities for disabled visitors. We understand that everywhere is fully accessible by wheelchair including the grounds, swimming pool (having a gentle ramp), sunbathing areas, restaurant, bar, lounge, television room, etc.

The main rooms and services are situated in the central building, while private rooms are dotted over the estate but mostly near the swimming pool.

Special diets/vegetarian, diabetic, gluten-free, fat-free can be catered for. In addition, a fully equipped clinic is available with a nurse on day duty Monday to Friday to give injections, dressings and first aid. Aids available include hoists, toilet height raisers, blocks for raising beds, urine bottles, bed pans, crutches, wheelchairs and walking frames.

Prices: (1984) 1 week £335, 2 weeks £460, 3 weeks £625, 4 weeks £770.

Further information from Lanzarote Villas, 37 East Street, Horsham, Sussex RH12 1HF (Tel: Horsham (0403) 51304).

DENMARK (EEC)

Danish Tourist Board, Sceptre House, 169 Regent Street, London W1R 8PY (Tel: 01-734 2637).
Will provide information to travellers with disabilities of any special facilities.

The Board also supplies a manual to travel agents covering a great deal of information including general travel details, transport, accommodation, places of interest and a range of useful information. It would be worth asking your travel agent to consult this.

National Association of the Disabled in Denmark (Landsforeningen af Vanføre), Kollektivhuset, Hans Knudsens Plads 1, 10, DK-2100 Copenhagen Ø, Denmark (Tel: (010 45) 01-29 35 55).
This organisation will provide information and advice. They also have a few folding wheelchairs which they will loan provided they are collected and returned to the office. They will also hire pushchairs and they have one electric wheelchair.
Europe for the Handicapped Traveller (section on Denmark) – for details see Mobility International, page 203.
Orange badge scheme, reciprocal arrangements, *see* page 209.

EUROPE

Details about individual countries appear under the name of the country concerned in this section.
Europe for the Handicapped Traveller is a most imaginative series of country guides. Further details are given on page 203 under Mobility International.

FINLAND

Association for the Disabled, Kumpulantie 1A, 00520, Helsinki 52, Finland (Tel: (010 358 0) 718 466). Publishes *Majoitus-ja Matkailuopas Vammaisille* – a guide covering suitably accessible accommodation of every type. Although it is in Finnish, there is an English key, and therefore it does have some positive use.
Finnish Tourist Board, 66 Haymarket, London SW1Y 4RF (Tel: 01-839 4048).
The FTB welcomes enquiries about holidays in Finland by disabled holiday makers.
Europe for the Handicapped Traveller (section on Finland) – for details see Mobility International, page 203.
Peurunka is a 'rehabilitation and motion centre' which also caters for holidays. Situated at Peurunka Lake in the vicinity of Laukaa Village, not far from Jyvaskyla. For further details write to Kuntoutumis-ja Liikuntakeskus, Peurunka 41350 Laukaa, Finland (Tel: (010 358) 41 831 601), or enquire at the FTB as above.

Medical treatment on holiday
Consultations at health centres are free for holders of UK passports. You will have to pay some charges for hospital treatment, dental treatment, ambulance travel, and prescribed medicines. Some charges may be partially refunded by the Finnish Sickness Insurance Institution. This must be claimed before you leave.
Orange badge scheme, reciprocal arrangements, *see* page 209.

FRANCE (EEC)

Comité national français de Liaison pour la Réadaptation des Handicapés, 38 boulevard Raspail, 75007 Paris, France (Tel: (010 33 1) 548-90-13).
French Government Tourist Office, 178 Piccadilly, London W1 (Tel: 01-499 6911 (recorded message)). Has a special information sheet for disabled travellers. Please enclose s.a.e.

Access Guides
Pauline Hephaistos Survey Projects, 39 Bradley Gardens, West Ealing, London W13. This organisation is justly famous for its access guides which are compiled by boys and old boys from the Hephaistos School near Reading and St Paul's School, Barnes. The compilers, some of whom are handicapped (including a number in wheelchairs), in each case carried out the research and survey work in a very practical way. Nearly all the places included in the guides – public buildings, sights, hotels, etc., have been walked into and wheeled over by one of the survey teams.

The guides are very thorough in their coverage and are written in the usual encouraging and informal style as the other guides in the series.
Guides for France: Access in Brittany, Access in the Loire and in 1984 a new *Access in Paris. See also* details of the book *Access at the Channel Ports*, page 205.
Available free (though a donation towards postage and printing would be appreciated).
Association des Paralysés de France, 22 Rue du Père Guerin, 75013 Paris, France (Tel: (010 33 1) 580 82 40). This organisation has produced a hotel guide price F 30.
Europe for the Handicapped Traveller (section on France) – for details see Mobility International, page 203.
Michelin Red Guide to France uses the wheelchair access symbol. Available from bookshops or by post from Hachette Bookshop, 4 Regent Place, London W1R 6BH (Tel: 01-734 5633). Price £5.95 plus £1.55 postage.
Michelin Guide to Paris H and R (in English). Available from Hachette Bookshop. Price £1.30 plus 75p postage and packing.
Hachettes also recommend two other guides from their stock: *Voyager Quand Même* which is a French government publication in French on France. Price approximately £6 plus £1.25 postage and packing; and *Guide Officiel Camping/Caravaning* published by the Fédération Française de Camping et de Caravaning for £3.50 plus £1.25 for postage and packing. In addition they stock a guide entitled *Les*

Vacances des Personnes Handicapées edited by the Ministère de la Jeunesse des Sports et des Loisirs. Price £3.95 plus 95p postage and packing. This guide gives information on how to arrange holidays for disabled people and describes literature which includes *Tours en fauteuil roulant, Où ferons nous étape, Service échanges voyages.*

Cottage Holidays in Rural France
VFB (Vacances Franco – Britanniques Ltd), 15 Rodney Road, Cheltenham, Gloucestershire GL50 1HX (Tel: Cheltenham (0242) 26338).
Looking through the brochure is almost a holiday in itself. If you enjoy France and fancy tucking yourself away in a rural idyll, this might be just right for you. An access symbol is included against certain of the properties as a guide that they may be more suitable than others for those with access problems but the General Manager says 'we prefer to discuss by telephone or letter the requirements of any particular enquirer before the booking is made; some requirements can vary so widely, and we may have on file rather more detailed information than could be included in a brochure'.
Prices vary considerably depending on location, season, mode of travel, etc. A price list will be sent with the brochure.
Guide des Autoroutes à L'usage des Personnes à Mobilité Reduite is a 48-page guide containing information on accessible facilities throughout the network of French highways. The guide is available free of charge from Ministère des Transport, Direction des Routes, Service du Contrôle des Autoroutes, BP 70-69672 Bron Cedex, France.

Holidays in Brittany
Contact: Mr W.C. Millow, The Spinney, St Peter's Valley, Jersey, Channel Islands (Tel: Jersey (0534) 20896).
Holidays for physically handicapped people and their families are arranged by Mr and Mrs Millow and Mrs E. Ashton-Edwards at Jugon-les-lacs in Northern Brittany from April to June. Guests stay in lakeside bungalows in a camp site. Excursions are arranged each day. Prices (1983) range from £112 in April (10 days) to £184 in June (14 days).

Aéroport de Paris – Assistance to Disabled Persons
Available free from Aéroport de Paris, 291 boulevard Raspail, 75675 Paris, Cedex 14, France. The leaflet is bilingual.

Medical treatment on holiday
You must pay for treatment and medicines but you will be able to claim partial refunds. The doctor or

dentist will give you a signed statement of treatment given (feuille de soins). The chemist will hand you back the prescription which is then attached to the feuille de soins. You will receive about 75 per cent of the medical or dental fees and about 70 per cent of the cost of most prescribed medicines. For treatment in an approved hospital you will receive about 80 per cent refund of costs.

For information or refunds you go to local sickness insurance offices (Caisses Primaires d'Assurance-Maladie) or in Paris to the Central local sickness fund for the Paris area (Caisse Primaire Centrale d'Assurance Maladie de la Région Parisienne) Centre 461, 84 rue Charles Michels, 93525 St Denis. Tel: 820 61 05. You ask for International Relations Service (Services des Relations Internationales).

It is important to remember that refunds are not paid at once, even if you call in person. It will be some six to eight weeks before a money order arrives at your home. (See Leaflet SA 36; details on page 190.)

Orange badge scheme, reciprocal arrangement, *see* page 209.

GERMANY (EEC)

Bundesarbeitsgemeinschaft Hilfe für Behinderte eV, Kirchfeldstrasse 149, 4 Düsseldorf 1, West Germany (Tel: 010 49 211 320085) publishes *Ferienführer der Bundesarbeitsgemeinschaft Hilfe für Behinderte*. A very comprehensive and helpful guide to hotels and guest houses throughout West Germany giving detailed information on the accommodation and on the surroundings. A list of access guides to 43 West German cities is also included in *Ferienführer*. There is an English version of the guide.

Europe for the Handicapped Traveller (sections on East and West Germany) – for details see Mobility International, page 203.

Other Access Guides

Frankfurt/Main Access Guide – *Behinderten-Weg-weiser: Frankfurt/Main*. Available free from Kontaktstelle für Korperbehinderte und Langzeitkranke, 6000 Frankfurt am Main 50, Eschersheimer Landstrasse 567, Federal Republic of Germany (Tel: (010 49 611) 5302 257). In German.

The Postillion

Contact: Miss Lore Herold, Löwenstrasse 12, 2000 Hamburg 20, West Germany (Tel: (010 49 40) 462184).

This is a world-wide contact circle to bring people who may be lonely into contact with each other. They also have a Hamburg Tourist Service for handicapped people. They will arrange accommodation, sightseeing, tours, etc. When enquiring, please include an International Postal Reply Coupon.

German National Tourist Office, 61 Conduit Street, London W1R 0EN (Tel: 01-734 2600).

Apart from general literature the office has a leaflet *Autobahn Service für Behinderte* which gives a guide to the services available on German motorways for disabled people. In German, but the map has an English and French key and is easy to understand for non-German speakers.

Michelin Red Guide to Germany. Uses the wheelchair access symbol. Available from bookshops or direct from Hachette Bookshop, 4 Regent Place, London W1R 6BH (Tel: 01-734 5259/ 734 5633). Price £7.05 plus £1.55 postage and packing.

Medical treatment on holiday

Hospital treatment in a public ward is free. Other medical and dental treatment is free if you go to a doctor or dentist who practises within the sickness insurance scheme. You may have to pay a fee in the first place but you will be able to claim a refund.

For information you go to local sickness insurance offices (Allgemeine Ortskrankenkassen – known as AOK), normally open Monday to Friday, mornings only. In Berlin: AOK Area Office 3A (Bezirksstelle 3A – Ausland) at Muellerstrasse 143, 1000 Berlin-Wedding. Tel: (010 49 30) 465071. Ask for the Overseas Department (Auslandsdienstelle). (See Leaflet SA 36: details on page 190).

Orange badge scheme, reciprocal arrangements, page 209.

GUERNSEY

Access guide available from the Royal Association for Disability and Rehabilitation, 25 Mortimer Street, London W1N 8AB (01-637 5400). Price 45p.

Access in Guernsey

Published by the Chamber of Commerce, it can be obtained from the Tourism Department, PO Box 23, States Office, Guernsey. Free of charge.

HONG KONG

A Guide for Physically Handicapped Visitors to Hong Kong. This guide gives access and general information on hotels, restaurants, churches, transport, places of interest and recreational facilities. We understand the information will be updated every six months.

Copies of the free pamphlet are available from the Hong Kong Tourist Association, 14–16 Cockspur Street, London SW1Y 5DP (Tel: 01-930 4775).

Medical treatment on holiday
In-patient treatment in general wards of public hospitals is normally free, also casualty services at certain listed hospitals and clinics, and emergency dental treatment at certain government dental clinics. You must show your passport or NHS medical card.

IRELAND (REPUBLIC OF) (EEC)

Irish Tourist Board, Ireland House, 150 New Bond Street, London W1Y 0AQ (Tel: 01-493 3201).
This office has a good deal of information for disabled travellers and welcomes enquiries. It has two particularly useful publications: *Accommodation and Facilities for Disabled Persons*; *Activities and Facilities for Disabled Persons* (available free).
Irish Wheelchair Association, Frances Genockey, Blackheath Drive, Clontarf, Dublin 3 (Tel: Dublin (0001) 338241). Will loan wheelchairs given sufficient advance notice, providing they can be picked up at the above address.

An Irish Holiday
Contact: Mrs E. Ashton-Edwards, 4 Cherry Tree Court, Dee Road, Richmond, Surrey TW9 2JW (Tel: 01-940 2276/940 4406 (messages)).
Autumn holidays are arranged in a modern ranch-type bungalow $3\frac{1}{2}$ miles from the town of Killarney. Horses stabled on the farm may be hired for riding or pony trekking.
Prices (1983) range from £11.50 per day in late August and September to £10.50 per day in October. (all 14-day holidays).
Europe for the Handicapped Traveller (section on Republic of Ireland) – for details see Mobility International, page 203.
Michelin Red Guide to Great Britain and Ireland. Uses the wheelchair access symbol. Available from bookshops or direct from Hachette Bookshop, 4 Regent Place, London W1R 6BH (Tel: 01-734 5259/ 734 5633). Price £4.95 plus £1.55 postage and packing.

Medical treatment on holiday
Information from the Health Board of the area in which you are staying. Hospital treatment in public wards and other medical care and prescribed medicines are free if you ask for treatment under the EEC social security regulations. (See Leaflet SA 36: details on page 190.)

ISRAEL

Access in Israel: A Tourist's Guide for the Disabled and for those who have problems getting around. Compiled by boys and old boys from the Hephaistos School near Reading and St Paul's School, Barnes.

The compilers, some of whom are handicapped (including a number in wheelchairs) carried out the research and survey work during 1979. Practically all the places included in the Guide – public buildings, sights, hotels, etc., have been walked into and wheeled over by one of the survey teams.
The book is as thorough as possible and is written in the usual encouraging and informal style as the other guides in the same series.
Available free (though a donation towards postage and printing would be appreciated) from Pauline Hephaistos Survey Projects, 39 Bradley Gardens, West Ealing, London W13.

ITALY (EEC)

Italian State Tourist Department (ENIT), 201 Regent Street, London W1 (Tel: 01-439 2311).
Europe for the Handicapped Traveller (section on Italy) – for details see Mobility International, page 203.
Michelin Red Guide to Italy. Uses the wheelchair access symbol. Available from bookshops or direct from Hachette Bookshop, 4 Regent Place, London W1R 6BH (Tel: 01-734 5259/734 5633). Price £5.95 plus £1.55 postage and packing.
Project Phoenix Trust Fund – Overseas Study Tours for the Disabled, 68 Rochfords, Coffee Hall, Milton Keynes MK6 5DJ. The Trust has compiled pocket booklets on Rome and Florence (1983). The information is based on actual experience, and does not contain lists of hotels (unless they are personally known to the Trust). It is therefore selective information based on what study groups have done (and what they were unable to do), what they have seen and why they went to see it. The information will be of interest to those holidaymakers who want something more than just sitting on a beach. The booklets cost £2.00 inclusive of postage (£2.75 for overseas).
Centro Studie Consulenza Invalidi, Via Gozzadini 7, 20148 Milano, Italy (Tel: (010 392) 4045485).
This organisation is concerned with providing information for disabled people concerning aids, laws, education, etc. They will also supply information on holidays and have a leaflet (in Italian only) *Turismo – Vacanze per Disabile*. The letter from the Co-ordinator of CSCI was most warm in answer to our enquiry.

Medical treatment on holiday
Medical and dental treatment is free from doctors or dentists on a prescribed list. Standard charges will be made for medicines. You are entitled to free treatment in certain hospitals.
Further information from the local Health Unit (Unita Sanitoria Locale USL).

(See Leaflet SA 36: details on page 190.)
Orange badge scheme, reciprocal arrangements, *see* page 209.

JERSEY

Access in Jersey – a guide for those who have problems getting around. Available free from Jersey Tourism, Weighbridge, St Helier, Jersey.

Medical treatment on holiday (for stays of three months or less)
Hospital in-patient, out-patient and casualty treatment are free.
Further information may be obtained from the DHSS or from the Scottish Home and Health Department or in Jersey from: Hospitals (Group) Administrator, The General Hospital, St Helier, Jersey.

THE NETHERLANDS (EEC)

National Orgaan Gehandicaptenbeleid, Postbus 323, Oude Gracht 136, 3500 AH-Utrecht, The Netherlands (Tel: (010 31 30) 33 11 21). The Netherlands abound with facilities for handicapped travellers, for instance camp sites which are so designed as to be accessible to wheelchair users, and where integration is automatically accepted. In addition there is a wealth of other accommodation from holiday bungalows and caravans to four-star hotels. Intending travellers are strongly recommended to contact The Netherlands National Tourist Office, 143 New Bond Street, London W1Y 0QS (Tel: 01-499 9367), who have all this information at their finger tips, and are very ready to give advice.

In addition a condensed guide in English is available free from the Tourist Office which provides useful information for handicapped visitors on hotels, camp sites, hostels, restaurants, places of interest, yacht harbours, horse riding, boat trips, fishing sites, swimming facilities, filling stations with adapted toilets and travelling facilities for disabled people by rail, plane, taxi or touring car. The book has been compiled by ANWB, the Dutch sister organisation of the Automobile Association, and the Netherlands Society for Rehabilitation.

ANWB has also prepared a map of day recreation facilities. This is in Dutch but its use of symbols including the wheelchair symbol, makes it easy for foreign visitors to understand. It is available free, but only to members of the AA from the Automobile Association, Fanum House, Basingstoke, Hampshire RG21 2EA (Tel: Basingstoke (0256) 20123).
Europe for the Handicapped Traveller (section on the

Netherlands) – for details see Mobility International, page 203.

Travelling by train in the Netherlands
Again the Tourist Office will be glad to advise. Travelling by train in the Netherlands is made as easy as possible and the following facilities are available:
1. If applied for in time, assistance will be given, where possible, at stations of departure, changing and arrival by a member of the railway staff. This assistance may also be given when changing to other forms of connecting public transport.
2. Those whose handicap makes it difficult to buy a ticket at the ticket window can obtain a ticket from the guard in the train without extra cost.
3. A wheelchair or other invalid conveyance is transported free of charge.
4. At many stations a Red Cross wheelchair is available free of charge.
5. At all main stations and many other stations a movable ramp is available free of charge.
6. The assistance mentioned under 1 and 5 can be applied for on working days between 8 a.m. and 4 p.m., telephone (010 31 30) 33 12 58. Written applications can be addressed to NV Nederlandse Spoorwegen, Dienst van Exploitatie, Afd 6, Postbus 2025, 3500 HA Utrecht. Assistance has to be applied for at least 24 hours in advance, before 12 a.m. Applications for Saturday, Sunday and Monday have to be made on Friday before 12 a.m. If no application for help has been made in advance, usually no asistance by railway personnel can be given. For those who require assistance on their journey because of their handicap, an application can be made for a (male or female) Red Cross helper. Applications can be sent to the Netherlands Red Cross, 27 Prinsessegracht, 2514 AP Den Haag (Tel: (010 31 70) 46 95 95 ext. 131). No charge is made for this help, but the fare and expenses of the helper will be charged.

Orange badge scheme, reciprocal arrangements, *see* page 209.

Travelling by plane
At Schiphol Airport necessary assistance will be given to handicapped passengers. When you book it is necessary to state your handicap. Adapted lavatories are available at the airport. If you need more specific information you could ask for the brochure *Schiphol's Helping Hands*, a publication of NV Luchthaven Schiphol, External Relations Department. (Tel: (010 31 20) 517 24 77).

Motoring in the Netherlands

Seriously handicapped visitors in the Netherlands may apply for a parking badge (well in advance of the journey) to Ministerie van Verkeer & Waterstaat, Koningskade 4, Den Haag. A fee would be charged for any medical examination which it was felt necessary to carry out. Orange badges supplied in the United Kingdom are also valid in the Netherlands.

Holland Tourist Hotels, Hyacinthstraat 138, 9713 XJ Groningen, The Netherlands.

This chain of hotels includes the wheelchair access symbol against those hotels listed in their brochure which they consider partially or entirely suitable for guests in wheelchairs.

Medical treatment on holiday

Medical treatment is free if you are treated by a doctor within the ANOZ scheme. You may have to pay part of the cost of dental treatment. Hospital treatment is free under the scheme, as well as some prescribed medicines. Further information from The Netherlands General Sickness Insurance Fund (Algemeen Nederlands Onderling Ziekenfonds – ANOZ), Kaap Hoorndreef 24–28, Utrecht. (See Leaflet SA 36: details on page 190.)

LUXEMBOURG

Tourist Office, 1010 Luxembourg, PO Box 1001, Luxembourg (Tel: (010 352) 48 79 99). 36-37 Piccadilly, London W1V 9PA (Tel: 01-434 2800).

An attractive range of literature makes this small mountain country seem very inviting. A general guide to the Grand Duchy of Luxembourg; a colourful leaflet on camping which includes the wheelchair access symbol; a booklet – *Aero-port de Luxembourg* with plans for arrivals and departures showing elevators for handicapped travellers; a brochure listing hotels, auberges, restaurants and pensions including the wheelchair access symbol showing bedrooms accessible to physically handicapped guests. (It would be as well to ask about the accessibility of the rest of the building.)

Europe for the Handicapped Traveller (section on Luxembourg) – for details see Mobility International, page 203.

MALTA

Physically Handicapped Rehabilitation Fund, Rehabilitation Centre, Corradino, Paolo, Malta (Tel: (010 356) 27518).

Organises exchange visits with groups of physically handicapped people in the United Kingdom and other countries. Also provides the loan of wheelchairs and other walking aids to handicapped tourists visiting the island. The Fund even advises handicapped visitors of hotels and accessibility to places of interest.

Europe for the Handicapped Traveller (section on Malta) – for details see Mobility International, page 203.

NORWAY

Norges Handikapforbund, Nils Hansens Vei 2, Oslo 6 (Tel: (010 47 2) 67 92 05).

The Norwegian Association for the Disabled has a *Travel Guide for the Disabled* which provides information on access regarding hotels, camp sites and tourist sites as well as public transport including railway stations, airports and taxis. Price N.kr. 58 plus postage and packing.

Norwegian Tourist Board, 20 Pall Mall, London SW1Y 5NE (Tel: 01-839 6255).

The Board can supply all the usual tourist information including a general guide to holidays in Norway with lots of useful information. It also has a hotel guide which includes the wheelchair access symbol for accommodation considered to have barrier-free facilities for wheelchair-bound holidaymakers.

Travel guide for the disabled. A complete list of transport, accommodation, camp sites and general attractions in Norway especially accessible to disabled people. There is a separate map section. Price N.kr. 65 (pay by international money order). Available from Forlagssentralen, Box 6005, Etterstad, Oslo 6, Norway. Price N.kr. 58.

Norwegian Youth Hostels, Landslaget for Norske, Ungdomsherberger, Dronningensgt 26, Oslo, Norway.

The Guide to Norwegian Youth Hostels is published in Norwegian, except for a brief introduction and an explanation of the symbols. We understand that certain hostels have given particular priority to the needs of disabled travellers. These are Fauske, Kalvatn, Kragerø, Stavanger, Svolvaer and Voss. These are all mentioned in the Guide.

Europe for the Handicapped Traveller (section on Norway) – for details see Mobility International, page 203.

Travelling by train in Norway

Norwegian State Railway – specially designed coach for disabled persons. The NSR have introduced a railway coach which has been specially designed to provide facilities on long-distance trains to better suit the needs of disabled people. The coach contains a compartment for stretcher cases and a compartment specially adapted to take two wheelchairs by the window by removing the normal seating. Double sliding doors provide good access from the corridor.

Close to this compartment there is a toilet fully accessible by wheelchair. The coach is also provided with a transport chair which can be used when travellers with restricted mobility wish to be moved to an ordinary coach or to the restaurant car. The loading of wheelchairs into coaches has always been a problem, in this case the difficulty is solved by means of two lifting platforms which make it possible to wheel the chair into the luggage compartment and thence into the disabled person's compartment. The lifting platforms are easy to operate and are capable of lifting 250 kg. Coaches are operating between Oslo and Bergen, Oslo and Trondheim, Oslo and Stavanger, Trondheim and Bodø. Further information may be obtained from Norwegian State Railways Travel Bureau, Stortingsgata 28, Oslo 1, Norway (Tel: (010 47 2) 42 94 60).

Medical treatment on holiday
As a resident of the United Kingdom you will receive reimbursement of part of the cost of treatment by a general practitioner or as an out-patient at a public hospital (poliklinikk); free treatment as an in-patient in a public hospital; reimbursement of part of the cost of some dental treatment; reimbursement of the full cost of transport necessarily incurred in obtaining treatment. A receipt (Legeregning refusjonssystemet) should be obtained at the time of payment and before you leave Norway this should be produced, with your UK passport, at the social insurance office (Trygdekasse) of the town where treatment was obtained. Drugs and medicines are normally paid for by the patient except when he is an in-patient in a hospital. Enquiries about the Norwegian health services can be made of the local social insurance office (Trygdekasse) or the National Insurance Office (Rikstrygdeverket), Oslo, or the Ministry of Social Affairs (Sosial-departementet), Oslo.

PORTUGAL

Portuguese National Tourist Office, 1-5 New Bond Street, London W1Y 0NP (Tel: 01-493 3873).
There is, as yet, no published accommodation guide suggesting accommodation suitable for people using wheelchairs. However, the tourist office will be glad to send you general guidelines together with a sheet *Information for the Disabled* which lists hotels they have been informed are in some way accessible. They are mainly de luxe or first-class hotels. You would, of course, have to contact the hotels direct to ask for more information.
Europe for the Handicapped Traveller (section on Portugal) – for details see Mobility International, page 203.

SPAIN

Michelin Red Guide to Spain and Portugal. Uses the wheelchair access symbol. Available from bookshops or direct from Hachette Bookshop, 4 Regent Place, London W1R 6BH (Tel: 01-734 5259/734 5633). Price £4.95 plus £1.55 postage and packing.

Medical treatment on holiday
Full costs will have to be paid.

Europe for the Handicapped Traveller (section on Spain) – for details see Mobility International, page 203.

SWEDEN

Hotels in Sweden marks with an 'H' those hotels which have special rooms with facilities for handicapped people. These rooms have especially large doors, no doorsteps, handles in the bathrooms and are integrated with the other rooms in the hotel. There are also lifts and easy access from the street level. A fact sheet is also available containing holiday information for disabled people. For both publications contact Swedish National Tourist Office, 3 Cork Street, London W1X 1HA (Tel: 01-437 5816). *Europe for the Handicapped Traveller* (section on Sweden) – for details see Mobility International, page 203.

Medical treatment on holiday
Svenska Turistföreningen Vasagatan 48, Box 25, 101 20 Stockholm, Sweden (Tel: (010 46 8) 22 72 00).
Will provide a range of general tourist information. This includes the *Swedish Youth Hostels Handbook* (1983) which is in Swedish but under the heading 'Rörelsehind' (R) from page 78 are listed those which are considered suitable for disabled people.
Orange badge scheme, reciprocal arrangements, *see* page 209.

Medical treatment on holiday
The Swedish medical services provide free in-patient treatment in the public ward of a State or municipal hospital and a refund of up to three-quarters of the cost of general medical practitioners' fees. Charges may be made for certain drugs. Dental treatment for children is free (50 per cent fee for adults). You will need to show your UK passport to prove entitlement.
Further information about the Swedish medical services may be obtained from Riksforsakringsanstalten, Adolf Fredriks Kyrkogata 8, Stockholm 3, Sweden.

199

SWITZERLAND

Swiss Hotel Guide for the Disabled. Written in German, French and English, this is a very helpful guide to accommodation throughout Switzerland indicating precisely those premises considered suitable for:
(a) wheelchair users;
(b) those who are severely handicapped in walking;
(c) those who are slightly handicapped in walking.
Information is given on spas, climatic conditions and on the general facilities of the accommodation listed including sporting activities. Available from Swiss National Tourist Office, Swiss Centre, 1 New Coventry Street, London W1V 8EE (Tel: 01-734 1921).
Schweiz Arbeitsgemeinschaft für Körperbehinderte (SAK) and Mobility International Switzerland, Postfach 129, 8032 Zürich, Switzerland (Tel: (010 41 1) 251 05 31).
The following guides are available:
Swiss holiday guide for the Handicapped throughout Switzerland;
Motel Guide with Youth Hostels and Camping Places. Additional information on barrier-free restaurants and toilets on the Swiss highways.
Both guides with explanations in Italian, French and English.
Holiday for the Handicapped. This brochure appears every year and contains:
(a) tips for the independent traveller through Switzerland and abroad;
(b) aids to plan holidays;
(c) organised holiday camps for handicapped children and adults;
(d) organised holidays for adults abroad.
An excellent series of pocket *City Guides* in which five symbols are used to denote varying degrees of accessibility. These are explained in German, French, Italian and English. Baden, Basel, Bern, Glarus, Grenchen, Luzern, Schaffhausen, Solothurn, St Gallen, Thun, Winterthur, Zürich (German); Geneva, Lausanne, La Chaux de Fonds, Le Locle, Neuchâtel (French).
All guides are free of charge.
Europe for the Handicapped Traveller (section on Switzerland) – for details see Mobility International, page 203.
Michelin Red Guide to Switzerland. This guide which in 1984 is in course of preparation, will use the wheelchair access symbol. It will be available from Hachette Bookshop, 4 Regent Place, London W1R 6BH (Tel: 01-734 5259/5633).
The *Swiss Youth Hostel Guide* has a splendid map and gives full details of youth hostels including where they are accessible to wheelchair travellers. Available from Swiss Youth Hostel Federation, Postfach,

Hochhaus 9, 8957 Spreitenbach, Switzerland (Tel: (010 41 056) 71 40 46).
Orange badge scheme, reciprocal arrangements, *see* page 209.

Medical treatment on holiday
Full costs will have to be paid.

UNITED STATES

Access Guides
Access National Parks: A Guide for Handicapped Visitors. Wherever possible, extra facilities within the parks are made to assist disabled people (including chair-users and the blind and deaf) to enjoy the opportunities offered. Available from the Superintendent of Documents, US Government Printing Office, Washington DC 20402 (quoted stock number 024-005-00691-5). Price $8.15 including international handling. Cash in advance via international money order which may be obtained from banks at a cost of about 40p.
Access New York. Available from the Institute of Rehabilitation Medicine, New York, University Medical Centre, 400 East 34th Street, New York, NY 10016. Price $2.
Access New York City covers 400 public buildings in Manhattan including hotels and restaurants, museums and galleries, places of worship, parks and sports centres, transportation, tourist sites, theatres, cinemas, hospitals and department stores. Also included is a specially prepared fold-out map of Manhattan and compilation of special services for disabled people. Available from The Junior League of the City of New York, Inc., 130 East 80th Street, New York, New York 10021, USA. Price $2.
Information for Handicapped Travellers (1979). This reference circular includes information on travel information centres in the United States, special transportation services in the United States, travel information in other countries and details of some travel guides. Available free from Reference Section, National Library Service for the Blind and Physically Handicapped, Library of Congress, Washington DC 20542.
Highway Rest Areas for Handicapped Travellers. This guide has been produced by the President's Committee on Employment of the Handicapped, Washington DC 20210, in co-operation with the Federal Highway Administration. It gives route numbers, directions served, location, etc., of over 800 rest areas claimed to be 'barrier free' to wheelchair users and others severely disabled.
Los Angeles: Around Town with Ease. Available for 55¢ (postage) from Junior League of Los Angeles, Farmers Market, Third & Fairfax, Los Angeles, Ca

90036. (A bus company in Los Angeles recently purchased 200 buses which have an entrance for wheelchair users.)

Access Washington: A Guide to Metropolitan Washington for the Physically Disabled. Available from Information Center for Handicapped Individuals, Inc., 605 G Street, NW, Suite 202, Washington DC 20001.

The Wheelchair Traveller. For details *see* page 207.

Rehabilitation Gazette, International Journal and Information Service for the Disabled, 4502 Maryland Avenue, St Louis, Missouri 63108 (Tel: (010 1 314) 361 0475). The *Rehabilitation Gazette* serves as the international clearing house and co-ordinator of post-polio persons interested in sharing information and forming support groups.

Gini Laurie, the inspiring and marvellously enthusiastic editor of the *Gazette*, writes to us in her usual helpful way on travelling within the United States. 'Regular *Gazette* readers will have no trouble finding congenial disabled persons in the United States since all the many vignettes and profiles include the names and addresses. I would suggest picking a congenial-sounding person in the location wanted and writing for assistance with holidaying in the area. Americans are hospitable!' Gini also says she will be happy to help regular readers. She will also be glad to help respirator users whom she will put in touch with other respirator users and equipment representatives all over the country. To become a subscriber to the *Rehabilitation Gazette*, write to Gini for details of subscription rates.

US car hire

As might be expected, hiring cars in the United States is made as easy as possible, and while we have been personally unable to check these facts we understand that the 'Big Three' rental car agencies – Avis, Hertz and National – offer cars in many places with hand controls. We also understand there is no charge for hand controls at any of the three companies, but Hertz requires a $25 deposit when renting on a cash basis, though the deposit is waived when renting in the State of Florida.

Without personal checking, we can only offer guidance and since, in any case, there are different rental rates for different cities and agencies, and special rates for groups, also discounts for certain times and mileage, we would urge you do your own checks.

Avis reservations. In the United Kingdom contact: Reservations Department, Trident House, Station Road, Hayes, Middlesex UB3 4DJ (Tel: 01-848 8733). Toll-free number for international reservations (for use only in USA): 800-331-2112.

Locations available: all major US cities.
Cars with hand controls: any available car.
Advance notice: 14 days.

Hertz reservations. In the United Kingdom contact: Central Reservations, 44 The Broadway, London SW19 (Tel: 01-540 5265). Toll-free number (for use only in USA): 800-654-3131.

Locations available: over 40 cities and virtually all locations in Florida.
Cars with hand controls: all American cars and vans.
Advance notice: 5 days.

Medical treatment on holiday

Full costs will have to be paid – be warned! Armed with medical insurance, you will be safe from the very high charges made by medical and nursing services.

YUGOSLAVIA

Yugotours Ltd, Chesham House, 150 Regent Street, London W1R 5FA (Tel: 01-734 7321).

This organisation is always very glad to help disabled people plan holidays in Yugoslavia and, with their extensive knowledge of the country, they are able to cater for individual needs and tastes.

Medical treatment on holiday

People insured under the United Kingdom insurance scheme (including retirement pensioners, full-time students, apprentices and trainees) and their dependants, may receive Yugoslav medical benefit on presentation of a UK passport under the same conditions as people insured under Yugoslav legislation who are ordinarily resident in the country. The free service includes hospital treatment, some dental treatment as well as some other medical treatment. You will have to pay for prescribed medicines.

Enquiries about the Yugoslav scheme should be sent to Savezni Zavod Za Socijalno Osiguranje, Nemanjina br 34, Belgrade, Yugoslavia.

Interest and Specialist Holiday Organisations

The British Ski Club for the Disabled
See details in Section 11, page 227.

Camping
See details in Section 9, page 171.

Central Bureau for Educational Visits and Exchanges
Seymour Mews House, 26–37 Seymour Mews, London W1H 9PE (Tel: 01-486 5101) and 3 Bruntsfield Crescent, Edinburgh EH10C 4HD (Tel: 031-447 8024) and 16 Malone Road, Belfast BT9 5BN (Tel: Belfast (0232) 664418).

Educational travel and exchange projects are run on an integrated basis whenever possible, encouraging opportunities where handicapped people can mix freely and as a right with able-bodied people. The Bureau is a member of Mobility International. The Bureau will answer any queries regarding foreign travel of an instructional or educational nature, and in many instances it acts as a clearing office, bringing together people with like-minded needs and leaving them to make their own arrangements. Leaders are always welcome who are prepared to take a party of disabled people abroad. Groups of people are usually aged between 16 and 30, but general queries regarding travel abroad will always be dealt with, regardless of age: *see also* Books and Publications, page 201.

CHIVE (Council for Hearing Impaired Visits and Exchanges)
This is the national voluntary agency for the general development of educational travel and exchanges with other countries giving advice to groups of young deaf people who wish to visit another country and learn about different ways of life. CHIVE also arranges some special projects itself. The secretariat is provided by the Central Bureau for Educational Visits and Exchanges.

CHIVE can help young hearing-impaired people to find friends and contacts in different countries; can arrange travel; can tell you about the country you wish to visit; may be able to advise about money for your visit.

Contact them c/o The Central Bureau for Educational Visits and Exchanges, Seymour Mews House, 26–37 Seymour Mews, London W1H 9PE (Tel: 01-486 5101).

Evergreen Travel Service Inc
19505L 44th Avenue West, Lynnwood, Washington 98036, USA (Tel: (010 1 202) 776-1184).
While the group holidays arranged by this company, in the persons of Betty and Jack Hoffman, are mostly intended for holidaymakers in the United States, nevertheless they would be glad to welcome others on their tours where this is geographically possible. For instance British people could join a European tour, by joining the group at a convenient airport. Their 'Wings on Wheels Tours' make exciting reading (though the tours may sound expensive). Betty and Jack personally accompany the tours and would welcome enquiries from Directory readers. They point out that when people from the United Kingdom go on their tours and join them in Europe, they have a decided advantage because of the airfares.

Holiday Care Service
2 Old Bank Chambers, Station Road, Horley, Surrey RH6 9HW (Tel: (029 34) 74535).
The Service has established a central clearing house of information on holiday opportunities for disabled people. For further details *see* page 176.

The Les Evans Holiday Fund for Sick and Handicapped Children
183a St Mary's Lane, Upminster, Essex (Tel: Upminster (040 22) 22920/28103).
Free holidays abroad are made available to children aged 8 to 15 years suffering severe illness and/or disability. Applicants are accepted and their holidays granted in accordance with medical priority. The Fund aims to provide 'the holiday of a lifetime'. A doctor and nurses accompany the children. Parents or guardians are only required to provide conveyance of the child to and from the airport.

Uphill Ski Club
See page 227.

Workcamps
See page 174 in Section 9 for information.

PILGRIMAGES TO LOURDES

Across Trust
Crown House, Morden, Surrey SM4 5EW (Tel: 01-540 3897).
The Across Trust has especially designed and equipped coaches, named the Across Jumbulances, and with these vehicles the Trust has been able to realise its objective to provide suitable transport for the severely handicapped and seriously ill person to go on pilgrimage to Lourdes or on holidays through Europe. Travellers can be lying down, if necessary, or wheelchair users. For details write to the Secretary.

Catholic Touring Association Ltd
122 Coombe Lane, London SW20 0BA (Tel: 01-947 6991).
The Association organises large diocesan pilrimages to Lourdes which always cater for sick and disabled people belonging to a particular diocese. In addition they arrange travel for individuals providing they have someone to attend to them at all times where this is necessary. People who are very disabled (needing to travel lying down) would need to be attached to one of the big pilgrimages where they travel by train in ambulance cars and are under full medical supervision the whole time.

HCPT (Handicapped Children's Prilgrimage Trust) and Hosanna House Trust
119 Westmead Road, Sutton, Surrey SM1 4JH (Tel: 01-643 4431).
HCPT takes over 1,500 children (usually between the ages 7 and 18) on the annual pilgrimage. The groups stay in the Lourdes hotels to enable the handicapped children to lead as full a life as possible in Lourdes. Parents are encouraged to make a contribution to the cost where possible.

In addition, handicapped adults may stay at Hosanna House near Lourdes where weekly groups of 35 including helpers fly from Gatwick and Manchester airports.

YOUTH HOSTELS

All other information in this Directory is checked at source by the authors. However, we were unable to check details of accessible Youth Hostels abroad. We are therefore grateful to the Northern Ireland Council for the Handicapped for the following information. In Israel, the Bet Yatziv Youth Hostel at Beersheba is to have a specially adapted wing constructed; in Switzerland, facilities for handicapped guests are automatically taken into account when planning new buildings or converting existing ones, so that nine hostels in Switzerland are now able to accommodate people using wheelchairs; and in Hungary, it is understood that there are two youth centres with facilities for guests with handicaps. These are Verocemaros, 40 km from Budapest by the River Danube, a centre with 1,000 beds in one- or two-bedded bungalows, two restaurants, sports grounds, a swimming pool and large recreation rooms, and Kiliantelep Youth Centre, 150 km from Budapest on the shores of Lake Balaton. This centre offers similar facilities plus water sports.

Mobility International
62 Union Street, London SE1 1TD (Tel: 01-403 5688).
Mobility International exists to encourage the integration of handicapped with non-handicapped people by arranging international projects of wide appeal, which vary from youth festivals and activity programmes, where the accent is on leisure, sport and culture, to more professional conferences and seminars on specific themes. In the last ten years MI have helped several thousand people to travel to different parts of the world by encouraging them to join their projects or by giving advice to those who wish to travel alone.

Mobility International publishes *Mobility International News* packed with details of world-wide organisations and travel; also a set of booklets under the title *Europe for the Handicapped Traveller*. Each country is well described and sources of information and help are given. Interesting to read in their own right, they are not to be missed if you are holidaying in Europe.

Annual subscription £5. MI will be glad to send you details of current projects.

Young Disabled on Holiday
See page 179.

General Holidays

The following holiday suggestions do not fall into any particular category, and some indeed depart from our usual practice of not listing hotels, since it would be impossible to do so comprehensively in a book of this kind. However, some of the information we received seemed so generously given, and some was so frankly exotic and therefore not of the type to be found in any other guide, that we make no apologies for printing such information.

HELPFUL TRAVEL AGENTS

Association of British Travel Agents
55–57 Newman Street, London W1P 4AH (Tel: 01-637 2444).
The travel industry generally is becoming more aware of the needs of disabled travellers, and travel agents are beginning to pay more attention to the wishes of their disabled clients by providing specialist information where required. You would be well advised to seek out those agents who are members of ABTA and who conform to a common code of practice. In the event of difficulties and if the agent has proved unco-operative over a complaint, you may then approach ABTA, who will offer free conciliation facilities.

Best Western Hotels International
26 Kew Road, Richmond, Surrey TW9 2NA (Tel: 01-940 9766).
The hotels within the Best Western organisation are, in the main, independently owned and run, meaning that hotels have to apply to join and have to maintain certain standards. Their glossy brochures show hotels throughout the United Kingdom and abroad. Among the welter of symbols indicating facilities are two wheelchair symbols, one showing access for wheelchairs in all areas and the other showing access for wheelchairs in some areas.

Chalfont Line Holidays – for disabled people and their friends
4 Medway Parade, Perivale, Middlesex UB6 8HR
Telephone: 01-998 2143/6516.

This company seeks to provide integrated holidays which are barrier free and worry free. They have their own specialised coaches and on each holiday they provide a party leader/courier, a state registered nurse (on all overseas holidays) and an able-bodied helper who is generally available.

Disabled people are invited to bring a companion for whom a £10 discount will be allowed. Also, members of the family are also encouraged to participate in these holidays. Holiday insurance is included in the price and is compulsory.

Holidays have been arranged for destinations in the United Kingdom, Spain, Switzerland, the Netherlands, Hungary and the United States.

Cosmos Air Holidays Ltd
Cosmos House, Bromley Common, Bromley, Kent BR2 9LX (Tel: 01-464 3444).
This company will advise individual clients on the suitability of the hotels featured.

Hideaway Holidays
Villas Portuguesas, 67 Marylebone High Street, London W1N 1HA (Tel: 01-486 1168).
This organisation provides furnished villas and apartments for holidays in Europe, the Americas, Far East, Near East, Australia and New Zealand. We have been assured by Alan Bainbridge that he is happy to provide facilities for handicapped holidaymakers. Each individual enquiry is judged on its merits and costed accordingly.

Horizon
Broadway, Edgbaston Five Ways, Birmingham B15 1BB (Tel: 021-643 2727).
In addition to Horizon's usually enticing and holiday-packed brochure they have produced a splendid companion volume entitled *Hotel Guide to Easy Access Holidays for the Disabled and the Infirm*. This describes accessibility features of hotels in Austria, Greece, Italy, Malta, Morocco, Portugal, Spain, Spanish islands and Yugoslavia. Interestingly it also lists those hotels it considers unsuitable and describes why. A helpful feature we thought.

The Guide may be available free from your nearest Horizon Travel Centre or you could send for it from the above address. It is free.

Kuoni Travel Ltd
Kuoni House, Dorking, Surrey RH5 4AY (Tel: Dorking (0306) 885954).
This company arranges holidays in distant places, and went to considerable trouble to list hotels which they considered reasonably convenient to disabled travellers, being accessible throughout, including to pool and beach (with the exception of Nassau Beach, which has two or three steps at the front entrance). Kuoni would be glad to make the necessary arrangements. They stipulate that all disabled travellers needing any personal help should be accompanied. The following hotels are recommended:
Hawaiian Regent, Honolulu, Hawaii – has a special bedroom.
Bali Hyatt, Bali, Indonesia – has wheelchair for hire.
Nassau Beach, Nassau, Bahamas.
Rasa Sayang-Penang, Malaysia.

Out and About – Holidays for the Disabled
112 Eskdale Avenue, Chesham, Buckinghamshire HP5 3BD (Tel: (0494) 775377).
This organisation specialises in arranging holidays for people who for one reason or another, experience difficulty in taking an 'ordinary' holiday as set out in travel brochures. Consideration is not always given to slow walkers or those who are in wheelchairs.
There are three types of holiday:
1. By coach, using a new luxury vehicle with side lifts so that no steps are involved.
2. By air, on holidays co-ordinated with Thomas Cook and Wings.
3. Self-catering apartments on the sea front at Calpe in the Costa Blanca.
Holidays have been arranged in Yorkshire, Scotland, France, Germany, Switzerland, Belgium, Malta and Minorca.

Threshold Travel
Wrendal House, 2 Whitworth Street West, Manchester M1 5WX (Tel: 061-236 9763).
This firm provides European and world-wide holidays especially chosen for physically handicapped people travelling with families and friends.

Holidays include: motoring, fly-drive, coach tours and group holidays. A glossy brochure describes facilities available and locations. Applicants are required to state the nature of their disability in the booking form and to give the name and address of their doctor.

Travelwell
Carlisle House, 8 Southampton Row, London WC1B 4AE (Tel: 01-405 9481).
A new specialist company providing largely group holidays for disabled people abroad and in the United Kingdom. They will only arrange holidays in those destinations they have researched thoroughly as having suitable accommodation and transport. However, they have already arranged touring and one-centre holidays in Britain and in North America, Denmark, Malta, Southern Ireland, North Africa, Belgium, Holland and the south of France.

Thomsons have stated that they are able to arrange holidays for physically handicapped holidaymakers to any one of a number of hotels they consider suitable. They say that any travel agency will supply details of the best-equipped hotels. They ask for good advance warning of any special requests, and where necessary a doctor's certificate should be provided stating that the person is fit to fly. Contact local agents for further information.

Books and Publications

See also Access Guides listed under Country by Country.

Access at the Channel Ports: A guide for disabled people and those who have problems getting around (1982). Prepared by a group of old students of the Hephaistos School near Reading and St Paul's School in London. Half the group are disabled and half able-bodied and many of the entries in the book have been walked into and wheeled over by various survey teams. Other information has been supplied by the port authorities and ferry companies.

This is a wonderfully practical and friendly book, a positive encouragement to have a go. There is a good deal of general information and there is detailed information on the ferry and hovercraft services, and, of course, on the ports themselves.

The guide is free although a contribution towards postage and printing would be appreciated. Available from Pauline Hephaistos Survey Projects, 39 Bradley Gardens, West Ealing, London W13.

Central Bureau for Educational Visits and Exchanges
Seymour Mews House, 26–37 Seymour Mews, London W1H 9PE (Tel: 01-486 5101).
CBEVE publish a number of useful travel books, some of which indicate those organisations which welcome disabled participants whether physically, visually or hearing impaired. As symbols, the letters PH, B and D are used. Unfortunately there are not too many PHs and even fewer Bs and Ds, but you may find just what you are looking for!
1. *Working Holidays*. The authoritative guide to working around the world compiled by Hilary Sewell for CBEVE. A marvellously challenging book opening up opportunities for the adventurous to turn their hand to a wide variety of jobs around the world, from archaeology to farmwork. This book shows you the way to pick hops in Kent or grapes in France, teach crafts to American children or English in Japan,

restore Roman roads in Italy or *châteaux* in France. In the domestic section there are opportunities to work as housekeeper, bookkeepers, laundry and bar staff, food buyer, chef and cashier in a number of locations including Club Méditerranée villages (provided you can speak French). The guide also gives practical information on cheap accommodation and travel insurance and work permits. Available from CBEVE, price £2.95.

2. *School Travel and Exchange.* A guide for parents, teachers and youth leaders listing world-wide education and adventure activities for those aged 8 to 18. Opportunities are many and varied including painting and drawing in Italy, jazz dancing in Finland, camping in Iceland and exploring the Netherlands by barge. There is also a section on Great Britain. The guide gives details of home-to-home exchanges and paying-guest visits, advice on programme planning and cheap travel, and much more. Available from CBEVE, price £1.50.

3. *Adventure and Discovery.* A guide giving details of many exciting and original sports, special interest, language and study holidays all over the world. Opportunities include travelling through seven time zones on the Trans-Siberian Express, husky sledging in Greenland, trekking in India, restoring paintings in Florence, and learning French in Cannes or Danish in Copenhagen. The guide also includes advice on cheap accommodation, travel, practical information and useful publications. Available from CBEVE, price £2.50.

The Disabled Traveller's International Phrasebook (1978) compiled and edited by Ian McNeil. Available from Royal Association for Disability and Rehabilitation, 25 Mortimer Street, London W1N 8AB (Tel: 01-637 5400).

Words and phrases specially relevant to the disabled traveller are listed under the headings aids, ailments, the human body, parts of a wheelchair, materials, utensils and medicaments, sources of help, access, wheelchair, motoring and repairs. The *Phrasebook* contains English, French, German, Italian, Spanish, Portuguese, Swedish and Dutch. Price 90p including postage and packing.

Holiday Inns provide a guide to their hotels listing those in Great Britain and abroad with special facilities. Each hotel has a room (if possible on the ground-floor) with access facilities incorporating a bathroom, and including helpful details such as handrails, low mirrors, etc. Available from Holiday Inn, 128 King Henry's Road, London NW3 3ST (Tel: 01-722 7711).

Holidays for the Physically Handicapped, published by the Royal Association for Disability and Rehabilitation, 25 Mortimer Street, London W1N 8AB (Tel: 01-637 5400), has a very adequate section on holidays abroad (*see* page 180 in Section 9 for information regarding this book).

International Directory of Access Guides prepared by the staff of *Rehabilitation World – the US Journal of International News and Information*. This is a well-recommended and helpful directory covering Australia, Austria, Belgium, Bermuda, Canada, Denmark, Finland, France, Germany, Hong Kong, Republic of Ireland, Israel, Italy, Japan, Luxembourg, the Netherlands, New Zealand, Norway, Portugal, Spain, Sweden, Switzerland, the United Kingdom and the United States, and including air and rail guides. Available free from Travel Survey Department, Rehabilitation International USA Inc., 20 West 40th Street, New York, NY 10018, USA.

International List of Travelling Holiday and City Guides for the Disabled. Fourth revised edition compiled May 1981. Provides a country-by-country list. Available from Rehabilitation International Information Service, c/o Stiftung Rehabilitation, 6900 Heidelberg 1, Postfach 101 409, Federal Republic of Germany. Price DM 20 per copy – prepayment is requested.

Motoring and Mobility for Disabled People by Ann Darnbrough and Derek Kinrade. The book includes a chapter on holiday motoring, giving information on ferries, Motorail, Hovercraft services, toll concessions, etc. For full details of the book *see* page 167.

Rollin' On: A Wheelchair Guide to US Cities (1978). Maxine H. Atwater. Published by Dodd, Mead and Company, 79 Madison Avenue, New York, NY 10016. Price $9.95. This guide offers detailed sightseeing itineraries for Chicago, Honolulu, New York, Philadelphia, San Diego, San Antonio, San Francisco and Washington DC as well as giving information on other cities – Boston, Denver, Miami, New Orleans, Phoenix and Seattle. Additionally, an introductory chapter provides basic travel information that applies to any US city.

Travelability. A Guide for Physically Disabled Travellers in the United States by Lois Reamy. We have not had the pleasure of seeing this book, but the *New York Times* says of it: 'probably the most comprehensive, thoughtful and useful guidebook on the subject yet written'.

Available from Accent Special Publications, Box 700, Bloomington, Illinois 61701, USA. Price $13.95 plus $1.35 postage and packing. We understand it is also free on loan as a talking book from Recording for the Blind, 215E 58th Street, New York 10022 but we are unable to check this.

The Wheelchair Traveller by Douglass Annand. A directory of over 6,000 listings from the 50 US States, plus Canada, Mexico, Puerto Rico and more. Lists accessible hotels, motels, restaurants and sightseeing attractions that can be enjoyed by handicapped travellers. This guide was compiled by a paraplegic who has travelled extensively. Price $8.25 including postage and packing. Available from The Wheelchair Traveller, Ball Hill Road, Milford, NH, 03055, USA.

Rail Travel

Railway travel abroad can be a hazardous business. It must be remembered that Continental trains are very high up from the platform and there are steep steps to negotiate. Also disabled people who cannot travel in a normal train carriage are usually not allowed to travel in their wheelchairs in the guard's van.

See under the Netherlands, Norway and the United States for special railway services in those countries.

MOTORAIL SERVICES

See Section 8.

World-wide Travel Manual for the Handicapped. We have not had the opportunity of seeing this manual but we understand it has been specifically designed to assist the travel agent to book the holiday/travel arrangements most suited to the disabled person. It contains details of over 5,000 hotels, motels and camp sites in 100 countries and gives full details of facilities available at international airports. The book is only available to travel agents, but you might find it helpful to ask your nearest agent if she has a copy as a guide to help you arrange your holiday.

Air Travel

Airlines require disabled people to contact them well in advance of their journey, in order that any necessary special arrangements may be organised. Depending on the severity of the disability, the airline may require a 'medical certificate of fitness for air travel', to be completed by the traveller's doctor. Not all airlines want this, and it is important to check at the time of booking.

It is worth noting that folding wheelchairs are carried on aeroplanes free of weight restrictions.

Some airlines will allow disabled people to stay in their wheelchairs, arranging a space near the rear of the plane. The *Who Looks After You* leaflets give details of the special facilities available to the disabled traveller and may be obtained for the following airports: Heathrow, Gatwick, Stansted and Scottish Airports. All are available free of charge from the External Relations Department, British Airports Authority, Head Office, Gatwick Airport, West Sussex RH6 0HZ (Tel: Gatwick (0293) 517755).

Teesside Airport Authority's leaflet *Disabled Passengers' Guide to Teesside Airport and Hotel* is free from Airport Director, Teesside Airport, Darlington, Co. Durham DL2 1LU (Tel: Dinsdale (0325) 332811).

Care in the Air – Advice for Handicapped Passengers. This little booklet very encouragingly starts out by pointing out that British Airways carries around 50,000 handicapped passengers every year – two-thirds of them using wheelchairs. It goes on to provide a practical guide to air travel discussing prior preparations, fares (blind persons are entitled to special concessions on UK domestic routes), arrival at the airport, facilities at the airport, boarding and leaving the aircraft, etc. Available free from the Air Transport Users Committee, 129 Kingsway, London WC2B 6NN (Tel: 01-242 3882).

Cardiff-Wales Airport has issued a booklet *Advice for Disabled Passengers*. Further details from Cardiff-Wales Airport, nr Cardiff CF6 9BD (Tel: Rhoose (0446) 710296).

Access Travel: Airports, A Guide to Accessibility of Terminals. The booklet lists design features, facilities and services at 282 airport terminals around the world that are important to handicapped travellers. Available from National Clearing House of Rehabilitation Training Materials, 115 Old USDA Building, Oklahoma State University, Stillwater, OK 74078, USA. Price $1.25.

Access to the Skies. An international project, Access to the Skies aims to make airlines more accessible for disabled travellers. That includes making the lavatories accessible, providing foldable arm-rests, developing boarding and on-board wheelchairs (some of which are already in commercial production), among a number of other objectives.

A number of major airlines are making important initiatives in this area. SAS (Scandinavian Airlines System) was the first air carrier in the world to equip its entire fleet with movable aisle arm-rests. KLM, the Dutch airline, is rapidly moving to make its fleet of aircraft accessible.

The *Access to the Skies* programme plans to publish a list of such facilities offered by each airline and how the disabled traveller may request them.

Incapacitated Passengers Air Travel Guide. Published by IATA (International Air Transport Association), this booklet provides basic information on all aspects of air travel for 'incapacitated' persons. It includes an introduction to the standard IATA forms and procedures, and much useful information on what the airlines require of incapacitated passengers and how to make a trouble-free airline trip. Published in English and French. Available free of charge for five copies or less. Available from Publications Officer, International Air Transport Association, 26 chemin de Joinville, 1216 Cointrin, Geneva, Switzerland.

Motoring

CAR FERRY SERVICES

As is obvious, there are quite a number of ferries operating across the channel offering different routes, different prices, different levels of service and each with its own advantages and disadvantages. Many car ferry companies offer some measure of facilities, including financial concessions to disabled drivers whose cars have been adapted to suit their particular needs.

We give brief details below, but we would strongly recommend you send for a copy of the book *Access at the Channel Ports* which gives very full information on the ferry services (*see* page 205).

We divide the companies into three distinct groups:
GROUP 1 – those allowing eligible vehicles free passage.
GROUP 2 – those allowing varying discounts in respect of eligible vehicles.
GROUP 3 – those making no concessions, but nevertheless providing accessible features.
As you will see the concessions normally apply *only* to the eligible vehicle and represent either a total or partial reduction in charges. So far as we know there is only one exception, that of a Scottish ferry which allows discounts on passenger fares; otherwise driver and passenger fares are paid at normal rates.

In order to qualify for the concessionary rates all but one of the ferry companies (the exception is Sealink which has special arrangements) require drivers to be authorised by either the Disabled Drivers Association (DDA) or the Disabled Drivers Motor Club (DDMC). Details of these clubs are given on page 157.

Both the DDA and the DDMC have leaflets ex-

plaining the application procedures and precise criteria; also outlining in detail the policies of shipping companies which offer concessions and on which routes the concessions are applicable. It will be necessary, when writing to your club, to give brief details of your disability and the adaptations fitted to your vehicle, to indicate whether you are in receipt of mobility allowance and to enclose a stamped addressed envelope.

GROUP 1. The following ferries carry eligible vehicles free of charge, subject to authorisation as described above.

Sealink – British Rail. Disabled drivers may now be granted free conveyance of their cars without being members of the DDA or the DDMC. You should send for an application form to Sealink UK Ltd, Eversholt House, 163–203 Eversholt Street, London NW1 1BG (Tel: 01-387 1234). The form has to be signed by a director of a local authority social services or social work department who must certify that the applicant is a severely disabled driver. You are asked to make sure that you apply well in advance of your journey so that all documentary procedures can be completed smoothly.
Routes: France, Belgium, Holland, Isle of Wight, Ireland, Isle of Man and the Channel Islands.
Townsend Thoresen. 1 Camden Crescent, Dover, Kent CT16 1LD (Tel: Dover (0304) 203388).
Routes: Dover/Calais; Dover/Zeebrugge; Felixstowe/Zeebrugge; Southampton/Le Havre; Southampton/Cherbourg; Portsmouth/Le Havre; Portsmouth/Cherbourg; Cairnryan/Larne.
P & O Ferries – Channel Services. Arundel Towers, Portland Terrace, Southampton SO9 4AE (Tel: Southampton (0703) 34141).
Routes: Southampton/Le Harvre; Dover/Boulogne.
B + I Line. Reliance House, Water Street, Liverpool L2 8TP (Tel: Liverpool 051-227 3131).
Routes: Liverpool/Dublin; Pembroke/Cork; Holyhead/Dublin; Pembroke/Rosslare. We are informed these routes may be changed.
North Sea Ferries Ltd. King George Dock, Hedon Road, Hull HU9 5QA (Tel: Hull (0482) 795141).
Routes: Hull/Rotterdam and Zeebrugge.
Olau Line Ferries. Sheerness, Kent ME12 1SN (Tel: Sheerness (0795) 666666).
Routes: Sheerness/Flushing and Vlissingen.
Brittany Ferries. Brittany Centre, Wharf Road, Portsmouth PO7 8RU (Tel: Portsmouth (0705) 27701).
Routes: Plymouth/Roscoff and St Malo; Portsmouth/St Malo.
GROUP 2. The following shipping lines are among those offering varying discounts, mostly ranging

from 20 per cent to 50 per cent off the cost of carrying the car. In addition, many of the Scottish island and other national ferry services offer concessions. It is always worth enquiring before setting sail.

The Isle of Man Steam Packet Co. Ltd. PO Box 5, Imperial Buildings, Douglas, Isle of Man.

P & O Ferries. PO Box 5, P & O Ferries Terminal, Jamieson's Quay, Aberdeen AB9 8DL.

Routes: Aberdeen/Lerwick; Scrabster/Stromness.

DFDS Danish Seaways. Passenger Department, Latham House, 16 Minories, London EC3N 1AD (Tel: 01-481 3211).

Routes: Harwich/Newcastle and Esbjerg; Newcastle and Gothenburg operated jointly with Tor Line.

GROUP 3. The following ferry services make available facilities to disabled passengers and drivers, but do not at present offer any financial concessions. However, it would always be worth asking in case they have changed their policy or to encourage them to do so.

DFDS Prins Ferries. Latham House, 16 Minories, London EC3N 1AD (Tel: 01-481 3211).

Routes: Harwich/Hamburg. It is possible to join connecting ferries from Hamburg to Finland (Helsinki) via Finnlines. You should ask Prins Ferries about these arrangements.

DFDS Tor Line. Anzani House, Trinity Avenue, Felixstowe IP11 8EX (Tel: Felixstowe (0394) 273131).

Routes: Harwich/Gothenburg; Newcastle/Gothenburg operated jointly with DFDS (Danish Seaways).

Fred Olsen Travel. 11 Conduit Street, London W1R 0LS (Tel: 01-491 3760 – administration; 01-409 2091 – reservations).

Routes: Harwich and Newcastle/Kristiansand, Oslo, Bergen and Stavanger. (This service is now operated by DFDS (Danish Seaways).)

HOVERCRAFT SERVICES

These are alternatives to the ferry services and can be used by private cars as well as coach and rail operators. Unfortunately, the service is more vulnerable than the ferry to changes in the weather.

Hoverspeed

(a) International Hoverport, Ramsgate BT12 5HS (Tel: Thanet (0843) 54881).

Approximate crossing time to Calais – 40 minutes. There is fairly good access throughout the terminal, except for the restaurant which is up 25 stairs. Lavatory cubicle doors are 22 in. wide. At Calais they are a spacious 27 in. There are five steps up from the car deck to the seating area on board the hovercraft. The lavatory on board is not accessible to wheelchair-bound people.

(b) Dover International Hoverport, Kent CT17 9TG (Tel: Dover (0304) 208013).

Routes: Dover/Boulogne (39-45 minutes); Dover/Calais (35 minutes). There is good access throughout the newly designed terminal. Lavatory cubicle doorways are 26 in. A specially adapted and accessible unisex lavatory is situated in the departure lounge. The lavatories on board are not accessible to wheelchair-bound people.

Reservations for Hoverports: Thanet (0843) 55555; London 01-499 9481; Birmingham 021-236 2186; Manchester 061-228 1453. Prior notification of any special requirements is needed by the company when they will do all they can to help.

TAKING YOUR INVALID TRICYCLE ABROAD

Your three-wheeler may be taken outside the United Kingdom for the purpose of holiday travel and for no longer than 31 days, only to the Republic of Ireland or certain countries on the continent of Europe. It is necessary first to have the formal permission of the Department of Health and Social Security. At least three weeks' notice must be given to enable insurance arrangements to be made. Similarly, users on the mainland of Great Britain must obtain permission from the Department to take their three-wheelers to Northern Ireland.

An additional premium which will include Accidental Damage, Fire and Theft in respect of your three-wheeler will be payable by you for each visit made to the continent of Europe and Republic of Ireland. In the event of an accident in these places you will be required to pay the first £10 of any claim. On payment of the premium, an International Motor Insurance Card (Green Card) will be issued, the production of which is necessary in most Continental countries and it must be obtained before the start of a journey.

To start the official procedure you should contact in England and Wales: Department of Health and Social Security, Disablement Services Branch, Government Buildings, Warbreck Hill Road, Blackpool, Lancashire FY2 0UZ. In Scotland: Scottish Home and Health Department, Room 205, St Andrew's House, Edinburgh EH1 3DE.

ORANGE BADGE SCHEME

Reciprocal arrangements with European countries
Since December 1981, holders of orange badges who visit some European countries which provide parking concessions for their own disabled citizens may take advantage of the concessions made by the host country by displaying their orange badge. The concessions vary from one country to another, but they

usually allow for an extension of the time limit where waiting is restricted and an entitlement to use special parking places reserved for disabled people.

Apart from the United Kingdom, 12 countries are participating. They are Austria, Belgium, Denmark, Finland, France, West Germany, Italy, Luxembourg, Netherlands, Portugal, Sweden and Switzerland. The concessions available in Northern Ireland under their orange badge scheme are also open to orange badge holders from Great Britain, and from 1 April 1982 the Jersey orange badge scheme has been available to holders of UK badges.

It should be noted that in some countries responsibility for introducing the concessions rests with individual local authorities so that they may not be generally available. In such cases badge holders should enquire locally, as they should whenever they are in any doubt as to their entitlement. Moreover, as in this country, the arrangements apply only to badge holders themselves and the concessions are not for the benefit of able-bodied friends or relatives. Non-entitled people who seek to take advantage of the concessions in Europe by wrongfully displaying an orange badge will be liable to whatever penalties apply for unlawful parking in the country in question.

A summary of the parking concessions available to disabled people in each country is given below. Queries about these arrangements may be sent to the Department of Transport, Room S1/10, 2 Marsham Street, London SW1P 3EB (Tel: 01-212 5252).

Austria

The Austrian scheme of parking concessions allows badge holders to park without time limit where indicated and they may stop (even where double parked) where the relevant sign is displayed.

A sign is also used to indicate that badge holders may park in a pedestrian zone when loading and unloading is permitted. In addition, the authorities may set aside special parking places for disabled people's vehicles near such places as hospitals and public service facilities for the care of disabled people.

Belgium

Special parking places are reserved for disabled people. These are indicated by sign with the addition of the international symbol.

Badge holders may also park without time limit where parking time is otherwise restricted:
(a) by road signs;
(b) in blue zones;
(c) by parking meters (most local authorities do not require badge holders to pay at meters).

Under no circumstances are badge holders allowed to park in places where parking is prohibited.

Denmark

Badge holders are allowed to park for up to one hour where a shorter time limit applies to other motorists and unlimited parking is permitted where a time limit of one hour or longer would otherwise apply.

Finland

Badge holders are allowed to park in places where parking is prohibited by road signs and they will be exempt from parking charges. Concessions have not yet been extended to include disabled visitors.

France

Responsibility for parking concessions in built-up areas rests with local mayors and not central or regional authorities. Apart from reserved parking places for the disabled (indicated by the international symbol) there is no formal system of concessions in operation although it is understood that, in practice, a good deal of latitude is given, since the police have instructions to show consideration where parking by disabled motorists is concerned.

In some towns or cities, such as Paris, disabled people are allowed to park at meter bays and pay only the initial charge.

West Germany

Badge holders are allowed to park:
(a) for a maximum of three hours where indicated (the time of arrival must be shown on a parking disc);
(b) beyond the permitted time in certain areas;
(c) beyond the permitted time where a sign is displayed with an additional panel restricting parking time;
(d) during the permitted periods for loading and unloading in pedestrian zones;
(e) without charge or time limit at parking meters;
These concessions apply unless other parking facilities are available within a reasonable distance.

Reserved parking places for disabled people are also provided; these are indicated by a sign with the international symbol or in exceptional cases where the symbol is marked on the highway.

Italy

Responsibility for the concessions rests with the local authorities. In general, public transport is given priority in town centres and private cars may be banned, but the authorities are required to take special measures to allow badge holders to take their vehicles into social, cultural and recreational activity areas as well as to their work places.

Reserved parking bays are provided, indicated by signs with the international symbol (a small number of spaces are reserved for particular vehicles and in such cases the sign will show appropriate registration number).

Luxembourg

In most urban areas reserved parking places are provided and indicated by signs with the international symbol. Generally speaking, however, badge holders are not allowed to exceed the parking time limit.

Netherlands

Badge holders are entitled to the following concessions:

(a) the use of a car park set aside for handicapped people (the parking place must be signed and there is no time limit);
(b) indefinite parking in blue zones;
(c) indefinite parking at places marked with a sign in conjunction with an additional panel stating parking time;
(d) parking at places properly marked for a maximum of two hours. A handicapped person's parking disc must be used. This concession does not apply where other parking facilities exist within a reasonable distance. An extension of this time limit, particularly after 6 p.m. is being considered.

Portugal

Parking places are reserved for badge holder's vehicles. These are indicated by signs with the international symbol.

Badge holders are not allowed to park in places where parking is prohibited by a general regulation or a specific sign.

Sweden

Badge holders are allowed to park:

(a) for three hours where parking is banned or allowed only for a shorter period;
(b) for a period of 24 hours where a time limit of three hours or more is in force;
(c) at reserved parking spaces, indicated by signs with the international symbol;

In general, parking charges must be paid although there may be local exemptions. Concessions have not yet been extended to include disabled visitors.

Switzerland

Badge holders are allowed to park:

(a) without time limit at parking places where time limits are in force or within a blue or red zone;
(b) without time limit at parking meters on payment of the minimum charge;
(c) where parking is otherwise banned, provided no obstruction or danger is caused and that no other parking spaces are available. (Parking is not allowed where stopping is prohibited);
(d) at reserved parking places indicated by signs with the international symbol.

Coach Travel

Greyhound Lines, International Sales
14–16 Cockspur Street, London SW1 (Tel: 01-839 5591).

This firm offers a Helping Hand Service for handicapped people which is exceptionally considerate in the provision it makes for disabled travellers in the United States and Canada. Where a disabled person requires the assistance of a companion, on production of a medical certificate, only one ticket will be charged; an imaginative range of facilities and services is also offered.

Emergency Travel

Trans-Care International
193–195 High Street, Acton, London W3 9DD (Tel: 01-992 5077).

A world-wide get-you-home commercial 24-hour service for the seriously injured and disabled. Trans-Care will take over all the necessary arrangements with a doctor in attendance and with official bodies – Foreign Office, customs, police, immigration authorities, airlines, consuls, etc. – and will organise the fastest and most suitable travel arrangements. There are standard charges; *i.e.* a private ambulance to and from Heathrow to a London hospital costs £60, including one hour waiting time. The crew helps with luggage, documentation and, in most cases, transfers direct from ambulance to plane or vice versa.

The St John Ambulance Aeromedical Services
1 Grosvenor Crescent, London SW1X 7EF (Tel: 01-235 4633 (24-hour service)).

Provides volunteer medical practitioners and qualified nurses specially trained in in-flight care who also have the necessary aeromedical equipment. They will escort sick and injured people by air to and from any part of the world. This voluntary service is available to any company, organisation or private individual. It is able, at short notice, to provide qualified Aeromedical attendants to escort patients travelling on scheduled flights and, when necessary, to arrange the charter and the equipping of aircraft as air ambulances ranging from light aircraft to executive jets. In addition to escorting patients by air the service will, if necessary, undertake all the booking arrangements and supply an ambulance to or from the airport.

The St John Aeromedical Attendants are all volunteers who do not charge or receive any fees for their services. The cost of their return fare on scheduled flights, their expenses incurred in travelling to and from the United Kingdom and any overnight accommodation and incidental expenses and, in the case of chartered aircraft, the cost of chartering, are the responsibility of the patient, his agents or the person requesting the service. Further information from the Director, St John Ambulance, Aeromedical Services.

Air Ambulance Service
Bilbao House, 36–38 New Broad Street, London EC2M 1NH (Tel: 01-588 3578/4207).
The international service is available to individuals, national and international organisations, travel and shipping companies, government departments, embassies and health services. Teams of specialist medical officers, nursing officers and paramedical attendants, who are trained to care for intensive therapy patients, are on call 24 hours a day. The Service will also be glad to offer quotations for those disabled people who simply require the privacy of their own aircraft without necessarily having their own attendant medical facilities.

SECTION 11
SPORTS AND LEISURE

The spice of life is provided by all those numerous activities we follow by inclination, and seemingly because, unlike our work, they are voluntarily chosen we pursue them with that extra degree of zeal. In these areas we are expressing hidden facets of ourselves and perhaps more fully developing our personalities than is possible in any other way. For disabled people the choice can be narrower, but, perhaps because the challenge is harder, the achievements are so often that much greater.

Where they are satisfied that there is real need, local authorities are empowered by the Chronically Sick and Disabled Persons Act 1970 to help disabled people who are resident in their areas to enjoy a wide range of recreational activities. For instance, they may provide or help people to obtain radio, television or similar leisure facilities. They may also provide lectures, games, outings and many other leisure pursuits including social and youth clubs. Many local authorities operate a travelling library service which will call regularly at the homes of those who are confined to them.

The arrangements differ considerably from area to area but it is certainly worth making full enquiries as to the opportunities in your own locality. We would urge that you never be put off too easily if your own particular interests appear not to be provided for. This may merely be the result of a lack of demand; for instance almost any subject can be covered by an evening class when that need is demonstrated. Our experience is that requests from disabled people are received with more than usual consideration. Nor should it be forgotten that many voluntary organisations provide recreational activities, and specialist sporting and hobby clubs will often go out of their way to welcome and help a disabled person.

In addition many sports centres and outdoor pursuits centres provide opportunities for disabled people to participate in their programmes. Many sports centres now run sports clubs especially for disabled people, and the local centre manager should be approached for details.

The British Sports Association for the Disabled will also be glad to provide information on local facilities and the local BSAD representative would be glad to offer individual advice.

For details of holiday courses in a wide variety of subjects, *see* Section 9.

Amateur Radio

The Radio Amateur Invalid and Blind Club
Secretary: Frances Woolley, 9 Rannoch Court, Adelaide Road, Surbiton, Surrey KT6 4TE.
The Club was founded in 1954 as a self-help organisation to enable blind and handicapped people to pool their knowledge, skills and spare radio components and to benefit from each other's experience. Over the years the Club has grown considerably, and has links with similar organisations, both in this country and abroad. Membership is by a normal subscription to *Radial* the Club newsletter.

Members wishing to obtain their transmitting licences are helped in their studies by local amateurs and clubs. Cassettes are available for the use of blind members, and Morse code lessons are also taped. Local helpers undertake to keep equipment serviceable and advise members.

Radial is issued eight times a year at a minimum annual subscription of £1.50. It contains news of and from members and articles on many subjects. Also available on cassette.

The Radio Society of Great Britain
35 Doughty Street, London WC1N 2AE (Tel: 01-837 8688).
The national society of radio amateurs in the United Kingdom. Members of the RSGB receive the monthly edition of *Radio Communication* and are provided with information on technical matters and on the various activities and events of concern to amateurs. There are regional and area representatives who can provide advice on the hobby and also supply information on local club meetings.

How to Become a Radio Amateur
Copies of this pamphlet may be obtained without charge from the OCCA Division, Dept of Trade and

Industry, Radio Regulatory Division, Waterloo Bridge House, Waterloo Road, London SE1 8UA (Tel: 01-275 3000).

Citizen's Band Radio
See page 217.

Angling

People with a wide range of disabilities are able to enjoy angling. The different types of fishing and the range of techniques available provide a spread of options to suit individual needs and tastes. The three forms of angling – coarse fishing, game fishing (salmon and trout) and sea fishing can be enjoyed from bank or shoreline, landing stages, piers or boats.

The Water Sports Division of BSAD (*see* page 229) will be glad to advise. *See also* details of their publication *Water Sports for the Disabled. See also* Section 9, Interest and Specialist Holidays.

National Anglers' Council
11 Cowgate, Peterborough PE1 1LZ (Tel: Peterborough (0733) 54084).
The Council will advise on facilities throughout the country. It has set up a Committee for Disabled Anglers and has published a *Guide to Fishing Facilities for Disabled Anglers* which lists over 100 fishing sites (coarse, sea and game) in England and Wales where both ambulant and disabled anglers may fish. Details of relevant officials to contact, species of fish, parking and shelter facilities, and of special equipment available are covered. Price £1.

Committee for the Promotion of Angling for the Disabled
Aims to develop angling facilities for disabled people in Scotland. A member of the Committee has designed a purpose-built seat and gantry. Anyone who would like to make use of special angling facilities is invited to register with the Committee. The person will be issued with a registration card entitling him or her to the concessionary rates available on various lochs and rivers in Scotland.

The Committee, together with the Scottish Sports Association for the Disabled (*see* page 235) has produced an access guide to fishing areas describing a range of information of concern to disabled fisherpeople including whether a special gantry is available.
For information contact Tom Mackenzie, 17 Nicholson Street, Edinburgh EH8 (Tel: 031-667 2288 – daytime Monday to Saturday).

FILMS
Able to Fish, in three parts:
1. *Coarse Angling* (16 mm, colour, 34 minutes)
2. *Game Fishing* (16 mm, colour, 32 minutes)
3. *Sea Angling* (16 mm, colour, 23 minutes)
These films on angling for disabled people are available from Town and Country Productions, 21 Cheyne Row, Chelsea, London SW3 5HP. The hire charge in each case is £11.50 to be sent with order. The films are now also available for hire on VHS or Betamax at £11.50 and for sale at £39.95 including VAT.

Archery

The Grand National Archery Society
National Agricultural Centre, Stoneleigh, Kenilworth, Warwickshire (Tel: Coventry (0203) 23907). For information on national activities contact the Secretary.

Archery for Disabled People
7 New Street, Shefford, Bedfordshire SG17 5BW. This is part of the Grand National Archery Society and aims to help those disabled people who are keen to take up the sport and also to provide solutions experienced by existing archers. Help can be given with release aids, special adaptations and where to seek tuition. A new archery round was initiated in 1981, The Elizabethan, specifically for the novice and severely disabled person. For further information, physically disabled people should contact the National Co-ordinator John Burgess at the above address – please enclose a 4 in. × 9 in. s.a.e.
See also BSAD book on archery, page 236.

Arts and Crafts

Trust Fund for the Training of Handicapped Children in Arts and Crafts
94 Claremount Road, Wallasey, Merseyside L45 6UE (Tel: 051-638 1422).
Any parent, guardian or teacher who believes that a handicapped child would benefit by extra art tuition, a supply of art materials and equipment should apply. Financial help is available.

Conquest – The Art Society for the Physically Handicapped
3 Beverley Close, East Ewell, Epsom, Surrey KT17 3HB (Tel: 01-642 0473/393 6102).
Conquest aims to encourage physically handicapped adults to take up and pursue artistic, creative activity. For this purpose groups have been formed and a magazine and pamphlets produced. In addition, ex-

hibitions are held, talks are given and information is available.

Athletics

Advisory Notes for Track and Field Officials at Sports Meetings for the Disabled
Available from Moira Gallagher, Amateur Athletic Association, 26 Banfield Crescent, High Ash, Leeds LS17 8RU (Tel: Leeds (0532) 689043).
Athletics by Moira Gallagher. Produced by the British Sports Association for the Disabled. Chapters include: Athletes for all Disabilities, The Rules of Athletics and How to Officiate; Organising an Athletics Meeting; Athletics Awards to Young Athletes. Price £1.75 including postage and packing.

Available from BSAD, Sir Ludwig Guttmann Sports Centre for the Disabled, Stoke Mandeville, Harvey Road, Aylesbury, Buckinghamshire HP21 8PP.

Basketball

The Great Britain Wheelchair Basketball Association
76 Leicester Road, Failsworth, Manchester M35 0QP (Tel: 061-682 9521).
The Association is the governing body of wheelchair basketball in the United Kingdom and is affiliated to the English and Scottish Basketball Associations. The aim of the Association is to promote and encourage the game, particularly through its various Leagues and Competitions. The National League is made up of a First Division and regional divisions playing matches between October and April each year. Playing membership is open to those 'who have a severe permanent physical disability of one or both lower extremities which excludes their participation in the regular game of basketball'. The Association encourages all levels of the sport organising coaching and tournaments for youngsters: the age limit for the Senior National League is a minimum of 14 years. Teams are mixed with women and men playing together. We are told that it is very likely that by the 1988 Olympics for the Disabled there will, in fact, be a very good Women's GB team. All information concerning rules, coaching and League entry to the above.

Billiards and Snooker

While, because of the regulation height of the tables, there are obvious difficulties in playing these games from a wheelchair, some disabled people can overcome this handicap. From another point of view, wheelchairs benefit from the fact that it is necessary to have considerable space around the table to handle the long cues. For details of snooker playing by disabled people contact the British Sports Association for the Disabled, Ludwig Guttmann Sports Centre for the Disabled, Stoke Mandeville Hospital, Harvey Road, Aylesbury, Buckinghamshire HP21 8PP (Tel: Aylesbury (0296) 27889).

Billiards and Snooker Control Council
Coronet House, Queen Street, Leeds LS1 2TN (Tel: Leeds (0532) 440586).
The Council is responsible for the organisation and running of all national billiards and snooker events for non-professional players. It jointly sponsors the Billiards and Snooker Foundation and as such administers a national coaching scheme.

Board Games

Some of the most popular games, such as Scrabble, Mastermind, backgammon, chess and draughts, are available in specially adapted versions which make them suitable for blind, partially sighted, or sighted players, from the Royal National Institute for the Blind, 224 Great Portland Street, London W1N 6AA (Tel: 01-388 1266).

John Slade, 170 Cambridge Road, Seven Kings, Ilford, Essex IG3 8NA (Tel: 01-599 4256) has both redesigned board games and devised new ones with playing pieces which are both visual and tactile. He has produced an explanatory leaflet.

QED
1 Prince Alfred Street, Gosport, Hampshire PO12 1QH (Tel: Gosport (070 17) 81179).
The Stalkerboard Games Machine enables up to four disabled players to enjoy board games, including chess, draughts, backgammon, ludo, noughts and crosses, and solitaire using only one switch for each player. The metal games pieces are carried about the board by an electromagnet that is controlled by each player in turn.

Price £325 plus switch if required £5, plus freight and VAT.

QED also produce a simpler steel chess board with magnetic rubber chess pieces and a mains-operated dice thrower for disabled players.

WAVES
Corscombe, nr Dorchester, Dorset DT2 0NU (Tel: Corscombe (093 589) 248).
Manufacture and supply a variety of magnetic board games at prices from £3.40 to £18.12. These include some dual purpose boards, which have on the reverse the relatively unfamiliar but absorbing game, Nine Men's Morris (mentioned by Shakespeare).

Boating

See also Section 9, Peter Le Marchant Trust.

Useful guidance is contained in the publication *Water Sports for the Disabled*. This covers power boating, canal cruising, coracles, inflatable boats, model boats, and a specially built catamaran 'Sparkle' (this was provided by *Sparks*, the sportsman's charity and is accessible for up to ten people in wheelchairs). Enquire as to summer locations and group bookings (Tel: 01-637 5400). Early booking is recommended. For details *see* page 229, under British Sports Association for the Disabled – Water Sports Division.

Boating for the Handicapped: Guidelines for the Physically Handicapped by Eugene Hedley who is himself a physically handicapped boater. The guide deals largely with safety for the handicapped boater and lists the types of boating activities which may be considered suitable. The book discusses personal flotation devices, emergency equipment and procedures to follow if a boat capsizes or a person falls overboard. Also covered are procedures for transference of disabled boaters to and from the dock and handling special equipment for individual needs. One unique feature of the book is a section on boating safety written in braille. While the first print-run lasts, copies are free. Available from the Human Resources Centre, I. U. Willets Road, Albertson, New York 11507.

Bowling

English Bowls Council
Eric Crosbie, 150 Wellington Road, Enfield, Middlesex EN1 2RH (Tel: 01-360 7669).

With the help of portable ramps designed to prevent damage to greens, wheelchair bowlers can manoeuvre into position with efficiency. Specifications may be obtained from the British Sports Association for the Disabled (*see* Sports Associations, page 232).

Camping

See details in Section 9.

Canoeing

See also Section 9, the Calvert Trust Adventure Centre and the Multi-Activity Adventure Centre.

British Canoe Union
Flexel House, 45–47 High Street, Addlestone, Weybridge, Surrey KT15 1JV (Tel: Weybridge (0932) 41341).

Canoeing is a sport in which it is possible for people with certain disabilities to take part, very often at a standard comparable to an average canoe club member and occasionally to a far higher standard. The British Canoe Union considers that disabled people should be encouraged to play an active part as normal members of the sport. However, there are several groups which make special provision for disabled people, and many kayaks and canoes which are eminently suited or can easily be adapted for special needs. The BCU will give advice on all of these aspects. They also have a publication *Canoeing for the Disabled*, price 65p.

See also Spastics Society, page 236.

Useful guidance for disabled canoeists is contained in the publication *Water Sports for the Disabled*. For details on water sports *see* page 229, under British Sports Association for the Disabled – Water Sports Division.

Chess

British Chess Federation
9a Grand Parade, St Leonards-on-Sea, East Sussex TN38 0DD (Tel: Hastings (0424) 442500).

An 'umbrella' organisation to which is affiliated a multitude of local chess clubs and specialist societies. Carries information on chess by correspondence.

British Postal Chess Federation
22 Birley Road, London N20.

The principal objects of the Federation are to encourage the playing of chess by correspondence and to harmonise the efforts of the many chess organisations which are affiliated to it. There are five major affiliated correspondence chess organisations, details of which will gladly be provided by the Federation.

Braille Chess Association
59 Sefton Street, London SW15 1NA (Tel: 01-785 9844).

The Association offers its members a wide variety of services, including participation in international team and individual championships; braille correspondence chess between blind and sighted players; over the board chess against sighted teams; discussion groups on tape; publications of the BCA *Gazette* in braille or on tape; a cassette tape service of chess books and other chess publications (small copying charge on members' own tapes); a library of braille chess books; the sale of a braille book *The ABC of Chess*. Annual subscription is £4 or *pro rata*. For further details contact the Secretary, Jack Horrocks.

Friedreich's Ataxia Group Postal Chess Club
Organiser R. G. Hughes, 4 Lambs Hill Close, Thornton, Blackpool, Lancashire FY5 5JS.

The Chess Club is open to all members of FAG, for whom there are no fees.

Magnetic Chess, Draughts or Checkers with Boards
Details from WAVES, Corscombe, nr Dorchester, Dorset DT2 0NU (Tel: Corscombe (093 589) 248).

Cinemas and Theatres

Just the Ticket – Access to Theatres and Cinemas in Central London
A list compiled by the Greater London Council and available from the Royal Association for Disability and Rehabilitation, 25 Mortimer Street, London W1N 8AB. Price 25p.

Those disabled people who would like to visit local theatres or cinemas should contact the manager, as even where special facilities do not exist it may well be possible to make special arrangements. Likewise, the manager may be prepared to make arrangements for a disabled child to attend the Saturday morning cinema club.

Citizen's Band Radio

For many people, including those who are disabled or housebound, elderly, agoraphobic, shy or lonely, CB has made a significant contribution to their life-styles. CB is the instrument by which you can talk to people up to a few miles away free of charge (except for original equipment and licence costs) from home, car or trike.

Many individuals benefit from CB's relaxed, informal attitude. People who have previously found themselves isolated have developed new relationships through CB which have resulted in invitations to CB clubs or other breakers' (CB users') homes.

Motoring with CB also has its advantages. Not only can it provide company on the road but it can also be used to summon help. There is a 'Good Buddy' image which most CBers are proud of and it may be possible to find help with changing a tyre, phoning a garage or asking directions. A few small, enterprising electronic engineering companies have spent time working on refinements which make CBing easier for people with handicaps. The most useful adaptation for the mobile rig user is the Vox operated switch incorporated into a boom-type microphone. By merely speaking, the CB set automatically goes into transmit which saves both having to hold a microphone and having to press a button. Another adaptation made for blind people is a rig which actually speaks out the channel number to the user, which is obviously very useful.

If you decide you want to become more involved with CB as a hobby but would like more information

you could contact CiBTA (Citizen's Band Trade Association), PO Box 6, Hayes, Middlesex UB4 0SS (Tel: 01-561 5778). There may also be a CiBTA member near you selling the equipment.

A set of seven Citizen's Band Radio Information Sheets has been produced by the Department of Trade and Industry. Licensing, and its conditions, frequencies, modulation, antenna, together with details of illegal equipment and interference, are covered in detail in these fact sheets. Available from Department of Trade and Industry, OCCA Division, Waterloo Bridge House, Waterloo Road, London SE1 8UA (Tel: 01-275 3000).

Cookery

Cooking Made Easy for Disabled People by Audrey Ellis (with a Foreword by Anne Davies). Cooking should be enjoyable, even for those of us who have disabilities which make it difficult to move around in the kitchen or follow tiring recipe instructions. This 32-page booklet, specially produced by Sainsbury's in their popular Food Guides series, shows how problems can be overcome by streamlined cooking techniques. The recipes have been tested by disabled people themselves, and the booklet also contains helpful advice on planning a convenient kitchen, choosing equipment and easier shopping. Available from Sainsbury's stores at a price of 30p or from the Royal Association for Disability and Rehabilitation (RADAR), 25 Mortimer Street, London W1N 8AB, at 50p including postage.

The Cook's Lifeline by Joy Montague. Published by Exley Publications Limited, 16 Chalk Hill, Watford, Hertfordshire WD1 4BN.
This book of 256 pages, illustrated with dozens of line drawings is a useful 'shopping by post' way of choosing from a wide range of ideas for tableware, furniture and fittings, unusual foods, aids for disabled people in the kitchen, cookers, freezers, luxuries, novelties, courses, wallcharts and utensils. Price £4.95 paperback; £9.95 hardback, plus postage and packing.

Cycling

Tandem Club
25 Hendred Way, Abingdon, Oxfordshire OX14 2AN.
The Club has 2,500 members and exists to encourage tandem cycling by sending a bi-monthly magazine to all full members, by providing a comprehensive spare parts service and technical advice, by organising day runs and touring weekends and by running both open and club trials.

The Club has a Liaison Officer for handicapped members who is glad to offer help to blind, partially sighted people or those with, say, balancing problems or only one leg. The annual subscription of £3.25 covers up to two people (one full and one joint member).

Cyclists' Touring Club

Cotterell House, 69 Meadrow, Godalming, Surrey GU7 3HS (Tel: Godalming (048 68) 7217).
This Club has a scheme for enabling blind or partially sighted people to take part in cycle rides on the rear of a tandem. The Club would also be glad to explore other ways in which handicapped people could take part in local cycling activities. If anyone would like to explore such opportunities we have been assured that he or she will receive every assistance.

Drama

BBC Television Play Synopses. Printed by the BBC and distributed by RNID free of charge to deaf people to help them follow TV series transmitted by the BBC. Apply to The Royal National Institute for the Deaf, 105 Gower Street, London WC1E 6AH (Tel: 01-387 8033).

Fencing

Wheelchair Fencing Association

Leslie Veale, 14 Kingsley Park Grove, Sheffield S11 9HL (Tel: Sheffield (0742) 362194).
The WFA co-ordinates and assists the development of wheelchair fencing activities throughout Great Britain and is affiliated to the Amateur Fencing Association of Great Britain. They can supply information on local clubs, coaches, copies of the rules for fencing, plans for chair stabilising frames (£1 per set), and general information on the sport. Membership is £2 per annum. Associate membership for able-bodied people is £1 per annum.

Flying

Contact: Dawn Marler, 28 Addenbroke Drive, Wylde Green, Sutton Coldfield, West Midlands B73 5PY (Tel: 021-355 4384).
Coventry airport in Baginton, we are told, provides good facilities for disabled people interested in flying. It is hoped that other airports will show a similar interest and they are being encouraged to do so. Many more disabled people will be able to learn to fly when hand controls, which are in the course of production, become available. Anyone interested in learning to fly should contact Dawn Marler, who will do her best to advise.

Football

See Access Guide *Sports and Leisure*, page 239.

Gardening and Horticulture

See also Section 9, Field Centres.

The Alpine Garden Society

Lye End Link, St John's, Woking, Surrey GU21 1SW.
For all who are interested in rock gardening and alpine plants. The Society offers: a quarterly bulletin; a list of some 4,000 species of seeds; shows for exhibition; local groups; and tours to overseas mountain resorts under the guidance of expert leaders. Single membership is £6.50 per year (family £8).

Blind gardeners

RNIB's booklet *Gardening without sight* by Kathleen Fleet for blind people who enjoy growing flowers or vegetables in their garden, allotment or indoors is available in print, braille or on tape. Contact the Royal National Institute for the Blind, 224 Great Portland Street, London W1N 6AA for details.

The Gardener Magazine and the Cassette Library for Blind Gardeners

An annual subscription of £1 covers receipt of *The Gardener* magazine each quarter and use at any time of the Cassette Library for Blind Gardeners. Cheques and postal orders should be made payable to *The Gardener* or to the Cassette Library for Blind Gardeners. They should be sent to Kathleen Fleet, 48 Tolcarne Drive, Pinner, Middlesex HA5 2DQ (Tel: 01-868 4026). When writing you are asked to supply your own name and address in block capitals and not to send cassettes as you will be given full particulars about these in reply to your subscription.
The Gardener magazine is circulated quarterly in braille and on C90 cassette. The braille copies are small-sized volumes and the taped copies require only one cassette. The cassette copies are on loan, so must be returned each quarter. Subscribers should state whether they wish to receive braille or cassette copies. Slow braille readers often find that their speed in touch reading can be helped by having both braille and taped copies.
The Gardener is administered through the medium of the Cassette Library for Blind Gardeners. Every reader, whether taking braille or taped copies, can have free access to all the Library recordings at any time, but to obtain copies of these additional recordings magazine readers must send their own cassettes. A library catalogue list will be supplied to every subscriber and additions to the

Library announced in *The Gardener* magazine. Catalogue lists are sent in braille to braille readers and in typescript to those who receive the magazine on tape. Anyone wishing to have a cassette copy of the list can send a C60 cassette to the Library Copying Service, the address of which is given in the magazine. The magazine consists of short articles about all aspects of gardening, so readers will be able to find something for individual use and personal interest in every issue. The contents contain answers to readers' questions, news of recent products and ideas for helping gardeners without sight. Communication with readers is considered to be of great importance, as the magazine articles are based on their requests.

The Cassette Library for Blind Gardeners – the existing master tapes in the Library cover a wide range of gardening subjects and include Royal Horticultural Society Handbooks and other small specialist booklets. With the revival of *The Gardener*, additions to the Library are now chosen as supplements to the magazine which is available to registered blind and registered partially sighted people.

The Library points out that certain simple rules must be observed by subscribers, for example poor quality cassettes cannot be accepted for making copies as they damage the equipment.

The Federation to Promote Horticulture for Disabled People

The Drove, Gillingham, Dorset (Tel: Gillingham (074 76) 2369).

The Federation aims to identify the benefits which can be gained by disabled people from out-of-doors pursuits and to influence all concerned to recognise those benefits and to provide solutions to the problems that arise.

The Federation is a forum through which the many organisations and individuals involved in outdoor activities for disabled people keep in touch. To this end courses, conferences and meetings are arranged. Papers presented at these activities are published as annual proceedings. A mailing list subscription to a selected list of people interested in or concerned with the promotion of horticulture and land use for disabled people is available at an annual fee of £2.

The Garden Club

Honorary Secretary: Mrs M. Haines, Church Cottage, Headcorn, Kent TN27 9NP (Tel: Headcorn (0622) 890467).

A nationwide body affiliated to the Gardens for the Disabled Trust. It aims to encourage gardening by disabled people both for enjoyment and as a therapy. Members receive a quarterly newsletter and there is a comprehensive advisory service on disabled gardening. Grants are made for the adaptation, planning and equipment of disabled members' gardens, including the provision of suitable tools. Applications for grants must be supported by the local social services department. The Club is building up local representation so that local groups can be formed as needed.

Membership is open to any disabled person who enjoys gardening of any kind, from tending a bedside pot plant to managing a large garden. Individual membership is £1 a year. Life membership is £15. Membership for institutions is £2 a year. Able-bodied and disabled members are also sought to act as local advisers/helpers/representatives in all areas.

Gardens for the Disabled Trust

Honorary Secretary: Mrs M. Haines, Church Cottage, Headcorn, Kent TN27 9NP (Tel: Headcorn (0622) 890467).

Gives practical help with gardening for the disabled, with special interest in gardens which are cared for by a group such as hospitals, special schools, handicapped centres and so on. The Trust will consider a grant towards the suitable adaptation of equipment, raising of flower beds and so on.

Garden Research Department

Mary Marlborough Lodge, Nuffield Orthopaedic Centre, Headington, Oxford OX3 7LD (Tel: Oxford (0865) 64811).

The Centre will give advice and information on all aspects of gardening for the disabled and it is here that experiments and research are undertaken to continue to find the best possible ways of helping disabled gardeners to enjoy their hobby. The department will be glad to answer written enquiries but please enclose a s.a.e.

Horticulture training

If you want to train seriously to the extent of considering some kind of garden work, then the courses offered by the four national colleges for the disabled might be worth investigating. *See* Finchale Training College, Portland Training College, Queen Elizabeth's Training College and St Loye's College for Training the Disabled in Section 6.

The Royal Horticultural Society

Vincent Square, London SW1P 2PE (Tel: 01-834 4333).

The RHS welcomes disabled gardeners. If you are keen to learn more about the delights of horticulture many evening classes are of a very high standard and include the general examination of the RHS. If you prefer to study at home, the RHS would be glad to advise you as to which correspondence schools are prepared to teach the subject by post. The RHS also has a garden at Wisley, Surrey where they have erected a garden for disabled people which includes many helpful ideas. A useful publications list is available. For details of the garden, write to Royal Horticultural Society Garden, Wisley, Woking, Surrey.

The Society for Horticultural Therapy and Rural Training
Goulds Ground, Vallis Way, Frome, Somerset BA11 3DW (Tel: Frome (0373) 64782).
Horticultural Therapy is an organisation which offers practical help, through its services, to disabled gardeners and those who work with them. It publishes a most imaginative magazine *Growth Point*, which sets a very high standard in magazine publication. It includes articles and information of interest to the small-scale gardener and the professional horticulturist both in this country and abroad. The layout of interestingly organised print, spiced with pictures, cartoons and other graphics makes it a joy to read.

HT offers the following services:

Project development provides specialist staff to help and work on sites which may be managed by an NHS hospital, a social service department or a voluntary organisation.

Design service. A landscape architect can help in identifying the potential of a site. After that she can provide on site planning, design, construction planting and maintenance.

Land Use Volunteers (LUVs) are qualified or experienced young horticulturists. They can help a project by providing enthusiastic and competent help for up to 12 months as long as the project can supply board, lodging and pocket money.

HT Training Centre meets the special needs of those who work with disabled or handicapped people. The Centre offers practical study days throughout the year at its base at the Warwickshire College of Agriculture. Courses can also be offered at other venues.

International project development. HT contributes a service to help disabled farmers in developing countries and has a full-time member of staff based in Zimbabwe.

Information service. This provides a wide range of information either as a direct answer or by linking up the enquirer with other sources of information. A series of information sheets and special papers is available.

Gardening Unit. This aims to provide a garden advisory service to help individual disabled gardeners

with their problems. The Unit will also provide support for local groups where disabled gardeners will have the opportunity to discuss their problems and make their needs known.

GARDEN TOOLS FOR DISABLED PEOPLE

A wide range of tools is available on mail order and in garden shops. A few of these have been designed for people with disabilities while many others are simply designed to make gardening a lot easier for the great numbers of people with physical frailties who otherwise would not be able to indulge themselves in this absorbing hobby. The Society for Horticultural Therapy and Rural Training has a booklet entitled *Gardening for Everybody* which is a very useful source of information listing tools, aids and books.

Horticultural Therapy, as it is popularly known, can be contacted at Goulds Ground, Vallis Way, Frome, Somerset BA11 3DW (Tel: Frome (0373) 64782).

GARDENING BOOKS AND PUBLICATIONS

The following three books on gardening are available from the Disabled Living Foundation and may be obtained from: DLF Sales Ltd, Book House, 45 East Hill, Wandsworth, London SW18 2QZ.

1. *The Easy Path to Gardening*. A great deal of gardening research, knowledge and experience has been gathered in this book, and apart from advice on plants there is information on suitable tools and general planning, with a view to minimum effort and maximum effect. There is a wealth of comprehensive information and chapters are included on raised beds, chemical weed control, laying a garden path, lawn maintenance, window boxes, greenhouses, etc. Published by *Reader's Digest* in conjunction with the Disabled Living Foundation. Price £1.85.

2. *Gardening for the Disabled*. A set of papers including a list of suggested garden tools and plants and plans for making raised flower beds. Price £1 inclusive of postage.

3. *The Garden and the Handicapped Child* by Patricia Elliott. Deals with the practical and educational aspects of gardening for physically or mentally disabled children. Also covers vocational possibilities and gardening as a hobby. Fully illustrated. Price £4.10.

Gardening for the Physically Handicapped and Elderly by Mary Chaplin. A very full guide, with illustrations, covering aids and adaptations, species, indoor gardening, outbuildings, gardening in day centres and hospitals, facilities, tools and publications. Available from B. T. Batsford Ltd, 4 Fitzhardinge Street, London W1H 0AH (Tel: 01-486 8464). Price £5.95.

Gardening is for Everyone: A Week-by-Week Guide for People with Handicaps by Audrey Cloet and Chris Underhill. Published by Souvenir Press.
In this imaginative and detailed guide keen would-be gardeners will find a host of ideas for every week of the year, and within the scope of those whose mobility may be restricted. Designed with beginners in mind, it explains every technique with text and clear drawings, showing how to grow potatoes in containers, how to create a garden indoors, how and when to sow and plant, and how to make decorative pictures from pressed flowers, seedheads and grasses. Price £4.95 paperback; £6.95 hardback. Available from Horticultural Therapy, Goulds Ground, Vallis Way, Frome, Somerset BA11 3DW.

Gardens to Visit published by Gardeners' Sunday, who celebrated their Silver Jubilee in 1981. The booklet gives details of many gardens open in spring and summer; it gives a clear indication of their accessibility and was one of the first outdoor guides to encourage disabled visitors. It can be obtained from many booksellers price 50p or direct from Mrs K. Collett, White Witches, 8 Mapstone Close, Glastonbury, Somerset BA6 8EY. The price by post is 70p inclusive of postage and packing.

Leisure and Gardening is one of the books in the series *Equipment for the Disabled*. For details *see* page 237.

Shopping by Post for Gardeners (1980) by Joy Montague. Published by Exley Publications Limited, 16 Chalk Hill, Watford, Hertfordshire WD1 4BN. This guide to suppliers, seedsmen and services is usefully cross-referenced and also includes details of societies, books and holidays. It is useful to know that almost every kind of garden produce can be delivered to your home. Price £3.95 paperback; £7.95 hardback, both plus 50p postage and packing.

Golf

See also Section 9, Multi-Activity Adventure Centre.

Society of One-Armed Golfers
Don Reid, 11 Coldwell Lane, Felling, Tyne and Wear NE10 9EX (Tel: Felling (0632) 694742).
Founded in 1932, the Society holds regular meetings. Apart from a week-long annual championship, weekend and one-day events are organised by regional conveners in England, Scotland and Ireland.

Members pay an annual subscription of £3 and there is provision for junior members (under 18) at 50p.

Handbell Ringing

Handbell Ringers of Great Britain
36 Kensington Drive, Bury, Lancashire BL8 2DE (Tel: 061-764 0604).
The Society's aim is to promote the art of handbell tune ringing, and to achieve this aim arranges events bringing together handbell ringers. Seven regional associations promote local events and issue newsletters. The national magazine *Reverberations* is published bi-annually. Annual subscription is £2.

Mayola Music Ltd
205 High Street, Clapham Village, Bedfordshire MK41 6AJ (Tel: Bedford (0234) 62474).
This firm publishes a book *Handbell People* which includes amongst its 'people' those who are physically handicapped, blind, deaf or mentally handicapped, providing helpful information on how to help people with different needs enjoy handbell ringing. Price £1 plus 30p postage.

Handicrafts

Fred Aldous Ltd
PO Box 135, 37 Lever Street, Manchester M60 1UX (Tel: 061-236 2477).
This firm will be glad to send you a catalogue selling masses of DIY items for the home handicraft enthusiast. Pewter and copper, enamelling, jewellery accessories, flower making, handbag handles, lampshade materials and so on. In fact, the firm handles all those little things it is usually so difficult to buy.

Bradley Inkle Looms
82 North Lane, East Preston, Sussex BN16 1HE (Tel: Rustington (090 62) 70108).
A table Inkle loom is available which is relatively easy to use, even for those with limited movements. Each one is hand made and the design has been perfected for simplicity and ease of operation so that even the partially sighted can cope. The usual table model costs £15.50 plus carriage.
Inkle Weaving: A Comprehensive Manual has been written by Lavinia Bradley and published by Routledge & Kegan Paul Ltd (1982). Price £3.95, the manual shows how to use the loom to its full potential.

221

Campden Weavers
16 Lower High Street, Chipping Campden, Gloucestershire GL55 6DY (Tel: Evesham (0386) 840864).
A small handweaving firm supplying handweaving yarns, handweaving and spinning equipment, books on spinning, weaving and dyeing, fancy embroidery threads, knitting wool and accessories, and hand-woven articles. A shop with easy parking facilities is at the above address (early closing Thursday). *Loomcraft*, a practical magazine for handweavers, is published quarterly at £2.50 for four issues (inclusive of postage and packing). Send s.a.e. for catalogue of books and equipment supplied by mail order.

Craftsman's Mark Yarns
Tone Dale Mill, Wellington, Somerset TA21 0AW (Tel: Wellington (082 347) 7266).
This firm supplies undyed woollen yarns in natural colours specially designed for the use of hand-weavers, also plain cotton, jute, sisal and natural linen. For samples and details of prices apply to the firm.

Needlework by Post and Household Linens Catalogue. Produced by Copeland Linens Ltd, PO Box 95, 59 Boundary Street, Belfast 13. A very comprehensive catalogue selling all the necessary materials and designs for table linen, tapestry pictures, fire screens and embroidery pictures including frames. In addition there are bargain parcels of linen cloths, traced ready for hand embroidery, and remnants to make a variety of items. Price 60p.

Dressmaking for the Disabled. This book shows how to adapt paper patterns to individual physical disabilities, how to deal with materials, and how to alter and adapt ready-made clothes. There is also information on fastenings, aids and equipment for sewing and a list of useful books and publications. Published by the Disabled Living Foundation and available from: DLF Sales Ltd, Book House, 45 East Hill, Wandsworth, London SW18 2QZ. Price 80p.

Jigsaws

The British Jigsaw Puzzle Library
Old Homend, Stretton, Grandison, Ledbury, Herefordshire HR8 2TW (Tel: Trumpet (053 183) 462).
This is a lending library and puzzles are exchanged by post. All the puzzles are wooden without guide pictures and have varying numbers of pieces. Subscription rates on request and on receipt of a s.a.e.

Judo

British Judo Association
16 Upper Woburn Place, London WC1H 9QH (Tel: 01-387 9340).
The BJA is the official governing body for judo in Great Britain, and it has formed a working party to take into account the needs of disabled people interested in the sport.
Anyone interested in membership or in learning judo or a group requiring a coach at either national, area or local level, or requiring any other information, should contact the Chairperson of the working party at the above address.

Modelling

British Model Soldier Society
Honorary Secretary: D. Pearce, 22 Lynwood Road, Ealing, London W5.
The Society has a number of groups throughout the country and publishes a quarterly bulletin. The subscription for adults is £5 per annum, for young people under 17 £2.50.

International Plastic Modellers' Society
Membership Secretary: 85 Sycamore Drive, Ash Vale, Hampshire GU12 5JY.
The Society, which caters for all aspects of plastic modelling, has over 40 UK branches which meet monthly and 25 branches overseas. It publishes a bi-monthly magazine and offers a technical advisory service to all members. Send 50p (including postage and packing) for further details and sample magazine. Annual subscription £7.50 first year and £7 thereafter.

Model Railways

The Model Railway Club
Keen House, 4 Calshot Street, London N1 9AT.
The Club was founded in 1910 and is thus the oldest model railway society in the world. Purpose-built club rooms were opened at Keen House in 1960 and weekly meetings are held there on Thursday evenings. In addition there are frequent Saturday afternoon meetings organised in conjunction with some of the 140 or so clubs affiliated to the Model Railway Club. A bi-monthly bulletin is distributed to members and affiliated clubs. A most important feature of the Club's activities is the building and exhibiting of model railways and currently the club has projects in 'O' gauge, 'S' gauge 'OO' gauge and 'N' gauge. These provide scope for members to produce items of rolling stock, buildings and scenic features, as well

as to build its baseboards, install the track and the necessary electrical wiring.

The Model Railway Club is the organiser of the annual 'Imrex' International Model Railway Exhibition held each Easter at the Wembley Conference Centre. Subscription for adults living or working within 35 miles of London is £12.50 and £7 for others. Junior rates are half of those for adults.

Music

See also Section 9, Holiday Courses.

British Society for Music Therapy
Guildhall School of Music and Drama, Barbican, London EC2Y 8DT (Tel: 01-368 8879).
Membership is open to all who can further the Society's object, which is to promote the use and development of music therapy in treatment, education, rehabilitation and training of children and adults suffering from emotional, physical or mental handicap. Publishes papers, available to the general public, and a journal for members. It has several regional branches, and offers a diploma course in music therapy at the Guildhall School of Music, London.

Disabled Living Foundation
380–384 Harrow Road, London W9 2HU (Tel: 01-289 6111).
The DLF has a Music Advisory Service which is available to disabled people, whatever their age or disability, and to all those involved with them. Information covers the whole range of music interests and includes: details of music organisations; advice on instruments, instrumental aids and adaptations, aids for those who are visually handicapped; recommended books, sheet music, songs and records; library services available; checklists for the accessibility of concert halls; employment opportunities for disabled people in the music industry; the planning of training courses; opportunities for working in music with handicapped people and training available.

To assist in the exchange of information an experimental newsletter *Music News 1* was produced in November 1982. It is hoped that two or three issues will be published each year and that it will be sent free of charge. Anyone wanting to go on the mailing list should write to the Music Adviser.

The book *Access to Music for the Physically Handicapped Schoolchild and School-leaver* is a valuable source of information and encouragement and is written by Daphne Kennard who is the Music Adviser to the DLF. The book is available from DLF Sales Ltd, Book House, 45 East Hill, Wandsworth, London SW18 2QZ. Price £4.25.

The Chromaharp
Kate Baxter, 6 Esher Grove, Mapperley Park, Nottingham NG3 5DR (Tel: Nottingham (0602) 609528).
The Chromaharp is an easy to play chordal zither and is, we understand, a proven success with many disabled people. The recommended model is the 15-chord one (gives primary chords in seven keys), price £83 (approximately). Also available is the *Comprehensive Tutor* (large print and flip-back pages) which suspends for bed and wheelchair players, price £3.85. Available from Kate Baxter.

The Soundpost
Musical Instrument Co-operative Limited, Unit 122, 31 Clerkenwell Close, London EC1 (Tel: 01-250 1164).
This is a co-operative of musical instrument makers and repairers who also try to meet the needs of disabled people needing instrument modifications. They have modified both wind and string instruments and also have the capability of making or designing instruments from scratch if someone feels that is the most suitable solution. They can also build instruments, conventional or unconventional, for use in music therapy.

Prices are, of course, very variable as every modification is unique, but as a co-operative they do try to keep prices reasonable and will sometimes subsidise this work from more profitable jobs or from any other finance which may be available. Soundpost are specialists in woodwind, guitar, brass and violas.

BOOKS AND PUBLICATIONS

Oxford University Press
Music Department, Ely House, 37 Dover Street, London W1X 4AH (Tel: 01-629 8494).
The OUP publishes a number of music therapy books; we include brief details of five of them:
1. *Just Me* by Jean Turnbull (songs) and Steve Storr (pictures) contains 24 illustrated songs with piano or guitar (with chord chart) for handicapped and pre-school children in nurseries and playgroups. The songs are intended to assist the child to develop body awareness, to promote simple learning concepts and to overcome perceptual difficulties. Price £5.
2. *Music for the Handicapped Child* by Juliet Alvin. There are chapters on music in relation to mentally and physically handicapped children and those who are blind and deaf, price £3.75.
3. *Music Therapy for the Autistic Child* by Juliet Alvin. This book, based on the author's original research with a representative sample of autistic

children analyses the effects of music therapy on their whole development, price £3.75.

4. *They Can Make Music* by Philip Bailey. The author considers that if music can be made available to children with serious handicaps, whether mental or physical, it not only gives great pleasure and satisfaction but also, in some cases, provides an incentive to overcome disabilities, price £3.50.

5. *Up, Up and Away* by Derek Pearson. This songbook is the first of its kind (published in the United Kingdom) to provide material which can be used in the classroom, specially selected with the needs of handicapped children in mind. Price £4.95.

Music for Mentally Handicapped People by Miriam Wood. Published by Souvenir Press in their Human Horizons Series. Price £7.95.

The author shows how a parent or teacher, even if she or he is a non-musician, can work out music programmes for a child at home or for a group of pupils in a school. The book is full of suggestions on how to make simple instruments, write songs, work out musical dramas and how to encourage pupils to join in. A useful book for those who recognise the benefits music therapy can bring, but who need advice and ideas on how to approach the subject.

Nature Study

See also Section 9, Field Studies.

The Countryside and Wildlife for Disabled People: A regional access guide to nature reserves, country parks and open spaces throughout the United Kingdom. Compiled by Anthony Chapman. Published by the Royal Association for Disability and Rehabilitation, 25 Mortimer Street, London W1N 8AB (Tel: 01-637 5400).

Each entry gives a precise description of the location and of the facilities. It also gives details of the natural wonders which may be found. It serves to remind us of all the many places there are to visit and it provides the encouragement to go and look and enjoy. Price £1.60 including postage and packing.

National Trust Properties. Guides are available which include information on those properties which are accessible to disabled visitors. *See* Section 9 for details.

The Royal Society for the Protection of Birds
The Lodge, Sandy, Bedfordshire SG19 2DL (Tel: Sandy (0767) 80551).

The RSPB is Europe's largest voluntary nature conservation organisation with some 360,000 members.

It owns or leases 93 nature reserves covering about 108,000 acres of woods, heaths, marshes, lakes, cliffs, moors and meadows throughout the United Kingdom. Most of them are open to visitors and some have facilities *e.g.* bird-watching hides, paths and information centres, accessible to disabled people. A free leaflet is available.

The RSPB produces booklets and leaflets on such topics as making a garden attractive to birds, feeding birds, bird projects, making a DIY nestbox, etc. A free mail order sales catalogue includes practical items such as nest boxes and bird tables as well as domestic gifts, books and records. Members receive the colour magazine *Birds* quarterly, have free entry to reserves and are encouraged to join local groups whose activities include talks and film shows, bird-watching outings and fund-raising events. Disabled members are welcome. Subscription £9 (reduced on application by OAPs).

Photography

Photography for the Disabled
190 Secrett House, Ham Close, Ham, Richmond, Surrey (Tel: 01-948 2342).

This organisation is pioneering the development of specially adapted equipment and it is possible to obtain cameras where the shutters can be clicked by a mouth-operated pneumatic shutter or an adapted camera to fit on to a wheelchair. Other innovations can also be made for operation by the disabled photographer. The Secretary would also be glad to receive any unwanted photographic equipment to be adapted or sold to raise funds. There are area clubs in process of formation.

An annual exhibition of work by disabled photographers is held each year in July/August. Entry forms from the Secretary.

Playing Cards

Piatnik Large Index Playing Cards
These are designed for people with reduced eyesight and are available from Benno Partners and Products Ltd, 27 Little Russell Street, London WC1 2HN (Tel: 01-405 7030). Price £1.14.

Waddingtons
Castle Gate, Oulton, Leeds LS26 8HG (Tel: Leeds (0532) 826195).

Waddingtons produce 'Easy to See' playing cards (stock no. 3281) and the suggested selling price is £1.65 per pack.

Playing Card Holder
Designed for the use of players with only the use of

one hand, and it is free standing on a table. A privacy screen is incorporated into the bench of the holder to prevent other players seeing the cards or the order into which they are arranged.

For further details contact: D. C. Williams, 170 Lytham Road, Warton, nr Preston, Lancashire PR4 1AH. Price £5 plus £1.50 postage and packing.

Poetry

The Poetry Society exists for anyone interested in writing, reading or listening to poetry. Members receive copies of the *Poetry Review* and are entitled to half-price admission to events which take place at 21 Earls Court Square. These include the Thursday night 'Poets-in-Person' readings and different workshops. Occasional festivals are held throughout the year.

The bookshop specialises in poetry from the small and independent presses, and there is a mail-order catalogue for distribution to members.

The Society administers a programme of 'Poets in Schools', and verse-speaking examinations. It also organises several poetry competitions, some for members only.

The National Poetry Secretariat is incorporated in the Poetry Society, and exists to sponsor and encourage poetry readings throughout the country.

The Society's aim is to produce a lively, comprehensive programme, and to make poetry available to as many people as possible through the channels of voice, print and personal creativity.

Annual membership: London £12; country, £9; associate/student members, £5; life £250; corporate/affiliated £9. Further details and membership application forms from Belinda Walker, the National Poetry Centre, 21 Earls Court Square, London SW5 (Tel: 01-373 7861).

Puppetry

Puppetry for Mentally Handicapped People by Caroline Astell-Burt. Published by Souvenir Press, 43 Great Russell Street, London WC1B 3PA (Tel: 01-580 9307).

The author describes the special contribution puppetry can make to the lives of mentally handicapped people, helping them to act and speak for themselves through the medium of the puppet and providing the excitement and stimulation of theatre.

Intended for use by parents, teachers, therapists and care staff, the book explains how to make puppets of all kinds, from simple sock puppets to elaborate marionettes, and how to perform with them in play and learning situations. Price £4.95 paperback; £6.95 hardback, plus 56p and 72p respectively for postage.

Radio and Television

TV licences are available to registered blind persons from local post offices at a special reduction.

British Wireless for the Blind Fund
226 Great Portland Street, London W1N 6AA (Tel: 01-388 1266).

Radios are available on free 'permanent' loan to registered blind persons aged 16 or over. Distributed on behalf of BWBF by the local voluntary organisation for the blind, or social services department.

Wireless for the Bedridden
81b Corbets Tey Road, Upminster, Essex RM14 2AJ (Tel: Upminster (040 22) 50051).

This organisation aims to provide, on free loan, radios or televisions to disabled persons. The radios are high-quality transistor sets; televisions are on free rental/maintenance from one of the leading rental companies. A licence will be provided only in cases of exceptional need. Those who would like to make an application should send for the necessary form.

Royal National Institute for the Deaf
The RNID produces a comprehensive leaflet describing aids for listening to radio and television, with a list of manufacturers.

Reading

Dillons Bookshops
This company has a number of bookshops around the country, some on University campuses.

Personal callers: Dillons, 1 Malet Street, London WC1E 7JB (Tel: 01-636 1577). The shop is very accessible with ramps and lifts and holds stock on most subjects, academic and general.

Mail order: Dillons University Bookshop, c/o The Library, University of Kent, Canterbury, Kent CT2 7NG (Tel: Canterbury (0227) 62450).

The company operates an account system for personal and institutional customers through its shops and mail order department. Details of this can be obtained from Pentos Bookselling Group, 12 Ethel Street, Birmingham B2 4BQ.

Riding

See also Section 9.

Riding for the Disabled Association
Avenue R, National Agricultural Centre, Kenilworth, Warwickshire CV8 2LY (Tel: Coventry (0203) 56107).

Each of the 550 groups throughout the United Kingdom consists of an organiser, secretary, riding instructor, usually a physiotherapist and some 30 helpers. Basically the riding is free but where schools are concerned, and individuals can afford it, contributions are welcomed.

Riding for the Disabled Association Northern Ireland Region

Regional Chairperson: Angela Wilson, 70 Ballygarvey Road, Ballymena, Co. Antrim BT43 7JX.

Aims to provide the opportunity of riding to disabled people who might benefit in their general health and well being.

Riding for the Mentally Handicapped. Published by MENCAP – The Royal Society for Mentally Handicapped Children and Adults, 123 Golden Lane, London EC1Y 0RT. Price 5p.

FILMS

Riding Towards Freedom, 16 mm, colour, 33 minutes. This film was produced by the Riding for the Disabled Association and depicts the pleasure achieved by handicapped people when riding. Available from Town and Country Productions Ltd, 21 Cheyne Row, London SW3 5HP (Tel: 01-352 7950). Hire charge £11.50 to be sent with order (film or video – VHS or Betamax).

The Right to Choose, 16 mm, colour, 35 minutes. This film shows individual adult riders, with a number of severe physical disabilities, who have nevertheless learned to ride with varying degrees of independence and accomplishment. Available from Town and Country Productions Ltd, 21 Cheyne Row, Chelsea, London SW3 5HP. Hire charge £11.50 to be sent with order (film or video – VHS or Betamax).

Sailing

See also Section 9.

Useful guidance for disabled sailors is contained in the publication *Water Sports for the Disabled*. For details *see* page 229 under British Sports Association for the Disabled – Water Sports Division.

Jubilee Sailing Trust

Atlantic Road, Eastern Docks, Southampton, Hampshire SO1 1GD (Tel: Southampton (0703) 31388).

The Trust gives disabled people a unique opportunity to find fulfilment as working crew members and to share on an equal basis with their able-bodied counterparts the integrating and challenging experience of sailing an ocean-going square-rigged ship at sea. Eventually the Trust hopes to build its own specially designed 135 ft barque, the STS *Lord Nel-*

son, but as an intermediate step it is chartering the brigantine *Soren Larsen* and running a series of trial cruises for up to 22 volunteers on each cruise, ranging from a weekend to a fortnight in duration. This will enable the Trust to carry out further research and also to test various items of prototype equipment which, if successful, will be transferred to the STS *Lord Nelson* later. The challenge is open to all would-be sailors from 14 to 60 years old with or without experience. Anyone interested in helping to fund-raise or sailing with the Trust should contact the above address.

RYA Seamanship Foundation

Victoria Way, Woking, Surrey GU21 1EQ (Tel: Woking (048 62) 5022).

The Foundation's aims are:

(a) to improve the knowledge and seamanship of yachtsmen and other pleasure-boat owners by better training;

(b) to provide opportunities for young people, especially those from deprived areas, to benefit from activities directly connected with sailing and the sea;

(c) to organise courses and to provide special equipment to enable handicapped people to learn to sail and afterwards to participate on equal terms with the able-bodied;

(d) to promote research into the design of craft and equipment with a view to improving safety and efficiency.

They Said We Couldn't Do It edited by John Chartress is a well-illustrated and marvellously descriptive account of how individual sailors have overcome their handicaps to enjoy 'messing about in boats'. In among these accounts we learn of the wide variety of solutions found to overcome specific problems. Also included are details of instructional techniques. It concludes by saying that sailing is fun and that is what this book is all about. Available from RYA as above, price £1.

The Wheelyboat

A project is going ahead to produce a boat which has been specially designed to enable people in wheelchairs to get afloat in their own chair to fish, row or sail or use an outboard motor. It is being designed so that minimum assistance is required, possibly to help launch and beach the boat.

At the time of writing funding was still being sought to produce the prototype. It is expected that after, say, the first five boats are in operation the project will be self-financing. Further information from A. A. Faulkner, Slivericks Farm, Ashburnham, Battle, East Sussex TN33 9PE (Tel: Rushlake Green (0435) 830571).

Skiing

The British Ski Club for the Disabled
Corton House, Corton, nr Warminster, Wiltshire (Tel: Warminster (0985) 50321).
The Club was formed in 1974 to provide skiing facilities for disabled people. It is affiliated to the English Ski Council, the Ski Club of Great Britain and the British Sports Association for the Disabled.

Special training is often necessary and facilities and equipment have to be suitable if the maximum benefit and proficiency is to be achieved. The Club has sessions at ski centres in Britain and acts as an information and advisory centre to all interested in cross country (Nordic) downhill (Alpine) skiing, sledging and skating as well as being responsible for training teams to compete in national competitions. Teams are also trained to compete in the Winter Olympic Sports for the Disabled. Skiing holidays are arranged annually.

Instructors and guides are always required, so the Club welcomes and needs able-bodied members willing to qualify. Membership £5 per annum.

The Uphill Ski Club
12 Park Crescent, London W1N 4EQ (Tel: 01-636 1989).
This is an independent club affiliated to the Spastics Society which takes spastic and other motor-impaired people on winter sports holidays. Equipment is available to compensate for the user's disabilities and to enhance their abilities. Paraplegics, being unable to use their lower limbs, usually ski on short skis and a pair of outriggers, the skis often being tied together to prevent the 'splits'. Hemiplegics have difficulty in exerting equal pressure on both skis and particularly in unweighting the spastic limb. Some hemiplegic skiers therefore use a short ski on their weakened leg and a standard length ski and outrigger on their good side.

The Arroya Sled
Arroya V is a manoeuvrable sled with specific human factors and design considerations for persons with disabilities. It is lightweight and said to be extremely durable. Its special strap system secures the skier to the sled much like a foot to a ski boot. The contour-moulded seat cushion provides maximum comfort over rough terrain. Stainless steel edges give Arroya skiers the ability to carve controlled turns. Arroya can be used in a variety of snow conditions and it is compatible with existing lift facilities. Having said all that, the makers issue a warning to the effect that the Arroya is potentially a dangerous device. It cannot compensate for lack of competence whether disabled or not.

For further information contact Beneficial Designs Inc., 5858 Empire Grade, Santa Cruz, CA 95060.

Spinning

Dingle Hill Products
Mid-Cowden, Comrie, Perthshire PH6 2HU (Tel: Comrie (0764) 70667).
Some disabled people have found that they have had to give up spinning because disablement prevented their pedalling a traditional spinning wheel. There are also many who have not considered spinning as an occupation or hobby due to disablement.

This firm has developed the Dingle Hill Spinner which is powered by a small electric motor enabling anyone with more-or-less normal manual dexterity to spin, and derive the same satisfaction as when using a normal spinning wheel. We are assured that the Spinner has been tested by two well-known spinning instructors both of whom are said to be delighted with its action and have recommended it for use by disabled people. The price of the Dingle Hill Spinner is only £49 against £84 for their traditional foot operated wheel.

Sub-aqua Sports

The British Sub-Aqua Club
16 Upper Woburn Place, London WC1H 0QW (Tel: 01-387 9302).
While the BSAC does not actively recruit disabled persons as members, it gives the branches every encouragement to accept and train them as divers where the branches are prepared to do so. The Club has recently published a comprehensive set of guidance notes for the use of branches wishing to train disabled people, and for the disabled members themselves. Copies of these notes are available from BSAC HQ.

The Club has a co-ordinator on its Technical Committee who is responsible for giving advice on diving for disabled people and he too can be contacted via BSAC HQ.

Scottish Sub-Aqua Club
16 Royal Crescent, Glasgow G3 7SL (Tel: 041-332 9291).
An organisation independent of the British Sub-Aqua Club. Physically handicapped people are welcome to join any branch, subject to confirmation of fitness and suitability.

Swimming

The baths managers of many swimming pools make special provision for disabled people, either for organised groups by allocating special times, or to individuals by making general facilities accessible. Further details of local facilities are available direct from the local swimming pools, or from area officers of the British Sports Association for the Disabled (*see* page 232). *See also* Spastics Society, page 236.

Amateur Swimming Association
National Development Officer for the Disabled, c/o Harold Fern House, Derby Square, Loughborough, Leicester LE11 0AL (Tel: Loughborough (0509) 230431).

Association of Swimming Therapy
Secretary: Bill Wood, Treetops, Swan Hill, Ellesmere, Shropshire SY12 0LZ (Tel: Ellesmere (069 171) 3542).
The Association aims to teach safety, swimming and 'happiness' in the water, regardless of the severity of handicap, provided that medical approval is given. It encourages handicapped people to take part in swimming and water recreation, the formation of swimming clubs and swimming competitions. A team of lecturers is always prepared to advise, help or train in any area on request. Instructors and helpers are trained within their clubs.

The AST works through regional associations to which local clubs can affiliate and on whose experience, advice and instructor training they can call. Audiovisual slide programmes on techniques for handling handicapped people in water can be purchased, and two films are available for hire. The AST can also arrange insurance cover granting indemnity to AST members against liability for bodily injury to third parties or accidental damage to property.

A publication is available, *Swimming for the Disabled*, covering safety in dressing room and at bathside, as well as in the water; the four stages through which a learner must work – adjustment to water, rotations, buoyancy and balance, propulsion; games to develop expertise and aid progress; and how to form and operate a swimming club. There is also a section describing in layman's terms the various disabilities which can be encountered by an instructor working with disabled people. Published by EP Publishing Ltd. Price £3.95. For further details of AST send a s.a.e.

National Association of Swimming Clubs for the Handicapped
Rosemary Leeson, 219 Preston Drove, Brighton BN1 6FL (Tel: Brighton (0273) 559470).
The Association acts as a co-ordinating body for member organisations. It encourages, promotes and develops swimming among handicapped people.

The following booklets are available:
Register of Swimming Clubs for Handicapped People, price 50p.
Teaching Disabled People to Swim:
Part 1 – *Disabilities*, price 25p.
Part 2 – *Balance, Buoyancy and Propulsion*, price 25p.
Part 3 – *Pupil and Teacher*, price 25p.

Swimming for Disabled People. A programme of three tape/slide sequences designed to illustrate some important techniques for handling handicapped people in water – position and balance, movement, and group activities and formations. Any or all of the three sequences may be obtained from Town and Country Productions Ltd, 21 Cheyne Row, Chelsea, London SW3 5HP. Price £20 each, plus 15 per cent VAT to be sent with order.

Water free, 16 mm, colour, 35 minutes. This film is presented by the Association of Swimming Therapy and shows how, by simple though scientifically proven methods, people of all ages with different disabilities are able to enjoy a remarkably high degree of mobility in the water. Available from Town and Country Productions Ltd, 21 Cheyne Row, London SW3 5HP (Tel: 01-352 7950). Hire charge £11.50 to be sent with order (film or video – VHS or Betamax).

Toys and Play Aids

Fair Play for Children
248 Kentish Town Road, London NW5 (Tel: 01-485 0809).
Provides a pack which includes information aiming to provide basic information and contacts for people interested and involved in play and handicapped children. Information is mostly concerned with charitable and voluntary groups including toy libraries, national play organisations, etc. Also included is a publications list.

Play Matters – The Toy Libraries Association for Handicapped Children
Seabrook House, Wyllyotts Manor, Darkes Lane, Potters Bar EN6 2HL (Tel: Potters Bar (0707) 44571).
The Association is the parent body for over 1,000 toy

libraries in the United Kingdom, many of which lend toys to handicapped children for recreational use and to develop skills. As well as giving advice on how to set up and run a toy library, it maintains links at the national level with therapists, psychologists, teachers and researchers; with toy manufacturers, art colleges and toy designers; with children's societies and between the toy libraries themselves.

Information and guidance on toys and play is passed on to members through a regular journal, *ARK*, conferences and a wide selection of booklets (*see* Noah's Ark Publications, page 238). A permanent display of toys at Potters Bar can be viewed by appointment.

In 1981, the Association merged with ACTIVE, which promotes a do-it-yourself approach to leisure, learning and communication aids for severely handicapped children and adults. (For further details of ACTIVE, see page 60.)

Membership of Play Matters costs £8 per year to toy libraries, £50 per year to groups of toy libraries and £6 for individual members.

Handicapped Persons Research Unit (HPRU)
Newcastle upon Tyne Polytechnic, 1 Coach Lane, Coach Lane Campus, Newcastle upon Tyne (Tel: Newcastle upon Tyne (0632) 664061).
A *Playaids Catalogue* is available as a result of a national exhibition of playthings and other aids organised by HPRU in June 1982. It contains illustrated descriptions of over 150 items suitable for handicapped children. The ideas range from variations on existing playaids and innovative ideas to unique designs made from throwaway materials. Price £1.50 including postage and packing.

Toy Aids Projects
Lodbourne Farmhouse, Lodbourne, Gillingham, Dorset (Tel: Gillingham (074 76) 2256).
Makes available some battery-operated remote-control toys, with specially enlarged switches suitable for handicapped children who would find ordinary controls difficult to operate. The toys are adapted by handicapped people and are sold at normal retail prices.

Choosing Toys and Play Activities for Handicapped Children (36 minutes).
Playthings for the Handicapped Child (38 minutes).
Nottingham University Toy Library for Handicapped Children (18 minutes).
Three tape/slide programmes prepared by Nottingham University and available for hire or for sale from Graves Medical Audiovisual Library, Holly House, 220 New London Road, Chelmsford, Essex CM2 9BJ (Tel: Chelmsford (0245) 83351).

BOOKS ON TOYS

Easy to Make Toys for Handicapped Children by Don Caston. Published by Souvenir Press Limited, 43 Great Russell Street, London WC1B 3PA (Tel: 01-580 9307).
The author provides detailed instructions for making 60 imaginative toys that will aid development and skills. They are all considered to be within the scope of the beginner. Price £5.95 plus 80p postage and packing.

Let's Make Toys by Ray McConkey and Dorothy M. Jeffree. Published by Souvenir Press Limited, 43 Great Russell Street, London WC1B 3PA (Tel: 01-580 9307).
The book discusses the role of toys in play and the importance of having the right toy. There is a chapter on choosing toys and then there are guidelines on the tools and materials you will need for making junk toys, wooden ones and some with electrical components in them. Price £6.95 plus 72p postage and packing.
See also reference to *Let Me Play*, page 237.

Toys for Handicapped Children, 16 mm, black and white, 6 minutes. A filmed extract from a BBC science programme on suitable toys which can develop simple abilities. Available from Concord Films Council Ltd, 201 Felixstowe Road, Ipswich, Suffolk IP3 9BJ. Hire charge £4.40 plus carriage and VAT.

Water-based Activities

British Sports Association for the Disabled, Water Sports Division (formerly the Sports Council Advisory Panel)
National Co-ordinator Water Sports: L. D. Warren, 29 Ironlatch Avenue, St Leonards-on-Sea, East Sussex TN38 9JE (Tel: Hastings (0424) 427931 Monday to Friday from 2 p.m. to 5 p.m.).
The Water Sports Division is responsible for developing water sports among disabled people. Activities include: canal cruising, canoeing, coarse fishing, game fishing, sailing, sea fishing, snorkelling, sub aqua diving, rowing, water skiing, power boating and model boating. The Division provides information on any of the above water sports activities, including facilities, training programmes, special aids and a wide range of technical information. The Division has its own excellent publication *Water Sports for the Disabled* (1983) giving essential advice to disabled participants in all types of water sports. Price £9.95. For information of a general or specific nature relating to any of the above sports or for details of publications, leaflets or films, contact the

National Co-ordinator. When writing please enclose a s.a.e.

Water Sports and Epilepsy

A pamphlet written by Norman Croucher (see his book *Outdoor Pursuits for Disabled People*) aimed at encouraging and helping people with epilepsy to enjoy more water sports and to enjoy them more fully. Price 50p. Available from the Disabilities Study Unit, Wildhanger, Amberley, Arundel, West Sussex BN18 9NR.

The British Disabled Water Ski Association

c/o Maeve Edge, Warren Wood, The Warren, Ashtead, Surrey KT21 2SN (Tel: Ashtead (0322) 73046).
This specialised club has been formed to help disabled people to water ski. The Association is based mainly in the South and now has its own water facilities west of London near Staines. In addition, courses are held at ski clubs in other parts of the country. There is a small annual subscription. An information sheet is available plus *Additional Code of Practice for Disabled*.

Port Edgar

South Queensferry, Edinburgh EH30 9SQ (Tel: 031-331 3330).
Lothian Regional Council Department of Planning arrange a watersports programme every year and disabled people are welcome on the courses, including canoeing and boardsailing. There are also courses arranged especially for disabled people. Port Edgar is the base for a specially designed *Challenger Trimaran* which we understand can be sailed safely by those with restricted mobility.

Water Authorities Association

1 Queen Anne's Gate, London SW1H 9BT (Tel: 01-222 8111).
The Association publishes a leaflet *Facilities for the Disabled*.

Wheelchair Dancing

National Wheelchair Dance Association

Contact: Pam Griffin, Thomas Delarue School, Shipbourne Road, Tonbridge, Kent TN11 9NP (Tel: Tonbridge (0732) 354584).

Wheelchair Dances. Diagram of action and main turns for 12 dances adapted for wheelchair dancing. From the Spastics Society, 12 Park Crescent, London W1N 4EQ. Price Book 2, 60p; Book 3, £1.50 plus postage and packing.

Wine Making

A monthly magazine is available at an annual subscription of £10.50 or at 55p a copy. By post from *Amateur Winemaker*, South Street, Andover, Hampshire (Tel: Andover (0264) 3177). This is a lively and interesting magazine for those who delight in providing their own tipples. Plenty of helpful hints and suggestions, a readers' queries page and a section devoted to club news. The Winemakers' Mart advertising section provides copious information on equipment, etc. Apply to *Amateur Winemaker* for details of local clubs and the following books:
First Steps to Winemaking by C. J. Berry. Price £2 plus 71p postage.
Straightforward Winemaking by Professor Gerry Fowles. Price £1.95 plus 40p postage.
Both these books are helpful and informative and include a number of recipes for both 'by ingredient' fruit, flower and vegetable wines, and for 'by purpose' aperitif, table, social and dessert wines.
The third book, *Making Inexpensive Liqueurs* by Ben Bellis, is full of ideas and is eminently readable. Price £2.20 plus 51p postage.
Free book list available on application.

Writing

Disabled Writers' Quarterly – The International Literary Magazine of Physically Disabled Writers

The copy of the magazine (in the shape of a book) we read had some really challenging and interesting articles and it has an attractive international flavour. Manuscripts are welcome and you should also send an international reply coupon for return.

Details of subscription from Disabled Writers' Quarterly, 2495 Major Street, St Laurent, Montreal, Quebec, Canada H4M 1E5.

National Association of Disabled Writers

British Section of the International Association of Disabled Dissident Writers, 18 Spring Grove, Harrogate, North Yorkshire HG1 2HS.
This is described as a Human Rights organisation having the aim of freedom of thought, enquiry and expression. They publish a bi-monthly *International Newsletter* and maintain links with similar organisations in other countries.

Membership is £5 per year to those who can afford it and free to those writers who cannot.

The Writers' and Artists' Yearbook is published annually by A. & C. Black, 35 Bedford Row, London WC1R 4JH. This reference book (available in paperback, price £4.50, 1984 edition) has an extensive list of journals and magazines both in this country and abroad, together with other useful information about publishers, copyright, etc. The details about journals and magazines include the type and length of articles or stories which are normally published.

Yoga

Yoga for Health Foundation
Ickwell Bury, Biggleswade, Bedfordshire SG18 9EF (Tel: Northill (076 727) 271).
The practice of yoga has special advantages for disabled people, developing control of movements and of breathing, and ameliorating the effects of some physical disabilities.

Yoga for the Handicapped by Barbara Brosnan. This practical handbook for teachers, parents and specialists explains how to introduce yoga to a handicapped person, how to adapt the poses to suit each type of disablement and how the individual can obtain benefit and pleasure from the exercise. Published by Souvenir Press, 43 Great Russell Street, London WC1B 3PA (Tel: 01-580 9307/637 5711). Price £4.95 paperback; £6.95 hardback.

Sports Associations and Others

Artists with Disabilities
Primarily a support group for people with disabilities who practise the arts including painting, drawing, sculpture, drama, music and writing. They have organised a festival of artists with disabilities and four members have exhibited together at the People's Gallery in London under the title of 'No Need for Glass'.
Contact: Keith Armstrong, 22 Seymour House, Church Way, Somers Town, London NW1. Send s.a.e. with enquiry. The Group may also be contacted c/o Housmans Bookshop, 5 Caledonian Road, Kings Cross, London N1. Send s.a.e. with enquiry.

Arts for Disabled People in Wales
Wales Council for the Disabled, Caerbragdy Estate, Bedwas Road, Caerphilly, Mid Glamorgan CF8 3SL (Tel: Caerphilly (0222) 887388).
An initiative of the Regional Arts Association of Wales and the Wales Council for the Disabled, committed to introducing programmes of creative activity to areas of special needs. It operates through three Regional Panels, complementary to the Arts Association areas in Wales, and sees its priority in offering advice and training to existing statutory and voluntary agencies, in value and use of creative activity, and in recruiting, placing and supporting creative people in work situations with disabled and handicapped people.

Artsline
5 Crowndale Road, London NW1 1TU (Tel: 01-388 2227/8).
Available for telephone calls from 10 a.m. to 4 p.m. Tuesday to Friday and from 10 a.m. to 2 p.m. on Saturday.
Artsline helps make art and entertainment more accessible in London by providing information on what's on; about steps into venues; about access into arts and entertainment buildings; about whether there are lifts and how easy and close the parking is. It can tell you whether there is an induction loop for those who are hard of hearing or even whether there is a price concession for the hard up. Then there is information on lavatories and whether you can get transport to and from where you want to go.
Artsline can help with suggestions for arts activities to interest experienced enthusiasts and novices alike. Anything from workshops in drama and music to silk-screen printing, from crafts or talking newspapers for blind people to dance or puppetry for people with mental handicaps. If, in addition, you think you might be good enough to go professional Artsline even advises you where to train.

British Amputee Sports Association
Secretary: Dr G. Thomas, 110 Speed House, Barbican, London EC27 8AU.
BASA is a national organisation responsible for the development and co-ordination of amputee sport. The organisation is run by amputees for amputees. Membership can be as one of an amputee group, or if there is no group nearby then there is individual membership.
BASA holds annual amputee games where athletes from all over the country compete in track and field events, table tennis, snooker, bowls, pistol shooting, badminton and swimming. Annual subscription is £1.

The British Association of Sporting and Recreational Activities of the Blind
Mr Frank McFarlane, 11 Ovolo Road, Liverpool L13 3DR (Tel: 051-220 2516).
This national organisation keeps members in touch with sporting and recreational activities arranged for blind people in the United Kingdom and abroad. The quarterly magazine *Participation* is available in braille and print. Individual membership subscription £1 a year; organisation fee according to size.

British Deaf Sports Council
Mr R. Haythornthwaite, 38 Victoria Place, Carlisle CA1 1UH (Tel: Carlisle (0228) 20188).
Through its 120 clubs and 11 Regional Councils, the

BDSC organises sporting activities locally, regionally, nationally and internationally. The Council is involved in promoting a wide range of sports.

Through its affiliation with the CIDS (International Committee for Deaf Sport) the Council sends British representative teams to European and World Games every four years. The BDSC is keen to point out, however, that it is not an elitist body but is concerned that all deaf people are catered for – from a local game of dominoes to promoting world-class competitors.

More detailed information may be obtained by contacting your Regional Office (Regional Officers are themselves deaf). Addresses are available from the above address.

British Paraplegic Sports Society
Ludwig Guttmann Sports Centre for the Disabled, Hayward House, Barnard Crescent, Aylesbury, Buckinghamshire HP21 8PP (Tel: Aylesbury (0296) 84848).
The BPSS is the governing body of sport for those who are spinal cord paralysed (paraplegics and tetraplegics). It is responsible for organising the annual National Stoke Mandeville Games (in conjunction with the International Stoke Mandeville Games Federation) and the annual International Stoke Mandeville Games.

The BPSS maintains and administers the Ludwig Guttmann Sports Centre for the Disabled which provides extensive sporting and residential facilities for disabled sportspeople for training and leisure as well as for competitive events. In accordance with the objects of the BPSS, the integration of disabled people with their able-bodied fellows is encouraged by extending Club membership of the Centre to able-bodied sports enthusiasts. We understand that this is the only Sports Centre in Great Britain that is able to offer especially built residential accommodation with comprehensive sports facilities for disabled people. The Centre includes a large sports hall, swimming pool, indoor bowls green, halls for table tennis, fencing, weight-lifting and snooker.

The British Sports Association for the Disabled
Ludwig Guttmann Sports Centre, Hayward House, Barnard Crescent, Aylesbury, Buckinghamshire HP21 8PP (Tel: Aylesbury (0296) 27889).
The BSAD exists to bring the joys of sport and physical recreation to people, young and old, with many different kinds of disability, who may not have thought they could experience them. The BSAD helps to inform statutory and voluntary agencies of what is already done in many sports and activities for

the disabled and what still needs to be done. The BSAD is recognised by the government and the Sports Council as the co-ordinating body for all types of sport for all types of disablement and its aims are:
(a) to encourage, promote and develop sport and recreation amongst disabled people and so enable them to compete with each other and with the able-bodied;
(b) to endeavour to secure the provision and improvement of facilities for sport and recreation for disabled people by the government and local authorities;
(c) to tell disabled people of the benefits of recreation through sport.
The Centre includes a large sports hall, swimming pool, indoor bowls green, halls for table tennis, fencing, weight-lifting and snooker.

The BSAD has representatives throughout the country organising regional sport, and these agents are always glad to advise and instruct, and will arrange talks and lectures to clubs together with showings of the BSAD films (*see* page 239).

Support is given to local authorities and other bodies to form new sports clubs for disabled people and to encourage integration into existing able-bodied sports clubs. For further details and advice on aids and equipment for sporting activities write direct to the above address. (*See also* BSAD books, page 236.)

The Country Landowners' Association Charitable Trust
16 Belgrave Square, London SW1X 8PQ (Tel: 01-235 0511).
The CLA Charitable Trust was founded in 1980 by the Country Landowners' Association with the main purpose of encouraging and helping landowners to provide facilities on their land for those who are physically or mentally handicapped to enjoy sport and recreation. A number of projects supported have included nature trails, bird-watching, rides, self-catering farm holidays and an indoor riding school. At the time of writing (1984) the Trust is publishing a guide to sport and recreation in the countryside for disabled people.

CPISRA (The Cerebral Palsy International Sports and Recreational Association)
General Secretary: Mr A. L. Hessels, Balyeweg 26, 6874 AJ Wolfheze, The Netherlands.
CPISRA is an organisation concerned with providing greater opportunities for people throughout the world suffering from cerebral palsy and allied conditions to take part in and enjoy a wide variety of sports

and recreational activities at all levels. The organisation was responsible for the International CP games held in Denmark in 1982 and for organising games in the USA in June 1984. To participate in CPISRA events, CP sportspeople must pass the minimum standards as laid down by CPISRA and should be in membership through an organisational body in their country.

CRYPT

Creative Young People Together sets out to help and develop disabled people with creative talent. The Trustees plan to achieve the following:

1. Buy and equip bungalows, each for 2, 3, or at the most 4 creative young disabled people. Dwellings would be near – but not necessarily next door to – each other, so that each would have to be part of the larger community.
2. Provide one or more workshop areas where other disabled people with talent could share in the creative work on a daily basis.
3. Appoint helpers (for the special needs arising from the disabilities) and leaders/tutors/aides to further the creative work.
4. Provide publishing facilities and act as a 'clearing house' through which the talents can find a wider audience (from exhibiting to public musical and dramatic performances).
5. Show that disablement is no barrier to creative achievement.

The Disabled Drivers' Association
Ashwellthorpe, Norwich NR16 1EX.
The Association has produced a leaflet setting out information on a range of recreational activities which may be of interest to disabled people.

GENERAL INFORMATION

The three organisations below provide broadly similar information services which include extensive resource material on sports and general recreational activities, details of relevant aids and publications.

Disabled Living Foundation
380–384 Harrow Road, London W9 2HU (Tel: 01-289 6111).

Scottish Council on Disability
Information Department, 5 Shandwick Place, Edinburgh EH2 4RG (Tel: 031-229 8632).

Northern Ireland Council for the Handicapped
2 Annadale Avenue, Belfast BT7 3JH (Tel: Belfast (0232) 640011/649555).
A publication is available free: *Sport and Leisure Opportunities for the Disabled in Northern Ireland.*

This lists the wide range of voluntary organisations concerned with sport and leisure opportunities, as well as leisure centres, swimming pools, universities and colleges of further education, education and library boards, health and social service addresses and finally the addresses of Secretaries of governing bodies of sport in Northern Ireland from aeromodelling to cycling and from darts to yoga.

Wales – see Welsh Sports Association for the Disabled, page 236.

The Duke of Edinburgh's Award Scheme
This Scheme involves service, expeditions, skills and physical recreation, and welcomes the participation of physically handicapped young people (aged 14 to 25). Provision is made where necessary for appropriate adjustments to accommodate their individual handicaps. The Award's *Guide for the Handicapped* gives details of these and is available from all Award offices. The criteria for entry are that young people will gain something from participating in Award activities and will not suffer physical deterioration in the process. Further information from the Adviser for the Handicapped, Duke of Edinburgh's Award, 5 Prince of Wales Terrace, London W8 5PG (Tel: 01-937 5205).

EXTEND (Exercise Training for the Elderly and/or Disabled)
Director: Penny Copple, 5 Conway Road, Sheringham, Norfolk NR26 8DD (Tel: Sheringham (0263) 822479).
EXTEND is an organisation run in association with the Women's League of Health and Beauty. It aims to improve the health and vitality and mobility and thus the quality of life of elderly and mentally or physically disabled people through recreational movement. With help from government, local authorities and other sources, EXTEND is actively promoting special training and encouraging the setting up of local classes in various parts of the country. Further information from the above address. Please send a s.a.e.

Friends for the Young Deaf
FYD Communication Centre, East Court Mansion, Council Offices, College Lane, East Grinstead, Sussex RH19 3LT (Tel: East Grinstead (0342) 23444 (voice); 21488 (teleprinter)).
Among its activities (*see also* page 303), FYD has continued to develop the Communication Through Sport Project. A wide variety of sporting and leisure events is organised, including training courses, coaching courses, water sports, tennis, badminton,

squash and camping weekends, drama, drawing and painting classes, etc.

FYD liaises with CCPR (Central Council for Physical Recreation) to promote among young deaf people the CCPR community sports leaders award. The young people may then be encouraged to progress further and obtain qualified coaching awards.

The Girl Guides Association
17–19 Buckingham Palace Road, London SW1W 0PT (Tel: 01-834 6242).
Any disabled girl over the age of 7 may join the Girl Guides Association provided she can make and understand the Promise and its implications. She works on the same programme and takes the same badges as any other girl. There are two leaflets, *Enabled Though Disabled* and *Guiding with the Handicapped*.

Handicapped Adventure Playground Association (HAPA)
Fulham Palace, Bishops Avenue, London SW6 6EA (Tel: 01-736 4443).
HAPA has built and equipped five adventure playgrounds which are for the use of all physically, mentally or otherwise handicapped children and young people. Brothers and sisters may join in during school holidays. Playgrounds are in Chelsea, Wandsworth, Islington, Fulham and Lambeth. Further details on request from HAPA office. HAPA has also published a guide *Adventure Playgrounds for Handicapped Children*. Price £1.40.

Interlink
358 Strand, London WC2R 0HS (Tel: 01-836 5819).
This organisation is concerned with promoting creative activities internationally with disabled and elderly people, with prisoners and with other disadvantaged people. Any nation, organisation or individual can become part of the service.

A lively quarterly magazine *Positif* is published providing interesting accounts of self expression through the creative medium of theatre, dance, clay modelling, painting, sculpting, music, singing and so on.

Details of subscriptions to the above address, but if payment would cause hardship to an organisation or individual this may be waived.

International Blind Sports Association
Secretariat: Postboks 5947, Hegdehaugen N Oslo 3, Norway.
The Association publishes the quarterly periodical *Blind Sports International*. It is supplied free of charge and is available in English, French, German and Spanish. It provides very precise information on the various sporting events played at international level. Essential information for serious sportspeople.

MENCAP – Royal Society for Mentally Handicapped Children and Adults
MENCAP Centre, 123 Golden Lane, London EC1Y 0RT (Tel: 01-253 9433).
The Society's National Federation of Gateway Clubs provides clubs throughout the United Kingdom, all giving mentally handicapped people the opportunity to take part in an exciting range of leisure activities. Some clubs take their members rambling, fell walking, rock climbing, horse riding and even canoeing. Others concentrate on team sports like football and rounders, and on athletics and swimming. There are facilities for painting, craft work, music and dancing, drama and various indoor games. A 25-minute colour film *Gateway* shows various aspects of the Gateway movement.

PHAB (Physically Handicapped and Able-Bodied)
Tavistock House North, Tavistock Square, London WC1H 9HX (Tel: 01-388 1963).
Through over 400 PHAB Clubs throughout the United Kingdom, this organisation seeks to extend the opportunities for physically handicapped people to enjoy a wide range of leisure and recreational activities alongside and with able-bodied members. Holiday courses are run on such subjects as art, pottery, crafts, music, drama, photography, sailing, riding, swimming and canoeing (*see* Section 9).

Royal National Institute for the Blind
Sports and Recreation Officer, 224 Great Portland Street, London W1N 6AA (Tel: 01-388 1266).

SCAD (Scottish Committee for Arts and Disability)
Scottish Council on Disability, Princes House, 5 Shandwick Place, Edinburgh EH2 4RG (Tel: 031-229 8632).
A voluntary organisation set up to improve disabled people's awareness of, and participation in, the arts. Practical projects include promoting workshops and other arts events for disabled and able-bodied people in the community, running training courses for staff working with disabled people and sponsoring national projects which will increase the public's awareness of the field of arts and disability. An information centre will help artists to find out what institutions, day centres and other care facilities will welcome their work. The centre will also help individuals and organisations who wish to know what provisions and resources exist for disabled people in

the arts. The Development Officer and Administrative Secretary are based at the offices of the Scottish Council on Disability.

Scottish Centre for the Tuition of the Disabled

Queen Margaret College, Clerwood Terrace, Edinburgh EH12 8TS (Tel: 031-339 5408).

As well as providing tutors in academic subjects, the Centre can provide tutors in leisure/sporting pursuits. It can also provide information on local and national opportunities for sport and leisure pursuits. (*See also* section on Further Education page 116.)

The Scottish Council for Spastics

22 Corstophine Road, Edinburgh EH12 6HP (Tel: 031-337 9876).

This organisation, independent of the Spastics Society which covers England and Wales, organises active sporting and recreational programmes (*See also* Section 16.)

Scottish Paraplegic Association

Honorary Secretary: Jean Stone, 3 Cargil Terrace, Edinburgh EH5 3ND (Tel: 031-552 8459 (office hours); ansafone service outside office hours).

The Association organises regular events to cater for all abilities – from the novice to the international athlete. Popular activities are archery, table tennis, bowls, swimming, chess, basketball, fishing, arts and crafts. Continental group holidays are organised. The Association also provides an information and welfare service for members.

Scottish Sports Association for the Disabled

Honorary Secretary: Bill Fenwick, 14 Gordon Court, Dalclaverhouse, Dundee DD4 9DE (Tel: Dundee (0382) 40263).

The SSAD, the co-ordinating body for all sport for all disabled people in Scotland, can offer a comprehensive specialist advice service on most aspects of participation in sport and recreation by people with disabilities. The Association has the services of a full-time officer who has at his disposal a large range of films, videos, books and information, and experience which can be made available to any group, club, organisation, governing body of sport or statutory agency wishing to include disabled people in its activities.

Additionally, SSAD operates a number of branches throughout Scotland, some with full-time officers who can be contacted to provide more local advice and information.

The Scottish Sports Council

1 St Colme Street, Edinburgh EH3 6AA (Tel: 031-225 8411).

The Scottish Sports Council is the national agency responsible for encouraging the development of sport and physical recreation among the public at large in Scotland, for fostering the provision of facilities and for promoting the attainment of high standards. The Council employs a Development Officer, Ron Stuart, for sport and physical recreation for disabled people. He works closely with the Scottish Sports Association for the Disabled.

The Scout Association

Training Department, Gilwell Park, Chingford, London E4 7QW (Tel: 01-524 5246).

The Scout Association accepts disabled boys to join in membership. This extension of Scouting is outlined in *Extension Activities Handbook*. Available from Scout Shops Ltd, Churchill Industrial Estate, North Lancing, Sussex. Price £1.50 plus postage.

Shape

9 Fitzroy Square, London W1P 6AE (Tel: 01-388 9622/9744).

Shape is a unique and imaginative service introducing programmes of creative activities to areas of special needs. Much of its work involves initiating regular arts workshops in dance, drama, music, visual arts, crafts, etc., for people who are physically disabled, mentally handicapped, elderly, mentally ill or socially disadvantaged in hospitals, homes, day centres, clubs and hostels, and in the open community. In this Shape acts as a catalyst providing the initial expertise and funding then, once the activity is established, encouraging the setting to take over responsibility for it. Shape also organises performances by professional artists and companies in such places as hospitals, hostels, day centres, etc. It runs a ticket scheme which offers reduced price tickets and free booking service for events in London's theatres, concert halls, galleries and museums to groups and individuals with special needs; undertakes special projects such as murals, reminiscence, liberal arts, tours and exhibitions of contemporary prints to hospitals and day centres; helps produce performances by integrated companies of disabled and able-bodied performers; runs training courses, etc. Shape's register of over 400 professional artists and its staff of four full-time administrators are always available to respond to requests for art projects of any description from groups with special needs. Shape started in London in 1976 but there now exists a network of ten independent but associated services throughout Great Britain.

Spastics Society – Sports and Leisure
The Spastics Society's Sport and Recreation Officer is Stephen Williams, 16 Fitzroy Square, London W1P 5HQ (Tel: 01-387 9571).
Many sporting activities are arranged for people suffering from cerebral palsy and these include sporting meetings, swimming galas, archery, canoeing, rifle shooting, and wheelchair dance festivals. In addition, indoor meetings are held, providing such activities as table tennis, draughts, chess, Scrabble, whist, etc.

See also Churchtown Farm Field Studies, Lanlivery, Cornwall, where courses are provided for all types of handicapped people in adventure pursuits, including sailing, pony trekking, and a wide variety of leisure activities such as photography, brass rubbing, stone polishing and bird-watching. Details in Section 9.

The Sports Council
16 Upper Woburn Place, London WC1H 0QP (Tel: 01-388 1277).
Through its headquarters, nine regional offices, six national centres and the many agencies in the field, the Sports Council seeks to provide increasing opportunities for disabled people to take part in the activity of their choice at top international or at recreational level, either integrated into community sport or in separate clubs. The staff are always prepared to provide details of local facilities and contacts with other organisations at local or national level.

The Sports Council of Northern Ireland
House of Sport, Upper Malone Road, Belfast BT9 5LA (Tel: Belfast (0232) 661222).

Sports Council for Wales
National Sports Centre for Wales, Sophia Gardens, Cardiff CF1 9SW (Tel: Cardiff (0222) 39751).

Plas Menai National Outdoor Pursuits Centre (formerly known as Plas y Deri), Caernarfon, Gwynedd LL55 1UE (Tel: Caernarfon (0248) 670964).
Outdoor pursuits centres are available and are specially designed to accommodate small groups of physically handicapped people. Specific bookings may be made through the Principal.

United Kingdom Sports Association for People with Mental Handicap
c/o The Sports Council, 16 Upper Woburn Place, London WC1H 0QP (Tel: 01-388 1277).
The Association has in membership voluntary, statutory and professional organisations concerned. Its prime aim is to coordinate the work of its member organisations, to provide a national forum, to represent the UK internationally and to develop the training of leaders and coaches. Its regional structure has the same boundaries as BSAD.

Voluntary Council for Handicapped Children
National Children's Bureau, 8 Wakley Street, Islington, London EC1V 7QE (Tel: 01-278 9441).
The Council produces a number of fact sheets. The one on *Water Sports for Handicapped People* lists relevant organisations.

Welsh Sports Association for the Disabled
This body is now the main contact for sport in Wales. WSAD has three regional organising committees: in north, west and south-east Wales. For further information contact the Secretary, Mrs L. Roberts, 'Crosswinds', 14 Cae Garn, Heolycyw, Bridgend, Mid Glamorgan (Tel: Pencoed (0656) 860854).

Books and Publications

Aids and Games for the Blind. An illustrated catalogue produced by and available from the Royal National Institute for the Blind, 224 Great Portland Street, London W1N 6AA. All kinds of aids for communication, employment and leisure are included.

Arts Centres – Facilities and Amenities for the Handicapped. Edited by Struan Simpson, published by RADAR, and jointly produced with the Arts Council of Great Britain and the Disabilities Study Unit. Available from RADAR, 25 Mortimer Street, London W1N 8AB (Tel: 01-637 5400), price £1.15.

British Sports Association for the Disabled, Ludwig Guttmann Sports Centre, Harvey Road, Aylesbury, Buckinghamshire HP21 8PP (Tel: Aylesbury (0296) 27889). BSAD are producing a series of books 'Sport and Leisure for Disabled People'. The first two are available now, while others are being planned. We understand number 3 may be on snooker.
1. *Archery* by Alf Webb. Price £1.75 including postage and packing.
2. *Athletics* by Moyra Gallagher. Price £1.75 including postage and packing.

Disability, Theatre and Education by Richard Tomlinson. Published by Souvenir Press, 43 Great Russell Street, London WC1B 3PA (Tel: 01-580 9307). The author describes, from his own experience, the essential factors for setting up a company of professional standard (he had been involved with setting up the Graeae Theatre Company), and discusses the work of other companies now being formed throughout the country. He shows how theatre work in workshops and schools can be used to bring disabled people more fully into the community, and how material can be adapted from existing scripts as well as written specially for the occasion. Price paperback £4.95; hardback £6.95 plus 56p and 72p respectively for postage.

Gateway Clubs. Published by MENCAP – The Royal Society for Mentally Handicapped Children and Adults, 123 Golden Lane, London EC1Y 0RT, price 5p.

Give Us the Chance by Kay Latto. A guide to sport and physical activities with mentally handicapped people. The book gives general guidance on teaching methods, choosing an activity and making the most of available outdoor activities. It also gives examples of all types of sport and physical activities that can be undertaken by mentally handicapped people and includes useful hints on teaching and how the activities can be adapted. Available from DLF Sales Ltd, Book House, 45 East Hill, Wandsworth, London SW18 2QZ. Price £9.50.

A film and video of the same name and covering the same subject is available from Town and Country Productions Ltd, 21 Cheyne Row, London SW3 5HP. Hire charge £11.50 to be sent with order.

Help Yourself to the Arts is a 41-page booklet by Annie Delin giving detailed information on the facilities offered by 96 venues in the counties of Derbyshire, Leicestershire, Nottinghamshire, Northamptonshire, and the borough of Milton Keynes. The details given take account of various disabilities. Available free on receipt of s.a.e. (A4 size, 17p in stamps) from East Midlands Arts, Mountfields House, Forest Road, Loughborough, Leicestershire LE11 3HU.

Informal Countryside Recreation for Disabled People (1981). Number 15 of an Advisory Series published by the Countryside Commission. This book aims to provide countryside recreation site managers and providers with the advice and ideas which will help them to encourage disabled people to enjoy the countryside. The book first looks at the nature of disability relating to those who are mobility impaired, those with a loss of sensory perception and those with a mental handicap.

Advice is given on diversional and other requirements which need to be followed if common features such as car parks, footpaths, lavatories, gates and stiles are to be usable by disabled people. Other parts deal with recreation in the countryside and the problems of transport.

There is also a useful list of addresses and interesting lists of plants with aromatic foliage, plants with highly fragrant or scented flowers, and trees and shrubs with ornamental bark or twigs. The book is available from the Countryside Commission, John Dower House, Crescent Place, Cheltenham, Gloucestershire GL50 3RA.

Integrating the Disabled (Chapter 7 of the *Snowdon Report: Sport and Leisure*) (*see* Appendix A).

Joining In – Integrated Sport and Leisure for Disabled People. In this booklet, Norman Croucher discusses the question of the integration of disabled and able-bodied people in sporting activities and provides useful information on angling, camping, croquet, darts, canoeing, flying, skiing and rock climbing. Available from the Disabilities Study Unit, Wildhanger, Amberley, Arundel, West Sussex BN18 9NR. Price £1 to be sent with order.

Leisure and Gardening, one of the books in the series 'Equipment for the Disabled', containing the following sections:
Leisure: information; resource centres; access to places of entertainment; sports centres; the countryside; channel ports; travel; holidays, UK and abroad; associations and clubs; outdoor activities; sport; artistic activities; hobbies and games; educational activities; select bibliography; address/telephone numbers; alphabetical index.
Gardening: garden design; tool handles; hand tools; soil cultivation; staking and tying; flower gatherers; watering and spraying; frames and greenhouses; grass cutting; wheelbarrows; garden grabs; pruning; accessories; sources of information and advice; select bibliography; address/telephone numbers; alphabetical index. Available from Equipment for the Disabled, Mary Marlborough Lodge, Nuffield Orthopaedic Centre, Headington, Oxford OX3 7LD. Price £3.50 plus postage and packing (send no money with order).

Let Me Play by Dorothy M. Jeffree, Roy McConkey and Simon Hewson. A programme of games devised to encourage motor and sensory skills, intellect, imagination and social confidence in severely handicapped children. The authors have recognised that in handicapped children the spontaneous wish to play often needs to be encouraged. The book helps teachers and parents to introduce the experience of play and to build on it from basic exploratory games to quite complex perceptual, discriminatory, manipulative and memory games. Published by Souvenir Press, 43 Great Russell Street, London WC1B 3PA (Tel: 01-580 9307/637 5711), price £2.75.

Outdoor Pursuits for Disabled People by Norman Croucher. The author has scaled Mont Blanc, the

Matterhorn, the Eiger, and most recently, Peru's highest mountain, Huascaran (21,820 feet) on his two metal legs, and is an inspiration by personal example, to all other would-be disabled sportsmen. The new and expanded edition of this guide is intended to encourage people, with whatever type of disability, to experiment with outdoor pursuits they had thought beyond their abilities. The information covers a wide range of sports and there are useful appendices listing helpful organisations, etc. Published by Woodhead-Faulkner, Fitzwilliam House, 32 Trumpington Street, Cambridge CB2 1QY, in association with the Disabled Living Foundation. Price £6.95.

Noah's Ark Publications. Obtainable from Play Matters – The Toy Libraries Association, Seabrook House, Wyllyotts Manor, Darkes Lane, Potters Bar, Hertfordshire EN6 2HL (Tel: Potters Bar (0707) 44571). The range of publications is the response to queries from parents, professionals and toy libraries on various aspects of play. They are intended to give advice and stimulate ideas on play for all children, with particular reference to the needs of handicapped children.

1. *The Good Toy Guide.* The toys described have been tested and recommended by the Association's professionally qualified Advisory Panel. A one-page chart details a child's development and suggests appropriate toys for each stage. Price £2.95.
2. *Do-it-yourself.* Ideas and instructions for DIY toys ranging from simple, cheap ideas to more complex designs. Includes designs to meet the special needs of handicapped children, which are not yet available commercially. Price £1.
3. *For Busy Hands.* Detailed DIY instructions on how to make noisy, rewarding play material which will appeal to the child who steadfastly ignores all 'toy shop' toys. Price £1.
4. *Hear and Say.* A much extended and now fully illustrated new edition of *Toys for Children with Speech, Hearing and Language Difficulties.* Price £1.10.
5. *Design and Make Magnetic Board Toys.* Price £1.
6. *Encouraging Language Development.* Price £1.
7. *I Can Use My Hands.* Price £1.
8. *Positions for Play.* Price £1.10.

No Handicap to Dance: Creative Improvisation for People with Handicaps by Gina Levete. Published by Souvenir Press, 43 Great Russell Street, London WC1B 3PA (Tel: 01-580 9307). The author shows how people with even severe physical and mental disability can take part in dance, creative improvisation, music and movement if they are encouraged to respond to music and ideas in their own way. Gina Levete describes in detail method classes and workshops that she has used with her own classes of children and adults, showing the immeasurable benefits they can bring to people whose lives are confined by handicap or institutional restrictions. Price paperback £4.95; hardback £6.95 plus 56p and 72p respectively for postage.

Out of Doors with Handicapped People by Mike Cotton. Published by Souvenir Press, 43 Great Russell Street, London WC1B 3PA (Tel: 01-580 9307). As a result of the author's years of experience he is able to outline a wide range of projects that can be enjoyed by people without the full use of their limbs, both in city and country environments. Bird-watching, pond studies and fishing are combined with more energetic pursuits like visiting a farm and camping. Price paperback £4.50; hardback £6.95 plus 64p and 80p respectively for postage.

A Philosophy of Leisure in Relation to the Retarded by Kenneth Solly. Available from MENCAP – the Royal Society for Mentally Handicapped Children and Adults, 123 Golden Lane, London EC1Y 0RT (Tel: 01-253 9433). Price 35p.

Physical Education for the Physically Handicapped. Published by HMSO (Department of Education and Science). Price £1.20.

Play for the Handicapped Child by Joan Hill. Price 50p plus 15p postage and packing from the Education Department, Wiltshire County Council, County Hall, Trowbridge BA14 8JB. This short booklet is addressed to parents of a handicapped child: How does play help? How do I decide the kind of play my child needs? Of particular interest are the development charts which follow the main text. Here, types of play for five different stages of development between birth and six years are suggested, although these ages relate to the stage of development reached by a child, not his chronological age.

Sports Centres and the Disabled (second edition). A directory of sports centres in England and Wales with their facilities for disabled people. Compiled and published in collaboration with the Sports Council and the Royal Association for Disability and Rehabilitation. Price 75p. Available from the Disability Study Unit, Wildhanger, Amberley, Arundel, West Sussex BN18 9NR.

Sports and Leisure. An access guide for disabled spectators. Compiled by Peter Lawton. Covers a variety of sports venues such as football, rugby and cricket grounds, horse riding, greyhound racing, speedway and motor racing tracks and tennis clubs. Published by RADAR, 25 Mortimer Street, London W1N 8AB (Tel: 01-637 5400), price £1.35.

Textbook of Sport for the Disabled by Sir Ludwig Guttman. This first modern comprehensive illustrated textbook is written for doctors, physiotherapists, remedial gymnasts, physical instructors, coaches, referees, administrators and all others involved in competitive sport for the physically handicapped. It covers the disabilities of amputation, blindness, cerebral palsy, deafness and spinal paralysis, with particular emphasis on spinal paraplegia and tetraplegia, and the applications of the results of many years' research to the development of sporting activities of disabled people. The medical aspects of sport are covered in some detail with considerable stress on the assessment and classification of physical deficit and on the physical, psychological and social effects of sporting activities upon disabled sportsmen and women. Available from booksellers or direct from HM & M Publishers, John Wiley & Sons Ltd, Baffins Lane, Chichester, Sussex PO19 1UD. Price £14 plus postage.

Films

Give Us the Chance, 16 mm, 36 minutes, presented by the Disabled Living Foundation. The film aims to promote some positive ideas and approaches to recreative physical activities which are being carried out successfully in hospitals, adult training centres, special schools, sheltered communities, Gateway clubs and in the home by leaders who, by imaginative use of facilities, are helping mentally handicapped people to enjoy a range of leisure activities. Available from Town and Country Productions Ltd, 21 Cheyne Row, Chelsea, London SW3 5HP (Tel: 01-352 7950). Hire charge for film or video – VHS or Betamax, one showing is £11.50 (including VAT). Also for sale, film £275; video cassette £39.95.

It's Ability That Counts, 16 mm, colour, 25 minutes. A film made for the British Sports Association for the Disabled to show the opportunities that exist for handicapped people to partake in a variety of sporting activities. Available from BSAD Regional Officers – addresses from BSAD, Ludwig Guttmann Sports Centre for the Disabled, Hayward House, Barnard Crescent, Aylesbury, Buckinghamshire HP21 8PP.

Not Just a Spectator, 16 mm, colour, 35 minutes. This film produced by the Disabled Living Foundation concerns recreative physical activities for people with a wide range of disabilities. Among the activities depicted are climbing, basketball, cycling, wheelchair dancing, canoeing, sailing and birdwatching. Available from Town and Country Productions Ltd, 21 Cheyne Row, London SW3 5HP (Tel: 01-352 7950). Hire charge to be sent with order (film or video – VHS or Betamax).

16 mm Entertainment Films for the Deaf and Hard of Hearing. This catalogue of captioned films is supplied by Rank Film Library, PO Box 20, Great West Road, Brentford, Middlesex TW8 9HR (Tel: 01-568 9222). Includes comedies, westerns, drama, musicals, adventure, animated features, mysteries and thrillers.

SEX AND PERSONAL RELATIONSHIPS

Ignorance is not bliss, and at last we are coming to an understanding of the vital importance sexual pleasure and love-making have for all our lives. The need for physical closeness to other beings is, after all, as natural as breathing. As we grow up we learn to put a distance between ourselves and others, and there are periods when there is just no one near. But as sexual expression and warmth and closeness can be the well-spring of some of our greatest happinesses, so its frustration can lead to the most profound and unremitting misery.

For people with disabilities sexual problems may well be compounded by physical difficulties. However, many of these problems can be overcome given a little practical advice and by the exercise of imagination and tolerance between partners.

Disability can affect our sexual activities in a number of different ways, either directly or indirectly. There is a direct effect when the spinal cord is damaged and nerves passing to the sexual organs are affected. If messages from the brain intended to stimulate sexual responsiveness are not able to travel effectively all the way down the spinal cord until they reach the sexual organs, then depending on the severity of the damage, the functions and the feelings of those organs will be affected to a greater or lesser degree. This would impair, for instance, those with spinal injuries through accidents or those with multiple sclerosis – a disease of the nervous system where the sheaths surrounding nerves in the brain and spinal cord are damaged, thus affecting the function of the nerves involved, or people with spina bifida whose spinal cord has not developed properly.

Indirect effects may include: incontinence; pain (which if prolonged will naturally diminish the sex drive, and is especially liable to affect people with arthritis); fear of further physical damage, for instance, after a hip replacement operation or after a heart attack; lack of body control as occurs with spasms; fear of inducing fits in those with epilepsy.

For some, intercourse is not possible or only rarely attainable, but it can be a great mistake to see the goal of intercourse as the only reason for making love – it is, in fact, only a part of our sexual activity. Gentle and prolonged love-making with no 'goal' necessarily in sight, where sexual activity is less of a tumultuous release and more of a prolonged sharing can bring wonderful and satisfying experiences to the couple willing to experiment in this way.

Alex Comfort, in his foreword to *Sexual Options for Paraplegics and Quadriplegics* (*see* page 249) says: 'Virtually nobody is too disabled to derive some satisfaction and personal reinforcement from sex – with a partner if possible, alone if necessary. When a disabled person is unable to enjoy sex, the greatest obstacle to enjoyment usually isn't the difficulty or impossibility of making particular movements, but the social convention that sex consists of putting the penis in the vagina and that all the rest of the rich range of human and mammalian sexual responses – oral, manual and skin stimulation – are abnormal. Human sex is widely versatile and not limited to the genitalia.'

We all know how easily love lives can go stale with the same old boring routine and it is only by being imaginative and varied in our activities that we can ensure this does not happen to us. Finding new ways to enjoy sexual activities can be very rewarding and is marvellous for releasing inhibitions. Willingness to experiment can be a great asset for everyone and especially for anyone with limited movement. Different positions padded up with pillows, prolonged caressing and massage, oral sex, masturbation, varying the surroundings, warm shared baths and showers, gently lit beds in a cosy room with drinks at hand can all add a new dimension and be especially helpful to people whose bodies have parts which do not respond in the way they would wish.

We would urge people experiencing difficulties to seek help. SPOD (*see* page 243) will always be glad to help and may be able to recommend someone you can talk to locally. In the following pages we describe a few books and publications you may find helpful. Those seeking partners may like to try joining the Outsiders Club; they have a very useful book of practical suggestions aiming to help people who are feeling socially and sexually outside the mainstream of life. Somewhere in all this information there may be the answer to the quest for your own fulfilment.

Sex need not be disabled, it only feels like it when practical (and psychological) difficulties remain unsolved.

Helpful Organisations

We list below organisations which provide specialist services and also some of the general organisations which have indicated they would be glad to help with questions on sexuality whenever they can.

Action for Research into Multiple Sclerosis (ARMS)
71 Gray's Inn Road, London WC1X 8TR.
ARMS Telephone Counselling Service:
England and Wales: 01-568 2255 (London), 021-476 4229 (West Midlands);
Scotland: 041-637 2262 (Glasgow);
Northern Ireland: (0247) 63378 (Bangor).
ARMS run a very good 24-hour counselling service with trained counsellors who know about MS from personal experience. They are there to listen to any problems concerning MS and will be glad to help with sexual problems. The counsellors help callers cope with their distress, fears and anger and try to help them find hope for the future.

British Pregnancy Advisory Service
Head Office: Austy Manor, Wootton Wawen, Solihull, West Midlands B95 6DA (Tel: Henley-in-Arden (056 42) 3225).
A non-profit-making charitable trust which offers help, information and counselling for any problems connected with pregnancy, contraception, infertility or sexuality. At some of its branches a special counselling service for disabled people with sexual problems is available.

Brook Centres
The Centres welcome disabled people, but only their Centres in London: 233 Tottenham Court Road, London W1P 9AE (Tel: 01-323 1522/580 2991); Coventry: Gynaecological Out-Patients, Coventry and Warwickshire Hospital, Stoney Stanton Road, Coventry (Tel: Coventry (0203) 412627); and Edinburgh: 2 Lower Gilmore Place, Edinburgh EH3 9NY (Tel: 031-229 5320) are accessible. The Centres offer a contraception service (including routine screening); pregnancy testing, diagnosis and counselling (including, where appropriate, referral to NHS or voluntary charitable agencies for further advice and/or help with motherhood, adoption or abortion); counselling for emotional or sexual problems; advice on sex education courses and speakers.

Disdate
This is basically a penfriend/dating agency for disabled, lonely and understanding people and was founded by disabled people. The life registration fee is £8 to cover advertising, printing and other expenses. This covers a minimum of three introductions – more if you are not satisfied. For further details contact Bruce Brown, 56 Devizes Avenue, Bedford (Tel: Bedford (0234) 40643).

The Family Planning Association and The Family Planning Information Service
27–35 Mortimer Street, London W1N 7RJ (Tel: 01-636 7866).
The Family Planning Information Service was set up to ensure that people know about and use the free NHS family planning facilities. An extensive range of free leaflets, posters, and information sheets can be obtained from the FPIS office. There are also telephone and mail enquiry services, a walk-in information bureau and a library.

There are 11 regional offices which act as information and activity centres for the whole of the country. Details of all these and other services are available from the address above.

Gemma
For details of this organisation for disabled lesbians, *see* page 303.

Independent Consultant
Bill Stewart, first Development Officer of SPOD – Association to aid the Sexual and Personal Relationships of the Disabled – and author of a number of publications on sex and handicapped people, now operates as an independent consultant working in the fields of sexual and psycho-sexual dysfunction, including that relating to physical and mental disability. Bill Stewart maintains his writing and lecturing activities and is available as organiser/tutor for courses on advice/counsel in the sexual problems of disability. He is unable to provide personal advice and counsel for individual disabled clients.

For further information contact him at 1 Winnersh Grove, Winnersh, Wokingham, Berkshire RG11 5EQ (Tel: Wokingham (0734) 791032).

Muscular Dystrophy Group of Great Britain and Northern Ireland
Nattrass House, 35 Macaulay Road, London SW4 0QP (Tel: 01-720 8055).
The Group has a Patient Care Officer to advise people with muscular dystrophy and their carers. She is happy to answer specific welfare queries and can also provide details of the nearest genetic counselling

centre. Two leaflets are produced: *Inheritance and the Muscular Dystrophies*, providing a brief summary of the complex genetics of these conditions; and *Sexuality and Neuromuscular Disease*, which gives a brief description of the problems and provides a resource list of helpful organisations, books, films, etc. For further details of the Group *see* page 312.

National Marriage Guidance Council
Herbert Gray College, Little Church Street, Rugby CV21 3AP (Tel: Rugby (0788) 73241).

NMGC services are available to all, of any age, of either sex, in any circumstances, who are worried about personal relationships, regardless of whether they are married or not. It can be a couple or a woman or man alone.

Counselling normally takes place in the NMGC premises, some of which are accessible. Sessions are usually arranged weekly to last for an hour, free from interruptions, for as long as is necessary for clients to talk through their problems. If there is a sexual problem as distinct from purely a relationship problem, it may be appropriate, with the client's agreement, to seek the help of one of the NMGC's Sexual Dysfunction Clinics.

There is no obligatory charge for counselling help, but naturally the NMGC as a voluntary organisation, hopes that clients will contribute to the cost of the work and this is something the counsellor will discuss with you.

The NMGC operates in England, Wales and Northern Ireland. It is independent and is not attached to any sectarian, denominational or cultural institution. There are now over 500 counselling centres throughout the country, with a total complement of more than 1,750 counsellors. Some counsellors have specialist knowledge of disability where this is needed.

To make an appointment, telephone, write or call in to your local MGC. Telephone numbers and addresses for MGCs are listed in telephone directories under 'Marriage Guidance'.

Scottish Marriage Guidance Council
58 Palmerston Place, Edinburgh EH12 5AZ (Tel: 031-225 5006).

The SMGC is constitutionally separate from the NMGC, but close working links are maintained. It operates in a similar way and has virtually the same objectives. In addition, sex therapy is available in Aberdeen, Edinburgh and Glasgow. NHS domiciliary family planning services operate in a number of areas. If you are seeking birth control advice and services and have difficulty in reaching a clinic, arrangements could be made for the domiciliary service to visit you. Your social worker or family doctor could advise about this or you could contact your local family planning clinic (in telephone directory under 'Family Planning').

The Outsiders Club
This is an independent group who aim to rescue others who have become emotionally stranded, and help each other find partners to love.

People who have been pretty much discarded by society as being 'loners', those who do not fit the 'Martini-set' image, the unattractive, inarticulate people who were born, or have become, disabled or disfigured, people crippled with shyness or suffering phobias, those weakened by illness – everyone is welcome to join. They help each other to build up their confidence, go out on dates and hopefully find the kind of partner they are looking for.

To most people, emotional stability and sexual satisfaction are essential for them to function properly in their work or socially. The Outsiders Club hopes that it will contribute to making its members happier and better able to function. It has found that some members cheer up so dramatically that even their disabilities are lessened; speech is improved, depressions are lifted and medicines are no longer required.

The Club provides a system in which people can meet each other. People get together who have similar difficulties, offering each other comfort and practical help. They can swap ideas on how to cope with shared handicaps; shy people can team together to go out and enjoy themselves; those who are lonely can offer each other company.

There are hundreds of members in the Club, living all over the country and abroad, too, but it tries to keep small, so that it can be responsive to each member as he or she joins. Sexual tastes are not questioned or condemned; members are encouraged to become relaxed about themselves and uninhibited. The club runs a postal library of books on emotional, personal and sexual topics and lends book-tapes and erotic tapes to blind members. Every member receives lists, a booklet of practical suggestions (*see* page 248) and details of contacts as well as newsletters about forthcoming events and parties. Blind people receive all this on tape.

A charity has been formed to operate alongside the Outsiders Club called the Social Habilitation and Integration Trust for Disabled People. The aims include: to help people who are handicapped in any way make happy and fulfilling relationships; to help counter the loneliness or emotional isolation felt by some people with handicaps.

The Club and the Trust were founded by Tuppy Owens and continue to be generally inspired by her. They are run from her London offices. Contact Box 4ZB, London W1A 4ZB (Tel: 01-741 3332).

Spinal Injuries Association
Yeoman's House, 76 St James's Lane, Muswell Hill, London N10.
The SIA has a marvellously refreshing attitude to its members and this is best reflected in its newsletter, which deals practically and imaginatively with all aspects of living with a disability. In contrast to many other magazines in the field of disability, it is above all else reader responsive and indeed, its readers set the tone by writing frankly and fully of their difficulties and of their achievements. Sexual matters, artificial insemination, management of incontinence and all other matters of daily living are discussed regularly and fully.

The Welfare Service (Tel: 01-380 0232), with 24-hour answerphone for members, aims to provide friendly counsel and advice, to help solve problems (including those of a personal and sexual nature), sometimes by putting people in touch with other individuals or organisations. For further details of SIA *see* page 328.

SPOD: Association to Aid the Sexual and Personal Relationships of the Disabled
286 Camden Road, London N7 0BJ (Tel: 01-607 8851).
SPOD was set up in 1972 by the National Fund for Research into Crippling Diseases, with the object at that time of studying and advising on sexual problems that might be experienced by disabled people. In a few years a great deal has been achieved with regard to changing people's attitudes by bringing discussion into the open and showing that disability doesn't rule out sexual feelings, sexual needs or, usually, sexual capabilities.

SPOD provides information on disability and sexuality, including a range of publications (*see* page 251). SPOD has a country-wide network of counsellors and can usually put disabled people in touch with a counsellor near to their home. SPOD also arranges study days on the subjects of 'Sexuality and Disability'; 'Sex Education for Physically Handicapped Young People'; and 'Sex Education for Mentally Handicapped People'. A teaching pack on sex education for mentally handicapped people is also available.

For further information contact Morgan Williams, the General Secretary.

Voluntary Council for Handicapped Children
National Children's Bureau, 8 Wakley Street, London EC1V 7QE (Tel: 01-278 9441).
The Council provides a number of information sheets, one of these entitled *The Sexual Needs of Handicapped Young People* lists useful organisations and relevant publications and films. For further details of the Council's work *see* page 330.

Incontinence and Sexuality

Incontinence refers to a loss or a weakening of control of the bladder or bowel, or of both. There can be any number of causes of incontinence which may be temporary or permanent. These may include temporary illness, childbirth, local conditions affecting the bladder or womb including infections, complications of artery disease, or disease or injury of the spinal cord.

The management of incontinence is improving all the time. This is not to say that it is ever easy, but a greater understanding and awareness of the individual needs of people who suffer in this way and an understanding of the universality of the problem have led to the development of techniques of management and the production of more acceptable equipment.

At the same time there is increasing recognition of the sexual needs and aspirations of disabled people and the difficulties, in sheer practical terms, which incontinence can pose. There is no simple answer and it is vital that the disabled person should seek professional help and advice in this matter as much can be done to bring the problems within manageable limits. With proper diagnosis and management techniques it has been found that only a small proportion of people need to use appliances on a long-term basis. In seeking help it is important to persist even if the first doctor or nurse approached does not provide the advice needed. The general practitioner and/or consultant should be prepared to help not only in better overall management of an incontinence problem but also with regard to its relevance to sexual activity. It is worth noting that attached to some District General Hospitals are Urological Assessment Clinics, with sophisticated equipment for diagnosis. The importance of seeking medical advice before adopting any particular procedure cannot be emphasised too strongly.

Fluid intake
While an adequate overall intake of fluids must be maintained (it is vital as a means of combating infection) it is often possible to regulate this to fit in with sexual activity.

Control exercises

In some cases of urinary incontinence a great deal can be done to improve the condition by a programme of simple physical exercises. This mostly applies in the case of stress incontinence where it may be possible gradually to strengthen the appropriate muscles. Stress in this context is a purely physical condition, when a slight leakage occurs during some minor exertion such as sneezing, laughing or coughing. Suitable exercises are described in Dorothy Mandelstam's book *Incontinence*: *see* page 68.

Emptying the bladder

Some people are able to use what is known as the Credé method to make sure the bladder is totally empty at a particular time. This involves taking a deep breath, folding arms across the abdominal area and bending forward at the waist to increase the pressure in the lower abdominal area. Another method known as 'percussion' is simply banging the abdomen with palm or fist. (This can be very frustrating if it does not work and is not worth the trouble of persisting for too long!)

Emptying the bowel

Maintaining a regular bowel programme is the best protection against accidents; however, a degree of flexibility in routine can be achieved where this is needed to fit in with a personal lifestyle. The frequency of bowel management varies considerably from person to person – commonly once a day, sometimes twice a week, with some people reporting once-weekly evacuation with no visible ill effects. For those people using suppositories, a suppository inserter can be a great help.

Equipment

There is a wide variety of equipment on the market. The best possible advice, combined with trial and error, should usually determine the most appropriate equipment for individual needs. The Disabled Living Foundation has a fairly comprehensive list of incontinence aids. Their incontinence adviser will be glad to answer queries. (*See* page 54 for details.)

Intermittent or self-catheterisation

In the past few years this system of regularly emptying the bladder has gained a wider acceptance and indeed has been found preferable where retention of residual urine is a problem. Intermittent self-catheterisation is a clean, non-sterile method of introducing a catheter into the bladder every two to four hours, depending on the doctor's guidance and individual requirements.

Considering Genetics

It is natural for everybody to worry a little about the possibility of having a baby who may be handicapped. It is also natural that parents who are handicapped themselves should be particularly concerned. Very often there is no real cause for concern, but in any event, it is important to seek advice. For instance, if it is decided to go ahead with a pregnancy, there are a number of diseases and abnormalities which can be detected by a simple test early on in the pregnancy. Your doctor should be consulted initially for referral to a local genetic advisory centre which may provide diagnosis, a biochemical testing service and genetic counselling. *See* page 246 for references to *Human Genetics*; *The Genetics of Down's Syndrome*; *Know Your Genes*; the Association to Combat Huntington's Chorea's publications; *Genetic Counselling in Mental Handicap*; and *Sex and Young People with Spina Bifida and Cerebral Palsy*.

Aids and Equipment

The use of sex aids is frowned on by many people. The manner of their selling does not help. The sleazy shops and the off-putting (for some people) brochures confirm the feelings that they can be no part of a 'normal' relationship. But within reason, and provided inhibitions can be overcome, an introduction to the use of sex aids can transform people's relationships. Quite apart from their potential for harmless fun in bed, many such aids can be positively helpful in overcoming sexual problems and have a special place where disability has adversely affected sexual function and sensation.

Easily the best aids catalogue that we have seen is that of the Xandria Collection, PO Box 31039, San Francisco, CA 94131, California, USA. Ray and Judi Lawrence, who produce it, believe that 'sexual aids can enhance a relationship and provide a positive influx of new and pleasurable sensations for each partner'. In a philosophical foreword, they give a personal testimony to the efficacy of aids in bridging the gap between hurried, non-communicative sex and the more satisfying experience of a fully sensual and understanding relationship. Used individually, they say, sex aids can help to bring an understanding of one's own sensitivities. Used together, they can help partners to learn more about performance and allow a relaxed approach to love-making in which partners can 'take the time and pleasure of seeing, feeling and understanding each other's responses'. The catalogue goes on to provide a basic explanation of the male and female genital organs and the sexual response cycles of the two sexes. The aids themselves are illustrated by 'soft' drawings and are fully described. There is also a special edition for disabled people.

Blakoe Ltd
229 Putney Bridge Road, London SW15 (Tel: 01-870 4251).
This firm produces a range of sexual aids, and, bearing in mind the consideration that there are still many people who feel that the use of artificial aids to achieve sexual satisfaction is unnatural, Blakoe have carefully chosen to market those aids which they consider have a purpose in a therapeutic sense, and none is included purely because it contributes to eroticism. It is claimed that all assist the natural processes of the sexual act and so contribute towards attaining satisfactory and happy relationships. Among the aids available, which are tailored to individual requirements, are for women: clitoral and vaginal stimulators; for men: erection promoters and penis supports and substitutes. It is stressed, however, that the use of these appliances should follow medical and psychological examination to identify remedial physical and psychological causes. (*See The Blakoe Manual of Mechanotherapy* below.)

Harmony (Bulkcourt) Ltd
41 Cross Street, Manchester 2.
This mail order company is sensitive to people with sexual problems and supplies prosthetics to the National Health Service and various medical groups. Its catalogues, though explicit, offer useful explanations. Discounts are available to disabled customers.

Disabled Living Foundation
380–384 Harrow Road, London W9 2HU (Tel: 01-289 6111).
A small display of sexual aids and prostheses which may be useful in varying forms of disability is on show at the DLF. The display is not, of course, dramatic or sensational but gives an opportunity for those who are interested to see some of the aids outside the usual setting of the sex shop. An appointment should be made for the visit, but the DLF would like to make it clear that they are not able to offer counselling help.
For further details about the DLF service *see* page 53.

The William Merritt Aids and Information Centre for Disabled People
St Mary's Hospital, Green Hill Road, Armley, Leeds LS12 3QE (Tel: (0532) 793140).
The Centre has a small display of sex aids and

manufacturers' catalogues. These aids can be ordered direct from the Centre on the client's behalf. Counselling is not available, but a referral system to other agencies is available.

SPOD (*see* page 243) would also be glad to advise on aids.

Books and Publications

There are so many publications dealing with the subjects of sex and family relationships that it would be impossible to list them here; therefore only specialist books relating to disablement have been included. However, for further reading, the National Marriage Guidance Council and the Family Planning Association publish lists of books by well-known authors, covering a wide variety of views and offering information, advice and encouragement to all, in whatever particular dilemma or situation they find themselves.

Association to Combat Huntington's Chorea, Borough House, 34a Station Road, Hinckley, Leicester LE10 1AP (Tel: Hinckley (0455) 615558). Helpful publications include:
Huntington's Chorea: a Booklet for Families, which describes the disease and its effects and carefully illustrates the inheritance factors. Every child born to a parent with Huntington's Chorea (the symptoms of which usually do not appear until mid-life) has a 50 per cent chance of inheriting the defective gene and therefore of developing the disease in later life. Price 35p plus postage.

Is It in the Family? A leaflet designed to inform young people of the basic problems of Huntington's Chorea and to encourage them to seek advice. Free on receipt of a self-addressed envelope.

Tomorrow's Child? A booklet discussing the problems of and alternatives to parenthood in a Huntington's Chorea family. Free on receipt of a self-addressed envelope.

What is HC? A comprehensive question-and-answer leaflet on Huntington's Chorea. Free on receipt of a self-addressed envelope.

Better Lives for Disabled Women by Jo Campling. Discusses sexuality and sexual needs of disabled women (*see* Appendix A for further details).

The Blakoe Manual of Mechanotherapy: A concept in the treatment of sexual dysfunction is written by the makers of Blakoe sexual aids and is intended mainly for members of the medical profession. It discusses very briefly some of the reasons for physical and psychological sexual problems and naturally goes on to recommend use of the firm's sexual aids where these would be suitable. Published by Medical Division, Blakoe Ltd, 229 Putney Bridge Road, London SW15 (Tel: 01-870 4251).

Disabled – an Illustrated Manual of Help and Self-help by Dr Philip Nicols with Ros Haworth and Joy Hopkins. Published by David & Charles (1981). Available from David & Charles, Brunel House, Newton Abbot, Devon (Tel: Newton Abbot (0626) 61121). Price £7.95. Among the subjects covering every aspect of disabled living, is a short chapter on personal relationships which includes brief details on contraceptive methods and also describes a few positions for sexual intercourse.

Disabled Eve: Aids in Menstruation by Brenda McCarthy. Published by the Disabled Living Foundation (1981) and available from DLF Book Sales Ltd, Book House, 45 East Hill, Wandsworth, London SW18 2QZ. Price £3.50 including postage and packing. A practical guide, well illustrated, which describes the techniques, sanitary aids and devices which should help to alleviate or solve the difficult management problems facing disabled women during menstruation. The chapter on techniques is very informative, describing first the use of tampons, with a variety of tampon inserters to suit various disabilities. These are all clearly illustrated.

Entitled to Love: the Sexual and Emotional Needs of the Handicapped by Dr Wendy Greengross. Available from SPOD (*see* page 243). Price £2.90 including postage and packing. The author sets out to challenge at all levels the widely accepted view that people with disabilities do not, or should not, have sexual feelings. This is not a handbook on sex, but a discussion weaving understanding and concern into readable patterns. She makes the point that we all have to take emotional risks and being over-protective to people with disabilities is never kind and may often be cruel.

Dr Greengross goes on to discuss the problems of handicapped people in institutions (*e.g.* having little privacy), as well as the problems of staff who may find difficulty in coming to terms with the sexual needs of those in their care. She deals with sex education and the sexual problems of the adolescent, and also makes a plea that couples, where movements are restricted, should be ready to consider experimentation to widen the scope of their love-making.

Female Sexuality following Spinal Cord Injury by Elle Friedman Becker. Personal interviews with

disabled women and professionals with substantial experience in this field provide technical and scientific information in a practical, understandable manner. Published by Accent Special Publications, Box 700, Bloomington, Illinois 61701, USA, price $10.95 plus $1.15 shipping.

Genetic Counselling in Mental Handicap by Brian Kirman. Published by the Royal Society for Mentally Handicapped Children and Adults (MENCAP). Available from MENCAP Bookshop, 123 Golden Lane, London EC1Y 0RT. Price 50p plus 25p postage.

The Genetics of Down's Syndrome (An Account for Parents). The aim of this account is to explain the genetic mechanisms whereby Down's syndrome occurs so that parents can understand why their child has this condition, and the likelihood of a similar abnormality in further children. Available from Down's Children's Association, Quinborne Community Centre, Ridgacre Road, Birmingham B32 2TW (Tel: 021-427 1374).

Handicapped Married Couples by Michael and Ann Craft. This is an excellent and moving account of 40 mentally handicapped couples as discovered through the authors' careful analysis of a survey carried out by them. Dr Craft is a consultant psychiatrist and Mrs Craft is a social worker. The idea that mentally handicapped men and women are capable of normal sexual feelings, and are entitled to express these, has until recently been totally unacceptable to all but an enlightened few. Michael and Ann Craft have now published the evidence showing that marriage between mentally handicapped people, under the right conditions, has a high chance of success and should be encouraged rather than forbidden. Published by Routledge & Kegan Paul Ltd. Price £9.25.

Human Genetics is a helpful booklet prepared by the DHSS. It is concerned with the medical implications of human genetics and in particular the role of genetic counselling. It is presented in a simplified form and gives the bare outline of the subject only. The main types of inheritance: dominant, recessive (including the implications of marriage between blood relatives), sex linked (X-linked) are explained and some examples given. Also discussed are conditions due to chromosomal abnormalities and those with partial and complex inheritance. While this booklet is primarily intended to alert doctors to the problem of genetic disease in the community and to the number of persons who would find genetic counselling of benefit, and therefore presumes a knowledge of medical terms, it could well be of interest to those who are concerned about possible genetic problems within their own families.

The Joy of Sex by Alex Comfort. Published by Quartet Books (new full colour illustrated paperback edition, 1982). Price £6.50. During our research this was a book that seemed to be on everyone's list of favourites. Indeed, it is now so well known as to scarcely need recommendation. It gains considerably from its new larger format which does better justice to the black and white illustrations of Charles Raymond and Christopher Foss, while the new colour plates greatly enhance the sensuality of a book which is itself a hymn to sensuality.

Know your Genes by Aubrey Milunsky. Information about hereditary disorders and your personal risks and options. This is a most readable layman's guide to genetics, setting in sensible perspective the fears and worries we all have regarding the effects our own genetic inheritance may have on any children. The important thing is that we should understand any possible risks. The result for many people will be to put their minds at rest. For those with real problems the author seeks to inform and encourage them in their difficult decisions. Apart from all the useful details on chromosomes and genes, information is given on superstition and birth defects, drugs and their danger, genetic counselling, artificial insemination by donor, ethics, morality, the law and pre-natal diagnosis, heredity, race and learning disorders, test-tube babies.

This book is written for an American audience but translates well to our own culture. Warmly recommended. A Pelican Book, price £2.50.

Images of Ourselves (for details *see* page 340).

Life Together compiled by Inger Nordqvist. This book is essentially an account of the symposium on the intimate relationships of handicapped persons, arranged by the Swedish Central Committee for Rehabilitation in 1969. Its purpose is to outline and study the factors that complicate the relationships of physically handicapped people of all ages – practical problems, prejudices, complexes – and where possible suggest solutions. The emphasis on sexual problems is due, of course, to those being the most charged with prejudice, and involving considerable practical difficulties. Chapters include amongst others: 'The parent relationship to a handicapped child'; 'The liberation of handicapped young people'; 'Physically handicapped adults and their contacts with others'; 'The sexual life of the physically handicapped'; 'Contraceptive methods'. Available from Royal Association for Disability and Rehabilitation,

25 Mortimer Street, London W1N 8AB (Tel: 01-637 5400). Price £1.20 inclusive of postage.

Living with a Colostomy by Margaret Schindler. Published by Thorsons Publishers Ltd (1981). Price £3.50. This book is written to provide reassuring advice on returning to normal life after a colostomy operation. It gives guidance on diet, appliances, travel and personal relationships. The discussion on sexuality comes alive through the words of people who have themselves had colostomies. They are a source of considerable encouragement in the way they tell of their experiences.

Marriage, Sex and Arthritis. Produced by the Arthritis and Rheumatism Council, 41 Eagle Street, London WC1R 4AR (Tel: 01-405 8572). Price 20p including postage. A short, clearly written booklet containing information on sex, family planning, pregnancy, childbirth and inheritance of arthritis.

MENCAP – The Royal Society for Mentally Handicapped Children and Adults publishes several leaflets relating to sex, they are:
(a) *Sex Education and the Mentally Retarded* by George W. Lee, including short sections on parent involvement, programme planning objectives and curriculum. Price £1.
(b) *Sex and Social Training in an Adult Training Centre* by Lindsey Lowes. Price 30p.
(c) *The Sexual Rights of the Retarded* by George W. Lee and Gregor Katz. Price 50p.
(d) *Help your Child to Understand Sex* by Victoria Shennan. Straightforward and helpful seven-page pamphlet written especially for parents. Price 50p. Add 25p per £1 of order.
Available from the Bookshop, MENCAP Centre, 123 Golden Lane, London EC1Y 0RT (Tel: 01-253 9433).

Multiple Sclerosis: a Self-help Guide to its Management by Judy Graham. Published by Thorsons Publishers Ltd (reprinted 1982). Price £3.95. There has been very little information of a practical nature available to people with MS. The matter of diets has been dealt with in a piecemeal way, but it has always been very difficult for those with MS to get hold of facts. This is a complete lifestyle book of inestimable value to individuals who want to run their own lives and want to try regimes or diets which may not have been fully proved to defeat MS, but which have nevertheless been shown to be of benefit to many people.

Naturally, the author writes about relationships and sex, woven in as they should be in her recommendations for managing MS and for establishing a pattern for more satisfactory living. The book now also includes a chapter on childbirth.

Not Made of Stone. The following is a quote from the book: 'The invalid doesn't sit on stone where a healthy person sits on flesh.' The book was compiled by three doctors in Holland – Dr U. Heslinga, an educationalist, in association with Dr A. M. C. H. Schellen, a gynaecologist-andrologist, and Dr A. Verkuyl, a specialist in rehabilitation.

As might be expected, the book has a very medical bias with lots of diagrams and essentially professional descriptions of different conditions and diseases. Chapters are included describing the reproductive system, while other subjects covered are genetics; specific disabilities and their consequences as far as sexual life is concerned; sexual and related problems in people with respiratory disorders and skin diseases; sexual education; adults and sexuality; marriage and family planning. The final chapter makes ethical suggestions on the subject of the sexuality of today's handicapped people. For the general reader there is no doubt that the chapters on marriage and whether to have children will have the greatest significance, offering personal stories and a good deal of considered wisdom in helping to determine these problems.

A good deal of information and encouragement is given in the use of aids such as vibrators, penile aids and quasi-vaginal tubes. These aids, it is suggested, can often restore sexual relations where the partners may have considered their physical intimacy at an end. Where an impotent man is able to wear an artificial penis and so satisfy his wife, this will do much to restore his ego and build up his confidence, and will form a basis for a continuation of a happy relationship for both of them.

The book is a serious study of sexuality in all its aspects and is intended primarily for doctors, nurses, physiotherapists, social workers, etc., but its caring and concerned approach makes it also suitable for the serious lay reader. In addition, there is a glossary of medical terms to help the uninitiated. Available from Woodhead-Faulkner (Publishers) Ltd, Fitzwilliam House, 32 Trumpington Street, Cambridge CB2 1QY. Price £12.50.

The Outsiders Club booklet *Practical Suggestions*, available from Box 4 ZB, London W1A 4ZB (Tel: 01-741 3332). This booklet is positively jam-packed with advice and practical suggestions on meeting and keeping partners. All the questions we ask ourselves but mostly do not dare to express are here brought out into the open with suggestions on how to cope with the problems. There are sections on home truths; the problems of meeting people; other people's attitudes; our attitudes to ourselves; physical barriers; feeling trapped in a situation; establishing a sexual and social identity. Also included are lots of addresses for sources of help and useful organisations. Available to members of the Outsiders Club.

Paraplegia. A handbook of practical care and advice by Michael Rogers. Mental adjustment to the many problems the individual paraplegic will have to face is discussed in chapters on sex and the psychological aspects of paraplegia. For further details on this book *see* Appendix A.

Personal Relationships, the Handicapped and the Community edited by D. Lancaster-Gaye. This book looks at some of the solutions to the problems of long-term residential care of disabled people and amongst others describes the relatively integrated flats accommodation of the Swedish Fokus system as well as the Dutch Het Dorp Village Settlement. It also covers the problems which arise in personal relationships between disabled people and between them and the community. These are mostly first-hand experiences, and for this reason have added depth and understanding. The writer discusses love, sex and companionship and looks in general at the emotional needs of disabled young people. Available from the Spastics Society, 12 Park Crescent, London W1N 4EQ. Price £1 plus postage.

Sex and the Handicapped Child by Dr Wendy Greengross, published by National Marriage Guidance Council (1980). Erection, masturbation, homosexuality and contraception present particular problems to the parents of handicapped children. Yet there is very little help available. This book examines the reasons for this and suggests positive ways of helping. The book ends with two useful lists, one of helpful reading, the other of helping organisations for disabled people. Available from SPOD, 286 Camden Road, London N7 0BJ (Tel: 01-607 8851). Price £1.20 including postage and packing.

Sex and the Mentally Handicapped by M. and A. Craft. Written for professionals and parents caring specifically for the mentally handicapped – the authors look at many of the questions, anxieties and fears raised by the sexuality of this group. They examine myths and misconceptions, and offer guidelines for those wishing to plan health and sex education programmes for mentally handicapped youngsters and adults, including a review of the audiovisual resources available. They give the results of their research into marriages where one or both partners are mentally handicapped, and conclude that, with adequate counselling and support, a partnership can relieve much tension and loneliness and also enrich the quality of life enjoyed by handicapped people. Published by Routledge & Kegan Paul Ltd. Available from bookshops and from SPOD, 286 Camden Road, London N7 0BJ (Tel: 01-607 8851). Price £5 inclusive of postage.

Sex and Young People with Spina Bifida and Cerebral Palsy. This is a wonderfully straightforward book with sensitive line drawings by Liz McQuiston which illustrate the text perfectly. There are of course illustrations which are helpfully explicit without being too clinical. In addition there are some delightful drawings showing the joy of loving and coupling where the lines of the bodies merge in a manner which would be difficult to portray so gracefully in photographs.

Essentially this is a book for the young and uninitiated and for their parents. It explains carefully all those aspects of growing up which disabled youngsters may well find perplexing, cut off as they so often are from the sort of contact and communication their able-bodied peers take for granted. There are full descriptions of the bodies of men and women and their functions including how conception takes place and how a baby grows. Worries about having a handicapped baby and genetic counselling are also discussed. There is helpful advice on menstruation and coping with incontinence in order to be able to enjoy sex. There are brief references to abortion and sterilisation and useful information about some of the methods of contraception. Masturbation is discussed and reassurance given about this very natural form of sexuality. Homosexuality is also mentioned along with the very usual mixed-up emotions most teenagers have with regard to their feelings for their own and the opposite sex. Finally there is a useful dictionary of terms and some helpful names and addresses and a brief list of further reading. We would warmly recommend this book to young disabled people who are seeking to understand their own sexuality. While written specifically for those with spina bifida and cerebral palsy it would be a useful book for those with different handicaps.

Available from the Association for Spina Bifida and Hydrocephalus, 22 Upper Woburn Place, London WC1H 0EP. Price £1.52 including postage and packing.

The Sex Directory by Ann Darnbrough and Derek Kinrade. Published by Woodhead-Faulkner Ltd, Fitzwilliam House, 32 Trumpington Street, Cambridge CB2 1QY (Tel: Cambridge (0223) 66733).

A directory in two parts. The first describes the sort of sexual problems people encounter and provides information on the national agencies (some with local branches) offering help and advice. The second part lists, county by county, local agencies and individual counsellors providing a range of services to assist people with sexual problems. The needs of disabled people are considered throughout and there is, in addition, a chapter devoted to disability and sexuality.

Sex Education for the Physically Handicapped. A survey of the sex education currently provided for physically handicapped children in England and Wales. The author, Bill Stewart, describes the deficiencies in this branch of sex education. Price £3.50. Available from the Disability Study Unit, Wildhanger, Amberley, Arundel, West Sussex BN18 9NR.

Sexual Adjustment: A Guide for the Spinal Cord Injured. While written mainly about sexual adjustment for the paraplegic male, this book offers useful information to individuals with other physical disabilities as well. The guide also contains an anthology of professional observations of paraplegia, what it is and what effects it has on individuals. Published by Accent Special Publications, Box 700, Bloomington, Illinois, 61701, USA. Price $4.95 plus $1.15 shipping.

Sexual Aspects of Social Work by Bill Stewart. Aims to help social workers, both professional and voluntary, towards a better understanding of the sexual aspects of their work. One chapter specifically relates to the sexual problems experienced by handicapped people. Available from Woodhead-Faulkner Ltd, Fitzwilliam House, 32 Trumpington Street, Cambridge CB2 1QY. Price £9.95, plus postage and packing.

Sexual Options for Paraplegics and Quadriplegics by T. O. Mooney, T. M. Cole and R. A. Chilgren, with a foreword by Alex Comfort. This book is written by a spinal-cord-injured person with the assistance of two doctors experienced in human sexuality research and rehabilitation. Included are 65 photographs showing spinal-cord-injured people preparing for sex and participating in various kinds of sexual expression, with special attention devoted to the problems of people who must wear catheters or stoma bags and who cannot move their arms and legs, or both. Readers are warned that the pictures are very explicit and, while many people would find the book helpful, some may find its frankness disturbing. Published by Little, Brown and Company, Boston, USA. Promotional agents in the United Kingdom are Quest Publishing Agency, 145a Croydon Road, Beckenham, Kent BR3 3RB (Tel: 01-650 4929). Available from major bookshops. Price approx. £6.55.

Sexual Problems and Their Management. By Christopher G. Fairburn, Mark G. Dickerson and Judy Greenwood. Published by Churchill Livingstone. Price £3.95. This book is intended for doctors wishing to manage common sexual problems without undergoing a formal training in sex therapy. However, professional language does not 'cloud' the information for the lay person and it is therefore useful for all those who want a reasonably succinct and clear explanation of sexual problems and their management. A fair amount of space is given over to the sexual aspects of disease and disability. The majority of conditions are covered. There is also a table listing drugs and their possible effects on sexual appetite and sexual excitement.

The Sexual Side of Handicap: A guide for the caring professions by Bill Stewart. The aim of this book is to provide guidance and practical information for those working with physically or mentally handicapped people. Though primarily intended for members of the caring professions, the book should also be useful to voluntary workers and to those who are handicapped themselves.

The first section of the book examines the sexual problems experienced by handicapped people and sets these in the context of relationships and social outlook. Sexual education, counselling, problems of the institutional setting and legal aspects of sex and disability are also discussed. In the second part the author describes some typical disorders and their effect on relationships, sexual capacity and parenthood.

In the past a failure to provide adequate practical advice on sexual matters has often resulted in handicapped people being 'doubly disabled'. The intention of this book is to indicate the sort of help which can be provided in order to prevent this occurring. Available from Woodhead-Faulkner (Publishers) Ltd, Fitzwilliam House, 32 Trumpington Street, Cambridge CB2 1QY. Price £9.95 plus postage and packing.

Sexuality and Multiple Sclerosis by Michael Barrett of the MS Society of Canada. Reprinted by SPOD, 186 Camden Road, London N7 0BJ (Tel: 01-607 8851). Price 50p plus postage and packing. (Free to people with MS.) This booklet describes itself as 'an exploration of sexual possibilities, expectations and concerns

and of ways to communicate them'. As such, it has a warm and encouraging way of discussing sexuality and of helping people with MS to cope with the frustrations, tensions and fatigue which all too often characterise the condition. The author emphasises the need to discover and use imaginative ways of love-making to enhance sexual activity which may otherwise be restricted.

Sexuality and the Physically Handicapped: an Introduction for Counsellors. Available from SPOD, 186 Camden Road, London N7 0BJ (Tel: 01-607 8851). Price £1.50 plus 20p postage and packing. Many professionals are reluctant to consider problems in the personal and sexual relationships of disabled people as part of their concern. This can be because they do not have relevant information easily available to them.

The aim of this booklet is to provide information on various disabilities, outlining possible implications for sexual and personal relationships. Subjects considered include masturbation, sex aids, drugs and sex, incontinence and, to help the reader gain further information, a resource list and a list of helpful organisations.

Sexuality and Physical Disability: Personal Perspectives (1981). Edited by D. G. Bullard and S. E. Knight. Published by C. V. Mosby Company, St Louis, Missouri, USA. While not having seen this book it has nevertheless been recommended very warmly to us by SPOD and others. In fact it was described as an excellent read. The various contributors (47 in all) give a very personal perspective on coping with disability. A variety of issues are discussed including women's issues, family issues and professional issues. Price £17.95. (You could obtain a copy through your library.)

So You're Paralysed ... by Bernadette Fallon. This book has been written for the newly paralysed, and, while it has been written for those who have sustained injury, it would be most helpful to all who have a degree of paralysis however caused. The approach is sensitive but down to earth to help people who find themselves in the bewildering position where responsibility for the most intimate bodily functions seems to have been handed over to medical staff. Sex is just one of the subjects covered in this book; it takes its place, as of course it should, with all the other physical (and mental) functions of life. Available from The Spinal Injuries Association, Yeoman's House, 76 St James's Lane, Muswell Hill, London N10. Price £3. Greek members of the Association in the United Kingdom can obtain a copy of the new Greek edition of *So You're Paralysed*. This has been produced by the Cyprus Paraplegic Association together with SIA from whom it is available at £3.

SPOD Advisory Leaflets
All available free for disabled clients from SPOD, 186 Camden Road, London N7 0BJ (Tel: 01-607 8851).
Physically handicapped people and sex. A very reassuring leaflet, pointing out that sexuality is concerned with the mind and the emotions as well as the body, and that if you are disabled and are having sexual problems, you are not alone. Indeed 'even for those who are unable to have sexual intercourse, it is often possible not only to obtain sexual pleasure but also to satisfy a partner'.
Physical handicap and sexual intercourse – positions for sex. For too long many people have felt that adventurous love-making involving different positions and a degree of planning was somehow wrong. For disabled people, experimenting with different positions may be vital and this leaflet discusses positions, and questions the reluctance to try new ways.
Physical handicap and sexual intercourse – methods and techniques. We rather expect to know all about sex as a normal matter of course, but in any case if in doubt, would be ashamed to admit our ignorance. We rather suspect that this is so because we feel there is a very limited amount to know – the lights out, under the blankets, one position routine. In fact, lack of knowledge about sex can be blamed for a great deal of unhappiness among both able-bodied and disabled people. This leaflet discusses some helpful techniques.
Aids to sex for the physically handicapped. The leaflet explains that 'for those disabled people who meet with physical difficulty in their sexual relationships, a number of aids can be used. They may vary from such everyday articles as pillows or cushions to specially made appliances'. We are further reassured that the use of aids need not be seen as 'wrong' or 'kinky', but of value where they meet a need. A warning is given to avoid sharp suppliers who may con you into buying useless articles at fancy prices.
Sex for the severely disabled. The leaflet reassures that many severely disabled people do achieve intercourse, but that where this is not possible, there are many other ways of fulfilling a loving and caring relationship.
Mentally handicapped people and sex. This leaflet is provided mainly for parents and others involved in the care of mentally handicapped persons, for as we know, myths about the sexuality of mentally handi-

capped people abound. The leaflet discusses the fears concerning this sexuality, putting them in a proper perspective and asks not whether a mentally handicapped child or adolescent should have sex education, but how and from whom.
Your handicapped child and sex. To many parents of handicapped children, the dawning realisation that their child is becoming sexually adult, can come as quite a shock. Their reactions may be ones of denial and over protection. In fact to deny young people sexual knowledge can make life very difficult for them. This leaflet broadly discusses attitudes and problems and recommends seeking further advice where necessary.
Your disabled partner and sex. The problems are different for those whose partners are already disabled when they married or those who became disabled after marriage. For some people there are no problems at all. This leaflet discusses the questions and the difficulties of those who find it hard to be both nurse and lover.
Physically handicapped people and contraception. Disability does not usually affect fertility, and so disabled people who do not wish to have children, or want to plan their family, need to choose a method of contraception appropriate to their state of health, lifestyle, physical and mental capabilities, and personal preference.

Sex and the Person with an Ostomy. Some reassuring facts, including: What is an ostomy? How does it affect sex? What if the man can't get an erection? Fertility and some practical suggestions.
 SPOD also has a range of resource lists which give details of books, papers, films, tapes, etc., on particular subjects. These are listed below and may be obtained by sending a stamped addressed envelope:
 1. *Arthritic Disorders*.
 2. *Attitudes Towards Sex and Disabled People*.
 3. *Disabled People and Marriage*.
 4. *Friendship, Dating and Marriage*.
 5. *Multiple Sclerosis*.
 6. *Sexual Concerns of Disabled Women*.
 7. *Sex Education for Mentally Handicapped*.
 8. *Sex Education for Physically Handicapped*.
 9. *Sex Education for Physically Handicapped: Teachers' Notes*.
10. *Spinal Injury*.

Toward Intimacy: Family Planning and Sexuality Concerns of Physically Disabled Women by The Task Force on Concerns of Physically Disabled Women, edited by Susan Shaul, Jane Bogle and others. The booklet is dedicated to exploring the various relationships within a disabled woman's life.

It explores a woman's relationship to her body and how this image affects her personally and her relationships with others. A major section is devoted to a thorough exploration of sexuality as it relates to specific disabilities, and there is a detailed investigation of contraceptives related to these disabilities. Menstruation, masturbation and the many forms of sexually related disease are covered. Also included are discussions of the important relationships with parents and health care practitioners. The booklet contains personal statements of disabled women discussing their own experiences including the joys and frustrations of sexuality and disability. This sensitively illustrated manual acknowledges the unique concerns of disabled women and provides the reader with the comfort of sharing other disabled women's similar experiences. Published by Human Sciences Press, 3 Henrietta Street, London WC2E 8LU (Tel: 01-240 0856). Price £3.50.

The Wheelchair Child by Philippa Russell. Contains information and guidance on sex. (*See* Appendix A.)

Within Reach: Providing Family Planning Services to Physically Disabled Women by The Task Force on Concerns of Physically Disabled Women, edited by Julia Hale-Harbaugh, Ann Norman and others. The companion volume to *Toward Intimacy* examines the health and family planning clinic's responsibilities toward working with the physically disabled woman. Special sections include providing for in-service training of staff, counselling, administering physical examinations and providing for physical accessibility to the grounds of the clinic. Also examined are the medical aspects of physical disabilities, especially those which occur most frequently among women of child-bearing age, including spinal cord injury, cerebral palsy, poliomyelitis, rheumatoid arthritis and multiple sclerosis. The final section delineates in chart form the many aspects of female sexuality, reproduction and special considerations for contraceptive use for each specific disability. Published by Human Sciences Press, 3 Henrietta Street, London WC2E 8LU (Tel: 01-240 0856). Price £3.50.

Films

Like Other People, 16 mm, colour, 37 minutes. Made in 1972 under the auspices of the Mental Health Council, it depicts the problems of two severely disabled spastic people in a residential home. They want to establish their right to work and to love and live 'like other people'. All the characters are 'real' people. What they say about their need for fulfilment applies equally to people handicapped in other ways. Available on hire from Concord Films Council Ltd, 201 Felixstowe Road, Ipswich, Suffolk IP3 9BJ (Tel: Ipswich (0473) 76012).

SECTION 13

LEGISLATION AFFECTING DISABLED PEOPLE

To an unthinking recipient of any of our many national welfare benefits it might appear that 'authority' is inspired by a touching benevolence and is devoted to charitable purposes and good works. In fact, of course, every aspect of professional social welfare in this country rests firmly upon parliamentary legislation. A basic knowledge of such legislation is indispensable in two respects:

(a) To ascertain the extent to which benefits and services *should* be available.
(b) To enable a disabled person to secure those benefits and services to which he is entitled.

We therefore make no apology for the fact that this chapter is heavy going. It is not, of course, intended to be an exact statement of the law. Our summaries and interpretations of the statutes are intended as a guide. We have avoided altogether the complex legislation on which tax reliefs, and social security and National Insurance benefits are based, preferring to rely on the practical explanations of the working arrangements given in Section 2 on Financial Benefits and Allowances.

There is little doubt that any major advances in provision for disabled people, whether to protect their rights as citizens or to afford the practical and financial help which they need to overcome disadvantage, must come through either new or amended legislation. Those who need to keep right up to date with details of current social and industrial legislation may wish to subscribe to CANS, the Citizens' Advice Notes Service of the National Council for Voluntary Organisations. Subjects covered include: education, employment, health and welfare, housing, social security and transport. The main body of information is presented in a loose-leaf binder and costs £48. This is updated by three supplements in each subscription year (1 April to 31 March). A renewal subscription (currently £35) is charged for subsequent years. Available from NCVO, 26 Bedford Square, London WC1B 3HU.

Access

See Disabled Persons Act 1981 and Chronically Sick and Disabled Persons Act 1970 under the heading Statutory Services.

Education

EDUCATION ACT 1944 (England and Wales only)

Section 8 (as amended by the Education Act 1981, Section 2)
This requires that schools to be provided by local education authorities (LEAs) must be 'sufficient in number, character, and equipment to afford all pupils opportunities for education offering such variety of instruction and training as may be desirable in view of their different ages, abilities and aptitudes'. In particular, Section 8(1)(b) requires that there shall be sufficient schools ... 'for providing secondary education, that is to say full-time education, suitable to the requirements of senior pupils'. These are defined by section 114 as pupils who have reached the age of 12 but not the age of 19. This means that local education authorities have a duty to provide for young people up to and including the age of 18. Such education may be provided in school or in an establishment for further education.

Later in the same section, among the duties to which the LEAs must have particular regard is 'the need for securing that special educational provision is made for pupils with special educational needs'. *Taken together, these provisions mean that local education authorities are required by law to provide education for pupils with special educational needs up to and including the age of 18, where this is wanted.*

Section 36 (as amended by the Education Act 1981, Section 17)
Imposes a duty on the parent of every child of compulsory school age to cause him/her to receive efficient full-time education suitable to his/her age, ability and aptitude, and to any special educational needs the child may have, either by regular attendance at school or otherwise.

Section 37 (as amended by the Education Act 1981, Section 16 and Schedule 4)

Deals with the arrangements for making school attendance orders to secure education for a child suitable to his/her age, ability or aptitude or to his/her special educational needs.

Section 55

Local education authorities are required to make transport arrangements to facilitate the attendance of pupils at school, county colleges or further education classes free of charge; if such transport is not provided, the authority must pay (wholly or partly as it thinks fit) reasonable travelling expenses.

Section 56 (as amended)

Provides that if a local education authority is satisfied that because of 'extraordinary' circumstances, a child or young person cannot attend a suitable school to receive either primary or secondary education, it has the power (subject to the Secretary of State's approval) to make special arrangements for education otherwise than at school. Or, if the authority is satisfied that it is impracticable for the pupil to receive full-time education, it may (if the Secretary of State approves) arrange for education similar in other respects, but less than full-time.

EDUCATION (MISCELLANEOUS PROVISIONS) ACT 1953
(ENGLAND AND WALES ONLY)

Section 6

Empowers local education authorities, with the approval of the Secretary of State for Education, to arrange the provision of primary or secondary education for pupils to be at non-maintained schools.

Where education is so provided, or is provided under the Education Act 1981 (see page 255), the authority is responsible for the payment of the whole of the fees in respect of the education in three defined cases. These include:

(a) where because of a shortage of reasonably convenient schools, education suitable to the pupil's age, ability and aptitude, and special educational needs he/she may have cannot be provided by the local education authority except at a school which is not maintained by that or another authority, and

(b) where the authority is satisfied that the pupil has special educational needs and that it is expedient in his/her interests that the required special educational provision should be made for the pupil at a school not maintained by it or another LEA.

If, further, the authority is satisfied that residence at the school is necessary in order that the pupil should receive education suitable to his/her age, ability, aptitude and to any special educational needs he/she may

have, it will also pay for the cost of board and lodging.

NOTE: Under the Education Act 1976, Section 5(1) the Secretary of State has power to revoke any approval given under the above Section.

EDUCATION (HANDICAPPED CHILDREN) ACT 1970

Provided (in England and Wales) for the discontinuance of classifying handicappedn children as being unsuitable for education at school. 'No further use' to be made of the powers under Section 57 of the Education Act 1944 for classifying children suffering from mental disability as children unsuitable for education at school. Local health authorities relieved of their powers and their duty to make arrangements for training such children.

Comparative Scottish legislation: Education (Mentally Handicapped Children) Act 1974 similarly gave education authorities responsibility for the education of children previously categorised as ineducable and untrainable.

EDUCATION ACT 1980

Section 8

Requires a wide range of information to be provided by local education authorities. Regulations made under the Act (The Education (School Information) Regulations 1981 – SI 1981 No. 630) set out in detail the information to be provided by English and Welsh authorities. This includes, by Schedule 1, Part II:

The authorities' detailed arrangements and policies in relation to:

(a) the identification and assessment of children with special educational needs and the involvement of parents in that process;

(b) the provision made in county, voluntary and special schools maintained by them for pupils with special educational needs and the use made by them of special schools maintained by other authorities;

(c) special educational provision otherwise than at school.

The authorities' arrangements and policies as respects the use of non-maintained special schools and of independent schools providing wholly or mainly for pupils with special educational needs.

The arrangements for parents who consider that their child may have special educational needs to obtain advice and further information.

The authorities' general arrangements and policies in respect of transport to and from maintained and non-maintained special schools and such independent schools as are mentioned above.

The arrangements for parents to obtain the information set out in Schedule 2 of the Regulations (details of individual schools including special curricula and other arrangements made for particular classes or descriptions of pupil including those with special educational needs) in the case of special schools used by the authority which are maintained by them or other authorities.

Changes in respect of any matter mentioned in this Part which have been determined to be made after the start of the school year to which the information relates.

Schedule 2, paragraph 4 of the Regulations indicates that information relating to special education is to be published in two ways:

(a) by copies being available for distribution without charge to parents *on request* (our italics), and for reference by parents and others at the offices of the relevant local education authority; and

(b) by copies being available for reference by parents and other persons:
   (i) at every school maintained by the authority; and
   (ii) at the public libraries in the area of that authority.

EDUCATION ACT 1981 (ENGLAND AND WALES ONLY)

This Act is based on the proposals of the Warnock Report, *Special Needs in Education* (1978). It replaces the previous system of 'ascertainment' – assignment to a particular category of handicap based on medical assessment – by a new concept of certain children having special educational needs of whom a small percentage require 'careful multi-professional assessment to reveal the totality of their special educational needs'.

Throughout the Act, by Section 114(1) of the Education Act 1944, references to 'parent' include a guardian and every person who has the actual custody of the child or young person. Where a child is in the care of a local authority, it will be for the Director of Social Services to involve the child's natural parent according to the circumstances of each case.

References in our text to Regulations refer to the Education (Special Educational Needs) Regulations 1983 (SI 1983 No. 29). Department of Education and Science Circular 1/83 to local education authorities considers the implications of the Act and its procedural application.

Section 1

Defines 'special educational needs' in terms of learning difficulties which call for 'special educational provision'. A child is deemed to have a 'learning difficulty' if:

(a) he has significantly greater difficulty in learning than the majority of children of his age; or

(b) he has a disability which either prevents or hinders him from making use of educational facilities of a kind generally provided in schools, within the area of the local authority concerned, for children of his age; or

(c) he is under the age of five and is (or would be if special educational provision were not made for him) likely to fall within paragraph (a) or (b) when over that age.

However, special educational provision can vary with circumstances: if the child is under 2 years of age, it can be any kind of educational provision, but in relation to a child of 2 years or over it means provision which is additional to, or otherwise different from, the educational provision made generally for children of the same age in schools maintained by the local education authority concerned.

NOTE: A child is not taken as having 'learning difficulties' simply because the language taught is foreign to that which has at any time been spoken in the child's home.

Section 2

(1) & (4): These sub-paragraphs amend Section 8(2) of the Education Act 1944 to require local education authorities, in securing the availability of schools for their areas, to have regard to the needs of pupils requiring special educational provision and obliges authorities to keep their arrangements for special educational provision under review.

(2) & (3): In subsequent sections, the Act lays down formal procedures for the assessment of certain children (in practice, those with severe or complex learning difficulties) whose needs are, or probably are, such as to require local education authorities to determine their special educational provision and to have the protection of a Statement. Section 2 (2) and (3) require that where an authority arranges special educational provision for a child who is the subject of a Statement, it is to secure that the child is educated in an ordinary school, provided that the views of the child's parent have been taken into account. However, this provision is made subject to a number of 'escape clauses' in that the arrangements should be compatible with:

(a) the child receiving the special educational provision he requires;

(b) the provision of efficient education for the children with whom he will be educated; and

(c) the efficient use of resources.

(5): Duties are also imposed by this section which are intended to secure that individual county and voluntary schools, and maintained nursery schools, are conducted in a way which will meet the special educational needs of their pupils.

Section 3
Empowers local education authorities, if satisfied that it would be inappropriate for special educational provision (or part of that provision) required for a child with special educational needs to be made in a school, to arrange, after consultation with the child's parent, for it to be made elsewhere.

Sections 4 and 5
These sections deal with the duty of local education authorities to identify and assess children aged 2 or more for whom they are responsible and who have special educational needs which call for the authority to determine the special educational provision that should be made for them. DES Circular 1/83, paragraphs 13/16 offers guidance on the children who should be so identified. As a preliminary to assessment, the local education authority must notify the child's parent:
(a) that it proposes to make an assessment;
(b) of the procedure to be followed in making it;
(c) of the name of the local education authority officer from whom further information may be obtained; and
(d) of the right to make representations, and submit written evidence, to the authority within a specified period (not less than 29 days).

A copy of the notification must also be sent to the local social services department and district health authority.

After the expiry of the specified period, the authority shall, if it considers it appropriate after taking parental views into account, proceed to assess the educational needs of the child concerned, first notifying the parent in writing of its decision and the reasons for making it. Alternatively, if having notified a proposal to assess, the local education authority decides not to proceed with assessment, it must notify this decision to the parent in writing. The assessment procedures are set out in Schedule 1, Part 1 of the Act and in regulations made thereunder.

Where a local education authority proposes to make an assessment, it is empowered to serve a notice on the child's parent to require the child's attendance at a stated time and place for examination. Parents must, however, also be informed of their right to attend the examination, and to submit any information they wish.

Under Regulation 4, in order to make an assessment, local education authorities must seek educational, medical and psychological advice and any other advice which they consider desirable. The

authority must provide the person whose advice is being sought with any parental representations or evidence submitted by or at the request of the parent. The adviser may consult others, and must give his/her advice in writing. Regulations 5, 6 and 7 specify from whom educational, medical and psychological advice may properly be taken. DES Circular 1/83, paragraph 23 offers guidance on the approach to be adopted by professional advisers. Where a child has moved from one education area to another, Regulation 12 allows such advice to be obtained from the old authority.

In making an assessment, the local education authority is required (by Regulation 8) to take a number of matters into account, *viz*:
(a) any representations made by the child's parent;
(b) any evidence submitted by, or at the request of, that parent;
(c) the advice obtained under Regulation 4; and
(d) any information relating to the health or welfare of the child from any district health authority or social services department.

If, having made an assessment, the local education authority concludes that it does not have to determine special educational provision, it must notify the parent of his or her right of appeal to the Secretary of State for Education, who may, if he thinks fit, direct the local education authority to reconsider its decision.

Section 6
Empowers local education authorities, with the consent of a parent, to assess the special educational needs of children *under* the age of 2, and requires authorities to do so at the parent's request.

An assessment under this section can be made in whatever manner the local education authority considers appropriate, whereupon it may 'make a Statement' of the child's special educational needs and thereafter maintain that Statement as it considers appropriate.

Section 7
Where an assessment has been made under Section 5, local education authorities are required to make and maintain a Statement of special educational needs for any child determined as requiring special educational provision. Thereupon, it is a duty of the local education authority to arrange that the specified provision is made, unless a parent has made suitable arrangements.

Form and Content of Statements
In addition to setting out special educational needs (Section 7(1)), Statements must, by Regulation 10:

(a) specify the special educational provision (in terms of facilities and equipment, staffing arrangements, curriculum or otherwise) which the local education authority considers appropriate to meet the child's special educational needs.
(b) without prejudice to the generality of (a) above, specify either:
  (i) the type of school which the local education authority considers would be appropriate for the child and, if it considers that a particular school would be so appropriate, the name of that school, or
  (ii) if they consider it appropriate that the child should be provided with education otherwise than at school, particulars of what they consider appropriate;
(c) specify any additional non-educational provision:
  (i) which, unless proposed to be made available by the local education authority, they are satisfied will be made available by a district health authority or social services department or some other body, and
  (ii) of which, in their opinion, advantage should be taken if the child is properly to benefit from the special educational provision specified at (a) and (b) above; and
(d) set out the representations, evidence, advice and information taken into consideration in pursuance of Regulation 8.
A model form of Statement is appended to the Regulations.

Parental Rights
Before making a statement of a child's special educational needs, the local education authority must serve the parent with a copy of the proposed Statement and a written explanation of the right to:
(a) make representations about the content of the proposed Statement;
(b) require a meeting to discuss the proposed Statement. If, having required and attended such a meeting, a parent disagrees with any part of the assessment, there is an additional right, within a specified period, to require the local education authority to arrange further meetings as they consider will enable the parent to discuss the professional advice on which the proposed Statement is based in so far as it is relevant to the disagreed matters, either with the person who gave the advice or with another person who is, in the opinion of the authority, appropriate to discuss it with the parent.

After considering a parent's representations, the local education authority may take any one of three courses. They may:
(a) make a Statement as originally proposed;
(b) make a Statement in a modified form;
(c) determine not to make a Statement.
Again, this decision must be notified in writing to the parent. If a Statement is made, the local education authority must provide the parent with a copy and a written notice advising a right of appeal (*see* Section 8 following) and the name of the person to whom application can be made for information and advice about the child's special educational needs.

Review
Statements must be reviewed at least annually (Schedule 1, paragraph 5). DES Circular 1/83, paragraph 55 offers guidance and recommends the involvement of parents.

Reassessment
A reassessment will, in practice, normally be appropriate if and when there has been a significant change in the circumstances of the child, and may arise as a result of a review or in response to a parental request. Where a local education authority maintains a Statement for a child whose educational needs have not been assessed since a date prior to him/her reaching the age of $12\frac{1}{2}$, then those needs must be reassessed within one year of the child reaching the age of $13\frac{1}{2}$, Regulation 9 (*see also* Section 9 below).

Confidentiality
Statements are confidential to prescribed persons. Regulation 11 places restrictions on disclosure without parental consent except in limited, specified circumstances, and requires that they be kept, so far as is reasonably practical, secure from access by unauthorised persons.

Amendment or Cessation
Before it amends or ceases to maintain a Statement, a local education authority must notify parents in writing, advising them of their right to make representations within 15 days. Local education authorities must consider any such representations and inform parents in writing of their subsequent decision (this does not apply where Statements are lapsed because a child ceases to be a responsibility of a local education authority, nor to amendments which arise from the making, amendment or revocation of a school attendance order). (Schedule 1, paragraph 6.)

Section 8
Provides for parents to appeal to appeal committees constituted under the Education Act 1980, against

what is being proposed by way of special educational provision. Such committees may require authorities to reconsider their decisions, and there is a final right of appeal to the Secretary of State for Education.

Section 9

Enables parents to request that the special educational needs of their children be assessed.

Where no Statement has been made under Section 7, such a request must be met unless it is, in the opinion of the local education authority, unreasonable. If a Section 7 Statement is being maintained, a request for an assessment must also be complied with if an assessment has not been made in the six months prior to the request, unless the authority is satisfied that an assessment would be inappropriate.

Section 10

Requires District Health Authorities to inform parents and the appropriate local education authority when they consider that a child under the age of 5 has special educational needs.

Comparative Scottish legislation is contained in the Education (Scotland) Act 1980, Sections 60/65 (as substituted by the Education (Scotland) Act 1981, Section 4) and in the Education (Scotland) Act 1981, Section 3.

Up to the time of writing, no similar legislation has been introduced in Northern Ireland, though there is pressure that urgent steps should be taken to remedy this disparity.

Employment

DISABLED PERSONS (EMPLOYMENT) ACT 1944

(does not apply in Northern Ireland)

This Act defines a 'disabled person' as one 'who on account of injury, disease (including a physical or mental condition arising from imperfect development of any organ), or congenital deformity, is substantially handicappedn in obtaining or keeping employment, or in undertaking work on his own account, of a kind which apart from that injury, disease or deformity would be suited to his age, experience and qualifications' (Section 1).

The main provisions of the Act are:

(a) To set up a Register of 'disabled persons'; in consultation with 'District Advisory Committees', the Secretary of State for Employment is empowered to regulate the conditions of entry to, retention on and disqualification or withdrawal from the Register. The aim is 'to secure that the fact that a person's name is in the Register will afford reasonable assurance of his being a person capable of entering into and keeping employment, or of undertaking work on his own account'.

(b) An employer who normally has or even temporarily has a workforce of 20 or more must, subject to certain exceptions, give employment to a quota (*i.e.* a proportion of his total staff wherever employed – staff who work less than 10 hours a week are disregarded; staff who work from 10 to 30 hours a week are treated as one half) of registered disabled persons (currently 3 per cent). The proportion may be 'standard' or (and this is rarely used in practice) 'special' (for specified types of work) or a combination of the two, and the percentages are set by Ministerial Order.

There are two restrictions upon employers:

(i) If, when a vacancy occurs, an employer who is subject to the quota scheme is below that quota or if taking on an unregistered person would bring him below the quota, then he must not engage or offer to engage an unregistered person, unless he obtains a permit to do so *or* the prospective employee is entitled to employment under an Act of Parliament. (Permits might be issued if, for example, the vacancy was unsuitable for a disabled person, or it could be demonstrated that no disabled person was available to fill it.)

(ii) An employer who is and could remain subject to the quota scheme must not discharge a registered person if he is below his quota or if to do so would bring him below his quota, unless there is reasonable cause. Penalties are prescribed for breach of these restrictions, but there is provision for referral to an advisory committee and for representations by the employer before prosecution is considered (Sections 9–10).

(c) The Secretary of State for Employment may designate certain categories of employment so as to reserve further entry into them for registered disabled persons. (Rarely used in practice. Only car park attendants and electric lift operators are designated at present.) It is an offence for an employer to engage, offer to engage, or transfer an unregistered person for such work unless he obtains a permit to do so or the prospective employee is entitled to employment under an Act of Parliament (Section 12).

(d) The Secretary of State for Employment may provide special facilities for the employment of persons so seriously disabled as to be unable to obtain normal employment or to sustain a business of their own in competition with able-bodied people (Section 15).

NOTE: A more detailed interpretation of the Act may be obtained from the Department of Employment.

DISABLED PERSONS (EMPLOYMENT) ACT 1958 (as amended)

(does not apply in Northern Ireland)

This Act amends the 1944 Act of the same name in two main respects:

(a) It allows a registered disabled person to have his name removed from the Register on written application (Section 2).

(b) It imposes a duty upon local authorities to provide the facilities referred to in Section 15 of the 1944 Act (*i.e.* 'sheltered' employment) for registered disabled persons resident in their areas, to such extent as the Secretary of State for Employment may direct (it also *empowers* local authorities to provide such facilities for non-residents).

NOTE: The provisions under (b) above are in lieu of similar requirements in Section 29 of the National Assistance Act 1948 and Section 12 of the Health Services and Public Health Act 1968.

EMPLOYMENT AND TRAINING ACT 1973 (as amended)

A Commission established by the Act (now known as the Manpower Services Commission) is charged with a duty to make such arrangements as it considers appropriate to assist persons to select, transfer, obtain and retain employment suitable for their ages and *capacities* (Section 2). Section 12 makes it clear that this includes consideration of physical handicap, and requires the Commission in such cases to give preference to disabled people, of either sex, who have served whole-time in the armed forces, merchant navy or mercantile marine, in line with Section 16 of the Disabled Persons (Employment) Act 1944 (as amended by the Armed Forces Act 1981, Schedule 5).

It is unlawful for the MSC to discriminate against women or on racial grounds in providing courses or other facilities (Sex Discrimination Act 1975 and Race Relations Act 1976 as amended by the Employment and Training Act 1981).

THE COMPANIES (DIRECTORS' REPORT) (EMPLOYMENT OF DISABLED PERSONS) REGULATIONS 1980

These regulations require, with effect from 1 September 1980, that every directors' report of a company to which the regulations apply (*i.e.* those with more than 250 employees) shall contain a statement describing such policy as the company has applied during its financial year:

(a) for giving full and fair consideration to applications for employment by the company made by disabled persons, having regard to their particular aptitudes and abilities;

(b) for continuing the employment of, and for arranging appropriate training for, employees of the company who have become disabled persons during the period when they were employed by the company; and

(c) otherwise for the training, career development and promotion of disabled persons employed by the company.

Comparative legislation for Northern Ireland became effective on 28 February 1983.

The Regulations do not apply to nationalised industries, health authorities, local government or the Civil Service, but Department of the Environment Circular 28/81 states 'the Government are concerned that public sector employers should publish similar statements about their policies, and authorities are asked to make arrangements to do so'.

The following policy statement was made in the January 1983 issue of the magazine *Independent*:

The Civil Service policy on the employment of disabled people is as follows:

Although the Disabled Persons (Employment) Act 1944 is not binding on the Crown, the Government has nevertheless undertaken to accept the same responsibilities as other employers. The basic policy followed is that disablement is of itself no bar to recruitment to, or advancement in, the Service. The test applied is ability to do the job, and the Government is very concerned to ensure that in the Civil Service every opportunity to employ disabled people is taken. Accordingly the following action is taken by government departments.

The Management and Personnel Office issues a Code of Practice which advises departments of the steps they should take to help both disabled entrants and newly disabled serving officers. Each department is required to designate an officer or officers to have full responsibility for the recruitment and career development of all disabled people in their department. An annual publication *Independent*, which deals with the employment of the disabled in the Civil Service, is issued to interested bodies (both inside and outside the Service) and to all the Departmental Disabled Persons/Liaison Officers. Six-monthly meetings of groups of these officers are also arranged to give them an opportunity to discuss problems encountered and to pool experience.

Recruitment

Unless the point is covered in some other way, all applicants for employment are sent a note with the application form which states that disability would not in itself be a bar to employment provided that it would not prevent the candidate from carrying out the duties of a grade satisfactorily. Registered Disabled People who apply for clerical posts without the prescribed educational qualifications can take a written test instead. Special arrangements are made for disabled candidates to attend tests and interviews, and the policy is that where the merits of candidates are evenly balanced preference should be given to a registered disabled person, if a department is below quota.

Disabled civil servants

Suitable jobs are identified for disabled staff in consultation, as necessary, with the Disablement Resettlement Officers/Blind Persons Resettlement Officers, according to their particular skills and taking into account their special problems. Where possible jobs are restructured to enable disabled people to work with the maximum convenience and efficiency and, where appropriate, special aids are provided.

Staff who become disabled while employed by departments are retained, and arrangements are made for the appropriate rehabilitation and training. If a suitable vacancy cannot be found by the parent department, the MPO makes efforts to transfer or re-post the officer concerned.

The general career development policy seeks to make the most effective use of staff, taking account not only to work needs and of people's abilities now, but also of future likely needs. As far as promotion is concerned, the successful candidates should be those best fitted in terms of knowledge, skills and experience to carry out the duties of the higher grade. Within this framework disabled staff are provided with equal training, retraining and promotion opportunities; they have the means to discuss their careers with central personnel staff who can take a longer-term view of individual needs and opportunities, whilst paying special attention to the problems which staff may experience in taking advantage of such opportunities.

For general guidance on employment legislation, *see An A-Z of Employment and Safety Law* by Peter Chandler (Kogan Page), price £16.95.

Housing

LAND COMPENSATION ACT 1973

Section 45

Compensation for compulsory requisition of a dwelling constructed or substantially modified to meet the needs of a disabled person shall, if the person whose interest is acquired so elects, be assessed 'as if the dwelling were land which is devoted to a purpose of such a nature that there is no general demand or market for that purpose'. The effect of this provision is to allow the assessment of compensation to be made under Section 5(5) of the Land Compensation Act 1961 on the basis 'of the reasonable cost of equivalent reinstatement' rather than the normal basis of Section 5(2), *viz*. 'the amount which the land

if sold in the open market by a willing seller might be expected to realise'.

HOUSING ACT 1974 (as amended by the Housing Rents and Subsidies Act 1975 and the Housing Act 1980)

Part VII of the Act deals with the financial assistance available towards works of improvement, repair and conversion (other than by a housing authority). A general explanation is given in Section 4, House and Home. The Act makes special provision for disabled people in a number of places:

Section 56

Provides for a number of grants, including:

(a) improvement grants for works to provide dwellings by the conversion of houses or other buildings or for the improvement of a dwelling, except as are wholly covered by (b) below. 'Improvement' is defined in Section 84 (as amended) as including: 'alteration and enlargement and in relation to a dwelling for a disabled occupant, includes the doing of works required for making it suitable for his accommodation, welfare or employment';

(b) intermediate grants in respect of:

(i) works required for the improvement of a dwelling by the provision of standard amenities which it lacks; *or*

(ii) works required for the provision of a dwelling for a disabled occupant of any standard amenity where an existing amenity of the same description is not readily accessible to him/her, by reason of his/her disability.

NOTE: Numerous examples of items which may be accepted by local authorities as eligible for inclusion in an application for improvement grant when proposed for a disabled person (as well as being admissible for housing subsidies in the case of public sector housing) are given in Department of the Environment Circular 59/78.

Improvement grants for owner-occupiers are normally confined to dwellings with rateable values which fall below prescribed limits. However, by the Housing Act 1980, Section 107 and Schedule 12, paragraph 7, these limits do not apply where the application is made in respect of a dwelling for a disabled occupant and it appears to the local authority that the works are needed to meet a requirement arising from the particular disability from which the disabled occupant suffers.

Improvement and intermediate grants are normally given only in respect of buildings erected up to and including 2 October 1961, but Section 56(4) of the 1974 Act indicates that, subject to the overriding directions of the Secretary of State, local authorities have discretion to allow grants for dwellings built after that date 'if they consider it appropriate to do so'. In fact, the Secretary of State has given directions which enable authorities to consider such discretionary action in the case of dwellings for disabled people.

Section 65(3)(a)
The condition that standard amenities must have been missing for at least a year to qualify for grant is waived in the case of a disabled applicant.

NOTE: Department of the Environment Circular 21/80 advises local authorities in paragraph 10 that 'favourable consideration should generally be given to applicants whose financial resources would qualify them for supplementary benefit or family income supplement, even if such benefit has not been claimed', and that 'although criteria related to income, upon which eligibility for rate rebate [now housing benefit] is assessed, are not necessarily a true reflection of ability to meet capital expenditure, many of those qualifying for rate rebate [housing benefit] are unlikely to have adequate savings to meet their normal share of the cost or have sufficient income to bear without stress the loan charges that would arise if they resorted to borrowing'. Finally, the paragraph concludes, 'very sympathetic consideration should be given to any applicant whose principal source of income consists of a state retirement or disability pension'. We have outlined special provisions in the Housing Act 1974 for the benefit of disabled people. They may, of course, qualify for grants in the ordinary way on grounds unrelated to disability.

HOUSING RENTS AND SUBSIDIES ACT 1975

This Act includes amending the Housing Act 1974, and these changes have been incorporated in the summary of that Act as given above. In addition it defines certain expressions in the 1974 Act (as amended) which are of importance to disabled people.

'Disabled occupant' means a disabled person for whose benefit it is proposed to carry out any of the relevant works.

'Disabled person' means:
(a) any person who is registered in pursuance of arrangements made under subsection (1) of Section 29 of the National Assistance Act 1948; and
(b) any other person for whose welfare arrangements have been made under that subsection or, in the opinion of the welfare authority, might be made under it.

'Dwelling for a disabled occupant' means a dwelling which:
(a) is a disabled occupant's only or main residence when an application for a grant in respect of it is made, or

(b) is likely in the opinion of the local authority to become a disabled occupant's only or main residence not later than the expiry of a reasonable period after the completion of the relevant works.

RATING (DISABLED PERSONS) ACT 1978

Section 1
This section provides for a rebate of rates in respect of certain 'hereditaments' (broadly, property) situated in England and Wales possessing special facilities (which are prescribed) required for meeting the needs of a resident disabled person. As well as facilities within a home, the Section extends to garages, carports or land used (other than temporarily) to accommodate a vehicle used by and required for meeting the needs of a disabled person.

A 'disabled person' is defined as anybody who is blind, deaf or dumb or who suffers from mental disorder of any description or who is substantially and permanently handicapped by illness, injury or congenital deformity or any other disability for the time being prescribed for the purposes of Section 29(1) of the National Assistance Act 1948.

'Required for meeting the needs' is also carefully defined as being essential or of major importance to the well-being of the disabled person because of the nature and extent of that person's disability.

A resident disabled person includes one who is 'usually' resident in the hereditament.

The rebate may be allowed to either the disabled person himself, if he is the occupier of the property or if he pays all or any of the rent, or to anybody who belongs to the same household as the disabled person, who, similarly, is the occupier or pays all or any of the rent of the property.

Section 2
Provides for rebates of rates for institutions for the disabled in England and Wales.

Section 3
Procedures for application and appeal in England and Wales. The rating authority is given the right to determine the 'rebate period'. Application must be made by the entitled person (see Section 1) to the rating authority. Appeal against refusal may be made to the county court.

Schedule 1
Provides for the determination of the amount of rebate under Section 1.

Section 4
Comparative legislation to Section 1, applicable in

Scotland. This is broadly similar, but there are differences in the way the rebate is assessed (Schedule 1 does not apply).

Section 5
Provides for rebates of rates for institutions for the disabled in Scotland.

Section 6
Comparative legislation to Section 3, applicable in Scotland. Broadly similar, save that appeals are the province of the sheriff.

A general outline of the rebate scheme is given in Section 4 of this Directory, House and Home.

Relief is determined in accordance with the following table:

Item	Description	England and Wales Rebate is equal to the rates that would be chargeable on the property for the rebate period if its rateable value were:	Scotland Rebate is calculated as follows:
(a)	A property which includes a room (other than a bathroom or lavatory) predominantly used (whether for therapy or other purposes) by and required for meeting the needs of a resident disabled person (*see* Note 1).	£30 (*see* Note 2).	So much of the rates chargeable on the property for the rebate period as is attributable to the special facility (*see* Note 3).
(b)	A property which includes an additional bathroom or lavatory which is required for meeting the needs of a resident disabled person (*see* Note 1).	(i) £20 where the facility is a bathroom (*see* Note 2). (ii) £10 where the facility is a lavatory (*see* Note 2).	As item (a) above
(c)	A property which includes a heating installation to provide, in two or more rooms, heating which is required for meeting the needs of a resident disabled person (*see* Note 1).	So much only as is attributable to the heating installation (*see* Note 3).	As item (a) above.
(d)	A property which includes any other facility which is required for meeting the needs of a resident disabled person (*see* Note 1), *e.g.* a lift or escalator.	So much only as is attributable to the facility (*see* Note 3).	As item (a) above.
(e)	A property which includes floor space to permit the use of a wheelchair used by and required for meeting the needs of a resident disabled person (*see* Note 1).	£30 (*see* Note 2).	The rates that would be chargeable on the special facility for the rebate period if its rateable value were £30 (*see* Note 2).
(f)	A property which *includes* a garage, carport or land used (other than temporarily) to accommodate a vehicle used by and required for meeting the needs of a disabled person (*see* Note 1).	*Either:* 1 (i) £25 where the facility is a garage (*see* Note 2); (ii) £15 where the facility is a carport (*see* Note 2); (iii) £5 where the facility is land (*see* Note 2). *Or:* 2 (If the applicant so elects.) So much of its rateable value as is attributable to the garage, carport or land (*see* Note 3). If, however, the garage, carport or land is also used for other purposes, the rating authority has discretion to reduce any rebate under this alternative proportionately or by any lesser amount.	As item (a) above.

Item	Description	England and Wales Rebate is equal to the rates that would be chargeable on the property for the rebate period if its rateable value were:	Scotland Rebate is calculated as follows:

(g)	Property which *consists* of a garage, carport or land used (other than temporarily) to accommodate a vehicle used by and required for meeting the needs of a disabled person (*see* Note 1).	*Either:* 1
		  (i) £25 where the facility is a garage (*see* Note 2);
		  (ii) £15 where the facility is a carport (*see* Note 2);
		  (iii) £5 where the facility is land (*see* Note 2).
		Or: 2
		(If the applicant so elects.) The rates chargeable on the property for the rebate period.
		If, however, the garage, carport or land is also used for other purposes, the rating authority has discretion to reduce any rebate under this alternative proportionately or by any lesser amount.
			As item (a) above.

NOTE:

1. 'Required for meeting the needs of', 'resident' and 'disabled person' are all clearly defined (*see* page 261).
2. The Secretary of State may by order vary any of these amounts. Also, the rating authority has discretion to increase the rebate allowed by one-fifth in respect of items (a), (b), (e) and (f)(1). (However, by Section 69 of the Local Government, Planning and Land Act 1980, no government aid attaches to any such increase, so that local authorities may be reluctant in practice to use this discretionary power.)
3. The amount attributed must be certified by the valuation officer (in Scotland, the assessor). There is a right of appeal.
4. Where the property qualifies for rebate for only part of a rebate period, the rating authority has discretion to reduce any rebate proportionately or by a lesser amount.
5. In England and Wales, in respect of items (a), (b) or (f), if the valuation officer certifies that no part of the rateable value of the property is attributable to the room which is predominantly used by the disabled person, the additional bathroom or lavatory or, as the case may be, the garage, carport or land used for accommodating the vehicle, the rebate is nil.

RATES AMENDMENT (NORTHERN IRELAND) ORDER 1979

Extends to Northern Ireland similar provisions to those of the Rating (Disabled Persons) Act 1978. However, relief is not fixed; in all cases the District Valuer has to certify the value of any qualifying facility.

Mental Health

The Mental Health Act 1983 has replaced The Mental Health Act 1959 and makes considerable changes in the law. MIND (*see* page 310) has published *A Practical Guide to Mental Health Law* by its former Legal Director, Larry Gostin. It comprises a review, explanation and analysis of the new legislation and its implications for patients, relatives and professionals. Available from MIND Bookshop, price £2.50 including postage and packing.

Comparative Scottish legislation is contained in the Mental Health (Scotland) Act 1960 and the Mental Health (Amendment) (Scotland) Act 1983 pending consolidation.

Motoring and Mobility

NOTE: Fuller details on the law as it affects disabled drivers will be found in *Motoring and Mobility for Disabled People* by Ann Darnbrough and Derek Kinrade (Royal Association for Disability and Rehabilitation, 1983), price £1 plus postage and packing and available from RADAR at 25 Mortimer Street, London W1N 8AB.

ROAD TRAFFIC ACT 1972

With Regulations, this Act, among other things, sets out the conditions of holding a driving licence. In the United Kingdom, you must hold a licence before driving most categories of vehicle on the road. The licence may be 'provisional' if you are learning to drive, or 'full' if you have passed a test of competence to drive. The minimum age for driving a car is 17, but this is reduced to 16 if the vehicle concerned is an 'invalid carriage'. (*Invalid carriage* is defined in Section 190(5) as a mechanically propelled vehicle with an unladen weight not more than 254 kg (5 cwt) which is specially designed and constructed, not merely adapted, for the use of a person suffering from some physical defect or disability, and used solely by that person. For the purposes of Part II of the Act, however – relating to the licensing of drivers – the maximum weight is increased to 508 kg (10 cwt) by the Motor Vehicles (Driving Licences) Regulations 1981. Certain kinds of invalid carriage, however, are treated as not being motor vehicles and are wholly outside the licensing provisions – *see* page 265.) The minimum age is likewise reduced to 16 if the driver is in receipt of mobility allowance.

Sections 87/87A

With Regulations made thereunder (Motor Vehicle (Driving Licences) Regulations 1981, Regulation 22, as amended by the Motor Vehicles (Driving Licences) Amendment No. 3 Regulations 1982), this section contains powers to refuse, revoke or limit a licence to people suffering from certain disabilities, referred to as being either 'relevant' or 'prospective'.

'Relevant' disabilities are broadly as follows:
(a) epilepsy;
(b) severe subnormality or mental deficiency (both closely defined in the 1981 Regulations);
(c) liability to sudden attacks of disabling giddiness or fainting resulting from:
   (i) any disorder or defect of the heart, as a result of which the person concerned has a device implanted in his/her body (commonly called a cardiac pacemaker) designed to correct the disorder or defect (but see page 265);
   (ii) any other cause;
(d) inability to read in good daylight (with the aid of glasses if worn) a registration mark fixed to a motor vehicle at a distance of 75 feet (where the letters and figures are $3\frac{1}{2}$ in. high) or 67 feet (where the letters and figures are $3\frac{1}{8}$ in. high) (less stringent standards apply for a licence restricted to Group K vehicles only – *i.e.*, mowing machines or pedestrian-controlled vehicles);
(e) any other disability likely to cause the driving of a vehicle to be a source of danger to the public.

'Prospective' disabilities are those which, by virtue of their intermittent or progressive nature or otherwise, may in time become 'relevant' as described above.

Notification of a Disability

Applicants for licences are under a legal obligation to declare a disability (either relevant or prospective) as required by the appropriate section of the licence application form.

A licence holder is similarly required by law to inform the Licensing Centre 'forthwith' if during the currency of a licence he/she becomes aware that he/she is suffering from a relevant or prospective disability not previously disclosed, or if a previously notified disability becomes worse. The notification is required in writing and should advise the nature and extent of the disability. Failure to notify without reasonable excuse is an offence under section 170 of the Road Traffic Act 1972.

Temporary disabilities (those reasonably expected to last less than three months) which the licence holder has not previously suffered are outside this obligation. A licence must, in law, be refused or revoked if the applicant or licence holder is suffering from a relevant disability (as previously defined) unless the disability is one of the following:
(a) A disability which is not progressive in nature and which consists solely of any one or more of the following:
   (i) the absence of one or more limbs;
   (ii) the deformity of one or more limbs;
   (iii) the loss of use (including a deficiency of limb movement or power) of one or more limbs.
   (Reference to a limb includes reference to a part of a limb.)
   Provided in this case either that the application is for a provisional licence or, if a driving test has been passed at any time, it does not appear that the disability has arisen or become worse since that time or was, for whatever reason, not disclosed at that time.
(b) Epilepsy which in a particular case is appropriately controlled.
   The applicant must satisfy the conditions that:
   (i) he/she has been free from any epileptic attack during the period of two years immediately preceding the date when the licence is to have effect (or, if not, that he/she has had such attacks only whilst asleep during a period of *three* years immediately preceding the date when the licence is to have effect); and
   (ii) the driving of a vehicle by him/her in pursuance of the licence is not likely to be a source of danger to the public.
(c) Any disorder or defect of the heart, which has been controlled by implanting a cardiac pace-

maker (see (c) (i) of the list of relevant disabilities on page 264). The applicant must satisfy the conditions that:

(i) his/her driving of a vehicle in pursuance of the licence is not likely to be a source of danger to the public; and

(ii) he/she has made adequate arrangements to receive regular medical supervision by a cardiologist throughout the period of the licence, and is conforming to those arrangements.

Where a disability is such as not to necessitate refusal or revocation of a driving licence, any licence issued may nevertheless be restricted in duration and/or the description of vehicles which may be driven. Such restrictions are typically worded: 'Entitled to drive... with all controls so fitted that they can be correctly and conveniently operated with/without/despite (followed by a description of disability, *e.g.* loss of left leg).'

Because some disabled drivers overcome their disabilities more successfully than others it is not considered practicable to specify what adaptations, if any, are required. The restriction on driving licences is, in fact, so worded that it places the onus on the driver to ensure that the practical effect of his disability does not affect the safe control of his vehicle. It is for the licence holder to decide in the light of this, what, if any, adaptations are required. Essentially, he/she must be satisfied that if stopped by a police officer it could be demonstrated that the terms of the licence were being met. (An explanatory leaflet is issued with all restricted licences.)

Disabled people whose full licence authorises them to drive only an invalid carriage or a vehicle of special construction or design are not entitled to drive any other type of vehicle. If they wish to drive a vehicle of a type not covered by their full licence, they should contact the Licensing Centre about amending their licence.

NOTE: It is important to be aware that it is an offence under Section 5 of this Act to drive or attempt to drive a motor vehicle on a road or other public place if 'unfit to drive through drink or drugs'. Conviction carries an automatic disqualification from driving. An offence could arise from a normal and prescribed use of a medicine, if thereby a driver was so affected as to be unfit to drive.

There is a separate offence of being 'in charge' of a motor vehicle on the road or other public place when unfit to drive through drink or drugs. You would not be regarded as in charge of a vehicle if you could prove that the circumstances were such that there was no likelihood of you driving while you remained unfit to drive, but clearly this could be difficult to establish.

EEC Harmonisation

EEC Directive 80/1263EC, Article 6, indicates that from 1 January 1986 new driving licences will be granted only to those who have passed a practical and theoretical test set out in Annex II of the Directive, and who meet medical standards, the minimum requirements of which may not be substantially less stringent than those set out in Annex III of the Directive. These 'Minimum Standards of Physical and Mental Fitness' are set out more precisely than in current UK law, but will affect only *new* applicants after 1 January 1986. It will be for our own government to make or amend regulations, if necessary, to accord with Article 6 of the Directive.

Licences for 'Trike' Drivers who Change to a Standard Car

The law does not permit the grant of a full licence to drive a car unless:

(a) the applicant can satisfy the Secretary of State that he has held a licence, valid within the last ten years, for the class of vehicle for which he/she is applying; or

(b) the applicant has passed a driving test for the relevant class of vehicle(s) within the last ten years; or

(c) the applicant can satisfy the Secretary of State that he/she has held an appropriate licence valid within the last ten years which was issued in Northern Ireland, the Isle of Man or the Channel Islands.

If a 'trike' driver is not thus entitled to a full licence for the vehicles he/she now wishes to drive, he/she would have to apply for provisional entitlement to be added to his or her Group J licence in order to take the appropriate driving test. Such applications would, of course, be subject to medical enquiries. However, no fee is payable for either the restoration of previous entitlement or the addition of provisional entitlement.

Vehicles which can be Driven without Licence

By the Chronically Sick and Disabled Persons Act 1970, Section 20, as amended by the Road Traffic Act, Schedule 7, an invalid carriage which complies with the Use of Invalid Carriages on Highways Regulations 1970 (SI 1970 No. 1391) and which is being used in accordance with the conditions prescribed by those Regulations, is exempted from a number of statutory requirements. For this purpose, an invalid carriage is defined as a vehicle, whether mechanically propelled or not, constructed or adapted for use for the carriage of one person, being a person suffering from some physical defect or disability. The conditions which must be met are that the invalid carriage must:

(a) not exceed 250 lb unladen weight;

(b) if mechanically propelled, be so constructed as to be incapable of exceeding four m.p.h. on the level under its own power;

(c) if mechanically propelled, have brakes which comply with the current regulations;

(d) when used during the hours of darkness, have a front light, rear light and rear reflectors.

In the case of an invalid carriage which fulfils all these conditions:

(a) no statutory provision prohibiting or restricting the use of footways shall prohibit or restrict the use of that vehicle on a footway;

(b) if the vehicle is mechanically propelled, it shall be treated for the purposes of the Road Traffic Regulations Act 1967 and the Road Traffic Act 1972 as not being a motor vehicle;

(c) whether or not the vehicle is mechanically propelled, it shall be exempted from the requirements of sections 68 to 81 of the Road Traffic Act 1972 (relating to lighting).

Such vehicles are not liable to vehicle excise duty and need not be registered.

NOTE: The invalid tricycle, or 'trike', is of course outside this exemption. Nor does it fall into the classification of 'invalid carriage' in Section 190(5) of the Road Traffic Act 1972 (*see* page 264) or the identical definition in Section 253(5) of the Road Traffic Act 1960. It is, therefore, subject to all normal legislation relating to motor vehicles, but equally is not prohibited from motorways or subject to speed restriction.

MOTOR VEHICLES (WEARING OF SEAT BELTS) REGULATIONS 1982 and MOTOR VEHICLES (WEARING OF SEAT BELTS BY CHILDREN) REGULATIONS 1982

These Regulations are made under the *Road Traffic Act 1972*, as amended by the Transport Act 1981. Since 31 January 1983, they have required seat belts to be worn by anyone aged 14 or more when travelling, as driver or passenger, in the front seats of certain vehicles, *i.e.*:

cars and three-wheeled vehicles (weighing 408 kilograms or more unladen) with not more than 12 passenger seats, made after 30 June 1964 and first registered after 31 December 1964 (usually C or later number plates),

light vans (with an unladen weight not exceeding 1525 kilograms or a laden weight of 3500 kilograms) made after 31 August 1966 and registered on or after 31 March 1967 (usually E or later number plates),

three-wheeled motor vehicles (exceeding 255 kilograms unladen weight) made after 28 February 1970 and first registered after 31 August 1970

(usually J or later number plates) and

any vehicle which has belts fitted (although not required by law) because of the use being made of the vehicle.

The seat belt must comply to standards prescribed by regulations both as regards the belt itself and its anchorage, but the normal requirements are somewhat relaxed for vehicles specially constructed or adapted for physically disabled people. Nevertheless, such special seat belts must be worn, and if you are using a vehicle fitted with the normal design of seat belt, you will have to wear this unless exempted in one of the ways described below.

There is also a responsibility upon drivers to ensure that children under 14 do not ride in a front seat of any vehicle covered by the adult regulations unless they are wearing a seat belt or are in an approved child restraint. (Further guidance is given in a free leaflet *Child Safety in Cars* available from your local road safety officer or from the Department of Transport, Distribution, Building No. 3, Victoria Road, South Ruislip, Middlesex HA4 0NZ.)

Exemptions

You do not have to wear a seat belt:

If you are sitting in a middle front seat (*e.g.* a bench seat) and two passengers (including yourself) are sitting in front. (When the passenger in a middle front seat is a child under 14, exemption applies only if there is no belt fitted to the child's seat and *all* other front and back seats are occupied.)

If you are driving a vehicle and carrying out a manœuvre which includes reversing.

If you have a valid medical exemption certificate (*see* below) (also applies to children).

If you are making a local delivery or collection round using a vehicle constructed or adapted for that purpose.

If your seat belt has become defective on your journey; or previously and you have already arranged to have the belt repaired or replaced.

If your inertia reel seat belt has, for the moment, locked because your vehicle is or has been on a steep incline. But you will have to put the belt on as soon as the mechanism has unlocked.

If you are a qualified driver and you are supervising a learner driver who is carrying out a manœuvre which includes reversing.

If you are the driver of a taxi which is being used for seeking hire or answering a call for hire or carrying a passenger for hire. (You will only be exempt if you carry the plate showing your vehicle is licensed as a taxi.)

If you are the driver of a private hire car vehicle which is being used to carry a passenger for hire. (You will only be exempt if you carry the plate showing that your vehicle is licensed as a private hire car vehicle or that it is licensed at the hackney carriage rate under the Vehicles (Excise) Act 1971.)

If you are riding in a vehicle and you are looking into or repairing a mechanical fault. You will only be exempt if the vehicle is on trade plates.

(These are the main exemptions to the law. Others are only for people in special jobs and in certain circumstances, for example the police.)

The exemption which is significant for disabled people is contained in Regulation 5(d) and requires the holding of a statutory form of certificate, signed by a registered medical practitioner, to the effect that it is inadvisable on medical grounds to wear a seat belt. If, as the holder of such a certificate, you are told by a police officer that you may be prosecuted for a seat belt offence (maximum penalty £50) and cannot produce the certificate then and there, you need to do so within five days to establish your exemption from the law.

It would be a gross error, however, to suppose that disability will confer an automatic right to exemption. On the contrary, guidelines for doctors prepared by the Medical Commission on Accident Prevention conclude that there are very few people who ought not to wear a seat belt because of their health. 'Doctors', the Commission observes, will 'wish to *balance very carefully indeed* the advantages to their patient of reducing the risk of injury or death against any reason the patient may give for seeking exemption from wearing a seat belt'. The position of disabled drivers is analysed in some detail and there is a general conclusion that the available medical evidence shows that a person fit to be in control of a vehicle is fit to wear a seat belt and that in some medical conditions and in many disabilities, the wearing of a seat belt is a positive advantage to comfort and to the safe control of the vehicle. *A possible implication is that unfitness to wear a seat belt could call into question fitness to drive.*

THE DISABLED PERSONS (BADGES FOR MOTOR VEHICLES) REGULATIONS 1982

These Regulations are made in pursuance of Section 21 of the *Chronically Sick and Disabled Persons Act 1970*, and are generally known as the orange badge scheme. For a general description of the arrangements *see* Section 8 of this Directory.

TRANSPORT ACT 1968

Section 138
Empowers local authorities to make travel concessions for:
(a) men over 65 and women over 60;
(b) people so blind as to be unable to perform any work for which sight is essential;
(c) people suffering from any disability or injury which, in the opinion of the local authority (or any of the local authorities by whom the cost incurred in granting the concessions falls to be reimbursed), seriously impairs their ability to walk.

NOTE: The same power has been extended to the Greater London Council by The Travel Concessions (London) Act 1982.

Residental Homes

THE RESIDENTIAL HOMES ACT 1980

Consolidates legislation relating to the registration, inspection and conduct of residential homes for disabled, old or mentally disordered people.

Statutory Services

NATIONAL ASSISTANCE ACT 1948 (as amended by Local Government Act 1972)

Section 29
This Section of the Act deals with the promotion of the welfare of handicapped persons by local authorities. In respect of *residents*, the authority is *required* to make the necessary arrangements, to such an extent as the Secretary of State may direct. In respect of *non-residents*, the authority *may* make such arrangements, subject to the approval of the Secretary of State. The definition of those benefiting under the Section is important, *viz.* 'persons who are blind, deaf or dumb, and other persons who are substantially and permanently handicapped by illness, injury or congenital deformity or such other disabilities as may be prescribed by the Minister'.

The arrangements which authorities may make include:
(a) advice on available services to those concerned;
(b) instruction in ways of overcoming the effects of disabilities;
(c) provision of workshops and hostels for handicapped workers*;
(d) provision of work for handicapped persons*;
(e) assistance in the disposal of the produce of such work;
(f) provision of recreational facilities;
(g) compilation and maintenance of a register of handicapped persons.

* But see Disabled Persons (Employment) Act 1958.

Section 30

Allows local authorities to use certain voluntary organisations for disabled people's welfare as their agents in making the above arrangements, and to contribute to the funds of such organisations.

NATIONAL HEALTH SERVICE ACT 1977

Section 5(2)(a)

Under this section, the Secretary of State *may* 'provide invalid carriages* for persons appearing to him (her) to be suffering from severe physical defect or disability and, at the request of such a person, may provide for him (her) a vehicle other than an invalid carriage'. By Schedule 2 of the Act, the Secretary of State also has power, in respect of any such invalid carriage or vehicle so provided or which belongs to any person such as is mentioned in Section 5(2)(a), on such terms and subject to such conditions as he/she may determine:

(a) to adapt it so as to make it suitable for the circumstances of that person;
(b) to maintain and repair it;
(c) to insure it and pay the vehicle excise duty;
(d) to provide a structure in which it may be kept, and to provide all necessary materials and works to that purpose;
(e) make payments by way of grant towards costs incurred by any such person as is mentioned in Section 5(2)(a) in respect of:
　(i) taking action under (a) to (d) above;
　(ii) the purchase of fuel for the vehicle (so far as the cost of the purchase is attributable to the excise duty thereon);
　(iii) taking instruction in driving the vehicle.

* Defined as 'a mechanically propelled vehicle specially designed and constructed (not merely adapted) for the use of a person suffering some physical defect or disability and used solely by such a person'.

In practice, no vehicles are now issued to new applicants.

Schedule 8, paragraph 3

Lays a *duty* upon local social services authorities to provide or arrange to provide 'on such a scale as is adequate for the needs of their area', home-help for households where such help is required in a variety of circumstances, including situations where help is needed because of the presence of a person who is suffering from illness, lying-in, an expectant mother, aged, or *handicapped as a result of having suffered from illness or by congenital deformity* (our italics).

Every such authority also has the *power* (not the duty) to provide or arrange for the provision of laundry facilities for households for which home-help is being, or can be, provided under this sub-para-

graph. The authority is, however, entitled to recover 'reasonable' charges for such services, having regard to the means of the beneficiaries.

CHRONICALLY SICK AND DISABLED PERSONS ACT 1970 (as amended)

Section 1

Local authorities must:

(a) take steps to inform themselves of the numbers and needs of disabled persons* in their areas;
(b) publish information as to the services they provide under Section 29 of the National Assistance Act 1948 (but only 'from time to time at such times and in such manner as they consider appropriate');
(c) ensure that disabled persons* are informed of any available services which in the opinion of the authority are relevant to their needs.

* As defined in Section 29 of the National Assistance Act 1948.

Section 2

Where a local authority which acts under the said Section 29 is satisfied that in order to meet the needs of a disabled person (as defined in Section 29) resident in its area it must make arrangements for any or all of the matters set out below, then it is duty bound, under the general guidance of the Secretary of State, to do so:

(a) The provision of practical assistance for that person in his home.
(b) The provision of that person of, or assistance to that person in obtaining, wireless, television, library or similar recreational facilities.
(c) The provision for that person of lectures, games, outings or other recreational facilities outside his home or assistance to that person in taking advantage of educational facilities available to him.
(d) The provision for that person of facilities for, or assistance in, travelling to and from his home for the purpose of participating in any services provided under arrangements made by the authority under the said Section 29 or, with the approval of the authority, in any services provided otherwise than as aforesaid which are similar to services which could be provided under such arrangements.
(e) The provision of assistance for that person in arranging for the carrying out of any works of adaptation in his home or the provision of any additional facilities designed to secure his greater safety, comfort or convenience.
(f) Facilitating the taking of holidays by that person, whether at holiday homes or otherwise and

whether provided under arrangements made by the authority or otherwise.

(g) The provision of meals for that person whether in his home or elsewhere.

(h) The provision for that person of, or assistance to that person in obtaining, a telephone and any special equipment necessary to enable him to use a telephone.

NOTE: A Code of Practice on the proper implementation of Section 2 has been drawn up by 15 national charities. Criteria for each of the services listed above are suggested. Copies of the Code are available from the Royal Association for Disability and Rehabilitation, 25 Mortimer Street, London W1N 8AB in response to a s.a.e. (minimum 9 in. × 6 in.).

Section 3

Extends the requirements in Section 91 of the Housing Act 1957 for local authorities to consider housing needs in their areas to the consideration of the special needs of the chronically sick and disabled.

Sections 4, 5, 6, 8, 8A and 8B

Require that in providing buildings open to the public, provision must be made for the needs of disabled visitors in the external and internal means of access and in any parking facilities or lavatories. Similarly, where lavatories are provided for the public by local authorities, or under local authority notice in buildings such as hotels, restaurants and theatres, account must be taken of the needs of disabled people. Comparable requirements apply to universities, colleges, schools and further education institutions and to new office, shop, railway or factory premises. All such provision is required only 'in so far as it is in the circumstances both practicable and reasonable' (*but see* Note to Section 6 of the Disabled Persons Act 1981 on page 270).

A new Section 8B was added by Section 7 of the Disabled Persons Act 1981, requiring the Secretary of State to report to Parliament on his proposals for ensuring the improvement of means of access to buildings and premises referred to in Sections 4, 8 and 8A of the 1970 Act, to public lavatories, to lavatories in places used or to be used for entertainment, exhibitions or sporting events to which the public is admitted, to places selling food and drink for consumption on the premises and to betting offices.

Section 7 (substituted by Section 5 of the Disabled Persons Act 1981)

Requires that where any provision required by or under Sections 4, 5, 6, 8 or 8A of the Act is made at buildings or premises:

(a) a notice or sign indicating that provision is made for disabled people must be displayed outside;

and

(b) signs must be displayed inside to show both the route to and location of such provision.

Lavatories provided elsewhere than in a building, and not in themselves buildings, must also carry a notice as at (a).

Where parking is provided for disabled people under Section 4, notices or signs must be displayed indicating an appropriate route for disabled people between the parking place and the related building or premises.

Sections 9 to 15 and 23

Provide for disabled persons or those experienced in working with disabled persons to serve on advisory bodies and local authority committees wherever possible.

Section 16

Requires the National Advisory Council of the Disabled Persons (Employment) Act 1944 to provide for the training of those who train or find employment for disabled people.

Sections 17 and 18

Requires the Secretary of State to use his best endeavours to secure that, as far as practicable, disabled and long-term patients under the age of 65 are not cared for in any part of the hospital which is normally used, wholly or mainly, for the elderly (65 plus) and to present an annual statement to Parliament in this regard. Local authorities are required to supply statistics about the numbers of disabled persons under 65 in old people's homes.

Section 20

Wheelchairs, etc., whether or not motorised, may be used on footpaths, bridle paths and pavements and do not have to carry lights in these circumstances.

Section 21

Covers the issue of orange badges by local authorities for motor vehicles 'driven by, or used for the carriage of, disabled persons'.

Comparative legislation was enacted by Northern Ireland on 31 July 1978 through the Chronically Sick and Disabled Persons (NI) Act 1978. This is broadly similar to the preceding legislation.

NOTE: *A Charter for the Disabled* by Eda Topliss and Brian Gould, published by Basil Blackwell, describes vividly and with inside knowledge the way Alf Morris, MP, fought to bring the Chronically Sick and Disabled Persons Act 1970 to the statute book. It goes on to analyse the impact of the Act on the lives of disabled people and how it has been interpreted and implemented. Available from the publisher at 108 Cowley Road,

Oxford OX4 1JF, or from good bookshops. Price £6.50 paperback; £15 hardback.

The following leaflet is available from RADAR, 25 Mortimer Street, London W1N 8AB (Tel: 01-637 5400): *Chronically Sick and Disabled Persons Act 1970*. Free, but 15p postage and packing.

CHRONICALLY SICK AND DISABLED PERSONS (AMENDMENT) ACT 1976

Inserts a new Section 8A into the Chronically Sick and Disabled Persons Act 1970 (*see* page 269).

DISABLED PERSONS ACT 1981

This Act amends and inserts provisions into various other Acts aimed at ensuring that better provision is made for the needs of disabled people using highways, buildings and other public places.

Section 1

Inserts a new Section 175A into the Highways Act 1980 (also serves as a new Section 27A to the Roads (Scotland) Act 1970). The new section requires statutory authorities responsible for highways to consider the needs of disabled or blind people when carrying out, in a street, works which may impede their mobility. Specific attention is drawn to the placing of lampposts, bollards, traffic signs, apparatus or other permanent obstructions, and to the proper protection of 'holes in the road', be they temporary or permanent.

Highway authorities are also directed to have regard to the needs of disabled people when considering the desirability of providing ramps at appropriate places between carriageways and footways.

Section 2

Amends the Road Traffic Regulation Act 1967 in three places:

New subsections are inserted in Sections 31 and 42 which have the effect of creating additional parking offences when an infringement is committed in a parking place reserved for a disabled person's vehicle either in a car park or on the highway.

NOTE: Parking places reserved for disabled badge holders cannot be enforced unless they are backed up by a traffic regulation order under Sections 31 or 42.

Anyone found guilty of such an offence is liable on summary conviction to a fine of up to £200 (Criminal Justice Act 1982). A new Section 86A is inserted, whereby a person found guilty of an offence under the Act, commits a secondary offence if at the relevant time a disabled person's orange badge was being wrongfully used. The secondary offence carries a fine on summary conviction of up to £200.

Section 3

Inserts new Sections 29A and 29B into the Town and Country Planning Act 1971. These concern grants of planning permission in respect of premises covered by Sections 4 to 8A of the Chronically Sick and Disabled Persons Act 1970 (*see* page 269) and require attention to be drawn to the relevant provisions of that Act and either the British Standards Institution Code of Practice BS 5810:1979 (Access for the Disabled to Buildings) or Design Note 18 (Access for the Physically Disabled to Educational Buildings) as appropriate.

NOTE: Design Note 18 is relevant only in England and Wales. It is of lesser scope than BS 5810:1979 and fails to meet the requirements of disabled staff or disabled visitors. In Scotland, BS 5810 applies equally to educational buildings as to other premises.

Section 4

Amends Section 20 of the Local Government (Miscellaneous Provisions) Act 1976 by the insertion of three new subsections 11, 12 and 13, designed to ensure that when a notice is served to provide, maintain, keep clean or make available 'sanitary appliances' at a place of entertainment, attention is drawn to Sections 6(1) and 7 of the Chronically Sick and Disabled Persons Act 1970 and to the British Standards Institution Code of Practice BS 5810:1979 (Access for the Disabled to Buildings).

Section 5

Substitutes a new Section 7 in the Chronically Sick and Disabled Persons Act 1970 (*see* page 269).

Section 6 (England and Wales only)

Further amends the Chronically Sick and Disabled Persons Act 1970, Sections 4(1), 5(1), 6(1), 8(1) and 8A(1), from a date to be announced. The words 'in so far as it is in the circumstances both practicable and reasonable' would be deleted in favour of a requirement of 'appropriate provision' in accordance with British Standards Institution Code of Practice BS 5810:1979 (Access for the Disabled to Buildings) or Design Note 18 (Access for the Physically Disabled to Educational Buildings), *unless* it can be shown to the satisfaction of a body appointed by the Secretary of State, that 'in the circumstances it is either not practicable to make such provision or not reasonable that such provision should be made'.

NOTE: The difference may appear slight, but the amendment, if brought into force, would both specify the kind of provision required and make non-provision exceptional and subject to the satisfaction of an expert body. However, at the time of writing, it is uncertain whether Section 6 will be brought into effect. Consideration is being given, as an alternative, to the incorporation of access provisions into the Building Regulations with BS 5810:1979 enjoying the status of an approved document.

(*See* Appendix A for further details of BS 5810.)

Section 7

Inserts a new Section 8B into the Chronically Sick and Disabled Persons Act 1970 (*see* page 269).

NOTE: Guidance on the implementation of the Disabled Persons Act 1981 is contained in Department of Health and Social Security Circular to local authorities, LAC(82)5.

Comparative Northern Irish legislation is contained in the Disabled Persons (Northern Ireland) Order 1982 (SI 1982 No. 1535).

LOCAL AUTHORITY SOCIAL SERVICES ACT 1970 (as amended)

This Act requires every local authority to establish a social services committee to deal with (amongst other things) the following:

(a) Provision of residential accommodation for the aged, infirm, etc. (National Assistance Act 1948, Sections 21 and 27).

(b) Welfare of persons who are blind, deaf, dumb, or otherwise handicapped or are suffering from mental disorder; use of voluntary organisations for administering welfare schemes (National Assistance Act 1948, Sections 29 and 30).

(c) Provision of facilities to enable disabled persons to be employed or work under special conditions (Disabled Persons (Employment) Act 1958, Section 3).

(d) Prevention of illness and care and after-care of the sick* (Health Services and Public Health Act 1968, Section 12).

(e) Provision of home-help and laundry facilities for certain households (Health Services and Public Health Act 1968, Section 13).

(f) Promotion of welfare of old people (Health Services and Public Health Act 1968, Section 45).

(g) Financial and other assistance to voluntary organisations (Health Services and Public Health Act 1968, Section 65).

(h) Obtaining information as to the need for, and publishing information as to, the existence of certain welfare services (Chronically Sick and Disabled Persons Act 1970, Section 1).

(i) Provision of welfare services (Chronically Sick and Disabled Persons Act 1970, Section 2).

* Excluding matters which the Minister directs as being mainly medical in nature (see Section 25 (3(b)) and (4)).

LOCAL GOVERNMENT ACT 1972

Section 195(2)

Provides for consultation by district councils in non-metropolitan counties with respect to the nature and extent of the accommodation needed for people who, because of infirmity or disability, need accommodation of a special character.

CONTACT AND TAPE ORGANISATIONS

Postal Concessions

The Post Office has advised the following details:

ARTICLES FOR THE BLIND (BY INLAND POST)

Packets containing literature and other articles specified below, specially adapted for the use of the blind, will be transmitted by the first-class letter service under the following conditions:

Rate of Postage
Free.

Weight and Size
The maximum weight is 7 kg.
The limits of size are 610 mm (2 feet) in length, 460 mm (1 foot 6 inches) in width and 460 mm (1 foot 6 inches) in depth; or if made up in the form of a roll, the length plus twice the diameter should not exceed 1.040 m (3 feet 5 inches) and the greatest dimension should not exceed 900 mm (2 feet 11 inches).

Permissible Articles
 1. Books, papers and letters to or from blind persons impressed or otherwise prepared for the use of the blind.
 2. Paper posted to any person for the purpose of being so impressed or prepared.

Also the following articles specially adapted for the use of the blind:
 3. Relief maps.
 4. Machines, frames and attachments for making impressions for the use of the blind.
 5. Pencil writing frames and attachments.
 6. Braillette board and metal pegs therefor.
 7. De Braille instructional devices.
 8. Games (including card games).
 9. Mathematical appliances and attachments.
 10. Voice records on discs, film, tape or wire of readings from books, journals, newspapers, periodicals or other similar printed publications (that is 'talking books') and apparatus designed to play such records.
 11. Metal plates impressed, or posted for the pur-

pose of being impressed, for the use of the blind.
 12. Wrappers and labels for use on postal packets for the blind – bulk supplies.
 13. Braille watches, clocks and timers.
 14. Tools, aids and precision instruments.
 15. Rules and measures.
 16. Sectional or collapsible walking-sticks.
 17. Harness for guide dogs.

Articles 8 to 17 inclusive may be sent only to blind persons by institutions which have entered into special arrangements to the satisfaction of the Post Office for the transmission of such articles, or to such institutions by blind persons. Article 10 must not contain any personal messages or communications.

Conditions
A packet may consist only of articles described above for the use of the blind, and may not contain any communication, either in writing or printing, in ordinary type, except:
(a) a title, date of publication, serial number, names and addresses of printer, publisher or manufacturer, price and table of contents of a book or paper, or any key to or instructions for, the use of the special type or of any enclosed article; and
(b) a printed label for the return of the packet.

A packet must be posted either without a cover, or in a cover which can be easily removed for the purpose of examination.

A packet must bear on the outside the indication *ARTICLES FOR THE BLIND*, and the written or printed name and address of the sender. The use of a printed label with the necessary indication is recommended.

If these conditions are not fulfilled, the packet will either be charged as an unpaid letter, or transferred to the parcel post and charged as an unpaid parcel.

LITERATURE FOR THE BLIND

Definition
Periodicals, books, and papers of any kind including unsealed letters, impressed in Braille or other special type for the use of the blind, may be sent.

Rate of Postage
Postage free (surface only). For air rates of postage see Postal Rates Overseas Compendium.

Weight
The limit of weight is 7 kg.

Size
The limits of size are:

Normal-shaped Packets (other than in the form of a roll)

Minimum:

One surface must be at least	90 mm × 140 mm ($3\frac{1}{2}$ inches × $5\frac{1}{2}$ inches).

Smaller items with tied on address labels are not permitted.

Maximum:

Length, depth and width combined	900 mm (3 feet).
Greatest single dimension	600 mm (2 feet).

Roll-shaped Packets

Minimum:

Length plus twice the diameter	170 mm ($6\frac{3}{4}$ inches).
Greatest single dimension	100 mm (4 inches).

Smaller items with tied on address labels are not permitted.

Maximum:

Length plus twice the diameter	1040 mm (3 feet 5 inches).
Greatest single dimension	900 mm (3 feet).

Packing and Make-up
The packets should conform to the regulations applicable to printed papers. In addition, in the upper left-hand corner of the address side, they should be clearly marked *LITERATURE FOR THE BLIND (CÉCOGRAMMES)*. The name and address of the sender should also be shown.

Registration
Packets sent in the registration service must be packed in the same way as ordinary literature for the blind items, as under *Packing and Make-up* above. Literature for the blind items cannot be insured.

Admissible Articles
The following articles are also admitted free of postage as literature for the blind:
Plates for embossing blind literature: and
Discs, tapes or wires bearing voice recordings and special paper intended solely for the use of the blind provided that they are sent by or addressed to an

officially recognised institution for the blind. Leaflets explaining how this may be done are obtainable from The Royal National Institute for the Blind, 224 Great Portland Street, London W1N 6AA.

Although in the inland service various additional articles are admitted free of postage, the only articles other than papers impressed for the use of the blind which are transmissible as literature for the blind in the Overseas Post, are those indicated above.

Contact Clubs

Braille Correspondence Club
Linda Watts, Special Unit Blind, Social Services Department, Civic Centre, Newcastle upon Tyne NE1 8PA.
This club links braillists both in the United Kingdom and abroad. Anyone interested should contact the above address, giving personal details including interests and standard of braille.

Friends by Post
Mrs Ilse Salomon, 6 Bollin Court, Macclesfield Road, Wilmslow, Cheshire SK9 2AP (Tel: Wilmslow (0625) 527044).
Aims at putting in touch like-minded people in order to have a 'Conversation by Correspondence'. Those restricted in their social life may not have an understanding friend at hand when needed most, but pen and paper are always available. Those interested may contact the organisation for explanatory leaflets. Apart from a stamped addressed envelope, the service is entirely free of charge.

The Friendship Register
Organiser: Joan Mertens, 29 Goldstone Way, Hove, East Sussex BN3 7PA.
This organisation provides information to contact personal friends and pen-friends nation-wide. On joining, a member receives a register of current members and can make a personal choice of friends. Further lists are published at two-monthly intervals, each accompanied by a newsletter. The subscription for the first year is £2.50 plus 50p for forwarding letters to those members who do not wish to have their addresses published.

Inter-Nations Friendship Circle
Mr T. L. Simmons, 30A Wellington Parade, Blackfen Road, Sidcup, Kent DA15 9NF.
A pen-friendship organisation with members all over the world. It relies on voluntary donations. Friends of the INFC receive a list of members each year. Mr Simmons believes that 'a spirited mind will not be content to remain within itself'.

Penfriends World-wide
June Maughan, 60 Ellesmere Road, Benwell, Newcastle upon Tyne NE4 8TS (Tel: Newcastle (0632) 736732).
This correspondence club was formed in 1977 and is open to anyone. A number of members correspond by cassette tape and more visually handicapped and physically disabled people would be welcomed. Mrs Maughan will be pleased to put any person in touch with a pen-friend in a similar age group or with similar interests, and is also willing to include your name for one free listing in the quarterly magazine *June's Penpal Circle*. This service is free to visually handicapped and physically disabled people, but a stamp for reply would be appreciated.

Brenda Perridge
8 Dukes Close, North Weald, Epping, Essex CM16 6DA.
Correspondence groups arranged linking people of similar age or with interests in common, either in writing or by cassette. Send 25p plus s.a.e. for complete list.

The Postillion
Miss Lore Herold, Löwenstr. 12, 2000 Hamburg 20, West Germany (Tel: (010 49 40) 46 21 84).
A world-wide contact circle for handicapped, ill or lonely people. The organisation has been active since 1975 and has contacts in Germany, Austria, Switzerland, England, America, Canada, New Zealand, Africa, Sri Lanka and Indonesia. Some of the contacts have resulted in marriage.

A newsletter is published every two months, and includes details of all new contacts. Membership is free, but applicants are asked to send with their letter an international postal reply coupon.

'Sugar' Correspondence Club
Jo Stead, Room 7054, BBC, Broadcasting House, Portland Place, London W1A 1AA.
This popular club is organised by the BBC branch of the Citizens' Advice Bureau in association with *Does He Take Sugar?*, the radio programme for disabled people. It aims to put listeners in touch with others who share their interests and problems. All facilities of the club are free and include a membership card, badge and occasional newsletter.

Wider Horizons
Mr. A. B. Fletcher, 'Westbrook', Back Lane, Malvern, Worcestershire WR14 2HJ.
This society has the following aims:
(a) the improvement of the condition of life for persons who are handicapped by physical disabilities;

(b) to promote wider interests, new friendships and the exchange of information and views between members;
(c) to publish six times a year a magazine containing the work of members;
(d) to assist disabled members to obtain, through a Modern Aids Fund, aids to communication and daily living, where these are not available through other sources.

The contents of a typical issue of the Wider Horizons magazine *WH* include articles on varied topics, verse, stories or anecdotes, ideas and experiences, book reviews, cookery or plant-growing items, a free advertisement service for readers and a crossword or competition. *WH* also contains special sections including *Christian Horizons*, *Watching Wildlife*, and a hobbies page. Efforts are made to link up members by correspondence or cassette with others having similar interests, or through 'special interest' folder groups.

The annual subscription is £3. For those on limited incomes, payment is reduced to what can be afforded, with a minimum of £1.

The '62 Clubs
Despite their name these clubs are intended for adults from the age of 18 years upwards. While spastic people have priority, all handicapped people are welcome. There are over 35 of these organisations throughout the country and each arranges its own programme of activities. The aim of the clubs is that handicapped people themselves should make their own decisions and organise their own programmes. For further details apply to the Regional Office, The Spastics Society, 12 Park Crescent, London W1N 4EQ (Tel: 01-636 5020).

Tape Organisations

Tape recordings offer an alternative means of communication for many visually handicapped people, and a wide range of organisations now exists (and is growing) to facilitate their circulation. There are some which encourage fellowship between members, others which send out tape books, newspapers and magazines, and invaluable stalwarts who will record letterpress material for you.

In this short section we can offer no more than a selection of the many services in this field. For more detailed information, particularly of local services, we recommend:

The Talking Newspaper Association Tape Information Service
Rosemary Millar, 12 Aynhoe Road, London W14 0QD (Tel: 01-602 2617).

This service was set up in 1981 to provide information about what is available on tape for blind people to anyone who asks. The information (which in the first instance was an updated version of Catherine Ireland's study, *see* page 280) is stored on index cards, and individual enquiries can be made by telephone, letter (including braille) and on tape to the above address. There is also a printed version of the information available: *TNAUK Guide to Tape Recordings for the Handicapped*, price £3.50, post free, to non-members of TNAUK; free to members. This can be obtained from Ted Davis, Honorary Treasurer TNAUK, Woodhatch, Heathfield, East Sussex TN21 0UP (Tel: Heathfield (043 52) 2883). An abbreviated version of the Guide is available on tape to members of TNAUK: enquiries to Dunfermline Sound, PO Box 3, Dunfermline, Fife.

The TNAUK Tape Information Service is free, but a self-addressed, stamped envelope is always appreciated.

TAPE FELLOWSHIP SOCIETIES

Chatterbox Recording Club
Secretary: Dick Armstrong, 1 Chestnut Drive, Holme-on-Spalding-Moor, York YO4 4HW.
CRC exists to bring together people of similar interests, providing information necessary to make the initial contact. Each new member is provided with a directory of members, and contacts can then be selected at will. Members who are interested in specific subjects, *e.g.* photography, steam engines, jazz, have formed their own circle of friends, meeting on tape to swap ideas and experiences.

A quarterly printed magazine brings news and views, and provides a technical service, alternating with a sound magazine obtainable through the Area Representatives. Blind members can receive the printed magazine on tape. In addition, a library of sound, covering a wide variety of subjects, is available to all members. Annual subscription (UK) £3.50.

Muriel Braddick Foundation (incorporating Tapes for the Handicapped Association)
14 Teign Street, Teignmouth, South Devon (Tel: Teignmouth (062 67) 6214).
The Foundation seeks to enrich the lives of housebound and isolated handicapped people by providing specially prepared cassette tapes directed to the specific tastes and interests of the recipient, and, where necessary, easily handled cassette recorders. For those who do not possess such machines, and are unable to provide them for themselves or with the assistance of social services departments, the Foundation provides recorders on a free loan basis. These may be either battery or mains operated. The organisation has a number of county branches and publishes a magazine *Focus* (20p per copy plus postage and packing).

Membership: not less than £2 per annum (which includes *Focus*).

Surrey Tapes for the Handicapped Association
Mrs Jean Woodiwiss, 34 Tudor Close, Cheam, Surrey.
This Association was formed under the Muriel Braddick Foundation and is now a registered charity in its own right. Sixty-minute cassettes are circulated among members. The Association could be described as a talking family circle intended for the housebound who have difficulty communicating because of their isolation.

Tape Programmes for the Blind
President/Founder: Maurice Chambers, 'Kingsmead', Blackfirs Lane, Marston Green, Solihull, West Midlands B37 7JE (Tel: 021-779 3202).
Offers cassettes from a large library of recorded material and opportunities for joining a growing circle of people keeping contact by round-robin conversation tapes. There is no subscription, but voluntary donations are always welcome. All material is post free in both directions. The founder is a former RAF squadron leader who would be interested to hear from any ex-Service personnel who are visually handicapped, as well as civilians.

World-wide Evangelical Tape Fellowship
Secretary: Mike Cox, 99 Pilgrim's Way, Kemsing, nr Sevenoaks, Kent TN15 6TD (Tel: Sevenoaks (0732) 61447).
The Fellowship has an extensive library of tape cassettes relating to the Christian religion, including Bible studies, church services, music and books. These tapes are available to members on free loan. Further tapes are circulated at regular intervals throughout the year, and members are encouraged to correspond, by tape or letter, on a personal basis.

Membership is restricted to people who are 'sincere believers in the Christian faith' who must adhere to an 11-point fundamentalist 'Declaration of Faith' prescribed by the Fellowship. Minimum annual subscription £1.50.

World-wide Tapetalk
Secretary: Charles Towers, 35 The Gardens, West Harrow, Middlesex HA1 4HE.
This organisation aims to promote, through exchang-

ing tapes (cassette or open-reel), contacts and friendships between people of all nationalities – able-bodied or disabled, no distinction is made. On joining the club a member receives the latest comprehensive *Tape Station Directory*, hints on successful tape-talking, a copy of the magazine *Sound Advice*, and a personal tape station identification card. Annual membership is £4 plus £1 enrolment fee.

Religious Tapes

Bible Society
Publishing Division, Stonehill Green, Westlea, Swindon SN5 7DG (Tel: Swindon (0793) 486381).
Produces the New Testament (Good News Bible) on 23 cassettes. Price £2.99 per cassette (inc. VAT). The entire set is available in a presentation case for £65.55 (inc. VAT). Orders under £5 add handling charge 80p. Postage and packing are not charged.

One
8 Dukes Close, North Weald, Epping, Essex CM16 6DA.
A quarterly Christian magazine with articles, book reviews, pen friends, tape library, etc. Normally printed, but available on tape. Price 46p plus large s.a.e. Tapes are also loaned from a tape library for cost of postage.

The Torch Trust for the Blind
Torch House, Hallaton, Market Harborough, Leicestershire LE16 8UJ (Tel: Hallaton (085 889) 301).
The Trust extends its facilities to those who are registered blind or partially sighted, and will supply Christian literature in braille, Moon type, very large print and on small cassettes and Talking Book Cassettes. Lending library facilities for these and magazines are free. There is, however, a nominal charge for some of the literature. There are Torch Fellowship groups all over the country for both blind and sighted people, which meet usually once a month, whenever possible in an easily accessible room. A one-year course is run for young (aged 18 to 30) visually handicapped people to encourage them to use their time in Christian service.

Talking Address Book
A system based on two C60 cassettes with pre-recorded alphabetical cues which allow the user to record information such as telephone numbers and addresses in sequential sections. Instructions for use are also pre-recorded. Available from The Royal National Institute for the Blind, 224 Great Portland Street, London W1N 6AA (Tel: 01-388 1266), price £1.20 per pair.

Talking Books for the Handicapped (National Listening Library)
12 Lant Street, London SE1 1QR (Tel: 01-407 9417).
A registered charity which provides a postal library of books recorded on long-playing cassettes for handicapped people who are unable to read a book for reasons other than blindness. There is a long list of books covering a wide range of interests, including books for children. Members are asked to contribute £15 a year towards the costs of the service. Further information from the above address.

Taped Books

British Library of Tape Recordings for Hospital Patients
12 Lant Street, London SE1 1QR (Tel: 01-407 9417).
Operates a scheme to provide taped books for patients in hospital.

British Talking Book Service for the Blind
Mount Pleasant, Wembley, Middlesex HA0 1RR (Tel: 01-903 6666).
Books representative of those available in public libraries are recorded by professional readers in the RNIB's own studios. Membership of the Talking Book Library service is open to any visually handicapped person who can provide a certificate from a consultant ophthalmologist, ophthalmic optician or family doctor to the effect that the applicant has defective reading vision (N12 or worse with spectacles). Persons registered as blind with their local authority do not have to provide this certificate. An annual subscription is payable; this includes the free loan of the play-back machine and its maintenance. Contact the Wembley address for further details. (For the Student Tape Library *see* Section 6.)

Calibre
Aylesbury, Buckinghamshire HP20 1HU (Tel: Aylesbury (0296) 32339).
Calibre is a lending library of books on standard compact cassettes for anyone who cannot read printed books either through poor sight or through difficulty in handling or reading. Members use their own cassette recorders and receive book cassettes by post. There is also a free quarterly cassette magazine with Calibre news, book reviews and articles of general interest. Through the magazine, members can contact each other, make friends and form clubs.

No subscription is charged for ordinary membership (though donations are always needed). Applications should be accompanied by a doctor's certificate confirming that you are unable to read printed books in the ordinary way.

In Touch
The BBC's *In Touch* book is available on tape from Tape Recording Service for the Blind (*see* page 65 and Appendix for details).

Jewish Guild for the Blind
15 West 65 Street, New York, NY 10023, USA.
The Guild has an extensive cassette library of current works of fiction and non-fiction, with particular emphasis on books not easily obtained elsewhere. The books are recorded on standard cassettes. The service is free and the loan period is up to 90 days. Further details and a catalogue in ink print available from the Librarian, Bruce Massis.

Tape Magazines and Newspapers

The Alternative Talking Newspapers Collective (ATNC)
Box 35, 136 Kingsland High Street, London E8 2NS.
Frustrated by the unaware censorship of their reading matter, a group of blind people and sighted allies have formed a collective to produce two magazines on tape: *Left Out*, a collection of articles from the Left and Alternative Press, and *Women Tape Over*, a magazine for blind women interested in feminism.

Association of Talking Newspapers in Northern Ireland
Secretary: Peter Craddock, 36 Circular Road, Castlerock, Co. Londonderry, Northern Ireland.
The Association was founded in 1980 to unite organisations in Northern Ireland which undertake the systematic provision of news and other material by recorded tapes to those who are blind or find conventional reading a strain. Meetings and workshops are arranged and advice is available to new groups.

Birmingham Tapes for the Handicapped Association
Honorary Secretary: Derek L. Hunt, 20 Middleton Hall Road, Kings Norton, Birmingham B30 1BY (Tel: 021-459 4874).
This Association sends out a regular monthly magazine on tape (reel or cassette) all over the British Isles and overseas on a round-robin basis. Its contents include stories, poems, news, interviews and music. There is a 25p registration fee on joining, plus a membership fee of 50p payable annually. A free tape library service is now available to members.

Blind Centre for Northern Ireland (The)
65 Eglantine Avenue, Belfast BT9 6EW (Tel: Belfast (0232) 664544).
The Blind Centre provides information through its tape magazines on free C90 cassettes. *Soundvision*

Ulster is distributed throughout the Province, in Eire and to others now living on the mainland. The magazine is sent monthly to over 700 recipients and deals with sport, cooking, drama, yoga and an Ulster news round-up. *New Dimension* is specially designed for visually handicapped teenagers.

Global Radio Blind Services
4 Claremont Road, Folkestone, Kent CT20 1DL.
This service started in 1960 and offers members a stereo or mono sound magazine once a month. A world-wide, free service is provided and discounts can be negotiated on blank tapes (o/r and cassette) and component parts. Life membership £2.

In Touch
The BBC's *In Touch* quarterly bulletin is available on tape from Tape Recording Service for the Blind (*see* page 65 and Appendix A for details).

Link Up
Trevor Rathbone, 55 High Street, Lower Easton, Bristol BS5 6DW (Tel: Bristol (0272) 520398).
Link Up produces a monthly tape-recorded magazine for disabled and lonely people. This includes stories, music, interviews and information on aids and services for people with disabilities. Religious items are also featured and a large number of members are of the Christian faith.

There is no membership fee, but members are encouraged to support the work by making donations from time to time.

National Tape Magazine for the Blind
Lilac Cottage, Moorhouses, New Bolingbroke, Lincs PE22 7JL (Tel: Coningsby (0526) 42918).
NTM was formed in November 1976 in an effort to keep isolated visually handicapped people in touch with developments in services, aids, etc. A tape magazine is sent out at monthly intervals (except August) and this is supplemented by a weekly library service of features which are too long for the magazine tape.

The editor, W. F. Cox, is himself blind. Cassettes are despatched in wallets containing a reversible 'Articles for the Blind' label so that postage is free. Subscription to the magazine is £1.25 per annum, and to the supplementary library service £1.50 per annum.

Possibility
Contact: Mike Tennison, 31A Northfield Close, West End, South Cave, Brough, North Humberside (Tel: North Cave (043 02) 2809).
This is the quarterly magazine of *Sequal* (*see* page 326) and is available on tape.

Radio Churchtown/Radio Camelot
2 High Park Road, Southport, Merseyside PR9 7QL (Tel: Southport (0704) 28010).
Provides a number of tape services on cassettes to blind and other handicapped people; music for the blind, light music, short stories, plays and humour; science news, folk and popular music of Russia – from various short-wave radio stations; thrillers and documentaries; plus music from the BBC, Radio Israel and Voice of America. A completely free service. Applications to the Director, Derek Mills.

Soundaround
61 Church Road, Barnes, London SW13 (Tel: 01-741 3332).
Launched in 1975, *Soundaround* is a national news magazine for visually handicapped people, produced monthly on compact cassette. It now reaches up to 30,000 listeners throughout Britain. *Soundaround*'s editor, Nigel Verbeek, himself blind, is a well-known broadcaster. He brings together a fascinating combination of news, views, letters, hobbies, pen-pals, features and celebrity spots. Above all, the magazine is in tune with its listeners and the issues which affect them. *Soundaround* is available entirely free to visually handicapped people.

The Talking Newspaper Association
Secretary: Cyril Cocks, 130 Chester Road, Watford, Herts (Tel: home, Watford (0923) 46621; work, 01-951 3811).
Voluntary groups in over 300 areas in the United Kingdom produce cassette versions of local newspapers and magazines for distribution to visually and physically handicapped people in the area.
Tape versions of Sunday newspapers and *Radio Times* are produced on a national basis.

Commercial Recordings

A number of voluntary organisations produce tape cassettes either in specialist areas of interest on a 'home-made' magazine/news basis and we include a selection of these. But by far the widest range of interest is provided by professionally made, commercially marketed tape cassettes which are readily available to mail order or can frequently be borrowed from public libraries. The best guide to the vast amount of material which is available is provided by the publications of General Gramophone Publications Ltd, 177–179 Kenton Road, Harrow, Middlesex HA3 0HA (Tel: 01-907 4476), *viz.*
Gramophone, a monthly magazine founded in 1923, price 70p.

Gramophone Classical Catalogue, quarterly £2 (£2.55 by post).
Gramophone Popular Catalogue, quarterly and cumulative, March 50p, June 70p, September 90p, December £1.40 (then starts again) (postage and packing extra).
Gramophone Spoken Word Catalogue, annual £1.50 (£1.77 by post).
Gramophone Recommended Recordings, £1 (£1.22 by post).

TalkTapes
13 Croftdown Road, London NW5 1EL (Tel: 01-485 9981).
TalkTapes supplies a very wide range of educational, spoken word and entertainment recordings on standard compact cassettes. The general catalogue covers poetry, drama, fiction, critical studies, English and foreign languages, religion, science, business studies, radio comedy, etc. from leading audio publishers. Many additional special lists provide more detailed subject listings.
All items are for sale (no loan service). Mail order only. Send two 13p stamps for catalogue and full details of service. Terms: cash with order (special terms to organisations).

Reading Services

GENERAL SERVICES

A number of local voluntary organisations for the blind are known to be prepared to record material for blind people in their area.
Many other voluntary societies may well be able to help with reading on to tape or cassette, and we are sure that they will always respond helpfully to any reasonable request. If you are uncertain of where to contact your nearest society, ask the RNIB, 224 Great Portland Street, London W1N 6AA (Tel: 01-388 1266).

SPECIALIST SERVICES

If, as a blind student, you need whole books to be recorded, you should contact the RNIB Student Tape Library (*see* page 108).

ADA Reading Services for the Blind, 12 Renhold Road, Wilden, Bedford MK44 2QA (Tel: Bedford (0234) 771693).
This is a family service set up to encourage visually handicapped people to enjoy their work and their hobbies and to live as normal a life as possible. The founders believe that it is extremely important to facilitate communication between blind and/or handicapped and sighted persons.

There are now many readers available in the service agreeable to record anything, from religious works to computer manuals, including books in some foreign languages. Requests should be accompanied by a blank cassette(s) of suitable length and a self-addressed label. Audrey Artus reads the CPSA magazine for blind civil servants each month and sends out some hundred taped copies.

The service is also responsible for the copying of the cassettes for members of the Cassette Library for Blind Gardeners (more information on this society can be obtained from Mrs A. Artus at the above address in response to a s.a.e. *Gardening without Sight* is available to everyone, whether members or not. Requests for copies should be sent to the above address with two C90 cassettes and a s.a.e. All services are free.

Express Reading Service (RNIB), Tarporley Recording Centre, 79 High Street, Tarporley, Cheshire CW6 0AB (Tel: Tarporley (082 93) 2115 or 2729). This service offers to record and send back an hour's recording by return of post. In the case of longer items, the service tries to record an hour a day until the reading is completed. Material may be connected with work, study, or leisure pursuits: the only rule for acceptance is that rapid access to the material is really needed and cannot wait for one of the other tape reading organisations to deal with it.

If you think that this service might be of use, write or telephone the Centre, giving some idea of the type and length of material you would want read, and the likely frequency of your requests. The Centre will let you know if it has the capacity to deal with your needs (do not send in material without this preliminary contact).

Items can be recorded on cassette at standard or half-speed, on two or four tracks, and can add tone-indexing. The Centre will record on your own C60 or C90 cassettes or can provide good quality tapes at very moderate cost. There is no charge for the actual recording, though any donations towards running costs are most gratefully received.

RNIB Customer Liaison Unit, Braille House, 338–346 Goswell Road, London EC1V 7JE (Tel: 01-837 9921).
Distinct from the British Talking Book Service (*see* page 276) which issues catalogued 'talking books', and the Student Braille and Tape Libraries which also lend particular titles from their stocks, the RNIB Customer Liaison Unit serves as a *producer* of required material in braille or on tape. It acts as the first point of contact between the clients and other services, and all requests for books and other material, apart from stock 'talking book' items are dealt with by the Unit.

The Unit is very much involved in producing material for individual needs, but the response to requests is, of course, constrained by limited resources, and a blanket 'on demand' service cannot realistically be offered.

The Unit is also building up a bibliographical record of all material available in braille or on tape throughout the world, including the considerable resources of the United States Library of Congress and Recording for the Blind Inc. Though this information will be (indeed already is) far too vast ever to be put into any sort of comprehensive catalogue or series of catalogues which can be made available to the public, it will none the less provide an invaluable resource, identifying the growing body of literature available to blind people under appropriate subject headings.

Tape Recording Service for the Blind
48 Fairfax Road, Farnborough, Hampshire GU14 8JP (Tel: Farnborough (0252) 547943).
The Service undertakes to record on to cassette any printed material for visually handicapped individuals, with the exception of party political work or religion. Fiction will be accepted only when it is required for personal study or is not available in the current libraries. The scope runs from instruction manuals for domestic appliances to text book and study courses.

Printed matter for recording should be sent to the above address, together with sufficient tapes or cassettes and a self-addressed label for the return of work.

The work is forwarded to a volunteer reader, who will record and return it as soon as possible. Personal or confidential papers are given special attention.

Certain material is kept in readiness for copying or supply including holiday phrase language courses in French, German, Italian, and Spanish; touch typing; braille; the *Radio Amateurs Examination Manual*; the BBC Handbook *In Touch*, the *In Touch* quarterly bulletin; and *New Beacon*, the monthly journal of the RNIB.

Details of any specific item can be obtained by sending a s.a.e. There is no specific charge for carrying out work, although voluntary donations are always acceptable. Copies of works will be supplied for the cost of the cassettes.

Tape Services

Foundation for Audio Research and Services for Blind People

12 Netley Dell, Letchworth, Herts SG6 2TF (Tel: Letchworth (046 26) 74052).

This Foundation, in conjunction with the Audio Reading Trust, offers high quality compact cassettes specially designed for blind people. They have tactile markings to indicate tape length and are sold at substantial concessionary prices, being zero-rated for VAT. Please send s.a.e. for price list and VAT exemption certificate for blind people or organisations serving their needs to the Audio Reading Trust, Spirella Building, Bridge Road, Letchworth, Herts SG6 4ET (Tel: 046 26 77331 – Supplies Department).

A range of variable-speed tape recorders and accessories is also available from the Audio Reading Trust. It includes the American Printing House variable speed, four-track recorder which has tone-indexing and allows for eight hours' recording on an ART 2 C105 cassette. It also accepts standard cassettes and those recorded in the US Library of Congress format, essential for students wishing to join the Recording for the Blind Inc., 215 East 58th Street, New York, NY 10022, USA.

This cassette recorder also enables visually handicapped school children to assimilate information more rapidly and improves retention of the material. The multi-track facility allows questions recorded by a teacher to be answered by a pupil without any danger of obliterating the original recording.

Tape Services to the Blind and Physically Handicapped in England and Wales by Catherine Ireland, published by LLRS Publications (1980). This is a 'study of user requirement and existing provision'. It contains basic information on the handicapped reader, libraries, broadcasting, copyright, postal regulations, etc., together with a directory of all known tape services and indexes of taped journals and places (now somewhat out of date: *see* TNAUK Tape Information Service on page 274). Available from the publisher at City of London Polytechnic, Calcutta House Precinct, Old Castle Street, London E1 7NT (Tel: 01-283 1030). Price (prepaid only) £10 (£5 to blind or physically handicapped people or organisations concerned with them).

INFORMATION, LEGAL AND ADVISORY SERVICES

Information Services

Most organisations of and for disabled people run some sort of information service, usually geared to their specific areas of concern. Some of these are sophisticated and highly responsive, and the reader is referred to Section 16, Helpful Organisations, for details of the services available. In this section we mention those information services which have a more general function, unrelated to particular disabilities.

DIAL-UK – National Association of Disablement Information and Advice Services
DIAL House, 117 High Street, Clay Cross, Chesterfield, Derbyshire S45 9DZ (Tel: Chesterfield (0246) 864498): *see also* Section 16, Helpful Organisations. DIALs are autonomous local self-help groups of disabled people with the primary aim of providing information for other disabled people or those concerned with disability. At the time of writing, the following groups are known:

List of groups

	Hours of opening
DIAL ABERDEEN, Denburn Health Centre (Room 64), Rosemount Viaduct, Aberdeen AB1 1QB (Tel: Aberdeen (0224) 634786).	2 p.m. to 4 p.m. Tuesday and Thursday 11 a.m. to 1 p.m. Wednesday
AYRSHIRE Information on Disablement Service, Carrick Street Halls, Ayr (Tel: Ayr (0292) 264716/ 262872).	2 p.m. to 4.30 p.m. and 7.30 p.m. to 8.30 p.m. Mondays 6.30 p.m. to 8.30 p.m. Wednesday
DIAL BANGOR, 372 High Street, Bangor, Gwynedd (Tel: Bangor (0248) 52197).	10 a.m. to 5 p.m. Monday to Friday
BIRMINGHAM Handicapped Children's Information Service, 260 Broad Street, Birmingham B1 2HF (Tel: 021-643 6267).	9 a.m. to 5 p.m. Monday to Friday
DIAL BLACKBURN, Mill Hill Day Centre, Mill Hill Street, Mill Hill, Blackburn, Lancs (Tel: Blackburn (0254) 64004).	10 a.m. to 4 p.m. Monday to Friday

	Hours of opening
DIAL BRADFORD, 103 Dockfield Road, Shipley, West Yorkshire BD17 7AR (Tel: Bradford (0274) 594173).	10.30 a.m. to 3.30 p.m. Monday to Friday
BRIGHTON – CWISH, (The Charley White Information Service for the Handicapped), 8 Hawkins Close, Shoreham-by-Sea, West Sussex (Tel: Shoreham-by-Sea (0273) 593322).	Day-time answering service which gives a number to phone in the evenings between 6 p.m. and 9 p.m.
BRISTOL Disabled Advice Centre, 127 Pembroke Road, Clifton, Bristol 8 (Tel: Bristol (0272) 733282).	9.30 a.m. to 4.30 p.m. Monday, Tuesday and Thursday 9.30 a.m. to 1 p.m. Wednesday and Friday
DIAL BUCKS, Tindal Hospital, Tindal Road, Aylesbury, Bucks HP20 1HU (Tel: Aylesbury (0296) 33937).	10 a.m. to 4 p.m. Monday, Wednesday and Friday
BURY Disabled Advisory Service, 12 St George's Court, Unsworth, Bury (Tel: 061-796 7077).	10 a.m. to 4 p.m. Monday, Wednesday and Friday 7 p.m. to 9 p.m. Tuesday and Thursday
CARDIFF The Disabled Person's Information Service, 45 Park Place, Cardiff CS1 33B (Tel: Cardiff (0222) 398058).	10 a.m. to 4.30 p.m. Monday to Friday
DIAL CORBY, The Stonehouse, South Road, Corby, Northants (Tel: Corby (053 63) 4742).	10 a.m. to 12 noon and 2 p.m. to 4 p.m. Monday, Tuesday and Friday 10 a.m. to 12 noon Wednesday 2 p.m. to 4 p.m. Thursday
CORNWALL Hi-Line, 56 Lemon Street, Truro TR1 2PE, Cornwall (Tel: Truro (0872) 2314).	1 p.m. to 5 p.m. Monday to Friday
DIAL COVENTRY, c/o Mrs P. Orson, 159 Belgrave Road, Coventry (Tel: Coventry (0203) 612890, ansaphone).	10 a.m. to 12 noon and 2 p.m. to 4 p.m. Monday to Friday

Hours of opening

DIAL CWMBRAN, Disability Advice Centre, c/o CEP Association, 17 Caradog Road, Cwmbran, Gwent (Tel: Cwmbran (063 33) 62951).

9 a.m. to 5 p.m. Monday to Friday

DIAL DAVENTRY, The Welfare Foundation Centre, New Street, Daventry, Northants (Tel: Daventry (032 72) 4223).

11 a.m. to 4 p.m. Tuesday to Friday

DIAL DERBYSHIRE, Cressy Fields, Cressy Road, Alfreton, Derbyshire (Tel: Alfreton (0773) 833220).

9 a.m. to 5 p.m. Monday to Friday

DIAL DUMFRIES AND GALLOWAY, Loreburn Hall, Newall Terrace, Dumfries (Tel: Dumfries (0387) 65599).

10 a.m. to 4 p.m. Monday to Friday

DIAL ESSEX, 90 Broomfield Road, Chelmsford, Essex CM1 1SS (Tel: Chelmsford (0245) 87177).

10 a.m. to 4 p.m. Monday to Friday Answering service after 4 p.m.

EXETER Disability Rights Advisory Service, 3 Palace Gate, Exeter, Devon (Tel: Exeter (0392) 59336).

2 p.m. to 4.30 p.m. Monday to Friday

DIAL GLENROTHES, Preston Centre, Glenrothes, Fife (Tel: Glenrothes (0592) 753891).

10 a.m. to 4 p.m. Monday to Friday

DIAL GRANGEMOUTH AND DISTRICT, c/o Grangemouth Community Council, Station Road, Grangemouth FK3 8DG (Tel: Grangemouth (0324) 483386).

10 a.m. to 4 p.m. Wednesday

DIAL HARLOW, Aneurin Bevan Centre, Garden Terrace Road, Harlow, Essex (Tel: Harlow (0279) 412020).

10 a.m. to 4 p.m. Monday to Friday

HULL Disability Rights Advisory Service, Crown Chambers, Land of Green Ginger, Hull HU1 2EN (Tel: Hull (0482) 226234).

9.45 a.m. to 4 p.m. Monday to Friday

DIAL KENT, 7 Victoria Road, Canterbury, Kent (Tel: Canterbury (0227) 50001).

10 a.m. to 4 p.m. Monday, Tuesday and Friday
4 p.m. to 8 p.m. Thursday

DIAL LEEDS, The William Merritt Centre, St Mary's Hospital, Green Hill Road, Leeds 12 (Tel: Leeds (0532) 795583).

10.30 a.m. to 3.30 p.m. Monday to Friday

DIAL LEICESTERSHIRE, Medical Aid Department, 76 Clarendon Park Road, Leicester LE2 3AD (Tel: Leicester (0533) 700666).

10 a.m. to 4 p.m. Monday to Friday

DIAL LIVINGSTON, Braid House, Morriss Square, Almondvale, Livingston, West Lothian (Tel: Livingston (0506) 414472).

10 a.m. to 4 p.m. Monday to Friday

LONDON – ARCH (Advice and Rights Centre for the Handicapped), St John's Day Centre, 113 St John's

10.30 a.m. to 3.30 p.m. Monday to Friday

Hours of opening

Way, London N19 3RS (Tel: 01-263 8622).

LONDON Handicapped Help Line, c/o Community Links, 81 High Street South, East Ham, London E6 (Tel: 01-472 6652).

7 p.m. to 9 p.m. Monday to Friday

LONDON – Lambeth Disabled Advice Phone-in Service, c/o A. Higgins, 115 Clapham Road, London SW9 (Tel: 01-582 4352).

1 p.m. to 3 p.m. Tuesday and Thursday

LONDON – DIAL Waltham Forest, Old School Building, 1A Warner Road, Walthamstow, London E17 (Tel: 01-520 4111).

10 a.m. to 4 p.m. Monday to Friday

LONDON – Wandsworth Disablement Advice Service, Atheldene Centre, 305 Garrett Lane, London SW18 (Tel: 01-870 7437).

10 a.m. to 4 p.m. Monday to Friday

MANCHESTER Telephone Advice Bureau, c/o Community Development Section, Solway House, Aytoun Street, Manchester (Tel: 061-228 211 ext. 200).

1 p.m. to 5 p.m. Monday to Friday

MANSFIELD Council for Voluntary Service, Community House, 36 Wood Street, Mansfield, Nottinghamshire NG18 1QA (Tel: Mansfield (0623) 25891/2).

10 a.m. to 4 p.m. Monday to Friday

DIAL MERTHYR TYDFIL, c/o Ty Gwyn Day Centre, Church Street, Merthyr Tydfil, Mid Glamorgan (Tel: Merthyr Tydfil (0685) 79769).

10 a.m. to 4 p.m. Tuesday and Friday

MIDDLESBROUGH Rehabilitation Information Service, The Information Centre, Middlesbrough General Hospital, Ayresome Green Lane, Middlesbrough, Cleveland TS5 5AZ (Tel: Middlesbrough (0642) 813133 ext. 133).

10 a.m. to 4 p.m. Monday to Friday

DIAL MIDDLETON AND DISTRICT, Parkfield Parish Hall, Sarah Street, Middleton, Nr Manchester (Tel: 061-653 2729).

11 a.m. to 4.30 p.m. Monday to Friday

DIAL MIDHURST, The Court House, Grange Road, Midhurst, Sussex (Tel: Midhurst (073 081) 3962).

10 a.m. to 4 p.m. Tuesday

DIAL MID SUSSEX, The Health Centre (Room 213), Heath Road, Haywards Heath, West Sussex RH16 3BB (Tel: Haywards Heath (0444) 416619).

10 a.m. to 4 p.m. Tuesday and Friday
2 p.m. to 4 p.m. Wednesday

DIAL NEWCASTLE UPON TYNE, Mea House, Ellison Place, Newcastle upon Tyne NE1 8XS (Tel: Newcastle upon Tyne (0632) 323617).

10 a.m. to 4 p.m. Monday to Friday

DIAL NEWPORT, 78 Chepstow Road, Newport, Gwent (Tel: Newport (0633) 58212).

9.30 a.m. to 4.30 p.m. Tuesday to Friday

Hours of opening

ASK NORWICH (Advice for Handicapped Children Only), Gaffers Cottage, Grange Farm, Spixworth, Norfolk (Tel: Norwich (0603) 51061).

24-hour service. Seven days a week. The operator will give an alternative number on certain days.

NUNEATON AND BEDWORTH Council for the Disabled, 17 Newtown Road, Nuneaton, Warwicks (Tel: Nuneaton (0203) 349954).

10 a.m. to 4 p.m. Monday to Friday

DIAL OXFORD, Ritchie Russell House, Churchill Hospital, Headington, Oxford (Tel: Oxford (0865) 750190).

2 p.m. to 5 p.m. Monday to Friday

DIAL PERTH, Letham Clinic, Marlee Road, Off Rannoch Road, Perth, Tayside (Tel: Perth (0738) 36358).

11 a.m. to 3 p.m. Monday, Thursday and Friday

DIAL PORTSMOUTH AND DISTRICT, Disabled Living Centre, Prince Albert Road, Southsea, Hants (Tel: Portsmouth (0705) 824853).

10 a.m. to 3 p.m. Monday, Wednesday and Friday

DIAL ROTHERHAM, Central Library, Walker Place, Rotherham (Tel: Rotherham (0709) 73658).

10 a.m. to 3 p.m. Monday to Friday

DIAL SHEFFIELD, Park Grange, 100 Park Grange Road, Sheffield S2 3RA (Tel: Sheffield (0742) 27996).

11.30 a.m. to 3 p.m. Tuesday to Friday

DIAL SOMERSET, 8 Albemarle Road, Taunton, Somerset (Tel: Taunton (0823) 78067).

10 a.m. to 4 p.m. Tuesday to Friday

SOUTHAMPTON Help for Health, South Academic Block, Southampton General Hospital, Southampton SO9 4XY (Tel: Southampton (0703) 777222 ext. 3753).

9 a.m. to 5 p.m. Monday to Thursday
9 a.m. to 4.30 p.m. Friday

STOCKPORT Telephone Advice Bureau, c/o Mr J. E. Luke, Metropolitan Borough of Stockport, Liaison Group of Volunteers, c/o Social Services Division, Town Hall, Stockport SK1 3XE (Tel: 061-480 0101).

1 p.m. to 5 p.m. Monday to Friday

DIAL STOKE-ON-TRENT, 25 Regent Road, Hanley, Stoke-on-Trent (Tel: Stoke-on-Trent (0782) 279149).

10 a.m. to 4 p.m. Monday to Friday

DIAL SUNDERLAND, 241 Southwick Road, Sunderland (Tel: Sunderland (0783) 492844).

9 a.m. to 5 p.m. Monday to Friday

TAMWORTH Support and Advice for the Disabled, Tamworth Youth Centre, Spinning School Lane, Tamworth (Tel: Tamworth (0827) 66393).

2 p.m. to 4 p.m. Monday only

SOUTH TYNESIDE Disablement Advisory Service, 25 Flagg Court, South Shields NE33 2LS (Tel: South Shields (0632) 540232).

10 a.m. to 4 p.m. Monday to Friday

DIAL WEST LANCS, c/o Mrs C.

1 p.m. to 5 p.m.

Hours of opening

Jones, 13 Cobbs Brow Lane, Newburgh, Wigan, Lancs (Tel: Wigan (025 76) 2761/3921).

Monday to Friday

DIAL WESTON SUPER MARE, 5 Roselawn, Walliscote Road, Weston-super-Mare, Avon BS23 1UJ (Tel: Weston-super-Mare (0934) 419426).

2 p.m. to 4 p.m. Tuesday and Thursday

DIAL WIGAN, Heath Road Day Centre, Ashton-in-Makerfield, Wigan, Lancs (Tel: Wigan (0942) 714111).

10.30 a.m. to 3.30 p.m. Monday to Friday

DIAL WREKIN, c/o Mr E. Harvey, 21 Haybridge Avenue, Hadley, Telford (Tel: Telford (0952) 48376).

9 a.m. to 4 p.m. Monday to Friday

The Disability Alliance Educational and Research Association
25 Denmark Street, London WC2 8NJ (Tel: 01-240 0806).
See Section 2 for a general note. The Alliance operates a Welfare Rights Information Service which offers free advice and information on social security matters. Enquiries, from 2 p.m. to 4.30 p.m. by telephone, or in writing. The Alliance publishes the well known and much respected *Disability Rights Handbook* (£2 post-free) which is particularly useful in dealing with the complexities of benefits and allowances.

Disabled Living Foundation
380–384 Harrow Road, London W9 2HU (Tel: 01-289 6111).
The DLF provides a comprehensive information service for those professionally concerned with disabled people, voluntary organisations and other groups and individuals requiring up-to-date information. It is particularly strong on aids (*see* page 53) but also covers all relevant aspects of disability, with specialist advice in the areas of incontinence, clothing, visual impairment, music, physical recreation and skin.

Information is provided free of charge to occasional enquirers, or, if sought on a regular basis, against an annual subscription. Subscribers to the service receive a complete set of information lists and subsequent bi-monthly bulletins. The lists are regularly updated.

Any member of a subscribing group is entitled to make unlimited use of the enquiry service. Enquiries on any relevant subject, except purely medical matters, are answered by telephone or letter with any appropriate trade literature or information. Subscribers are also entitled to borrow DLF publications.

NOTE: A slide set is available from Graves Medical Audiovisual Library which describes the work of the DLF Information Service – how the information is collected, stored and made available to users.

Greater London Association for Disabled People
1 Thorpe Close, London W10 5XL (Tel: 01-960 5799).
Primarily concerned with handicapped people in the Greater London area, GLAD's information service also covers a range of national news about services and facilities for disabled people. Information on benefits, aids, housing, employment, parking, education, insurance, services for the blind and social activities is made available to association secretaries, voluntary and statutory agencies, and individual applicants.

Health Education Council
78 New Oxford Street, London WC1A 1AH (Tel: 01-637 1881).
See Section 16 for a general note. The HEC has an information service on all health-related matters which is available to individual enquirers, and maintains an excellent library and resources centre. A free publications catalogue lists and illustrates the many leaflets and posters which are available, and resource lists are available on a variety of subjects including one under the title *Handicap*.

Help for Health: Patient Care Information Service
Wessex Regional Library Unit, South Academic Block, Southampton General Hospital, Southampton SO9 4XY (Tel: Southampton (0703) 777222 ext. 3753; Southampton (0703) 779091 (24-hour Ansaphone)).
A resource centre of information to enable patients to understand health problems, to look after themselves and to make full use of the help available from statutory and voluntary sources. Although primarily a local service it will deal with enquiries from elsewhere and is greatly respected for its expertise.

Help for Health provides an enquiry service by telephone, letter or personal visit. The centre keeps addresses of voluntary organisations and self-help groups, both national and regional, and has a large collection of relevant literature. It publishes a regular newsletter, and will compile information sheets on request.

An information series has been devised to provide information on a range of disease or handicap categories. The general plan of each is to list organisations of direct relevance to the subject field; then to give an annotated list of publications (books, leaflets, audio-visual materials) which are easily available and written for patients; and finally a brief list of suggested background reading. The following titles are available: *Diabetics* (1/78) 50p; *Stroke* (9/78) 50p; *The Hearing Impaired* (11/78) 50p; *Paraplegics* (10/79) 50p; *Cystic Fibrosis* (3/80) 50p; *Breast Cancer*

(1/81) £1.50; *Migraine and Headaches* (10/81) £1.50; *Haemophilia* (11/81) £1; *Epilepsy* (10/82) £1.50; *Multiple Sclerosis* (10/82) £1.50; *Premenstrual Syndrome* (10/82) £1.50.

Help for Health has also published a valuable information package under the title *Getting Started*, based on the experience of the Wessex Help for Health Information Service and directed towards all those involved in the provision of health information for patients and the public. It advises on the setting up of a basic collection of health information for patients, disabled people in the community and the public at large. It details what to collect, how much it costs, how to store the information, index it and retrieve it for use. Price £12.

The In Touch Scheme
Ann Worthington, 10 Norman Road, Sale, Cheshire M33 3DF (Tel: 061-962 4441).
This Scheme (not to be confused with the BBC's *In Touch* programme/book for blind people) was founded in March 1968 to provide contacts for parents of mentally handicapped children. Membership has grown steadily to include both parents and professionals and there is increasing emphasis on the provision of information, both through a quarterly newsletter and in response to specific requests. A useful handbook of addresses for parents with a handicapped child has recently been published, price £1 (*see* Appendix A).

Because the membership is both national and international, it is often possible to link families who have children affected by rare mental handicap conditions. Annual subscription: £2 for professionals, £1 for parents. The latter charge is, however, optional and no other charges are made.

NOTE: Ann Worthington is the author of *Coming to Terms with Mental Handicap* and *Glossary of Terms used in mental handicap and allied disorders* (*see* Appendix A for details).

Line 81 on Disability
252 Western Avenue, London W3 6XJ (Tel: 01-992 5522).
Line 81, which was set up initially as part of the International Year of Disabled People, is a nationwide public information service covering all aspects of disablement. It is organised by *Broadcasting Support Services* which has links with a wide range of television and radio programmes, and provides producers with back-up and research facilities as well as a follow up service for the individual viewer and listener. Individuals can contact Line 81 by telephone (any weekday between 9.30 a.m. to 5.30 p.m.) or letter (to Line 81, PO Box 7, London W3 6XJ) for information and advice. The service has access to

over 1,500 separate sources of help, both national and local, and will try to put you in touch with the organisation or local group best able to help you. Enquirers can also be referred to information services in other parts of the country.

Line 81 also publishes a series of leaflets for disabled people as follows:

1. *Guidance for Parents*:	information for the parents of mentally handicapped children including advice on how to set up a self-help group.
2. *Holidays*:	details of who to ask and where to look for advice on holidays for the physically and mentally handicapped, both in the United Kingdom and abroad.
3. *Benefits*:	a guide to the range of benefits and allowances for disabled people, plus further sources of help.
4. *Help with Projects*:	for school students and others who want more information about disablement.
5. *Sport and Recreation*:	lists activities open to disabled people, ways in which disabled people can participate together.
6. *Aid for the Hard of Hearing*:	information about lip-reading classes, aids, useful organisations, a simple loop system and other sources of help.
7. *Advice for Disabled Women*:	a practical guide to coping with the many difficulties faced by women who live at home.

Single or multiple copies of any leaflet are 20p each. Leaflets 1 to 5 are available as a set, 'Information for Disabled People', Price 85p a set or two sets for £1.50.

Further discounts on larger quantities are available on request.

Orders should be sent to Line 81, PO Box 7, London W3 6XJ.

Cheques or postal orders are to be made payable to *Broadcasting Support Services*.

Mobility Information Service
See Section 8.

Northern Ireland Information Service for Disabled People
2 Annadale Avenue, Belfast BT7 3JH (Tel: Belfast (0232) 640011).
Runs a comprehensive information service in Northern Ireland similar to that provided by the Disabled Living Foundation in England. For details *see* Section 3. An excellent newsletter.

Scottish Council on Disability, Information Department
5 Shandwick Place, Edinburgh EH2 4RG (Tel: 031-229 8632).
Runs a comprehensive information service in Scotland similar to that provided by the Disabled Living Foundation in England. For details *see* Section 3. An excellent newsletter.

Scottish Health Education Group
Woodburn House, Canaan Lane, Edinburgh EH10 4SG (Tel: 031-447 8044).
Fulfils a role in Scotland similar to that of the Health Education Council in England. For details *see* Section 16.

Scottish Telephone Referral Advice and Information Network
Dowanhill, 74 Victoria Crescent Road, Glasgow G12 9JQ (Tel: 041-357 1774).
A media-linked service similar to that offered by Broadcasting Support Services in England (*see* Line 81, page 284). Network acts as the referral agency for Scotland and has developed links with local referral points throughout Scotland so that enquirers responding to a broadcast on radio or television can be given information and passed on to the appropriate agency. Network works very closely with the Scottish Health Education Group, the Scottish Centre for the Tuition of the Disabled and the Scottish Council on Disability Information Service.

Wales Council for the Disabled (Cyngor Cymru i'r Anabl)
Caerbragdy Industrial Estate, Bedwas Road, Caerphilly, Mid Glamorgan CF8 3SL (Tel: Caerphilly (0222) 887325/6/7).
Among its activities, the Council has established an information service. Support is also being given to the establishment of a network of local disability advice centres throughout Wales. *See also* Section 16.

Legal Advice and Aid

Nowadays, no one need be deterred from seeking legal advice or assistance from a solicitor because their means are limited. Solicitors commonly offer general advice in special sessions at legal advice centres and law centres. Legal advice centres are staffed by volunteer lawyers and have limited opening hours, but offer a free service. Law centres are manned on a full-time basis by lawyers and ancillary staff. They will handle a client's case in the ordinary way, but normally also offer a free advice service.

(Legal Action Group, 28a Highgate Road, London NW5 1NS, publish a directory of all such centres in England, Wales, Scotland and Northern Ireland, price £1.25.)

Assistance of most kinds can also be sought from any solicitor operating under the legal aid system, and dependent on financial circumstances can be obtained either free of charge or against a contribution. Lists of solicitors willing to accept legal aid cases can be seen in public libraries, Citizens' Advice Bureaux, law centres, magistrates' and county courts, town hall information centres, housing advice centres or consumer advice centres.

Three free leaflets on legal aid have been prepared by the Central Office of Information, The Law Society and the Lord Chancellor's Department. These are *Legal Aid Guide, Legal Aid – Financial Limits* and *Legal Aid Could Help You*, available either from Citizens' Advice Bureaux, The Law Society or direct from the Central Office of Information, Publications Division (LH 502), Hercules Road, London SE1 7DU.

The Law Society

The Law Society's Hall, 113 Chancery Lane, London WC2A 1PL (Tel: 01-242 1222).

The Law Society is the solicitors' professional association representing the 41,500 practising solicitors in England and Wales. It administers the civil Legal Aid Scheme. The Society can help and advise persons who have a complaint as to the professional conduct of a solicitor; or who consider that a solicitor has made an excessive charge in non-contentious matters. The Legal Aid and Advice Scheme ensures that persons eligible under it may receive legal advice or assistance for nothing or for a substantially reduced charge. Additionally most solicitors throughout the country operate a 'fixed fee interview' scheme, whereby a person may have an initial diagnostic interview with a solicitor at a fee of £5.

For further information as to these and other services, contact The Law Society at the above address.

Lay Observer

Royal Courts of Justice, Strand, London WC2.
Complaints against solicitors that are rejected by the Law Society can be taken to the Lay Observer. Representations should be made in writing. There are separate Lay Observers, located in Edinburgh and Belfast, dealing with complaints about solicitors in Scotland and Northern Ireland respectively, *viz*:
Lay Observer for Scotland, 22 Melville Street, Edinburgh EH3 7NS.
The Lay Observer (NI), 64 Chichester Street, Belfast BT1 4JX.

Motoring Organisations

The AA and RAC give free legal assistance to members on relevant matters (*see* pages 155 and 158 for further information).

Network for the Handicapped

16 Princeton Street, London WC1R 4BB.
Network is a free law and advisory centre for disabled and handicapped people and their families. It was formed by various action groups in an attempt to clarify the legal rights and obligations which exist within present legislation and to give practical guidance to the implementation of those laws and directives.

Specialised help is given on all aspects of social security including: attendance allowances, mobility allowance, NCIP, dietary and heating allowances, exceptional needs payments, the Chronically Sick and Disabled Persons Act 1970, patients' rights, rights to elective surgery and the protection therefrom, bus passes, consumer rights, wills, trusts and settlements, charity law, etc., educational problems of juniors and adults.

The centre is open to any person, parent or guardian or relative who falls within the category catered for under the Mental Health Act and the Chronically Sick and Disabled Persons Act 1970 and any organisation directly involved in this field.

All problems within the law such as attendance allowance claims, etc., wills and trusts, neglect by authorities and ministries, etc., will be advised upon by lawyers. Other advisers will be present to give general guidance and apply their practical knowledge in informal chats, if required. Where the law is not enforced, Network will be able to help you. Network is open by appointment only during the day and on Thursdays from 7.30 p.m. For appointments please telephone Helen Berent on 01-831 7740. Thursday evening appointments are at Bedford House, 35 Emerald Street, London WC1.

Patients' Rights Handbook

A basic guide for mental patients, their relatives and friends, and professionals and volunteers working in the mental health field, published by MIND (*see* page 310) and available from its bookshop at 155-57 Woodhouse Lane, Leeds LS2 3EF, price £1.95, post and packing free. Written by MIND's former Legal Director, Larry Gostin, the Handbook offers a wealth of advice about self-advocacy and rights issues based on the MIND Legal Department's experience of maintaining an information service for patients over a period of six years.

The Handbook discusses informal and formal admission to hospital, Mental Health Review Tribunals, consent to treatment, rights in hospital and in the community, duties of social services and housing departments, and complaints procedures. It also includes a directory of advice and information centres, a list of suggested further reading and an explanation of the major psychiatric treatments.

In the Handbook, MIND is guided by the philosophy that patients are entitled to a high quality of life, that their dignity and legal status must be fully protected and that, if their rights are removed, they should have unqualified access to an independent review body. Patients, Larry Gostin believes, must be their own principal advocates. The Handbook pre-dates the Mental Health Act 1983 and the changes are of substance. However, MIND has prepared a series of leaflets on the new Act. A book is also available entitled *Mental Health: Tribunal Procedure*, price £8.95. (*See also* Section 13, page 263.)

Trade Unions and Professional Bodies
Provide advice and assistance to members, including, if necessary, representation by an advocate at tribunals.

You and Your Rights
Published by the Reader's Digest Association Ltd, price £13.95 including postage and packing. An A to Z guide to the law. Thousands of legal situations are illustrated and explained for the lay person.

Other Advisory Services

Accent Buyer's Guide – 1984/5 Edition
An American publication from Accent on Living (*see* Appendix B) providing information on products for disabled people. It gives US company names and addresses for over 450 items, cross-indexed under product names for easy reference, and backed up by a computerised retrieval system. Available from Accent Special Publications, Box 700, Bloomington, Illinois 61701, USA. Price $10 plus $1.15 postage and packing.

Citizens' Advice Bureau Service
Administrative Headquarters: National Association of Citizens' Advice Bureaux, 115/123 Pentonville Road, London N1.

Citizens' Advice Bureaux will advise on most subjects, often providing leaflets and pamphlets. They offer guidance on most simple preliminary legal matters, referring clients to a solicitor where necessary, or to their own legal sessions. They will supply the names of individuals or centres where legislative advice may be sought and obtained, and advice on the qualifying requirements for legal aid. They will also supply a list of solicitors who accept legal aid work. There are over 800 Citizens' Advice Bureaux, the addresses of which can be found in the telephone directory or at the library.

About one-third of Citizens' Advice Bureaux have facilities for specialist financial advice provided by chartered accountants under a voluntary aid programme run by the Institute of Chartered Accountants. The service is free to those who need financial advice but cannot afford to pay for professional help. Problems about income tax, hire purchase, mortgages, insurance, credit arrangements, budgeting to meet financial difficulties and similar money matters can be dealt with. Those CABs which do not have a specialist service should nevertheless be approached: they will do all they can to help, making special arrangements if necessary. The staff of the bureaux can give much sound advice themselves, particularly on such matters as welfare benefits.

In cases of special difficulty, contact Peter Gilbert, Institute of Chartered Accountants in England and Wales, PO Box 433, Chartered Accountants' Hall, Moorgate Place, London EC2P 2BJ (Tel: 01-628 7060).

Community Health Councils
See Section 1 on Statutory Services. Addresses of local councils appear in telephone directories.

Lloyds Bank Services for Visually Handicapped People
Statements in braille and large print are two of the services offered by Lloyds Bank for visually handicapped customers. A braille correspondence service is also available. The Bank supplies cheque and envelope addressing templates as well as a note gauge to help identify banknotes and a tape cassette giving general banking information. Lloyds has adapted three of its 'Black Horse Guides' to braille and large print: *Managing Your Money*, *Retirement*, and *Buying and Improving Your Home*. In addition, two more booklets, one dealing with basic banking services and the other with specialist services such as advice on wills, investment and tax are similarly

available. All these items are free of charge and can be obtained through branches or from the Public Relations Department, Lloyds Bank plc, 71 Lombard Street, London EC3P 3BS (Tel: 01-626 1500).

Medico-Legal Service: Compensation for Personal Injury

A London-based firm specialising in medico-legal services offers free telephone advice to help people who have suffered personal injury to evaluate whether they might have a valid claim for compensation and, if so, what action to take. Claims may arise in relation to any accident where another person is to blame, or where injury results from medical negligence. The service does not offer *legal* advice, but has a directory of solicitors who are expert in this area. The advice line is open daily on 01-580 9798.

National Federation of Consumer Groups

12 Mosley Street, Newcastle upon Tyne NE1 1DE (Tel: Newcastle upon Tyne (0632) 618259).
Local consumer groups are voluntary organisations which aim to search out information about local goods and services, campaign for their improvement and represent the interests of local consumers. Some groups help solve individual complaints. Addresses may be obtained from the National Federation office, who can also help people start groups or enrol them as direct members.

Office of Fair Trading

Field House, 15–25 Bream's Buildings, London EC4A 1PR (Tel: 01-242 2858).
A government agency whose job is to keep watch on trading practices in the UK for the protection of both consumers and traders against unfair practices. The Office of Fair Trading cannot deal directly with complaints about such things as faulty goods, or goods or services which are misdescribed, but does collect information about trading practices and can, if appropriate, suggest changes in the law or other remedies. We believe that disabled people who are housebound are a particularly vulnerable consumer group, being unable to 'shop around', compare prices and evaluate competitive goods. They are also open to exploitation by firms operating on a mail order or door-to-door basis who offer relief for their disabling conditions and pain, but whose real concern is to sell products which may be overpriced and inappropriate to the needs of the individual.

The Office of Fair Trading publishes advisory leaflets to inform people about their rights and obligations. These include:

Fair Deal, previously issued free of charge, and now available from bookshops and many newsagents, priced 95p, is a handy 68-page booklet covering shopping problems and consumers' rights, buying on credit, how to obtain redress, where to get advice, useful addresses, etc.

How To Put Things Right (leaflet). Explains consumers' legal rights on faulty goods (in England and Wales) and where to get help and advice.
Dear Shopper In Scotland (leaflet). Describes shoppers' rights under Scottish law.
Dear Shopper In Northern Ireland (leaflet). An explanation for Northern Ireland consumers of their legal rights, taking account of differences in advisory and legal procedures in Northern Ireland.
How To Cope With Doorstep Salesmen (leaflet). Highlights some of the selling methods used, and how to deal with problems.
Stop And Think (leaflet). Warns consumers about risks involved in making 'contracts' and paying deposits.
No Credit? Your right to know what credit reference agencies are saying about you (leaflet). Explains consumers' rights under credit reference agency regulations.
There's More To Credit Than Just HP (leaflet). A quick guide to 'Never Never Land'. Essential reading for anyone thinking of buying on easy terms or taking out a loan.
Buying By Post. Deals with Codes of Practice and other schemes operated by trade associations in the mail order industry.

There are also special leaflets on buying cars, double-glazing, electrical goods, funerals, furniture, laundry and dry-cleaning services, package holidays, photography and shoes, all available from local Citizens' Advice Bureaux.

Social Security and Other Benefits

For relevant advisory services *see* Section 2.

Welfare Rights

For relevant advisory services *see* page 10 and Child Poverty Action Group (Welfare Rights Department), page 298.

HELPFUL ORGANISATIONS

It must be true to say that there are few problems for which a society has not been established to try to solve the difficulty. Where a need has been recognised an organisation has grown to offer help. In less enlightened times, charitable enterprises tended to concern themselves more with ethical standards than with individual well-being. In this age, we are all more aware of our own fallibility and concerned to a much greater extent with mutual dependence. Thus we can, as of right and with dignity, apply for help and advice to those who offer such aids in the particular area of our difficulties. This section lists such helpful organisations – if you have difficulty in finding the name of an organisation concerned with a particular problem, consult the index at the end of the Directory. We would urge readers never to struggle alone; there is help, but only you can make the need known, and that is halfway to finding a solution.

Abdominal diseases
See Kingston Trust.

Access Committee for England
126 Albert Street, London NW1 7NF (Tel: 01-482 2247).
The Committee is served by the Centre on Environment for the Handicapped and was formed in 1984 to achieve an accessible environment for people with physical, sensory or mental disablement. Its aim is to work towards the removal of the physical and attitudinal barriers which prevent full participation in the life of society.

Action Against Allergy (AAA)
43 The Downs, London SW20 8HG (Tel: 01-947 5082).
An association to further the study of the role of modern foods, chemicals and biological materials in the causation of the allergic illnesses increasingly afflicting people in the western world. Send s.a.e. for further information and recommended reading.

Action for Dysphasic Adults (ADA)
Northcote House, 37a Royal Street, London SE1 7LL (Tel: 01-261 9572).

Dysphasia is a serious communication handicap usually resulting from a stroke or head injury, which affects some or all of a person's ability to speak and write, and to understand the spoken and written word.

ADA grew out of the Association of Speech Clubs set up by Diana Law (who is herself dysphasic as a result of a brain haemorrhage). It aims to facilitate and extend long-term rehabilitation for dysphasic adults in association with the speech therapy services and to create awareness among professional groups and the general public, both of the nature of dysphasia and the needs of dysphasic adults.

In order to achieve its aims Action for Dysphasic Adults will:
provide information services for dysphasic patients and their families;
put volunteer organisations and groups in touch with dysphasic adults and their families;
give support and assistance to speech therapists in the setting up of speech clubs;
support speech therapists in the provision of facilities to extend the scope of their professional service, *e.g.* organising relatives' groups, social clubs, etc.;
seek to make provision for recreational, vacational, domiciliary and residential facilities for dysphasic adults and their families;
collect statistics about the prevalence and incidence of dysphasia in adults, its treatment, follow-up and rehabilitation facilities;
seek to have dysphasia recognised by the DHSS and other bodies as a registered handicap;
inform the general public and professional groups about dysphasia and the needs of dysphasics;
provide sources of information for patients, relatives, professionals, volunteers and other interested people through newsletters, reading lists and a library of books and journals;
organise workshops, conferences, study days, meetings and any other activity that will provide up-to-date information about research in the field of dysphasia for speech therapists, doctors and other interested professionals;

encourage research into dysphasia and its treatment and endeavour to make funds available for this.

Action Research for the Crippled Child

(National Fund for Research into Crippling Diseases), Vincent House, North Parade, Horsham, West Sussex RH12 2DA (Tel: Horsham (0403) 64101).

Promotes and supports medical research into all aspects of crippling diseases regardless of cause. Current emphasis is on prevention, especially in the child, but ways of alleviating the effects of an existing handicap in all age groups are included.

A quarterly magazine *Action Research* is written so as to be understood by people with little medical knowledge. It describes the latest developments in medical research in the very wide field covered by this charity.

Action for the Victims of Medical Accidents (AVMA)

Director: Arnold Simanowitz, 135 Stockwell Road, London SW9 9TN (Tel: 01-737 2434).

An organisation set up in October 1982 to help those who have suffered medical accidents to assess what has happened to them. If negligence is a possibility, it will put victims in touch with solicitors, and solicitors with medical experts. The Advice Centre at Stockwell Road also works closely with Community Health Councils.

As well as assisting with personal cases, AVMA hopes, in the fullness of time, to approach the problem of medical accidents in a broader way, by providing information, publicising what is at present a neglected social problem, promoting discussion among groups with special responsibilities (such as medical social workers), producing statistics which are currently lacking, publishing details of previous out-of-court settlements, and generally increasing awareness of the problem both among the general public and within the medical profession.

There is no wish to promote unnecessary litigation, but AVMA seeks to make it easier for ordinary people to perceive and pursue necessary litigation to which they have a right. AVMA believes that ultimately compensation for medical accidents should be available without the need to prove negligence, and will support any scheme to achieve this.

Subscription £4 for individuals, £8 for organisations, entitling you to receive newsletters and published information.

Advocacy Alliance

2nd Floor, 115 Golden Lane, London EC1Y 0TJ (Tel: 01-253 2056, for messages 01-253 9433 ext. 22/23).

An exciting and innovative project sponsored by MIND, MENCAP, The Leonard Cheshire Foundation, The Spastics Society and One-to-One. The scheme is working in three hospitals at present: St Ebba's in Epsom, Normansfield in Teddington and St Lawrence's in Caterham.

Residents without relatives or regular visitors now have the opportunity to have their own advocate, an ordinary citizen who befriends a person with mental handicap on a one-to-one basis and represents her or his interests as if they were their own. Training is given to prepare prospective advocates for this very special role, and includes information on legal rights, services and benefits available to people with mental handicap.

For further information contact the Co-ordinator, Sally Carr at the above address.

Age Concern England (National Old People's Welfare Council)

Bernard Sunley House, 60 Pitcairn Road, Mitcham, Surrey CR4 3LL (Tel: 01-640 5431).

A national organisation established 'to promote the welfare of old people'. Over 1,300 independent local groups provide a wide range of services. The Age Concern movement also campaigns on issues of concern to elderly people. Age Concern England provides central co-ordination and information services. The wide variety of publications includes *Your Rights* and the journal *New Age*.

Allergy

See Action Against Allergy.

Alzheimer's Disease Society

Central Office: Bank Buildings, Fulham Broadway, London SW6 1EP (Tel: 01-381 3177).

Alzheimer's disease is a condition which causes intellectual disturbance by damaging some of the cells in the brain. The cause is unknown and treatment is, at present, limited to amelioration of its effects.

The Society, founded in 1979, aims to give support to families by linking them through membership; to provide information about the disease and available aids; to ensure that adequate nursing care is available when it becomes necessary; and to promote research and the education of the general public. A newsletter is published; meetings and symposia are arranged.

The ADS has a network of relatives' self-help groups and contact people throughout the United Kingdom. At the time of writing, eight regional offices are being established. Minimum subscription £2 per annum.

Amputees
See British Limbless Ex-Service Men's Association, National Association for Limbless Disabled, Reach.

Ankylosing Spondylitis
See National Ankylosing Spondylitis Society.

ARMS (Action for Research into Multiple Sclerosis)
71 Gray's Inn Road, London WC1X 8TR (Tel: Information – Bishop's Stortford (0279) 53863; Scotland: 34 Brooklea Drive, Glasgow G46 6AS; Counselling (England/Wales) – 01-568 2255 or 021-476 4229 (Scotland) – 041-637 2262).
ARMS is a vigorous organisation run by people with personal experience of multiple sclerosis providing information to others who suffer from multiple sclerosis. Its *Newsletter* is particularly good: direct, relevant, informative and non-patronising. The organisation seeks to encourage research and education on multiple sclerosis. A 24-hour counselling service is operated.

Arthritis Care
6 Grosvenor Crescent, London SW1X 7ER (Tel: 01-235 0902).
The Association caters for the social and welfare needs of rheumatism and arthritis sufferers. It has over 240 branches throughout the United Kingdom (*i.e.* including Northern Ireland) which hold regular social meetings.

The Association administers five specially adapted holiday centres and a residential home with nursing care. A welfare department advises on a variety of subjects, *e.g.* holidays, aids, transport and equipment for use at home. Publishes a quarterly newspaper, *Arthritis News*.

Arthritis and Rheumatism Council
41 Eagle Street, London WC1R 4AR (Tel: 01-405 8572).
Aims to inspire and encourage medical research into the causes and cure of arthritis and rheumatism, ensure that the beneficial results of the research are made available to sufferers as quickly as possible and raise the funds necessary for the research to continue.

Publishes a quarterly magazine called *ARC Magazine* which can be obtained for a nominal annual subscription and contains many short articles on interesting aspects of medical research and arthritis.

ASBAH
See Association for Spina Bifida and Hydrocephalus.

Association For All Speech Impaired Children (AFASIC)

347 Central Markets, Smithfield, London EC1A 9LH (Tel: 01-236 3632/6487).

AFASIC is an association of parents and professionals which seeks to draw to the attention of the public, and local and central government, the special needs of children and young people with specific speech and language disorders. The Association believes that regular speech therapy and education by specially trained teachers (preferably in a language unit attached to an ordinary school) are essential if these children are to achieve their potential and to participate fully in society.

AFASIC provides an advice and information service, fund-raises for mobile speech therapy clinics and organises activity week holidays for the children. It campaigns for more language units attached to ordinary schools and improved speech therapy services, runs courses and symposia and was instrumental in setting up the first training course for teachers of language disordered children. It is currently investigating the field of employment training for speech and language disordered young people. The Association has a network of 16 regional groups and six area correspondents. Publishes a newsletter for members.

The Association of Carers

Lilac House, Medway Homes, Balfour Road, Rochester, Kent (Tel: Medway (0634) 813981).

While the needs of disabled people have increasingly attracted attention and support, the needs of those who care for them to have lives apart from disability, to fulfil their own personal aspirations and interests and not to be wholly confined to their dedicated role is insufficiently recognised. The Association of Carers, established in September 1981, fills this gap.

It aims to unite carers in local groups to bring relief from the extreme stress, both physical and emotional, which can result from looking after physically and mentally handicapped people and the elderly over lengthy periods. It assists in the formation of groups, offers an information service and a holiday and respite care service for those wishing to find suitable holiday accommodation for a disabled dependant. The bi-monthly newsletter is a forum for members' views and an information exchange.

Association to Combat Huntington's Chorea

Director: Dick Bates, Borough House, 34a Station Road, Hinckley, Leicestershire LE10 1AP (Tel: Hinckley (0455) 615558). London Office and Family Counselling Service: 108 Battersea High Street, London SW11 3HP (Tel: 01-223 7000).

The United Kingdom National Association – Combat – was founded in 1971 and devotes its energies to promoting and supporting research; identifying areas of special need; minimising the effects of the disease in any possible way; educating and influencing professionals and the general public into an awareness of the realities of the condition; sustaining and comforting those who suffer; providing and running a holiday and short-term care home for patients; developing a branch network to meet local needs; providing a National Social Worker to give specialised aid and counselling; carrying out clinical trials of aids and appliances applicable to the disease; initiating social research intended to improve the quality of life of HC families; publishing and distributing appropriate literature; and raising funds so that this disease can finally be eradicated.

Association of Crossroads Care Attendant Schemes Ltd

Chief Executive Officer: Pat Osborne, 94 Coton Road, Rugby, Warwickshire CV21 4LN (Tel: Rugby (0788) 61536).

(A similar trust operates in Scotland: Crossroads (Scotland) Care Attendant Scheme Trust. Director: Mr A. Murray, 24 George Square, Glasgow G2 1EG (Tel: 041-226 3793).)

With a grant from the DHSS, this scheme became a national organisation in April 1977, following a three-year pilot project in Rugby. It represents a bold, imaginative (but totally practical) and much needed strategy to improve the care of disabled people within the community. The scheme's primary objective is to relieve stress in the families or carers of disabled people and to avoid their admission to hospital or residential care should a breakdown or other failure occur in the household. To achieve this objective the Association promotes the establishment of domiciliary support services in local areas, managed by local committees and manned by 'care attendants' who are paid for their time and provided with appropriate training. Attendants are not professional people, but act rather as 'substitute' relatives, providing care in a homely and friendly way, in a manner to which the disabled person is accustomed. An important aspect of an attendant's work is that attendance is provided on a flexible basis, if necessary outside what are considered normal working hours. The Association emphasises that such teams supplement and complement, not replace, existing statutory services and work closely with them, striving for the highest possible standards of care.

Many physically handicapped people are able to

live at home only because of the support they get from other people – friends, housekeepers or relatives. Those who care for disabled people in this way are often under great strain themselves and the support provided by care attendants can make all the difference. Equally, if for any reason a breakdown in normal support occurs, the help of a care attendant, for a few hours a week, can fill the gap and save the situation. The Association has published a guide to the scheme which is available from the Royal Association for Disability and Rehabilitation, 25 Mortimer Street, London W1N 8AB, or from the headquarters address given above (price 40p including postage). A useful publications list is available free on request.

Association of Disabled Professionals
The Stables, 73 Pound Road, Banstead, Surrey SM7 2HU (Tel: Burgh Heath (073 73) 52366).
The Association is a self-help group seeking to improve the rehabilitation of disabled people. Members can help other members with advice on education/training and employment problems. Publishes occasional *Newsletter* and a quarterly *House Bulletin*. Its sub-group Home Opportunities for Professional Employment (HOPE), provides information to people who have had to give up professional careers and must work at home (*see* Section 7).

Association of Parents of Vaccine Damaged Children
2 Church Street, Shipston-on-Stour, Warwickshire CV36 4AP (Tel: Shipston-on-Stour (0608) 61595).
Represents, through parents, those children who have suffered handicaps as a result of vaccination, and campaigns for state provision for them.

Association of Professions for the Mentally Handicapped
126 Albert Street, London NW1 7NF (Tel: 01-267 6111).
Founded in 1973 to promote the general welfare of mentally handicapped people and their families, by encouraging high standards of care and development, by facilitating co-operation and the sharing of knowledge among professional workers, by offering a unified professional view on the strategies of mental handicap and by educating the public to accept, understand and respect mentally handicapped people.

The Association now embraces over 40 different professions in the fields of health, education, social service and voluntary services. It is consulted by government departments, has held regular congresses and 'workshops' and has published a number of relevant reports and papers.

Association for Research into Restricted Growth
c/o Pamela Rutt, 24 Pinchfield, Maple Cross, Rickmansworth, Herts. WD3 2TP.
Since its foundation in 1970, the Association has been concerned chiefly to provide, through a newsletter, meetings and conventions, a forum for communication among people of restricted growth. It thus brings together people with common problems and needs, providing opportunities for social contact and discussion. There is a special children's committee, a medical committee and a clothing officer, all able to offer relevant advice.

The Association has established a regional panel of specialists to whom GPs can refer parents for competent medical advice about any form of restricted growth. Publications include the *Layman's Guide to Restricted Growth* and *Coping with Restricted Growth*.

Association for Spina Bifida and Hydrocephalus (ASBAH)
22 Upper Woburn Place, London WC1H 0EP (Tel: 01-388 1382).
Northern Ireland Association: 23 Dalboyne Park, Lisburn, Co. Antrim BT28 3BU (Tel: Lisburn (084 62) 6023).
Over 80 local associations in England, Wales and Northern Ireland. Also Scottish Spina Bifida Association: 190 Queensferry Road, Edinburgh EH4 2BW (Tel: 031-332 0743).
A welfare and research organisation. The Association provides information, advisory and welfare services and practical assistance, supports the work of the local associations. Social workers and field officers serve in some areas. Short-term and permanent care home in Yorkshire. Sponsorship of research into causes and treatment. Bi-monthly magazine, *Link*.

LIFT, a group for young members (13 to 25 years) within the Association, has information on social and leisure activities, a quarterly free newsletter and training programmes on personal care and social independence.

Autism
See National Autistic Society.

Back Pain Association
Grundy House, 31–33 Park Road, Teddington, Middlesex TW11 0AB (Tel: 01-977 5475/5).
The Association raises funds for research into the causes and treatment of back pain. It seeks to help

prevent damage by teaching people to use their bodies sensibly and to form local branches to help disseminate useful information and provide neighbourly help to sufferers. Publishes quarterly magazine *Talk Back*, available on subscription, and various literature on back pain and lifting to help reduce the heavy toll which now affects four out of five people at some time during their lives. Information will be provided upon receipt of a large s.a.e., but the Association regrets that it cannot deal with enquirers' specific complaints.

Blindness and Partial Sight
See: Guide Dogs for the Blind Association; Jewish Blind Society; London Association for the Blind; National Association for Deaf-Blind and Rubella Handicapped; National Deaf-Blind Helpers League; National Federation of the Blind of the United Kingdom; National League of the Blind and Disabled; National Library for the Blind; Optical Information Council; Partially Sighted Society; Royal Commonwealth Society for the Blind; Royal National Institute for the Blind; St Dunstan's.

Breakthrough Trust Deaf/Hearing Integration
Charles W. Gillett Centre, Selly Oak Colleges, Birmingham B29 6LE (Tel: 021-472 6447).
Promotes a variety of projects, social activities and cultural pursuits which bring deaf and hearing children and adults into harmonious contact with each other in a natural way through practical self-help ventures, *e.g.* regional group activities, integration weekends, communication workshops and communication holiday projects. (*See also* Section 3).

The Trust's Roughmoor Centre at Shaw, Swindon, Wiltshire SN5 9PW (Tel: Swindon (0793) 771021) offers the use of its farmhouse accommodation for a variety of projects which may be ideal for integration projects for deaf and hearing children, families, young people and deaf people with additional handicaps. Advice and information on deafness is offered to local people and groups.

British Association of the Hard of Hearing
7–11 Armstrong Road, London W3 7JL (Tel: 01-743 1110/1353, Vistel 01-743 1492).
Promotes the formation of local groups, of which there are 220 in Great Britain and Northern Ireland, and provides a wide range of educational, cultural and social activities. Gives advice on hearing problems and encourages the improvement of speech and lip-reading. Co-operates with statutory and voluntary bodies to advance measures to prevent and cure deafness and to provide better services for the hard of hearing. Publishes a quarterly magazine *Hark* (annual subscription £1.50).

British Association of Myasthenics
38 Selwood Road, Brentwood, Essex (Tel: Brentwood (0277) 218082).
Seeks to help families and social workers to know more about this rare disease. Chapters have been and are being established and quarterly bulletins issued. Purposes include contact, welfare, education, publicity and, by fund raising, the support of research in conjunction with the Muscular Dystrophy Group.

British Council of Organisations of Disabled People
Yeoman's House, 76 St James's Lane, Muswell Hill, London N10.
BCODP was established in November 1981 to act as a co-ordinating body for national organisations *of* (*i.e.* controlled by) disabled people. Its main purpose is to provide a forum for the free exchange of information, ideas and views with the object of enabling disabled people to develop and express their own needs in order to carry out particular projects. The Council's general aim is to promote the active participation of people with disabilities in securing equal opportunities for full integration into society.

National action plans have been drawn up to tackle specific social barriers to integration into the community. Standing committees of people with disabilities have been set up to assess and campaign for:
1. Their housing needs (*see* page 79).
2. Their educational needs (aimed at reducing by half the number of children attending special schools over the next decade).
3. The growth of centres of independent living.
These plans highlight the need for people with disabilities to participate in decision making, service delivery and professional training. The BCODP aims to become a strategic central channel for official representation of people with disabilities into the decision-making bodies of society.

Membership is open to those national organisations which are controlled by disabled people.

The British Deaf Association
38 Victoria Place, Carlisle CA1 1HU (Tel: Carlisle (0228) 48844, Vistel (0228) 28719). London sub-office: 311 Gray's Inn Road, London WC1X 8PY (Tel: 01-278 1005, Vistel 01-278 1007).
Local branches throughout the country. Organises a variety of group activities for deaf people and is able to advise individuals and parents on development and education. Organises special holidays for deaf senior citizens. Financial assistance can be given in suitable cases. Organises courses for school leavers, outdoor adventure and travel courses for young deaf people plus an annual summer school and short special interest courses for all age groups. Produces educational material (including sign language video tapes) and a monthly news magazine.

British Diabetic Association
10 Queen Anne Street, London W1M 0BD (Tel: 01-323 1531).
Safeguards the interests of diabetics and provides them with information and advice. Raises money for research. Organises holidays for diabetic children and elderly diabetics. Publishes a bi-monthly newspaper, *Balance*, sent free to all members and provides cassette recordings of the newspaper for the registered blind. A series of four video films (VHS) is now available covering all aspects of diabetes and is intended for patients.

British Dyslexia Association
Church Lane, Peppard, Oxon RG9 5JN (Tel: Rotherfield Greys (049 17) 699).
The British Dyslexia Association represents and co-ordinates the activities of local Dyslexia Associations. It co-operates with the Department of Education and Science, and with local education authorities. Corporate members of the BDA are involved in research, assessment and teaching. The BDA provides counselling and advice to parents and other people in obtaining remedial help for those handicapped by dyslexia.

British Epilepsy Association
Crowthorne House, Bigshotte, Wokingham, Berkshire RG11 3AY (Tel: Crowthorne (0344) 773122).
Northern Ireland Regional Office, Claremont Street Hospital, Belfast BT9 6AQ (Tel: Belfast (0232) 248414).
Leeds Regional Office, 313 Chapeltown Road, Leeds LS7 3JT (Tel: Leeds (0532) 621076).
Birmingham Regional Office, Guildhall Buildings, Navigation Street, Birmingham B2 4BT (Tel: 021-643 7740).

Promotes increased public understanding of epilepsy. Provides an information and advisory service. Raises money for research. Publishes periodical *Epilepsy Now*, and keeps a continually updated list of relevant films. There is a national network of mutual support groups – addresses can be obtained from the above addresses.

British Heart Foundation

102 Gloucester Place, London W1H 4DH (Tel: 01-935 0185).
Primarily a medical research charity working in the field of cardiovascular disease. Activities include provision of Heart Research Series leaflets free of charge to heart patients and their families. No funds are available for welfare or rehabilitation grants to individuals.

British Institute of Mental Handicap

Wolverhampton Road, Kidderminster, Worcestershire DY10 3PP (Tel: Kidderminster (0562) 850251).
The BIMH aims to raise standards of treatment, care and management of mentally handicapped people both in hospital and in the community. An Information and Resource Centre answers queries on all aspects of mental handicap. Conferences and workshops on many aspects of mental handicap are organised on a national basis. Publications include, *Mental Handicap*, a quarterly journal covering themes in mental handicap (£8 per annum), *Mental Handicap Bulletin*, a quarterly collection of topical articles (£10.50 per annum) and a monthly Current Awareness Service to keep those who are interested informed on the latest books and articles (£10 per annum). BIMH also publishes books on various aspects of mental handicap. Individual membership, which includes *Mental Handicap*, and entitles the member to reduced charges when attending BIMH courses and a discount on publications, costs £11 per annum and is open to anyone. Details of other forms of membership are available on request.
See also Appendix A: Directories/Bibliographies – BIMH Current Awareness Service.

British Kidney Patient Association

Bordon, Hampshire (Tel: Bordon (042 03) 2022; appeals office: Bordon (042 32) 3430).
Gives advice and help to sufferers, and raises funds. Seeks to extend the donation of kidneys by healthy people. Membership is open to all kidney patients at a fee of £1 for life membership. This entitles them and their immediate family to financial help.

British Legion

See Royal British Legion.

British Limbless Ex-Service Men's Association

Frankland Moore House, 185-87 High Road, Chadwell Heath, Essex RM6 6NA (Tel: 01-590 1124/5). Has local branches. Advises on pensions, employment and welfare matters. Safeguards the interests of members and runs two residential convalescent homes. Publishes a magazine *Blesmag*.

British Nursing Association

5th Floor, 470 Oxford Street, London W1N 0HQ (Tel: 01-629 9030).
With 50 branches in Great Britain (13 in London), the BNA offers fully qualified nursing care to private patients. This need not be on a full-time basis if the need is for short-time help. A trained nurse can be provided for as little as an hour at a time. If the patient does not have private health insurance, it is possible that attendance allowances may be available to offset some of the cost. The service is able to respond at very short notice and both male and female nurses are available. The national network is in operation round the clock every day of the week to cover both routine and emergency needs. Nurses are also available to act as escorts to patients who cannot travel alone and can provide specialist care where this is needed. If there is a branch in your area, it will be listed in the telephone directory. Otherwise, contact the above address/number.

British Polio Fellowship

Bell Close, West End Road, Ruislip, Middlesex HA4 6LP (Tel: Ruislip (089 56) 75515).
Has local branches. Encourages mutual support, service and recreation. Provides personal welfare and advisory services and aims at rehabilitation through training. The Fellowship has a residential/holiday establishment as well as self-catering accommodation (a bungalow, holiday flat and holiday caravans). Publishes quarterly newspaper *The Bulletin*.

British Red Cross Society

9 Grosvenor Crescent, London SW1X 7EJ (Tel: 01-235 5454).
Dedicated to the relief of suffering whether through war, disaster or accident. Provides first-aid and auxiliary nursing services, and many welfare services in hospitals and the community. There is also a youth and junior section. Publishes *Red Cross News*.

British Retinitis Pigmentosa Society

Secretary: Mrs L. M. Drummond-Walker, 24 Palmer Close, Redhill, Surrey RH1 4BX (Tel: Redhill (0737) 61937).
Retinitis Pigmentosa (RP) refers to a group of hereditary diseases of the retina, in which the light sensitive tissue of the eye slowly degenerates,

progressively restricting vision. BRPS, formed in 1975, aims chiefly to counsel, support and encourage those who have RP and to pursue measures towards finding the cause, effective treatment and cure of the disease. It further seeks to increase public awareness of RP, and to co-operate with government, statutory and relevant voluntary organisations and professional workers, nationally and internationally. It will press for more government-funded research as well as raising money on its own account for this purpose.

The Society has a branch structure covering over a thousand members, and provides a regular flow of information relating to the disease.

British Sports Association for the Disabled
See Section 11, Sports and Leisure.

British Tinnitus Association
c/o The Royal National Institute for the Deaf, 105 Gower Street, London WC1E 6AH (Tel: 01-387 8033).
The BTA was formed in July 1979 to bring together sufferers and other interested people for discussion of problems, experiences and any matters of mutual interest that might help to relieve suffering in day-to-day living. The Association also seeks to enlist financial and other support, sympathy and understanding from the general public, and to bring pressure to bear on MPs and other relevant persons and organisations to encourage the channelling of funds into the relief and cure of tinnitus.

Subjective tinnitus is an extremely common complaint affecting a large number of people with normal hearing as well as those with varying degrees of hearing impairment. Very small abnormalities in the hearing nerve can generate sounds, inaudible to other people, but which can take the form of a great variety of ringing, whistling, buzzing or other more complicated sounds which plague the affected person.

The Association conveys information to members through the *BTA Newsletter*, published four times a year, price £2.50 for four issues. A reprint of Newsletters 1-19 contains much basic information including a section on tinnitus maskers and their availability through the NHS and commercially, and an authoritative article on tinnitus research and current treatment. There are nearly 80 local groups throughout the country.

Brittle Bone Society
112 City Road, Dundee DD2 2PW (Tel: Dundee (0382) 67603).
The Society seeks to promote research into the causes, inheritance and treatment of osteogenesis imperfecta and similar disorders, characterised by excessive fragility of the bones. It also provides advice, encouragement and practical help for patients and their relatives facing the difficulties of living with brittle bones. Raises funds for research and acts as a contact organisation for those affected.

The Campaign for Mentally Handicapped People
16 Fitzroy Square, London W1P 5HQ (Tel: 01-387 9571).
Established as an independent group in 1971. Campaigns for greater integration of mentally handicapped people in ordinary society and the abolition of specialist subnormality hospitals. The group both collects and disseminates information to evaluate needs and promote improvements in provision. Organises conferences and meetings and publishes a quarterly newsletter. Other publications include policy statements, discussion and enquiry papers, conference reports, evidence to government bodies and specialist studies. These are available from CMH Publications, 5 Kentings, Comberton, Cambridgeshire CB3 7DT.

Cancer
See Marie Curie Memorial Foundation; National Society for Cancer Relief; Women's National Cancer Control Campaign.

Cardiac Spare Parts Club
c/o National Westminster Bank Ltd, 2 High Street, Olney, Buckinghamshire MK46 4BB.
A support club for those who have undergone or who require heart surgery, and for those with pacemakers. Founded in 1969 by heart patients, the club seeks to assist patients prior to their operation, to provide any help required afterwards, to raise funds for cardiac research equipment, and to give advice in these areas.

Carers
See Association of Carers; National Council for Carers.

CARE (Cottage and Rural Enterprises Ltd)
9A Weir Road, Kibworth, Leicester LE8 0LQ (Tel: Kibworth (053 753) 3225).
CARE is an organisation whose aim is to care for mentally handicapped adults of both sexes in village-type communities where they can work and live as normal a life as possible. 'Villages' exist at East Anstey (North Devon), Petworth (West Sussex), Leicester, Samlesbury (nr Preston, Lancashire), Sevenoaks (Kent) and at Ponteland (Newcastle upon Tyne). Elsewhere, groups are exploring the possibility of further development.

Residents of mixed handicaps and abilities live in cottage-type units for up to fourteen people, and work in pottery, agriculture, horticulture, printing, woodwork and craft workshops. The aim is to provide necessary care, support and guidance and the opportunity to realise expectations of a useful, secure and enjoyable life.

CARE raises its own funds to meet capital costs, while the day-to-day expenses are largely met by fees paid by the residents' home local authorities.

Catholic Handicapped Children's Fellowship
2 The Villas, Hare Law, Stanley, Co. Durham DH9 8DQ (Tel: Stanley (0207) 34379).
This fellowship stresses the difficulty of providing both for the spiritual and special physical needs of handicapped children and the need for parents to have a 'friendly hand'. Organised in independent Diocesan Fellowships in Roman Catholic dioceses in England, each Diocesan Fellowship has its own order of priorities, but there is a general pattern in all – family care, meetings and activities for children and parents, social activities, holidays and pilgrimages, religious instruction and help in taking handicapped people to Mass.

Central Bureau for Educational Visits and Exchanges
See Section 10, Holidays Abroad.

Centre for Clinical Communication Studies
86 Blackfriars Road, London SE1 8HA (Tel: 01-928 4563).
As part of the City University, the Centre offers a four-year degree training in speech therapy. The Blackfriars Dysphasic Group provides intensive, long-term treatment for dysphasics and there are two-week intensive courses for young stammerers (10 to 18 years). The work of this group was featured in the BBC 2 *Open Door* series, and a film or video version of this is available.

Centre on Environment for the Handicapped
See Section 4, House and Home, page 80.

Centre for Policy on Ageing
Nuffield Lodge Studio, Regent's Park, London NW1 4RS (Tel: 01-586 9844/9).
CPA issues a range of publications intended to be of practical help to professionals concerned with direct services/policies for older people. Some publications are intended to provide a regular monitoring of current research, publications and events; others provide analysis of policy and practice in given fields. Publications list available.

Cerebral Palsy
See Scottish Council for Spastics, Spastics Society.

Chest, Heart and Stroke Association
Tavistock House (North), Tavistock Square, London WC1H 9JE (Tel: 01-387 3012).
Northern Ireland: 28 Bedford Street, Belfast BT2 7FE (Tel: Belfast (0232) 20184).
Scotland: 65 North Castle Street, Edinburgh EH2 3LT (Tel: 031-225 6527).
Promotes a wider knowledge of chest, heart and stroke illnesses. Publishes educational literature, cassettes and a magazine *Hope*. Sponsors research into chest and stroke illnesses.

Child Poverty Action Group
1 Macklin Street, London WC2B 5NH (Tel: 01-242 3225/9149).
Promotes relief of poverty among children and families. Although not directly concerned with disablement, this can obviously be a prime cause of hardship. Has a Welfare Rights Department which will advise on welfare benefit problems, including benefits for the disabled (Tel: 01-405 5942). Publishes the *National Welfare Benefits Handbook*.

Children's Society, Church of England Children's Society
Old Town Hall, Kennington Road, London SE11 4QD (Tel: 01-735 2441).
Provides help and support to families through family and day care centres and community and neighbourhood centres. Many of the Society's homefinding teams specialise in placing children with special needs. Specific services for disabled people include: residential centres, holiday schemes, respite care, further education and training, and community support. For further information about the Society's services, please contact the Social Work Director, at the above address.

Citizens' Advice Bureau Service
See Section 15.

College of Speech Therapists
Harold Poster House, 6 Lechmere Road, London NW2 5BU (Tel: 01-459 8521).
Provides a number of pamphlets for parents and relatives and will advise on the location of qualified speech therapists.

Colostomy Welfare Group
38–39 Eccleston Square, London SW1V 1PB (Tel: 01-828 5175).
Seeks to help people through the anxiety before and after colostomy operations by giving a free advisory

service and providing all patients with the opportunity to meet and talk to an ex-patient who is well rehabilitated, and who has been trained to give help, relief and comfort to others facing the same experience.

Combat
See Association to Combat Huntington's Chorea.

Community Health Group for Ethnic Minorities
28 Churchfield Road, London W3 6EB (Tel: 01-993 6119).
CHGEM is an independent national charitable organisation formed in 1977 by the combined efforts of health workers and ethnic community leaders who felt that health was one of the areas of deepest racial inequality in our society.

The main aim of CHGEM is thus to resolve some of the health and social problems that arise in ethnic communities, especially as a consequence of migration. To this end, the Group offers a variety of helpful services both to ethnic communities and to statutory and voluntary service agencies, through two main channels:

Ethnic Switchboard offers instant, free, multilingual interpreting and translating services. It offers basic advice to and acts as a referral agency for non-English speaking people with problems in the areas of health and social services, local authorities, community services, etc. The interpreting services are designed for National Health and Social Services' employees who are in the caring sections of these services. It aims to benefit doctors, nurses, midwives, health visitors, etc., who experience linguistic barriers with their clients, or when a diagnosis is hampered by communication problems.

For health workers who have other responsibilities, the Switchboard offers an immediate translating service. The Switchboard operates in more than 20 languages and is available between 9.30 a.m. to 5.30 p.m. In cases of *extreme* urgency (*i.e.* emergencies) there is a 24-hour Aircall Service on 01-834 7334 Blip ext. 0277.

Centre Link is a resource/information centre on the health and social aspects of race, ethnic minorities and migrants in Britain and other developed/developing countries.
CHGEM has collected information covering all aspects of health and social services provisions for ethnic minorities in Britain and elsewhere for over 15 years. Its overall aim is to develop a greater awareness of the health and social problems of minority groups, particularly those which arise as a result of migration. A fully computerised information service

is available to District Health Authorities, health professionals, local authorities, voluntary organisations and individuals.

A variety of publications is available in a reference library and a conference is held annually in December. *CHGEM would be particularly useful for disabled people who cannot speak English.*

Community Service Volunteers
See Section 7, Employment, page 125.

Contact a Family
Director: Noreen Miller, 16 Strutton Ground, Victoria, London SW1P 2HP (Tel: 01-222 2695/3969).
Contact a Family aims to promote the formation of local self-help groups of families who share the problem of having a physically or mentally handicapped child living at home. Parents thus have the chance to meet socially, exchange ideas and give each other practical help, mutual support and understanding.

Membership of a group gives parents a better opportunity to press collectively for improved services and to express their common needs. Families are encouraged to organise services themselves with the help of volunteers and in some cases full-time community workers. Family events such as holiday play schemes, baby-sitting, swimming clubs, and family holidays are the sort of activities arranged through *Share an Idea* newsletter. Contact a Family now links its own and independent self-help groups nation-wide and provides groups with an opportunity to meet at annual 'Share a Weekend' events.

A film and set of guide-lines for the formation of a group are available.

Council for the Advancement of Communication with Deaf People
3 Compton Street, Carlisle CA1 1HT (Tel: Carlisle (0228) 48572).
A representative body of all major national organisations concerned with deafness set up because of a concern that the number of hearing people in the United Kingdom with good sign communication skills is declining, while in certain other countries advancements in research, legislation and provision have shown increasing recognition of the needs and aspirations of deaf people.

The objects of the Council are to promote training and assessment in communication skills, and to administer a register of qualified interpreters.

Counsel and Care for the Elderly
General Secretary: John Hobart, 131 Middlesex Street, London E1 7JF (Tel: 01-621 1624).
This charity exists to provide a comprehensive counselling service and to give advice on any matters to all

persons of pensionable age in the United Kingdom and those returning to the United Kingdom from abroad.

It exists to enable these persons to have the care they need in suitable homes and to assist them financially towards the cost of fees in nursing homes and care in their own homes.

Crossroads Care Attendant Schemes
See Association of Crossroads Care Attemdant Schemes.

CRYPT, Creative Young People Together
See Section 6, Further Education.

Cystic Fibrosis Research Trust
5 Blyth Road, Bromley, Kent BR1 3RS (Tel: 01-464 7211).
Scottish Council Offices: 39 Hope Street, Glasgow G2 6AE (Tel: 041-226 4244).
Northern Ireland Region: Anchor Lodge, Cultra, Co. Down (Tel: Holywood (023 17) 3178).
Cystic fibrosis (CF) is an inherited disease affecting the lungs and digestive system which threatens the lives of many thousands of children in this country from birth onwards.

The Cystic Fibrosis Research Trust was founded in 1964 to finance research to find a cure and, in the meantime, to improve treatment, to help and advise parents and to educate the public, and to promote earlier diagnosis in young children. The Trust is currently funding over 50 major research projects. There are over 280 branches and local groups throughout the United Kingdom. Publishes a wide range of relevant literature and a quarterly magazine *Cystic Fibrosis News*.

Deafness
See Hearing Impairment.

Depressives Anonymous
83 Derby Road, Nottingham NG1 5BB.
Depressives Anonymous is an association of people who have personal experience of depression. At present there are three facilities for members:

1. Local groups are available in a few areas. Work is proceeding to form new groups where there is a demand and sufficient support. (However, DA is opposed to the practice of group therapy without a trained therapist.)
2. Open meetings are held several times a year up and down the country, usually at weekends. These give people without groups a chance to meet each other and to meet the committee.
3. A quarterly newsletter is published containing contributions by depressives, including book reviews, articles, poems and letters. News of groups, including new ones formed and news of all meetings is also published.

The organisation has a strong emphasis on confidentiality and, partly for this reason, prefers to operate through meetings, national and local, and the newsletter rather than person-to-person contacts.

A single copy of a newsletter, as soon as available, will be sent to enquirers on receipt of a s.a.e. (foolscap) or a label. Regular copies may be obtained by writing to the above address enclosing £2.50 per annum, 50p if unwaged (s.a.e. with all enquiries please).

Depressives Associated
Janet Stevenson, 19 Merley Ways, Wimborne Minster, Dorset BH21 1QN (Tel: Wimborne (0202) 883957).
A self-help service for anyone suffering from depression, run by ex-depressives with an understanding of the mental and emotional anguish so commonly experienced by ordinary people in all walks of life.

The main aim is to encourage people to befriend each other so as to break down isolation. The organisation seeks to remove the stigma associated with depression, to provide help for depressives and to carry out research on the problems of depression. Members will be encouraged to become more involved with others around them, to stop looking at the past and to be positive again, preferably without resorting to pills.

As far as possible, letters are answered personally, but many problems are so similar that leaflets have been prepared to cover them, including one under the title *Some of the Problems of the Physically Handicapped*. This and most other leaflets cost 10p each, plus a suitable s.a.e.

A membership fee of £4 per annum includes a quarterly newsletter. Wherever possible, members are put in touch with one of the local groups which are now building up over the country. All enquiries to the above address. A stamped addressed envelope is requested.

Diabetes
See British Diabetic Association; National Diabetes Foundation.

DIAL UK – National Association of Disablement Information and Advice Services
Victoria Buildings, 117 High Street, Clay Cross, Chesterfield, Derbyshire S45 9DZ (Tel: Chesterfield (0246) 864498).
The first Disablement Information and Advice Line (DIAL) was set up early in 1977. DIALs are

autonomous local self-help groups of disabled people with the primary aim of providing information for other disabled people or those concerned with disability. DIALs prefer to give information direct to disabled people to enable them to help themselves, with back-up services, where necessary, *e.g.* advocacy and supportive counselling.

DIALs work in close co-operation with other services to meet a special need – the impaired person who vitally needs open access to specialist information and relevant local services. Although disability is no qualification to provide such a service, it has been found that it often breaks down barriers between caller and information provider and affords a natural kinship which encourages communication. The National Association, formed in 1980, unites, supports and represents over 60 groups throughout Britain, as well as providing training opportunities for DIAL volunteers. *See also* Section 15.

The Disability Alliance

25 Denmark Street, London WC2 8NJ (Tel: 01-240 0806).

The Disability Alliance is a federation of over 80 organisations of and for people with disabilities who have joined together to press for the introduction of a comprehensive income scheme for disabled people, replacing the existing patchwork of social security benefits with a rational system based on severity of disability alone.

The sister organisation, the Disability Alliance Educational and Research Association, publishes yearly *The Disability Rights Handbook* costing £1.80 post-free, and runs a Welfare Rights Information Service which will give free advice and information on social security matters. Enquiries from 2 p.m. to 4.30 p.m. daily by telephone or in writing.

The Alliance seeks to encourage the take-up of existing benefits by those entitled to them and presses for improvements in the way they are operated (notably a strenuous campaign to abolish the 'household duties' test in determining eligibility for the non-contributory invalidity pension for married women).

A publications list, which includes a number of research pamphlets concerned with the financial implications of disability, is available on request.

Disabilities Study Unit

Director: Dr Duncan Guthrie, Wildhanger, Amberley, Arundel, West Sussex BN18 9NR (Tel: Bury (079 881) 406).

The objects of the Disabilities Study Unit are the relief of disabled people generally, whether of individuals or of groups, and in particular for the conduct or promotion of research or studies into the needs of disabled people in their living conditions, and ways of relieving these needs, and the application and publication of the result of such research and studies for the benefit of disabled people.

To these ends, the DSU is willing to undertake projects submitted to it, but the unit's financial resources are strictly limited and projects from outside the unit will normally have also to be funded from outside. The DSU is a non-profit-distributing organisation and all projects are costed on this basis.

The DSU has already produced a number of notable publications in the field of disability, including a directory of sports centres in England and Wales with their facilities for disabled people (see page 238), a collection of essays under the title *Disability – Legislation and Practice* (*see* Appendix A), *One of the Family*, a booklet for brothers and sisters of children with handicaps (*see* Appendix A), *Loneliness – The Other Handicap* (*see* Appendix A), *Water Sports and Epilepsy* (*see* page 230) and *Sex Education for the Physically Handicapped* (*see* page 249). A useful free leaflet *Dear Councillor*, which is a guide to the Chronically Sick and Disabled Persons Act 1970 for local authority councillors, was distributed in 1981 and is still available.

Disabled Drivers' Association
See Section 8, Mobility and Motoring.

Disabled Drivers' Motor Club Ltd
See Section 8, Mobility and Motoring.

Disabled Living Foundation
380–384 Harrow Road, London W9 2HU (Tel: 01-289 6111).

The DLF is a charitable trust concerned with all disabilities (mental, physical and sensory) including multiple handicaps and the infirmities of age. The Foundation works to help disabled people in those aspects of ordinary life which present special problems and difficulties. Its activities embrace a comprehensive information service, a permanent collection of aids of all kinds, and incontinence and clothing advisory services. Fuller details and particulars of the Foundation's many helpful publications are given in Section 3. Other studies made by the Foundation include sport and physical recreation, music, gardening, employment, further education and the problems of those with partial sight.

Disabled People's International
Box 36033, S-100 71 Stockholm, Sweden.

This international coalition of consumer organisations of disabled people was conceived in Winnipeg, Canada at the 1980 World Congress of Rehabilitation International. The First World Congress of Disabled People's International, 30 November to 4 December 1981 in Singapore, formally established the organisation and elected its first World Council. Organisations of disabled people from more than 50 countries were represented at this founding congress. Similar organisations from 25 countries are now represented on the World Council and DPI presently has such affiliations in more than 70 nations. DPI has divided the world into 5 regions (Africa, Asia, Europe, Latin America and North America) and is now in the process of developing its regional infrastructure of regional assemblies and councils.

The representative for Europe, who is also a vice-chairperson of DPI, is Liam Maguire, Irish Wheelchair Association, Clontarf, Dublin 3, Ireland.

Disablement Income Group (DIG) and Disablement Income Group Charitable Trust
Attlee House, 28 Commercial Street, London E1 6LR (Tel: 01-247 2128/6877).
Disablement Income Group (Scotland): 152 Morrison Street, Edinburgh EH3 8BY (Tel: 031-228 1666).
DIG is a pressure group, with 50 local branches, whose aim is to promote the economic and social welfare of all disabled people in the United Kingdom through legislative reform. Publications include a journal, *Progress*, three times yearly and a directory for disabled people (*see* Appendix A). The Charitable Trust operates an advisory service which is freely available to all disabled people for advice on benefits and services available. The Trust is also concerned with research, collection and dissemination of information about the economic and social problems of disabled people.

Disfigurement Therapy Research Unit
Wester Pitmenzies, Auchtermuchty, Fife, Scotland. *See* Society of Skin Camouflage and Disfigurement Therapy.

Distressed Gentlefolk's Aid Association
Vicarage Gate House, Vicarage Gate, London W8 4AQ (Tel: 01-229 9341).
Provides financial help, clothing, comforts and holidays in suitable cases. Runs 13 nursing/residential homes.

Down's Syndrome
See below and Scottish Down's Syndrome Association.

Down's Children's Association
4 Oxford Street, London W1N 9FL (Tel: 01-580 0511/2).
Advice on the developmental management of children with Down's Syndrome and the promotion of research into care and education of such children.

Dr Barnardo's
Tanners Lane, Barkingside, Ilford, Essex IG6 1QG (Tel: 01-550 8822).
Barnardo's aims to provide and develop, in consultation with statutory authorities and other agencies, selected services for children in need and their families. Residential work provides for children who are handicapped physically, mentally and emotionally. Field social work projects include highly concentrated efforts to find homes for the 'hard to place' child; sustained programmes for the training of social work volunteers; support projects for those who are bereaved and for one-parent families. Day care centres for pre-school children, for the non-school attenders and for unemployed youth are available. Holiday play schemes are in operation and also holiday placements for mentally handicapped children. The services are operated on a devolved divisional basis (eight divisions).

Dyslexia
See British Dyslexia Association; Scottish Dyslexia Association.

Dysphasia
See Action for Dysphasic Adults; Centre for Clinical Communication Studies.

Dystrophic Epidermolysis Bullosa Research Association (DEBRA)
Secretary: Winnie Foster, 38 Cornwall Avenue, Clayton, Newcastle-under-Lyme, Staffordshire (Tel: Newcastle (0782) 6200028).
DEBRA is a self-help organisation which offers friendship and support to parents and sufferers of all forms of epidermolysis bullosa. The Association also promotes research into the cause, nature, treatment and cure of this disease, and offers a Peer Counselling Service to members.

Eczema
See National Eczema Society.

Educational Visits and Exchanges
See Central Bureau for Educational Visits and Exchanges.

Elderly Invalids Fund
See Counsel and Care for the Elderly.

Epilepsy
See British Epilepsy Association; National Society for Epilepsy; Scottish Epilepsy Association.

Ex-Services Mental Welfare Society
37 Thurloe Street, London SW7 2LL (Tel: 01-584 8688).
A specialist organisation concerned with the welfare of those ex-servicemen and women from all ranks of HM Forces and the Merchant Navy who suffer from psychiatric disabilities, more particularly those with active or long regular service. The Society operates throughout the United Kingdom and Eire, with headquarters in London, and offices in Manchester and Glasgow. Great emphasis is placed on domiciliary visiting, and the closest liaison is maintained with mental hospitals. The Society runs a convalescent home, a hostel for single men, cottages for married people and their families, and a veterans' home. Application to the General Secretary.

The Family Welfare Association
501–505 Kingsland Road, London E8 4AU (Tel: 01-254 6251).
An independent social work agency providing a professional counselling service to people in difficulties. There are nine FWA social work centres in London, one in Milton Keynes and one in Northampton. Offers training programmes for social workers. Publishes annually *Guide to the Social Services* and *Charities Digest*.

Friedreich's Ataxia Group
Burleigh Lodge, Knowle Lane, Cranleigh, Surrey GU6 8RD (Tel: Cranleigh (0483) 272741).
The Group works to raise money for research into the cause and treatment of Friedreich's ataxia, a crippling disease of childhood. It also maintains a small welfare fund to help sufferers and their families. It publishes a quarterly newsletter, an information folder and other literature useful to sufferers, their families, social workers, etc., and has on free loan a 25-minutes, 16-mm colour, optical sound film.

Friends for the Young Deaf Trust
East Court Mansion, Council Offices, College Lane, East Grinstead, Sussex RH19 3LT (Tel: East Grinstead (0342) 23444).
This Trust was established in 1967. It promotes the general welfare of deaf people, especially the deaf child and school-leaver. FYD addresses itself to the needs of deaf children and young deaf people in the community where they can often experience severe isolation due to their special communication needs. The aim of FYD is to encourage the self-esteem, self-confidence and independence of deaf children, school-leavers and young deaf people so that they can learn the value of self-help and helping their fellows in society.

The combined head office and resource centre organises educational and recreational activities. It provides a central office of information and a focal point of contact for the deaf, hard of hearing and those wishing to help them within Sussex, Surrey, Kent and London.

Activities include leadership courses; opportunities to participate in the Duke of Edinburgh's Award Scheme (which, in addition to advancing personal achievement among young deaf students, encourages young hearing people to acquire communication skills, such as sign language, in pursuit of awards); international educational visits and exchanges; sport and leisure pursuits (*see* Section 11); holidays; and speech and language development. Communication and personal relationship courses/communication workshops can be arranged in any area where not otherwise available, for parents, teachers, social workers, audiometricians, doctors, nurses and students.

A research project, *Deaf-Fax*, concerned with the development of electronic aids for people with impaired hearing and/or speech, is linked to similar developments in Europe.

Gay Men's Disabled Group
c/o Gay's the Word, 66 Marchmont Street, London WC1N 1AB.
Aims to provide close support for gay men with disabilities and to bring them and gay men without disabilities together; to make gay groups and society at large more aware of the needs of disabled people; and to further gay liberation and the liberation of people with disabilities.

A newsletter is produced about four times a year and includes a pen-friend/contact section. This operates on a box number system and all correspondence is treated as strictly confidential. From time to time throughout the year, meetings of the Group are held; these vary quite a bit – some are social, some discussion groups and so on.

Annual membership £5 (£2.50 for OAPs, students and the unwaged).

Gemma
BM Box 5700, London WC1N 3XX.
Gemma is a group for disabled/able-bodied homosexual women aiming to lessen the isolation of those whose disability hinders appropriate relationships and access to homosexually orientated litera-

ture. The group stresses that it is not a dating agency, nor a ghetto of disabled lesbians, nor even a counselling service; simply a group of friends with some understanding through personal experience providing a bridge into a wider friendship circle.

Pen-friends, meetings and socials. Quarterly newsletter is on tape. Publishes *Disabled Gay's Guide (Britain)* (new edition 1983/4) and *London Disabled Gay's Guide* (1983).

Gingerbread
35 Wellington Street, London WC2 (Tel: 01-240 0953).

An association with over 370 local groups which seeks to encourage and promote the interests of people who, for whatever reason, have to support and care for their families on their own. Group meetings are held and a wide range of advisory literature is available.

The Girl Guides Association
17–19 Buckingham Palace Road, London SW1W 0PT (Tel: 01-834 6242).

The Girl Guides Association makes provision for handicapped young people. The aim of the movement is to provide a programme of activities which girls enjoy, and which at the same time helps each girl to develop physically, mentally, and spiritually. The handicapped girl works on the same programme and takes the same badges as any other girl; she is encouraged to share in every Guide activity within her capacity. There are special units which offer facilities so that even children who are housebound or in hospital may take part in activities. Any disabled girl over the age of 7 may join the Guides provided that she can make and understand the Promise and its implications. They produce the leaflets *Enabled Though Disabled* and *Guiding with the Handicapped*.

Glaucoma
See International Glaucoma Association.

GRACE (Mrs Gould's Residential Advisory Centre for the Elderly)
PO Box 71, Cobham, Surrey KT11 2JR (Tel: Cobham (093 26) 2928/5765).

Co-ordinates information about nursing homes, privately run residences and some hotels and guest houses, all of which are regularly visited by GRACE staff. Offers experienced and careful advice regarding available accommodation to suit the individual needs of clients, whether for permanent or short-stay residence and with or without nursing care. To defray some of the cost a booking fee is charged,

which is returnable if accommodation is secured in one of the residences suggested by GRACE.

Property of a kind handled by estate agents, and self-catering accommodation, are not covered. The service covers 25 counties of England south of a line from Norfolk to Hereford and Worcester, but excludes London.

Greater London Association for Disabled People (GLAD)
1 Thorpe Close, London W10 5XL (Tel: 01-960 5799).

Aims to be a source of authoritative information on local and national welfare legislation, and to press for improvements in the quality of life of disabled Londoners. It publishes a directory of clubs in London for physically disabled people, a quarterly magazine, information sheets on specific subjects and other specialist publications.

The Guide Dogs for the Blind Association
Alexandra House, 9–11 Park Street, Windsor, Berkshire (Tel: Windsor (075 35) 55711).

Provides guide dogs and training in their use for registered blind people aged 18 and over. The Association's work has expanded considerably in recent years. There are now six training schools and about 3,000 guide dog owners. Some 500 owner and dog 'units' are trained each year.

Guild of Aid for Gentlepeople
10 St Christopher's Place, London W1M 6HY (Tel: 01-935 0641).

The Guild's aim is to make grants and special gifts to gentlefolk in distress as a result of old age, disability or misfortunes not of their making. Applications to be made to the Secretary.

Haemophilia Society
PO Box 9, 16 Trinity Street, London SE1 1DE (Tel: 01-407 1010).

Advice and information are available through various publications or in response to enquiries. The Society seeks to promote and protect the interests of haemophiliacs and to represent their special needs to government and local authorities, both generally and in specific cases. Financial help is given in suitable cases. Local groups provide social fellowship, and raise funds for research.

Handicapped Adventure Playgrounds Association (HAPA)
See Section 11, Sports and Leisure.

Handicapped Persons Research Unit
Newcastle upon Tyne Polytechnic, 1 Coach Lane,

Coach Lane Campus, Newcastle upon Tyne NE7 7TW (Tel: Newcastle upon Tyne (0632) 664061).

An interdisciplinary research and consultancy unit concerned with realistic problems as they occur in the field of handicap. To this end it undertakes professional and postgraduate research into a wide range of subjects concerned with mentally and physically handicapped people. Many research reports have been published including the *Directory of Non-Medical Research relating to Handicapped People* (1982) (*see* Appendix A).

Handicapped Students
See National Bureau for Handicapped Students.

Headway (National Head Injuries Association)
Secretary: 17–21 Clumber Avenue, Sherwood Rise, Nottingham NG5 1AG (Tel: Nottingham (0602) 622382).

A voluntary organisation which seeks to provide support for head injury patients and their families in the problems they have to face.

Self-help support groups have been formed throughout the United Kingdom (including three in London). These groups are generally hospital based and supported by caring medical and para-medical personnel, but are fundamentally for people involved to meet with each other.

A new series of publications has been launched to provide information for patients, families and professionals. A list is available. A booklet on *Starting a Group* is already available, price 60p.

Health Education Council
78 New Oxford Street, London WC1A 1AH (Tel: 01-637 1881) (for Scotland, *see* Scottish Health Education Group).

The HEC was set up by the government as a national centre of expertise in health education, 'to promote and encourage ... education and research in the science and art of healthy living...'. At its head office in New Oxford Street, the Council runs an information service for the general public. A library and resources centre are open to all for more detailed enquiries. Publishes a quarterly journal containing scientific articles of interest to professionals in the field and a helpful publications catalogue (free).

Hearing Impairment
See: British Association of the Hard of Hearing; British Deaf Association; Council for the Advancement of Communication with Deaf People; Friends for the Young Deaf Trust; Link, the British Centre for Deafened People; National Association for Deaf-Blind and Rubella Handicapped; National Deaf-Blind Helpers League; National Deaf Children's Society; Royal Association in Aid of the Deaf and Dumb; Royal National Institute for the Deaf.

Heart Disease
See: British Heart Foundation; Cardiac Spare Parts Club; Chest, Heart and Stroke Association.

Help the Aged
32 Dover Street, London W1A 2AP (Tel: 01-499 0972).

International organisation for the relief of distress amongst old people both in the United Kingdom and overseas. In the United Kingdom it publishes a monthly newspaper, *Yours*, and promotes day centres, work centres, day hospitals, rehabilitation units and medical research, and provides minibuses to transport elderly housebound and disabled people to social centres. It is active in extending and improving housing provision for the elderly.

Home and School Council
81 Rustlings Road, Sheffield S11 7AB (Tel: Sheffield (0742) 662467).

Aims to encourage the spread of good practice in home and school relationships.

Horticultural Therapy
See Section 11, Sports and Leisure.

Huntington's Chorea
See Association to Combat Huntington's Chorea.

Hydrocephalus
See Association for Spina Bifida and Hydrocephalus.

Hyperactive Children's Support Group
Secretary: Sally Bunday, 59 Meadowside, Angmering, West Sussex BN16 4BW.

The HACSG was formed in November 1977 to help and support (other than financially) hyperactive children and their families. It encourages the formation of local groups where parents may get together for mutual support and understanding. It aims to persuade the medical profession and the health and education authorities to take more interest in the day-to-day problems of hyperactive children and adolescents, to promote urgent research into the causes, treatment and management of hyperactivity, to press for its early and proper diagnosis, and to disseminate information to all interested people.

While recognising various causes of hyperactivity, the Group is particularly concerned to explore sensitivity to chemical food additives and to offer advice on basic diet. A booklist is available, and newsletters are published three times a year. Membership fee £3 (January/December). Those joining in the last three months of the year need not renew until the following December.

The Ileostomy Association of Great Britain and Ireland

Central Office: Amblehurst House, Chobham, Woking, Surrey GU24 8PZ (Tel: Chobham (099 05) 8277).

The Ileostomy Association (IA) was formed in 1956 as a mutual-aid association by a group of people with ileostomies. The primary aim has always been to help others facing ileostomy surgery to return to a fully active and normal life as soon as possible. There are over 60 branches in Great Britain – including three in Wales, three in Scotland and one in Northern Ireland – plus one branch in the Republic of Ireland. There are also honorary officers with a range of advisory services. A quarterly journal is sent free of charge to all members, and local members' meetings are arranged at which the latest ileostomy equipment and skin-care preparations are displayed. The Ileostomy Association supports and works closely with the Kingston Trust.

Independent Development Council for People with Mental Handicap

126 Albert Street, London NW1 7NF (Tel: 01-267 6111).

Established in the summer of 1981 with the support of the King's Fund Centre at the instigation of six leading organisations working in the field of mental handicap – Royal MENCAP, The Spastics Society, Dr Barnardo's, MIND, Campaign for Mentally Handicapped People and Association of Professions for the Mentally Handicapped to promote nationally the development of appropriate services for people with mental handicap and their families.

The Council aims to establish effective new means of providing at national level informed and independent policy advice on all aspects of service provision. It builds on the previous work of the National Development Group for the Mentally Handicapped. Strategic advice will be offered to relevant government departments and other concerned bodies on policies for the development of services and how such policies can best be practically implemented. Equally, looking towards the field, the Council will offer advice on good practices and the local action necessary to introduce and sustain better services.

In pursuing these objectives, the Council will be guided by the general belief that services for mentally handicapped people should:

(a) affirm and enhance the dignity, self-respect and individuality of mentally handicapped people who are people first and mentally handicapped second;

(b) pay due regard to what people with mental handicap and their families want and be informed by their views; enable them to share in and contribute to community life, including family life;

(c) assist them to lead as normal a life as possible, where necessary providing extra help to enable them to do so.

The Council's Secretary, David Towell, and Administrator, Andrea Whittaker, can be contacted at the above address for further information.

Infantile Hypercalcaemia Parents Association

Lady Cooper, Mulberry Cottage, 37 Mulberry Green, Old Harlow, Essex.

The IHC seeks:

(a) to help parents of children with William's Syndrome and Infantile Hypercalcaemia, by providing information about the condition, putting parents in touch with each other and enabling their children to meet;

(b) to acquire background information to assist research;

(c) to stimulate interest, particularly among the medical profession, in the condition.

A record of affected children is maintained by the Association. The Infantile Hypercalcaemia Foundation, a registered charity, has commenced research into this very complex condition. Anyone interested in the Association or who knows of a child with the condition is invited to write to Lady Cooper at the above address.

International Glaucoma Association

William Bowman Ward, King's College Hospital, Denmark Hill, London SE5 9RS (Tel: 01-274 6222). The patient-based IGA aims to encourage general awareness and understanding of glaucoma, thus improving the chance of early diagnosis as well as providing and stimulating increased resources for a high standard of management for glaucoma patients. The IGA holds discussion forums, answers written enquiries (s.a.e. please) and helps to support important clinical research. Newsletters, information booklets and posters are also issued and information films loaned. All those interested in the prevention of glaucoma blindness are welcome as members.

Intractable Pain Society

Derbyshire Royal Infirmary, London Road, Derby. This is a Society for those doctors concerned with the treatment of chronic pain in the United Kingdom and Ireland. It exists to enable experience to be exchanged and advice to be given concerning methods and research as to the best modes of treatment. Referrals to pain relief clinics can only be made by members of the medical profession, but information concerning their location can be obtained from the Honorary Secretary.

Invalid Children's Aid Association
126 Buckingham Palace Road, London SW1W 9SB (Tel: 01-730 9891).
Provides free help and advice for parents with handicapped children. This is given through its information service which deals with general enquiries, its secretary for schools who will advise on educational problems, and its social work service (which operates in parts of London and Surrey). ICAA runs four residential schools; one for severely asthmatic boys and three for children with speech and language disorders. They also have a publications list, with particular emphasis on speech and language disorders.
See also Section 5, Education.

Invalids at Home Trust (IAHT)
23 Farm Avenue, London NW2 (Tel: 01-452 2074).
Provides money to help invalids to live at home:
(a) by making special grants to meet the heavy additional costs of living at home and to cope with inevitable emergencies;
(b) by providing equipment to help ensure their safety, comfort and independence or to help them earn a living; and
(c) by granting interest-free loans to help them to buy specialised equipment or to meet temporary financial difficulties.

Jewish Blind Society
1 Craven Hill, London W2 3EW (Tel: 01-262 3111).
Welfare organisation for Jewish blind in the United Kingdom, with both residential and holiday homes, day centres and clubs. Members receive braille versions of interesting articles from the Jewish press and other publications.

From May 1983, the Society extended its activities to assist, in addition to the visually handicapped, all disabled groups in the Jewish community within the age group 18–60.

Jewish Welfare Board
315–317 Ballards Lane, London N12 8LP (Tel: 01-446 1499).
The Jewish Welfare Board (JWB) is the largest Jewish social work agency. It is a generic agency, but at present is concentrating on work with two major client groups: the very old and their families, and mentally ill people and their families.

The Board undertakes work with other client groups in partnership with smaller Jewish welfare organisations. It has three area social work teams based at Redbridge, Hackney and Finchley, serviced by a small team of social workers in each area.

JWB has, as its major resources, 12 homes for elderly people, one mental after-care hostel, one rehabilitation hostel for mentally handicapped people, and several group homes for both mentally ill and mentally handicapped people. It also runs four day centres for elderly people and one for people suffering from mental illness.

John Grooms Association for the Disabled
10 Gloucester Drive, London N4 2LP (Tel: 01-802 7272).
Provides care and accommodation for severely disabled people and elderly ladies. Runs a craft centre with associated homes on a garden estate at Edgware; holiday hotels for wheelchair users in Somerset and North Wales, and self-catering holiday units on 12 sites in other areas. Through a housing association promotes the provision of purpose-built flats for disabled people.

Kidney Disease
See: British Kidney Patients' Association; National Federation of Kidney Patients' Associations; Renal Society.

King's Fund Centre
126 Albert Street, London NW1 7NF (Tel: 01-267 6111).
Maintained by King Edward's Hospital Fund for London, an independent charity which seeks to encourage good practice and innovations in health care through research, experiment, education and direct grants.

The Centre provides a forum for discussion and study in conferences, exhibitions and meetings, with a view to accelerating improvements in the planning and management of health services.

One focus of the Centre's work is long-term community care, an aspect of which is the development of services which better meet the needs of people with mental handicap, physical handicap, psychiatric problems or simply growing older.

An extensive library can be used by anyone interested in health services, and there is a parallel information service for those who are unable to visit the Centre. (Books are not available for loan, but there is a limited lending service which incorporates cuttings from periodicals, etc., on specific subjects.)

Kingston Trust

The Drove, Kempshott, Basingstoke, Hampshire RG22 5LU (Tel: Basingstoke (0256) 52320).
Founded 1961. Provides homes for all types of 'stoma' patients (or those with other abdominal diseases) in need of permanent and short-stay accommodation. Homes established in Leigh-on-Sea, Leeds and Filey Bay. Problems are understood, and treated with sympathy and care.

Kith and Kids

Carol Schaffer, 27 Old Park Ridings, Grange Park, London N21 2EX (Tel: 01-360 5621).
An organisation which provides opportunities for families with handicapped children to meet informally on a regular basis. The children are able to enjoy social activities with able-bodied friends in a family atmosphere and in addition volunteer helpers provide a back-up service at four-weekly intervals aimed at training the young people and children to cope with their disabilities. Although London-based, Kith and Kids has served as a model for similar groups up and down the country, and has been able to carry out effective work as a national pressure group seeking to improve provision for handicapped children. A book *Kith and Kids* by Maurice and Doreen Collins was published in 1977. Price £2.50.

Lady Hoare Trust for Physically Disabled Children

7 North Street, Midhurst, West Sussex GU29 9DJ (Tel: Midhurst (073 081) 3696).
A professional visiting staff of medical social workers provide welfare support of every kind to the families of physically handicapped children.

L'Arche UK

Secretariat: 14 London Road, Beccles, Suffolk NR34 9NH (Tel: Beccles (0502) 715329).
Since 1964, L'Arche has established over 50 communities in various parts of the world where mentally handicapped people live and work together with non-handicapped assistants. The organisation aims to provide a home and to develop self-respect, independence, spiritual values and a sense of being useful. Wherever possible handicapped members are encouraged to work in open employment. In the United Kingdom there are communities at Barfrestone (Kent), Inverness, Liverpool, Lambeth and Bognor Regis. Admissions, when vacancies become available, are normally arranged through local authority social services departments. Films and publications list obtainable from the Secretariat.

Laryngectomy

See National Association of Laryngectomee Clubs.

Laurence-Moon-Beidl Syndrome

Although there is no separate organisation representing those affected by this condition, the British Retinitis Pigmentosa Society (*see* page 296) will endeavour to advise on visual problems, the present state of research, provide information on aids and put enquirers in touch with others who are similarly affected.

Leonard Cheshire Foundation

26–29 Maunsel Street, London SW1P 2QN (Tel: 01-828 1822).
Runs 75 residential homes in the United Kingdom, mainly for severely physically handicapped men and women. Of these, one caters for mentally handicapped adults, four for mentally handicapped children, and three offer a half-way home for patients discharged from long-stay psychiatric hospitals who need time to acquire sufficient confidence before living independently in the community. Has also set up 16 Family Support Services in England offering part-time help to disabled people living in their own homes.

Also runs 147 residential homes for mentally and physically handicapped men, women and children in 45 countries overseas. Publishes quarterly journal *The Cheshire Smile*.

Leukaemia Research Fund

43 Great Ormond Street, London WC1N 3JJ (Tel: 01-405 0101).
Apart from its major role of raising funds for research, this organisation runs an information service and has published a number of booklets on leukaemia and allied blood diseases for patients and their families, covering the nature of the diseases, symptoms, diagnoses, treatments and the outlook for the future.

Leukaemia Society

PO Box 82, Exeter, Devon EX2 5DP (Tel: Exeter (0392) 218514).
Operates throughout the United Kingdom. The Society aims to promote mutual assistance among its members. This may take the form of information about the disease, friendship and understanding, or practical help. Limited financial assistance can be offered in cases of need. The Society does not itself raise funds for research but maintains close contact with the Leukaemia Research Fund, 43 Great Ormond Street, London WC1N 3JH.

The Liberation Network of People with Disabilities

Secretary: Micheline Mason, Flat 4, 188 Ramsden Road, Balham, London SW12.

The Liberation Network is a group run by people with disabilities who believe that the problems associated with disability are largely created not by the disability itself but by the social structures in which we live.

Its aims are: to unite people with disabilities around a liberation policy; to form local groups of members; to give each other personal support and friendship; to educate the able-bodied about disability; to initiate or support campaigns on particular issues; to fight for the rights of people with disabilities as equal members of the human race.

Liberation Network now has a number of active groups. It publishes a Liberation magazine, *In from the Cold*, written by people with disabilities, three times a year (also available on tape).

There are two types of membership: full (open to people with disabilities) and associate (open to people who consider themselves to be able-bodied). Associate members are fully involved, but do not have voting rights. Both types of membership cost £2.50 a year (£3.50 overseas). Subscription to *In from the Cold* costs £1.50 a year to individuals, £2 a year to organisations. Members need not subscribe to *In from the Cold* as they receive it automatically.

Link – The Neurofibromatosis Association
Secretary: Clare Peperell, Pepperpots, 11 Crescent Drive, Maidenhead, Berkshire SL6 6AQ (Tel: Maidenhead (0628) 27549).
Neurofibromatosis (nf) is a genetic disorder affecting roughly 1 in every 3,000 people, although only some 10 to 20 per cent of sufferers will ever need medical treatment for the condition. Neurofibromatosis is still poorly understood and many milder cases remain undiagnosed. It can, however, be progressive during lifetime and in its severest form can have very serious physical and mental effects.

Link is a national association with emergent local groups. It seeks to provide mutual support, linking sufferers with each other and with the medical profession. It provides information on nf and promotes awareness and understanding of the problems encountered in the disorder. Finally, it sponsors medical research into the treatment, prevention and cure of nf.

The officers and management committee of Link are all voluntary workers and include a doctor and other professional people who work in close liaison with a medical advisory board, a panel of doctors with expert knowledge of different areas of nf. A newsletter is published four times a year, and fact sheets are available. Membership subscription £1.50 per annum.

Link, The British Centre for Deafened People
19 Hartfield Road, Eastbourne, East Sussex BN21 2AR (Tel: Eastbourne (0323) 638230).
Provides residential courses for adults who have become deafened together with member(s) of family. Payment including travelling expenses may be met through social services, health authorities or voluntary sources.

London Association for the Blind
14/16 Verney Road, London SE16 3DZ (Tel: 01-732 8771).
The Association operates nationally. It has hotels at Bognor Regis and Weston-super-Mare providing holidays for registered blind and partially sighted people, their families and escorts, at which guide dogs can be accommodated; two homes in Surrey for elderly blind and partially sighted men and women; 54 warden-supervised flats in Epsom, Surrey, for single and married blind people; and hostel accommodation in single bedsitting rooms in south-east London for single working blind people. The Association also provides sheltered employment in a modern factory in south-east London for work in PVC and injection moulding.

Grants in the form of annuities and lump sum payments can be given in appropriate cases to registered blind or registered partially sighted applicants. Over 600 people all over the country benefit every year. Applications can be made either through a social worker, local organisation for the blind, or other impartial organisation. A form is available for this purpose.

Marie Curie Memorial Foundation
28 Belgrave Square, London SW1X 8QG (Tel: 01-235 3325).
The Foundation is concerned with the welfare of cancer patients. Its nation-wide services include 11 residential nursing homes (431 beds), day and night domiciliary nurses, welfare needs in kind, advice and helpful leaflets on care and aspects of the cancer problem, and a research institute. Information freely available from the Secretary.

Mastectomy Association
26 Harrison Street, London WC1H 8JG (Tel: 01-837 0908).
Aims to help women who have recently had, or been advised to have, a breast removed. The service is strictly non-medical and aims to complement medical and nursing care by giving information about various types of prostheses, and to provide mutual understanding and encouragement. The Association has published a number of helpful booklets and leaf-

lets and has a permanent exhibition of mastectomy aids.

Medic-alert Foundation
11–13 Clifton Terrace, London N4 3JP (Tel: 01-263 8597).
Provides a service to people with unseen medical problems. They wear a warning emblem to alert anyone who may attend them in circumstances which preclude normal communication. A central reference office, able to provide more detailed information, is on call round the clock. It is available by reverse call charge from anywhere in the world.

MENCAP – The Royal Society for Mentally Handicapped Children and Adults
123 Golden Lane, London EC1Y 0RT (Tel: 01-253 9433).
Northern Ireland region: Segal House, 4 Annadale Avenue, Belfast BT7 3JH.
MENCAP operates in England, Wales and Northern Ireland and provides a wide range of services for mentally handicapped people, their families and the professionals who work for them. The Society has consistently worked to improve provision for mentally handicapped children and adults by increasing public knowledge and concern and by seeking to persuade local authorities and central government to provide desperately needed services. Over the years, it has mounted pioneer demonstration projects to point the way ahead and to show that mentally handicapped children and young people can be trained to expand their capabilities, go out to work, earn their own living and make a real contribution to the community where they live and work.

It is above all an organisation of parents. Over 500 local societies run pre-school play groups, nurseries, hostels and clubs, backed up by 12 regional officers who undertake welfare counselling and liaison with statutory authorities. The following services are provided:
for mentally handicapped people:
two social training units providing a bridge between school and the outside world;
a rural training unit where young people are taught agricultural and horticultural skills;
holidays, many of them for the very severely handicapped;
through the National Federation of Gateway Clubs to cater for the leisure-time needs of the mentally retarded (these are now nation-wide with over 10,000 members who enjoy sports, handicrafts, outings and other activities);
four residential homes for very severely handicapped children;

the Trustee Visitors' Service, a personal visiting service for mentally handicapped people after the death of their parents;
Pathway, a unique work training scheme;

for parents:
a welfare visiting scheme run by local society voluntary welfare visitors;
a welfare and counselling service;
help and support through a nation-wide network of regional offices;
books, pamphlets and leaflets on all aspects of mental handicap;
a quarterly magazine *Parents Voice*;
advice and information;

for professionals:
a specialist information service;
conferences, seminars, in-service and day-release courses;
publications and quarterly *Journal of Mental Deficiency Research*.
An entirely separate organisation, the Scottish Society for the Mentally Handicapped, operates in Scotland (*see* page 325).

Mental After-Care Association
Eagle House, 110 Jermyn Street, London SW1Y 6HB (Tel: 01-839 5953).
Provides homes and hostels, long- and short-stay, for adults recovering from mental illness under the care of trained staff; and also offers accommodation for recuperative holidays.

Mental Handicap
See: Association of Professions for the Mentally Handicapped; British Institute of Mental Handicap; The Campaign for Mentally Handicapped People; CARE; Independent Development Council for People with Mental Handicaps; L'Arche UK; MENCAP; Scottish Society for the Mentally Handicapped.

Mental Health
See: Ex-Services Mental Welfare Society; Mental After-Care Association; MIND; Psychiatric Rehabilitation Association; Richmond Fellowship; Scottish Association for Mental Health.

Metabolic Diseases
See Research Trust for Metabolic Diseases in Children.

MIND (National Association for Mental Health)
22 Harley Street, London W1N 2ED (Tel: 01-637 0741).

Regional Offices
Northern MIND, 158 Durham Road, Gateshead, Tyne and Wear NE8 4EL (Tel: Gateshead (0632) 784425).
Yorkshire MIND, 2 Blenheim Terrace, Woodhouse Lane, Leeds LS2 9JG (Tel: Leeds (0532) 446666).
Wales MIND, 23 St Mary Street, Cardiff CF1 2AT (Tel: Cardiff (0222) 395123).
North West MIND, Room 223, Miller House, Miller Arcade, Preston, Lancashire PR1 2QA (Tel: Preston (0772) 21734).
Trent MIND, 69/71 Wilkinson Street, Sheffield S10 2GJ (Tel: Sheffield (0742) 21742).
West Midlands MIND, Princess Chambers, 3rd floor, 52–54 Lichfield Street, Wolverhampton WV1 1DG (Tel: Wolverhampton (0902) 24404).

MIND runs an advice service which offers advice, referrals and short-term help to patients and their families; also an information service for both mental health professionals and the general public.

MIND has pioneered a variety of community-based projects and presently aims to support people in the community who would otherwise be in psychiatric hospitals. Feversham School in New-castle – a residential school for children with emo-tional problems – and Bryn Estyn – a holiday home in Rhyl for people in mental handicap and psychiatric hospitals – are two of their projects.

The Association runs a legal and welfare rights service to protect the rights of patients and mental health workers and to press for changes in the law. It also runs a mental health review tribunal service. In the community MIND supports and co-ordinates over 170 local mental health associations and organises regional meetings and conferences.

MIND aims to stimulate research, and keeps up sustained pressure for improvements in the mental health services, putting forward practical proposals and submitting evidence to government committees and enquiries. It produces a wide range of publica-tions on all aspects of mental health (a list is avail-able). It publishes a bi-monthly magazine called *Open Mind* and a series of fact sheets on mental illness, mental handicap, manic depression, and schizophrenia.

A holiday list will be provided free on receipt of a large s.a.e.

Motability
See Section 8, Mobility and Motoring.

Motor Neurone Disease
See below and Scottish Motor Neurone Disease Association.

Motor Neurone Disease Association
National Director: M. Roy Price, 38 Hazelwood Road, Northampton NN1 1NL (Tel: Northampton (0604) 22269).
Motor neurone disease, often shortened to MND, is the name given to a group of diseases in which the nerve cells which control the muscles of movement, known as motor neurone and located in the brain and spinal cord, are slowly destroyed. With no nerves to control them, the muscles gradually weaken and waste away, hence the muscles to be affected are those involved in giving a patient movement and with time weakness spreads to the arms and legs and to the throat and chest resulting in difficulties with speech, swallowing, breathing and a general immobility.

No one yet knows the cause of MND. It does not affect the senses or the intellect and the patient is able to think, reason and experience emotion at all stages of the disease. Most patients have passed their 40th birthday but there have been cases as young as 20 and an average course for the disease might be four years, though there are sufferers who have lived with MND for 20 years.

The Association aims to provide moral support to those suffering from motor neurone disease and their families; to provide financial help where this is needed to obtain aids and equipment not readily available from the usual caring agencies; to collect and spread information about the disease; and to foster interest in and provide funds for further research. There are local groups in various parts of the country. The Association also employs two Pa-tient Care Officers who are in touch with, and advise, professionals and sufferers and their families.

Mucopolysaccharide Diseases
See Society for Mucopolysaccharide Diseases.

Multiple Sclerosis
See below and ARMS.

Multiple Sclerosis Society of Great Britain and Northern Ireland
286 Munster Road, London SW6 6AP (Tel: 01-381 4022/4025 *or* 01-385 6146/7/8).
Northern Ireland Branch: 34 Annadale Avenue, Belfast BT7 3JJ (Tel: Belfast (0232) 648379).
Association of Scottish Branches: 27 Castle Street, Edinburgh EH2 3DN (Tel: 031-225 3600).
Promotes research into the cause and cure of multi-ple sclerosis; its many local branches spearhead the raising of funds and are also the primary means of bringing welfare, advice, encouragement, help with holidays, aids, etc., and a wide range of social activi-

ties to members, according to local needs Headquarters provides back-up information and welfare services.

Crack MS is the younger members' arm of the Society and helps them to meet their particular needs through self-help groups within the parent branches. The Society publishes a quarterly magazine, *MS News*, and a monthly bulletin which incorporates news for Crack MS members. (*See also* Section 9).

Muscular Dystrophy Group of Great Britain and Northern Ireland

Nattrass House, 35 Macaulay Road, London SW4 0QP (Tel: 01-720 8055).
Primarily a medical research charity, but also provides, in liaison with statutory and voluntary bodies, welfare services and social contacts through over 400 local branches. Provides informative literature about the neuromuscular diseases and helpful handbooks for sufferers and their families. Also publishes a quarterly newspaper the *Muscular Dystrophy Journal*. Has published a useful series of books on aids – see Section 3.

Myalgic Encephalomyelitis Association

Secretary: Mrs P. Searles, The Moss, Third Avenue, Stanford-le-Hope, Essex SS17 8EL.
The Association was formed in 1978. It offers support to those affected by this debilitating and capricious disease. It promotes research to try to establish a diagnostic test and to effect a cure, and works to make people aware of the disease and its effects. A major object is to pass on information obtained from the medical profession.

Myasthenia

See British Association of Myasthenics.

National Ankylosing Spondylitis Society

Director: Fergus Rogers, 6 Grosvenor Crescent, London SW1X 7ER (Tel: 01-235 9585).
Ankylosing spondylitis is a painful condition of the spine and associated joints. The Society's prime objects are research into the causes of ankylosing spondylitis, the relief of suffering and the education of patients and the public. Cassette tapes are available for patients to learn and do beneficial exercises. The Society promotes the welfare of patients, and deals with individual enquiries. Support groups are being formed.

The National Association for Deaf-Blind and Rubella Handicapped

311 Gray's Inn Road, London WC1X 8PT (Tel: 01-278 1000).

NADBRH provides advice and support to deaf-blind and Rubella handicapped children and adults, their families and professionals in the field. Information and guidance is available on benefits, education provision, community placements, aids and equipment. A quarterly *Newsletter* is published to members.

The SENSE Campaign was launched to increase public awareness of this problem, and to raise funds to support the Association's activities. The Family Centre at Ealing provides teaching and support to pre-school deaf-blind children and their parents throughout the country, through a programme of Residential Parent/Baby Courses, home visits and training weekends. Information and courses for professionals working with deaf-blind children are also provided.

The Manor House in Market Deeping provides assessment, residential care and training for 17 deaf-blind adolescents and young adults. Individual programmes include communication, social skills, leisure activities and vocational skills.

An Education Department runs regular conferences for teachers of deaf-blind children. The Regional Organisation enables parents that want support to be put into contact with other families who have experienced similar problems. Local information and advice is also available through this network.

NADBRH is in the forefront of the campaign to increase uptake of Rubella vaccination and therefore reduce the incidence of Congenital Rubella Syndrome.

National Association of Laryngectomee Clubs

4th floor, 39 Eccleston Square, London SW1V 1PB (Tel: 01-834 2857).
Many of those who have undergone surgical removal of the larynx find it extremely difficult to master the technique of producing alternative speech from the oesophagus. The result is often a retreat from communication into loneliness. In an attempt to meet this problem, laryngectomee clubs have been formed in many areas, in association with speech therapy clinics. Members meet regularly to try out their new voice techniques and give and receive confidence and fluency in a congenial, sympathetic and social atmosphere. The National Association of Laryngectomee Clubs encourages the formation and affiliation of clubs, and collects, co-ordinates and disseminates information concerning the rehabilitation of members. It advises on the availability of speech aids and medical supplies, demonstrates speech aids and lectures on mouth to neck resuscitation on request of

professional bodies. Arrangements can also be made for an experienced oesophageal speaker to visit pre-operative and post-operative patients.

National Association of Leagues of Hospital Friends

Secretary-General: Gordon Palliser, 38 Ebury Street, London SW1W 0LU (Tel: 01-730 0103).

Membership is open to all Leagues of Hospital Friends (or kindred bodies) whose objects are, in general, to support the charitable work of the hospitals and, in particular, to assist the patients, former patients and staff of their hospitals by giving their time, their talents and their money. The National Association is the central organisation to which are affiliated over 1,300 Leagues of Hospital Friends. Its functions are to assist existing Leagues by providing common services and by the exchange of information, and to encourage the expansion of the Hospital Friends movement, including the giving of advice and practical help to Leagues in the process of formation. *The Hospital Friend* magazine (circulation 4,650) is published quarterly.

National Association for Limbless Disabled

203A Uxbridge Road, West Ealing, London W13 9AA (Tel: 01-579 4918).

Founded in 1983, the Association aims to relieve and promote the rehabilitation of persons who have suffered the loss of a limb or part of a limb.

Membership is open, from age 16, to those who have lost one or both legs, or one or both arms, or hands or feet. An advisory service seeks to ensure that members receive their proper entitlements under existing legislation and to assist needy dependants wherever possible. The Association also seeks to help members to secure suitable employment, to combat discrimination and to provide opportunities for a better, fuller social life for its members.

The Association works to facilitate the sharing of knowledge and experience to help all limbless members of the community, and co-operates with other organisations and government departments to improve services, including advances in the design and fitting of artificial limbs.

Membership fee £3.50 per annum, which includes the cost of a newsletter.

National Children's Bureau

8 Wakley Street, London EC1V 7QE (Tel: 01-278 9441).

A voluntary and independent organisation concerned widely with children's needs in the family, school and society, and their all-round development and well-being. Membership includes statutory and voluntary organisations as well as individuals. It has four basic aims: to make existing knowledge on children's development and needs readily available through its information service, library, and numerous publications; to improve communication and co-operation between education, medical and social workers and between statutory and voluntary services; to evaluate existing services and encourage new developments; to contribute to new knowledge and to assist others wishing to do so.

The Bureau undertakes an extensive research programme and its information service and library handles about 6,000 enquiries a year. The Voluntary Council for Handicapped Children (*see* page 330) was established and operates under its aegis.

Its booklist is impressive and includes works on the social, emotional and educational adjustment associated with various specific forms of handicap affecting children, as well as the more general *Living with Handicap* (1970, reprinted 1971).

National Children's Home

Principal: Rev. Gordon E. Barritt, 85 Highbury Park, London N5 1UD (Tel: 01-226 2033).

The National Children's Home, which looks after some 7,000 children a year in over 100 residential homes, schools and family centres, also makes provision for disabled children. It runs one residential school for physically handicapped children at Chipping Norton, Oxfordshire; two homes for severely subnormal children at Limpsfield, Surrey, and Ebley, Gloucester; and three residential schools for educationally subnormal children at Bramhope, West Yorkshire, Edgworth, Lancashire, and Hildenborough, Kent.

National Association for the Relief of Paget's Disease

Secretary: Ann Stansfield, 413 Middleton Road, Middleton, Manchester M24 4QZ.

Paget's disease involves thinning of bone followed by unregulated new bone formation. It is quite common in the older age groups and in a small proportion of cases can be progressive, leading to pain, deformity or other associated disabilities. The disease is now being diagnosed in younger sufferers.

The Association was founded in 1973 to raise funds for research and to increase public awareness of the disease. It has subsequently helped to fund a number of important research projects, and has established branches in various parts of the country. Members are regularly kept in touch with progress and new ideas about treatment.

National Association for the Welfare of Children in Hospital
Exton House, 7 Exton Street, London SE1 8UE (Tel: 01-261 1738).
Helps children in hospital and their parents. Supplies books, leaflets and all kinds of information. Local groups give practical help.

National Autistic Society
276 Willesden Lane, London NW2 5RB (Tel: 01-451 3844).
Northern Ireland Society, 13a Seahill Drive, Craigavad, Holywood, Co. Down (Tel: Holywood (023 17) 3807).
Runs an advisory and information service. Publishes literature on the education and management of autistic children, and a quarterly periodical *Communication*. With affiliated regional societies, provides special schools and residential services for adults in various parts of the United Kingdom.

National Bureau for Handicapped Students
See Section 6, Further Education and Training.

The National Childbirth Trust
9 Queensborough Terrace, Bayswater, London W2 3TB (Tel: 01-221 3833).
An attempt to form a group for parents who are disabled, under the name *Nurture*, has, despite considerable publicity, not yet received sufficient support. However, the Trust would be interested to hear from disabled parents and, with the help of Jenny and Danny Estermann, will respond to correspondence about motherhood with disability. It would also be keen to print articles from disabled parents in its magazine *New Generation*.

National Council for Carers and their Elderly Dependants
29 Chilworth Mews, London W2 3RG (Tel: 01-262 1451).
Helps and advises carers of elderly and infirm people at home; provides a service of information and guidance for carers and their dependants; studies legislation affecting their problems and promotes policies to improve their circumstances; campaigns for increased domiciliary services; provides some warden-serviced housing for working carers with dependants; promotes holiday and other relief services; circulates a bi-monthly *Newsletter* giving advice and information.

The Council can also supply information about nursing homes offering short-term care for elderly and infirm people. It handles some 12,000 queries a year and has 46 branches throughout the United Kingdom.

National Council for One Parent Families
255 Kentish Town Road, London NW5 2LX (Tel: 01-267 1361).
Gives free, confidential advice and practical help (including representation at tribunals) to lone parents and single, pregnant women, publishes informative pamphlets and booklets, and presses the needs of one-parent families and their children to the government, local authorities and society in general.

Single parents living in the 12 south London boroughs should contact *One Parent Families*, South London Office, 20 Clapham Common South Side, London SW4 7AB (Tel: 01-720 9191).

National Council for Voluntary Organisations
26 Bedford Square, London WC1B 3HU (Tel: 01-636 4066).
NCVO is a national resource centre providing advisory and information services for voluntary organisations. On matters of common interest, it speaks on behalf of the voluntary sector to the government and other sections of society. It also attempts to promote new forms of voluntary social action.

Membership comprises about 350 national voluntary organisations – including almost all of those representing or working on behalf of disabled people – and some 200 local development agencies such as the councils for voluntary service, whose national secretariat is based at NCVO. All member organisations in the disability field come together in the Health and Handicaps Group, which meets quarterly to discuss specialist issues.

Advice and information – for example on charity law, tax affairs, fundraising, management, publishing, and relations with government departments and local authorities – is available, usually without charge, to all voluntary organisations, whether local or national, NCVO members or not. NCVO is particularly pleased to hear from new or would-be voluntary organisations.

Several units may be of particular interest to disability groups: for example the Inner Cities Unit, which advises voluntary bodies on how to make the most of Urban Programme funds; and the Community Schemes Unit, which does the same for the MSC's training and temporary employment programmes. A new Community Health Initiatives Resource Unit began work in July 1983.

Recent studies by NCVO's Policy Analysis Unit include *Disabled People – A Right to Work?* and *Housing and Community Care*. NCVO's publishing imprint, the Bedford Square Press, has a range of other relevant titles in its 1984 catalogue. Copies of the catalogue are available from the Sales Manager,

Bedford Square Press, at the NCVO address above.

The latest (1984/85) edition of *Voluntary Organisations: An NCVO Directory* contains details of 700 national bodies. It can be obtained for £5.90 (postage and packing included) from MEDS Ltd, Estover Road, Plymouth PL6 7PZ.

National Deaf-Blind Helpers' League

18 Rainbow Court, Paston Ridings, Peterborough PE4 6UP (Tel: Peterborough (0733) 73511).

Offers hope and encouragement to deaf-blind people, bringing them together through regional group activities, rallies and *The Rainbow*, quarterly magazine in braille, Moon type and ordinary print. Provides private self-contained flats for deaf-blind people capable of running their own home, a small guest house and short stay centre, where deaf-blind people are encouraged towards re-integration into the normal community. Help is given as and where needed.

National Deaf Children's Society

45 Hereford Road, London W2 5AH (Tel: 01-229 9272).

Main aims are to stress for the need of early diagnosis; to press for the provision of adequate education for all deaf children; to explore the whole field of suitable employment for deaf school-leavers; to publicise the needs of deaf children; to assist in the training of teachers and other staff to care for deaf children in and out of school. Activities include: personal advice to parents on education and employment of their deaf children, also through correspondence and circulation of literature; bursaries to student teachers; assistance with publication of books for deaf children; consideration of medical and technical research projects in the field of deafness in children; provision of grants, holidays and equipment; welfare counselling of parents of deaf children.

National Diabetes Foundation

177a Tennison Road, London SE25 5NF.

This organisation has recently been formed with the support of the Juvenile Diabetes Foundation International of America. The main aims are as follows:

1. To fund research into the causes and complications of diabetes including blindness, heart and kidney disease, gangrene; while the primary objective of the Foundation will be to find a cure for diabetes.
2. To provide a programme of public awareness and education.
3. To raise funds to supplement hospitals with equipment and other help required for diabetic care.

4. To represent the interests of all diabetics in the United Kingdom.

The Foundation issues an interesting quarterly magazine, *Diabetic Life*, for the understanding of diabetes, with regular mailings to members of the most recent progress in diabetic research work. In addition, the Foundation has a panel of doctors and allied members of the medical profession who are able to give general help and advice to diabetics and especially the parents of diabetic children.

A 24-hour telephone answering service is operated to give non-medical advice with co-ordinators appointed throughout the country as local contacts.

Annual membership £3.50 (£2 for pensioners).

National Eczema Society

Tavistock House North, Tavistock Square, London WC1H 9SR (Tel: 01-388 4097).

The Society was formed in 1975 to act as an information centre and mutual support organisation for eczema sufferers and their families and others concerned with their welfare. The Society now has branches and groups of members throughout much of the British Isles. Its publications include a quarterly magazine *Exchange*, and a detailed leaflet *What is Eczema?* both sent free to members. In addition, the Society acts as a source of information on eczema for the public and the news media, and it is raising funds for research into the causes and treatment of the condition.

National Elfrida Rathbone Society

11a Whitworth Street, Mancheser M1 3GW (Tel: 061-236 5358).

The Society seeks to develop all forms of social work with the educationally handicapped (the so-called ESN(M) group), including club activities for school-children and young adults, play groups, holiday schemes, family casework, the provision of hostel accommodation, unemployment schemes and training workshops. It also aims to increase public awareness of the problems which the educationally handicapped have in integrating into the community and to show how voluntary effort can help them. In addition to its central organisation, the Society has two regional officers – one in Leeds and one in Coventry – and carries out a great deal of work through a network of voluntary committees. Publications include a newsletter, *Rathbone News*.

The National Federation of the Blind of the United Kingdom

Chairperson, Environment and Social Services Committee: Jill Allen, 59 Silversea Drive, Southend, Essex (Tel: Southend (0702) 74059). Public Relations Officer: Peter Westwood, 24 The Wheatings, Ossett, Wakefield, West Yorkshire.

Founded in 1947, the Federation believes that no one understands the problems of blind people better than themselves, and plays a pre-eminent role in providing a means by which blind people can effectively bring their collective views to bear on the development of relevant services.

To achieve a better understanding between blind people and those who are able to see so as to bring visually handicapped people fully into the life of society, the Federation campaigns on six fronts: education; employment; environmental safety; financial compensation; appropriate and sensitive social services; and representation and involvement in the administration of relevant welfare services. There are local branches throughout the United Kingdom and one which is postal-linked for those who are not within easy reach of an ordinary branch. A quarterly journal *Viewpoint* is free to full members and a booklet, *Looking for Jobs*, has been published (one copy free; bulk supplies at 15p each; braille version 25p).

The Federation can already claim to have had a significant impact in a number of policy areas, having been concerned for example with the introduction of the blind person's tax allowance, various concessions regarding guide dogs and travel concessions. Full membership is open to all blind and partially sighted people, and associate membership is available to sighted friends, relatives, or anyone else who is interested.

National Federation of Kidney Patients' Associations

Acorn Lodge, Woodsetts, Worksop, Nottinghamshire (Tel: Worksop (0909) 562703).

The NFKPA was started in October 1978 to provide a strong, well-informed national 'voice' for all kidney patients. It aims to promote a wider knowledge of the problems of kidney patients, to co-operate with local organisations and statutory bodies with a view to improving the facilities for kidney patients, to further and assist the work of local Kidney Patients' Associations and to raise funds for these purposes.

The Federation is governed by a Council drawn from member Associations, at least 60 per cent of whom are themselves kidney patients. A quarterly *Newsflash* is produced with information of interest to all patients and those working in the field of renal medicine. A Medical Advisory Panel is available for advice and opinions.

Membership is open to all Kidney Patients' Associations attached to renal units within the United Kingdom, and associate membership is available to constituted organisations whose objects are in accordance with the aims of the Federation. The Federation can put people in touch with their local Kidney Patients' Association.

National Fund for Research into Crippling Diseases

See Action Research for the Crippled Child.

National Housewives' Register

National Organiser: Antoinette Ferraro, 245 Warwick Road, Solihull, West Midlands B92 7AH (Tel: 021-706 1101).

NHR offers women of all ages with enquiring minds the opportunity to meet in each other's homes to participate in stimulating and wide-ranging discussion, leading to friendship and activities. Disabled women are welcome.

The National League of the Blind and Disabled

2 Tenterden Road, London N17 8BE (Tel: 01-808 6030).

A trade union of blind and disabled people formed in 1899, and affiliated to the TUC since 1902. Membership is open to any registered blind or partially sighted person of either sex over the age of 16, and to any severely disabled sighted person being trained or employed in Workshops for the Blind.

Broadly, the objects of the League are to secure improvements in education and the economic and social conditions of blind and disabled people. Of particular help to many members over the years has been the provision of legal assistance in a variety of circumstances, notably in relation to accidents at work, and, more often, accidents outside work such as falling in unguarded holes.

There are 60 branches of the League in various parts of Great Britain, and a membership of around 3,500.

A challenging and well-produced printed journal, *The Advocate*, is published quarterly at 15p per issue, and a braille journal, *The Horizon*, is issued bi-monthly at £1 per annum.

National Library for the Blind

Cromwell Road, Bredbury, Stockport, Greater Manchester SK6 2SG (Tel: 061-494 0217/8/9).

Provides a lending service, free and post free, of books in embossed and enlarged types for visually handicapped readers. For further details apply to the Library.

National Schizophrenia Fellowship

78–79 Victoria Road, Surbiton, Surrey KT6 4NS (Tel: 01-390 3651).

NSF (Scotland), 67 York Place, Edinburgh 3 (Tel: 031-557 4410).

Schizophrenia is a term used to describe a group of severe mental disorders. The symptoms occur in widely different combinations and with varying intensity, but among them are deep disturbances or distortions of feeling, thinking, perception and conduct which lead to a kind of withdrawal from the outside objective world.

The National Schizophrenia Fellowship is a national organisation for all matters concerning the relief of sufferers from schizophrenia and the support of their families and dependants. In particular it works to:

(a) encourage sufferers and their families to help each other and themselves;
(b) secure, by pressure on government and statutory authorities, the improvement of community care facilities of all kinds;
(c) spread a greater understanding of the special problems arising from the illness;
(d) sponsor important research projects into the cause of schizophrenia and into ways to improve facilities for sufferers from schizophrenia.

There are now 145 local NSF groups throughout the United Kingdom as well as an increasing number of contacts overseas and around the world. The Fellowship publishes a wide range of books and pamphlets on the problems associated with schizophrenia.

National Society for Cancer Relief

Michael Sobell House, 30 Dorset Square, London NW1 6QL (Tel: 01-402 8125).

Founded in 1911 by Douglas Macmillan, the National Society for Cancer Relief is the oldest national cancer charity in Great Britain. Its main objective is to give every possible kind of practical help to those with cancer. Such help is given in four ways:

1. Benefits. Financial aid is given to alleviate the problems which can arise when a cancer patient has to be cared for at home.
2. Macmillan Continuing Care Homes. The Society, with the National Health Service, has established twelve homes throughout the country. These homes have been built and equipped by the Society and given to the NHS, which now runs them. They provide specialist care for patients, mainly with cancer, who cannot benefit from treatment aimed at cure. All patients receive individual attention, and medical and nursing skills are employed to relieve pain and improve the quality of the patient's life. Support is also given to relatives, who are encouraged to take an active part in the patient's nursing care.
3. Macmillan Home Care Services. Most patients prefer to be cared for at home and many families can look after them well, given the right support. The Society is therefore establishing home care services nation-wide. Macmillan nurses work with family doctors, health visitors and district nurses, advising on medical or nursing care and giving social support both to the patient and the family. The Society helps to set up the services by financing them for the first three years, after which the Health Service or a local charity takes over responsibility.
4. Education. The Society has now started an education programme designed to pass on the special skills of cancer care to nursing and medical students. The programme includes the funding of training courses for nurses, and extended facilities in Macmillan homes so that they can become education centres. This will not only ensure that trained staff are available for the Society's own Macmillan services, but also for general hospitals, where most cancer patients are cared for.

Cancer Relief also works in association with the Colostomy Welfare Group, the National Association of Laryngectomee Clubs and the Mastectomy Association.

The National Society for Epilepsy

Chalfont Centre for Epilepsy, Chalfont St Peter, Gerrards Cross, Buckinghamshire SL9 0RJ (Tel: Chalfont St Giles (024 07) 3991).

This Centre provides long-term residential care for over 400 adults, and short-term accommodation for 45 adults for observation, assessment and drug control. The emphasis is on rehabilitation, and employment is provided for those whose condition necessitates long term accommodation.

The Education and Information Service also offers lectures and literature to those involved in the professional management of epilepsy.

The National Society for Phenylketonuria and Allied Disorders

14 Newfound Drive, Cringleford, Norwich, Norfolk.
The Society is run by parents. It makes available a leaflet giving basic information about phenylketonuria and has published a number of booklets of dietary information/recipes. A quarterly newsletter keeps members up to date, and contacts for mutual support and advice are encouraged. An annual holiday conference and regional day conferences are organised. Annual subscription for voting members is £2; membership is otherwise free.

A more detailed account of the condition is given in the booklet *The Child with Phenylketonuria* by L. Tyfield and J. Holton, available from the Society – free to parents, otherwise 30p plus 20p postage and packing.

Neurofibromatosis
See Link – The Neurofibromatosis Association.

Northern Ireland Council for the Handicapped
2 Annadale Avenue, Belfast BT7 3JH (Tel: Belfast (0232) 640011).
NICH, a federal member of the Northern Ireland Council of Social Service, provides a forum for voluntary organisations concerned with disabled people and their carers. With 40 member organisations representing many forms of handicap and disability, the Council plays an increasing role in identifying needs, disseminating information and instigating action on behalf of disabled people throughout Northern Ireland, wherever this is possible.

A major activity is that of the Information Service for Disabled People in Northern Ireland, the only comprehensive service of its kind in the Province, and the work of the Regional Access Committee.

Northern Ireland Council for Orthopaedic Development
2nd floor, 7 Donegall Square West, Belfast BT1 6JD (Tel: Belfast (0232) 228378).
A voluntary organisation working in Northern Ireland to help those who are physically handicapped with conditions such as cerebral palsy, spina bifida, and muscular dystrophy to lead a full life.

NICOD is affiliated to and works very closely with the Spastics Society, and carries out the equivalent of its work in Northern Ireland. In addition, NICOD liaises closely with the Northern Ireland Association for Spina Bifida and Hydrocephalus.

The Council provides advice clinics for the treatment of all physically handicapped children from birth to 16 years. These are situated at Belfast, Erne, Londonderry and Omagh. Treatment is given by physiotherapists, occupational therapists, and speech therapists, and parents are made aware of the importance of correct handling and positioning of their child in the home. Advice and information is given on a variety of subjects, all aimed at helping parents to cope better with the problems associated with young physically handicapped children.

NICOD also provides a work centre at Balmoral (Belfast) for disabled school leavers, and a residential hostel in Belfast so that moderately handicapped young people from country areas can attend the work centre or obtain suitable employment in the Greater Belfast Urban Area.

Another residential hostel for severely physically handicapped people is being developed for completion in early 1985 (no other suitable accommodation is available in Northern Ireland at present). Fees are charged for residential accommodation, but sponsorship can be arranged through Health Boards. All other services are provided free to the handicapped person.

Northern Ireland Polio Fellowship
485 Antrim Road, Belfast BT15 3BP (Tel: Belfast (0232) 779476).
Independent of the British Polio Fellowship. Aims 'to provide a better life for the disabled... to give mutual help and encouragement in the fight of the polio disabled against the loneliness, and even hopelessness, that accompanies disability.'

Office of Health Economics
12 Whitehall, London SW1A 2DY (Tel: 01-930 9203).
Founded in 1962 by the Association of the British Pharmaceutical Industry. Undertakes research on the economic aspects of medical care; investigates health and social problems; publishes relevant information including data from other countries. It has produced a range of studies of current health problems and diagnosis papers.

The Officers' Association
48 Pall Mall, London SW1Y 5JY (Tel: 01-930 0125). (Scotland: 1 Fitzroy Place, Sauchiehall Street, Glasgow G3 7RJ (Tel: 041-221 8141/2).)
The Association exists to relieve distress among those who have held a Commission in HM Forces, and their widows and dependants, and to aid and assist and promote the interests of all such persons. Apart from giving financial help in appropriate cases, the Association can advise on the best method of finding accommodation for the elderly and sick in long-stay residential and nursing homes. In addition, the Association co-operates with the Housing Association for Officers' Families which provides housing for war disabled officers and their families. Ex-officers are also eligible to be considered for flats belonging to the Royal British Legion Housing Association.

Older people
See Age Concern; Centre for Policy on Ageing; Counsel and Care for the Elderly; Help the Aged.

One Parent Families
See National Council for One Parent Families.

Optical Information Council
418–422 The Strand, London WC2R 0PB (Tel: 01-836 2323).
Publishes a number of free leaflets giving information on the help available for the visual problems of the partially sighted, the use of low-visual aids, and methods of protecting the eyes against glare.

Outset
30 Craven Street, London WC2 5BR (Tel: 01-930 4255).
Outset is a national charity one of whose functions is in the field of disablement. Its main activity is to carry out identification surveys of the handicapped on behalf of government departments, local authorities, area health authorities, community health councils and any other organisations concerned about the implementation of the Chronically Sick and Disabled Persons Act 1970.

Outset will either act in an advisory capacity to someone wishing to carry out a survey, or construct and supervise surveys on behalf of the applicant, providing relevant training, conducting the analysis of all data, and publishing this material in report form at the end of the processing period. A fee is charged on the basis of £100 per 1,000 households surveyed.

Outset is always ready to investigate particular areas of concern for disabled people and is currently involved investigating employment opportunities for handicapped people. A Disablement Information Unit is also now in operation, the duties of which include monitoring the progress of local authorities since the implementation of the Chronically Sick and Disabled Persons Act.

Paget's Disease
See National Association for the Relief of Paget's Disease.

Parents for Children
222 Camden High Street, London NW1 8QR (Tel: 01-485 7526).
This is an adoption agency specialising in the placement of both older and handicapped children. Families who live within a 100-mile radius of London are welcome to enquire about becoming adoptive parents. Most local authority social service departments are also happy to hear from prospective adopters who will consider a child with a disability.

Parkinson's Disease Society of the UK Ltd
36 Portland Place, London W1N 3DG (Tel: 01-323 1174).
Provides an information and advice service at headquarters and through local branches around the country. Particular attention given to problems of

daily living for Parkinsonians and families. Raises funds for research and publishes a helpful quarterly *Newsletter* and other literature.

Partially Sighted Society
40 Wordsworth Street, Hove, East Sussex BN3 5BH (Tel: Brighton (0273) 736053).
Offers assistance to all people with impaired vision. Services include: information and advice; publications, including a bi-monthly magazine *Oculus* in large print; special printing and enlargement service; and aids to vision. The Society has over 20 local branches in the UK offering direct support and contact. Nationally, the Society represents the interests of partially sighted people to government bodies and other organisations. It organises conferences, runs exhibitions and displays, and contributes to the training of specialist workers. It maintains working committees in specific areas, like education, employment and mobility, and has access to special advisers on topics such as low vision aids and lighting.
Membership is open to all.

Patients' Association
Room 33, 18 Charing Cross Road, London WC2H 0HR (Tel: 01-240 0671).
An independent advisory service for patients, which also aims to represent and further their interests, and to make sure they are treated as people. It campaigns for improvements in the NHS and produces a number of information leaflets, *e.g.* on the legal rights of patients, changing one's doctor, going into hospital and using the NHS.

Pensioners' Link
17 Balfe Street, London N1 9EB (Tel: 01-278 5501).
A voluntary organisation which works with and provides services for pensioners, able-bodied or disabled. Their volunteers visit housebound, isolated people, helping out with odd jobs and in some cases with decorating. The organisation currently operates in 12 of the London boroughs.

Pet Concern
Animal Welfare Trust, Tyler's Way, Watford By-pass, Watford, Herts WD2 8HQ (Tel: 01-950 8215).
Established in 1979 to care for the pets of disabled and elderly people during hospital treatment or convalescence. If within easy reach of the Trust's London/Home Counties rescue centre, dogs can be boarded at £1 a day, cats at 60p a day.

Phenylketonuria
See National Society for Phenylketonuria and Allied Disorders.

Phipps Respiratory Unit Patients' Association (PRUPA)
Secretary: James Turner, 65 Gregory Road, Chadwell Heath, Romford, Essex (Tel: 01-599 2494).
Formed in 1979, PRUPA now has over 200 members, many of whom are pursuing active careers despite their breathing aids and equipment. The Phipps Respiratory Unit belongs to St Thomas' Hospital but is situated within the South-Western Hospital at Stockwell. Of the 300 or so patients who attend the ward, many live far away. The hope is that they can be made well enough to return to living reasonably active lives in the community.

The patients' association complements the work of the hospital by giving financial support for equipment when normal hospital funds are not available. It aims to promote the interests of patients in every way possible, keeping them informed of new developments, and to preserve the Phipps Ward as a centre of excellence.

The Phobics Society
4 Cheltenham Road, Chorlton-cum-Hardy, Manchester M21 1QN (Tel: 061-881 1937).
Founded in 1970, The Phobics Society is dedicated to promoting the relief and rehabilitation of sufferers from agoraphobia and other phobic illnesses. It offers immediate advice and understanding to those who desperately seek help, and tries to convince sufferers that they have a well-documented illness which can be treated and overcome.

There are now some 4,500 members, and branches have been formed in various parts of the United Kingdom, allowing phobics to discuss their problem and exchange views. The Society maintains contact with members through a regular newsletter. Annual membership £2.

PHAB (Physically Handicapped and Able-Bodied)
Tavistock House North, Tavistock Square, London WC1H 9HX (Tel: 01-388 1963).
Northern Ireland PHAB, Hampton House, Glenmachan Road, Belfast BT4 2NN (Tel: Belfast (0232) 768603).
This is a national organisation concerned with the integration of physically handicapped and able-bodied young people, largely through leisure activities. There are now over 400 clubs throughout the United Kingdom aiming towards equal numbers of both groups; the able-bodied being enrolled as full members rather than as 'helpers'. The clubs provide a setting in which barriers can be overcome and relationships established through the sharing of varied activities, so giving handicapped people the necessary confidence to take their full place in the community alongside their able-bodied peers.

The training of club leaders is an important aspect of PHAB's work and courses are arranged in different parts of the country. In addition to supporting and developing clubs and groups, PHAB arranges residential holiday courses in this country and abroad for people of all ages and for families.

Play Matters – The Toy Libraries Association
See Section 11, Sports and Leisure.

Polio
See British Polio Fellowship; Northern Ireland Polio Fellowship.

Possum Users' Association
See Sequal.

Professional Classes Aid Council
10 St Christopher's Place, London W1M 6HY (Tel: 01-935 0641).
The Council exists to help professional people and their dependants in times of distress by means of continuing grants and special gifts. Applications to the Secretary.

Psoriasis Association
7 Milton Street, Northampton NN2 7JG (Tel: Northampton (0604) 711129).
Collects funds for and promotes research, seeks to advance education, public acceptance and understanding and provides information and a point of social contact for sufferers from this skin condition. Publishes a triannual newsletter. A slide set, *The Social Effects of Psoriasis*, is available from Graves Medical Audiovisual Library (*see* page 345).

Psychiatric Rehabilitation Association
The Groupwork Centre, 21a Kingsland High Street, Dalston, London E8 2JS (Tel: 01-254 9753).
The purpose of the Association is to stimulate patients towards greater initiative and awareness of their environment and society. It prepares and encourages them to return and re-adapt to their community. At the same time, the Association attempts to improve attitudes towards the mentally ill and promotes practical measures and research for preventing and combating mental distress within the community. The Association pioneers community care projects and includes among its many services day centres, evening centres, industrial units, group homes and evening restaurant clubs, with a special emphasis on the needs of the isolated patient. The Association has concentrated for many years on the development of research programmes to study social problems associated with mental illness, and to assess methods and standards of rehabilitation required.

PRA has recently created a new company called PRA Aids for the Handicapped Limited, which, through PRA workshops, produces aids for the disabled and has built an assessment centre and permanent exhibition of aids at Mitchley Road, Haringey, London N17.

PRA is also producing a number of teaching aids for community care: in particular, tape/slide programmes on groupwork, day centres, industrial education units and residential care, which are used in conjunction with an updated manual, *An Aid to Community Care.*

Queen Elizabeth's Foundation for the Disabled

Leatherhead, Surrey KT22 0BN (Tel: Oxshott (037 284) 2204).

Comprises four units which provide assessment, further education, vocational training, residential sheltered work, holidays and convalescence. They are:

Banstead Place, Park Road, Banstead, Surrey SM7 3EE (Tel: Burgh Heath (073 73) 56222). Centre for total assessment (educational, social, medical, vocational) of physically handicapped boys and girls of school-leaving age (16 to 20) leading to placement. A Mobility Assessment Centre was opened in June 1981 (*see* page 153).

Queen Elizabeth's Training College: *see* Section 6, Further Education and Training.

Dorincourt Sheltered Workshop, Oaklawn Road, Leatherhead, Surrey KT22 0BT (Tel: Oxshott (037 284) 2599). Residential sheltered workshop (16 to late middle-age).

Lulworth Court, Chalkwell Esplanade, Westcliff-on-Sea, Essex SS0 8JQ (Tel: Southend-on-Sea (0702) 47818). Holiday and convalescent home for severely disabled men and women (17 plus). Enquiries to Leatherhead headquarters.

Raynaud's Association

Secretary: Anne Mawdsley, 40 Bladon Crescent, Alsager, Cheshire ST7 2BG (Tel: Alsager (093 63) 5167).

Raynaud's Phenomenon (or Syndrome) is a distressing condition in which blood is prevented from reaching the fingers and toes. People severely affected are constantly in pain. Ulcerations form on fingers and toes, which become gangrenous and can require amputation. Many sufferers are seriously disabled. There is, as yet, no cure.

The Association issues regular newsletters giving details of treatments which may alleviate the symptoms, and news of research. The Raynaud's Association Trust has been set up to raise funds to help finance research, and the Raynaud's Research Unit at King's College Hospital Medical School in London is trying to discover causes as well as ways of alleviating the pain.

The Association also facilitates communication between sufferers. It is hoped that by contacting each other, and discussing symptoms, treatments and tips found to be helpful, members may get support and comfort. There is at present no charge for membership.

Reach – The Association for Children with Artificial Arms

Secretary: R. Hendry, 11 Shelley Road, St Marks, Cheltenham, Gloucestershire GL51 7LE (Tel: Cheltenham (0242) 36552).

Reach is a society of parents of children with missing hands or arms. It aims to secure the best possible services and provision for such children; to gather and distribute information about new developments in artificial arms; to support parents of affected children (especially when they are first faced with the problem) and establish links between them; and to encourage research and the development of artificial arm technology.

Renal Society

64 South Hill Park, London NW3 2SJ.

Gives encouragement to kidney sufferers, particularly those coping with a strict diet. Issues periodic newsletter through which members can contact each other.

Research Trust for Metabolic Diseases in Children

Secretary: Lesley Greene, 9 Gerard Drive, Nantwich, Cheshire (Tel: Nantwich (0270) 626834).

Metabolic diseases are most generally described as inherited biochemical genetic disorders or inborn errors of metabolism. There are hundreds of such diseases. A few are well known and are catered for by other major charities, *e.g.*, diabetes, cystic fibrosis and muscular dystrophy. The vast majority, when named, mean nothing to most people, yet many of these inborn errors lead to severe physical and/or mental handicap and in all cases the conditions are degenerative.

RTMDC was founded in 1981 and has three basic aims: to promote research, to educate the public, and to act as a parent support group. The last-named is a very important aspect of the Trust's work, because many families of children with these conditions have previously felt very isolated, with nowhere to turn for support.

RTDMC runs a completely confidential parent-contact service, and holds an annual Parents' Conference where parents and specialists can meet, hear speakers and exchange their experiences.

Responaut
'Pen-Glyn', Beedon Hill, Beedon, Newbury, Berkshire.
This is the title of a periodical by, for and about respirator-aided and other gadget-aided people.

Restricted growth
See Association for Research into Restricted Growth.

Retinitis pigmentosa
See British Retinitis Pigmentosa Society.

Richmond Fellowship
8 Addison Road, London W14 8DL (Tel: 01-603 6373).
Provides residential short-term and long-term therapeutic care for people who have suffered or are on the verge of a nervous breakdown in 40 therapeutic communities and group homes throughout England, Wales and Scotland. The College runs courses for members of the caring professions and others who wish to gain skills in counselling and group work.

Royal Association in Aid of the Deaf and Dumb
27 Old Oak Road, Acton, London W3 7HN (Tel: 01-743 6187).
Operative in Greater London, Essex, Surrey and Kent. The Association provides trained staff to act as interpreters, and to advise and help with everyday problems; special churches, social clubs and recreational facilities; specialist social services for deaf patients in psychiatric and subnormal hospitals, and for blind-deaf people.

The Royal Association for Disability and Rehabilitation (RADAR)
25 Mortimer Street, London W1N 8AB (Tel: 01-637 5400).
RADAR acts as a co-ordinating body for the voluntary groups serving disabled people, and is able to provide information on relevant subjects. It seeks generally to investigate the causes and problems of disablement and to promote measures to eliminate or alleviate them. It is particularly active in promoting better access to public buildings and has published a number of Access Guides. Produces a helpful publications list, a first-class holiday guide, a quarterly journal *Contact* and a monthly *Bulletin*. (*See also* Section 3.)

The Royal British Legion
National Headquarters: 48 Pall Mall, London SW1Y 5JY.
With over 900,000 members in 3,500 branches, the Legion works for the welfare of ex-service people and their dependants. Each branch has a service committee of voluntary social workers.

The Legion provides financial assistance in cases of need; a pensions service for claims on behalf of those suffering from disabilities attributable to service in the Forces, and on behalf of widows; residential homes for the elderly and incapacitated; rest homes; holidays for severely disabled people. The Legion is the largest independent employer of disabled people in the United Kingdom and has a range of industries and retraining schemes. At the Legion Village in Kent is a treatment, rehabilitation and assessment centre for disabled people.

Welfare, as described above, is financed by the November Poppy Appeal, which is supplemented by fund-raising in the branches.

The Royal British Legion Housing Association, which is self supporting, has built 10,000 flats of sheltered accommodation for the elderly, some of which is suitable for disabled people.

Royal Commonwealth Society for the Blind
Commonwealth House, Haywards Heath, West Sussex RH16 3AZ (Tel: Haywards Heath (0444) 412424).
The Society promotes and co-ordinates education, training, rehabilitation, employment and welfare of blind people in the developing countries of the Commonwealth, and implements programmes for the prevention and cure of blindness.

Royal National Institute for the Blind
224 Great Portland Street, London W1N 6AA (Tel: 01-388 1266).
RNIB works for the better education, training, rehabilitation, employment and general welfare of Britain's blind people. It runs schools, training colleges, a rehabilitation centre, homes for elderly blind people and hotels for holidays. It sells specially adapted goods, publishes braille and Moon books and magazines, and runs students' braille and tape libraries and a Talking Book library. It helps blind people find commercial and professional jobs and funds research into the prevention of blindness. It publishes a monthly magazine, *New Beacon*, in print and braille, and a series of leaflets, including *Information for people losing their sight*.

The Royal National Institute for the Deaf
105 Gower Street, London WC1E 6AH (Tel: 01-387 8033).
Promotes the prevention and mitigation of deafness and seeks to ensure the welfare of all hearing-impaired people. Its range of special services for deaf

and deaf-blind people includes vocational training, rehabilitation and longer-term residential support. RNID offers comprehensive advisory, information and library services and carries out research in both medical and scientific spheres. It also provides a wide range of technical development to assist deaf people in their everyday lives and a personal welfare service.

Royal Society for Mentally Handicapped Children and Adults
See MENCAP.

Rubella
See National Association for Deaf-Blind and Rubella Handicapped.

St Dunstan's
191 Old Marylebone Road, London NW1 5QN (Tel: 01-723 5021).
Founded in 1915, this famous organisation exists to help men and women blinded in war or peacetime service in the forces, *or who become blind in later years as a result of injuries sustained during such service*. At Ian Fraser House, Ovingdean, East Sussex, a complete welfare service is provided and extra site facilities are available to rehabilitate and train men and women for employment, or if this is not possible because of age or health, to help them adjust to blindness and develop new interests. After training is completed, arrangements are made for placement and settlement, the provision of any necessary equipment and continuing support. The aim is not to shelter them in a 'home', but to put them back in the everyday world of the sighted community.

St Dunstan's is always ready to consider individual financial needs; grants and allowances can be made to meet special problems and other financial benefits are awarded automatically in appropriate circumstances. St Dunstan's estate department resolves many housing difficulties, purchasing suitable properties to rent to members or helping them to buy their own home with the help of a special mortgage scheme. The mortgage is at advantageous rates and is provided without the usual building society criteria.

A monthly magazine in letterpress, braille or on tape cassette is published for members. A film, *To Live Again*, produced by Jimmy Wright, depicts the work of St Dunstan's from its beginnings to the present day, and is available for hire from the above address.

St John Ambulance Brigade
1 Grosvenor Crescent, London SW1X 7EF (Tel: 01-235 5231).

Propagates knowledge of first-aid through training classes and instructional literature. The Brigade is organised into local divisions, the uniformed volunteers of which provide first-aid services wherever required. Many divisions run ambulances and they provide a variety of welfare help to sick and handicapped people. Publishes a magazine, *St John Review*, and many guides, including the helpful 40-page booklet *Simple Nursing at Home* (1980), which, with the help of clear illustrations and instructions, aims to help you to cope with some of the common problems of long-term illness, handicap and age. Available from the Supplies Department, Order of St John, St John's Gate, London EC1M 4DA, price £1.50 plus 80p postage and packing.

The Salvation Army Association for the Handicapped
101 Queen Victoria Street, London EC4P 4EP (Tel: 01-236 5222).
The aim of the Association is to provide spiritual fellowship, advisory and practical help to Salvationists and adherents. A monthly newsletter circulates the information received from the Royal Association for Disability and Rehabilitation and from other organisations. Blind and partially sighted members can receive the newsletter on tape.

Fellowship meetings are held four times a year at various places in the United Kingdom and a music school is run for both able-bodied and disabled people each year for a week.

The Samaritans
Administration: 17 Uxbridge Road, Slough SL1 1SN (Tel: Slough (0753) 32713, 9 a.m. – 5 p.m., *for administrative purposes only*).
The Samaritans, founded in 1953 to help the suicidal and the despairing, have 177 branches in the British Isles. Samaritans are ordinary people from all walks of life who devote part of their spare time to help people in distress. They are carefully chosen and prepared, and work under the guidance of a volunteer Director. The branches can be contacted at any hour of the day or night by telephone, or by personal visit any day or evening. Some people also contact by letter and a few are visited, when it seems particularly necessary, at their homes. The service is absolutely confidential and free. The telephone numbers and addresses of the branches are in local telephone directories.

The Samaritans will always try to help anyone: this, of course, includes people with disabilities, but it should be appreciated that not all branch premises are accessible to wheelchair users and the service is not specifically orientated towards the problems of disability. Indeed, in all their work The Samaritans focus upon the level of distress or despair rather than on specific questions posed.

Schizophrenia
See below and National Schizophrenia Fellowship.

The Schizophrenia Association of Great Britain
Centre for Schizophrenia, Bryn Hyfryd, The Crescent, Bangor, Gwynedd (Tel: Bangor (0248) 354048/6703791).

When founded in 1970, the Association was concerned only with the problems of schizophrenia. It now tries to help *all* people with psychiatric problems, whatever their diagnoses. We are impressed by the information which is made available to members, not least the twice-yearly newsletter which avoids trivialisation and keeps members informed on developments in the field.

As well as its prime task of helping sufferers, the Association aims to dispel the stigma attached to schizophrenia, and to this end seeks to educate the public about the condition through conferences, symposia, lectures, books and leaflets. Research projects are financed to examine the biochemical and nutritional factors involved in producing psychiatric symptoms of the disease and to advance treatment. Membership costs £1. Send remittance with large s.a.e. for papers and application form.

The Scoliosis Self-help Group
Mrs Ailie Harrison, 20 Prince Edward Mansions, Moscow Road, London W2 4EN (Tel: 01-229 1674). Scoliosis (or lateral curvature of the spine) affects about 2 per cent of secondary-school-aged children, although it can occur at any time between birth and maturity (it almost never develops in adults). Untreated, it may lead to severe deformity and lung damage, with serious consequences.

The Scoliosis Self-help Group (SSHG) is an independent national organisation which aims to promote information about the condition and also to act as a channel through which people with scoliosis (especially parents of children with scoliosis) can find and talk to the only people who can fully understand their concern: those who have had the same experience. A quarterly newsletter is produced, containing news, views, ideas, book reviews and much information for and from members about coping with scoliosis.

There is no charge for membership, SSHG being entirely dependent upon voluntary contributions.

Scottish Association for Mental Health
67 York Place, Edinburgh EH1 3JB (Tel: 031-556 3062).

SAMH is the only national Scottish organisation concerned with the development of services relating to mental illness and mental health, and with education and the promotion of mental health. It has developed a strategy based on three components:

1. The development of services and facilities within the voluntary sector. SAMH acts as a catalyst, a source of advice and information and as a direct instigator of action, working particularly through a network of local associations.

2. Co-operation with the statutory sector services in health, social work, housing and related fields; bringing together the statutory and voluntary services and influencing the allocation of resources and systems of planning in order that an *appropriate* mental health care service may emerge. In this context, SAMH acts as an intermediary, able to press, advise and challenge.

3. The promotion of, and contribution to, educational initiatives towards both the public and those providing services, aimed at giving a fundamental new impetus to the change in attitudes within society towards mental illness and to the recognition of the dignity and value of each individual and the quality of his/her life. The Association also develops education and action using its experience and understanding of mental illness and society to promote positive mental health.

Scottish Centre for the Tuition of the Disabled
See Section 6, Further Education and Training.

Scottish Council on Disability
5 Shandwick Place, Edinburgh EH2 4RG (Tel: 031-229 8632).

Provides a means of consultation and joint action among voluntary and statutory organisations in Scotland on such topics as employment, accessibility and mobility. Operates an Information Service and Mobile Aids Centre. (*See also* Sections 3 and 5.)

Scottish Council for Spastics
'Rhuemore', 22 Corstorphine Road, Edinburgh EH12 6HP (Tel: 031-337 9876).

The Council is directly responsible for the care, treatment, education, training, employment and shelter of more than 2,000 spastics in Scotland.

With the co-operation of statutory and local authorities, they operate three schools at Westerlea, Edinburgh (94 day pupils); Stanmore House, Lanark (65 severely handicapped resident pupils); and Corseford, Johnstone (40 resident and 20 day pupils).

Their multi-purpose New Trinity Centre in Edinburgh provides sheltered employment in laundry, metalwork, woodworking and gardening sections, occupational training and work centre activities, and occupational therapy services. There are facilities for assessment, further education, remedial work and speech therapy (accommodation: up to 200).

Hillington, Glasgow, is a well-equipped work centre with facilities for further education. It accommodates 160, while an adjoining day-care unit caters for 45.

Adult residences are in Paisley (28 men and women over 16 years of age and six from the surrounding area attending by day), and in Perth (48 flatlets, ultimately 72) for physically handicapped people capable of semi-independent living, with work and other facilities. A hostel at Erskine accommodates 30 men and 12 women.

Various forms of therapy are provided from the out-patient department in Edinburgh, while a mobile therapy unit operates from Paisley, both offering a home visiting service. Social workers are involved within the various establishments.

Scottish Down's Syndrome Association
Secretary: Rae Lamb, 478 Anniesland Road, Glasgow G13 1YH (Tel: 041-959 4305).
An independent organisation which sponsors local parent/child self-help groups, supports research into Down's Syndrome, provides a counselling service for new parents of Down's babies and for families with educational/social difficulties; there is a specialist information service for members and appropriate material is published. The Association promotes and supports a housing association for adult Down's persons, and holds seminars and conferences.

Membership fees are £3 per annum for parents and foster parents, and £5 per annum for all others.

Scottish Dyslexia Association
Department of Education, Dundee University, Dundee DD1 4HN (Tel: Dundee (0382) 78638).
A voluntary association for the study and treatment of dyslexia, with branches in Dundee, Edinburgh, Girvan, Glasgow, and Perth. The associations in Dundee (Tayside), Edinburgh and Glasgow all offer both assessment and teaching services, as well as a free advisory service. Tayside, in addition, has a resources centre for teaching aids and a lending library service for members.

The Scottish Dyslexia Association is separate from the British Dyslexia Association, but maintains close contact. It acts as a 'clearing house' for enquiries and as a co-ordinating organisation for the various dyslexia associations in Scotland.

Scottish Epilepsy Association
48 Govan Road, Glasgow G51 1JL (Tel: 041-427 4911).
Provides information and advice centres, and extensive casework services, runs clubs and holiday camps, provides a workshop, work centre and adult training centre in Glasgow, fosters parents' groups, organises conferences and arranges lectures. New branches able to extend this work have been established in Strathclyde, Tayside, Grampian and Central regions.

Scottish Health Education Group
Woodburn House, Canaan Lane, Edinburgh EH10 4SG (Tel: 031-447 8044).
The Scottish Health Education Group is part of the Scottish Health Service. It was formed in 1980 from the Scottish Health Education Unit and the Scottish Council for Health Education. It is responsible for the production and distribution of health education material throughout Scotland. It helps Health Boards and local education authorities in health education projects. It promotes concern for health education in the training of doctors, dentists, nurses, midwives, health visitors, teachers and others concerned with the promotion of health. It provides courses of instruction for persons involved in health education.

The Group has a library with a large collection of books, periodicals and audio-visual materials. The library is open to all those involved in health education in Scotland. A current awareness information bulletin is issued fortnightly.

Scottish Society for the Mentally Handicapped
13 Elmbank Street, Glasgow G2 4QA (Tel: 041-226 4541).
The Society's work parallels that of MENCAP – The Royal Society for Mentally Handicapped Children and Adults. It is based on parents of the mentally handicapped, and is concerned with all aspects of the welfare of the mentally handicapped. At present there are more than 70 branches throughout Scotland, and these provide a variety of services including social clubs, holiday facilities and day centres.

Nationally, the Society provides short-stay care at Viewpark Home, Alyth, Perthshire. It is also concerned with obtaining better services for mentally handicapped people in Scotland, and improving public attitudes towards the mentally handicapped. The Society has recently established the Key Housing Association to extend provision of accommodation for mentally handicapped people.

The Society has produced a number of leaflets and films, and has sponsored some research.

Scottish Motor Neurone Disease Association
c/o Volunteer Centre, 25 Wellington Street, Glasgow.
The SMNDA was set up in 1981 primarily to raise money for research. It is not part of the English Motor Neurone Disease Association but parallel with it, maintaining friendly contacts. A patient-care officer visits patients, giving advice on allowances etc., and informs the Association where there are needs not met by other welfare services. A variety of aids has been provided in cases of proven need, and the Association will represent people suffering from motor neurone disease in problems over local authority services, e.g. the need for ground floor accommodation.

Scottish Trust for the Physically Disabled
32 Inglis Green Road, Edinburgh EH14 2ER (Tel: 031-443 5634).
The primary object of the Trust is the establishment of facilities in groups of specially built houses, under the general supervision of wardens, to enable those who are physically handicapped to lead as nearly normal a life as possible. It also promotes and funds research in the field of disability.

The Scout Association
Gilwell Park, Chingford, London E4 7QW (Tel: 01-524 5246).
Both Scouts and Girl Guides make provision for handicapped children and young people. Integration in ordinary activities is encouraged wherever possible, working in the same programme and taking the same badges as any other boy or girl; but there are special units which offer facilities so that even children who are housebound or in hospital may take part in activities to the extent that they are able.

Sequal (formerly Possum Users' Association)
Co-ordinating office: 27 Thames House, 140 Battersea Park Road, London SW11 (Tel: 01-622 3738). Welfare Office: 160 De La Warr Road, Bexhill-on-Sea, East Sussex (Tel: Bexhill-on-Sea (0424) 217093).
This organisation provides communication aids of all kinds for severely physically disabled people. Electronic aids and microcomputers of all kinds provide the basis for the supply of equipment, with special emphasis placed on the inputs and activators. Two Welfare Officers (funded by the DHSS) cover the British Isles for the assessment of members, and the organisation is run by a voluntary group of severely disabled people who themselves make full use of new technology to remain independent. There is full information back-up on all aspects of disability

for members, plus a vehicle loan scheme. The quarterly magazine *Possibility* is another point of contact between members, and gives news of new equipment alongside general interest articles. Sequal has two classes of membership: full (for disabled people) £2 a year; associate £4 a year.

Sex
See SPOD.

Shaftesbury Society
Shaftesbury House, 112 Regency Street, London SW1P 4AX (Tel: 01-834 7444).
The Society maintains four residential schools for physically disabled children (one of which has an extended education unit), one further education centre, and four homes for young men and women suffering with muscular dystrophy and allied neuro-muscular diseases. Clubs and holiday centres are provided for the physically handicapped. In London, 29 mission centres practise Christian social work. An expanding housing association provides sheltered housing schemes, with special facilities for disabled people, in the south of England.
Publishes the *Shaftesbury Review* (April) and *Annual Report* (October).
Has a holiday centre for elderly and disabled people at Dovercourt.

Shape
9 Fitzroy Square, London W1P 6AE (Tel: 01-388 9622/9744).
An arts organisation working with and for all kinds of disadvantaged people through creative activities. For details *see* Section 11.

Shelter
See Section 4, House and Home.

Sickle Cell Society
c/o Brent Community Health Council, 16 High Street, Harlesden, London NW10 4LX (Tel: 01-451 3293).
The Sickle Cell Society has two main aims: to give help and support to affected families, and to inform the public and health professionals about the problems of sickle cell disease. The Society has produced a leaflet, *Sickle Cell Anaemia, Sickle Cell Trait* which is available free of charge, a report, *Sickle Cell Disease – The Need for Improved Services* (80p), and a guide for families, *A Handbook on Sickle Cell Disease* (£1). In addition to giving information, the Society gives support to families through home visits and, through a welfare fund, financial assistance when needed. Please send a s.a.e. for further information.

Sisters Against Disablement (SAD)
Contact: Lesley Wilde, 2 Mereworth Drive, Shooters Hill, London SE18 3EE.
A group of women with disabilities and able-bodied female allies have come together to look at how the oppression of women compounds the oppression of people with disabilities. They meet in London, produce a newsletter, and are particularly active in bringing the issues of disability to the forefront of the Women's Liberation Movement.

Skin Camouflage
See Society of Skin Camouflage.

Socialist Disability Action Group
Secretary: M. A. Barrett, c/o National League of the Blind and Disabled, 2 Tenterden Road, London N17 8BE (Tel: 01-808 6030).
Inaugurated on 2 July 1983, the Group welcomes into membership both individual members (over 15) and affiliated organisations. The Group recognises that there are people with physical, mental and sensory impairments, who are disabled *by society* from full participation in the social, economic and cultural life of the community. It therefore aims to encourage the political expression of such people, within the context of Socialist ideals, in order that they may gain control in directing every aspect of their lives. It also seeks to initiate and participate in campaigns on all issues affecting disabled people.

At the time of writing, local branches and twelve regional committees are being established throughout the country.

Individual membership fee £3 a year (£1 if unwaged).

The Society for Mucopolysaccharide Diseases
Secretary: Christine Lavery, 30 Westwood Drive, Little Chalfont, Buckinghamshire (Tel: Little Chalfont (024 04) 2789).
The Society has three main aims:
(a) to act as a support group for families of children and young adults suffering from any one of the seven Mucopolysaccharide diseases. Families in similar circumstances are put in touch with one another for their mutual benefit;
(b) to stimulate public awareness of these diseases and the plight of affected families;
(c) to raise funds to help to sponsor further research into MPS and to purchase a holiday caravan for sufferers and their immediate families.
Parent contact is maintained by letter and telephone, and a quarterly newsletter is published (free to affected families and available to professionals and other interested people for an annual subscription of £3 UK, £5 overseas).

Society of Skin Camouflage and Disfigurement Therapy
Wester Pitmenzies, Auchtermuchty, Fife, Scotland.
The Society is concerned with educating society into accepting disfigured people rather than regarding them as strange or threatening. Through discussion, counselling and self-help it also seeks to create a better understanding of how to overcome the problems and fears associated with disfigurement.

The Society strongly recommends that the parents of a disfigured child should seek its guidance at the earliest opportunity. The Society publishes a bulletin *Skin Deep* and holds a free, twice-weekly NHS Skin Camouflage Clinic at Perth Royal Infirmary.

It promotes and undertakes research, lectures and educational projects, and is helping to set up neighbourhood contacts throughout the United Kingdom. The Society's advice can often be of help in compensation or insurance claims which include disfigurement. Doreen Trust, founder of the Society, has written a sensitive book *Skin Deep* published by Paul Harris, 25 London Street, Edinburgh, price £4.50. Advice and guidance sheets available on a wide range of topics.

Sole-Mates
46 Gordon Road, Chingford, London E4 6BU (Tel: 01-524 2423).
This voluntary organisation helps people who have different sized feet by, wherever possible, partnering them with someone who takes reverse shoe sizes to themselves. Over 2,500 people are on the Sole-Mates' register to date. The organisation also caters for people who need only one shoe. Some pairs of 'odd' shoes in a variety of styles can be purchased from stock.

A free advisory service includes a list of relevant suppliers and services. Registration fee for the partnership scheme costs £1.50. S.a.e. with all enquiries, please.

The Spastics Society
12 Park Crescent, London W1N 4EQ (Tel: 01-636 5020).
The Spastics Society has extensive facilities for the assessment, treatment, training and education of children and adults who suffer from cerebral palsy (spasticity). It was founded in 1952 by a group of parents who were concerned about the neglected needs of their disabled children.

The Society runs 60 establishments, including eight residential schools (*see* Section 5) for children of differing intellectual abilities, 12 residential centres for severely handicapped adult men and women, and 16 residential hostels and adult house units which provide pleasant accommodation for adult spastic people who go out to work at a nearby work centre or are employed in open industry. It has 187 affiliated local groups throughout England and Wales who together run a further 100 establishments to help handicapped people in their own localities. These include workshops, day centres and holiday bungalows.

Eight industrial units give employment to spastic men and women who are too handicapped to compete in open employment. The Society also maintains an industrial training centre in Welwyn, Hertfordshire.

The Society has also established a special scheme in the new development town of Milton Keynes to provide independent living for up to 45 handicapped people along the lines of the Fokus Development in Sweden. The specially adapted flats are part of a regular housing estate and even severely handicapped people can enjoy living in their own homes with help on hand from a skilled care staff. An integral part of the scheme is the professional workshop where severely handicapped graduates work on computer technology.

In line with its belief that handicapped people should wherever possible be integrated into the community, the Society has built six specially adapted flats for disabled married couples in Cardiff.

The Society runs a library and bookshop, and a substantial list of the publications that are available can be obtained on application to: The Librarian, The Spastics Society, 12 Park Crescent, London W1N 4EQ. The Society's monthly newspaper *Disability Now* is obtainable from the Circulation Supervisor, The Spastics Society, 12 Park Crescent, London W1N 4EQ, on free distribution.

Family Help Units: The Society runs two Family Help Units, one for handicapped adults and the other for handicapped children:

Chiltern House Family Help Unit in Oxford offers short-term care in a homely atmosphere for nine spastic people aged 14 years and over. Most of those staying in the unit are severely handicapped physically and many are also mentally handicapped. While priority is always given to cerebrally palsied people, other handicaps are also welcomed when space permits.

The East Anglia Family Help Unit in Bury St Edmunds, Suffolk, provides expert care for 15 spastic children, many of whom may be mentally retarded, between the ages of 2 and 16. It also operates two mother and baby units where a mother can stay with her handicapped child to learn how to cope with the problems of caring for him or her. Day care facilities are also offered for handicapped children.

Family Services and Assessment Centre: The Society's Family Services and Assessment Centre at 16 Fitzroy Square, London W1P 5HQ (Tel: 01-387 9571) offers expert advisory and counselling services to spastic people and their families. Children, adolescents and adults are assessed by a small panel of professional staff in a pleasant environment so that advice may be offered on the many problems to be faced.

There is accommodation for up to 25 people at the centre, available to the families of handicapped children, or to cerebrally palsied people visiting for an assessment, or who may wish to stay in London overnight or for a short holiday. Other types of handicapped people can be accommodated when there are vacancies though those who need personal care are invited to bring a helper with them. A team of social workers provide support and counselling in the homes of spastic people throughout England and Wales. The Centre also offers advice on the planning of holidays and on toys, aids and equipment for handicapped children and adults.

Speech Impairment/Therapy
See: Association for all Speech Impaired Children; Centre for Clinical Communication Studies; College of Speech Therapists.

Spina Bifida and Hydrocephalus
See Association for Spina Bifida and Hydrocephalus.

Spinal Injuries Association
Yeoman's House, 76 St James's Lane, Muswell Hill, London N10 (Tel: 01-444 2121).
The SIA is run by wheelchair users and their friends for paraplegics and tetraplegics (spinal cord injured people) and their families, and aims to help individuals achieve their own goals, bring about the best medical care and rehabilitation, and stimulate scientific research into paraplegia.

The SIA provides information on all aspects of paraplegia to spinal cord injured, their families and everyone concerned with their welfare. It motivates members to set and meet objectives in such areas as home adaptations, wheelchair living, education, self-help aids and personal care.

The SIA Welfare Service maintains up to date information on all aspects of independent living. As well as advising on rights, and helping individuals to get the best out of local services, SIA is actively involved in projects to widen the choice of housing available to members. There is also a link scheme which introduces newly paralysed people to more experienced members. The SIA is committed to the idea of peer counselling and is actively engaged in encouraging training for this so that members can benefit from the skill and experience of others. The Welfare Office, headed by Frances Hasler, offers support, encouragement and advice and can be contacted by telephone on 01-380 0232 (Answerphone (24 hours) when out, also connected to main number 01-388 6840).

The SIA also seeks to develop communication between statutory and voluntary bodies on mobility, access, employment, integration and other problems common to all disability groups. It is consulted by government and has advised on the design of new spinal units.

The Association has two seven-berth *Kingfisher* narrowboats controllable from a wheelchair, and a holiday caravan in Sussex; these can be booked for active family holidays.

The Association has published a number of books and leaflets including *Nursing management in the general hospital: the first 48 hours following injury*, and the first of a new series, *People with Spinal Injuries: treatment and care* which offers guidance to professional and ancillary staff in general hospitals and the community medical and nursing services, who, though not specialists in the spinal injury field, may be called upon to deal with people who have sustained damage to the spinal column. *Able to Work* by Bernadette Fallon describes services for disabled people in the areas of training and employment (*see* Section 7) and *So You're Paralysed* by the same author gives guidance on coping with the problems of becoming paralysed (*see* Section 12 and Appendix A).

The SIA's quarterly newsletter is one of the best of its kind, is packed full of practical and useful ideas and serves as a very lively forum for members. Membership is open to all.

SPOD (The Association to Aid the Sexual and Personal Relationships of the Disabled)
See Section 12.

Sue Ryder Foundation
Cavendish, Suffolk CO10 8AT (Tel: Glemsford (0787) 280252).
Has 16 homes in the United Kingdom. One is a holiday/short-stay home for the handicapped and elderly, and others are for the handicapped, elderly, continuing care of cancer patients and the mentally ill. The Foundation is devoted to the relief of suffering on a wide scale and is active in a number of overseas countries. Domiciliary visiting is also undertaken from several of the Foundation's homes.

Task Force
See under new name, Pensioners' Link.

Tay-Sachs and Allied Diseases Association
17 Sydney Road, Barkingside, Ilford, Essex (Tel: 01-550 8989).
Tay-Sachs is an inherited disorder caused by the absence of a vital enzyme, resulting in the destruction of the nervous system. It is always fatal; to date, there is no cure. A Tay-Sachs baby develops normally for the first few months; then a relentless deterioration of mental and physical abilities begins. Death is inevitable, usually by the age of 5.

The Tay-Sachs Association was set up for the advancement of education and relief of suffering from Tay-Sachs and allied diseases, to promote screening to detect such diseases wherever possible, and to publicise the fact that screening facilities are available. When possible, it provides financial assistance to sufferers and their families, and makes available leaflets giving information about the disease and addresses where screening is carried out.

Tinnitus
See British Tinnitus Association.

Tourette Syndrome (UK) Association
734 High Road, Goodmayes, Ilford, Essex IG3 8QY (Tel: 01-599 1826).
The Association aims to help those who suffer from Gilles de la Tourette syndrome and their families, and to give them support. It seeks to reduce the estimated 7- to 14-year delay between the onset of symptoms, correct diagnosis and appropriate treatment, to promote research and to publish the results of that research.

A newsletter is circulated and information is provided about the syndrome and the educational needs of students with its associated learning disabilities. An American documentary film *Tourette Syndrome – the Sudden Intruder* has recently been acquired.

Toy Libraries Association for Handicapped Children
See Section 11, Sports and Leisure (Play Matters).

Tuberous Sclerosis Association of Great Britain
Secretary: Anne Underhill, Martell Mount, Holywell Road, Malvern Wells, Worcestershire WR14 4LF (Tel: Malvern (068 45) 63150).
The Association was formed in 1977 to act as a mutual self-help group for families concerned with the disease and to promote information about the condition and support research. Parents keep in contact through correspondence, magazines, an annual meeting and newsletters. Information leaflets, a

parents' 'contact' letter and reports of the talks on tuberous sclerosis are available from the Secretary.

Urinary Conduit Association

Secretary: Valerie Kings, 8 Coniston Close, Dane Bank, Denton, Manchester M34 2EW (Tel: 061-336 8818).

The UCA was formed in 1971 to help people before and after surgery resulting in a urinary diversion/ileal conduit. Advice can be given about appliances, housing, work situations, sexual problems, etc., to assist confident resumption of normal activities.

There are 22 branches in various parts of Great Britain, and the Association arranges visits both at home and in hospital. The UCA Journal is published twice yearly and provides a forum for the exchange of views and ideas.

Research into urinary conditions and the development of equipment is supported. Annual subscription £2.

Usher's Syndrome

This is one of the conditions associated with retinitis pigmentosa. A new awareness programme is being launched for young deaf people with RP. Information on this and any other queries should be addressed to the British Retinitis Pigmentosa Society (*see* page 296).

Vaccine Damaged Children

See Association of Parents of Vaccine Damaged Children.

Voluntary Council for Handicapped Children

National Children's Bureau, 8 Wakley Street, London EC1V 7QE (Tel: 01-278 9441).

The Voluntary Council for Handicapped Children is an independently elected Council established under the aegis of the National Children's Bureau. It provides information on all aspects of childhood disability and on services for handicapped children and their families, to parents and professionals. Holds regular seminars and workshops and has a range of information material including booklists, fact sheets (*see* Appendix A) and the free parents' booklet *Help Starts Here: for parents of children with*

special needs (an introduction to the intricacies of the welfare state).

Wales Council for the Disabled (Cynsor Cymru i'r Anabl)

Caerbragdy Industrial Estate, Bedwas Road, Caerphilly, Mid Glamorgan CF8 3SL (Tel: Caerphilly (0222) 887325).

The national co-ordinating body for disabled people living in Wales. It seeks to translate the general concern for disabled people into positive action on their behalf, and to further their full integration into society. The Council provides a forum for consultation amongst and co-operation between voluntary, professional and statutory organisations. It makes representations to local and central government and comments on proposed legislation on all matters affecting disabled people. It provides information on facilities and amenities for disabled people in Wales, and publishes a helpful guide for disabled visitors and the *Tidings* magazine at regular intervals.

See also Section 15.

Wireless for the Bedridden

81b Corbets Tey Road, Upminster, Essex RM14 2AJ (Tel: Upminster (040 22) 50051).

Provides, on free loan, radio and TV sets to needy invalids and the aged poor. Maintenance is covered, and in some cases the licence fee.

Women's National Cancer Control Campaign

1 South Audley Street, London W1Y 5DQ (Tel: 01-499 7532/4).

Concerned with measures for the prevention and early detection of cancers of the cervix and of the breast. Leaflets are available on request with s.a.e.

Women's Royal Voluntary Service

17 Old Park Lane, London W1Y 4AJ (Tel: 01-499 6040).

The WRVS, in addition to its other services for the community, provides care and practical help for the needs of disabled people of all ages, working in co-operation with local authority social services departments. Any disabled person in need of help or advice can contact their local WRVS office (listed in the telephone directory) or the Organiser, WRVS, Welfare for the Disabled, at the above address.

SELECTED FURTHER INFORMATION

(For publishers' and stockists' addresses see Appendix B.)

Information about particular aspects of disability will be found in other relevant sections of this Directory. Information which relates to specific handicaps is, in general, too vast to list here. The reader is advised to contact those organisations appropriate to his/her needs from Section 16; they will supply or recommend suitable literature etc.

Access/Restrictions/Discrimination

Access for Disabled People (Central Office of Information, 1978), hire £8.50 plus VAT, available from Central Film Library. This film which lasts $6\frac{1}{2}$ minutes, was made as a part of the campaign by the Silver Jubilee Committee on Improving Access for Disabled People, to increase awareness of the need for consideration of disabled people's requirements when providing or designing any public facility. It illustrates the difficulties commonly encountered by people in wheelchairs, and points out problems faced by those with other physical disabilities, such as impaired sight. Thoughtful design can help to avoid these problems and examples are shown of how this can be achieved.

Access in the High Street by Stephen Thorpe (Centre on Environment for the Handicapped, 1981), 50p including postage and packing. A practical guide offering advice on how to make shopping more manageable for handicapped people. Sections deal with entrance doors, counters, check outs, circulation and display, signs, and staff training. Well illustrated with photographs, sketch drawings, and cartoons (by Louis Hellman).

Code of Practice for Access for the Disabled to Buildings (BS 5810: 1979) (British Standards Institution, 1979), price £10.50 (half price to members). A high price for 16 pages! But this is the authoritative statement of 'appropriate provisions' for disabled people and is called up as such by both the Disabled Persons Act 1981 and the Local Government (Miscellaneous Provisions) (Scotland) Act 1981. There is, at the time of writing, a proposal to call up BS 5810 as deemed to satisfy the new Building Regulations.

The Code details the basic architectural provisions that need to be incorporated in new buildings to make them convenient for use by disabled people, including those dependent on wheelchairs and those with hearing or sight impairments. It incorporates design recommendations for dropped kerbs; level, ramped and stepped approaches to buildings; entrance doors and lobbies; and sets out criteria for internal planning, including changes of level, auditoria, lifts, doors, passageways, lobbies and staircases. There is a section on lavatories and another on general design recommendations, including car parking, approaches, floor and wall surfaces, handrails, doors, switches and controls, induction loops and telephones.

Finally, the now familiar access symbol is illustrated for display in buildings where provision for disabled people conforms to the Standard.

The following British Standards are referred to:
BS 5395: Code of Practice for Stairs
BS 5619: Design of Housing for the Convenience of Disabled People (*see* Section 4, House and Home)
BS 2655 and 5655: Lifts.

The CORAD Report (Committee on Restrictions Against Disabled People, 1982), available from DHSS Publications Unit, £5.35. CORAD was set up in January 1979 by the then Minister for the Disabled, the Rt Hon Alf Morris MP, to consider 'the architectural and social barriers which may result in discrimination against disabled people and prevent them from making full use of facilities available to the general public'. It completed its work in December 1981 and shortly afterwards presented its report to Hugh Rossi MP, then Minister of State for Social Security and the Disabled. The report is thus of the utmost significance as a record of the discrimination faced by disabled people in everyday living and a blueprint for the action needed to put matters right.

The evidence submitted to CORAD brought to

light instances of discrimination against disabled people in most aspects of life, including education, employment, entertainment and the transaction of domestic business and civic duties. Direct, personal, and very hurtful and damaging experiences of discrimination were reported, and the Committee concluded that the best way of combating them is by way of legislation, making discrimination against disabled people illegal and allowing them access to the law to secure the right to equal treatment. The Committee also concluded (and we wholeheartedly concur) that 'legislation has an important declaratory and educative effect, is a means of gaining the attention of the apathetic, and provides a foundation on which good practice can be built.'

The Report sets out 41 recommendations, the first three concerned with the call for anti-discrimination legislation, and the remainder covering education, employment, entertainment, access, pedestrianisation and parking, Codes of Practice, separate development, media presentation, insurance and the representation of disabled people's interests. As the expression of involved, concerned and expert consideration and a survey of first hand evidence, the Report should surely be taken up to guide a new policy for social justice in an area bedevilled by prejudice and misunderstanding.

Department of Health and Society Security Circular LAC(82)5
A circular issued to local authorities to draw attention to the Disabled Persons Act 1981 and to remind authorities of the importance of bearing in mind the needs of disabled people in discharging *all* their functions. In fact, the Circular expands somewhat beyond the strict terms of the Act, and in paragraphs 3.5 to 3.11 emphasises the importance attached by government to the provision of facilities and access for disabled people in buildings to which the Act applies, and the improvements which can be achieved through discussions and requirements at the planning stage. The Circular points out that 'where appropriate, conditions may be attached to a grant of planning permission to deal with the matter'. Although it is not normally made available to the general public, people concerned in this area should secure this Circular, which can be enormously useful in encouraging backward local authorities!

Getting Around: the barriers to access for disabled people (National Consumer Council, 1981), £2.50. This report considers the proposition that the opportunities for disabled consumers to realise their potential are circumscribed by legislation and regulations mainly devised for the protection and security of consumers who are not disabled. It draws on the advice of expert consultants, an advisory committee, and the views of disabled people who responded to an appeal for examples of discrimination. The report embodies an edited version of a challenging paper by David Carson, Lecturer in Law at the University of Southampton, *Disabled Consumers and the Law*.

The NCC looked at three main areas of concern: adaptations to the physical environment, the impact of public safety laws and regulations on disabled consumers, and the arguments for and against special measures to counter discrimination. The report is guided by four principles:
- that, in seeking to make the physical environment more hospitable to disabled people, the emphasis should be on the maximum possible encouragement.

With the *CORAD Report* (*see* page 331) this NCC report is a valuable contribution to a human rights issue which should surely be at the forefront of our national strategy.

assert the rights of disabled people, then the case for anti-discrimination legislation deserves serious examination;
- that, in seeking to make the physical environment more hospitable to disabled people, the emphasis should be on the maximum possible encouragement.

With the *CORAD Report* (*see* page 331) this NCC report is a valuable contribution to a human rights issue which should surely be at the forefront of our national strategy.

Guidelines for Improving Access for Disabled People by C. Wycliffe Noble (International Commission on Technical Aids, Building and Transportation, 1983), free, available from RADAR. A brief guide in French and English outlining the basic considerations to be taken into account in cities and buildings when developing planning policies.

Planning and Access for Disabled People (Centre on Environment for the Handicapped), 40p. A reading list.

Blindness and Partial Sight

BRAILLE PUBLISHERS
National Library for the Blind. See page 108.

Royal National Institute for the Blind. See page 332.

Scottish Braille Press
Publishes a wide range of material including the BBC *In Touch* bulletin (*see* page 333) and popular fiction.

BOOKS IN MOON EMBOSSED TYPE

The Royal National Institute for the Blind
Moon Branch, Holmesdale Road, Reigate, Surrey
RH2 0BA.
This is the only publisher in the world of Moon
books. The Moon system plays an important part
alongside braille, because its clear bold outline is
such that it can be learned and followed with ease. It
is particularly suited to introducing the newly blind
adult to the art of reading by touch: many adult
readers, having acquired confidence and a sense of
achievement by learning Moon, move on to the more
comprehensive braille system.

Because it is much slower to produce than braille,
there is far less literature available in Moon, but a
reasonably wide range is available on loan from lending libraries for blind people throughout the country.
The RNIB (Moon Branch) publishes a catalogue of
Moon books, and all new Moon publications are
advertised in the *New Beacon*, the *Braille Monthly
Announcements*, and the weekly *Moon Newspaper*.
Supplements are issued periodically.

All Moon books and periodicals are published free
of charge, but charges are required for playing cards,
greetings cards, private letters and contract work as
shown in the catalogue.

PUBLISHERS OF LARGE PRINT BOOKS

John Curley and Associates Inc. (distributors Magna
Print Books).
Bible Society (Bibles and New Testaments – AV and
GNB).
Eyre and Spottiswoode.
Magna Print Books (distributed to libraries, not
trade outlets).
Thorndike Press.
Ulverscroft Large Print Books Ltd.

OTHER INFORMATION FOR BLIND AND PARTIALLY
SIGHTED PEOPLE

(*See also* heading Children and Young People
below.)

Blindness and Partial Sight by Astrid Klemz
(Woodhead-Faulkner (Publishers) Ltd, 1977), £6.25
plus postage and packing. A guide for social workers
and others concerned with the care and rehabilitation of the visually handicapped.

In Touch (BBC Publications), printed version £2.95
available from BBC Publications; braille version
£17.60 (£1.76 to blind people in the UK) available
from Scottish Braille Press; tape version on standard
cassettes £6.30 (free in response to twelve C60 blank
cassettes – please enclose a self-addressed label)

available from Tape Recording Service for the Blind.

This book takes its title from a BBC Radio 4
programme for blind listeners. It is a very full and
helpful guide to aids and services available to blind
and partially sighted people.

A talking book version of *In Touch* by Thena
Heshel and Margaret Ford can be borrowed from the
British Talking Book Service for the Blind
(catalogue number 4400), and is also on sale at £2.95
for the two cassettes, which run for a total of 14
hours. Enquiries to the British Talking Book Service
for the Blind, Mount Pleasant, Alperton, Wembley,
Middlesex HA0 1RR (Tel: 01-903 6666).

Also available is the *In Touch* quarterly bulletin
free to blind or partially sighted people or to anyone
concerned either professionally or voluntarily with
their welfare. Send four s.a.e.s (not less than 8½ in. by
4½ in.) to *In Touch*, BBC, Broadcasting House, London W1A 1AA. The bulletin is also available in
braille free from Scottish Braille Press and on tape
from Tape Recording Service for the Blind, in
response to a blank C90 cassette and self-addressed
label. It is helpful to indicate which issues of the
bulletin are required.

Problems of the Blind (Graves Medical Audiovisual
Library, 1976). A series of eight cassettes, five with
slides, describing the problems encountered by a
blind housewife and mother when she lost her sight,
how she overcame them, and her experience of the
kind of help offered by various welfare services. The
whole programme lasts about 3½ hours.

Children and Young People

Adoption and the Handicapped Child (Graves Medical Audiovisual Library, 1978). Discusses the need
for skill, speed, sensitivity and service in the placement of a handicapped child for adoption. 23
minutes (tape only).

Facing the Future (Spastics Society, 1981), free. A
leaflet for parents of handicapped children, which
deals with some of the problems encountered as their
multiply handicapped children grow older. It also
includes the problems facing parents whose children
suffer handicap as a result of accident or illness.
Includes a recommended reading list. Please send
s.a.e.

The Hearing Impaired Child and the Family by
Michael Nolan and Ivan Tucker (Souvenir Press,
1981), £6.95 (hardback), £4.95 (paperback). Written
to help parents of hearing impaired children, but also
useful to professionals and students. The authors
explain the causes of deafness, how to assess the
hearing ability of young children, and how hearing

aids are fitted and used. They show how parents can help their child and prepare him or her for school. They stress that unnecessary deafness can be avoided by early diagnosis and careful therapy.

Helping your Handicapped Baby by Cliff Cunningham and Patricia Sloper (Souvenir Press, 1978), £4.95 (paperback). The authors describe in a positive and practical way a series of programmes for teaching and stimulating the handicapped baby through his or her first year of development.

More than Sympathy: the Everyday Needs of Sick and Handicapped Children and their Families by Richard Lansdown (Tavistock Publications Ltd, 1980), £3.50 (paperback). Nearly half the children in Britain have been in hospital by the age of 7; one in five is likely to require some form of special education. This book is concerned with the most seriously affected proportion of these children whose difficulties are likely to persist throughout their lives. It takes as a starting point the idea that many of the problems that arise can be predicted and that to know something of the child's condition and how it may affect behaviour is to be part way towards coping. Its well balanced, commonsense approach will be helpful to professionals and parents alike.

One of the Family (Disabilities Study Unit), 30p. A booklet for the siblings of disabled children.

Parents as Partners by Gillian Pugh and others (National Children's Bureau, 1981), £3.50 (concessionary price for members). This book examines schemes which support and guide parents to help children attain their maximum potential in the important early years of life. The so-called 'intervention' schemes, parent workshops and group work described are an interesting blend of research and practice and are useful 'blueprints' for similar new projects.

Physical Education for Handicapped Children by Sarah George and Brian Hart (Souvenir Press, 1983), £5.95 (paperback). The first book to deal with this subject, according to the publishers. The authors show how physiotherapy can be combined with physical education to benefit children with disabilities.

Picture Books for Blind or Visually Handicapped Children (William Collins & Sons Ltd). Collins currently have four books for visually handicapped children. These include *Red Thread Riddles* by Virginia Allen Jensen and Polly Edman (published by UNESCO), *What's That?* by Virginia Allen Jensen and Dorcas Woodbury Haller, and *Catching* by Virginia Allen Jensen alone. Ms Jensen is the joint winner with Margaret Marshall of the 1981 Eleanor Farjeon Award, given to those who have contributed to children's books over and above the call of their normal work. Both are deeply committed to helping disabled children through books.

These books, costing £4.95 each, are superbly produced and imaginatively conceived. They are designed to be read by both blind and sighted children. All the illustrations are both visually attractive and raised on the page as tactile shapes which can be 'read' by touch. *Red Thread Riddles* is supplemented by braille. A fourth book, *Roly goes Exploring* by Philip Newth, also at £4.95 is a picture book with illustrations made from various geometrical shapes cut out of bright green cardboard. The text is in print and braille.

Picture Books for Special Situations (The Bodley Head Ltd). The Bodley Head publish four titles in this series: *The Boy Who Couldn't Hear* by Freddy Bloom, illustrated by Michael Charlton, £3.25; *Ben* (a mentally handicapped boy) by Victoria Shennan, also illustrated by Michael Charlton, £3.25; *Suzy* (a partially sighted girl) by Elizabeth Chapman, illustrated by Margery Gill, £3.95; *Rachel* (a disabled girl in a wheelchair) by Elizabeth Fanshawe, £1.95. These books are for young children and aim to encourage a better understanding of the special needs of such children and to encourage their fullest possible participation in the everyday activities of childhood.

Play and Handicapped Children (Fair Play for Children), £1.50 including postage and packing. One of a series of information packs. It gives brief details of national play organisations, pre-school playgroups, toy libraries, adventure playgrounds, play in residential settings, playschemes, youth and junior clubs, toys and equipment, theatre, drama and inflatables, books and films, self-help groups and relevant organisations.

Shared Care (National Children's Bureau). This is a companion to *Parents as Partners* (*see* above) and is, as far as we know, the only convenient 'guide' to centres working with families of handicapped children. It is now out of print (for the second time) but photocopies are available from the NCB for £3 each.

Voluntary Council for Handicapped Children Fact Sheets
1. List of Independent Voluntary Establishments Providing Further Education, Social and Voca-

tional Training and/or Assessment and Sheltered Employment for Handicapped School Leavers (1981)
2. Water Sports for Handicapped People (1982)
3. Holidays for Handicapped Children (undated)
4. Village and Community Residential Homes for the Adult Mentally Handicapped (1980)
5. National Organisations Relating to Mental Handicap (1980)
6. The Sexual Needs of Handicapped Young People (1982)
7. Play and Toys for Handicapped Children (1982)
8. Art, Music, Drama and the Handicapped Child (1982)
9. Parent Workshops (1979)
10. Home-Based Intervention Programmes for Handicapped Children (1979)
11. Fostering Disturbed and Difficult Adolescents: Some Local Authority and Voluntary Agency Schemes (1980)
12. Long Term Fostering Schemes for Mentally and Physically Handicapped Children: Some Local Authority and Voluntary Agency Schemes (1982)
13. Short Term Respite Care Schemes for Mentally and Physically Handicapped Children (1982)

The Wheelchair Child by Philippa Russell (Souvenir Press, revised edition, 1984), £6.95 (paperback) plus £1.00 postage and packing. This book covers problems from early childhood to young adulthood. The author, Senior Officer of the National Children's Bureau's Voluntary Council for Handicapped Children, combines basic information on the main handicapping conditions, the medical and community services available to handicapped children and practical advice on aids, appliances and home adaptations and financial grants, with a thoughtful consideration of the developmental and emotional problems attached to disability. As well as the special needs for education and leisure, she deals with problems of depression for child and parent, the difficulties of siblings in a 'handicapped' family, dependency, adolescence and sex; and especially in relation to the degenerative handicap, the facing of early death.

You and Your Handicapped Child by Ann Purser (George Allen & Unwin, 1981), £6.95. This is a book written primarily for ordinary parents, to help them face and overcome both the initial shock of having a child who is physically or mentally handicapped, and the long-term effects upon their family life. Ann Purser writes from personal experience, and deals with the subject in a chronological way, from first hearing that your child is handicapped, through the various developments associated with growing up, education, finding a job, and questions of sex and marriage.

Your Deaf Child's Speech and Language by Mary Courtman-Davies (The Bodley Head, 1979), £7.50. This substantial book is written for parents. The author believes that the hearing impaired child achieves good speech through hard work and that parents are uniquely able to maintain support over the necessarily long period of training. In practice, parents all too often fail to understand their child's condition, and are at a loss as to how to interpret those aspects of behaviour which arise from hearing loss, or how to bring about the development of speech quickly enough to enable the child to join in with his/her peers.

This book aims to provide the answers to the questions which frequently puzzle parents, and to enable them to help their child to the fullest possible extent.

Directories/Bibliographies

BIMH Current Awareness Service (The British Institute of Mental Handicap), subscription £10 per annum.
CAS is an extensive bibliography of newly published books and journal articles relating to mental and multiple handicap. It covers over 300 sources each month from Great Britain, Europe, North America, Australia, and New Zealand, and also contains references from 3,000 journals derived from a monthly computer print-out. The information is classified under more than 30 subject headings. Books and journal articles are indexed separately. A photocopying service is offered for selected articles.

Charities Digest (Family Welfare Association, annually), £6.25 plus 50p postage and packing. A reference guide to charities and benevolent institutions and the work they do.

Compass – a direction finder for disabled people (Disablement Income Group, 1984), price £2.25. A guide to services, activities and organisations.

Directory of Agencies for the Blind (RNIB, 1980), £5.00. Contains over 1,300 entries covering the national government and voluntary agencies concerned with blind people as well as regional and local associations, schools, ophthalmic hospitals, homes and hostels. It includes information about periodicals in braille and Moon and about publishers of large print material. It also lists organisations and sources of funds which can provide financial help to blind individuals, and a few self-help groups of professional blind workers. Amendments are listed in RNIB's monthly journal *The New Beacon*.

Directory of Non-Medical Research relating to Handicapped People (Handicapped Persons Research Unit, 1982), £10.00 including postage and packing. 650 pages. The Directory consists of over six hundred detailed descriptions of non-medical research and design development projects in the handicap/disability field being undertaken in the United Kingdom. The projects cover such topics as: education, communication, training, employment, family, attitudes, community and institutional care, services, functional assessment, aids (*see also* BARD, page 55), equipment and microelectronic applications. Access to information is through a descriptive contents list and subject, worker and institution indexes.

Directory of Residential Accommodation for the Mentally Handicapped in England, Wales and Northern Ireland edited by Victoria Shennan. (MENCAP, 1982), £5.95 plus postage and packing. Contains over 1,000 entries, listing statutory and voluntary residential amenities for mentally handicapped children and adults.

Directory of Services for Visually and Mentally Handicapped People by David Ellis (Southern and Western Regional Association for the Blind, 1983), £1.00. Some 6–8 per cent of mentally handicapped people also suffer from visual handicap. A recent national survey conducted by the author showed that the proportion of visually handicapped people among residents of hospitals for the mentally handicapped is roughly ten times higher than in the general population. Sometimes, David Ellis believes, a person's dependency in self-care skills is assumed to have resulted from mental handicap, whereas it could be equally well due to visual handicap. The Directory is aimed at improving the services available to such people, and lists voluntary agencies, health and social services departments, and expert individuals throughout the country who can offer help to this group of people.

Directory of Voluntary Organisations of the Handicapped (Northern Ireland Council for the Handicapped, 1983), £1.00 plus 25p postage and packing. An easy reference guide to organisations and contacts in Northern Ireland, with the activities or services which each provides. The book also contains a list of contact addresses of all major organisations concerned with disabled people and which are not presently represented in Northern Ireland.

Employment for Handicapped People by Struan Simpson (Reedbooks Ltd, 1982), £6.50 plus 50p postage and packing, available from DLF (Sales) Ltd. An annotated bibliography of material relating to many aspects of employment and the work environment of handicapped people. It covers architectural and design requirements, including fire safety, community and group work, income and earnings, rehabilitation, sheltered employment, legislation and job classification.

Incontinence by Dorothy Mandelstam and Philippa Lane (Reedbooks Ltd, 1982), £6.50 plus 50p postage and packing, available from DLF (Sales) Ltd. A bibliography dealing with urinary and faecal incontinence in adults and children. Includes less easily found material concerned with practical management, as well as medical, surgical, social and psychological references.

The King's Fund Directory of Organisations for Patients and Disabled People (King Edward's Hospital Fund for London), available from the distributors, Oxford University Press (or booksellers), £5.00. Covers blindness, deafness, mental handicap and illness, physical disability, addictions, specific disorders, alternative medicine and the problems of children, women and elderly people.

Mental Health Year Book 1981/2 (MIND, 1981), £12.95 including postage and packing. This book (in fact, *not* a yearbook – there have been no subsequent editions) combines directory information and articles on various aspects of the mental health services in the United Kingdom. Part 1 includes information on government departments and statutory bodies with mental health responsibilities; national voluntary organisations working in the field, local authority mental health resources and sources of information on local voluntary services; research centres and training bodies with a mental health interest; and Mental Health Tribunal offices. There is also data on health authorities, CHCs, and mental illness and mental handicap hospitals.

Part 2 features authors with specialist knowledge of current services with articles on the development of mental health policy and provision. Their arguments are supported by data on hospital admissions and on mental health finance. Part 2 also includes information on statutory instruments and regulations relating to mental health, a glossary of psychiatric terms, and a selected reading list.

Finally, Part 3 looks at psychiatric day care, and a number of papers give instances of good practice in day care, and thoughts and feelings on the direction future day services should take.

National Voluntary Organisations in Scotland (Scottish Council of Social Service), £3.50 (£2.50 to members).

Partially Sighted People by Agnes Cameron (Reedbooks Ltd, 2nd edition, 1982), £6.50 plus 50p postage and packing, available from DLF (Sales) Ltd. Lists published material concerning the daily living problems of partially sighted people of all ages. Subjects covered include architecture and environment, employment, education and educational welfare. Includes sections on medical and ophthalmological material, social and welfare services and physical education. Appendices of aids and addresses.

Self-Help and the Patient (Patients Association, 8th edition 1982), £1.75 including postage and packing. A directory of national organisations concerned with various diseases and handicaps. It contains addresses, telephone numbers and brief particulars of over 170 organisations, systematically arranged under subject headings in eight sections. Indexed.

The Sunday Times Self-help Directory by Oliver Gillie and Angela Price (Granada, 1982), £3.95. This is the second, much enlarged edition of a helpful guide to national, local and specialist self-help organisations.

Useful Addresses for Parents with a Handicapped Child by Ann Worthington (In Touch (Sale)), £1.00. This directory provides contact addresses and some very brief details of organisations, aids, toys, education and further education, training, assessment, employment, residential homes, schools and communities, leisure, holidays and travel, finance, rights, legal advice and relevant publications.

Voluntary Organisations Concerned with Disabled People (Scottish Council on Disability, 10th edition, 1983), 75p. A listing of relevant organisations in Scotland, with a brief description of each.

Voluntary Organisations: An NCVO Directory 1984/5 (Bedford Square Press, 1984), £5.25 (or by post from the distributors, Macdonald & Evans Distribution Services Ltd, £5.90 including postage and packing). This edition has been revised and expanded to include some 700 national voluntary organisations. Names and addresses are listed alphabetically, with summaries of aims and activities.

Symbols indicate whether organisations are charities, have local branches, recruit volunteers, or have separate trading companies.

A list of useful addresses following the directory section includes professional and public advisory bodies which are relevant to the work of voluntary organisations. The index is classified according to the major subject interests.

General

Accent on Living (Accent Special Publications), subscribers outside United States: one year $6.50, two years $12, three years $17.50. Although primarily intended for the American market, this magazine for disabled people is a really excellent production and contains much material of the widest possible interest. It is published quarterly with over 18,000 paid subscribers in the United States and a few in some other countries. The Accent Special Publications Division has also produced several helpful booklets, including *Buyer's Guide* (products for disabled people) ($10), *Home Operated Business Opportunities* ($4.50), and *Sexual Adjustment* ($4.95). Add $1.15 per book for all orders to be mailed outside the United States.

Better Lives for Disabled Women by Jo Campling (Virago Ltd, 1979), also available from RADAR, £1.45 including postage and packing. This book concentrates on the special needs of disabled women and brings together a mass of relevant information, including not only the practical and financial help available but also a very frank appraisal of the social, psychological and sexual problems which can arise. There are particularly lucid chapters on contraception, motherhood and pregnancy. The book is one which could help to illuminate some of the darker corners of disabled living, enlightening those charged with the care of disabled people as much as speaking directly to handicapped women.

Breaking Barriers: Educating People about Disability by Roy McConkey and Bob McCormack (Souvenir Press, 1983), £5.95 (paperback). Looks to the full participation of disabled people in community life, and the removal of fears and inhibitions which hinder this goal.

Caring for the Sick, written under the authority of St John Ambulance Association and Brigade, St Andrew's Ambulance Association and the British Red Cross Society (Dorling Kindersley, 1982), £5.95 (hardback), £3.95 (paperback). In many respects an admirable book, attractively presented, logically ordered, clear, well illustrated and full of down-to-earth practical advice which will be invaluable to those who help people when they are sick or suffer from a disability. An enormous pity, therefore, that the anonymous authors have not avoided a tone of talking down to their readers. Right at the outset the prime target group is put firmly in its place: 'The professional members of the health team are responsible for the patient. As a volunteer, you are only there to assist them... You must recognise that you are privileged in being accepted as part of the caring team and you should be prepared in all things to put the patient first.'

The very title is unfortunate, conjuring up an image of 'the sick' as a genus who are to be 'done-to' (in fact, many of the people considered are not sick at all). There are constant references to 'the patient'. A difficult word to avoid in the context, admittedly, but it adds to the sense of patronage as between provider and recipient, expert and novice, master and subordinate.

The Charter for the 80s (Rehabilitation International, 1981), available from RADAR, 30p including postage and packing. The Charter is the work of an international committee that met under the chairmanship of the Rt Hon Alf Morris, MP. It presents an action plan that includes over 40 recommendations centred on four main aims:

- to save as many people as possible from becoming disabled by maximising the prevention of disability;
- to reduce the handicapping effects of disability by the provision of adequate rehabilitation services;
- to ensure that disabled people are a part of and not apart from society and that they can participate fully in the life of their communities;
- to promote full public awareness of the problems of disabled people and of their right to social equality.

With more than 500 million people disabled in the world today, a high proportion in developing countries, the Charter looks at the problems of disability from a global perspective. All of its aims are deeply important, but none more so than prevention. It identifies the pressing need to extend primary health care to all communities and step up the assault on the six major diseases of childhood.

The kind of society the Charter seeks to create is one where there is not pity but genuine respect for disabled people; where understanding is unostentatious and sincere; where it is the abilities of people, not their disabilities, that really count; and where disabled people have a fundamental right both to full citizenship and social equality.

Every country is urged by the Charter to adopt policies for the achievement of the fundamental aims *in this decade*. It is an historic document which challenges both our perspectives and our priorities.

Disability in Britain: A Manifesto of Rights by Alan Walker and Peter Townsend (Martin Robertson & Co, 1981), £15.00 (hardback) £5.25 (paperback).

Disability: Legislation and Practice (Macmillan Press, 1981), £8.95, available from Disabilities Study Unit. A collection of essays edited by Duncan Guthrie which look at the practical effect that specific legislation has had on the various aspects of a disabled person's life, including education, employment, financial benefits, mobility, aids and adaptations.

Disability – Whose Handicap? by Ann Shearer (Basil Blackwell), £14.00 (hardback), £4.95 (paperback). This book takes as its starting point the view that everyone has their personal share of ability and inability and that the line between 'able' and 'disabled' can be redrawn constantly. The author explores the significance of disability and of society's attitudes through a series of personal accounts of living with different impairments. These show that far from being the 'personal tragedy' so often assumed, disability is often a fact with which individuals will live in their own way. But they also show that living with disability is made easier or harder by the responses that individuals meet from other people, particularly professional workers and social institutions. Disabled people are unnecessarily handicapped by their exclusion from normal opportunities.

Disabled – An Illustrated Manual of Help and Self-Help by Philip Nichols, with Ros Haworth and Joy Hopkins (David & Charles, 1981), £8.95. A generously illustrated manual designed to meet the practical needs of disabled people and those who live and work with them. It begins with the fundamental means of personal mobility – walking aids and wheelchairs, lifts and other mechanical aids, and the associated planning of the home layout. The book then moves on to the routine tasks of housework and how organisation and minor modifications can improve efficiency and self-reliance. Special sections deal with bedrooms, bathrooms and kitchens, giving practical hints for disabled people and also for those giving assistance. Further sections discuss personal care and appearance, the development of personal relationships, the need for sexual fulfilment and the special problems encountered by handicapped parents and by the parents of a disabled child.

The final section of the book discusses the rights

and entitlements of the disabled person, outlining current legislation and providing a checklist of relevant central and local government departments and services. The directory section also lists many of the official and voluntary organisations offering social and recreational facilities, practical advice and personal counselling/advisory services.

The book wholeheartedly embraces the view that disabled people can, and should, play a full and rewarding role in the life of the community and that the most effective way of enabling them to achieve this goal is to help them to help themselves (our own view exactly). Confidence, self-reliance and independence of spirit are essential factors, but these can only be built on a firm foundation of practical advice and ready availability of information.

Disabled Gays' Guide (Gemma, 1981). Offers some useful addresses, telephone numbers and access information for physically handicapped gay men and women.

Gemma has more recently published *London Disabled Gays' Guide 1983/4*; price 50p plus 12½p postage and packing. It contains access details of London's lesbian and gay groups, women's centres, pubs, discos, bookshops, hotels and guesthouses, as well as information about recreation, travel, women's holidays, publications, health, counselling and services. Braille and cassette editions may be available.

Disabled We Stand by Allan Sutherland (Souvenir Press, 1981), £5.95 (hardback), £3.95 (paperback). It is the society we live in, not our physical handicap, that disables us, says the author of this angry, impassioned book. Through his own experience and that of other disabled people he criticises the stigmatisation of disabled people and the passive role that many of them have come to accept. He asks why organisations set up to 'help' disabled people allow them no voice in their policy-making; and he condemns institutions for failing to consider even such simple courtesies as mobility access.

Family Medical Adviser (Reader's Digest Association Ltd, 1982), £12.95 inclusive of postage and packing. A beautifully produced guide, copiously illustrated and set out in a clear and concise style. There is a section on disability, to which Ann Darnbrough was a major contributor, and another very useful practical guide to first aid.

First Aid Manual (written under the authority of St John Ambulance, the St Andrew's Ambulance Association and the British Red Cross), (Dorling Kindersley, 4th edition 1982), £5.95 (hardback),

£3.95 (paperback). A superb manual in which the information is presented in a straightforward, practical, concise and absolutely clear way with step by step illustrations in colour and a good index. It covers all aspects of first aid, from the basic principles of giving life-saving emergency mouth to mouth ventilation and external chest compression to the more supportive techniques of dealing with fractures or treating multiple injuries. There are sections on emergency childbirth, hernia, cramp, circulatory disorders; indeed the 18 chapters cover everything you need to know – from treating minor household mishaps to coping with emergencies on the road.

For Good by Christine Booth, hire £20.00, available from Circles or from Concord Films Council, (16 mm colour, 45 minutes). A documentary film in which three people, disabled by cerebral palsy, speak for themselves about what it is like to be disabled in an able-bodied society. They are shown at work and in the routines of daily living, revealing some of the real problems and frustrations of physical handicap. The film poses the question: how much are these problems and obstacles a direct result of the disability itself, and how much are they the result of ignorance and apathy in a society structured for and around able-bodied people?

Handicap in a Social World, edited by Ann Brechin, Penny Liddiard and John Swain (Hodder & Stoughton, 1981), price £6.75 (paperback). This is one of two books specially produced for the Open University course, *The Handicapped Person in the Community*, which itself has recently been completely revised and rewritten. It presents a selection of material from a wide range of sources on both sides of the Atlantic, together with seven articles specially commissioned. It is designed to evoke the critical understanding of its readers and is aimed at professionals, members of voluntary organisations, and disabled people and their families.

The General Introduction speaks of 'radical changes that have occurred in the prospects for a better quality of life for disabled people'. In practice, these changes are perhaps still rather more prospective than real, but the editors are right to set a tone which requires 'a re-examination of the assumptions underlying approaches to understanding disability and helping disabled people' and to suggest that 'the most fundamental questions challenge the assumption that the life-style and experiences of disabled people can be explained in terms of the mental and physical attributes of the individual'. They look to alternative definitions of 'disability' which 'focus on the restrictions that disabled people face in a particular combination of socially determined circumstances'. We are particularly heartened to see *choice* recognised as crucial to improved quality of life, and in the final article on DIAL UK to see *open information* described as 'the raw material of knowledge' and knowledge, in turn, as 'the basic tool needed to participate effectively in any activity or social organisation'. The book is arranged in four sections. The first two consider how and why disabled people are segregated in our society. The third looks at the role of professional help and support services, and possible changes in the relationship between those who provide and those who receive help. The final part explores the economics and politics behind the thrust for change, and particularly the participation of disabled people in the decision-making which shapes their lives.

Naturally, some of the articles are more radical than others, but it is overall a stimulating and challenging book, and full of insights – none better than Vic Finkelstein's historical review, which holds that 'it took the Industrial Revolution to give the machinery of production the decisive push which removed crippled people from social intercourse and transformed them into disabled people'. Think about it. This book will ask you to do so on almost every page.

Human Horizons Series. A library of books which explores new ways of helping and developing the abilities of handicapped children and adults. The aim is to present material clearly, without technical jargon, and in a way which is easy to understand and to adapt at home or school.

We have been able to include only a proportion of the available titles in this Directory, those which seem to us to have the most direct relevance to the parents of handicapped children or disabled people themselves. A complete catalogue is available from Souvenir Press Ltd.

Images of Ourselves edited by Jo Campling. (Routledge & Kegan Paul, 1981), £3.95 (paperback). 'Brief lives' of 24 disabled women. They range from adolescence to old age, and their disabilities are various. The contributors are allowed to speak for themselves and they write about their situations as women with disabilities and the attitudes they encounter. Thus the themes of relationships, sexuality, motherhood, education, employment and the practical problems of daily life emerge in a personal and essentially real way.

It cannot be said, however, that the 24 women are representative of disabled women in general. These are the 'fighters against the odds', the 'achievers', whose views tend to be correspondingly forthright, fiercely independent – even aggressive. There is, here and there, a tendency to draw general conclusions from particular circumstances (if does not follow, for example, that because one disabled women has muscles like an Olympic athlete this is commonly so, and that women as a group, and more especially disabled women, can dismiss help with physical limitations as cossetting). Nevertheless, a provocative and stimulating book which challenges conventional thinking.

It Could Happen To You by Nick Cance and the late Brian Line, 1981, hire £10.00 plus VAT (16 mm colour) or £7.00 plus VAT (video, all formats), available from Concord Films Council. (30 minutes). A film about the problems faced by physically disabled people. The production follows four main characters through rehabilitation, work, sport and leisure and emphasises that disability is something which can happen to anyone, sometimes very suddenly.

It's the Same World (Central Film Library, 1981), hire £9.50 plus VAT. This 20 minute film portrays the theme of IYDP: full participation, equality and solidarity for disabled people. Filmed on location in various parts of the world, the film recounts the day-to-day struggle for self-help of a number of handicapped people. A United Nations/UNICEF film made by Dick Young Productions.

Loneliness – the Other Handicap by W. F. R. Stewart (Disabilities Study Unit, 1983), £3.75. The report of a study of loneliness and its causes among physically handicapped people. Hopefully the interest this has attracted will encourage a more positive understanding of this widespread problem.

Lucky Break? by Graham Hurley (Milestone Publications, 1983), £2.50 (paperback). Neil Slatter was 19 when he broke his neck in a motor cycle accident, and became paralysed from the chest down. This book is notable both for the quality of the writing and the intensely human story of the young man's struggle against disability. As gripping to read as any fiction story, yet remarkable for the way it sheds a light of reality towards the better understanding of spinal cord injury.

The New Source Book for the Disabled edited by Glorya Hale (William Heinemann Ltd, revised edition, 1983), £9.95. This second edition of the Source Book now includes a good deal more information of specific relevance to readers in the United Kingdom and the text has been anglicised. As it was written with a US bias in the first edition, this is a welcome change for UK readers, since the health and social security systems in the two countries are so different.

The book's international flavour which remains provides an interesting context in which to view the progress being made in the provision of services for disabled people in other countries, as well as uniting the needs of disabled people wherever they live.

The book is written from a disabled person's point of view and its understanding of everyday problems reflects this.

The illustrations back up the text very helpfully, particularly when aids are being described. While the resources list at the back of the book is limited, due to its international nature, the book overall provides a wealth of discussion and information on all aspects of living with a disability.

Paraplegia – a handbook of practical care and advice by Michael A. Rogers (Faber & Faber Ltd, 1978), £2.95 (paperback). The author is himself paralysed from the neck down. He observes that before spinal injuries centres were founded, many paraplegics and even more tetraplegics failed to survive. Today, new techniques have evolved, research has progressed and the picture is completely different. Patients treated by modern methods in specialised centres can look forward to a normal life-span provided correct medical supervision continues. But they must learn a new way of living if they are to enjoy a worthwhile existence. Mr Rogers sets out the information which is vital to a return to a normal life within the community, and discusses the mental adjustments necessary. There is a chapter on sex, a most helpful one on transport, and a directory of useful organisations.

Physical Handicap: A guide for staff of social services departments and voluntary agencies by Lesley Bell and Astrid Klemz. (Woodhead-Faulkner (Publishers) Ltd, 1981), £12.50 (hardback), £7.50 (paperback) plus postage and packing. This book has been written in response to the many requests for information the authors have received from newly qualified social workers, social work assistants, day care and residential staff, home helps and others who have wanted to know more about ways of helping handicapped people.

The book is divided into four sections. The first section deals with common causes of physical handicap and outlines, in clear terms, the different diseases and disabilities, with an emphasis on how best to approach both the physical and mental problems of each disabled person. Part Two gives information on social security benefits, welfare legislation, the duties of social services and central government departments, and also gives an outline of the help offered by the major voluntary bodies. Part Three discusses the personal needs of handicapped people, describing aids and adaptations, and many possible solutions to the problems involved. Part Four is concerned with rehabilitation centres, employment services, housing, holidays and recreational facilities.

The authors – an occupational therapist and mobility officer – have written a book which is intended for use as an introduction, a guide, a source of reference, and even an inspiration when those who are disabled need help, support and advice.

Physical Handicap (Community Service Volunteers Advisory Service, reprinted 1979), £3.50 including postage and packing. A kit designed to arouse interest in and increase understanding of the problems faced by disabled people. It contains basic information, discussion material, project suggestions, and DHSS leaflets and gives many examples of school and college projects, together with articles written by people who are themselves disabled.

Rehabilitation Today edited by Stephen Mattingly (Update Publications Ltd, 2nd edition, 1977), £7.25 including postage and packing. This book provides a wide-ranging résumé of the various aspects of rehabilitation from a number of specialist contributors, mostly from the medical field (the editor is himself a consultant rheumatologist). The contents cover hospital services, medical rehabilitation and other special centres, community, employment and training services, and the support available in the process of resettlement within the community. The problems affecting particular disability groups are considered in an extremely practical way. There are also very useful sections on aids and appliances, wheelchairs and powered vehicles and on the principles of designing equipment and housing for disabled people. The book is well set out, generously illustrated with an index and appendices listing rehabilitation, artificial limb and appliance centres, and is notable for the amount of hard information which is given in a concise way. It is, perhaps, mainly intended for a professional readership.

Rehabilitation World (Rehabilitation World), non-US subscribers: individuals $35, non-profit organisations $45, commercial organisations $60; single copies $20. This is an American journal of international news and information for disabled people. It contains very punchy and imaginative articles often by disabled people themselves. Although produced in the United States, its contributors are multinational and its contents will interest English-speaking people all over the world, disabled and able-bodied alike. Its travel articles, in particular, are fascinating in their own right and no one should be put off by the rather forbidding para-medical title. Volume 7, No. 2 is entirely devoted to Travel and Disability.

Room for Manoeuvre (Central Film Library, 1980), hire £10.50 plus VAT. This 29-minute film presents six severely handicapped people of various ages who talk about their desire to live as normal lives as possible. It stresses the highly individual needs of disabled families, the importance of tailoring help to those needs, the time and patience needed while people adapt to disability. Sponsored jointly by the National Building Agency and the Crossroads Care Attendant Scheme.

The 'Snowdon Report', Integrating the Disabled, (National Fund for Research into Crippling Diseases, 1979), £2.50 plus 65p postage and packing. This report is a most significant contribution to the thinking of our time. In its philosophy it reflects the wisdom of those moral leaders who are concerned with the dignity of the individual, and in its recommendations in the fields of education, employment, transport, public buildings, and sport and leisure it serves to point the way ahead. Lord Snowdon himself defined integration as seen in this sense as implying the ability of handicapped people to enjoy life on the same terms as their able-bodied counterparts. The terms of reference were laid out as follows: 'To consider the areas in which disabled people are not fully integrated with the rest of society, to consider ways in which, in the different areas, the situation can be rectified so that the disabled person may, so far as his personal disabilities permit, have equal opportunities and appropriate facilities as his non-disabled fellows, and to make recommendations.'

NOTE: The evidence submitted to the Snowdon Working Party is available as a separate volume, price £2.50 plus £1.25 postage.

Social Work with Disabled People by Michael Oliver (Macmillan Press Ltd, 1983). Another title in the Practical Social Work series edited by Jo Campling, £12.50 hardback; £4.95 paperback. Michael Oliver, whose views are informed by a considerable personal experience of disability, has a refreshingly radical approach to his subject, challenging the traditional model of social work, with its package-deal response to preconceived need.

Oliver takes as his starting point the view that while arguments flourish for the limiting of social work to a scale which can be performed efficiently, the base of social work activity with disabled people needs to be broadened and informed with an awareness of the ways in which the feelings and aspirations of people with disabilities have changed radically in the past few years. He argues throughout the book that disability is not an individual problem, rather it is a social problem concerned with the effects of hostile physical and social environments upon impaired individuals. He stresses that by seeing their role too narrowly social workers have either ignored people's needs or have based their interventions on inappropriate assumptions about disability. He sees the approach of counting heads, compiling registers, and providing residential and day-care facilities, etc. as misconceived; what is needed is rather the development of ways in which the disabling effects of the physical and social environment can be measured: a social model of disability.

We were disappointed that a book so radical in its approach should put forward on page 77 the incredible proposition that disability may have less effect upon a wife's 'role' performance than that of a husband. Such blatant stereotyping of both women and the state of couples living together is unworthy of the book as a whole.

So You're Paralysed by Bernadette Fallon (Spinal Injuries Association, 1976), £3.00 including postage and packing. A guide to coping with the physical, social and psychological problems of becoming paralysed, whether through accident or illness. In a simple and direct way it gives the facts of paraplegia and tetraplegia and sets out the route to independence.

Who are you Staring At? (Community Service Volunteers Advisory Service with the Mental Health Film Council, 1980), £7.50 including postage and packing. A kit showing, through 36 poster-sized photographs, tape-recorded interviews and other material, how six young people with various handicaps share the challenges, frustrations, joys and difficulties they experience in life. It explores their individual response to handicap, and looks at the ways in which it affects their education, job prospects, independence and social life.

Mental Handicap/Health

BIMH Current Awareness Service : *see* Directories, page 335.

Beginning to Listen by David Brandon and Julie Ridley (MIND, 1983), 85p including postage and packing.
Beginning to Listen was inspired by the principle of 'normalisation', which the authors define as the

'revaluing of devalued people'. They stress that in this country research on mental handicap provision is dominated by the perceptions of professionals and of relatives of mentally handicapped people, despite the fact that handicapped people have views of their own. Brandon and Ridley believe that mentally handicapped people 'should be given every opportunity to make choices for themselves', and embarked on this study to discover the ideas and opinions of a group living in a local authority hostel. The residents talked in particular about the hostel, the training centre associated with it, and what it feels like to be handicapped. What emerges from the expression of their own views is that many mentally handicapped people see their future in *ordinary* housing and *ordinary* jobs. Although hostels offer a valuable local service, Brandon and Ridley conclude that 'it is extremely difficult to integrate people into a neighbourhood from a relatively segregated facility.'

Camera Talks Ltd distribute an extensive range of audiovisual aids including a series of slide/tape sets under the title *Mental Health*.

Coming to Terms with Mental Handicap by Ann Worthington (Helena Press, 1982), £4.95 including postage and packing. Written by the founder/ organiser of the handicap contact and information service *In Touch* (*see* page 333) and based on a long (14 years) and extensive correspondence with parents of mentally handicapped children and her personal experience as a mother whose children have included one with mental handicap. Topics include: breaking the news to parents; the needs of brothers and sisters; stress in the family; parents as teachers; speech, play, mobility, feeding, toileting; further education; social and sexual difficulties. There is also an information section, giving names and addresses of organisations, publications and a list of aids.

T. W. Pascoe in *Parents Voice* (the Journal of the National Association of Teachers of the Mentally Handicapped), June 1982, commented 'I . . . recommend and commend it unreservedly . . . as being "vital reading" – so get a copy *somehow* and read it soon!'

Graves Medical Audiovisual Library, Holly House, 220 New London Road, Chelmsford, Essex CM2 9BJ (Tel: Chelmsford (0245) 83351). The Library carries an extensive range of material relating to the care and understanding of mentally handicapped children and adults, including a number of tape/slide sets on sexual matters.

A Home of their Own by Victoria Shennan (Souvenir Press, 1983), £7.95 (hardback), £5.95 (paperback).

The author of *Mental Handicap Nursing and Care* describes the many schemes now being launched to establish mentally handicapped people in homes of their own as independent members of the community.

Mental Handicap – A Social View (Graves Medical Audiovisual Library, 1982). This programme aims to give an insight into the problems faced by parents of mentally handicapped children. Key issues are highlighted and constructive criticism is made of the current services for mentally handicapped people, with possible remedies for the shortcomings in both the community and hospital provision. The programme package contains two video cassettes (45 minutes each) two audiocassettes, one printed transcript from each part and a leaflet with suggestions for use. Available in VHS and Betamax formats (other video formats can be specially prepared).

Mental Health Year Book 1981/2: see Directories, page 336.

Overcoming Depression by Andrew Stanway (Hamlyn Paperbacks, 1981), £1.75 including postage and packing, available from MIND Bookshop. Offers practical and encouraging advice on the nature, cause, prevention and treatment of depression.

Social Work and Mental Illness by Alan Butler and Colin Pritchard. One of the titles in the Practical Social Work series edited by Jo Campling (Macmillan Press, 1983), £4.95. The aim of the book is not to debate the causes of mental illness but to provide a practical guide for social workers to work with mentally ill people. As such it is somewhat outside the remit of this Directory which is written for disabled people and their families. However, it seems to us to have a special interest not only to social workers but also to others concerned about the role of social workers and the supportive services they can offer to those who suffer from mental illness as well as their families.

A number of case studies are included, illustrating discussions on the meaning of mental illness, the impact of mental disorder, different approaches to work with mentally disordered people, drugs and physical treatment, social work and suicide, and the Mental Health Act legislation.

Trouble with Tranquillisers (Release Publications, 1982), 40p including postage and packing, available from MIND Bookshop. This pamphlet examines the most commonly prescribed group of drugs. It considers their effectiveness, side-effects, and gives practical advice on how to kick the habit.

We Can Speak for Ourselves by Paul Williams and Bonnie Shoultz (Souvenir Press, 1982), £7.95 (hardback), £5.95 (paperback). Human beings have a fundamental right to speak for themselves, but until now mentally handicapped people have been denied this right. Now, both in the United States and Britain, movements are growing to teach even severely mentally handicapped people the power of self-advocacy.

This book describes two successful projects in the United States and several in Britain where students at Adult Training Centres are learning skills necessary to take charge of their lives. It provides practical advice for ATC staff, hostel workers and parents who would like to set up their own self-advocacy schemes, and includes personal accounts by mentally handicapped participants.

ADDRESSES OF PUBLISHERS AND STOCKISTS MENTIONED IN THE MAIN TEXT

Film Distributors

Camera Talks Ltd
31 North Row, London W1R 2EN (Tel: 01-493 2761).
This company produces and distributes an extensive range of audio visual aids, including slide sets, 35 mm filmstrips, cassetted tapes, 16 mm films, and related equipment. A catalogue is available arranged by subject headings which include physiotherapy, occupational therapy, mental health, social services, and care of the aged. All programmes are available on approval (sale or return). The majority are slide/tape, with the tape pulsed for synchronisation with the slides if used with an automatic projector. Printed commentaries are also available. Boxed slide sets cost (at the time of writing) £10.95 per part, and the cassetted tape commentaries £6.95. Programmes are also available for hire at £7.50 up to a week, including a box of slides, tape and notes. Further details on request.

Central Film Library
Chalfont Grove, Gerrards Cross, Buckinghamshire SL9 8TN.

Concord Films Council Ltd
201 Felixstowe Road, Ipswich, Suffolk IP3 9BJ (Tel: Ipswich (0473) 76012).
This company makes available for hire an extensive range of documentary films with special emphasis on social issues. It is registered as a charity and now has the largest education film library in Britain. The films are selected primarily to promote discussion, for instruction and for training, many being used in the course of education or for training in the health service or social services. Many voluntary organisations have used Concord to distribute their films, in order to publicise their work and draw attention to the special needs of those people they exist to serve. A few of the films have been described elsewhere in the Directory but these represent only a fragment of the total stock. The library includes numerous documentary films on handicapped children, on children

in hospitals or institutions, on blindness and deafness, education, mental health, rehabilitation and physical handicaps.
Many of the films in the Concord library are also available as video cassettes. A free brochure giving details of approximately 100 programmes dealing with disablement (both physical and mental) is available on request. A comprehensive catalogue and index of all films and video cassettes costs £1.50 plus £1 postage. Inclusion on mailing list to receive regular supplements costs an extra £1.

Graves Medical Audiovisual Library
Holly House, 220 New London Road, Chelmsford, Essex CM2 9BJ (Tel: Chelmsford (0245) 83351).
This library carries a large stock of tape-slide programmes available for hire and sale. They are mostly of professional medical interest, but some bear on disability in a more general way.
At the time of writing the following hire charges apply:

Audio tape/slide programmes	£4.50 per tape for each period or part of 28 days
Teaching slide sets	£2.25 per set for each period or part of 28 days
Microfiche sets	£1.50 per set for each period or part of 28 days
Video tapes	£8.00 per tape per day

The Mental Health Film Council
22 Harley Street, London W1N 2ED (Tel: 01-637 0741).
Has a catalogue of over 600 films and videos concerned with all aspects of mental health and disability, price £3.75 including postage and packing.

Town and Country Productions Ltd
21 Cheyne Row, Chelsea, London SW3 5HP (Tel: 01-352 7950).
This company has a varied library of documentary films available for hire. Subjects include sport for disabled people (*see* Section 11), Citizens' Advice Bureaux, the work of the Invalid Children's Aid

Association, the Disabled Living Foundation, the Leukaemia Research Fund, and the St John Ambulance Brigade, and other social welfare issues. Catalogue available.

Publishers and Publishing Organisations

Accent Special Publications, PO Box 700, Bloomington, Illinois 61701, USA.

Age Concern England, Bernard Sunley House, 60 Pitcairn Road, Mitcham, Surrey CR4 3LL.

George Allen & Unwin Ltd, PO Box 18, Park Lane, Hemel Hempstead, Hertfordshire HP2 4TE.

BBC Publications, PO Box 234, London SE1 3TH.

Bedford Square Press, (NCVO), 26 Bedford Square, London WC1B 3HU.

Bible Society, Publishing Division, Stonehill Green, Westlea, Swindon SN5 7DG.

Basil Blackwell, 108 Cowley Road, Oxford OX4 1JF.

The Bodley Head Ltd, 9 Bow Street, London WC2E 7AL.

British Standards Institution, (Sales Department), 101 Pentonville Road, London N1 9ND.

Centre on Environment for the Handicapped, 126 Albert Street, London NW1 7NF.

Child Poverty Action Group, 1 Macklin Street, London WC2B 5NH.

Churchill Livingstone, Robert Stevenson House, 1–3 Baxter's Place, Leith Walk, Edinburgh EH1 3AF.

Circles, 113 Roman Road, London E2 0HU.

William Collins Sons & Co. Ltd, 8 Grafton Street, London W1.

Community Service Volunteers Advisory Service, 237 Pentonville Road, London N1 9NJ.

Consumers Association, (Subscriptions Department), Castlemead, Gascoyne Way, Hertford.

Croom Helm Ltd, St John's Chambers, 2–10 St John's Road, London SW11 1PN.

John Curley & Associates Inc., 23 Bass River Parkway, Bass River, Massachusetts 02664, USA.

David & Charles Ltd, Brunel House, Newton Abbot, Devon.

DHSS Publications Unit, PO Box 21, Stanmore, Middlesex HA7 1AY.

Disabilities Study Unit, Wildhanger, Amberley, Arundel, West Sussex BN18 9NR.

Disability Alliance Educational & Research Association, 25 Denmark Street, London WC2 8NJ.

Disabled Living Foundation, 380–384 Harrow Road, London W9 2HU.

Disablement Income Group, Attlee House, 28 Commercial Street, London E1 6LR.

DLF (Sales) Ltd, Book House, 45 East Hill, Wandsworth, London SW18 2QZ.

Dorling Kindersley Ltd, 9 Henrietta Street, London WC2E 8PS.

Equipment for the Disabled, Mary Marlborough Lodge, Nuffield Orthopaedic Centre, Headington, Oxford OX3 7LD.

Eyre & Spottiswoode Ltd, North Way, Andover, Hants SP10 5BE.

Faber & Faber Ltd, 3 Queen Square, London WC1N 3AU.

Fair Play for Children, 248 Kentish Town Road, London NW5.

Family Welfare Association, 501–503 Kingsland Road, London E8 4AU.

Gemma, BM Box 5700, London WC1N 3XX.

Granada, PO Box 9, Frogmore, St Albans, Hertfordshire.

Greater London Association for Disabled People (GLAD), 1 Thorpe Close, London W10 5XL.

Hamlyn Publishing Group Ltd, Astronaut House, Hounslow Road, Feltham, Middlesex TW14 9AR.

Handicapped Persons Research Unit, Newcastle upon Tyne Polytechnic, No. 1 Coach Lane, Coach Lane Campus, Newcastle upon Tyne NE7 7TW.

Health Education Council, 78 New Oxford Street, London WC1A 1AH.

William Heinemann Ltd, 10 Upper Grosvenor Street, London W1X 9PA.

Heinemann Educational Books, 22 Bedford Square, London WC1B 3HH.

Heinemann Medical Books, 23 Bedford Square, London WC1.

Helena Press, PO Box 2, Slaithwaite, Huddersfield HD7 5JF.

Hodder & Stoughton Ltd, Mill Road, Dunton Green, Sevenoaks, Kent.

In Touch Handicap Contact and Information Service, 10 Norman Road, Sale, Cheshire M33 3DF.

King Edward's Hospital Fund for London, 126 Albert Street, London NW1 7NF.

Longman Group Ltd, 6th floor, Westgate House, The High, Harlow, Essex CM20 1NE.

Macdonald & Evans Distribution Services Ltd, Estover Road, Plymouth PL6 7PZ.

Macmillan Press Ltd, 187 Fleet Street, London EC4.

Magna Print Books, Magna House, Long Preston, nr Skipton, North Yorkshire BD23 4ND.

Martin Robertson & Co., 108 Cowley Road, Oxford OX4 1JF.

MENCAP, 123 Golden Lane, London EC1Y 0RT.

Methuen & Co. Ltd, 11 New Fetter Lane, London EC4P 4EE.

Milestone Publications, Murray Road, Horndean, Hampshire PO8 9JL.

MIND Bookshop, 155–157 Woodhouse Lane, Leeds LS2 3EF.

National Children's Bureau, 8 Wakley Street, London EC1V 7QE.

National Consumer Council, 18 Queen Anne's Gate, London SW1H 9AA.

National Council for Voluntary Organisations, 26 Bedford Square, London WC1B 3HU.

National Fund for Research into Crippling Diseases, Vincent House, North Parade, Horsham, West Sussex RH12 2DA.

Northern Ireland Council for the Handicapped, 2 Annadale Avenue, Belfast BT15 3BP.

Office of Health Economics, 12 Whitehall, London SW1A 2DY.

Oxford University Press, 116 High Street, Oxford OX1 4BR.

Patients Association, Room 33, 18 Charing Cross Road, London WC2H 0HR.

Penguin Books Ltd, 536 King's Road, London SW10 0UH.

Pergamon Press, Headington Hill Hall, Oxford, OX3 0BW.

Frances Pinter (Publishers) Ltd, 5 Dryden Street, London WC2E 9NW.

Royal Association for Disability and Rehabilitation (RADAR), 25 Mortimer Street, London W1N 8AB.

Reader's Digest Association Ltd, 25 Berkeley Square, London W1X 6AB.

Rehabilitation World (Circulation Department), 1123 Broadway, New York, NY 10018, USA.

Routledge & Kegan Paul PLC, Broadway House, Newtown Road, Henley on Thames, Oxfordshire RG9 1EN.

Royal National Institute for the Blind (RNIB), 224 Great Portland Street, London W1N 6AA.

Royal National Institute for the Deaf (RNID), 105 Gower Street, London WC1E 6AH.

School Government Publishing Co. Ltd, Darby House, Bletchingly Road, Merstham, Redhill, Surrey RH1 3DN.

Scottish Braille Press, Craigmillar Park, Edinburgh EH16 5NB.

Scottish Council on Disability, 5 Shandwick Place, Edinburgh EH2 4RG.

Scottish Council of Social Service, 18-19 Claremont Crescent, Edinburgh EH7 4QD.

Southern and Western Regional Association for the Blind, 55 Eton Avenue, London NW3 3ET.

Souvenir Press Ltd, 43 Great Russell Street, London WC1B 3PA.

Spastics Society, 12 Park Crescent, London W1N 4EQ.

Spinal Injuries Association, Yeoman's House, 76 St James's Lane, Muswell Hill, N10.

Tape Recording Service for the Blind, 48 Fairfax Road, Farnborough, Hampshire GU14 8JP.

Tavistock Publications Ltd, 11 New Fetter Lane, London EC4P 4EE.

Thames Television, 149 Tottenham Court Road, London W1P 9LL.

Thorndike Press, Thorndike, ME04986, USA.

Tolley Publishing Co. Ltd, 209 High Street, Croydon CR0 1QR.

Ulverscroft Large Print Books Ltd, The Green, Bradgate Road, Anstey, Leicester LE7 7FU.

University of London Institute of Education, Bedford Way, London WC1H 0AL.

Update Publications Ltd, 33–34 Alfred Place, London WC1E 7DP.

Virago Ltd, 41 William IV Street, London WC2.

Woodhead-Faulkner (Publishers) Ltd, Fitzwilliam House, 32 Trumpington Street, Cambridge CB2 1QY.

INDEX